Lecture Notes in Computer Science 9172

Commenced Publication in 1973
Founding and Former Series Editors:
Gerhard Goos, Juris Hartmanis, and Jan van Leeuwen

Editorial Board

David Hutchison
  Lancaster University, Lancaster, UK
Takeo Kanade
  Carnegie Mellon University, Pittsburgh, PA, USA
Josef Kittler
  University of Surrey, Guildford, UK
Jon M. Kleinberg
  Cornell University, Ithaca, NY, USA
Friedemann Mattern
  ETH Zurich, Zürich, Switzerland
John C. Mitchell
  Stanford University, Stanford, CA, USA
Moni Naor
  Weizmann Institute of Science, Rehovot, Israel
C. Pandu Rangan
  Indian Institute of Technology, Madras, India
Bernhard Steffen
  TU Dortmund University, Dortmund, Germany
Demetri Terzopoulos
  University of California, Los Angeles, CA, USA
Doug Tygar
  University of California, Berkeley, CA, USA
Gerhard Weikum
  Max Planck Institute for Informatics, Saarbrücken, Germany

More information about this series at http://www.springer.com/series/7409

Sakae Yamamoto (Ed.)

Human Interface and the Management of Information

Information and Knowledge Design

17th International Conference, HCI International 2015
Los Angeles, CA, USA, August 2–7, 2015
Proceedings, Part I

 Springer

Editor
Sakae Yamamoto
Tokyo University of Science
Tokyo
Japan

ISSN 0302-9743   ISSN 1611-3349   (electronic)
Lecture Notes in Computer Science
ISBN 978-3-319-20611-0   ISBN 978-3-319-20612-7   (eBook)
DOI 10.1007/978-3-319-20612-7

Library of Congress Control Number: 2015941874

LNCS Sublibrary: SL3 – Information Systems and Applications, incl. Internet/Web, and HCI

Springer Cham Heidelberg New York Dordrecht London

Printed on acid-free paper

Springer International Publishing AG Switzerland is part of Springer Science+Business Media
(www.springer.com)

Foreword

The 17th International Conference on Human-Computer Interaction, HCI International 2015, was held in Los Angeles, CA, USA, during 2–7 August 2015. The event incorporated the 15 conferences/thematic areas listed on the following page.

A total of 4843 individuals from academia, research institutes, industry, and governmental agencies from 73 countries submitted contributions, and 1462 papers and 246 posters have been included in the proceedings. These papers address the latest research and development efforts and highlight the human aspects of design and use of computing systems. The papers thoroughly cover the entire field of Human-Computer Interaction, addressing major advances in knowledge and effective use of computers in a variety of application areas. The volumes constituting the full 28-volume set of the conference proceedings are listed on pages VII and VIII.

I would like to thank the Program Board Chairs and the members of the Program Boards of all thematic areas and affiliated conferences for their contribution to the highest scientific quality and the overall success of the HCI International 2015 conference.

This conference could not have been possible without the continuous and unwavering support and advice of the founder, Conference General Chair Emeritus and Conference Scientific Advisor, Prof. Gavriel Salvendy. For their outstanding efforts, I would like to express my appreciation to the Communications Chair and Editor of HCI International News, Dr. Abbas Moallem, and the Student Volunteer Chair, Prof. Kim-Phuong L. Vu. Finally, for their dedicated contribution towards the smooth organization of HCI International 2015, I would like to express my gratitude to Maria Pitsoulaki and George Paparoulis, General Chair Assistants.

May 2015

Constantine Stephanidis
General Chair, HCI International 2015

HCI International 2015 Thematic Areas and Affiliated Conferences

Thematic areas:

- Human-Computer Interaction (HCI 2015)
- Human Interface and the Management of Information (HIMI 2015)

Affiliated conferences:

- 12th International Conference on Engineering Psychology and Cognitive Ergonomics (EPCE 2015)
- 9th International Conference on Universal Access in Human-Computer Interaction (UAHCI 2015)
- 7th International Conference on Virtual, Augmented and Mixed Reality (VAMR 2015)
- 7th International Conference on Cross-Cultural Design (CCD 2015)
- 7th International Conference on Social Computing and Social Media (SCSM 2015)
- 9th International Conference on Augmented Cognition (AC 2015)
- 6th International Conference on Digital Human Modeling and Applications in Health, Safety, Ergonomics and Risk Management (DHM 2015)
- 4th International Conference on Design, User Experience and Usability (DUXU 2015)
- 3rd International Conference on Distributed, Ambient and Pervasive Interactions (DAPI 2015)
- 3rd International Conference on Human Aspects of Information Security, Privacy and Trust (HAS 2015)
- 2nd International Conference on HCI in Business (HCIB 2015)
- 2nd International Conference on Learning and Collaboration Technologies (LCT 2015)
- 1st International Conference on Human Aspects of IT for the Aged Population (ITAP 2015)

Conference Proceedings Volumes Full List

21. LNCS 9189, Distributed, Ambient and Pervasive Interactions, edited by Norbert Streitz and Panos Markopoulos
22. LNCS 9190, Human Aspects of Information Security, Privacy and Trust, edited by Theo Tryfonas and Ioannis Askoxylakis
23. LNCS 9191, HCI in Business, edited by Fiona Fui-Hoon Nah and Chuan-Hoo Tan
24. LNCS 9192, Learning and Collaboration Technologies, edited by Panayiotis Zaphiris and Andri Ioannou
25. LNCS 9193, Human Aspects of IT for the Aged Population: Design for Aging (Part I), edited by Jia Zhou and Gavriel Salvendy
26. LNCS 9194, Human Aspects of IT for the Aged Population: Design for Everyday Life (Part II), edited by Jia Zhou and Gavriel Salvendy
27. CCIS 528, HCI International 2015 Posters' Extended Abstracts (Part I), edited by Constantine Stephanidis
28. CCIS 529, HCI International 2015 Posters' Extended Abstracts (Part II), edited by Constantine Stephanidis

Human Interface and the Management of Information

Program Board Chair: Sakae Yamamoto, Japan

- Denis A. Coelho, Portugal
- Linda R. Elliott, USA
- Shin'ichi Fukuzumi, Japan
- Michitaka Hirose, Japan
- Makoto Itoh, Japan
- Yen-Yu Kang, Taiwan
- Koji Kimita, Japan
- Daiji Kobayashi, Japan
- Kentaro Kotani, Japan
- Chen Ling, USA
- Hiroyuki Miki, Japan
- Hirohiko Mori, Japan
- Robert Proctor, USA
- Ryosuke Saga, Japan
- Katsunori Shimohara, Japan
- Takahito Tomoto, Japan
- Kim-Phuong Vu, USA
- Tomio Watanabe, Japan

The full list with the Program Board Chairs and the members of the Program Boards of all thematic areas and affiliated conferences is available online at:

http://www.hci.international/2015/

HCI International 2016

The 18th International Conference on Human-Computer Interaction, HCI International 2016, will be held jointly with the affiliated conferences in Toronto, Canada, at the Westin Harbour Castle Hotel, 17–22 July 2016. It will cover a broad spectrum of themes related to Human-Computer Interaction, including theoretical issues, methods, tools, processes, and case studies in HCI design, as well as novel interaction techniques, interfaces, and applications. The proceedings will be published by Springer. More information will be available on the conference website: http://2016.hci.international/.

General Chair
Prof. Constantine Stephanidis
University of Crete and ICS-FORTH
Heraklion, Crete, Greece
Email: general_chair@hcii2016.org

http://2016.hci.international/

Contents – Part I

Information Presentation

Knowledge Management

Haptic, Tactile and Multimodal Interaction

Service Design and Management

User Studies

Contents – Part II

Information and Interaction for Driving

Information and Interaction for Learning and Education

Information and Interaction for Culture and Art

Supporting Work and Collaboration

Information Visualisation

Annotated Domain Ontologies for the Visualization of Heterogeneous Manufacturing Data

Rebekka Alm[1,2]($\boxtimes$), Mario Aehnelt[1], Steffen Hadlak[1,2], and Bodo Urban[1,2]

[1] Fraunhofer IGD, Joachim-Jungius-Str. 11, 18059 Rostock, Germany
{rebekka.alm, mario.aehnelt, steffen.hadlak,
bodo.urbang}@igd-r.fraunhofer.de
[2] University of Rostock, 18051 Rostock, Germany

Abstract. Manufacturing processes such as monitoring and controlling typically confront the user with a variety of heterogeneous data sources and systems. The cognitive efforts to summarize and combine the data from these different sources affect the user's efficiency. Our goal is to support the user in his work task by integrating the data and presenting them in a more perceivable way. Hence, we introduce an approach in which different data sources are integrated in an annotated semantic knowledge base: our domain ontology. Based on this ontology, contextually relevant data for a specific work task is selected and embedded into a meta-visualization providing an overview of the data based on the user's mental model. Two systems finally exemplify the usage of our approach.

1 Introduction

Advanced manufacturing promises an evolution of industrial production processes from management to the shop floor. It combines novel approaches, methods and technologies to increase the efficiency, effectivity as well as quality of industrial manufacturing. Visual computing plays a decisive role in making abstract data and connections between data visible and understandable for the user in order to enable well-founded work decisions. However, due to the growing complexity and heterogeneity of manufacturing data, we not only face the problem of visualizing *Big Data* but we also need to address the growing cognitive demands of the user accordingly.

For monitoring and control of manufacturing processes the user is confronted with a multitude of heterogeneous data sources and systems. *Enterprise resource planning* systems (ERP), *manufacturing execution systems* (MES) or even task-specific but isolated applications may help him to analyze large and complex data volumes from the manufacturing shop floor. Yet, their variety in providing different visualization and interaction approaches when working with data also challenges the user's mental model and reduces his efficiency [2].

For this reason, data visualizations need to incorporate and blend data from different systems as well as resemble familiar aspects and metaphors from the real

© Springer International Publishing Switzerland 2015
S. Yamamoto (Ed.): HIMI 2015, Part I, LNCS 9172, pp. 3–14, 2015.
DOI: 10.1007/978-3-319-20612-7_1

work domain in order to reduce the cognitive workload of perceiving, processing and applying the presented information embedded in manufacturing processes. Our work aims to address these issues for the data visualization on three levels:

- on the *contextual level*, we first transfer context knowledge about the working domain into a *domain ontology* to structure the typically unrelated data from ERP, MES, and other manufacturing data systems,
- on the *conceptual level*, we then use annotations as a central means to not only encode the contextual relationships between both abstract data and information concepts from the work domain ontology, but also to incorporate additional information not yet covered by existing systems, and
- on the *cognitive level*, we provide a meta-visualization based on the user's mental model of the work domain as an overview of the data and the interrelations in which contextual information of a work task are embedded.

The remainder of this paper details the related work in Sect. 2. In Sect. 3, we introduce our contextualized annotation approach. In Sect. 4, we illustrate two domain specific implementations of our concept for the concrete case of manufacturing. Section 5 concludes this paper and states ideas for future work.

2   Related Work

A fundamental problem of the multitude of heterogeneous data sources and applications is the *information overload* challenging the user's cognitive capabilities. This problem exacerbates the more data sources and thus the more applications handling them have to be used. Landesberger et al. [8] identified the lack of consistency as one of the major reasons for this problem making it a crucial design issue for integrated data visualizations. On the one hand, it can be addressed by using the same basic visualization and interaction means, e.g., from a standard library, if the heterogeneity of data allows for it. On the other hand, consistency is also a question of the user's perception. Here, research in *cognitive engineering* revealed that the user's *mental model* as well as his *macrocognitive context* plays a growing role in designing interactive applications [7]. Each user has an individual small-scale mental model of certain aspects of reality, which influences his understanding of and interaction with information. Conversely each information application is embedded into the user's cognitive processes of perception, understanding, decision making, learning, and behavioral control forming the macrocognitive context. Thus, each application has to resemble familiar metaphors in order to simplify its cognitive processing.

A common way for providing a more consistent and uniform access to the data is based on the introduction of an additional structure such as networks to link and connect the heterogeneous data sources. On the one hand, these structures provide overviews as given in [12] to select suitable data sources relevant for a specific task. On the other hand, they can be used as a guideline to access the different sources in a specific order during the analysis [11]. Especially in the manufacturing context where many hierarchical dependencies exist, more specific data structures such as ontologies have been used [6]. An ontology in this context describes an explicit specification of a shared conceptualization [5]. In cooperation with domain users, knowledge about a specific domain is gathered and usually formalized in a tree-like fashion that consists of concepts and different kinds of relationships between them. The main structure is often similar to a taxonomy representing hierarchical relationships between general concepts and their more specific counterparts. Additionally, the ontology establishes non-taxonomic relationships between concepts. This formal knowledge representation enables machine-interpretation and sharing of knowledge.

The practice of annotating documents is a familiar activity performed by diverse groups of people with the intention of classification, communication or documentation of information [3]. Students are writing annotations in their textbooks or people are putting sticky notes at objects to annotate them; the activity of annotating is easily done and useful to support information sharing and processing by human beings. In the context of machine-interpretability, annotations are defined as metadata objects that (semantically) enrich documents with additional information. The semantic enrichment of documents through annotations usually intends to support computers in processing the information context [9]. In this way, they support activities like searching for information, structuring and shaping a document, as well as enabling service interoperability.

In this paper, we intend to combine both: ontologies and annotations to support the cognitive and computational processing of heterogeneous manufacturing related data. In this sense, we extend the utilization of annotations from a mere mean for the automatic computational processing to a more flexible tool for providing additional information for a given task.

3   Contextualized Annotation and Visualization

Following our discussion in the previous sections, the visualization of abstract data requires suitable and familiar visual metaphors close to the work domain's original context in order to reduce the cognitive interpretation efforts. For this reason, we combine the contextualized visualization of heterogeneous manufacturing data with a conceptual annotation framework based on an interlinked domain ontology. Basically, this approach consists of five main components (an overview of the first four more data-related components is given in Fig. 1) that are grouped according to the aforementioned three levels:

Contextual level:
(1) all relevant contextual elements of the work domain are modeled with semantically interrelated concepts in a *domain ontology*,

Conceptual level:
(2) the *data* from systems like ERP and MES is attached to the ontology by annotations connecting data objects to corresponding domain concepts,
(3) *additional information* supporting the work process can be attached on the fly to both: concepts and data objects by manual annotations,

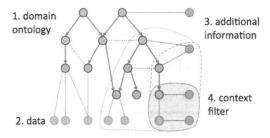

Fig. 1. Conceptual approach of linking context knowledge with manufacturing data as well as additional information. Context knowledge is covered by the domain ontology consisting of concepts (grey circles) that are connected by hierarchical (grey lines) and other relations (dashed grey lines). The data from manufacturing systems (orange circles) is attached to concepts (grey circles) of the ontology. Additional information (blue circles) may be attached to existing data and concepts. A context filter (green area) selects appropriate concepts and additional information based on the structure of the ontology. Here, a filter has been defined for a specific data object selecting its ontology concept and attached information (small green area). Following the ontology structure the filter has been extended (larger areas) to include related information (color figure online).

Cognitive level:
(4) the context of a given task is then used as a *context filter* for selecting the required information from the annotated domain ontology to be visualized,
(5) a *contextualized meta-visualization* provides a contextual overview of the data based on the user's mental model in which the task-specific information is embedded.

We detail the basic parts of our conceptual approach, after a brief introduction to the manufacturing domain context.

Our work addresses the general management of manufacturing work processes, focusing on the management of resources, their planning and monitoring. For us it is the *work task* (see Fig. 2) connecting the main context elements *people*, *places* and *things*, if we follow the classical definition of context from [1]. Furthermore, the users are used to dual information encodings. Working with information from the construction sub-domain, e.g. 2D drawings or 3D models, there is a close proximity between physical objects and virtual representations (see Fig. 3). However, working with production planning and monitoring applications leads to a break with the cognitive consistency. Real objects are represented by their abstract identifiers and numerical or discrete values. Analysis tasks which include the processing of both information types need to bridge this gap between the real or imaginable world and its abstract data representation, in order to keep both cognitive consistency and connectivity for the user.

Here we find the rationale for our proposed visualization approach which includes the visual adoption of metaphors and schemes from the contextual background of the work domain.

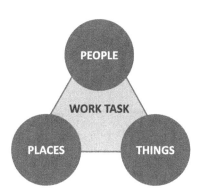

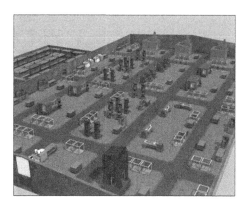

Fig. 2. Contextual dependency between people, places and things centered around the work task

Fig. 3. 3D virtual representation of a production hall containing different types of machines

3.1 Domain Ontology

To provide a consistent and uniform view on the data, all relevant contextual elements of the work domain are modeled by semantically interrelated concepts in an ontology. An ontology describes a shared conceptualization which formally represents a set of concepts (grey circles in Fig. 1) and the relationships (grey lines in Fig. 1). The domain ontology contains domain-specific knowledge as well as adaptions to the individual business. Especially general concepts and relations such as *manager assigns task to worker* or *product consists of parts* are transferable to businesses of the same domain. However, specific concepts such as a particular product is usually bound to an individual business. Our ontology is structured according to the manufacturing context as shown in Fig. 2:

- The *people* subgraph of the ontology formalizes the personas with their corresponding responsibilities and skills (e.g. planning engineers assign workers).
- The *places* subgraph of the ontology summarizes the local arrangements of the work places (e.g. the production hall contains different working groups).
- The *things* subgraph of the ontology summarizes all production-related materials such as tools, parts or products and also encodes their composition as specific interrelations.
- The *work tasks* subgraph formalizes the different work tasks, from general work tasks such as monitoring, planning and assembly to more specialized work tasks such as sticking and soldering.
  Moreover, the concepts of the *work tasks* subgraph connect all subgraphs.

Within these subgraphs, concepts are mainly ordered by hierarchical relationships, whereas non-hierarchical relationships encode more complex relations between concepts within a single subgraph and also connect concepts of different subgraphs. A small example for such a domain ontology showing these different

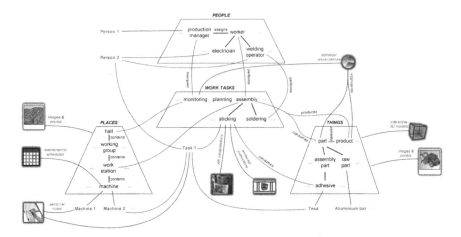

Fig. 4. Excerpt from an annotated example domain ontology. General context knowledge is covered by domain ontology concepts (black font) connected by hierarchical and other relations and grouped by the four context subjects: *people*, *places*, *things* and *work task*. The data from manufacturing systems (orange font) are attached to the corresponding ontology concepts. Additional information (blue font) may be attached to both, existing data as well as ontology concepts. While there are also relations connecting people, places and things (e.g. persons are usually working at a specific work station), they have been omitted from the figure for the sake of clarity (color figure online).

relations is given in Fig. 4 in which the concepts of these four subgraphs are colored in black. The assembly *work task* in particular relates to all other subgraphs as it is performed by a worker (*people*), at a work station (*places*) and consumes parts to produce a product (*things*). It is this powerful semantic knowledge base which allows for all of the following steps.

3.2   Connecting Data to the Ontology

Up to this point, the aforementioned domain ontology already provides a uniform way to describe the heterogeneous data that may stem from different manufacturing systems such as ERP and MES. Yet, to also provide access to this data in a consistent way it has to be integrated into our framework. For their integration, the data of the different systems is directly linked to the corresponding concepts of the domain ontology. This linking is performed on a per object basis connecting each object to the most specific related concepts (usually leaves) of the ontology (see the orange circles in Fig. 1). Here, a single object may be attached to multiple concepts (a worker for instance may fulfill multiple professions).

While all manufacturing systems together may present a heterogeneous data basis, each individual system is generally based on a more homogeneous and well-defined data storage for handling their information. Hence, all objects of a single data source can be linked in the same way and thus their linking needs only be defined once per manufacturing system. The basis of this definition is a simple object specification listing all properties with their description and type as well as a mapping function for linking objects to concepts according to their properties. In Fig. 4 the connected data is visualized in orange.

3.3 Additional Information by Annotations

Aside from the data provided by external systems such as ERP and MES there is much more knowledge in a business that also has to be formalized and contextualized for universal access. This knowledge may contain information related to business internal processes (e.g. maintenance schedules), documents supporting the execution of work tasks (e.g. handbooks, images, videos or even interactive visualizations), or feedback of workers (e.g. documentation with text and photos). This additional information can be related to abstract concepts or concrete data objects as symbolized by the blue circles in Fig. 1.

Because of its variety, the additional information ranges from well-defined and structured documents to not yet formalized individual knowledge of the work task and related objects. Additionally, personas may have different motivations, technical capabilities and resources for providing the annotations. For instance, a stressed worker on the one hand usually has only a handheld device and not enough time to provide a complete and structured documentation of his work that may be effectively reused. On the other hand, a planning engineer who is used to organize and distribute general resources often has more time to prepare the information in a more structured way. Therefore, it is reasonable to also provide personas with different ways of specifying annotations for different use cases ranging from rather simple interfaces to more rigid and stringent forms. In the following, some examples are given to underline the differences in the way additional information can be annotated.

Flexible Annotations. The knowledge an individual worker acquires by experience is rarely sufficiently documented in a way to make it beneficial for the efficient completion of future processes. It is especially valuable, because it is unique and not easily formalized and available, e.g. from external data sources. Manually created flexible annotations can be used to make this individual knowledge available to some extent to the whole business. The particular objective of this annotation activity is the documentation of the work tasks, arisen challenges and especially the solutions.

For the annotation activity it is important that the worker receives the flexibility to first and foremost capture all available information but not forcing him to annotate formally. A user-unfriendly static input mask might irritate and discourage him from giving additional interesting information. Therefore, he can take photos, write short texts and record audio or video documentations in a quick way without disrupting the workflow significantly. These flexible annotations are easily understandable for other humans and supports the cognitive understanding and collaborative work. However, the lack of standardization or formalization affects the computational processing of the data and thus the automatic reusability. For this reason, these annotations are in turn enriched by links to the current object, work task and related concepts of the domain ontology.

Structured Annotations. Information, already to some extent available, but not yet integrated into the framework, includes for instance manuals, guides, maintenance instructions, visual models, statistical visualizations and machine configurations. This information is extensive and general, so it is needed repeatedly for similar tasks. Yet, they are also more complex and more costly to integrate.

Therefore, the managing staff first links the information to the corresponding data objects and ontology concepts of the knowledge base. For instance, the machine configuration and its maintenance schedule are directly linked to the machine itself, whereas its manual is instead linked to the concept representing its machine type making it available for all other machines of that type. They then provide the type of the information, classifying whether it is for example a manual, a visualization, or a schedule resulting in a different visual reflection of the information. Depending on the chosen type different descriptions are required and filled in, such as the dates for a maintenance schedule or the work task to be performed according to this schedule. With these additional descriptions about the content of the documents, there are more possibilities for their automatic integration and visualization.

While the planning and managing staff are used to organize and distribute these resources, providing the necessary descriptions is nevertheless a burden that needs to be supported. For example, to aid a production manager in his monitoring task a statistical visualization can be attached as an annotation to his task providing him with an overview of the parts and products (as depicted by the annotation in the upper right of Fig. 4). However, for such an annotation one does not only have to specify which input parameters to show in a visualization, but also to select an appropriate visualization from a possibly large list, to actually support the given work task. While the selection of an appropriate visualization is still an open research question, there are first works that support this selection by ranking the visualizations according to their suitability for a given task [10].

3.4 Contextual Filtering

By linking the data objects to semantically meaningful concepts as well as by attaching additional annotations, we have enriched the pure manufacturing data with additional context information which was not included in their native management systems. However, we do not need to process all objects and annotations for specific work tasks, such as monitoring the current production state of a manufacturing site. In this case, we focus on the work task's subcontext only, meaning a subset of concepts directly related to the work task which requires a visualization or data analysis. In order to reduce the necessary data for the work task, we can use its context with its particular information demands as the main information filter.

At the same time, we can provide additional information on demand by following the relationships of the ontology. Here, the semantic relationships identify further concepts with connections to the main concepts in focus similar to the *contextualized network graphs* method as proposed in [4] which uses the semantic proximity to measure the relevance of connected network nodes (concepts). Following these relations, we can identify all relevant concepts with respect to the three other information hierarchies in our domain ontology (people, places, things) starting with the actual work task concept. Semantically close concepts are candidates to extend this filter for a more detailed data visualization and analysis as reflected by the green areas in Fig. 1. The domain ontology helps us here to interactively walk through the main information hierarchies in which we find the most detailed level at the leaves. Each time the user changes the work context, e.g. by switching between different analysis activities, the corresponding work task concept also changes and so do the other related information concepts to be visualized.

3.5   Contextualized Meta-Visualization

While the ontology and the attached information provides a uniform and consistent description of and access to the manufacturing data, for most persons it is too abstract to be used as an overview of the data. Hence, we utilize the user's mental model as a base to create such a meta-visualization for presenting a general overview of the work task's context. In general, most humans perform better in recognizing familiar faces or places instead of abstract data or concepts. Hence, a good basis for our meta-visualization are the *people* or *places* subjects of the manufacturing context (see Fig. 2). As we are especially interested in the work tasks and where they are performed, we focus primarily on the *places*. We therefore ground our meta-visualization on the spatial context of the manufacturing situations such as a 2D plan or a 3D representation. An example for a meta-visualization based on a 3D view of a production hall containing different types of machines is shown in Fig. 3. In this meta-visualization, we can then embed the information required for a specific work task. As the user has a high spatial understanding and knows where a specific machine is located, he can easily relate the presented information to the real world. How such an embedding of information can be realized is demonstrated for two concrete cases in the next section.

4   Plant@Hand and Plant@Hand3D

Our approach presented in the previous section was implemented in two different but conceptually similar manufacturing monitoring applications: *Plant@Hand* and *Plant@Hand3D*. Whereas Plant@Hand specifically addresses the monitoring and control of assembly works in shipbuilding industries, Plant@Hand3D focuses on the monitoring and control of production processes at a manufacturing site. Both systems integrate different data analysis and visualization functionalities,

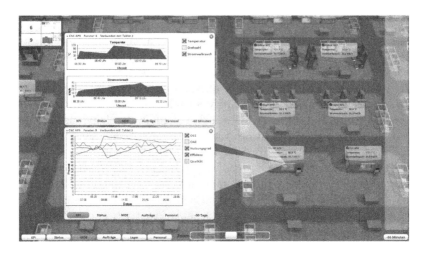

Fig. 5. Screenshot of the Plant@Hand3D System. A 3D model of the production plant serves as the meta-visualization representing the spatial context of the data. Embedded windows provide detailed information about the work task: Diagrams visualizing trends of temperature and electricity consumption of the selected machine (upper window) and a history of key performance indicators of the same machine (bottom window).

as they are usually provided by ERP or MES individually, within a consistent multi-touch user interface. Furthermore, the Plant@Hand solutions allow the connection of external displays, like big monitors, tablets, smartphones and smartwatches. While the multi-touch table generally gives an overview about the context of the work tasks, the distributed displays show the information that is most relevant for the current task and worker. In this way, they support multiple users working collaboratively with different contextualized data visualizations.

Plant@Hand aims at simplifying the central planning and supervision of installation works in ships to support the assembly across all stages of preparation, implementation and documentation. For this purpose, the relevant data and information from the leading manufacturing systems, such as ERP or MES, as well as planning documents and installation progress reports are merged and integrated with constructive models and drawings. A CAD construction plan serves as the meta-visualization representing the spatial context of the data and work tasks. The overall information is reduced to the essential details of the current task by selecting only information concerning the related area of the construction plan. Supplementary information can be accessed by clicking on objects directly in the construction plan or following links in the different windows where available. Further details can be manually added by the worker. For documentation purposes, he can annotate by text, photo, video or analogous on paper via smart pen.

Plant@Hand 3D is a centralized monitoring and controlling solution for production plants. The system visualizes data from manufacturing systems, databases and file systems in an integrative and comprehensible way by using a 3D model of the production plant as the base meta-visualization. The central environment for planning and controlling is a big multi-touch table which allows an intuitive and interactive access to the information (see Fig. 5). For each workplace detailed information can be retrieved, such as key performance indicators (KPI) or information about the machine status, work tasks, orders, stock or personnel. The mobile devices allow for a workplace independent visualization and interaction. In this system, the subjects of the context model from Fig. 2 are visualized by aggregating the information about *work tasks* (e.g. time schedule), *things* (e.g. parts in stock) and *people* (responsible personnel) and associating it to the corresponding work*place*. Accordingly, the displayed information is filtered primarily based on the selected *place* providing details of the related machine such as its status, KPI, or work tasks.

5   Conclusion and Future Work

In this paper, we presented an approach for a situation-based information delivery by integrating and visualizing heterogeneous information from different sources in one for the working environment familiar visual metaphor. We classified the data objects by their semantic context into people, things, places and work tasks and interlink them. For this purpose we used an ontology as the semantic knowledge base. Additional information is added by annotations. The contextualized information is then filtered according to the context of the work task and visualized intuitively using a familiar metaphor of the work environment. Here, a meta-visualization is used as an overview of the data in its spatial context in which we embed the information required for a specific work task. Our Plant@Hand solutions show how the application of big multi-touch tables and smaller displays support the information visualization from overview to detail.

The linked semantic knowledge base can enable proactive assistance and adaptive information visualization. By providing means to automatically identify a specific situation the user can be supplied with relevant information he did not know about and thus would not have searched for. While official manuals or other formalized information is ordinarily given for a work task, knowledge of colleagues is in most cases only inquired *after* encountering a problem (if at all). Early knowledge of challenges and their solutions obviates these problems. In this way, proactive assistance can increase the work processes. But as soon as there are too many information objects to similar topics, the filtering by the ontology concepts will most likely not be enough to prevent information overflow. Therefore, an additional ranking of the information is reasonable (e.g. by the expertise of the information composer and priority of information).

As manual formalization is inconvenient for users and easily neglected, due to the lack of motivation and time, a higher level of automation for context detection, annotating and linking of data is desirable. For instance, reliable activity recognition could enable an automatic documentation by annotations (e.g. tracking the steps of a work task). Further research should therefore take place in the area of automatic ontology evolution.

Acknowledgements. This research has been supported by the German Federal State of Mecklenburg-Western Pomerania and the European Social Fund under grant ESF/IV-BM-B35-0006/12.

References

1. Abowd, G.D., Dey, A.K.: Towards a better understanding of context and context-awareness. In: Gellersen, H.-W. (ed.) HUC 1999. LNCS, vol. 1707, p. 304. Springer, Heidelberg (1999). doi:10.1007/3-540-48157-5_29
2. Aehnelt, M., Schulz, H.-J., Urban, B.: Towards a contextualized visual analysis of heterogeneous manufacturing data. In: Bebis, G., Boyle, R., Parvin, B., Koracin, D., Li, B., Porikli, F., Zordan, V., Klosowski, J., Coquillart, S., Luo, X., Chen, M., Gotz, D. (eds.) ISVC 2013, Part II. LNCS, vol. 8034, pp. 76–85. Springer, Heidelberg (2013). doi:10.1007/978-3-642-41939-3_8
3. Cabanac, G., Chevalier, M., Chrisment, C., Julien, C.: Collective annotation: perspectives for information retrieval improvement. In: Procedings of the Large Scale Semantic Access to Content (Text, Image, Video, and Sound), pp. 529–548 (2007). dl.acm.org/citation.cfm?id=1931440
4. Ceglowski, M., Coburn, A., Cuadrado, J.: Semantic search of unstructured data using contextual network graphs. In: Preliminary white paper (2003)
5. Gruber, T.R.: A translation approach to portable ontology specifications. Knowl. Acquisition **5**(2), 199–220 (1993). doi:10.1006/knac.1993.1008
6. Kim, K.Y., Manley, D.G., Yang, H.: Ontology-based assembly design and information sharing for collaborative product development. Comput. Aided Des. **38**(12), 1233–1250 (2006). doi:10.1016/j.cad.2006.08.004
7. Klein, G., Ross, K.G., Moon, B.M., Klein, D.E., Hoffman, R.R., Hollnagel, E.: Macrocognition. IEEE Intell. Syst. **18**(3), 81–85 (2003). doi:10.1109/MIS.2003.1200735
8. Landesberger, T., Schreck, T., Fellner, D.W., Kohlhammer, J.: Visual search and analysis in complex information spaces–Approaches and research challenges. In: Dill, J., Earnshaw, R., Kasik, D., Vince, J., Wong, P.C. (eds.) Expanding the Frontiers of Visual Analytics and Visualization. LNCS, pp. 45–67. Springer, Heidelberg (2012). doi:10.1007/978-1-4471-2804-5_4
9. Lortal, G., Lewkowicz, M., Todirascu-Courtier, A.: Annotation: textual media for cooperation. In: Proceedings of the International Workshop on Annotation for Collaboration, pp. 41–50 (2005)
10. Schulz, H.J., Nocke, T., Heitzler, M., Schumann, H.: A design space of visualization tasks. IEEE Trans. Vis. Comput. Graph. **19**(12), 2366–2375 (2013). doi:10.1109/TVCG.2013.120
11. Streit, M., Schulz, H.J., Lex, A., Schmalstieg, D., Schumann, H.: Model-driven design for the visual analysis of heterogeneous data. IEEE Trans. Vis. Comput. Graph. **18**(6), 998–1010 (2012). doi:10.1109/TVCG.2011.108
12. Tshagharyan, G., Schulz, H.J.: A graph-based overview visualization for data landscapes. Comput. Sci. Inf. Technol. **1**(3), 225–232 (2013)

Evaluation of Data Display Methods in a Flash Flood Prediction Tool

Elizabeth M. Argyle[1]([⊠]), Chen Ling[2], and Jonathan J. Gourley[3]

[1] Cooperative Institute for Mesoscale Meteorological Studies,
Norman, OK, USA
emargyle@ou.edu
[2] University of Akron, Akron, OH, USA
cl99@uakron.edu
[3] National Severe Storms Laboratory/NOAA,
Norman, OK, USA
jj.gourley@noaa.gov

Abstract. Flash flooding can be difficult to predict using traditional, rainfall threshold-based approaches. New initiatives like the Flooded Locations and Simulated Hydrographs (FLASH) project provide real-time information using rainfall observations to force distributed hydrologic models to predict flash flooding events. However, in order to address the goal of creating a weather-ready nation, system designers must not only possess tools that relay useful information, but such tools must also be able to communicate environmental threats to stakeholders in a clear and easy-to-use interface. Where previous research has addressed the performance of forecasting models, the present study uses a human factors approach to enhance FLASH's ability to present information to decision-makers (i.e., forecasters).

Keywords: Flash flood · Decision Making · Forecasting

1 Introduction

The mission of the National Weather Service (NWS) is to "provide weather, water, and climate data, forecasts and warnings for the protection of life and property and enhancement of the national economy" [1]. One does not have to search very long or very hard in order to find examples of when forecasts have made a difference in public response to severe weather events. Events such as the May 20, 2013 tornado in Moore, Oklahoma or the September 2013 flash floods in Colorado show that timely forecasts can inform emergency managers, broadcasters, and the general public about weather-related risks.

Within the weather forecasting system, decisions must be made on many different scales. On a spatial scale, appropriate decisions may differ based on geographic region or between state or county borders. On a temporal scale, forecasters must synthesize information within strict deadlines each day; depending upon the role of the forecaster, forecasts may be for weather events in the very near term—i.e. 0–6 h forecasts, as in the case of severe weather—or in the longer term, such as for a

© Springer International Publishing Switzerland 2015
S. Yamamoto (Ed.): HIMI 2015, Part I, LNCS 9172, pp. 15–22, 2015.
DOI: 10.1007/978-3-319-20612-7_2

weekly forecast. In observations of forecasting operations, Morss and Ralph [2] found that lead time directly affected the weights that forecasters placed upon model guidance, model output statistics, radar observations, climatology, and personal background knowledge.

In addition, forecasters may apply events that match prototypes of weather phenomena more readily due to extensive training in class recognition [3]. Forecasters are trained to recognize "textbook" examples weather events, such as the synoptic patterns associated with tornado development [4]. This pattern matching technique is indicative of the representativeness heuristic, which can lead to errors if similar data sets are applied incorrectly to weather events. In a further example of this, Heinselman, LaDue, and Lazrus [5] found that a forecaster's prior experiences with a particular type of weather event affected the forecaster's ability to predict a similar weather event.

Another factor that may affect the forecaster's reasoning and judgment about the weather condition is the display method used in weather decision-making products. In this study, we explore how different display methods used for flash flood prediction affect judgments of the severity level of the event.

2   Flooded Locations and Simulated Hydrographs (Flash)

Many weather decision-making products exist to give forecasters information about potential weather-related threats. The Flooded Locations and Simulated Hydrographs (FLASH) project is one such product for flash flooding prediction. FLASH is a real-time system that uses rainfall observations to force hydrologic models to predict flash floods. Potential users would be forecasters at both the national and regional scales in the United States, including, but not limited to, National Weather Service Weather Forecast Offices, River Forecast Offices, and national centers. Both at the national and regional scale, FLASH is designed to assist national forecasters identify areas of risk and then work with local forecasters to predict specific threats.

In July 2013, the Hydrometeorological Testbed at the Weather Prediction Center (HMT-WPC) hosted the first Flash Flooding and Intense Rainfall (FFaIR) experiment [6]. The purpose of the experiment was to evaluate the utility of a set of experimental forecast models, including FLASH, on a sample of professional forecasters and weather researchers. Over the three-week period, forecasters assessed standard and experimental computational models to create probabilistic forecasts of heavy rainfall and flash flooding events in the United States. As part of the experiment, the researchers observed forecaster behavior when creating the forecasts and identified patterns of information processing. Through daily observations of three independently acting forecasters, the researchers observed that the design of the information display affected how well forecasters were able to interpret the data modeled in FLASH.

Of particular interest was a suggestion that FLASH's visual design led forecasters to predict false alarms. This comment was attributed to FLASH's sampling method and visualization design. Specifically, FLASH divides the continental United States into a 1 km-by-1 km grid. The model calculates a measure of flash flood risk, the return period, for every cell within the grid. However, when depicting the entire country, the system is not able to display each individual grid cell. The system developers solved this by developing an algorithm to sample the maximum grid cell value out of the collection of grid cells contained within one pixel, and the map of all the maximum values displays at the national level. In practice, this means that while the true predicted return period values are displayed when a viewer zooms in to a local level, the national view displays an adjusted value of the data by displaying the maximum value.

Forecaster comments from FFaIR led the researchers to hypothesize that a display algorithm which takes the average of sampled grid cells (henceforth called the average-based display) would produce different task performance than the maximum-based display. The present study seeks to identify differences in terms of error rate and task completion time when comparing two different display algorithms on the national-scale maps. It is hypothesized that the average method will produce fewer false alarms, but the maximum method will produce more hits. In terms of task completion time, it is hypothesized that the average display will take more time for participants to evaluate; it is thought that due to the color scheme and the larger size of represented regions, the design of the maximum-based display draws attention to events more rapidly than the average-based display would.

3   Method

3.1   Participants

A sample of 30 participants was recruited from the student and post-doctoral population at the University of Oklahoma. Participants were required to have a degree in meteorology or atmospheric science, or to be currently pursuing one. Though participants had little experience working with FLASH, this expectation ensured that they had adequate experience with reading weather prediction visualizations.

The sample consisted of 19 males and 11 females between the ages of 21–41 years old, with an average age of 25.0 years. Participants were randomly assigned to one of the between-subjects display conditions (the maximum-based algorithm or the average-based algorithm).

3.2   Materials

A set of 40 image pairs was created by taking screen captures of FLASH; each image pair consisted of one image of FLASH at a national, full-view level, and a second image of the same date and time, but zoomed in to a local, county- or state-level. It is important to note that while participants in the two display groups viewed different representations of the weather event at the national scale, the local images that participants viewed were identical between groups.

The dates and times were selected based on flash flooding events that were reported between April and July 2013 in the National Climatic Data Center Storm Events Database. When selecting the events from the database, the researcher categorized events into "severe" and "not severe" flash flooding. Unlike tornado events and the Fujita scale, there is not yet a standardized scale for flash flooding severity, so the research team defined severe flash flooding to be those that caused $500,000 or more of property and crop damage (n = 20, μ = $9.86 M; σ = $22.33 M). Events that were placed in the "not severe" category had less than $500,000 of property and crop damage (n = 20, μ = $38.75 K; σ = $84.59 K).

Images were randomly presented to participants using PsychoPy [7], an open-source software which allows researchers to present stimuli and collect data from participants. Each evaluation was conducted on an Asus A53U laptop with a 15-inch screen; each image was displayed at a size of 869 × 680 pixels.

3.3   Experimental Design

The between-subjects independent variable in the present study was the display algorithm which varied across two levels—the maximum-based display and the average-based display. Using a Signal Detection Theory framework [8], the error rates were calculated using a detection task. Though property damage was used as a measure of severity to select the image pairs, it was not an independent variable itself—within the study framework, participants had to detect which images represented severe events. Likewise, while participants viewed images at varied spatial scales, the local images were identical no matter which display algorithm each participant viewed at the national level.

3.4   Procedure

At the beginning of the study, participants were informed about the study's purpose and tasks. After completing an informed consent form, participants received an excerpt from the FLASH training manual that explained how to read and interpret the FLASH display. During the instruction stage, participants were given the opportunity to ask questions about FLASH, how to interpret the display, and what the study would involve.

Once participants stated that they felt comfortable with the FLASH interface, they answered a series of demographic questions (age, gender, and academic classification). Following this, a series of image pairs was presented in a randomized order. In each image pair, the first image showed an event in FLASH on the national-level (see Fig. 1A). Participants were asked, "Based on the information that is modeled in this image, would you expect for this event to produce flash flooding with severe levels of property damage? (> $500,000)." Participants reviewed the image, and then pressed "y" for yes or "n" for no after making their decision. The next image would be a representation of the same weather event, but the image would be zoomed in to a local scale (see Fig. 1C). The participants answered the same question about severity based on the new presentation of information. All forty image pairs were presented in a randomized order. When participants finished with the last pair, they were debriefed (Fig. 2).

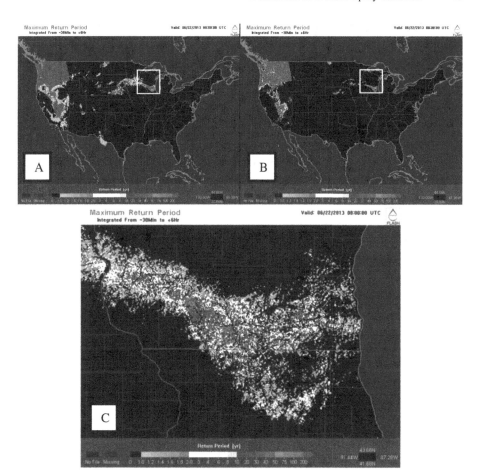

Fig. 1. Images showing the same severe hydrometeorological event, displayed at the national scale with the maximum-based display algorithm (A), the average-based display algorithm (B), and the local view associated with both (C).

4   Results

4.1   Error Rates

After collecting the participants' responses, an error rate in terms of the Signal Detection Theory framework [8] was calculated for the severity judgment associated with the average-based and maximum-based display styles and for the national and local images. The data were compared using t-tests. The results show that there is a significant difference between the display methods. A summary of the results is shown in Table 1. The maximum display produced a higher hit rate than the average display, but the average display minimizes false alarms.

Similarly, an analysis of participant judgments for the local-level images used the Signal Detection Framework. Though all subjects saw the same images in this

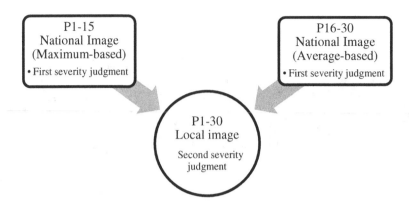

Fig. 2. Participants viewed pairs of national and local images of identical weather events. Half the participants viewed national images visualized with the maximum-based algorithm and the other half with the average-based algorithm.

Table 1. Comparison of average-based and maximum-based display types in terms error rates

	Hit rate	False alarm rate
Average-based	0.57	0.25
Maximum-based	0.85	0.50
p-value	<0.0001	<0.0001

Table 2. Error rates for viewing the local-level events (n = 30)

	Hit rate	Miss rate	Correct rejection rate	False alarm rate
Local	0.50	0.50	0.76	0.24

category, responses were compared between the maximum-based and the average-based participant groups in order to ensure parity. As expected, a t-test found no significant difference between how participants in either test group when judging the local-level images. Still, as shown in Table 2, participants did not make perfect judgments, which may in part be due to lack of participant experience with flash flood forecasting.

4.2 Task Completion Time

Task time was recorded from the time the national display was shown to the participant still they made a severity judgment on the national image. Though the original hypothesis was that the average display would produce slower response times than the maximum display, no significant difference was found between the two. A further analysis of task completion time for the time taken during hits, misses, false alarms, and correct rejections also failed to find any statistically significant differences. A summary of results is shown in Table 3.

Table 3 Average time (in seconds) taken to produce a hit, miss, correct rejection, or false alarm, analyzed with a t-test.

	Hit	Miss	Correct rejection	False alarm
Average-based	4.02	4.49	4.34	4.12
Maximum-based	4.63	5.23	5.81	5.45
p-value	0.58	0.81	0.12	0.57

5 Discussion and Conclusions

The results of this study show that there is a significant difference between display styles in terms of error rates, but not in terms of task completion time. Though the original hypothesis was that the average display would cause participants to review the image for a longer period of time, this in fact was not observed. When examining the images that participants commonly had trouble judging correctly, common causes of confusion occurred for events that had particularly different visual representations between the national and local level. For example, one event looked like a very small storm when visualized with the national-level average-based algorithm, but was actually very severe looking after zooming closer. Participants often judged the national image to be insignificant, but changed their minds after viewing the local level.

Design recommendations based on these results for future weather information displays must rely on the risk management values of the system designers. While the maximum display style maximized hits, it also produced many more false alarms than the average display. In weather forecasting, excess numbers of false alarms can consume valuable time that forecasters could be using to analyze true threats. However, while the average display style produced fewer false alarms, participants were much more likely to miss an event; this could also result in critical consequences.

In the case of a flash flooding prediction system such as FLASH, the recommendation from these results would be to use the maximum display algorithm. Flash flooding is by nature a rapidly occurring event that can have life-threatening consequences if not predicted with enough lead time. For such a system, having a design that promotes more hits, even at the expense of producing false alarms, would ensure that forecasters' attentions would be drawn to severe events in a timely manner.

In the future, more studies should examine the effects of a forecaster's first severity decision on the second severity decision; for example, understanding how the viewing the national map first affects how the forecaster interprets the local level information may shed light on other aspects of the forecaster's decision-making process. Additionally, future work could address limitations of the present study; namely, while participants all had some background in meteorology and forecasting, few had specifically studied flash flood forecasting. A similar study to the present work, but run with a sample of professional flood forecasters may produce new and valuable information.

References

1. National Weather Service Strategic Plan. http://www.nws.noaa.gov/com/stratplan/files/plan_v01.pdf
2. Morss, R.E., Ralph, F.M.: Use of information by national weather service forecasters and emergency managers during CALJET and PACJET-2001. Weather Forecast. **22**, 539–555 (2007)
3. Doswell III, C.A.: Weather forecasting by humans—heuristics and decision making. Weather Forecast. **19**, 1115–1126 (2004)
4. Johns, R.H., Doswell III, C.A.: Severe local storms forecasting. Weather Forecast. **7**, 588–612 (1992)
5. Heinselman, P.L., LaDue, D.S., Lazrus, H.: Exploring impacts of rapid-scan radar data on nws warning decisions. Weather Forecast. **27**, 1031–1044 (2012)
6. Barthold, F.E., Workoff, T.E., Cosgrove, B.A., Gourley, J.J., Novak, D.R., Mahoney, K.M.: improving flash flood forecasts: The HMT-WPC flash flood and intense rainfall experiment. Bull. Am. Meteorol. Soc. e-View (2015). http://dx.doi.org/10.1175/BAMS-D-14-00201.1
7. Peirce, J.W.: PsychoPy - psychophysics software in python. J. Neurosci. Meth. **162**, 8–13 (2007)
8. Wickens, T.D.: Elementary Signal Detection Theory. Oxford University Press, Oxford (2001)

Modernizing Exploration and Navigation in Enterprise Systems with Interactive Visualizations

Tamara Babaian$^{(\boxtimes)}$, Wendy Lucas, and Mengru Li

Bentley University, Waltham, MA, USA
{tbabaian, wlucas, l2_meng}@bentley.edu

Abstract. Enterprise Resource Planning (ERP) systems empower employees with access to vast amounts of data from across the organization. Learning how to navigate an enterprise system and explore the data within, however, can require herculean effort. Despite the efficacy of visualizations for enhancing knowledge discovery and exploration, they have yet to be applied to assisting users of ERP systems. In this paper, we present two visualization components designed specifically for those users. The first provides an easy-to-use search interface for visualizing relationships between data entities, while the second supports navigation via an interactive map. Both have been implemented in a prototype for validation in future studies.

Keywords: Interactive visualizations · Dynamic visualizations · Enterprise systems · ERP

1 Introduction

Contemporary visualization tools and techniques have been widely applied to visualizing data in various contexts. One domain in which they have not yet found broad applicability, however, is in Enterprise Resource Planning (ERP) systems, which integrate and manage data and processes from across the organization. While process visualizations have been applied to the off-line management of business workflows [14] and to navigating process repositories [5], they have not been integrated into leading ERP systems for assisting users of their notoriously difficult-to-use interfaces. The acknowledged usability issues users experience are in no small part due to the limited views provided of the underlying data and relationships, the overly complex menus used for navigation, and the lack of transparency concerning the processes being supported [1, 6, 7].

The primary contribution of the research presented here is in providing alternative means by which users can explore and navigate the transaction- and process-related data and relationships underlying ERP systems, which is typically presented to the user in the form of tables and lists. As noted by Shneiderman [2], effective visualizations contribute to the users' understanding of their data and support the discovery of relationships that would otherwise be difficult to perceive. These findings were recently

© Springer International Publishing Switzerland 2015
S. Yamamoto (Ed.): HIMI 2015, Part I, LNCS 9172, pp. 23–33, 2015.
DOI: 10.1007/978-3-319-20612-7_3

confirmed in studies specifically addressing ERP systems and tasks [6, 7, 9]. Our goal is to bring these benefits to enterprise system users by modernizing ERP interfaces with interactive visualizations.

In this paper, we present two types of visualization components for enterprise systems. These two visualizations address two different problems that users often experience: identifying data items related via complex many-to-many relationships and locating the correct functionality within the system. The first component, called an Association Map (AM), highlights associative relationships between the entities used in performing business transactions. Users are able to explore these relationships and perform selections of relevant data elements. The second component provides a novel means for task navigation via an interactive graph called a Dynamic Task Map (DTM). DTM is based on the transaction records derived from an SAP ERP system. It visualizes several measures that reflect aggregate user activity, thus depicting common usage patterns. Each of these components was implemented in D3 (see http://d3js.org). The utility and effectiveness of the developed approaches will need to be validated with user studies, which are planned for the future.

2   Related Work

The difficulties that ERP system users face in operating these complex data-based systems have been investigated and documented by several researchers. Topi and colleagues [13] first reported on a field study that included in-depth interviews of 10 users of a major commercial ERP system. Usability issues discovered from the analysis of the reported user experiences with the system were categorized according to a framework based on the system-user collaboration paradigm of human-computer interaction. These categories included identification of and access to the correct functionality, transaction execution support, system output limitations, support in error situations, terminology problems, and overall system complexity. Several of these problem classes have been confirmed later by different researchers using a variety of methodologies and examining a wider range of ERP systems [10, 11, 7]. Most recently, Lambeck and colleagues [7] conducted a survey of 184 users of different experience levels using a variety of ERP systems and confirmed that many of the identified problems still persist. Particularly relevant to the work presented here, this survey revealed that the "ability to locate desired enterprise functionality remains a general usability problem across different levels of experience" and that the "availability of useful visualizations improves perception of complexity" reported by the users.

There are fewer studies that attempt to create visualizations and other types of design interventions and investigate their efficacy in making ERP systems more usable [2, 4, 8]. In particular, Parush et al. [9] have performed an experiment with 85 users in which they compared user performance of ERP tasks of varying complexity in two different environments. In the first environment, system data was presented in a typical, tabular form, and in the second, the data was presented using visualizations. Two different types of visual displays were used for two different purposes: a Radial Hyperbolic Tree for depicting hierarchical data, and a Treemap showing quantitative data as bars for easy visual comparison. The findings of the experiment were that visualizations had a positive impact on the completion time for all task difficulty levels, with a greater impact on the more complex types of problems. Novice users benefitted more from the visual approach in this study, although in the aforementioned survey-based study by Lambeck and colleagues [7], the importance of visualizations was ranked similarly by novice and experienced users.

The same survey [7] also examined users' perceptions of navigational tools within ERPs. It revealed that users prefer in-context menus, i.e., those that provide access to a subset of tasks closely related to the currently performed task, to the tree-like ones, which present the overall task hierarchy regardless of the task in which the user is currently engaged.

A different stream of research, focused on business process mining [14, 15] and process visualization languages [3, 5], is also related to the problems of guiding the users through the "maze" of ERP screens. Process mining is concerned with identifying common paths through the system as manifested by users. Researchers have proposed using information on the commonly occurring task sequences discovered via mining to aid the users in selecting the next task, thus reducing navigational complexity by using a visual representation of business processes and common task transitions. The problem is exacerbated by the fact that business processes and, correspondingly, the visual languages used to represent them, are very complex, since they include a lot of details. Detailed information is needed to capture a variety of scenarios, yet an individual user typically needs to be aware of only a subset of the details surrounding the tasks he/she performs.

Creating a visual representation that can be quickly adapted to the required level of detail and is well suited to a user in a particular role [3] is the subject of ongoing research. Furthermore, Hipp et al. [6] describe Compass - a software system that allows navigation in a collection of process models and corresponding external information. In an experimental user study, subjects using a version of the system enhanced with a variety of dynamic, interactive, multidimensional visualizations reacted positively to it, showed a slightly better performance in terms of time, and made significantly fewer mistakes than those who used a similar system without the added visualizations.

There is a growing body of research that suggests the need for developing visualizations for complex data and navigational tasks within enterprise systems. We explore such visualizations in the remainder of this paper.

3   Visual Explorations of Master Data and Transactions

In this section, we present two visualization components developed for assisting users of ERP systems. We first describe the Association Map (AM) component, which offers various visualizations for discovering the relationships between associated data elements. The second component, the Dynamic Task Map (DTM), provides a novel means for supporting system navigation by providing interactive visualizations of the transactions performed by the system's users.

3.1 Association Map (AM)

The database at the heart of an ERP system stores vast amounts of data from across the enterprise. Knowledgeable users with sufficient expertise can pull the relevant information related to any transaction performed by the system. The learning curve for gaining that expertise is a very steep one, however, and even the most experienced users need to refresh themselves on the steps to take for performing tasks and running reports they don't access on a regular basis. Most users will only learn the small portion of the system that relates to their everyday tasks. Training focuses on step-by-step instructions concerning which transactions to access and what data to enter. The higher-level understanding of how tasks and data elements are related is often lost in the minutiae.

The Association Map (AM) visualizations presented here provide any user with a simple means for exploring the relationships between data elements. They offer a view of the data that is not readily evident from detailed reports and support the analysis and interpretation of the underlying, detailed data. An example of such data is shown in Fig. 1, which provides a view of purchasing documents for a particular vendor in an SAP ERP system. A vendor can supply one or more types of material that are maintained by one or more plants, and each material can be supplied by one or more vendors. From the report shown here, it is possible to pull out the materials supplied by a specified vendor and the plants that maintain them (the first two records in this report show that Vendor 101000 supplies Off Road Helmets and Road Helmets that are maintained in plant N00). Aggregating this data into a higher-level format highlighting all materials supplied by a particular vendor and maintained in a particular plant would typically involve a third party tool, such as a spreadsheet, or the creation of a customized report.

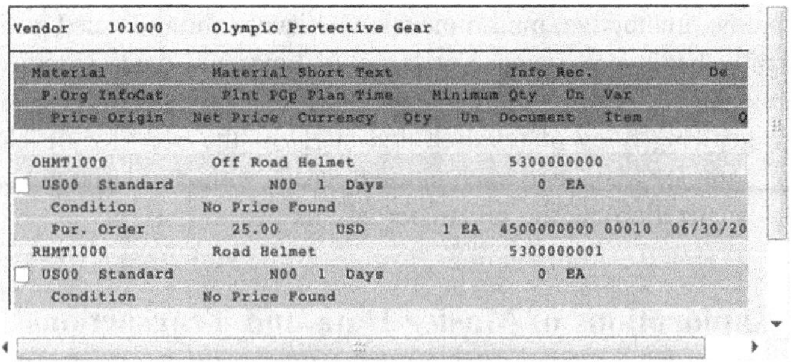

Fig. 1. SAP purchasing information records by vendor

The visualizations shown in Fig. 2 provide intuitive means for users to explore these types of higher-level relationships. While the related entities shown here are the plants, materials, and vendors used in the purchasing process, any entities in a many-to-many relationship could be visualized in the same ways.

Figure 2 shows the search interface. This visualization extends the D3 Concept Map (see http://www.findtheconversation.com/concept-map) by allowing the user to specify up to three search parameters. The light gray lines show all of the connections that exist in the data between the three entities.

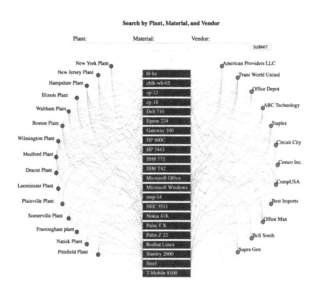

Fig. 2. Search interface for finding relationships between plants, materials, and vendors.

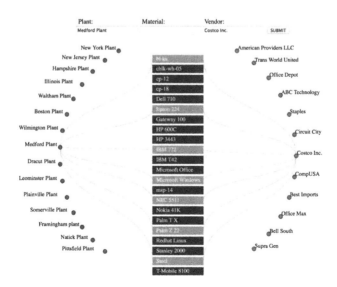

Fig. 3. Search by specific plant and vendor.

Figure 3 shows the results of a search in which the user has specified a plant and a vendor as search parameters. From this view, the user can easily see all of the materials maintained in the specified plant that have been supplied by the specified vendor.

This information can be helpful to a plant manager, for example, in analyzing vendor relationships.

Fig. 4. Selection of material from map

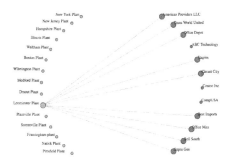

Fig. 5. Selection of plant from map

In Fig. 4, the user has clicked on a particular material in order to see all the vendors that supply that material and the plants where it is being maintained. This information is useful for a manager who is looking to consolidate inventory in fewer places or to find another plant that may be able to supply a particular material without having to order more from the vendor.

Figure 5 shows the visualization resulting from the user clicking on a particular plant, which reveals all of the vendors used by that plant. Similarly, the user could click on a vendor to show all of the plants with inventory supplied by that vendor. Both views support analysis of plant-vendor relations.

The information contained in all of these visualizations is available from ERP systems but, as noted above, it is likely to be presented in tables or reports with a degree of granularity similar to that shown in Fig. 1. While not part of the current implementation, the AM visualization component could be extended to allow the user to drill down from the higher level views shown in Fig. 2 to the detailed reporting data in Fig. 1.

3.2 Dynamic Task Map (DTM)

One of the difficulties most widely reported by enterprise system users concerns navigating to the desired task (a.k.a. transaction) interface. In addition, users, especially those new to the interface, often have trouble figuring out the next step; that is, what follows the task that they are performing. These difficulties stem from the sheer number of different functions implemented within an enterprise system and a general lack of guidance regarding the subset and sequence of transactions that form a specific business process.

The principal navigational tool in ERP systems is typically a menu structure. In addition to context-specific menus within each task interface, there is one main, all-encompassing expandable menu, which is displayed upon logging in and to which the user returns upon completion of a task to select the next one. Figures 6 and 7 present two views of the SAP main menu, which is called the Easy Access Menu. Figure 6 shows the full menu in its most compact, unexpanded form. Figure 7 shows the same menu with the Accounting branch partly expanded for accessing a specific task interface, such as Customer Sales. If the entire menu were to be expanded, it would take at least tens of pages to display. The nodes of the menu leading to a particular transaction can be up to seven levels deep in the hierarchy and are occasionally duplicated under different branches. The grouping of the transactions within menu branches is not always intuitive, even for expert users. It is not surprising that ordinary users experience difficulties and feel lost while looking for the right transaction using the menu, often giving up their search and turning to a colleague or to their notes for help [1, 13]. Users typically eventually learn to navigate to their most common transactions via an alphanumeric code, which they memorize or keep close by. Reliance on transaction codes, however, hinders users' independent exploration of the vast and powerful resources that the ERP system offers. The problem is exacerbated by the poor inter-task navigation options: when within a task interface, it is often difficult to locate the way to open a related task, such as when creating a new user account and needing to access an interface for testing it.

The SAP menu presented here is typical for the major vendors of ERP software. The menu structure can be configured to include a selection of favorite tasks and exclude entire categories for a specific user profile. Personalizing the menu mitigates navigation problems for some users; however, it does not alleviate them for those users who work with a relatively large set of ERP components. Nor does it help users in finding potentially useful parts of the system with which they are not familiar.

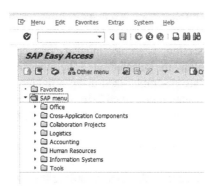

Fig. 6. SAP Easy Access Menu in its most collapsed form

Fig. 7. SAP Menu expanded for selecting a Customer Sales transaction

Researchers have applied process mining and process modeling approaches that we reviewed earlier to discover and visualize the task chains that comprise business processes performed within a specific organization. While these approaches can be used to guide users, they do not solve the problem of navigation entirely, since even when the users know what they should do next, it is still difficult to find how to navigate to the specific transaction unless the code is known.

We have developed a prototype of an alternative navigational tool called Dynamic Task Map (DTM). DTM depicts ERP tasks as a set of circular nodes, each labeled with its task name (Fig. 8). The DTM is composed from the task usage history, which is documented in the ERP system log. The size of each task circle is proportional to the task's frequency of use. Tasks that were performed by a user close together in time are positioned closer together.

The graph changes when a user selects a transaction, as shown in Fig. 9. The visualization automatically zooms onto the selected task, which is shown with a larger title. The selected task and those transactions that commonly co-occur or follow it are linked together and highlighted in a shade of red, thus helping the user identify and navigate to a related transaction. The color intensity of a connected transaction indicates how likely it is to follow the selected one. The other transaction nodes and their labels are still visible but are de-emphasized using a lighter shade of blue.

The prototype implementation presented here, while based on real ERP usage data, does not provide access to the respective task interfaces within an ERP system. If built into a system, it could be used as a navigational tool. Currently, the prototype does not group task nodes according to any relationship other than co-occurrence with the selected task, but different types of groupings can be added to further enhance the map and provide additional guidance to the user regarding the available transactions.

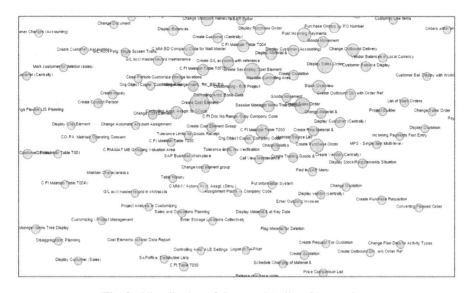

Fig. 8. Visualization of the complete list of transactions

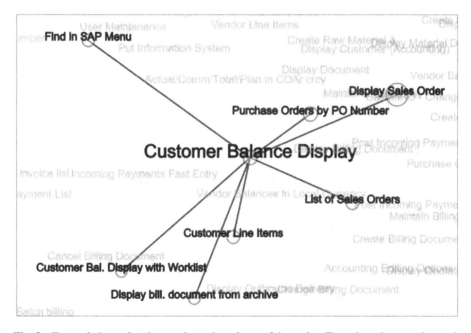

Fig. 9. Zoomed view, after the user has selected one of the nodes. The selected transaction node is shown with a larger title. The color of the connecting circle indicates the likelihood of transition to that transaction based on the past usage history.

4 Conclusions

In this paper, we have demonstrated the applicability of dynamic, interactive visualizations to guiding users in the ERP domain. These visualizations, which we have implemented using D3, address some of the difficulties users of these complex systems encounter, including insufficient means for data exploration, inadequate support for higher-level analysis, unwieldy menu structures that hinder navigation, and the lack of transparency concerning relationships between tasks.

The greatest limitation of the implementation we reported on here is that it is based on a relatively small data set compared to a significantly larger one that would be found in many organizations. However, just like with commonly used reports and tables, filtering and selection techniques that limit the set of items to a size that is relevant yet observable can be applied to visual representations. Furthermore, querying tools can be added to a visualization itself to focus on the data of interest and also display item details that are not shown in the high-level visualizations presented here.

The next step in this work will be to investigate the usefulness of our proposed visualizations with ERP system users. Findings will be applied to fine-tuning the AM and DTM components. User studies will also provide the opportunity to determine the optimal placement of these components within existing enterprise system interfaces for making them easily and obviously accessible to users.

References

1. Babaian, T., Lucas, W., Xu, J., Topi, H.: Usability through system-user collaboration. In: Winter, R., Zhao, J.L., Aier, S. (eds.) DESRIST 2010. LNCS, vol. 6105, pp. 394–409. Springer, Heidelberg (2010)
2. Babaian, T., Lucas, W.: Composing interface demonstrations automatically from usage logs. In: Cordeiro, J., Maciaszek, L.A., Filipe, J. (eds.) ICEIS 2012. LNBIP, vol. 141, pp. 376–392. Springer, Heidelberg (2013)
3. Bobrik, R., Reichert, M., Bauer, T.: View-based process visualization. In: Alonso, G., Dadam, P., Rosemann, M. (eds.) BPM 2007. LNCS, vol. 7447, pp. 88–95. Springer, Heidelberg (2007)
4. Goldberg, J.H., Helfman, J.I.: Enterprise network monitoring using treemaps. In: Proceedings of the Human Factors and Ergonomics Society Annual Meeting, vol. 49, no. 5, pp. 671–675. SAGE Publications (2005)
5. Hipp, M., Mutschler, B., Reichert, M.: Navigating in complex business processes. In: Liddle, S.W., Schewe, K.-D., Tjoa, A.M., Zhou, X. (eds.) DEXA 2012. LNCS, vol. 7447, pp. 464–480. Springer, Heidelberg (2012)
6. Lambeck, C., Fohrholtz, C., Leyh, C., Šupulniece, I., Müller, R.: Commonalities and contrasts: an investigation of ERP usability in a comparative user study. In: Proceedings of ECIS (2014)
7. Lambeck, C., Muller, R., Fohrholz, C., Leyh, C.: (Re-) evaluating user interface aspects in ERP systems–an empirical user study. In: Proceedings of the 47th Hawaii International Conference on System Sciences (HICSS), pp. 396–405. IEEE (2014)

8. Lucas, W., Xu, J., Babaian, T.: Visualizing ERP usage logs in real time. In: Proceedings of the 14th International Conference on Enterprise Information Systems (ICEIS 2013), pp. 83–90 (2013)

9. Parush, A., Hod, A., Shtub, A.: Impact of visualization type and contextual factors on performance with enterprise resource planning systems. Comput. Ind. Eng. **52**(1), 133–142 (2007)

10. Scholtz, B., Cilliers, C., Calitz, A.: Qualitative techniques for evaluating enterprise resource planning (ERP) user interfaces. In: Proceedings of the 2010 Annual Research Conference of the South African Institute of Computer Scientists and Information Technologists, pp. 284–293. ACM (2010)

11. Singh, A.: Designing adaptive user interfaces for enterprise resource planning systems for small enterprises. Doctoral dissertation, Nelson Mandela Metropolitan University (2011)

12. Shneiderman, B.: Creativity support tools: accelerating discovery and innovation. Commun. ACM **50**(12), 20–32 (2007)

13. Topi, H., Lucas, W., Babaian, T.: Identifying usability issues with an ERP implementation. In: Proceedings of the International Conference on Enterprise Information Systems (ICEIS-2005), pp. 128–133 (2005)

14. van der Aalst, W.M.P.: Process Mining: Discovery, Conformance, and Enhancement of Business Processes. Springer, Heidelberg (2011)

15. van der Aalst, W., et al.: Process mining manifesto. In: Daniel, F., Barkaoui, K., Dustdar, S. (eds.) BPM Workshops 2011, Part I. LNBIP, vol. 99, pp. 169–194. Springer, Heidelberg (2012)

Explorative Visualization of Impact Analysis for Policy Modeling by Bonding Open Government and Simulation Data

Dirk Burkhardt[1,2(✉)], Kawa Nazemi[1,2], Egils Ginters[3],
Artis Aizstrauts[3], and Jörn Kohlhammer[1]

[1] Fraunhofer Institute for Computer Graphics Research (IGD),
Darmstadt, Germany
{dirk.burkhardt,kawa.nazemi,
joern.kohlhammer}@igd.fraunhofer.de
[2] Department of Computer Science, TU Darmstadt, Darmstadt, Germany
[3] Sociotechnical Systems Engineering Institute,
Vidzeme University of Applied Sciences, Valmiera, Latvia
{egils.ginters,artis.aizstrauts}@va.lv

Abstract. Problem identification and solution finding are major challenges in policy modeling. Statistical indicator-data build the foundation for most of the required analysis work. In particular finding effective and efficient policies that solve an existing political problem is critical, since the forecast validation of the effectiveness is quite difficult. Simulation technologies can help to identify optimal policies for solutions, but nowadays many of such simulators are stand-alone technologies. In this paper we introduce a new visualization approach to enable the coupling of statistical indicator data from Open Government Data sources with simulators and especially simulation result data with the goal to provide an enhanced impact analysis for political analysts and decision makers. This allows, amongst others a more intuitive and effective way of solution finding.

Keywords: Information visualization · Visual analysis · Impact analysis · Simulation · Open Government Data · Policy modeling · Decision making

1 Introduction

One main factor for decision making in the domain of political policy modeling are data. The less data are available, the more challenging is the identification of the problem and therewith the solution finding. Currently most problems are identified based on statistical data, which are often called "indicator data", since data about a certain issue is measured all the time. Commonly a selected number of indicators are of special interest for decision makers. These indicators are called "key performance indicators" (KPI). Their changes are seriously observed and analyzed to identify expected or even not expected impacts. If a problem is identified, the analysis starts to retrieve the reasons for the underlying problem. Policy options are then worked out that aim to solve the identified problem.

© Springer International Publishing Switzerland 2015
S. Yamamoto (Ed.): HIMI 2015, Part I, LNCS 9172, pp. 34–45, 2015.
DOI: 10.1007/978-3-319-20612-7_4

In particular this solution finding is a challenging task in the policy modeling process, thus it is difficult to predict the most effective policy option for a certain problem. Obviously, decision makers and also analysts have a foundational and sufficient knowledge and expertise, but the problem context can be quite complex and solution finding can be complex and difficult too. This is due to the fact that multiple actions and repeated tasks are required for the decision making and problem solving process. A support for decision makers is the involvement of experts with the special expertise, but the involvement of experts can be cost intensive. An alternative technology is simulation, which allows simulating the impacts of possible policy options [1, 2]. The quality of such a simulator can be good enough, as far as the defined simulation model is well designed.

There exist already a number of simulators and also well-defined models for a variety of scenarios. Unfortunately most of these simulators are standalone software solutions and commonly not well integrated in the policy making lifecycle and in the analysis environment of the stakeholders. This increases the barrier to consider them within the analysis work with statistical indicator visualization solutions, due to their usage complexity.

We introduce in this paper an approach that combines visualization of statistical indicator data with the visualization of simulation data to provide an enhanced impact analysis. Therefore, we first introduce the general aspects and requirements of policy modeling and the policy making process, followed by an introduction of the usage of statistics in form of indicator statistics and simulation in policy modelling. Here, we also explain the benefits of Open Government Data bases, e.g. EuroStat that allows also the broader audience to perform analysis based on real political indicator data. Based on this reflection, we describe our main contribution, an approach to bond the indicator statistic visualizations with the simulation and in particular the simulation result visualizations to provide an enhanced impact analysis for analysts and decision makers. The concept is applied practically by bonding the statistic visualization based the EuroStat's data and the simulator system, which allows to simulate and generate results for a number of topics. The major benefit of this bonding approach is the explorative character in the elaboration of solution options where both, the statistics as is and the expected impact of a policy option can be shown and visualized simultaneously. This may lead to a more effective and efficient policy making, especially for local governments in municipalities, which do not have the budget to involve specific domain experts for almost all kinds of requisite policy decisions.

2 Analysis and Simulation in the Policy Modeling Lifecycle

The policy modeling lifecycle is an abstract term, which summarizes all necessary steps for a successful policy creation. The analysis phase becomes more important with the upcoming integration of ICT that allows in particular an interaction in graphical user-interfaces and is therefore easier to use. Likewise the visualization of political data benefit from the graphical representation, because complex aspect can be identified easier in visual charts than in large data tables. The inclusion of simulation in the policy domain is a relatively new approach, which allows predicting the impact and usage of policies based on mathematical models [25].

2.1 Policies and Policy Modeling Processes

The term policy is defined as "a theoretical or technical instrument that is formulated to solve specific problems affecting, directly or indirectly, societies across different periods of times and geographical spaces" [3]. In public and political context it can result in a new or changed law. In perspective of the creation of policies, policy modeling can be defined as "an academic or empirical research work, that is supported by the use of different theories as well as quantitative or qualitative models and techniques, to analytically evaluate the past (causes) and future (effects) of any policy on society, anywhere and anytime" [3]. So the major focus lays on the policy and the causes and effects on the society. The creation of policies consists of a number of tasks and involves a variety of stakeholders. To bring them in an efficient and effective order, policy modeling can be understood as a process, where it is defined what actor has what task at what certain time. This arrangement of task and stakeholders in relation to the development of policies is commonly named as policy modeling process.

The work in public authorities is majorly defined by concrete (administrative) processes. This should ensure an efficient and effective work. Conventional processes as they are defined in existing works [4–6, 28], are using ICT and new technologies in a more conservative manner. Modern processes with focus on the general alignment of ICT using majorly an abstract policy-making process, e.g. [7, 8, 28]. Most of these process definitions include a gap in bringing together the detailed policy definition and inclusion of ICT within the policy making process. This gap and thereby the solution is addressed in a couple of research projects, among others, in the European research project ePolicy (http://epolicy-project.eu) and FUPOL (http://fupol.eu). In FUPOL there already exists a detailed policy process definition [9, 10]. To each process step a number of ICT features are aligned. The process orients on conventional process definitions and were just enhanced for the inclusion of ICT, which should enable an easier installment in public authorities.

2.2 The Analysis Phase

Policy analysis can be defined according to Weimer and Vining [11, 12] as "policy analysis is client-oriented advice relevant to public decisions and informed by social values." There exist also other definitions that are similar to Weimer and Vinning, e.g. the definition by Gormley [13] or Meltsner [14]. The major goal of the analysis phase in the policy modeling life-cycle is the gathering of an understanding about an existing issue and the identification of possible solutions. The analysis is one of the most significant steps in the policy making where solution options are defined for the followed decision making.

Today established solution finding strategies in public authorities majorly focus on objective data, which are in most cases statistical indicator data. However, also modern

ICT features are going to be established in policy making, for instance the use of social media analysis. In contrast to objective (valid) data, social media data are subjective data, which represent only e.g. certain citizens' opinions. On the other hand these formulated opinions comprise alternative problems and solutions. Overall, the question in the analysis phase is not what kind of data is used; the question is what data is useful to identify the problem, the reason and what can be the best solution.

2.3   Open Government Data and Simulation Data

In most public authorities, the use of statistical indicator data is the common way to identify political problems. To provide an improved transparency, many governmental entities on national or communal level have initiated Open Government Data (sometimes also shortened as Open Data) initiatives where they provide the existing statistical indicator data to the public. Von Lucke [15] defines Open Government Data as open available data sets, which are of interest for public authorities and citizens without any limitation in its free use, redistribution and further use, and which are made available for free (Open-Access). The Open Knowledge Foundation mentions as a general requirement the provision of such data for free – also for commercial usage, and provides them in an open format, e.g. in CSV [16]. For this purpose the data needs to be open-accessible through a portal where the indicators are available in a simple statistical format, such as CSV, or in another open standardized format, such as SDMX (see [17, 18]). Some portals also provide basic visualization techniques to present the data in a graphical form too.

The creation of effective policies depends not only on the included data that is analyzed. It also depends on how identified solution options will be validated and "tested" before they will be ratified and applied. Normally decision-makers judging about the best option based on their experience. In particular local authorities in cities performing decisions based on experiences, especially because it would be too cost intensive to involve experts for each (also simple) problem. Only in complex topics they involve expertise and experts from the corresponding domain or they involve simulation techniques to determine the optimal (empirical) solution option.

The inclusion of simulation, based on mathematical models, allows testing the impact of a solution option under defined conditions as foresight. This does not guarantee any success of a new policy, since the simulation is only a mathematical prediction based on a mathematical model that covers only a limited number of conditions from the reality. However, the simulation is often a useful feature to avoid most useless or too ineffective policies, if the simulator is well designed and the used mathematical model is appropriate for the applied scenario.

Today a variety of simulators for different topics are available. Most of them are only available as very specific solution and using therefore a macro level model. These models are oftentimes precise, but they require high effort to define the conditions for the model. Complementary to these macro level simulators there is another group of simulator, the general simulators, which using a very basically mathematical model to calculate the forecast. These general models cover only the past indicator developments and a small number of dependencies to other indicators. The precision is often not that precise as macro level simulators, but these general models can be easily applied to other topics and used as very flexible impact analysis tools. The major benefit is their easy applicability to many other topics with less effort. However, the available simulators do rarely make use of involving Open Government Data in simulators, which would make it easier for analyst and decision makers to analyze a problem. A better inclusion of Open Government Data sources in simulators would allow a much easier simulation process, since the most actual date will be automatically included for the simulation purpose. In fact, simulation could be better involved for most of decision making processes so that it becomes more or less common to simulate first, before decisions were made.

3   Concept for Explorative Impact Analysis Visualizations

In the following part, we describe our approach of bonding the Open Government Data visualizations with the simulation data visualizations to enable an advanced explorative analysis.

3.1   Open Government Data as Major Data Foundation

The design of a statistics visualization dashboard that should include various types of static visualizations, consisting of two-, three, and multidimensional visualizations, needs to introduce the complexity to gather information from the data. Hereby we have to deal with existing Open Government Data portals and how this data can be used in these two- to multidimensional visualizations.

Existing Open Government Data portals, e.g. EuroStat, DEstatis, Data.gov and Da-ta.gov.uk, mostly structure the data into hierarchies of topics. For each topic a couple of so-called indicators are aligned. Furthermore, each indicator is defined by [26]:

- The name of the indicator, e.g. GDP, public growth, or public density.
- An assignment to a geographical region, i.e. a country, state/province, municipality, or city.
- A time-based data table, which consist of the indicator value by the measured time.
- Optional additional meta-information about the indicator, such as a description of influencing indicators or the used unit.

The introduced structure enables to model the given data in a technical manner by considering also their multidimensional characteristics for designing adequate statistics visualizations. Additionally, the data model needs to support interactive approaches, such as the option to link visualizations and to allow a further exploration of the data.

To allow an effective analysis, the personal orchestration of different visualizations is a beneficial approach. We entitle this visualization orchestration ability "cockpit" as described in our previous works [24, 26]. In general, the terms "cockpit" and "dashboard" [22, 23] are synonymously used, but we prefer the term cockpit, which focuses more on an active use in a very complex environment. For this purpose, the cockpit

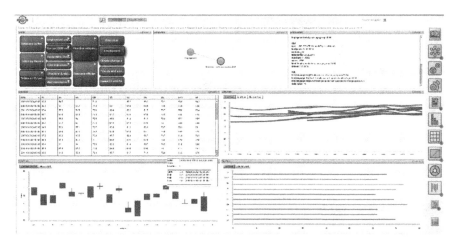

Fig. 1. Visualization of Open Government Data – here an indicator from EuroStat is shown

provides a higher degree of interaction and opportunities to orchestrate a personalized cockpit so that a given task can be solved more efficient (Fig. 1).

As a general design we consider a list of data sources, i.e. EuroStat and some local country and municipality data. The user can switch between these data sources. Next to the database options, the user can also search for one or more indicators that should be visualized. The user can compose his preferred cockpit by a number of available visualizations (simple chart visualization, as well as complex visualizations like Parallel Coordinates), which he can select and deselect. Any visualization can be configured in detail, e.g. decoupling the visualization for a comparative view. In order to focus on the most relevant visualization, the user can also resize the visualizations as needed.

3.2 The Simulator and the Simulation Data

The uses of simulators allow generating a forecast based on mathematical models [19–21, 25]. In perspective of policy modeling simulation is an effective method to test policy options before they will ratified and implemented to ensure its effectiveness (as far as possible with mathematical and therefore theoretical models). The challenge in visualizing simulations depends on its various parts that need to be combined. On the one hand we have the (mathematical) model that represents the simulation scenario based on the real world behavior. Based on this model a simulator must be used that allows generating the forecast based on given initial data and parameters. On the other hand we have the analyst and decision makers as users of these systems. To allow an interpretation of the performed simulation, visualizations are required that allow an intuitive and interactive exploration of the simulation results.

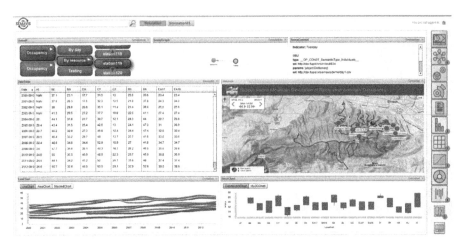

Fig. 2. Visualization of the Vodno Mountain Simulator [21]

From an abstract point of view the challenge of visualizing simulation is similar to default statistical indicator data. Therefore, similar approaches as also used for e.g. Open Government Data are appropriate. Also for this kind of data an explorative visualization based on a dashboard approach is beneficial (see Fig. 2).

In regards of simulation it is important to consider the best fitting kind of simulator. For the simulation of certain aspect a macro level simulator is used, which considers a number of relevant dependencies and influencing factors (Fig. 2 shows the visualization of macro-level simulation results). Such simulators are commonly very precise, but the definition of the models of such a simulator is difficult. Even more, such macro level simulators are only appropriate for the designed simulation scenario. In our approach we consider -in general- both kinds of simulators. For both kinds of simulators the inclusion of Open Government Data is useful, since the retrieval of the context is either beneficial.

3.3 Explorative Analysis and Impact Analysis Visualizations

The major aspect of our concept is the merging of Open Government Data visualization and simulation data visualization (Fig. 3). Especially through the inclusion of concrete indicator data coming from an Open Government Data source for the next simulation phase. Overall we can classify the benefits based on the different stages during policy modelling:

1. At the beginning of the policy modeling process, during the agenda setting, this merge supports to discover problems more precisely. During agenda setting phase decision makers aim to find problems based on negative indicator changes, e.g. the employment rate breaks down. Through the integration of simulation, it can be checked if this has major impacts also for the next time period, or if it is just a small incident around the normal trend.

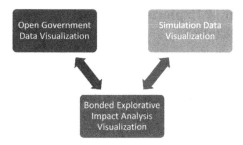

Fig. 3. The abstracted concept for the explorative impact analysis visualization that bonds the Open Government Data visualization with the simulation data visualizations.

2. During the analysis phase (where it is known that an indicator change is getting to be a problem) it can help to understand the context, why this is getting a problem. Even more it supports to allow testing of policy options based on parameter changes or testing of policies that aim to affect related/depending indicators, which in turn will solve the original problem and indicator.
3. During decision making, these combinations are also helpful, hence decision makers are able to trace and retrace the problem and solution finding process. This can be necessary since decision makers have experiences which can vary from the calculated simulation result. Even more political aspects, e.g. the agenda and program of the decision-makers/politicians party, can be included and if the consideration could increase the policy option impact.
4. But also after a policy was ratified and implemented it can be used for evaluation or monitoring purposes. Based on updated indicator data it can be validated if the policy has that impact as it was predicted. Even more, further impacts can be simulated for the next periods, which allow checking, if the policy solves the problem completely or if further investigations are necessary.

We can distinguish the benefit of this merge of Open Government Data visualizations and simulation data visualizations into (1) the enhanced exploration abilities through the parallel visualization of indicator data from Open Government Data sources and the simulation results. This allows the retrieval of the entire context of a current political problem as well as the forecast prediction. Another advantage (2) is the testing and elaboration of a planned policy. Thereby the parameters of the simulator will be adapted or a depending indicator can be changed in regards of the expected policy impact. Afterwards the simulation allows to predict the overall impact and if the aimed problem solution will be successful (in theory).

To enable the bonding of Open Government Data and simulation data visualizations, the indicator data from an Open Government Data will build the baseline. Based on a selected indicator the simulation will be performed. Afterwards the results of both data can be analyzed based on a cockpit approach where the user is able to select his preferred kind of data and visualizations.

4   Implementation of Explorative Impact Analysis Visualizations

The implementation follows the explained concept. In a first phase we considered the Open Government Data visualization based on EuroStat. EuroStat provides a large number of statistical indicators about countries and regions of Europe. The EuroStat indicator data building the baseline for the followed simulation, based on policy modeling simulators. The combined integration (technically and visually) builds the explorative impact analysis cockpit.

4.1   Open Government Data from EuroStat

In our approach we use EuroStat as Open Government Data source, because it covers the indicator data about all European countries and regions. EuroStat provides three technical features [26]: (1) it comprises a hierarchy of the available indicators, which allows users an easy exploration through the existing indicators. (2) It provides metadata about the included indicator data, e.g. date of update, information about the measurements and dependencies to other indicators. (3) Further it provides the indicator data for all European countries.

The technical inclusion follows the Open Government Data in SDMX[1] format. First of all we considered the available indicator hierarchy internally as semantic structure. Categories are internally represented as concepts and the concrete indicators are represented as instances. Such a network is beneficial for users, since the exploration through such networks is able with semantics visualizations.

The statistical data are also very similar to the provided data. We defined an internal data model that organizes the values and properties in indicator objects, which have as property the label/name, the geographic location and the data timetable (see detailed description in [26]). These data can then be shown in any kind of statistical visualization.

The meta-information is used to enhance and complete the internal representation either the indicator structure as well the statistical representation. In particular information to depending indicators can be considered in the structure visualization. Even more information about existing grouping capabilities can be considered, as e.g. the grouping in age groups or by gender.

4.2   Policy Modeling Simulators

For the visualization and inclusion of the simulators [19–21, 25] and the simulation result data, we adapted the used data models for Open Government Data to those simulator aspects [21]. For this purpose we specified a generic simulator API, over which the communication will be handled.

---

[1] More information about the SDMX format on: http://sdmx.org (accessed on 16/01/2015).

For the simulation result visualization we considered first of all a data structure, which is similar to EuroStat. The structure should allow an interactive elaboration of the concrete available result-set. Also the visualizations of concrete result indicators are similar handled as for EuroStat data. If the user selects a result indicator, the results will be shown.

The major benefit of the similar integration of simulation visualizations is the coherent use and visualization of the static data. This increases the usability for the users and enables the user both, the elaboration through the EuroStat data and parallel through the simulation result data. Another advantage is the further possibility to merge both kinds of data to a single visualization, where the forecast data of the simulation can be added to existing indicator data (of present and past).

In our current implementation we only include macro-level simulators and focus on the parallel visualization of the indicator from EuroStat and the result data from the simulator. In future we expect to include also the more generic simulators, which would allow providing simulation for most available EuroStat indicators.

4.3   Impact Analysis Cockpit

The combination of both is our so called impact analysis cockpit, where analyst and decision makers are able to analyze the indicator data and perform simulations to generate a forecast and compare the results with the indicator data. This enables analysts and decision makers to elaborate policies based on the current situation (past and present) and proposed situation (target/future). Figure 4 shows the result of the impact analysis cockpit.

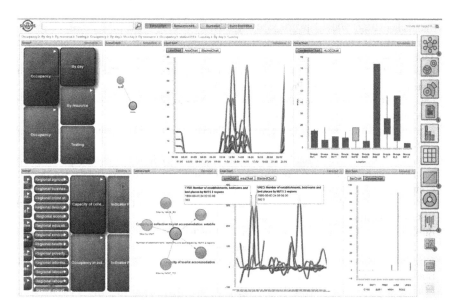

Fig. 4. The Impact Analysis Cockpit that bonds the EuroStat data and the simulation data for an enhanced and more interactive analysis.

5   Conclusion

In this paper we described a new approach to bond the visualization of statistical indicator data with the visualization of simulation data to provide an enhanced impact analysis for policy modeling. This enables analyst and decision makers an easier and explorative analysis of political problems for finding better solution options. The bonding of statistical indicator data and simulation data visualizations allows an effective policy making, since many options can be easily tested towards their impacts and thus allow identifying the (probabilistic/mathematical) best solution for an existing problem. As future work it can be interesting to merge it with other kind of data too, e.g. with Linked-Open Data [27].

Acknowledgment. Part of this work has been carried out within the FUPOL project, funded by the European Union under the grant agreement no. 287119 of the 7th Framework Programme. This work is majorly based on the SemaVis technology developed by Fraunhofer IGD (http://www.semavis.net). SemaVis provides an adaptive and modular approach for visualizing heterogeneous data for various users.

References

1. Kiker, G.A., Bridges, T.S., Varghese, A., Seager, T.P., Linkov, I.: Application of multicriteria decision analysis in environmental decision making. Integr. Environ. Assess. Manage. **1**(2), 95–108 (2005)
2. Rabelo, L., Eskandari, H., Shalan, T., Helal, M.: Supporting simulation-based decision making with the use of AHP analysis. In: Proceedings of the 37th Conference on Winter Simulation (WSC 2005), pp. 2042–2051 (2005)
3. Estrada, M.A.R.: Policy modeling: definition, classification and evaluation. J. Policy Model. **33**(4), 523–536 (2011)
4. Howlett, M., Ramesh, M., Perl, A.: Studying Public Policy: Policy Cycles and Policy Sub-systems. Oxford University Press, Oxford (2009)
5. Lasswell, H.D.: The Decision Process: Seven Categories of Functional Analysis. University of Maryland, College Park (1956)
6. Jones, C.O.: An Introduction to the Study of Public Policy, 3rd edn. Montery, Brooks/Cole (1984)
7. Macintosh, A.: Characterizing E-participation in policy-making. In: Proceedings of the 37th Annual Hawaii International Conference on System Sciences (HICSS 2004), vol. 5. IEEE Computer Society, Washington, DC (2004)
8. OECD: Promise and Problems of e-democracy – challenges of online citizen engagement. OECD Publication Service, Paris (2003)
9. Burkhardt, D., Nazemi, K., Sonntagbauer, P., Kohlhammer, J.: Interactive visualizations in the process of policy modeling. In: Electronic Government and Electronic Participation. Joint Proceedings of Ongoing Research of IFIP EGOV and IFIP ePart 2013. (LNI P-221), Bonn Köllen, pp. 104–115 (2013)
10. Sonntagbauer, S., Nazemi, K., Sonntagbauer, P., Burkhardt, D.: The FUPOL policy lifecycle. Handbook of Research on Advanced ICT Integration for Governance and Policy Modeling, pp. 61–86. IGI Global, Hershey (2014)

11. Weimer, D., Vining, A.R.: Policy Analysis: Concepts and Practice, 5th edn. Prentice Hall, Upper Saddle River (2011)
12. Vining, A.R., Weimer, D.L.: Policy analysis. In: Foundations of Public Administration Series, p. 17. ASPA (2010)
13. Gormley, W.T.: Public policy analysis: ideas and impacts. Annu. Rev. Political Sci. **10**, 297–313 (2007)
14. Meltsner, A.J.: Political feasibility and policy analysis. Public Adm. Rev. **32**(6), 859–867 (1972)
15. von Lucke, J., Geiger, C.P.: Open government data - frei verfügbare Daten des öffentlichen Sektors. Technical Report, Zeppelin University Friedrichshafen (2010)
16. Open Knowledge Foundation: Defining the open in open data, open content and open services (2009). http://opendefinition.org/okd/. Accessed 04 August 2014
17. Bunyakiati, P., Voravittayathorn, P.: Dissemination formats and major statistic data sets of the AEC countries: A survey. In: Information Science and Service Science and Data Mining (ISSDM), pp. 313-316 (2012)
18. Statistical Data and Metadata Exchange Initiative: SDMX Guidelines for the Use of Web Services (2005). http://www.sdmx.org/docs/2_0/SDMX_2_0%20SECTION_07_WebServices Guidelines.pdf
19. Zake, M., Ginters, E.: Migration among simulation paradigms and tools. In: Proceedings of European Modeling & Simulation Symposium. CAL-TEK S.r.l., Italy (2014)
20. Ginters, E., Aizstrauts, A., Eroles, M.-A.P., Buil, R.: Two stage simulation use in project verification and validation. In: Proceedings of European Modeling and Simulation Symposium. CAL-TEK S.r.l., Italy (2014)
21. Ginters, E., Aizstrauts, A., Baltruks, M., Nazemi, K., Burkhardt, D. et al.: FUPOL simulators and advanced visualization integration. In: Proceedings of European Modeling and Simulation Symposium, p. 7. CAL-TEK S.r.l., Italy (2014)
22. Few, S.: "Information Dashboard Design," overview article about dashboards (2012). http://blogs.ischool.berkeley.edu/i247s12/files/2012/01/Dashboard-Design-Overview-Presentation.pdf
23. Duval, E.: "Attention please! learning analytics for visualization and recommendation." In: Proceedings of the 1st International Conference on Learning Analytics and Knowledge (LAK 2011), pp. 9–17. ACM, New York (2011)
24. Nazemi, K., Burkhardt, D., Breyer, M., Stab, C., Fellner, D.W.: Semantic visualization cockpit: adaptable composition of semantics-visualization techniques for knowledge-exploration. In: Proceedings of International Conference Interactive Computer Aided Learning, pp. 163–173. University Press, Kassel (2010)
25. Ginters, E., Aizstrauts, A., Chinea, R.M.A.: Sociotechnical aspects of policy simulation. In: Handbook of Research on Advanced ICT Integration for Governance and Policy Modeling. IGI Global, Hershey, pp. 111–126 (2014)
26. Burkhardt, D., Nazemi, K., Stab, C., Steiger, M. et al.: Visual statistics cockpits for information gathering in the policy-making process. In: International Symposium Advances in Visual Computing, pp. 86–97. Springer, Heidelberg (2013)
27. Burkhardt, D., Nazemi, K., Retz, W., Kohlhammer, J.: Visual explanation of government-data for policy making through open-data inclusion. In: International Conference for Internet Technology and Secured Transactions, pp. 84–90. IEEE Computer Society, Los Alamitos (2014)
28. Burkhardt, D., Nazemi, K., Kohlhammer, J.: Policy modeling methodologies. In: Handbook of Research on Advanced ICT Integration for Governance and Policy Modeling, pp. 48–60. Information Science Reference, Hershey (2014)

Big Data Visualization for Occupational Health and Security Problem in Oil and Gas Industry

Daniela Gorski Trevisan[2], Nayat Sanchez-Pi[1(✉)], Luis Marti[3],
and Ana Cristina Bicharra Garcia[2]

[1] Instituto de Logica, Filosofia E Teoria Da Ciência (ILTC), Niterói (RJ), Brazil
nayat@iltc.br
[2] Computer Science Institute, Fluminense Federal University,
Niterói (RJ), Brazil
{daniela,bicharra}@ic.uff.br
[3] Department of Electrical Engineering, Pontifícia Universidade Católica do Rio
de Janeiro, Rio de Janeiro (RJ), Brazil
lmarti@ele.puc-rio.br

Abstract. Association rule learning is a popular and well-researched set of methods for discovering interesting relations between entities in large databases in real-world problems. In this regard, an intelligent offshore oil industry environment is a very complex scenario and Occupational Health and Security (OHS) is a priority issue as it is an important factor to reduce the number of accidents and incidents records. In the oil industry, there exist standards to identify and record workplace accidents and incidents in order to provide guiding means on prevention efforts, indicating specific failures or reference, means of correction of conditions or circumstances that culminated in accident. OHS's employees are in charge of analyzing the mined rules to extract knowledge. In most of cases these users has two main challenges during this process: (i) to explore the measures of interestingness (confidence, lift, support, etc.) and (ii) to understand and analyze the large number of association rules. In this sense, an intuitive visualization of mined rules becomes a key component in a decision-making process. In this paper, we propose a novel visualization of spatio-temporal rules that provides the big picture about risk analysis in a real world environment. Our main contribution lies in an interactive visualization of accident interpretations by means of well-defined spatio-temporal constraints, in the oil industry domain.

Keywords: Data visualization · Big data applications · Decision support systems · Oil and gas industry

1 Introduction

Occupational health and security (OHS) issues are priority matter for the offshore oil and gas industry. This industry is frequently in the news. Much of the time, it is because of changes in prices of oil and gas. Other |less frequent but perhaps more important| subject of media attention is when disasters strike, as is the case of offshore oil drilling platform explosions, spills or fires. These incidents have a high impact on

© Springer International Publishing Switzerland 2015
S. Yamamoto (Ed.): HIMI 2015, Part I, LNCS 9172, pp. 46–54, 2015.
DOI: 10.1007/978-3-319-20612-7_5

lives, environment and public opinion regarding this sector. That is why a correct handling of OHS is a determining factor in this industry long-term success.

There is an important effort of oil and gas industry to reduce the number of accidents and incidents. There are standards to identify and record workplace accidents and incidents to provide guiding means on prevention efforts, indicating specific failures or reference, means of correction of conditions or circumstances that culminated in accident. Besides, oil and gas industry is increasingly concerned with achieving and demonstrating good performance of occupational health and safety (OHS), through the control of its risks, consistent with its policy and objectives. Today, with the advances of new technologies, accidents, incidents and occupational health records are stored in heterogeneous repositories.

Similarly, the amount of information of OHS that is daily generated has become increasingly large. Furthermore, most of this information is stored as unstructured or poorly structured data. This poses a challenge, which is a top priority, for industries that are looking for ways to search, sort, analyze and extract knowledge from masses of data. Data mining can be applied to any domain where large databases are saved. Some applications are failure prediction [2], biomedical applications [7], process and quality control [6]. Association rule learning is a popular and well-researched set of methods for discovering interesting relations between entities in a large databases. It is intended to identify strong rules discovered in databases using different measures of interestingness. Many algorithms for generating association rules were presented over time.

Some well-known algorithms are Apriori [1], Eclat [14] and FP-Growth [9], but they only do half the job, since they are algorithms for mining frequent item sets. Another step needs to be done after to generate rules from frequent item sets found in a database.

In most of cases users has two main challenges during this process: (i) to explore the measures of interestingness (confidence, lift, support, etc.) and (ii) to understand and analyze the large number of association rules. In this sense, an intuitive visualization of mined rules becomes a key component in a decision-making process. In this paper we propose a novel visualization of spatio-temporal rules that provides the big picture about risk analysis in a real world environment.

Our main contribution lies in an interactive visualization of accident interpretations by means of well-defined spatio-temporal constraints, in the oil industry domain. The paper is organized as follows. After introducing the OHS problem, Sect. 2 briefly describes the state of the art on visualization techniques for association rules. After that, a case study involving rules visualization is presented in Sect. 3. Finally, Sect. 4 presents some conclusive remarks and outlines the current and future work been carried out in this area.

2 Foundations

Association rule mining algorithms typically generate a large number of association rules, which poses a major problem for understanding and analyzing rules. In this sense, several visualization techniques are proposed in order to facilitate this reasoning process.

Parallel coordinates, introduced by Inselberg in 1981 [12], represent a very useful graphical tool to visualize high dimensional data-sets in a two-dimensional space. They appear as a set of vertical axes where each axis describes a dimension of the domain and each case is represented by a line joining its values on the parallel axes. The Mosaic plots [10] and its variant of Double decker plots can be used to visualize the contingency table. They were introduced to visualize each element of a multivariate contingency table as a tile (or bin) in the plot and they have been adapted to visualize all the attributes involved in a rule by drawing a bar chart for the consequence item and using linking highlighting for the antecedent items.

The main drawback of Double Decker plot lies in the possibility to represent one rule at a time or at least all the rules generated from the different combinations of the items belonging to a given rule. In order to have the possibility to represent simultaneously many rules, Hofmann and Wilhelm [11] proposed the matrix of Association Rules with and without additional highlighting but in this case, only one-to-one rules are taken into consideration. In [8] the authors present and compare a set of visualization techniques implemented in arulesViz tool, which can be used to explore and present sets of association rules. The comparison criteria is based on the size of the rule set which can be analyzed, the number of interest measures which are shown simultaneously, if the technique offers interaction and reordering and how intuitive each visualization technique is. They found that Scatterplot (including two-key plots) and grouped matrix plot are capable to analyze large rule sets.

These techniques are interactive to allow the analyst to zoom and select interesting rules. Matrix-based can accommodate rule sets of medium size. Reordering can be used to improve the presentation. To analyze small rule sets the matrix-based method with 3D bars, graph-based methods and parallel coordinates plots [3–5] are suitable. Graphs for large rule sets can be analyzed using external tools and at last, double decker plots only can visualize a single rule. The techniques discussed in [8] can also be categorized based on the number of interest measures simultaneously visualized. Most methods can represent two measures and scatter plots are even able to visualize three measures for each rule in one plot. Scatter plot and graph based techniques are the most intuitive while matrix-based visualization with two interest measures, parallel coordinates and double decker require time consuming to learn how to interpret them correctly. It is important to note that most of these categories are only evaluated qualitatively, and the results presented are only meant to guide the user towards the most suitable techniques for a given application.

The only work that we have found reporting the user evaluation of the applied visualization techniques is described in [13]. They are using a matrix view to provide an overview of all of the association rules, allowing the user to filter and select rules that are potentially useful. The second visualization technique is a graph view and it shows the subset of rules selected from the matrix view, illustrating the relationships between the LHS (left-hand side) items and the RHS (right-hand side) items. At any time, the features of specific rules can be accessed within the detail view by highlighting the rules within the matrix or graph views. The matrix view, graph view, and detail view of the association rules are visualized separately since during association rule exploration, users often seek rules based on their interestingness measures first.

In this study they performed the user testing evaluation with 12 participants, which were, characterize as knowledgeable users, i.e. with knowledge on databases or data mining techniques.

These users should find the ten significant association rules in different dataset sizes. As results, they found that even though the number of rules increased by factors of 5 and 10 over the smallest group of rules, the time to find the required set of rules, the error rates, the perceived confidence, and the perceived ease did not change. In particular, the ability to filter the association rules using the matrix view, and then examines the rules using the graph view and detailed view made the task equally as easy even as the number of rules available for examination increased. The main drawback of such approach is the fact the users are not interpreting the rule itself they are mainly using a data mining visualization tool to filter and to find rules. We cannot conclude if experts users in the application domain but not in data mining techniques could be able to reach the same performance.

3   Visualization Approach

The approach proposed in this paper includes a visualization technique for mined association rules. It is applied in the post-processing stage in a straightforward way, and visualization results are used together with the mined rules. As already explained, the task of providing context-based information calls for the processing and extraction of information in the form of rules. One of the possible ways of obtaining those rules is to apply an association rule algorithm. In this work we employ Apriori [1] and FP-Growth [9] algorithms in parallel in order to mutually validate the results from each other. Association rules are not always simple to understand because results set are often very large and/or because the rule itself demands explanation. For the former problem, many techniques have been proposed to filter the most relevant set of rules. However, the later problem has received less attention.

Many techniques are quite difficult to understand and to correlate items making hard for the user to take a decision. In this direction, our work proposes two kinds of rules visualization. The first one is focused on visualization of one-to-one rules and the second one is focused on the n-to-n rules. In fact, for both visualizations we have two filters options, one filter that can be applied before mining, it is useful to filtering attributes to be mined, and the other filter can be applied after the mining process to filtering rules. For instance, the rule filter allows the user to choose to see all rules that have the ACCIDENT anomaly in the right hand (consequent) of the rule.

3.1   Visualization of Intra Association Rules

For the Intra association rules visualization we have chosen to show in two circular viewers all attributes involved in the mining process. The attributes are shown in the exterior part of each circle while their values are show in the interior area of each circle. There is a slider to navigate between rules and when the next rule is selected its correspondent attributes and values are highlighted in the circles indicating which are the antecedent and consequent items involved in that rule. As a result of the attributes filter we can see in Fig. 1 the visualization of 3 attributes involved in that rules while in the visualization illustrated in Fig. 2 shows only 4 attributes involved in that set of rules. Also it is possible to filter rules based on the number of occurrences (i.e. the lift criteria filter) and its confidence level.

The minimum values for these filters are defined before mining. Therefore, after mining the user can filter rules from this minimum predefined value until the maximum value while there are rules that can't these values well. An advantage of this visualization is to compare rules, it is easy to see which attributes has been changed along rules and which ones did not change.

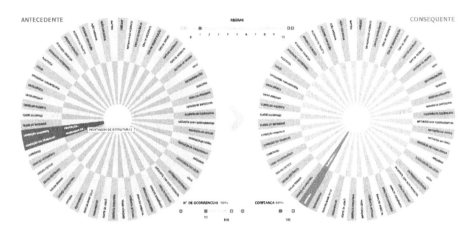

Fig. 1. Visualization of an Intra-anomaly rule with 3 attributes involved in that rule. The circle visualization is dealing with 60 attributes mined.

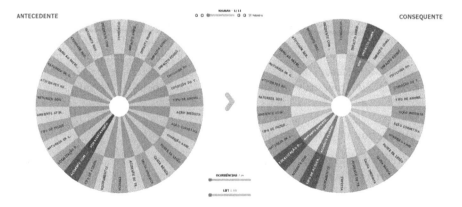

Fig. 2. Visualization of an Intra-anomaly rule with 4 attributes involved in that rule. The circle visualization is dealing with 30 attributes mined.

3.2   Visualization of Inter Association Rules

The visualization of spatiotemporal association rules calls for more complex interactive mechanisms in the attempt to explain the rules and its relationships once it can be any combination of *n-to-n* rules. An example of inter-anomaly mined rule interpretation is presented in Fig. 3 and its visualization is presented in Figs. 4 and 5. We start by defining three different colors to identify each kind of anomaly. Figure 6 is showing the three anomalies representation where blue color is related to the Deviation anomaly, the green color is related to the Incident anomaly and the red color is related to the Accident anomaly. For each rule, we visualize the anomalies (items) involved in the antecedent and consequent sides of rule. For instance, in Fig. 4 (see area 1) we have a visualization of *n-to-1* rule configuration and in Fig. 6 (see area 1) we can see visualization for *n-to-n* rule configuration. Area 1 is always showing the antecedent (left hand) and consequent (right hand) sides of the rule. Interactions with the consequent side of the rule (in area 1) will generate changes in the visualization of occurrences in area 2. Interactions with the antecedent side of the rule (in area 1) will generate changes in the visualization of occurrences in area 3.

By dragging and dropping one occurrence circle (for instance from the area 2 in Fig. 4) to the timeline area (area 3 in Figs. 4 and 5) the user can see all events involved in that occurrence according to the a given amount of precedence time. For instance, the user could have defined before mining that he would like to analyze events occurred 30 days before of this event happened. Also by selecting a circle anomaly in the consequent side (area 1 in Fig. 6) the user can see all correlated occurrences of that anomaly (see area 2 in Fig. 6). When the user selects a circle

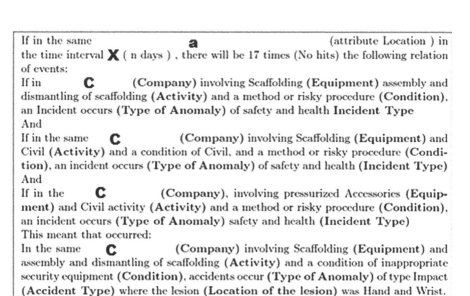

Fig. 3. Example of Intra-anomaly mined rule involving Incidents and Accidents anomalies

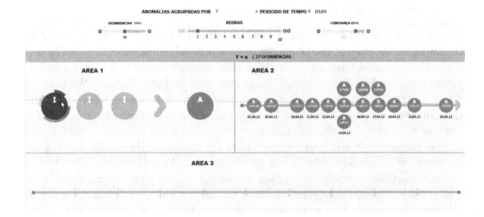

Fig. 4. Inter-anomaly interactive visualization of *n-to-1* rules (Color figure online)

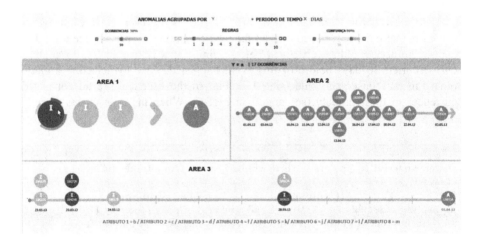

Fig. 5. Inter-anomaly interactive visualization of correlated events (Color figure online)

anomaly at the antecedent side (area 1 in Figs. 5 and 6) all occurrences in the timeline area which are shared with him are highlighted (see the highlighted circles in area 3 of Figs. 5 and 6).

Besides that, it is possible to investigate anomalies shared attributes. By clicking in one anomaly circle in the antecedent side (see Fig. 7) the user can see which are the attributes involved in that anomaly as well which of these attributes also appear in other anomalies. Finally, visualization resources for zoom in and zoom out in the timeline area are also available.

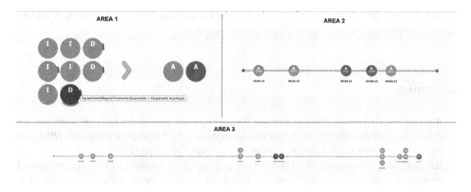

Fig. 6. Inter-anomaly interactive visualization of *n-to n* rules (Color figure online)

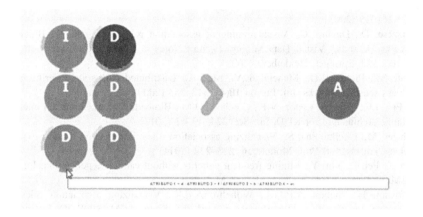

Fig. 7. Visualization of anomalies shared attributes (Color figure online)

4   Conclusions

In this work, we introduced a novel interactive visualization of association-mined rules specially devised to deal with massive problems. We have applied this interactive visualization to mined rules as part of Occupational Health and Security (OHS) in offshore oil extraction and processing plant. Although we have introduced and presented the interactive visualization of association rules problem itself, it must be pointed out that, this approach is currently deployed as part of a larger system that rely of the mining and classification modules. In addition, a set of usability tests will complement this study. The global system is currently in use by a major petroleum industry conglomerate of Brazil and is to be presented as a whole in a forthcoming paper. Readers must be warned that the results presented here had to be transformed in order to preserve the sensitive details of the data. Further work in this direction is called for and is currently being carried out. An important direction is the formal under-standing of the user-centric evaluation of the proposal.

References

1. Agrawal, R., Srikant, R.: Fast algorithms for mining association rules in large databases. In: Proceedings of the 20th International Conference on Very Large Data Bases. VLDB 1994, pp. 487–499. Morgan Kaufmann Publishers Inc., San Francisco (1994)
2. Borrajo, M.L., Baruque, B., Corchado, E., Bajo, J., Corchado, J.M.: Hybrid neural intelligent system to predict business failure in small-to-medium-size enterprises. Int. J. Neural Syst. **21**(04), 277–296 (2011)
3. Bruzzese, D., Buono, P.: Combining visual techniques for association rules exploration. In: Proceedings of the Working Conference on Advanced Visual Interfaces, pp. 381–384. ACM (2004)
4. Bruzzese, D., Davino, C.: Visual post-analysis of association rules. J. Vis. Lang. Comput. **14** (6), 621–635 (2003)
5. Bruzzese, D., Davino, C.: Visual mining of association rules. In: Simo, S., Bhlen, M., Mazeika, A. (eds.) Visual Data Mining. Lecture Notes in Computer Science, vol. 4404, pp. 103–122. Springer, Heidelberg (2008)
6. Conti, M., Pietro, R.D., Mancini, L.V., Mei, A.: Distributed data source verification in wireless sensor networks. Inf. Fusion **10**(4), 342–353 (2009)
7. De Paz, J.F., Bajo, J., Lopez, V.F., Corchado, J.M.: Biomedic organizations: an intelligent dynamic architecture for KDD. Inf. Sci. **224**, 49–61 (2013)
8. Hahsler, M., Chelluboina, S.: Visualizing association rules: introduction to the r-extension package arulesviz. R Proj. Module **16**, 223–238 (2011)
9. Han, J., Pei, J., Yin, Y.: Mining frequent patterns without candidate generation. In: ACM SIGMOD Record, vol. 29, pp. 1–12. ACM (2000)
10. Hofmann, H., Siebes, A.P.J.M., Wilhelm, A.F.X.: Visualizing association rules with interactive mosaic plots. In: Proceedings of the Sixth ACM SIGKDD International Conference on Knowledge Discovery and Data Mining, KDD 2000, pp. 227–235. ACM, New York (2000)
11. Hofmann, H., Wilhelm, A.: Visual comparison of association rules. Comput. Stat. **16**(3), 399–415 (2001)
12. Inselberg, A.: N-dimensional graphics, Part I - lines and hyperplanes. Harwood g. kolsky papers edn. International Business Machines Corporation (IBM). Los Angeles Scientific Center (1981)
13. Sekhavat, Y.A., Hoeber, O.: Visualizing association rules using linked matrix, graph, and detail views. Int. J. Intell. Sci. **3**, 34 (2013)
14. Zaki, M.J.: Scalable algorithms for association mining. IEEE Trans. Knowl. Data Eng. **12** (3), 372–390 (2000)

Affective Responses of Interpolated Sketches

Kun-An Hsiao[✉]

Industrial Design Department, National Kaohsiung Normal University,
No. 62, Shenjhong Rd., Yanchao, Kaohsiung, Taiwan
kahsiao@nknucc.nknu.edu.tw

Abstract. This study explored the expression differences between designer-interpolated shapes and computer-interpolated shapes under affective perceptual map. Multidimensional scaling (MDS) program was applied to construct product perceptual space as the basis to demonstrate the relationship among interpolation stimuli and affective adjectives. The designer-interpolated kettles have the tendency to design more fresh and modern images. Comparing the average distance between designer-interpolated kettles and midpoint of the source kettle, it is clear that the operations of interpolation image on the "simple-complex" axis are easier to create than the "contemporary-traditional" and "emotional-rational" axes. This study also proves the relationship between the computer-interpolated shapes and their affective responses to be nonlinear and non-uniform. The results showed under a condition of free design expression for the designer, the design purpose not only yields a finished product appearance but also represents the designer's will.

Keywords: Interpolation · Affective responses · Product shape · MDS

1 Introduction

Norman argued that the emotional side of design may be more critical to a product's success than its practical functions. Norman also considered this emotional aspect to be related to the complex brain structure at three emotional processing levels: visceral, behavioral and reflective [1]. Jordan observed that consumers expect a product to be not just a tool but a living object that expresses emotional image by its shape [2]. People could experience three different levels of affective responses toward a product – aesthetic experience, experience of meaning and emotional experience [3]. In addition to aesthetic pleasure, product forms provide a context for understanding all aspects of product design [4]. Helander and Tham indicated the most important task of affective research for human-factors design is to propose a satisfying survey method and theory. They also elucidated several significant issues in manipulating and researching affective design [5]. Manipulating affective images of product shapes thus becomes an increasingly important task for product designers.

Existing computer-aided tools only assist designers in drawing and modeling, and cannot offer much help in the challenge to develop products that convey specific affective meanings. There is a need for a computer-aided concept design system, with

© Springer International Publishing Switzerland 2015
S. Yamamoto (Ed.): HIMI 2015, Part I, LNCS 9172, pp. 55–66, 2015.
DOI: 10.1007/978-3-319-20612-7_6

which designers can rapidly explore a large number of product shapes and investigating their affective appeals. Many studies indicate that conventional media (such as design sketches) are simpler, intuitive and flexible than computers in concept-generation stages [6, 7, 8]. Although computer media could give immediately visualized feedback to the designer, these concrete images easily influence the designer and limit transformation in visual thinking and cognitive behavior [7]. Bilda and Demirkan [8] suggested a new invention-software package for computer-aided architectural conceptual design to fill the need for a natural cognitive process and stimulate interaction between mental imaging and digital-media simulation. Although CAD support is not currently appropriate in creative visual thinking, it is still a workable tool in automotive concept development [9]. In studies of the sketching behavior of designers, Lim et al. [10] indicated that integrating the advantages of paper drawings and CAD tools could provide a flexible sketching and modeling environment to help designers in the early stages of design. In exploring a new CAD system concept to represent and maintain vague geometric information of shapes in an early conceptual design stage, Lim, et al. [11] proposed morphing techniques as helpful for visualization, reuse and giving probability of shapes to support flexible conceptual design.

Among the many different ways of generating new shapes, interpolation is a technique that generates a series of gradually changing shapes from one shape to another. The morphing technique can generate highly realistic images to blend two objects. In the field of psychology, there has been much research on face perception where morphing techniques synthesized virtual faces for experimental studies [12–14].

Computer tools, such as Elastic Reality from Avid, can automatically generate a series of shapes from two given shapes (after specifying correspondences between them). Interpolating product shapes enables designers to quickly visualize varying shapes with gradually changing affective meanings. This technique may become a viable tool in a computer-aided concept design system.

Some proposals apply interpolation (or morphing) to automatically generate new designs. Chen and Parent proposed a "shape-averaging" method, where "averaged" wire-frame computer models create new shapes [15]. They suggested that shape averaging can predict the trend of a shape by averaging the different existing shapes, or extrapolating shapes to represent different views over time. Wang used shape interpolation to automatically create many in-between shapes in the design process for computer-aided styling [16]. Hsiao and Liu [17] applied three-dimensional morphing which automatically generates new product shapes based on desired affective-response specifications. Independently, Chen et al. proposed a set of visualization tools to explore affective product shapes by combining existing products that are successful in communicating certain affective meaning [18, 19]. These studies demonstrate the possibilities of applying the interpolation technique to realize and operate affective responses of product shapes.

Design examples from actual practice indicate that product designers sometimes derive new shapes by using interpolation techniques, particularly when specific styles or images need to be maintained. For instance, automobile designers from time to time apply interpolation techniques to bring in new styles while keeping a consistent brand or model image. Although the interpolation technique is employed by designers in practice, there have been few studies about exactly how designers interpolate between shapes. Do they operate directly on the overall shapes? Do they mix and match individual shape features? Do they operate strictly on the shapes? This study therefore analyzes sketches made while attempting to interpolate two product shapes, comparing these sketches to those generated automatically by computer software, to discover the similarities and differences. These investigations helped determine the requirements for a computer-aided concept design system that supports design thinking patterns.

2 Experiment Design

To investigate how designers interpolate shapes, designers were asked to sketch shapes that interpolate halfway between the two given product images. The two source products need to have very different characteristics to compare designer-interpolated shapes with the original shapes and uncover the interpolation method. To select very different source products, this study constructed a basic product perceptual space using a multidimensional scaling program, then selecting source products that lie at extremes of the perceptual space. Nine senior designers, each with at least five years' professional experience in product design, participated in the experiment. Each designer was expected to create his or her own interpretation of the interpolated shapes. On the other hand, the computer-generated interpolated shapes were free of designer's interpretations, allowing comparison of the designer-interpolated shapes to computer-interpolated shapes.

3 Stimuli Selection

A coffee kettle was the product for this research. A collection of sixty-four kettle images covered the range of variations in product shapes. Using these images, a survey elicited affective adjectives to describe these products. Twenty subjects (fifteen undergraduate students and five lecturers from Chang Gung University, Taiwan) participated in the survey. This yielded six hundred and forty-five affective adjectives for describing kettle shapes from voice recordings of the survey. After eliminating similar and unsuitable words, one hundred affective adjectives for kettles remained.

By applying our past study result (Hsiao et al. 2005), researchers used the twenty-one representative products as stimuli and ten adjective pairs to measure affective responses conducting a semantic differential survey to determine perceptions of the kettles (Fig. 1). A multidimensional scaling program (MDPREF) [20] was used to construct the perceptual map of the twenty-one kettles; a preference-mapping program (PREFMAP) [20] was also used to determine the vector locations corresponding to the adjective pairs. In this map, each point corresponds to a kettle and each vector corresponds to an adjective pair. As the stimuli for the experiment, this study selected three kettles A, B and C that lie towards the extremes of the map and far away from each other. The three kettles clearly exhibit very different characteristics, as required by the experiment.

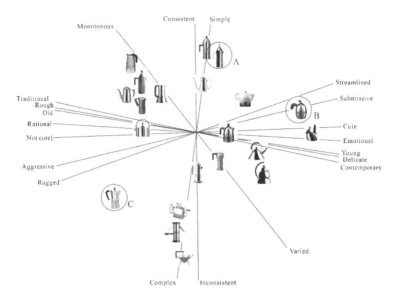

Fig. 1. Perceptual space of 21 kettles and 10 bipolar adjectives

4   Computer Interpolations

Because each designer may have his or her own interpretation of the interpolated shape between two given shapes, the computer-interpolated shape, free of any designer's interpretations, can serve as an analytical reference. Designer-interpolated shapes can be compared to computer-interpolated shapes to discover whether they share common features and in which aspects they are different. Researchers used a morphing software package, Elastic Reality from the AVID Company, to obtain the interpolated shapes between kettle pairs. The quality of computer interpolation depends on accurate definitions and correspondences of shape features between the two given kettles. This study defined the shape features of a kettle to be: (a) cap handle, (b) body handle, (c) cap, (d) opening, (e) upper half body, (f) bottom half body, (g) parting line of body and (h) light and shade. The last feature was needed because the kettles are made of metal which reflects light strongly. Figure 2 shows correspondence between two shape features (a. and b.) of kettles A and B for the morphing.

For pair-wise interpolation results of kettles A, B and C generated by the morphing software, in-between shapes are labeled A50/B50, to indicate respective weights (in percentages) of kettle A and B (Fig. 3). The image labeled A50/B50 corresponds to the "average" (interpolated) shape of A and B, and will be used as the comparison reference.

5   Designers' Interpolations

Nine senior designers, with at least five years of professional experience as product designers, participated in the experiment. One was from Phillip Design Center in Taiwan, two were from local design companies, two were lecturers teaching product

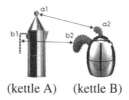

(kettle A)   (kettle B)

Fig. 2. Corresponding features between kettles A and B

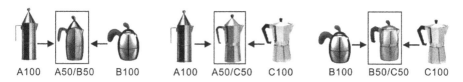

A100   A50/B50   B100   A100   A50/C50   C100   B100   B50/C50   C100

Fig. 3. Computer's interpolation between kettles A and B, A and C, B and C

design in the university, and the other four were in-house designers in computer companies. Each designer sketched the interpolated (50 % – 50 %) shape between one or two random pairs of kettles (A-B, A-C or B-C). The designer could freely express his or her interpretation in sketches, without any constraint on the number or the style of the sketches. Finally, from the numerous sketches, the designer chose a sketch that he or she felt best represented the interpolated shape between the two given kettles (Fig. 4, in arbitrary order). The designer-sketched interpolated shapes are more complex. Designers created many different interpolated shapes for the same pair of source products. Not all interpolated shapes are similar to the interpolated shapes computed by the morphing software. Some sketches emphasize particular elements from two source shapes; while, in some sketches, new elements different from those of the two source shapes were added to the interpolated shapes.

6   Perceptual Map of Sketches

To understand how people process the designers' interpolated shapes, an experiment interpreted the perceptual space of the source and interpolated kettles. Because the designer's sketches are drawn in very different styles that perhaps too abstract for subjects to envision as real products, these sketches formed the basis of three-dimensional digital models. Researchers used CAD software (Alias) to build the basic shapes and then used 3D Studio Max and VRay software packages to obtain highly realistic rendering of the sketched objects (Fig. 4).

In the same manner as described in Sect. 3, a multidimensional scaling program (MDPREF) was applied to construct the perceptual map and a preference-mapping program (PREFMAP) to determine the location of the vector corresponding to each adjective in the perceptual map using the twenty-one kettles (fifteen digital kettles, three source kettles and three halfway kettles with computer morphing) and ten

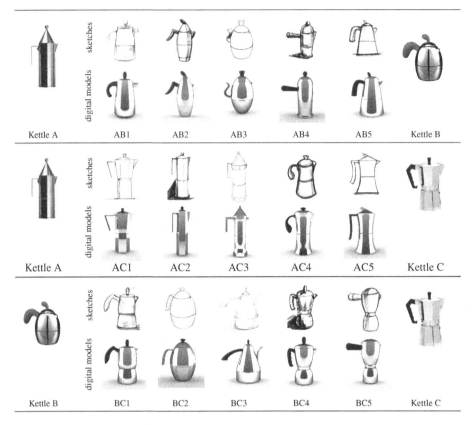

Fig. 4. Sketches and 3D digital models of designers' interpolations between two source kettles

representative adjectives. Forty subjects (twenty undergraduates and twenty post-graduates in Chang Gung University) participated in the experiment.

Figure 5 shows the perceptual space of the twenty-one kettles and the ten adjectives. Figures 6, 7 and 8 show the perceptual space between source kettles A-B, A-C and B-C respectively, which were isolated from Fig. 5. The distribution of designer-interpolated kettles from Figs. 5, 6, 7 and 8 shows that designers' interpolations do not exactly lie halfway between source kettles in this experiment. But some sketch kettles, such as AB5 for source kettles A-B, AC1 for source kettles A-C and BC1 for source kettles B-C, can be very close to the targeted halfway shapes in the perceptual space. Most kettles cluster to the right side of perceptual space, which represents more contemporary, emotional and simple imagery. This indicates that designers provided the products with more fresh and modern images, even though they were supposed to express the new kettle image halfway between the two source kettle images. This phenomenon is in contrast to the distribution of computer-morphed kettles which tend to express more complex and inconsistent images.

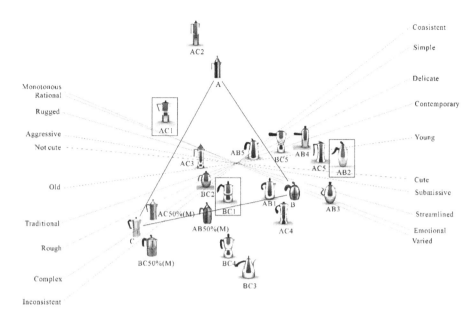

Fig. 5. Perceptual space of 21 kettles and 10 bipolar adjectives

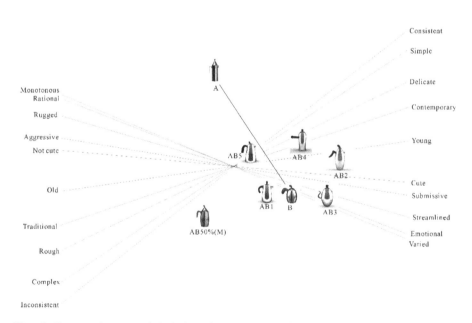

Fig. 6. Perceptual space of 5 designer-interpolated kettles and 1 computer-morphed kettle between source kettles A and B.

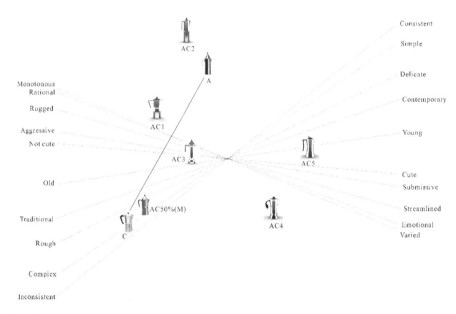

Fig. 7. Perceptual space of 5 designer-interpolated kettles and 1 computer-morphed kettle between source kettles A and C.

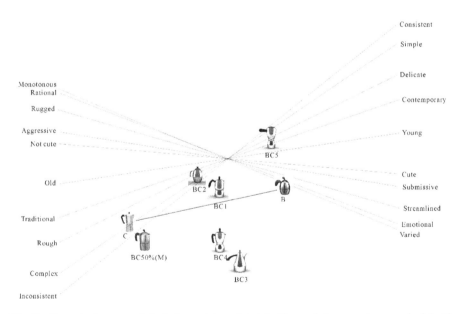

Fig. 8. Perceptual space of 5 designer interpolated kettles and 1 computer morphed kettle between source kettles B and C.

To examine the relationship between twenty-one different kettles and affective responses for each adjective, researchers vertically projected the points corresponding to the products to each vector of bipolar adjective and then calculated the *L-values* between the projections and the origin. Figure 9 shows an example of L-values for kettle B on the "simple-complex" axis. A large (resp. small) L-value indicates strong (resp. weak) of affective responses corresponding bipolar adjective. Positive (resp. negative) value indicates positive (resp. negative) effect on the corresponding adjective (e.g., contemporary, young).

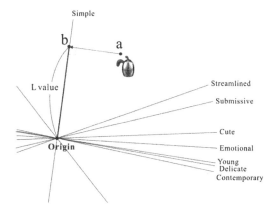

Fig. 9. L-value of kettle B on "simple-complex" axis

The L-value was calculated to further clarify the perceptions of the interpolated kettles in the perceptual space. The L-value of experimental kettles in three bipolar adjectives (Table 1): "contemporary-traditional", "emotional-rational" and "simple-complex" which were previously distilled as important fundamental dimensions of affective responses [21]. (1) The L-value of AB5, AC1 and BC1 are closest to the midpoint of source kettles A-B, A-C and B-C with respect to all three bipolar adjectives. Therefore, kettles AB5, AC1 and BC1 may most closely represent the halfway interpolation between the two given product images for the three bipolar adjectives. (2) The average L-distance of five designer-interpolated kettles is greater than the midpoint of source kettles for three bipolar adjectives. Thus, all designer-interpolated kettles have a more fresh and modern image. (3) Observing the distances between average (L-value) and the midpoint of the source kettles, researchers found that the shortest distance is in the "simple-complex" axis for all pairs source kettles: A-B, A-C and B-C. This result indicates that the operations of interpolation are easier to represent in "simple-complex" than in "contemporary-traditional" and "emotional-rational" axes.

7 Affective Responses of Interpolated Shapes

Figure 10 showed the Designer-interpolated shapes and computer-interpolated shapes between source kettles A-B, A-C and B-C. Previous study showed the relationship between the interpolation shapes created by computer and their affective

Table 1. L-values of experimental kettles in three bipolar adjectives

	A	AB1	AB2	AB3	AB4	AB5	B	Midpoint of source kettle A-B	Average distance of five sketch kettles	Distance between average and midpoint
Contemporary -traditional	−0.0083	**0.043**	0.2778	0.2538	0.1707	−0.0204	0.1564	0.074	0.14498	0.07098
Emotional -rational	−0.1727	0.1537	0.3075	0.2753	0.1949	**0.0186**	0.2187	0.023	0.19	0.167
Simple -complex	0.2343	0.0631	0.2691	0.0919	0.2834	**0.1266**	0.0971	0.1657	0.16682	**0.00112**
	A	AC1	AC2	AC3	AC4	AC5	C	Midpoint of A-C		
Contemporary -traditional	−0.0083	**−0.1693**	−0.0079	0.2035	0.1651	0.2797	−0.4054	-0.2069	0.09422	0.30112
Emotional -rational	−0.1727	−0.3107	−0.3053	**−0.1851**	0.2018	0.2013	−0.2558	−0.2143	−0.0796	0.1347
Simple -complex	0.2343	**−0.0301**	0.1489	−0.3827	0.0297	0.2119	−0.3868	−0.0763	−0.00446	**0.07184**
	B	BC1	BC2	BC3	BC4	BC5	C	Midpoint of B-C		
Contemporary -traditional	0.1564	**−0.1163**	−0.0884	−0.0318	−0.0666	0.1626	−0.4054	−0.1245	−0.0281	0.0964
Emotional -rational	0.2187	**0.0103**	−0.0792	0.1343	0.0686	0.1127	−0.2558	−0.0186	0.04934	0.06794
Simple -complex	0.0971	−0.0489	**−0.0927**	−0.2438	−0.2174	0.1613	−0.3868	−0.1448	−0.0883	**0.0565**

responses to be nonlinear and non-uniform [19]. This study also proves the phenomenon. The interpolation product shapes trends to show more traditional, old, inconsistent and complex. This probably caused by the image quality processed by morphing technique. Even if researchers move interpolation shapes to the right size (Contemporary, young, consistent and simple), their affective responses still not locate close to the midpoint between source kettles. The affective responses of interpolation shapes seem shifting to the side of complex shape. Taking A-B interpolation as example, the affective responses of interpolation shape (A50/B50) shifting to kettle B. Kettle A was created by straight line and showed concise style. Even though made a little adjustment to change the straight line into larger radian, the simple and concise style of straight line will be broken into different affective responses. AB5, sketched by designer, seems solve this problem. Appling trapezoid shape to maintain the straight line but flexible, and create more organic shapes on the handle to demonstrate curve image. The result shows both affective responses from Kettle A image (straight line) and Kettle B image (curve line). Therefore, the manipulation of affective responses on product shapes not only whole shape changing but also shape features effect. Designers' interpolating sketches showed diversified appearances and affective experiences than the morphing shapes by computer. Under a condition of free design expression for the designer, the design purpose not only yields a finished product appearance but also represents the designer's will. The design expression could include affective responses of product experiences as aesthetic experience, meaning and emotional experience [3]. That could explain why designers demonstrate diverse product appearances and affective experiences in a restricted design condition.

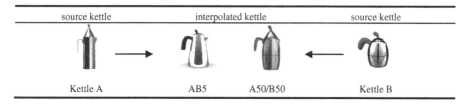

source kettle   interpolated kettle   source kettle

Kettle A   AB5   A50/B50   Kettle B

Fig. 10. Designer-interpolated shapes and computer-interpolated shapes between source kettles

8 Conclusions

This study explored the expression differences between designer-interpolated shapes and computer-interpolated shapes under affective perceptual map. By computing the perceptual map using realistic renderings of designer-interpolated kettles, computer-interpolated kettles and source kettles, three designer-interpolated kettles (AB5, AC1 and BC1) could most closely represent the halfway interpolation between the two given product images (source kettles A-B, A-C and B-C) for the three bipolar adjectives. The designer-interpolated kettles is also apparent that designers have the tendency to design more fresh and modern images, despite the request to express the new kettle halfway between two source kettle images. Comparing the average distance between designer-interpolated kettles and midpoint of the source kettle, it is clear that the operations of interpolation image on the "simple-complex" axis are easier to create than the "contemporary-traditional" and "emotional-rational" axes.

This study also proves the relationship between the computer-interpolated shapes and their affective responses to be nonlinear and non-uniform. The results showed computer-interpolated shapes could keep precisely blending contour shape but not for affective responses between two assigned product shapes. Comparing the computer-morphing method with the designer's interpolation, design sketches are much more flexible and interpolations performed on more than the shapes. The results suggest that a computer-aided concept design system based on the interpolation technique should include functions for computing morphing of overall shapes, and functions for combining shape features from different source shapes to create new shapes. The interpolation of concepts is difficult to implement in computers, at least with current technology.

Acknowledgment. The authors thank the National Science Council of Taiwan supporting this research under grant number NSC- 92-2213-E-011-007 and MOST 103-2410-H-017-028-MY2. They would also like to express appreciation for all designers who participated in the experiment.

References

1. Norman, D.A.: Emotional Design: Why We Love (or Hate) Everyday Things. Basic Books, New York (2004)

2. Jordan, P.W.: Designing Pleasurable Products. Taylor & Francis, London (2000)
3. Desmet, P., Hekkert, P.: Framework of product experience. Int. J. Des. **1**(1), 57–66 (2007)
4. Coates, D.: Watches Tell More Than Time. McGraw-Hill, New York (2003)
5. Helander, M.G., Tham, M.P.: Hedonomics-affective human factors design. Ergonomics **46** (13/14), 1269–1272 (2003)
6. Verstijnen, I.M., Hennessey, J.M., Leeuwen, C., Hamel, R., Goldshmidt, G.: Sketching and creative discovery. Des. Stud. **19**(4), 519–546 (1998)
7. Won, P.H.: The comparison between visual thinking using computer and conventional media in the concept generation stages of design. Autom. Constr. **10**(3), 319–325 (2001)
8. Bilda, Z., Demirkan, H.: An insight on designers' sketching activities in traditional versus digital media. Des. Stud. **24**(1), 27–50 (2003)
9. Tovey, M., Porter, S., Newman, R.: Sketching, concept development and automotive design. Des. Stud. **24**(2), 135–153 (2003)
10. Lim, S., Qin, S.F., Prieto, P., Wright, D., Shackleton, J.: A study of sketching behaviour to support free-form surface modelling from on-line sketching. Des. Stud. **25**(4), 393–413 (2004)
11. Lim, S., Lee, B.S., Duffy, A.: Incremental modelling of ambiguous geometric ideas (I-MAGI): representation and maintenance of vague geometry. Int. J. Artif. Intell. Eng. **15** (2), 93–108 (2001). Special Issue on Conceptual Modelling in Design Computing
12. Tiddeman, B., Burt, D., Perrett, D.: Prototyping and transforming facial textures for perception research. IEEE Comput. Graphics Appl. **21**, 42–50 (2001)
13. Busey, T.: Physical and psychological representations of faces: evidence from morphing. Psychol. Sci. **9**, 476–482 (1998)
14. Perrett, D.I., Lee, K.J., Penton-Voak, I., Rowland, I.D., Yoshikawa, S., Burt, D.M., Henzi, S.P., Castles, D.L., Akamatsu, S.: Effects of sexual dimorphism on facial attractiveness. Nature **394**(6696), 884–887 (1998)
15. Chen, S.E., Parent, R.E.: Shape averaging and its applications to industrial design. IEEE Comput. Graphics Appl. **9**(1), 47–54 (1989)
16. Wang, H.: An approach to computer-aided styling. Des. Stud. **16**(1), 50–61 (1995)
17. Hsiao, S.W., Liu, M.C.: A morphing method for shape generation and image prediction in product design. Des. Stud. **23**(5), 533–556 (2002)
18. Chen, L.L., Liang, J.: Image interpolation for synthesizing affective product shapes. In: Proceedings of the International Conference on Affective Human Factors Design, pp. 531–537. Asian Academic Press, London (2001)
19. Chen, L.L., Wang, G.F., Hsiao, K.A., Liang, J.: Affective product shapes through image morphing. In: Proceedings of the 2003 International Conference on Designing Pleasurable Products and Interfaces, pp. 11–16. ACM (2003)
20. Schiffman, S.M., Reynolds, L., Young, F.W.: Introduction to Multidimensional Scaling. Academic Press, New York (1981)
21. Hsiao, K.A., Chen, L.L.: Fundamental dimensions of affective responses to product shapes. Int. J. Ind. Ergon. **36**, 553–564 (2006)

An Approach to Spatial Visualizing Method for Information Structure to Enhance Remember to Look

Jae-Gil Lee[1] and Dong-Hee Shin[2(✉)]

[1] Department of Interaction Science, Sungkyunkwan University,
Seoul, Republic of Korea
firstmage@skku.edu
[2] Sungkyunkwan University, Seoul, Republic of Korea
dshin@skku.edu

Abstract. Individuals living in our information-driven society can feel overwhelmed by the amount of information as well as the myriad of technologies they can use to access it. Personal information management (PIM) is an activity in which an individual stores personal information items in order to retrieve them later. One ideal of PIM is that we always have the right information in the right place, in the right form, and of sufficient completeness and quality to meet our current needs. Personal information storage tends to become enormous over time. In addition, its structure can also become diversified and complex, resulting in information that is scattered in different forms across various devices and multiple versions. One way to solve the issue of information fragmentation is to emphasize the concept of remembering to look. Most information management system representations are using spatial metaphors, where virtual objects are displayed similar to physical objects in the actual world. The power of spatial metaphors lies in people's tendency to naturally use spatial metaphors.

Keywords: Spatial metaphor · Information structure · Personal information management

1 Introduction

Skills in the effective use of information are essential for individuals living in our information-driven society. Improvement to accessibility of information and communication technology (ICT) have placed new emphasis on both the quality of technology use as well as users' attitudes, thus going beyond the numbers of people who are able to access to use such technologies. Individuals living in our information-driven society can feel overwhelmed by the amount of information as well as the myriad of technologies they can use to access it. In addition to this, they often face much more information than can be consumed in current single session. Therefore, they must be able to identify information needs, to locate corresponding information sources, to extract and organize relevant information from each source, and to synthesize information from a variety of sources into cogent, productive uses [1]. Knowledge and attitudes, which are needed to carry out the above-mentioned activities, can be defined as 'information literacy' [2].

© Springer International Publishing Switzerland 2015
S. Yamamoto (Ed.): HIMI 2015, Part I, LNCS 9172, pp. 67–73, 2015.
DOI: 10.1007/978-3-319-20612-7_7

There is no argument that technology, such as computers have potential to improve people's ability to manage information. Researchers in the human–computer interaction (HCI) field have consistently suggested that technology can improve performance; however, new technologies often result in individuals focusing on the technology itself rather than its purpose (i.e., information). There are limitations to focusing a specific technology or device on an entire collection of information that already has been fragmented. Therefore, improving performance in a specific field would not be enough. In recent years, there has been increased discussion of human–information interaction (HII), which investigates how people interact with information [3]. Interest in HII is due in part to a realization that these interactions are more central to our lives than are our interactions with computers [4]. Combining HCI and HII will provide new opportunities for increasing storage, retrieval, and effective use of information, and could result in the examination of technology from an integrated perspective, which takes into account human aspects as well as information and technology.

2 Literature Review

2.1 Personal Information Management

Personal information management (PIM) is an activity in which an individual stores personal information items in order to retrieve them later [5]. Moreover, it places special emphasis on the organization and maintenance of personal information collections those are stored for later use and repeated reuse [4]. Ease of retrieval is a key aim of PIM; however, its purpose is not solely focused on being able to find material again. One ideal of PIM is that we always have the right information in the right place, in the right form, and of sufficient completeness and quality to meet our current needs [4]. Jones claimed three core activities for PIM such as finding/re-finding, keeping, and meta-level (Table 1).

Finding activity is based on the people's needs to information. People seek, search, and browse information to satisfy their own goal. This activity might be a sequence of interactions rather than a single stage. They scan through results to determine information items that relate to a need. It the result wasn't enough to satisfy their need, additional finding activity would be required.

Activity that related with keeping is the way to create connection between new and old information items. It is not only about information itself rather also includes channels of information. Tasks related with information activity used to produce much more information that can't be consumed in the single session. It generally leads people's fear to forget, kind of prospective memory failure.

Table 1. Three personal information management core activities

Activities	Description
Finding/Refinding	Retrieve information from personal or public information storage
Keeping	Store information into personal information storage
Meta-Level	Focus on the personal information storage for management and organization

Meta-level activities operate broadly upon information within the personal information storage and on the mapping that connects need to information for such information. The prefix of "meta-" contains the meaning of "beyond," and "about" as well as "after." This activity attempts to enhance user's controllability to their personal information storage by stressing proactivity.

These three activities are interrelated, and help people to establish, use, and maintain a map between information and need. For example, "Keeping" activity is closely related to how the user may organize and manage the information in their personal information storage (i.e., "Meta-level"), and how they retrieve it later(i.e., "Finding/Refinding"). Keeping information into the right place in accordance with future need has never been easy [6]. It is a cognitively difficult and error-prone activity due to the inconsistency of human memory. The definition or purpose of a folder is often unclear and may change over time; for example, people often forget about folders they previously created for the same purposes. Therefore, as information is fragmented in diverse places—often too many to keep track of— it becomes increasingly harder to find in the future.

2.2 Information Fragmentation

Personal information storage tends to become enormous over time. In addition, its structure can also become diversified and complex, resulting in information that is scattered in different forms across various devices and multiple versions. Moreover, the convergence of social and cloud computing, along with the growing presence of networked devices, are creating new opportunities for people to move personal files to online places [7]. This means that individuals have more places to store and to find their information, across technologies, devices, and services. It can be defined as "Information fragmentation", and it creates problems for keeping, finding, and meta-level activities such as maintenance and organization [4].

2.3 Remember Where to Look

PIM includes the management of information going into our own memories as well as the management of external information, or information going into our storages. One way to solve the issue of information fragmentation is to emphasize the concept of remembering to look. Jones [4] selected remembering to look as a starting point of finding activity (i.e., the sense that the information is "in there somewhere"). Greater sense of control and context over the search process lessens the cognitive burden associated with query articulation.

3 Research Proposition

3.1 Information Presentation with Spatial Metaphor

A useful information system will target people's natural understanding of information use. Most information management system representations are using spatial metaphors, where virtual objects are displayed similar to physical objects in the actual world. The power of spatial metaphors lies in people's tendency to naturally use spatial metaphors. The key to designing effective information navigation tools lies in discovering how people naturally conceive of information spaces, including the extent to which such spaces are thought of in terms of physical space [8]. It is easy to find virtual objects that following spatial metaphor such as a scroll bar and icons on desktop screen because their locations are intuitive. Most information spaces follow a two-dimensional (2D) desktop paradigm that uses a flat surface of display; however, the amount of information that has to be handled is increasing, and its structures are becoming increasingly complex, so this paradigm is approaching the limits of its own capacity.

Three-dimensional (3D) information space that replicates the way we live has also been suggested as a way to represent large amounts of information and to enhance the presence of that information. Application of spatial metaphors in 3D space can significantly improve individuals' recognition capabilities as well as the success of retrieval tasks. This is supported by empirical research studies for example, "data mountain" [9, 10]. Strengths and weaknesses of 3D space, however, both arise from the structure itself. A follow-up study that included a data mountain structure in actual physical space revealed that performance was lower in the 3D space than in a 2D space [11]. While 3D representations can convey more information, they consume much more human navigational capacity. These costs may take the form of additional cognitive load associated with the cognitive representation of three dimensions [12] or additional load associated with more complex procedures for generation of navigational commands. This means that 3D space requires people to make an extra effort.

Weaknesses of using 3D informational spaces are also associated with people's greater familiarity with 2D virtual interfaces [13]. For example, there is no word that represents exact direction to alert to someone who was in danger from being hit by a flying baseball immediately. In this aspect, free 3D space might require more effort to locate information, resulting in lowered performance. Formulaic information spaces that are in some way constrained might be better than a less structured 3D information space.

3.2   Visualizing Information Structure

Creating a structure for personal information storage through classification and organization is a fundamental part of PIM, because large environments cannot be viewed all at once. Indratmo and Vassileva [14] summarize organizational structure in information systems by dividing it into five types: hierarchical, flat, linear, spatial, and network (Table 2).

Table 2. Five structures of information organization

Structure	Example
Hierarchical	Folder and files
Flat	Tag
Linear	Alphabetically, chronologically ordered list
Spatial	Icons on the desktop
Network	Hypertext, link between items

These conceptual structures can be applied to the classification and organization of meta-data, and their representation can be visualized as an information space. Such a collection or visual inventory would allow these materials to be browsed through, giving users a sense of what they have [7] (Fig. 1).

Hierarchical structure is familiar to most people as folders and files. It visualizes hierarchical relationship between concepts and to help users to see such relationship. However, building a hierarchical structure in information can be a heavyweight cognitive activity due to our inconsistent memory. Concepts in information system are loosely related therefore information may be stored in multiple places in the system.

A flat structure can be represented as tags to label items. Several tags can be applied to a single item, so it may be more flexible than a hierarchical system. However, it is not surprising that these tags are often assigned inconstantly. It could be hard to search all relevant information with flat structure.

Linear structure arranges information items in an ordered list based on single attribute for example, time. It can be useful to maintain contextual aspect of information because people often arrange events in chronological ordering in their mind. Considering complexity in personal information system, property of linear structure that only single attribute can be applied at a time, can be a problem because relationship between items could not be captured. It is noteworthy that a linear structure such as time can be visualized in an information space. The domains of space and time are similar in their conceptual structure. People usually think about time using space as a metaphor. The spatial time metaphor is a one-dimensional, rather than a multidimensional, plain or space. This metaphor provides the relational information needed to organize events in time [15]. In our minds, past, present, and future occupy different positions on the line. This can be an intuitive and effective solution for locating time in space. When time is mapped onto the spatial dimension, its distance represents temporal duration, which allows people to estimate temporal duration using spatial distance [16]. It is also possible to predict a specific moment of time using a specific point in the spatial dimension. This means that people do not need to see a visual timeline at all times in order to estimate events in time. Partial information, such as hidden timelines

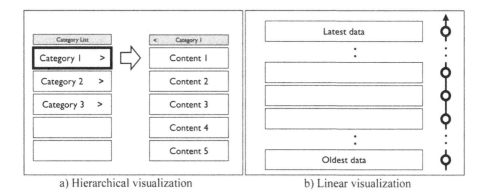

a) Hierarchical visualization   b) Linear visualization

Fig. 1. Hierarchical (a) and Linear (b) visualization

| a) Spatial visualization | b) Network visualization |

Fig. 2. Spatial (a) and network (b) representation

and a mid-point, are sufficient to recognize an event in time. This notion provides a guideline for constructing a timeline in information space (Fig. 2).

Spatial structure uses positions in display and user's mind in order to organize items. It is well known as computer desktop paradigm in a digital context with locating different types of information into different places. Visible items in desktop can be easily accessible, but it would not be efficient for large group of information items. There were several suggestions to overcome this problem with combining linear structure [17], but it is not widely used to store information.

Network structure is represented as a hypertext system. Providing link between different types of information items allows flexibility to system, meaning possibility to avoid structural constraint. However, it could be hard to see overview of whole structure, or navigate through it successfully. Hypertext, such as Internet document that is connected to a document via a link, also can be visualized in an information space. Moreover, this visualization can reduce users' cognitive effort in information activities. For example, individuals can connect information currently being viewed to information that was viewed previously; thus, spatial location can help individuals avoid "feeling lost" in complex information spaces. Much current research in hypertext appears to use the term "space" in its everyday sense, or as a physical relationship between objects [13], creating the notion that hierarchical and networked structures of information such as links between folder-contents or content-content can be visualized in information spaces. Other structures also have potential for visualization. Every possibility should be examined thoroughly.

4 Concluding Remarks

The primary motivation for this research came from a desire to leverage natural human capabilities to better understand information management. Based on prior research, new information management systems can be developed. Although a particular system will be developed and studied in this research, its concept can be applied to various types of information systems. The ultimate goal of this research is to make better use of people's valuable resources such as time, effort, and attention. In addition, might improve personal productivity and teamwork. In conclusion, improvements in information literacy programs are also expected. We live in a very complex and often overwhelming information world, and I personally believe that researchers who focus on information and information systems have a responsibility to help people make its retrieval, use, and application easier and more natural.

References

1. Moore, P.: Information problem solving: a wider view of library skills. Contemp. Educ. Psychol. **20**, 1–31 (1995)
2. Eisenberg, M.B.: Information Literacy: Essential Skills for the Information Age. DESIDOC J. Libr. Inf. Technol. **28**(2), 39–47 (2008)
3. Fidel, R.: What Is Human Information Interaction? Human Information Interaction: An Ecological Approach to Information Behavior, pp. 17–43
4. Jones, W.: Personal Information Management. Annu. Rev. Inf. Sci. Technol. **41**, 453–504 (2007)
5. Bergman, O.: Variables for personal information management research. Aslib Proc. **65**, 464–483 (2013)
6. Bruce, H.: Personal, anticipated information need. Inf. Res. 10(3) (2005). http://www.informationr.net/ir/10-3/paper232.html
7. Odom, W., Sellen, A., Harper, R., Thereska, E.: Lost in translation: understanding the possession of digital things in the cloud. In: Presented at the CHI 2012: Proceedings of the SIGCHI Conference on Human Factors in Computing Systems, New York, USA, May 2012
8. Maglio, P.P., Matlock, T.: The conceptual structure of information space. In: Höök, K., Benyon, D., Munro, A.J. (eds.) Designing Information Spaces: The Social Navigation Approach, 385–403. Springer, London (2003)
9. Jones, W.P., Dumais, S.T.: The spatial metaphor for user interfaces: experimental tests of reference by location versus name. ACM Trans. Inf. Syst. (TOIS). **4**, 42–63 (1986)
10. Robertson, G., Czerwinski, M., Larson, K.: Data mountain: using spatial memory for document management. In: Presented at the Proceedings of the 11th annual ACM symposium on User interface software and technology, New York, USA (1998)
11. Cockburn, A., McKenzie, B.: Evaluating spatial memory in two and three dimensions. Int. J. Hum. Comput. Stud. **61**, 359–373 (2004)
12. Barshi, I., Healy, A.F.: The effects of mental representation on performance in a navigation task. Mem. Cogn. **30**(8), 1189–1203 (2002)
13. Boechler, P.M.: How spatial is hyperspace? interacting with hypertext documents: cognitive processes and concepts. Cyber Psychol. Behav. **4**, 23–46 (2001)
14. Indratmo, J., Vassileva, J.: A review of organizational structures of personal information management. J. Digit. Inform. **9**, 1–19 (2008)
15. Boroditsky, L.: Metaphoric structuring: Understanding time through spatial metaphors. Cognition **75**, 1–28 (2000)
16. Casasanto, D., Boroditsky, L.: Time in the mind: using space to think about time. Cognition **106**, 579–593 (2008)
17. Lee, J.-G., Lee, K.C., Shin, D.-H.: A New Approach to Exploring Spatiotemporal Space in the Context of Social Network Services. In: Meiselwitz, G. (ed.) Social Computing and Social Media, pp. 221–228. Springer International Publishing, Cham (2014)

Visual Interactive Process Monitoring

Sebastian Maier[1]([✉]), Hannes Kühnel[2], Thorsten May[1], and Arjan Kuijper[2]

[1] Fraunhofer Institute for Computer Graphics Research,
Fraunhoferstr. 5, 64283 Darmstadt, Germany
{Sebastian.Maier,Thorsten.May}@igd.fraunhofer.de
[2] TU Darmstadt, Darmstadt, Germany

Abstract. Sensor data has been coined the oil of the 21st century. We present a technique for the visual analysis of multivariate sensor event log data. This technique tackles two challenges: Firstly, in a complex process the relation of causes and effects is often masked by indirections. Secondly, the metrics to measure success might be different from the measures that identify causes. Thus, our approach does not require that all sensor data is equal. Our techniques combines automated and interactive grouping to identify candidate sets sharing properties relevant for cause and effect analysis. Interactive visual probes offer immediate information on the statistical relevance of an identified connection.

1 Introduction

Large quantities of data are created nowadays by sensors embedded in larger systems. Sensor data is created in virtually any company, in an increasing number of devices, and even in our private lives. In an industrial setting, sensor data are often part of a complex production or service process. A single instance of such a process typically traverses a number of components. Many components are equipped with various sensors each creating additional data about this process instance. During process execution, these sensors create events containing a timestamp and further specific data. For example sensors are used to monitor input or output quality, operational parameters of the process component, like control parameters, throughput, resource consumption or wear. In our scenario, we assume that processes are executed multiple times. Thus, in summary they produce a large amount of data which can be used to evaluate process performance and cost.

Applying concepts from visual analytics to present and analyze this data helps to unveil those nuggets of information which have potential to improve the process and also the product. A key requirement is the ability to identify the root cause for a specific subset of process outcomes. For example, an operator might be interested in the cost-drivers for a specific industrial or service process. This can be further complicated as the effects might be expressed in one unit of measurement like revenue while the cause might be in another unit of measurement like execution time.

Given a process model and a reasonably large set of sensor data, it is difficult to find those interesting nuggets of information within such a sea of data.

© Springer International Publishing Switzerland 2015
S. Yamamoto (Ed.): HIMI 2015, Part I, LNCS 9172, pp. 74–85, 2015.
DOI: 10.1007/978-3-319-20612-7_8

Manyika et al. [11] have estimated the potential value for the US health care system to $ 300 billion. According to them this value can be created in several ways, two of them being creating transparency and by enabling experimentation to improve performance. Both ways require human access to the data.

In the following section we will give an overview of *related work* from the process mining and process monitoring community as well as previous works on visualizing temporal event sequences. In the *method* section we will discuss our approach in detail. Describing the visual representation as well as the analytical components. The *results* section will provide feedback from the user evaluation on specific visual design decisions and the overall application.

In summary, our contribution is a technique for the visual analysis of multivariate event logs data. This technique tackles two challenges: Firstly, in a complex process the relation of causes and effects is often masked by indirections. Secondly, the metrics to measure success might be different from the measures that identify causes. Thus, our approach does not require that all sensor data is equal. Our techniques combines automated and interactive grouping to identify candidate sets sharing properties relevant for cause and effect analysis. Interactive probes offer immediate information on the statistical relevance of an identified connection.

2   Related Work

As we consider this work to be at the corner of *process mining* and *visual analytics* we reviewed publications which are relevant to understand the field of process mining and those applying visual analytics techniques to process data.

2.1   Process Mining

Process mining is a combination of data mining, process modeling and analysis. As opposed to process design and operation, process mining is considered a "bottom-up" approach. This means, processes are modeled, evaluated and compared based on empirical measurement. The idea is to discover, monitor and improve real processes through extraction of information from event logs. The basis for process mining is an event log, with every event representing a sensor in a process step. Event typically include a timestamp and potentially multivariate information, depending on the sensor.

Van der Aalst et al. [3] distinguishes three high-level tasks for process mining - discovery, conformance and enhancement. *Discovery* is the task of building a process model based upon the patterns identified in the event logs. *Conformance* basically combines process mining and process design. Event data is mapped onto a specific process model. The result of a conformance test defines if and where the model matches the measurement. *Enhancement* aims at extending a process model to adapt to new measurements or newly emerging patterns.

Van der Aalst et al. defined six guiding principles for process mining in the Process Mining Manifesto [3], we will name those two we see as most important for our application:

- Log extraction should be driven by questions, because they give better understanding and meaning for event data.
- Models should be treated as purposeful abstractions of reality, because it is helpful to have multiple views on data because there can be multiple views.

In the same Manifesto they defined eleven challenges, we will focus on the challenges eight to eleven, which we do aim for with this paper:

- Provide operational support because process mining is not only an offline analysis but can also be used for online operational support, where three activities can be found: detect, predict, and recommend.
- Process Mining also should be combined with other types of analysis like e.g. visual analytics, simulation and data mining to get more information from event data.
- Usability for non-experts should be improved in form of user-friendly interfaces in front of the process mining and algorithms.
- Understandability for non-experts also has to be improved because there are problems by understanding the results of the analysis, so they should be clearly shown.

2.2 Process Visualization and Analysis

Process visualization techniques are a subclass of time-oriented data visualization techniques (see Tominski and Aigner for a survey [5]). In this section, we focus on techniques primarily aimed at *discrete* time-oriented data, such as event logs. With this focus, we may distinguish techniques that show explicit connections between discrete events (i.e. they show the process) and those that do not. Furthermore, we distinguish whether a technique shows a single instance or multiple instances. By "instance" we refer to either a process instance or an event series, in case a process is not defined. In these terms, our own technique is a process visualization for multiple process instances, each of which containing heterogeneous multivariate data. Visualization of process models actually have been first proposed outside the visualization community. In fact, visual business process design is part of a number of commercial tools. In virtually all cases, the visualization is a node-link diagram. Albrecht et al. [6] present an approach to layout models defined according to BPEL standard. However, the visualization of the model only, does not serve a direct purpose for a "bottom-up" approach. For visual process mining, the event data has to be included in the visualization.

Rind et al. [13] compare fourteen visualization techniques for electronic health records, which mostly consist of discrete event data. Most of the techniques surveyed do not show explicit connections between events. Events, like, diagnoses, therapies and outcomes are often arranged along a time axis. *Lifelines2* [18] is an example for such a visualization and temporal comparison of multiple patient records. Lifelines2 also features so called *temporal summaries*; these summaries present the distribution of durations or time between events over all patients in a specific group. This approach is similar to our probes, except that our probes are moved freely over the visualization to define events for analysis. In comparison, the *Lifeflow* [20] approach emphasizes the comparison of event sequences instead of time or durations. Such a sequence visualization offers a "middle ground" between anchoring events on a time axis and connecting events to a process model. Finally the Outflow [19] visualization anchors the patient data to the visualization of the model. Like our own approach, it combines properties from Sankey Diagrams [12] and techniques for layouting directed acyclic graphs [8]. Sankey Diagrams have originally been invented to visualize import and export volumes traded across the world. Riehmann et al. [12] present an interactive version to show an energy distribution network. Sankey Diagrams are directed graphs, whose edge thickness is defined by the volume of flow. With outflow and our approach, the edge thickness is defined by the number of instances. Directed acyclic graphs are easier to layout than general graphs. Thus, specific layout techniques have been proposed, and many layout techniques preserve the sequence of events, which we adopted for our technique. In comparison to Lifelines2 or similar approaches, the relative time is not preserved in the spatial layout. We capture time and duration in the nodes. *Sessionviewer* [10] is a visualization for web session logs, offering multiple levels of granularity. It relates views on different levels of aggregation. A model view, which is a state transition graph, an aggregate view over time and detailed information for all sessions. Most notably it is aimed at distinguishing sessions by different usage patterns.

Aside from the visualization itself, a number of approaches have focused on analytical challenges. One of these challenges is sequence aggregation and identification of patterns. For multivariate process data, patterns may be defined in terms of the process structure, in terms of node attributes or any combinations thereof. Fails et al. present a query interface for the comprehensive investigation of event patterns. Queries are edited in visual building blocks. Thus, the user must establish the correspondence between query and result on his own. Another approach to identify patterns between processes has been presented by Wongsuphasawat and Lin [21]. This approach analyses event logs, to identify different patterns of web client use for customer analysis. Specifically their visualization highlights changes of usage patterns for dynamic data. Usage patterns are distinguished by criteria with a predefined ordering. Our approach differs from Fails' approach that a query specification is done by interacting with probes in the process visualization. Our approach differs from Wongsuphasawat's and Lin's approach that patterns are defined as free combinations of node attributes and a specific process structure.

The *parallel sets* approach [9] has been proposed for multivariate categorical data instead of process data. However, parts of its design and behavior are similar to our approach. Most notably, parallel axes are connected by groups of data items, that can in turn be highlighted for detailed inspection. Furthermore the axes offer information about potential correlations between adjacent axes. We provide this function by means of virtual probes.

The idea of an interactive virtual probe has been mainly inspired from similar approaches in scientific visualization [16]. Probes are used to avoid clutter in complex three-dimensional views. In essence, they provide a pivot area (points, planes or volumes) of a domain, where detailed information is mapped onto. Typically, multiple probes of different types may be moved around freely, which is also supported by our approach.

3   Method

Following Shneidermans well known InfoVis mantra "Overview first, Filter and zoom, Details on demand" [15] we start with providing an overview of the process structure including the information about the event flow to the user. This process overview is provided using a customized Sankey diagram [7,14]. Each node in this diagram represents one of the sensors, see Fig. 1.

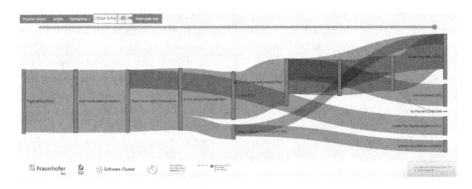

Fig. 1. Initial overview of the full process. The bars (in green) represent steps in the business process. We can immediately see that the process has different endpoints and various junctions (Color figure online).

This is the starting point for all analytical paths the user can choose to explore. We provide two complementing ways to explore the process data. One makes use of the identified event clusters while the other relies on the concept of data probes. A data probe is a small overlay visualization providing detailed information on the attribute(s) of a single sensor. Both ways enable the user to filter the data flow. We can filter based on cluster affiliation and based on the value at one or multiple sensors. For clusters we provide a means to compare two clusters based on their properties. Data probes allow us to perform what-if analysis to explore dependencies between different sensors and sensor attributes.

We will detail each of the described analytical paths in the following subsections after a quick discussion of the data preprocessing and the overview visualization.

3.1   Data Preprocessing

Most, if not all data analysis tools require some sort of data preprocessing to enable a reasonable (visual) presentation for the user.

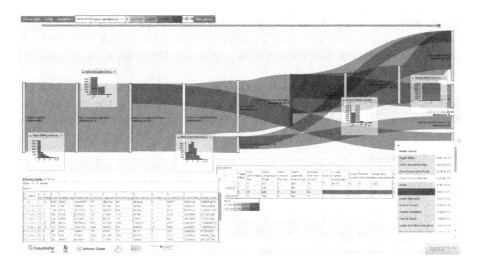

Fig. 2. Visualization of the entire process model with active filters and multiple overlays showing detailed information. Five probes have been places over the process visualization. They show the distribution of performance and cost indicators for a subset of event sessions.

The data consists of a process model, a directed acyclic graph, and a vector of readings for each sensor and session. Each reading is associated with a session id, enabling us to follow the flow of any session through the process model. The process model provides not only information about the relationship between sensors but also information about the split join semantics. Process and business model notations, as one instance of process models, usually provide two different split and join modes: *AND* and *XOR*. See Vergidis et al. for an overview of different business model notations and their supported patterns [17].

To collect sensor properties, like average duration, costs, etc. we attach the event data to the process model and calculate those metrics for each sensor. The two clustering steps are described in more detail in Subsect. 3.3. The overview visualization will be described in the following section (Fig. 2).

3.2 Overview

Providing users with an initial overview is considered good practice in the InfoVis community. Van der Aalst considers a good visual representation of a process model as one of the challenges of process mining [1,2]. We decided to use a *Sankey* diagram for the visualization of the events flowing through the process model. We decided against a standard node-link diagram to emphasize the amount of sessions following a certain path in the model. With a standard node-link diagram this would not be so explicit. As the maximum width of the links is restricted by the size of the nodes - it is not reasonable to draw the links larger then the attached nodes. Another option would have been a matrix visualization of the underlying graph. However, a matrix visualization masks the temporal ordering of the process. We assume, that preserving the ordering is helpful for cause and effect analysis.

The overview visualization provides zooming and panning for the user to adjust it to her needs. Additional overlays can be added to the overview to support the detailed analysis. They will be describes in the following subsections.

3.3   Clustering

As useful as it is to work on the event sessions, sometimes one is interested on a higher level of abstraction. Our approach offers a method to cluster the event series by their sequence. This is done with an modified *apriori* algorithm. The classical example for this is the identification of *items* which are bought together in the same *transaction* [4]. We interpret sensors as *items* and event sessions as *transactions*. This leads to a clustering of those event sessions that traverse the same set of sensors, independent of the sequence of traversal. In addition, it is possible to define custom clusters by selecting a set of sensors such that all event sessions traversing these sensors will be part of the custom cluster.

For each cluster a number of data attributes are calculated based on the event sequences. This includes information like the number of sequences in the cluster and the number of sensors traversed by this cluster. Also we aggregate each data attribute available for the events. This information is presented to the user in form of a data table.

An additional visualization is available to compare all clusters at once according to quantitative attributes, which has been calculated in the cluster creation phase (see Fig. 3).

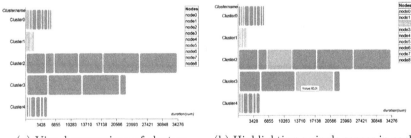

    (a) Visual comparison of clusters   (b) Highlighting a single sensor in each cluster

Fig. 3. The views are used to compare a quantitative attribute (here: duration) between different clusters (vertical axis). Every cluster defines a set of sensors, represented by green rectangles. The attribute is mapped on the width of a rectangle. Measurements on the same sensor, but different clusters can be compared as well (right) (Color figure online).

Cluster definitions can further be used to filter the full event dataset to only those events comprising a single cluster. This filtering is applied directly to the overview visualization, highlighting all sensors and event sessions which are part of the selected cluster (Fig. 4).

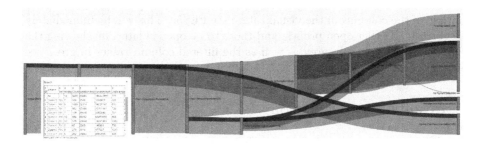

Fig. 4. Highlighting a single cluster

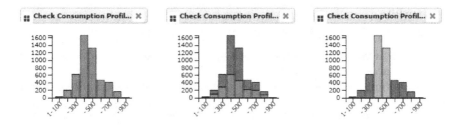

(a) No filter has been defined

(b) A filter has been defined on another probe

(c) A filter has been defined on this probe

Fig. 5. Data probe for a single sensor (here: consumption) in three different states. A value range can be chosen by selecting the corresponding bar of the histogram (Color figure online).

3.4 Data Probes

In contrast to the clustering, our concept of data probes provides a bottom up analytical access. Our user can start his analysis at any sensor, selecting any data attribute that is available for this sensor see Fig. 5a. A data probe will visualize the distribution of the selected attributes values for a single sensor.

There is no technical limitation - except available screen space - to the number of probes a user can attach to the process model. It is even possible to attach multiple probes for different attributes to the same sensor. As space is limited, we render the probes at about 200 square pixels, we perform an automated bucketing of the attributes values to reduce space requirements. To facilitate comparison the bucketing for any attribute is the same for all sensors.

Probes can either be linked to a sensor, in that case we can move them freely in the overview visualization and they will still show the linked sensors readings. Alternatively we can set them into *quick show* mode, in this case, they will always show the readings for the sensor currently touched with the mouse.

Data probes also allow the interactive definition of filters on sensor attributes. Uses can choose to select a single or multiple values by simply clicking on one or multiple of the columns in the visualization see Fig. 5c. This will be immediately reflected on all other open probes, and those to be opened later, by showing the original column values in grey as well as the filtered column values in green see Fig. 5b.

4   Results and Evaluation

We will give a quick overview of the results we obtained so far with this system and also give a summary of the evaluation we conducted with information visualization experts.

4.1   Results

The presented system allows us to analyze large sets of process instances. For our prototype we used different sets with up to five thousand artificially created process instances. Event attribute values have been generated using different stochastic distributions to model real world behavior. The generation of an custom event set has allowed us to work with a data set containing known correlations

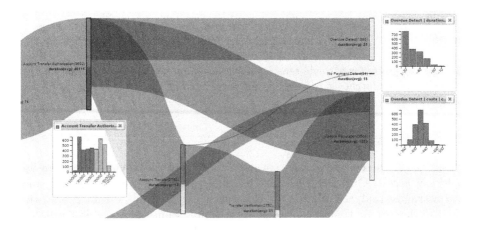

Fig. 6. Using our data probes to analyze correlations in the event data. We have mapped the average duration of events to the color of the sensors. For the leftmost sensor we selected those event sequences with the highest duration. We can see that the top right sensor is only visited by those long running sequences (Color figure online).

between attributes and sensors. The main data set shown in the included figures represents a billing process. The data set contained four dimensions for every event: duration, cost, resources and an invoice id. Parts of the user evaluation are based on smaller artificial sets to focus on specific aspects.

Figure 6 shows a dependency analysis highlighting the artificial correlation between high durations at one sensor and their final process step being *Overdue Detect*. The combination of two different techniques, clustering and data probes, allows to access the data from different perspectives, possibly answering different questions.

4.2   Evaluation

We conducted a two day evaluation with ten information visualization experts, all with an academic background. Most of them had previous experiences with graph visualizations but only a minority had been working with business processes in the past.

During design phase we identified that for a sankey diagram there exist multiple variants to split flows with *AND* or *XOR* semantic. As the split-join semantic is a central information for any process model we evaluated two different visualizations for *AND* and *XOR* splits, see Fig. 7.

All our participants of the evaluation identified 7a as *XOR* splits. And most of them identified 7d as *AND* splits. We subsequently used those representations for the *AND* and *XOR* split.

We also compared the usefulness of a visual mapping of a single sensor attribute to the color of the sensor with labels containing the exact attributes value. Hardly surprising the preference for one or the other depended largely on the task we asked the users to perform.

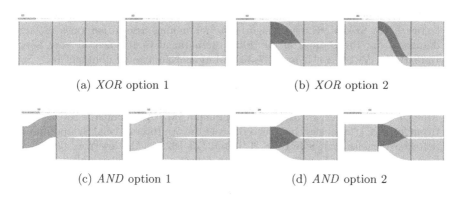

(a) *XOR* option 1   (b) *XOR* option 2

(c) *AND* option 1   (d) *AND* option 2

Fig. 7. Evaluation options for the visualization of a split (Color figure online)

5 Conclusion

We present a web-based system to enable human centered visual analysis of process based sensor readings. The application supports exploratory analysis on the aggregated process level as well as on the single sensor level. It is possible to explore the relation between cause and effect using our data probes. A top down approach using precalculated event clusters enables us to filter on process instances with a similar behavior. We evaluated different visual representations for process splits, providing an indication of understandability of those.

We have shown that it is possible to perform data intensive analysis of process log data within a browser. Using different visualization techniques for two distinct analytical paths. Using a sankey diagram for the process visualization has proven to be possible and understandable by experienced users.

Although we used a manually created process model, it would be possible to perform a process mining step on event data to create the process model needed for our approach.

Acknowledgements. This work was partially funded by the German Federal Ministry of Education and Research (BMBF) in the INDINET project under grant number 01IC10S04I.

References

1. van der Aalst, W.: Cartography and Navigation. In: Process Mining, pp. 321–335. Springer, Heidelberg (2011)
2. van der Aalst, W.: Epilogue. In: Process Mining, pp. 337–340. Springer, Heidelberg (2011)
3. van der Aalst, W., et al.: Process mining manifesto. In: Daniel, F., Barkaoui, K., Dustdar, S. (eds.) BPM Workshops 2011, Part I. LNBIP, vol. 99, pp. 169–194. Springer, Heidelberg (2012)
4. Agrawal, R., Srikant, R.: Fast algorithms for mining association rules in large databases. In: Proceedings of the 20th International Conference on Very Large Data Bases, VLDB 1994, pp. 487–499. Morgan Kaufmann Publishers Inc., San Francisco (1994)
5. Aigner, W., Miksch, S., Schumann, H., Tominski, C.: Visualization of Time-Oriented Data. Human-Computer Interaction Series. Springer, London (2011)
6. Albrecht, B., Effinger, P., Held, M., Kaufmann, M.: An automatic layout algorithm for BPEL processes. In: Proceedings of the 5th International Symposium on Software Visualization, SOFTVIS 2010, pp. 173–182. ACM, New York (2010)
7. Bostock, M.: Sankey Diagram (2012). http://bost.ocks.org/mike/sankey/
8. Gansner, E.R., Koutsofios, E., North, S.C., Vo, K.P.: A technique for drawing directed graphs. IEEE Trans. Softw. Eng. **19**(3), 214–230 (1993)
9. Kosara, R., Bendix, F., Hauser, H.: Parallel sets: interactive exploration and visual analysis of categorical data. IEEE Trans. Vis. Comput. Graph. **12**(4), 558–568 (2006)
10. Lam, H., Russell, D., Tang, D., Munzner, T.: Session viewer: visual exploratory analysis of web session logs. In: 2007 IEEE Symposium on Visual Analytics Science and Technology, VAST 2007, pp. 147–154, October 2007

11. Manyika, J., Chui, M., Brown, B., Bughin, J., Dobbs, R., Roxburgh, C., Byers, A.H.: Big data: the next frontier for innovation, competition, and productivity. Technical report, McKinsey Global Institute, June 2011
12. Riehmann, P., Hanfler, M., Froehlich, B.: Interactive sankey diagrams. In: 2005 IEEE Symposium on Information Visualization, INFOVIS 2005, pp. 233–240 (2005)
13. Rind, A., Wang, T.D., Aigner, W., Miksch, S., Wongsuphasawat, K., Plaisant, C., Shneiderman, B.: Interactive information visualization to explore and query electronic health records. Found. Trends Hum. Comput. Interact. **5**(3), 207–298 (2013)
14. Schmidt, M.: Der Einsatz von Sankey-Diagrammen im Stoffstrommanagement. Technical report 124, Hochschule Pforzheim (2006)
15. Shneiderman, B.: The eyes have it: a task by data type taxonomy for information visualizations. In: 1996 Proceedings. of IEEE Symposium on Visual Languages, pp. 336–343, September 1996
16. Speray, D., Kennon, S.: Volume probes: interactive data exploration on arbitrary grids. In: Proceedings of the 1990 Workshop on Volume Visualization, VVS 1990, pp. 5–12. ACM, New York (1990)
17. Vergidis, K., Tiwari, A., Majeed, B.: Business process analysis and optimization: beyond reengineering. IEEE Trans. Syst. Man Cybern. C Appl. Rev. **38**(1), 69–82 (2008)
18. Wang, T.D., Wongsuphasawat, K., Plaisant, C., Shneiderman, B.: Extracting insights from electronic health records: case studies, a visual analytics process model, and design recommendations. J. Med. Syst. **35**(5), 1135–1152 (2011)
19. Wongsuphasawat, K., Gotz, D.: Exploring flow, factors, and outcomes of temporal event sequences with the outflow visualization. IEEE Trans. Vis. Comput. Graph. **18**(12), 2659–2668 (2012)
20. Wongsuphasawat, K., Guerra Gómez, J.A., Plaisant, C., Wang, T.D., Taieb-Maimon, M., Shneiderman, B.: LifeFlow: visualizing an overview of event sequences. In: Proceedings of the SIGCHI Conference on Human Factors in Computing Systems, p. 1747. ACM Press (2011)
21. Wongsuphasawat, K., Lin, J.: Using visualizations to monitor changes and harvest insights from a global-scale logging infrastructure at Twitter. In: 2014 IEEE Conference on Visual Analytics Science and Technology (VAST), pp. 113–122, October 2014

Uncertainty Visualization Framework for Improving Situational Awareness in Emergency Management Systems

Natália Ferreira Oliveira[1(✉)], Leonardo Castro Botega[1,2], Lucas César Ferreira[1], and Márcio Roberto de Campos[2]

[1] Computing and Information Systems Research Lab (COMPSI), Marília Eurípides University (UNIVEM), Marília, São Paulo, Brazil
{nataliaoliveira,lucascesarf}@univem.edu.br
[2] Wireless Networks and Distributed Interactive Simulations Lab (WINDIS), Computer Department, Federal University of São Carlos (UFSCar), São Carlos, São Paulo, Brazil
{leonardo_botega,marcamposbr}@dc.ufscar.br

Abstract. Situation awareness (SAW) is the perception of environmental elements within a volume of time and space, the comprehension of their meaning, and the projection of their status in the near future. Processes of acquisition, maintenance and recovering of situation awareness, guided by information visualization methods, may be affected by problems related to the quality of information processing and display, undermining the decision-making process. Among such problems, uncertainty, general dimension and association with the complete gathering of information may arise from the acquisition to its processing and cognition in SAW-oriented systems. Thus, the present study describes the creation of a framework that integrates and disseminates issues related to quality of information and quality of representation, involving the application of graphical representation techniques of uncertainties generated by the dimensions of completeness, consistency and dimensions related to time, such as currently. A case study of emergency management information display will be discussed to illustrate the applicability of the representative framework to improve situation awareness, as well as the graphical representation techniques of uncertainty. Results of this study are discussed, and they point out the contribution to the process of situation awareness of emergency management makers.

Keywords: Uncertainty visualization · Situation Awareness

1 Introduction

The graphic representation of information for the emergency management decision-making presents challenges because of the need to provide expert decision makers, subsidies to understand the reality of the situation awareness in a real-time scenario [1].

To support SAW, the information display has been used as a manner to present products and by-products of processing steps of the emergency intelligence, called situation assessment. In each set of information produced, the expert observes and takes

© Springer International Publishing Switzerland 2015
S. Yamamoto (Ed.): HIMI 2015, Part I, LNCS 9172, pp. 86–96, 2015.
DOI: 10.1007/978-3-319-20612-7_9

guidance in the light of visualizations, and then makes the decision and acts according to the level of SAW.

These visualizations can be jeopardized when quality problems resulted in the acquisition, processing and interpretation of information are added to the SAW process. One of these problems is the uncertainty.

Pang et al. [2], it is described the uncertainty as a concepts which comprises inconsistency, doubt, reliability, inaccuracy and error, and may include statistics variations, errors, differences, noises, or missing data.

However, there is a consensus that uncertainty does exist and it is known, so it should be viewed and transmitted to the experts.

Thus, information visualization analysis is intended not only for evaluating available information and the way in which they are organized, but should also help guiding the expert as for the uncertainty of such information. To this end, quality metadata is used (metacues) to qualify the information. Such metadata can help inform the experts and help them measure the influence that each information has in decision making. When there is a lack of quality metadata, the visualization may allow some misunderstanding [1].

The state of the art in visualization uncertainties for situation assessment indicates that in order to graphically represent the information necessary for the SAW process, authors often describe visualization techniques for the dimensions specific to domains. However, the need to portray quality as a representation spread over several modules of acquisition, processing, and visualization of information in systems aimed at situation awareness, is still an area to be explored.

Every uncertainty information can directly change the decision-making process. This is due to the fact that there is no pattern to follow when it comes to issues of quality aggregated to information. The same thing happens with the data visualization process that does not follow any standard that indicates ideal data visualization for cognition under adverse conditions of uncertainty [2].

The present article introduces a new framework to orientate the creation of visualizations from uncertain information, propagated by processes of a group authorship situation assessment system. This framework also aims at demonstrating the impact of uncertainty on the graphical representation of information for the guidance of experts. To this end, it is evaluated methods of graphic representation of known uncertainties and new alternative proposals to make the framework feasible, specifically under the dimensions of completeness and dimensions related to time.

A case study in the analysis of context information for uncertain situation awareness of crime events is described. In this scenario, the framework is applied to the construction of visualizations in synergy with uncertain information propagated in the process, which is useful to the SAW process.

In Sect. 2 situation awareness applied to emergency management field is presented, as well as the importance of abstraction of situation information to the decision-making process. Section 3 presents the quality of data and information applied to the emergency management, as well as dimensions of quality and uncertainty. In Sect. 4, advances in visual representation of uncertainty are discussed. Section 5 illustrates in detail the processes that make up the framework. Section 6 presents the results of an implementation case study of the proposed framework for the design of uncertainty visualizations to the emergency. Finally, in Sect. 7, the findings of the case study results are presented and discussed, illustrating the contributions and future work.

2 Situation Awareness in the Emergency Management Systems

Situation Awareness (SAW) is a cognitive model which explains the understanding by an personal to dynamic and complex decision making systems. SAW can be modeled in three levels: perception, understanding, and projection.

The perception level is characterized by the identifying entities relevant of the environment. The level of understanding goes beyond the perception of the elements, including understanding the meaning and the evolution of states of these elements in view of the objectives. And the level of projection is characterized by the ability to project actions of the environmental features in the near future [3].

Since reaching the SAW state is a process that occurs in the operator's mind, it is very important to understand the level of knowledge they obtained in the use of a system, so that failures in cognition do not affect the decision-making process. In the representation level of information, the goal is to provide visualizations in order to assist in the understanding of what is happening in the scene for the user to abstract the current status in relation to the problem, so that the projection of the sequence of activities is faithful in what concerns the environment [3].

SAW is the basis for decision-making, and its performance is commonly applied to the emergency call situations. The higher the level SAW maintained, the greater the effectiveness of the decision-making.

These systems aiming to assist the understanding of the situation are dependent on the quality of the information so that the information provided to system operators is the best in relation to the current situation, thereby assisting in cognition and decision-making. The system operator can be subjected to uncertainty when uncertain information is provided to the SAW system, affecting the decision-making process.

Given that uncertainty can be contained in the information, the visualization of uncertain data must provide the user with a resource for the acquisition, maintenance and recovering of situation awareness. The goal is to provide the decision-maker with visualizations that help the abstraction of the current state of situation so that the projection of the activities sequence of resources is accurate related to the environment [4].

So that decision-makers acquire SAW of an specific mission by means of visual media, it is important to use charts, graphs, timelines, and visual distortion of the scene in the composition, in an integrated manner or in fusion, by adding glyphs, and visual metrics able to help prioritize future actions, then making useful visualizations to support the acquisition /maintenance of SAW and decision-making by reducing the analysis time of relevant information.

3   Quality of Information in Emergency Field

Quality is considered one of the most important factors in the decision-making systems, since information with quality problems reduce the effectiveness of a support system for cognition, hinders the formation of the mental model and affects SAW process, resulting in a wrong decision-making.

The quality of data is a multidisciplinary concept. In the emergency field, limitations are commonly reported regarding the completeness of size, accuracy, consistency, and time [5]. Emergency management systems, has quality of data as a decisive factor, since the process of awareness of the operator's situation is made based on the information that the system displays in real time. Such information, when lacking of quality, impairs creation of the mental model of the situation, which makes the projection of the activities sequence imperfect.

Although there is no consensus in general dimensions and metrics to be adopted in different fields that require knowledge of the quality of information, experts agree that both the presence of imperfect information and the lack of familiarity with quality meta-information knowledge can sacrifice all decision-making process, resulting in a decreased reliance on these systems.

According to Mecella et al. [6], you can define a basic set of dimensions that make up a definition of the quality of data and information in the emergency field, including the syntax accuracy, completeness, consistency, and time dimensions.

Pang et al. [2], describe uncertainty as a complex concept that encompasses several other concepts such as inconsistency, doubt, reliability, inaccuracy, and error. It can also include statistical variations, errors, differences, noise or missing data. More generally, the uncertainty of definitions implies that there are imperfections in the knowledge of users about a data set, process or outcome.

Among main sources of uncertainty in assessing situations, the main ones are the processes of acquisition and transformation of the data, steps where the data undergoes change from its initial shape [7].

The uncertainty in the emergency systems field is a process that takes place in the mind of an expert system due to quality problems above mentioned: imprecision, incompleteness, inconsistency, and time dimensions. When these factors are presented in the analysis of a situation, they can influence the system operator to an inaccurate and inconsistent opinion. Additionally, we consider uncertainty a generalization of such dimensions; an overall measure of quality information.

4   Advances in the Visualization of Uncertainties

Gouin and Evdokiou [4], present an advanced visualization developed for the program of the Future Command Post, called 'Circular Blobs', consisting of a three-dimensional terrain where circles represent the deployment force of the weapons base, the thickness of the line represents its strength, and the circle diameter represents the range of weapons. In this example, features such as color, size, shape, edges and thickness are used to represent the information.

Fricker and Macklin [8] introduce a map-based visualization in which resources are represented in different bases. All information is presented concerning quantity, resources and power level compared to other bases. In this example, colors in shapes and sizes are used to assist the representation, allowing the operator to easily understand the situation. The authors map routes that take the resources from allied bases to enemy bases. The information is presented in relation to criticality, amount of resources, power level (strength) of the base and whether it is running. This example conveys more information to the decision-maker since it uses color in the ground structure to transmit the degree of security of each region, which facilitates the recognition of the area to which the base belongs [8].

Pang et al. [2] present the results of the development of uncertainty visualization methods, among them radiosity, animation, interpolation, flow visualization, adding glyphs, adding geometry, geometry modification, attribute modification, sonification, and the use of psycho-visual techniques.

5   Uncertainty Visualization Framework for Improving Situational Awareness in Decision Making System

As part of a complete model of situation assessment, this paper aims to improve the process of SAW. To fulfill this objective, it was structured a framework that specifies the steps for the construction of visualizations aware of uncertainty which meet situation awareness requirements in management systems of emergency situations.

The framework was defined in order to support the phases of a situation assessment system, considering how each phase impacts on the representation of field information and on the observation /orientation of the expert.

The solution to be described aims to solve quality problems in emergency call decision-making, besides contributing to the acquisition, maintenance and recovering SAW state.

In order to do so, it is necessary that visualization assists the perception and understanding of the whole situation. Figure 1 shows how other assessment processes interact with the visual representation processes. In orange color, see the fundamental modules for the information visualization.

At first, it is necessary to relate specific sub-processes of information visualization with the acquisition phase at the beginning of the stream. This approach is relevant for two reasons: visually encode the raw data obtained from heterogeneous data sources, initially in transcribed audio of phone calls to the São Paulo State Police (PMES), or graphically represent objects and attributes identified in this step by natural language processing methods (NLP). This step of acquisition is best described by Junior et al. [9].

The visualization of raw data may be relevant to help the expert to infer entities not inferred by automated processes. In turn, encoding of objects and attributes is an essential part of SAW process, identified as a priority in the analysis of visualization requirements. According to [10] the needed objects to attend a robbery report are: criminal, victim, stolen object and event spot which are identified by the NLP [9]

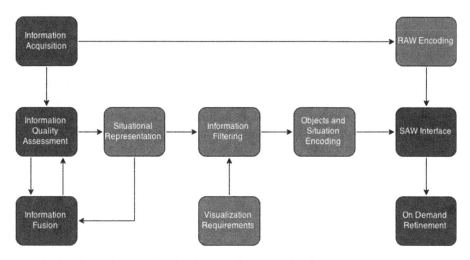

Fig. 1. Uncertainty visualization framework as part of a situation assessment process

When there is the need to visualize raw data, they are directly brought to the interface, without any prior review or quality assessment. In the case of the visualization of objects and relevant attributes identified via NLP and that are of interest to the expert, a JavaScript Object Notation (JSON) schema first transports them to an assessment of the quality of the inferred information, seeking a preliminary trial information.

In the primary evaluation phase, there is the analysis of synctactic accuracy, in which algorithms identify misspellings which can impair the assessment of the completeness dimension, measured by the attributes present in the complaint call. In addition to the completeness, timeliness is also inferred and scored. The return of this information is also in a JSON schema, this time also carrying quality indicators, useful for setting the visualization in the graphically represented quality [10].

The output generated by the acquisition and evaluation is regarded as a situation knowledge that should be represented. In the complete evaluation system, it was opted for the semantic model of ontologies to represent such knowledge. To date, objects, their attributes and possible relationships between objects are known. In situations assessment systems, it is appointed L1 and L2 levels of assessment, also corresponding to the levels of perception and understanding of SAW. This knowledge must be encoded in visualizations.

The process of abstraction and coding in visualizations is complicated when the representation contains a lot of information, since it may lead the expert to not notice all the elements in a given time interval. To mitigate these problems, a process of information filtering was used. Filtering is a process that helps determine which information should be represented, when it should be represented, how and where in SAW interface. This feature provides the user access to the high-level when available, and the low-level information when needed.

This abstraction is achieved by using graphics variables such as color, shape, size, animation, among others. When combined, these techniques allow the experts to easily get to the awareness of the situation due to the possibility to draw attention to the information that they consider important because of its quality score over others.

In addition to the acquisition processes for the generation of entities to be encoded, minings and integrations can be performed using the existing objects. This process, known as information fusion, is capable of producing, in a lesser extent, new objects and new semantic relations between them, which shall also be represented. The product of this step, called situation, is also subject to evaluations, enriches the existing situation awareness, and then encoded. Figure 2 shows an example of JSON schema to be encoded.

The encoding step results in visualizations of objects detected in the time of acquisition, fusion and evaluation, mapped in the visualization by using the above mentioned techniques of visualization of uncertain information such as colors, shapes, size, position, border, and transparency.

The requirements for the encoding of visualizations were defined based on the state of the art in visualization of uncertainties, and by mans of the rationale design methodology. This methodology helps the designer justify the interfaces and visualizations of design solutions for a given purpose. In addition, the authors have also been guided by the analysis result of the requirements of the PMESP in which the informational priorities have been defined to improve cognition. SAW global requirements were also considered, as described by Endsley [3].

The colors used in the representation of the instance vary according to the quality score of the information. The closer to 100 % sure, the darker the edge of the instance.

```
{"Situation": {
    "instance": "sit001",
    "data properties": {
      "uncertainty": "60"
    },
    "object properties": {
      "has_a": {
        "Complaint": {
          "instance": "den001",
          " data properties ": {
          }
        },
        "Criminal": {
          "instance": "crim_001",
          " data properties ": {
            "completeness": "70",
            " object properties ": {
              "runaway": {
                "site": {
                  "instance": "local_001",
                  " data properties ": {
                    " completeness ": "80"
}}}}}}}}}
```

Fig. 2. JSON schema generated by the previous steps to be encoded in visualizations

The warning connotation that this type of visualization impose on the data allows the expert to better understand it [12].

The variation of colors of objects are presented as in the use of red-green scale described by Ware and Jiang [11, 12], where the purest shade of red is the uncertainty, and green stands for certainty. Metrics of vibrant and dark colors and such as red, blue, shades of black, etc., represent the uncertainty of information, and green, yellow, and shades of white present the visualization of certainties.

The size of representations indicate the value of the data quality score entered into the information. The greater the size compared with the rest, the higher the quality score of the represented information.

The application of the transparency in information helps to identify the degree of reliability of the information. The greater the transparency score, the lower the quality. The application of transparency in instances of objects does not mean they do not have quality, but is a warning that there is a problem of quality added to information. Figure 3 shows the visualizations developed from the framework described, in two modes of representation: overlays in geo-referenced maps and in hierarchical graph.

The use of overlays in geo-referenced map is because PMESP operations dependent on the location attributes, especially to determine how to approach an occurrence. Thus, other objects that make up a situation complete the information with other objects and attributes such as information about criminals, victims, and stolen objects, each with its description.

The adoption of the graph structure is justified by the need of hierarchical knowledge about the formation of information objects and situations. It is necessary that PMESP operators know how each situation was composed, which objects and attributes.

The use of the graph structure is justified by the exploration of hierarchical knowledge about the formation of information objects and situations. It is necessary that PMESP operators know how each situation was composed, which objects and

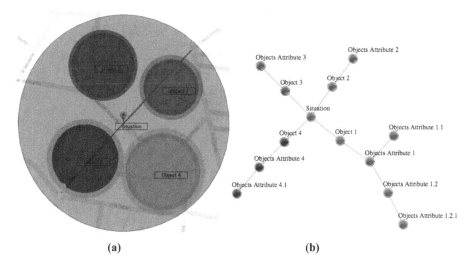

(a)   (b)

Fig. 3. Visualizations developed from the framework described, in two modes of representation: (a) overlays in geo-referenced maps and (b) situation attribute objects hierarchical graph.

attributes. This hierarchy was also obtained by analyzing the requirements by the PMESP. The situation is the central entity, constituted by the relationship between objects and their attributes, thus making its branches. Objects can have no relationship and, in this way, they may belong to independent hierarchies.

In our case study, a situation is a robbery event, and objects that constitute the situation are the victims, criminals, place, and stolen object, each with a set of characteristics called attributes

6   Case Study

The present case study aims to contribute to the decision-making process in the emergency field, more specifically to the decision-making process in the PMESP. The main objective of this study is to represent, by using visualizations, information that enable the identification of entities and situation compression of criminal charges, and also confirm the reported events. Since SAW is obtained, the expert has better subsidies to allocate resources and develop a better strategic plan of action. The acquisition of SAW in this context involves the identification of objects: criminal, victim, place, and stolen object and its attributes described in the complaint calls.

This case study specifically addresses situations of robbery, in which people make complaints by means of social networking posts or emergency calls. Such information is subject to the acquisition process, information fusion and quantification of quality. As an output of these processes prior to the visualization encoding, it was obtained the JSON schema shown in Fig. 4.

```
{"Situation": {
    "instance": "sit001",
    "data properties": {
      "date": "25/02/2015",
      "updateTime":"07:29 pm",
      "uncertainty": "60"
    },
    "object properties": {
    "has_a": {
        "Complaint": {
          "instance": "den001",
          " data properties ": {
            "dateComplaint": "25/02/2015",
            "transcribedCall": "good night ... black cap"
          }
        },
        "Criminal": {
          "instance": "crim_001",
          " data properties ": {
            "vehicle": "moto",
            "completeness": "70",
            " object properties ": {
              "runaway": {
                "site": {
                  "instance": "local_001",
                  " data properties ": {
                    "street": "avenue...",
                    " completeness ": "80"
}}}}}}}
```

Fig. 4. JSON schema generated by the previous steps which must be encoded in visualizations of the case study.

In visualization, situation is composed of edges that enable a relevant identification from the scores calculated by primary processing process.

The color information of the situation circle is applied in accordance with the total quality score received, where colors such as green, yellow, and shades of white are applied to represent the quality on a scale ranging from 0 to 100, where the closer to 100, the more quality; and the closer to 0, colors of blue, red, and shades of black in dark shades represent uncertainty.

The internal information regarding situation – instances of objects: victim, criminal, place, and stolen object – is classified under the same color scales described, as well as the use of size and edge, to which are also added transparency and shape.

In order to represent the fusion of information, visualization is attributed a higher score of opacity in color, indicating incidence of most significant amount. The use of shading around the representation is used to highlight the presence of information resulting from the fusion. To present the results of this process, a graph was created, as shown in Fig. 5, where the edges that concatenate the knots create an indicative of synergy information with potential to fuse. In this, attributes of quality are applied in the same way, using the sizes and colors of the knots to quantify the quality, as well as the use of edges.

The use of filters is aimed at showing or hiding information to or from the map. In visualization, this technique is applied by the expert, who has the option to visualize or not the data which was not processes in the visualization. Figure 5 shows the results of visualizations with the case study information.

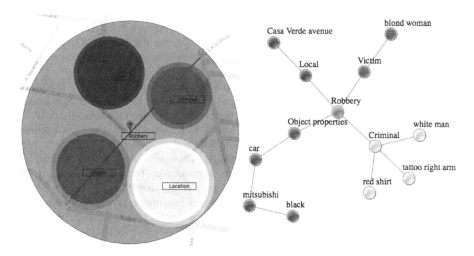

Fig. 5. Visualizations developed from the framework described and using case study information, in two modes of representation: (a) overlays in geo-referenced maps, (b) situation attribute objects hierarchical graph.

7 Conclusion

From the product resulting from the assessment steps, specifically acquisition and processing/fusion, it was possible to develop the framework in order to define uncertain information considering the phases of situation assessment and its impact on the graphical representation for the guidance of experts. Uncertain data visualization techniques were used, and the information generated by the use of the framework was encoded.

With this framework, it is expected that views dedicated to emergency rule can be created in synergy with the other steps of situation assessment.

So far, the results proved to be valid regarding the generation of such views in line with the assessment of the quality of information and information fusion.

The next steps include assessing the views generated regarding the acquisition and maintenance of SAW, together with decision makers from various levels of PMESP experience and expertise.

References

1. Thomson, J., Hetzler, E., MacEachren, A., Gahegan, M., Pavel, M.: A typology for visualizing uncertainty. In: Proceeding of the Electronic Imaging 2005, pp. 146–157. International Society for Optics and Photonics, March 2005
2. Pang, A.T., Wittenbrink, C.M., Lodha, S.K.: Approaches to uncertainty visualization. Vis. Comput. **13**(8), 370–390 (1997)
3. Endsley, M.R., Connors, E.S.: Situation awareness: state of the art. In: 2008 IEEE Power and Energy Society General Meeting-Conversion and Delivery of Electrical Energy in the 21st Century, pp. 1–4. IEEE, July 2008
4. Gouin, D., e Evdokiou, P.: A showcase of visualization approaches for military decision makers. Defence Research and Development Canadavalcartier (QUEBEC) (2004)
5. Wand, Y., Wang, R.Y.: Anchoring data quality dimensions in ontological foundations. Commun. ACM **39**(11), 86–95 (1996)
6. Meccella, M., Scannapieco, M., Virgillito, A., Baldoni, R., Catarci, T., Batini, C.: Managing data quality in cooperative information system. In: Meersman, R., Tari, Z. (eds.) CoopIS 2002, DOA 2002, and ODBASE 2002. LNCS, vol. 2519. Springer, Heidelberg (2002)
7. Huang, S.: Exploratory visualization of data with variable quality. Dissertation, WORCESTER POLYTECHNIC INSTITUTE (2005)
8. Fricker, L., e Macklin, C.: Improving Campaign Assessment and Decision Making in Command and Control Through the Use of Visualization Techniques. Qinetiq LTD Farnborough (United Kingdom) Centre for Human Sciences (2004)
9. Junior, V., et al.: Multi-criteria fusion of heterogeneous information for improving situation awareness on military decision making system. In: Yamamoto, S. (ed.) HIMI 2015, Part II. LNCS, vol. 9173, pp. 3–14. Springer, Heidelberg (2015)
10. Souza, J., et al.: Conceptual framework to enrich situation awareness of emergency dispatchers. In: Yamamoto, S. (ed.) HIMI 2015, Part II. LNCS, vol. 9173, pp. 33–44. Springer, Heidelberg (2015)
11. Ware, C.: Color sequences for univariate maps: theory, experiments and principles. IEEE Comput. Graph. Appl. **8**(5), 41–49 (1988)
12. Jiang, B., Brown, A., Ormeling, F.J.: Some perceptual aspects of colouring uncertainty. In: Advances in GIS Research II, pp. 477–90. Taylor & Francis, London (1996)

A Concept for Visualizing Psychophysiological Data in Human Computer Interaction: The FeaturePlotter

Falko Pross$^{(\boxtimes)}$, Dilana Hazer, Harald C. Traue, and Holger Hoffmann

Medical Psychology, University of Ulm, Ulm, Germany
falkopross@googlemail.com, {dilana.hazer,
harald.traue,holger.hoffmann}@uni-ulm.de

Abstract. This paper introduces a graphical concept and an implementation for visualizing psychophysiological data in human computer interaction. Psycho-biological measurements result in huge datasets, which are mandatory for the development of semi-automatic or automated emotion classification and hence a reliable planning and decision-making system called companion system. The mentioned amount of data calls for the need of making dependencies and coherences in those datasets visible for the human eye in addition to algorithmic pattern recognition and feature selection. Seeing through the data by exploring it playfully helps experts understanding the data structure and provokes non-specialists' curiosity.

Keywords: Data visualization · Psychophysiology · Companion systems · Emotion recognition · Human computer interaction

1 Introduction

Technical devices are getting faster and smaller by the week and computers affect the way we live more than ever. Invented as highly specialized machines and suitable for expertized operators only they migrated into our bags and pockets. They assist us in our daily routine and therefore must be able to perform a multitude of completely different functions. Hence the interaction between humans and machines becomes more complex and versatile, despite the steady enhancements by the efforts of user interface design and the technical development of more and more intuitive interaction possibilities like for example multitouch input.

This makes new steps in the evolution of interactions between humans and computing machinery possible – an evolution towards companion systems. Knowledge about the users' properties, current physical and emotional conditions and the environment, allows companion systems to anticipate the users' needs and wishes and to simplify the interaction by reducing its complexity [1]. Companion systems are reliable planning and decision-making systems depending on a large set of data. Especially the process of the analysis of naturalistic user behavior - which is often based on a multimodal approach combining the analysis of prosody, mimics, gestures and psychobiological measurements - has to deal with great quantities of data [2].

© Springer International Publishing Switzerland 2015
S. Yamamoto (Ed.): HIMI 2015, Part I, LNCS 9172, pp. 97–106, 2015.
DOI: 10.1007/978-3-319-20612-7_10

2   Materials and Methods

2.1   The Emergence and Structure of Feature Data

Psychobiological measurements depend on an elaborate setup and are therefore realized in controlled experimental settings or measured in quasi-experimental observational settings, during which a number of independent variables, like for example a variety of emotions or different pain levels are inducted [3]. Specialized hardware is measuring body functions and storing the values permanently over the course of time. Measured body functions are mainly skin conductance, blood volume pulse, electrocardiography, electroencephalography, electromyography or respiration.

During multiple processing steps a subset of the collected data is created: First the data is cut, so only the important sections shortly before and after the induction of an independent variable remain. Next the data is filtered to remove or reduce noise and undesirable frequencies [3]. Finally features are extracted from the preprocessed data, by performing a variety of mathematical functions on the dataset (e.g. amplitude, frequency) [4, 5]. The results are tables containing the feature values for each subject and measured point of time categorized by the inducted independent variable of that point of time.

In the further process of semi-automated emotion classification a subset of the feature data is used in classification algorithms like neural networks, k-nearest neighbor or support vector machines [6]. These algorithms train with part of the data and should afterwards be able to classify given datasets into independent variables. The success of correct classification highly depends on the applied subset of features.

The selected feature dataset is often more confusing than the initial amount of data, so it is still way too complex to be interpreted by humans and hence not possible for humans to choose the perfect set of features. For example there is one table for each subject – which means it is necessary to merge and compare a multitude of tables, which might be mentally stressing lots of cognitive capacity. In fact, not all the extracted features are relevant for the analysis. There are guidelines describing which features are suitable for which purposes and there are methods of algorithmic feature selection optimization [7]. Both aids are useful and necessary; nevertheless they still do not offer a possibility to understand the data directly.

2.2   Data Visualization

"Often the most effective way to describe, explore and summarize a set of numbers – even a very large set – is to look at pictures of those numbers" [8]. The previous sentence outlines the need for a visualization of the described feature data. Data visualization can be considered as external cognitive resources extending the human brain.

Following the state of the art and the proceedings in computer graphics as well as the rapid growing amounts of data, new approaches in data visualization have evolved over the last decades: Instead of specifying the entire representations of the data and its shapes, positions and colors, only a set of rules is determined [9]. These rules allow the user exploring the data actively and thus getting more involved. Important aspects for data visualization, meant to arouse interest and curiosity are: aesthetics, efficiency, information and novelty [10].

2.3 Graphical Concept

For visualizing multiple connected datasets in an easy and well structured way, a graphical concept based on the simplicity of a bar diagram has been developed. It starts with reducing the bars to simple points and then displaying them in one common scale (see Fig. 1). This way it is possible to consolidate all results of one subject, one feature and one independent variable in one figure.

Of course there exists way more than one feature. Also, it is important to compare the values of features with each other, so for the sake of intuitive visual comparison they have to be placed as close together as possible. To minimize the distance between an arbitrary amount of scales, they are arranged circular. And to keep track of a lot of small values, the null points of the scales are not unified in one point, but stretched apart in a circle (see Fig. 2).

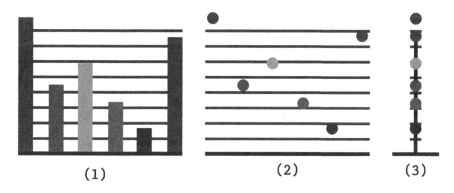

Fig. 1. Progression from bar diagram (1) to a simplified bar diagram (2) to a scale (3)

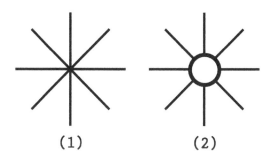

Fig. 2. Circular arranged scales (1) and scale circle with inner null circle (2) for better overview

Now each of those scale circles visualizes the values of all features of one subject and one independent variable, which provides a good overview over the feature values and makes it possible to answer the first question concerning the selection of features and the further processing towards classification and semi-automatic emotion recognition are:

1. Are the values of one feature, one subject and one independent variable all within a certain range or are they distributed randomly along the whole scale?

Randomly distributed values along a scale signify a feature which is not showing any methodic tendencies, like for example low values for an independent variable A and high values for an independent variable B. If the values of a feature do not show methodic tendencies, they can not be compared to other values. So the questions above answers if a feature is reliable and principally suitable for classification.

Further, there are two more important issues:

2. Do feature values of a subject vary among different independent variables? At which features do they vary? How do they vary?
3. Do feature values of an independent variable vary among different subjects? At which features do they vary? How do they vary?

It is not possible to answer these questions by use of the current form of representation, so the visualization concept has to be extended by another dimension: By arranging multiple scale circles on top of each other, feature values of either different independent variables (question 2) or different subjects (question 3) can be compared directly (see Fig. 3).

By adding a third dimension to the visualization, it is possible to change from the front view to the side view. This makes it possible to compare specific features in detail (see Fig. 4).

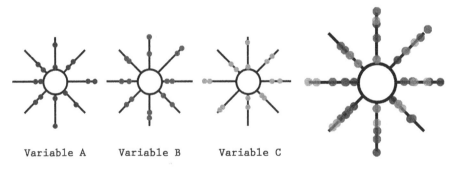

Variable A   Variable B   Variable C

Variable A,B,C

Fig. 3. Multiple scale circles on top of each other can be compared directly

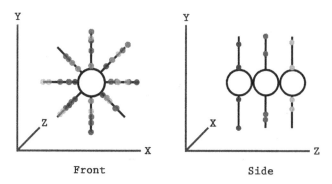

Fig. 4. Multiple scale circles on top of each other from front view and from side view

2.4   Fields of Application and Related Conditions

The FeaturePlotter application is not meant to be a static tool exporting static graphics. It is designed to create an interactive environment where it is possible to explore scientific data playfully. Therefore the data is visualized in a 3D-model, which can be manipulated in real-time by the user. Besides providing different perspectives and hence more possibilities of understanding the data altogether, the interaction involves the user and encourages to go beyond known boundaries.

Considering the qualities mentioned above, there are multiple fields of applications for the FeaturePlotter: Of course first of all it is a scientific tool for experts, helping them to understand data features. But it is also a tool for presenting, explaining and illustrating new or old feature data in front of an audience, for example in lectures or conventions. Furthermore, prearranged views of the data can be exported into static images and used in reports, documentations and journals. And on a final note it is a possible door opener in conversations with non-experts - for example at exhibitions or open house days: The application can arouse curiosity through its graphical design and its interactive capabilities.

2.5   Conditions

To meet all the expectations resulting from the fields of application, several conditions had to be considered during the implementation: Platform independence and an easy installation and handling are important features for providing a ready to use solution for displaying data without the need of having expert computer skills. This way it is possible for almost everyone to use the application on multiple different devices to show visualized content and share knowledge about it.

An innovative and attractive design arouses the curiosity of non-specialists and invites them to explore the graphical structures, shapes and colors. This is where an easy handling and detailed instructions and explanations guide a non-expert user through the application and introduce him to the topic and the context of the visualization.

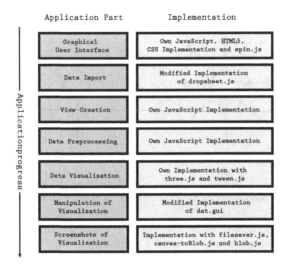

Fig. 5. Application structure and overview

2.6 Implementation

Using web technologies like HTML5, CSS, JavaScript and additional JavaScript libraries, all of the described conditions can be implemented smoothly. The application is developed as a web app, which is similar to a standard website but with an additional functionality. It is possible to run an instance of the application in every common browser without an installation or setup – just by visiting the corresponding domain online.

The application implementation is based on single page architecture: There exists only one HTML-File, which is dynamically filled with content via JavaScript. This avoids loading content from the server subsequently after each interaction and therefore increases the performance.

Additional to the browser version, there are desktop versions of the application for offline use on Mac OS and Windows. A similar version of the web app has been packed into a node-webkit container to provide server functionality for the web technologies without having to run a server locally. In Fig. 5 an overview over the structure and different parts of the application and used libraries is illustrated.

3 Features

3.1 Graphical User Interface

Because the application is not meant to be a scientific tool only, but a simple and inviting application for non-experts as well, the graphical user interface is structured in plain lucid sections and furnished with big self-explaining buttons and simple supervising texts (Fig. 6). In addition, there is a tooltip function explaining every

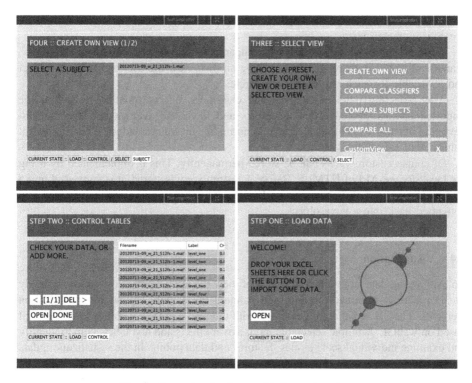

Fig. 6. Examples for the graphical user interface

button in the application. At the bottom of the application, there is an easy to use breadcrumb navigation showing the current state of the application and allowing to redo previous steps.

3.2 Data Import

The first step in the application is to import the feature data, which usually is available as CSV files or excel-sheets. The application allows to simply drag and drop one or more excel-files onto a denoted area, or to open the operating system's file explorer by a button. Afterwards the tables are parsed and converted into JavaScript-Arrays. The imported data is displayed in tables to enable the user to check if everything has been imported correctly.

3.3 Views

As mentioned before, a scale circle is created from a combination of a subject and a variable. In the second step of the application it is possible to choose from different predefined views, where combinations of subjects and variables are already picked, to create an own view by selecting combinations of subjects and variables or to pick a previously created view.

There are three predefined views: "Compare all subjects", "Compare all classifiers" (variables) and "Compare all". For creating an own view the user can select a subject and a variable for each requested scale circle.

After selecting pairs of subjects and classifiers, a corresponding subset of the imported data is created. Then the peaks and lows, the average and the standard deviation of each feature are calculated to normalize the values and wipe out discordant values.

Of course custom views can be stored permanently. This is implemented by using the localStorage-API of HTML5. Before a custom view is stored, it is converted into a single string object. When a view is loaded, the corresponding string is parsed and converted back into a view object.

3.4   Visualization

To explore the data from different points of view the application allows to move freely in 3D space by rotating, zooming and panning the camera around the visualization elements. The 3D scene is implemented with three.js, a graphics library for JavaScript based on webGL. Multiple selectable mouse-over effects and text labels help to identify and examine individual scale circles, features and data points. In the visualization, data points which are close to each other grow bigger to improve the visual illustration and emphasize similar measurements. The scaling factor can be changed by the user as well as the minimum distance between two points specifying if they are being scaled or not (see Fig. 7).

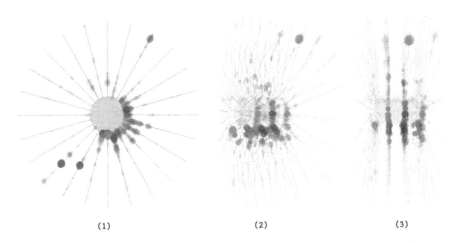

(1)   (2)   (3)

Fig. 7. Screenshots from the application showing a camera rotation from front view (1) to side view (3).

4 Restrictions and Suggested Improvements

The application performance is dependent on the number of elements to be visualized in the three-dimensional scene. Therefore it is not possible to visualize an arbitrary number of scale circles at once. The graphical concept is not meant for the visualization of many elements as well. It is designed to compare a preselected set of subject-variable-combinations. Of course improvements in the development of WebGL will improve the performance of the FeaturePlotter-Application too.

Especially on mobile devices the performance is not ideal, due to additional multiple browser-dependent problems: Some mobile browsers have problems displaying the application correctly when rotating the device or zooming in and out of different sections of the screen. Optimizing the application in terms of responsiveness on different devices, mobile platforms, screen sizes and computing power is necessary to enable a fully functional and stable mobile version of the application.

Data cannot be stored inside the application, so it has to be imported every time the application is started. In combination with customized views this can cause inconsistency when varying datasets have been imported. Storing the data inside the application is not possible regarding the underlying web technologies and their security restrictions. A simple way to simplify the data import and reuse of already imported data would be to store the path of already used data files locally and ask the user if certain datasets – which are required for the available or selected views – should be imported.

The formatting of the data tables is predefined and has to be strictly maintained to ensure correct import and further processing.

5 Conclusion

The FeaturePlotter-Application is the first iteration of a multifunctional tool helping people to overview, compare and understand big data sets with an intuitive visual data screening. It allows interacting with present data, exploring it playfully and discerning coherences and differences. Its simple, respectively unnecessary installation and its simple structure and design provide everyone with the possibility to use the application straightforward without the need of having experience in difficult scientific tools, complex programs or even the subject matter itself.

Of course the application has to be tested in the daily routine of experts and non-experts and there the actual benefit will become apparent as well as the need for further development, additional functionality or the redesign of specific parts of the application. There are already plans to add other modules and functions like for example animating the positions of the data points to illustrate the progression of the values over time during an experiment. So the FeaturePlotter-Application can be considered as a starting point for different researches and studies in the field of psychophysiological data visualization.

Acknowledgements. This research was supported by grants from the Transregional Collaborative Research Center SFB/TRR 62 Companion Technology for Cognitive Technical Systems funded by the German Research Foundation (DFG).

References

1. Wendemuth, A., Biundo, S.: A companion technology for cognitive technical systems. In: Esposito, A., Esposito, A.M., Vinciarelli, A., Hoffmann, R., Müller, V.C. (eds.) COST 2102. LNCS, vol. 7403, pp. 89–103. Springer, Heidelberg (2012)
2. Walter, S., Scherer, S., Schels, M., Glodek, M., Hrabal, D., Schmidt, M., Böck, R., Limbrecht, K., Traue, H.C., Schwenker, F.: Multimodal emotion classification in naturalistic user behavior. In: Jacko, J.A. (ed.) Human-Computer Interaction, Part III, HCII 2011. LNCS, vol. 6763, pp. 603–611. Springer, Heidelberg (2011)
3. Walter, S., Gruss, S., Limbrecht-Ecklundt, K., Traue, H.C., Werner, P., Al-Hamadi, A., Diniz, N., da Silva, G.M., Andrade, A.O.: Automatic pain quantification using autonomic parameters. Psychol. Neurosci. 7, 363–380 (2014)
4. Cao, C., Slobounov, S.: Application of a novel measure of EEG non-stationarity as "Shannon- entropy of the peak frequency shifting" for detecting residual abnormalities in concussed individuals. Clin. Neurophysiol. 122, 1314–1321 (2011)
5. Chen, W., Zhuang, J., Yu, W., Wang, Z.: Measuring complexity using FuzzyEn, ApEn, and SampEn. Med. Eng. Phys. 31, 61–68 (2009)
6. Hsu, C.-W., Chang, C.-C., Lin, C.-J.: A practical guide to support vector classification. BJU Int. 101, 1396–1400 (2008)
7. Kolodyazhniy, V., Kreibig, S.D., Gross, J.J., Roth, W.T., Wilhelm, F.H.: An affective computing approach to physiological emotion specificity: toward subject-independent and stimulus-independent classification of film-induced emotions. Psychophysiology 48, 908–922 (2011)
8. Tufte, E.R.: The Visual Display of Quantitative Information, 2nd edn. Graphics Press, Cheshire (2001)
9. Hidalgo, C.A., Almossawi, A.: The Visualization Revolution (2014). http://www.scientificamerican.com/article/the-data-visualization-revolution. Accessed 02 February 2015
10. Fry, B.: Visualizing Data. O'Reilly Media, Sebastopol (2008)

Proposal of a Visualization Method to Support Informal Communication Using Twitter Attributes

Ryota Sasajima[1]([✉]), Kohei Otake[1], Makoto Oka[2], and Akito Sakurai[1]

[1] School of Science for Open and Environmental Systems, Keio University, 3-14-1 Hiyoshi, Kohoku-Ku, Yokohama-Shi, Kanagawa-Ken 223-8522, Japan
{r.sasa0425,otake_koehi}@keio.jp,
sakurai@ae.keio.ac.jp
[2] Tokyo City University, 1-28-1 Tamadutsumi, Setagaya-Ku, Tokyo 158-8557, Japan
moka@tcu.ac.jp

Abstract. In this paper, we propose a method to visualize information regarding hobbies and interests of a person inferred from tweets on Twitter to support informal communication in the real world. Analysis of the current states and experiments on informal communication clarified that it is important and useful for a person to know information such as hobbies, interests and other attributes which indicate background of his/her partner to start and maintain a first and good meeting. Through experimental results, we demonstrated that our proposed social profile diagram was effective for informal communication.

Keywords: Social networking service · Informal communication · Visualization

1 Introduction

Along with development of the Internet technology, recently, people have communicated online by means of a wide variety of communication methods. In particular, SNSs and microblogging services (called social media services) that support interpersonal communication are popular these days. Use of social media services provides users with easy ways to transmit and collect information. The number of active users of such social media services has increased. The users of Facebook, which is one of the representative SNSs, actually exceeded 1.35 billion users across the world (2014). Under such circumstances, various studies using information that is posted on social media services have actively been made, such as motivation improvement based on gamification by using SNS [1], influence of SNS posts given to the service users [2], and categorization of posts on electronic bulletin boards based on Bayesian filters.

We consider that social media services have accumulated a wide variety of information necessary for conducting informal communication, such as tendencies and tastes of service users including their affiliations and locations. Therefore, presenting such information must serve as help to activate not only communication conducted on the Internet, but also face-to-face communication that is conducted in the real world.

© Springer International Publishing Switzerland 2015
S. Yamamoto (Ed.): HIMI 2015, Part I, LNCS 9172, pp. 107–114, 2015.
DOI: 10.1007/978-3-319-20612-7_11

2 Study Purpose

The purpose of this study is to clarify how to activate informal communication by focusing on one of the popular microblogging services, Twitter.

In this study, information communication (referred to as "IC" hereinafter) is defined as spontaneous communication with no specific purpose. Examples of IC include chatting at a lounge, and information exchange among friends in the same organization. This study focuses attention on university students, who belong to a main service user segment, having many opportunities to conduct IC. This is because, as indicated by Iizuka [2010], the communication skills of young people has tended to decline, while the enhancement of communication skills of students has become an important issue.

3 Analysis of the Current Conditions

We first explain about a questionnaire survey and a semi-structured interview survey targeting 70 university students we conducted in order to identify information that would be utilized for conducting IC and to clarify the usage situations of social media services. We, then, explain about Twitter that we focused on and the current conditions as a summary.

3.1 Analysis on Informal Communication

Analysis on Informal Communication based on Questionnaire Survey. In the beginning, we conducted a survey on the following items in order to clarify how the students felt about IC.

- Do you have any difficulty to talk to a stranger?
- What kind of things do you particularly feel when communicating with strangers?
- Do you need any cue to start to communicate with strangers?

The questionnaire survey results confirmed that those who feel that they are good at conducting IC had many friends in the real world, with a tendency to have positive feelings when communicating with strangers. On the other hand, those who feel that they are not good at conducting IC had negative feelings toward communicating with strangers, such as having trouble with choosing topics to start communication (Fig. 1). The questionnaire survey results also confirmed that both types of the students, who are good at and not good at conducting IC, tended to feel that common tastes or interests should be necessary for starting communication with strangers (Fig. 2).

Analysis on Informal Communication based on Face to Face Communication Experiments. Next, we conducted experiments related to IC in order to clarify the following items.

- Topics often picked up when IC is conducted
- Cues necessary for activating conversation

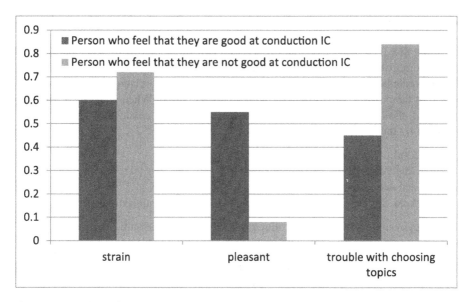

Fig. 1. Ratio of people who feel strained, pleasant, and difficult with choosing topics among those who think that they are good or not good at conduction IC when communicating with stranger.

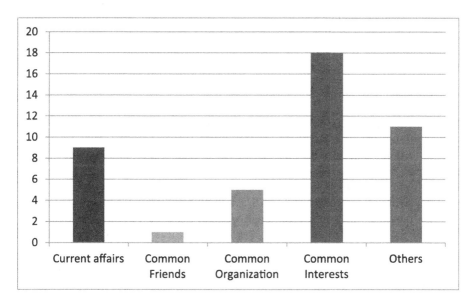

Fig. 2. The number of respondents who answered affirmative to questions what were cues to activate conversation with strangers.

The experimental subjects were divided into three groups consisting of a total of 11 students (8 males and 3 females), with 22 combinations of meeting for the first time. Assuming that IC would be conducted between two subjects, two subjects that met for the first time were placed in the experimental room along with movie cameras and voice recorders. Having them conduct IC without giving information of the other party to each of them, we recorded their IC with video and audio. When IC of each pair was completed, the questionnaire survey (feedback survey) was conducted. The questions answered by the subjects are as follows:

- What kind of topic did you talk with your partner?
- What was your impression of your partner?
- What activated your communication?
- What kind of clues or topics could have activated communication?

The survey results confirmed the following tendencies of the subjects.

- There is a correlation between how the subject satisfied with what they talked and how they felt how activated the communication was 0.77.
- In many cases, common interest or current situations serve as factors to activate communication
- As for factors that bring conversation down, in many cases, topics mismatched and bad first impression was created
- Common interest and friends in common are the factors that the subjects felt were important to activate communication

In this study, therefore, these results clarified that information of individual's interest and attribute information that indicates individual's background would be important keys for conducting IC.

3.2   Analysis on Twitter

The questionnaire survey on the usage situations of social media services showed that 74 % of the subjects were Twitter users. The survey also clarified that they use Twitter in order to communicate with their actual friends and collect information of their interests and tastes. It was also clarified that many of them post their tweets about what they are interested in or about their current situations.

As for posting frequency in other SNSs, 95 % of the users post five times or less per week. On the other hand, in Twitter, approximately 50 % of Twitter users frequently post tweets five times or more per week. While 13 % of users of other SNSs post what they are interested in, 52 % of Twitter users post tweets about it. This percentage for Twitter is apparently higher than that for other SNSs. These results clarified that there should be more information related to interests and tastes of service users on Twitter when compared to other SNSs.

3.3 Summary of the Current Conditions

As is described, we conducted the questionnaire surveys in order to identify information that would be utilized for conducting IC and the experiments targeting IC. The results clarified that information of individual's interest and attribute information that indicates individual's background serve as important factors for conducting IC. In addition, the questionnaire surveys and interview surveys on usage situations of Social media services clearly showed that Twitter is a service where which has more information regarding interests and taste of service users and many users are quite active in making posts. In keeping with the results of analysis on the current conditions, in this study, we propose a method to support IC by visualizing information of individual's interest and attribute information that indicates individual's background extracted from Twitter.

4 Proposal of an Informal Communication Support Method by Using Social Profile Diagrams

In this study, we propose a new communication support method based on social profile diagrams to visualize information of individual's interest and attribute information that indicates individual's background (Fig. 3).

Social profile diagrams are created by using information obtained from profiles of Twitter users along with those they follow as well as their followers. However, there still exist Twitter users that keep their profile blank. Additionally, it is difficult to identify individual user's interest and attribute that indicates their background only from profile of each Twitter user. Therefore, this study focuses on using profile of those that the user follows and his/her followers.

On Twitter, only the tweets of users you follow are displayed on your timeline; therefore, Twitter users tend to select and follow other users that they are interested in. For this reason, we consider that some attributes of users followed by the user might be related to certain factors that the user is interested in. In this study, therefore, we tried to obtain the information of the user's interest from the profiles of users followed by the user.

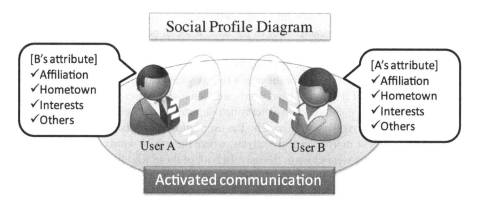

Fig. 3. An image of communication using social profile

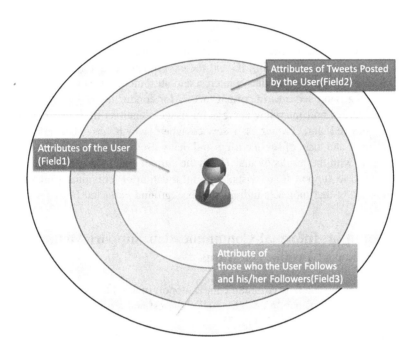

Fig. 4. A template of the social profile diagram with the layered fields that show attributes

Additionally, the questionnaire survey we conducted clarified that those users in a common affiliation or community tend to follow one another. With that, in this study, we attempted to obtain information of the user's attributes regarding their backgrounds from users in the relationship of following one another. These two types of information obtained from those who they follow and their followers were utilized for creating social profile diagrams. In order to obtain these types of information, we used API provided by Twitter. We also used Python as the development language.

To begin with, texts in the profile of a Twitter user were analyzed by conducting morphological analysis. Based on the result obtained, the frequency of each word was calculated. The top 10 words with high frequency were defined as the characteristics of the user. By using these characteristics of the user, a social profile diagram of the user was created. Here, those words that indicate the user's characteristics are displayed in Field 1 of the social profile diagram (Fig. 5).

Additionally, TF/IDF values for the user's tweets were calculated in order to extract characteristic words of the user. These words are then displayed in Field 2. The size of each word when it is displayed was determined depending on the TF/IDF scores.

Next, texts in the profiles of those who the user follows and his/her followers were analyzed by means of morphological analysis, where the top 10 words were defined as the characteristics that were close to the user. In both of those who the user follows and his/her followers, those highly-frequent words were treated that they were of high importance. Here, those words that indicate the characteristics of those who the user follows and his/her followers are displayed in Field 3.

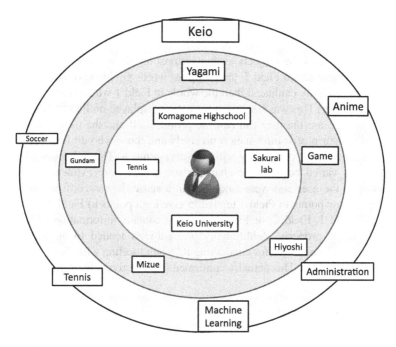

Fig. 5. An example of the social profile diagram using "Sasajima" data

The emphasis on each word that would be displayed in the social profile diagram was determined depending on the word's occurrence frequency. The stronger the interest was, the larger the word's font size was made, so that the level of interest reflected on words could be understood at first sight. Words were used for creating profile diagrams because many sentences contained in tweets on Twitter might include ungrammatical sentences; therefore, we considered that the user's characteristics would be accurately obtained on a word basis. Figure 4 shows a description of each field. Figure 5 shows a sample of profile diagram created.

5   Experiments and Results

We verified whether a group of words displayed in the social profile diagram would indicate information of users' interest and information of their attributes or not. The subjects were 10 students who have their own Twitter accounts. Targeting the subjects, we conducted a questionnaire survey on their own social profile diagrams. The evaluation was done on a five-point scale. The outline of the questions is described below.

- Does your social profile diagram indicate information of your interest and attributes properly?
- Can your social profile diagram serve as an effective information visualization when talking with others?

- Did you feel that this social profile diagram was easy to understand with its interface and the number and size of words?

The group of words that the subjects evaluated most highly was the one in Field 2. In order of Field 2, Field 1, and Field 3, the groups of words got high points. The words in Field 2 were more highly evaluated than the words in Field 1 which were derived from the profile of the user. This was because information displayed on Field 1 could contain significant bias because the user can edit the profile itself and the users vary between those who edits their profile information precisely and those who do not. On the other hand, Field 2 scored high on average without varying much. This is because the words in this field less varied because the characteristic words were extracted from many tweets related to the user and were smoothed in a sense. It was confirmed that those users who gave low points to Field 1 tended to give high points to Field 3. We can say that either of Field 1, Field 2, or Field 3 actually contains information of the user's interests and tastes properly. Additionally, the subjects tended to answer that this information would be effective for conducting IC when meeting with their conversation partners for the first time. This actually confirmed the effectiveness of this information.

6 Conclusion and Future Issues

Targeting university students, in this study, we proposed a communication support method with the aim to activate communication in the real world. Specifically, we created the social profile diagram that visualizes profile information of the user, those who the user follows, and his/her followers. In the future, we are going to implement a system including this proposed method and verify the effectiveness of this method. We are also going to classify those tweets related to interests and tastes collected as information of users' interest into topics so as to utilize such information for proposing topics when communication is developed.

References

1. Otake, K., Sumita, R., Oka, M., Shinozawa, Y., Uetake, T., Sakurai, A.: A proposal of sns to improve member's motivation in voluntary community using gamification. Int. J. Adv. Comput. Sci. Appl. **6**(1), 82–88 (2015)
2. Nakada, Y., Kamioka, E.: Analysis for Influential Postings on Twitter. IEICE, **3** (2014). (in Japanese)
3. Ichifuji, Y., Konnno, S., Sone, H.: Classification of BBS comment depending on the atmosphere of BBS. IEICE **3**, 125–128 (2010)
4. Okada, K.: Communication support and collaboration. IEICE **89**(3) (2006). (in Japanese)
5. Matsubara, T., Usuki, M., Sugiyama, K., Nishimoto, K.: Raison D'être object: a cyber-herarth that catalyzes face-to-face informal communication. IPSJ J. **44**(12), 3174–3187 (2003). (in Japanese)
6. Waki, H., Noto, T., Takeno, H.: Study of real world oriented informal communication support. Trans. IPSJ, **24**(11) (1997). (in Japanese)

A Team Hiring Solution Based on Graph-Based Modelling of Human Resource Entities

Avinash Sharma, Jyotirmaya Mahapatra, Asmita Metrewar,
Abhishek Tripathi, and Partha Dutta[(✉)]

Xerox Research Centre India, Bangalore, India
{Avinash.Sharma,Jyotirmaya.Mahapatra,Asmita.Metrewar,
Abhishek.Tripathi3,Partha.Dutta}@xerox.com

Abstract. As modern organizations become more agile and support more complex business processes, acquiring the right set of talent is becoming crucial for their operations. One of the key talent acquisition problems is staffing a team that has requirement for multiple job descriptions, from a pool of external candidates. This team hiring problem may arise for (i) a new organization, (ii) a new group in an existing organization, or (iii) an existing group that faces high attrition level. This paper presents a Talent Acquisition Decision Support System (TADSS) that provides decision support for team hiring. The system first builds a weighted graph based model for the three types of Human Resource (HR) entities in the problem setup (jobs, employees and candidates), and the inter-relationship among them. Next, an algorithm based on spectral embedding of the HR Graph is used to select teams. The system then provides an interactive team selection and comparison interface based on the HR Graph. Simulation-based evaluations show the effectiveness of the proposed system in team formation.

Keywords: Human resource graph · Graph embedding

1 Introduction

Motivation. Talent Acquisition is one of the key challenges in modern organizations. Many organizations face increasingly complex business operations, people-intensive business process or high attrition level, which makes the talent acquisition problem especially cumbersome. Not surprisingly, significant research effort has been devoted to analyzing and automating parts of the talent acquisition process. In particular, sourcing of candidates and screening them automatically for interviews has been the focus of multiple recent commercial and research projects [5, 7].

Although sourcing and screening of individual candidates is one of the central topics in talent acquisition, most business operations need a team of employees with different job descriptions (JD). Creating a cohesive team is often necessary for efficient business operations. In this context, this paper studies the *team hiring* problem, where given a pool of candidates and a team with talent requirements for different job descriptions, the organization needs to select a team of one of more candidates for each

© Springer International Publishing Switzerland 2015
S. Yamamoto (Ed.): HIMI 2015, Part I, LNCS 9172, pp. 115–126, 2015.
DOI: 10.1007/978-3-319-20612-7_12

job description in the team requirement while ensuring a certain level of cohesiveness or affinity among the team members.

The team hiring problem has two main aspects. First, for each job description in the team, the available set of candidates needs to be ranked with respect to the role, to aid in screening by the hiring manager. Second, given a possible team formation, one needs to evaluate how effective the group of candidates will be as a team. Although the first aspect can be addressed by earlier works, such as [5, 7], the challenges to address the second aspect are three-folds: (i) Modelling the key Human Resource (HR) entities that are involved in the team hiring problem and their inter-relationships, (ii) exploiting information from *indirect* relationship between HR entities, which may have important information about team's affinities, and (iii) obtaining a cohesiveness score for a team based on the pairwise strength of relationship between the team members, in order to recommend one team formation over another.

Contributions. This work presents an interactive decision support system for selecting a team of candidates for a given set of job descriptions such that, not only are the selected candidates suitable for their respective job descriptions, but also the formed team is as cohesive or compatible as possible. The paper proposes a natural graph-based representation of the HR eco-system (called HR Graph), where the nodes are the HR entities (job descriptions, current employees and external candidates), and links capture the relationship between these entities (see Fig. 1). The advantage of such a graph-based modelling is that the information used for candidate ranking and team selection is not restricted to a specific job description and candidate resumes, but takes into account the other entities (e.g., existing employees, common connections or peers), and the strength of the connections or affinities between all these entities. Then, a spectral embedding of HR Graph-based algorithm is proposed to select teams with high cohesiveness.

This work complements the proposed HR Graph modelling information with an interactive team selection (Fig. 2) and comparison interfaces (Fig. 3). The team selection interface assists the user (e.g., hiring manager) in selecting one or more candidates for each job description in the team by providing a ranked list of candidates. The comparison interface comprises of intuitive decision scales which works as a model of cohesion scoring of different teams. The interface allows user to provide simultaneous feedback in terms of different affinity weightages. It also captures the information with regards to different decision biases and exceptions added in team selection.

Finally, the proposed system is evaluated with a numerical simulation using synthetic data generated for 1500 candidates. Results on team formation show that the system provides a good trade-off between the compatibility of selected candidates to job descriptions and the cohesiveness of the formed team.

Related Work. The social network of job candidates has been studied in sociology. For example, [6] studied the effect of a job seeker's social network, and strengths of her relationship (affinity) in the network on the employment outcome. However, these studies do not propose a method to exploit the social network for job search or team formation. Recent works have presented some methods on how to use online social networks to search for a job. For instance, [7, 8] use social network profiles of candidates and employers to apply for jobs and find compatible jobs, whereas [9] ranks jobs for a candidate, based on the number of individuals in a candidate's social network who are employees of the corresponding organization. However, none of the above works considers hiring a team of candidates while taking candidate affinities into account, and the affinities that arise due to either indirect connections or connections that are not captured in social network (e.g., relationship between two job descriptions).

Although, employment rates for social groups have been modelled in economic sociology [10], this body of work does not consider how to hire a team based on the studied models. More recent works have considered affinity between employees while creating teams in an organization [11]. Team formation using existing employees of an organization under various resource constraints has been extensively studied under workforce optimization in Operations Research [1]. These papers, however, rarely consider the problem of hiring external job candidates, and affinities arising out of indirect relationship between candidates.

2   System Overview

This section gives an overview of the Talent Acquisition Decision Support System (TADSS) proposed in this work. Next, the construction of HR Graph in TADSS is described.

The nodes in the HR Graph are the job descriptions in the team, job candidates, and the existing employees in the organization. One of the challenges for the HR Graph construction is determining the link weights between the nodes. Table 1 presents the different kind of relationship considered in HR Graph, and the parameters that determine the weights of these relationship links. The strength of relationship between two HR entities is captured by link weights: higher edge weight indicates stronger affinity.

Table 1. Lists of functions used for computing link weights

JD-JD	f_{jj} (Job_Description)
candidate-candidate	f_{cc} (Candidate_Profile, Social)
employee-employee	f_{ee} (Employee_Profile, Job_Affiliation, Social)
JD-candidate	f_{jc} (Historical_Decision, Candidate_Profile, Job_Description)
candidate-employee	f_{ce} (Candidate_Profile, Employee_Profile, Social)
JD-employee	f_{je} (Historical_Decision, Employee_Profile)

Edge weighing functions are described below.

1. *Employee-employee* weighing function (*fee*) considers as parameters three meta-attributes, viz., Employee_Profile, Job_Affiliations and Social (Network Connections). Each of the meta-attributes has multi-level sub-attributes, e.g., Education as a sub-attribute of Employee_Profiles. An example formulation of *fee* is given below, where [0.4, 0.4, 0.2] are attribute importance factors that always sum

to one: *fee* (Employee_Profile, Job_Affiliation, Social) = 0.4* Employee_Profile + 0.4 * Job_Affiliation + 0.2 * Social.

2. Candidate-candidate weighing function (f_{cc}) formulation is very similar to f_{ee} with only two meta-attribute parameters and with different possible attribute importance factors, e.g., [0.7, 0.3].
3. JD-JD edge weighting function (f_{jj}) considers similarity in content of input pair of JD's in terms of skills and experience required.
4. JD-candidate weighing function (f_{jc}) considers Education, Experience and Skill overlap between JD and candidate profile. Although not considered in this work, historical hiring decisions, on candidates that were considered for the current JD or similar JDs, can also be used. Both these parameters can have real values and their weighted linear combination can be used to compute link weights.
5. JD-employee weighing function (f_{je}) has similar definition with different weights.
6. Candidate-employee weighing function (f_{ce}) computes a similarity score based on overlap in employee and candidate profiles as well as considering their social network connectivity, if available.

A detailed discussion on the practical aspects of the above edge weighing functions is presented in the section on HR Graph modelling parameters. Using these definitions, the HR Graph for TADSS can be induced which is then used for computing average connectivity (indicating the strength of relationship) among graph nodes. Figure 1 shows an example graph modeling of HRMS entities without link weights.

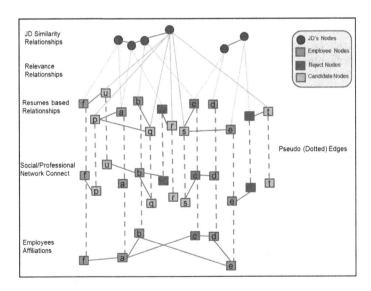

Fig. 1. Proposed graph representation

TADSS next computes an implicit representation of HR Graph known as *spectral or Laplacian embedding* [2]. The Laplacian embedding [3, 4] is a popular spectral representation technique where each graph node is mapped to a K-dimensional space spanned by the first K non-null eigenvectors of the graph Laplacian matrix. As described later, TADSS uses the Laplacian embedding of HR Graph to select teams, and exploits the property that the lower Euclidean distances in the embedding space reflect stronger average connectivity between two graph nodes in the original graph.

3   TADSS User Interface

This section illustrates the TADSS user interface through a use case, and describes the associated algorithms to select teams. Consider the case of John who is a hiring manager in a mid-sized Information Technology (IT) services delivery firm. John has to staff and manage the IT support requirements for their new client. This use case scenario below explains how John interacts with TADSS to hire the best team configuration for a given project.

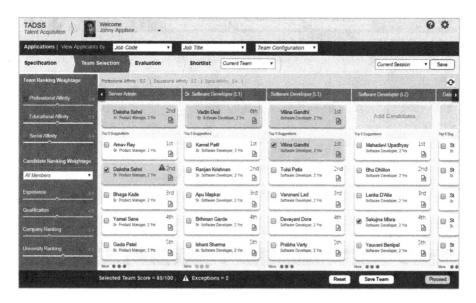

Fig. 2. Team selection interface

TADSS provides a four step wizard process for team creation. The first step, namely, the *specification interface* allows him to view, search, add and edit JD details against a large of pool of candidate profiles available with the company. He can use the application to specify his team configuration. In the second step, *team selection interface* as shown in Fig. 2, he can define Employee-Employee and JD-Employee weightage values for different HR entity attributes. Once John changes the affinity values, the preferred team-affinity weightages (Employee-Employee) and candidate ranking weightages (JD-Candidates) are used in the HR Graph construction.

Next top candidates with respect to each JD are found. The ranking algorithm considers John's preference on education, experience and skill competencies of all candidates and provides a ranking solution. In the team selection interface, he can select the default suggested candidate or add any exception by overriding system-suggested team member. For a given session a user can save multiple team compositions. While the user is selecting team members, the total cohesiveness of the team is computed simultaneously and shown as *selected team score*.

John can select one or multiple candidates for a given JD as per the requirement of team and thereby generate multiple such team configurations. Once John has selected and saved multiple team configurations, he can proceed to *team evaluation interface* as shown in Fig. 3. He can compare the different team configurations based on the affinity score. The affinity score is computed using the HR Graph embedding based algorithm described later.

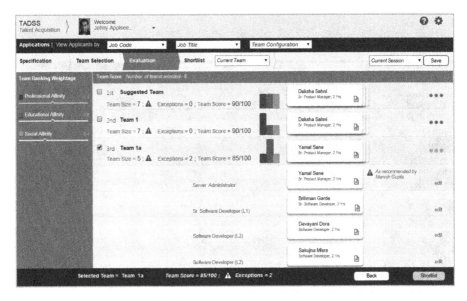

Fig. 3. Team evaluation interface

The team evaluation interface also provides the affinity visualization next to team cohesion score where he can compare the team capabilities. The suggested team and selected teams are shown as cluster packs which can be expanded and individual candidate resume can be seen along with any exception added to every candidate node. The interface can be further enhanced to include actions related to hiring decision workflow against every candidate card. The bar chart along with team score gives a quick preview of the cohesiveness value at various affinities. Next, the two main queries handled by the TADSS user interfaces are described.

Candidate Ranking Query: In this query, TADSS is asked to rank candidate profiles for a given job description. TADSS exploits the property that smaller Euclidian distance between two nodes in the Laplacian embedding of the HR Graph indicates stronger average connectivity (or stronger relationship) between the corresponding entities in the HR Graph. Thus, to answer the query for a given JD, TADSS simply ranks the candidates in increasing order of their distance from JD in the embedding space.

Team Hiring Query: In this query, TADSS system is asked to provide a cohesion score for a given set of candidates who are selected for a team. The system assumes the hypothesis that for forming a cohesive team, the members should have common or related academic background or past affiliation from previous jobs, or direct or indirect connections on social/professional media platforms. Based on the construction of the HR Graph, the closeness of the candidate nodes in the embedding space provides an indication of overall cohesion among them. Thus, this work proposes to compute the cohesion score as a 2-dimentional vector storing the standard deviation and average pairwise distance, of the embedded points associated with the set of candidates in the given team.

Let $\mathbf{X} = \{x_1, \ldots, x_n\}$ be the K-dim Laplacian embedding of HR graph where $x_i = \{x_i^1, \ldots, x_i^K\}$ represents K coordinates of a node. Let $\mathbf{T} = \{t_1, \ldots, t_p\}$ be the p teams configured by the hiring manager. Each team instance is represented by a set of candidates (associated with respective JDs) as $t_i = \{x_{\alpha(i,1)}, \ldots, x_{\alpha(i,m)}\}$ where the team has m members and $\alpha(i, :)$ is the index set of the respective selected candidates. Then the system computes the following for each team t_i.

$$mean(t_i) = \frac{1}{m} \sum_j x_{\alpha(i,j)} \tag{1}$$

$$sd(t_i) = \sqrt{\frac{\sum_j dist(x_{\alpha(i,j)} - mean(t_i))^2}{m}} \tag{2}$$

$$avg\_dist(t_i) = \frac{1}{m^2} \sum_{l=1}^{m} \sum_{j=1}^{m} dist\left(x_{\alpha(i,l)} - x_{\alpha(i,j)}\right) \tag{3}$$

$$score(t_i) = \begin{bmatrix} sd(t_i) \\ avg\_dist(t_i) \end{bmatrix} \tag{4}$$

On computing the cohesion score vector (where lower value in each dimension implies better team cohesion), the TADSS system either presents the vector as output to the query, or for ease of comprehension, a scalar normalized cohesion score value (as shown in Fig. 3) whose value increases with increased level of team cohesion, is obtained from the computed score vector.

4 Dataset Generation

This section describes the dataset generation for the numerical simulations. One of the challenges in talent acquisition analytics is the lack of public access to data due to privacy concerns. To overcome this challenge, this work uses synthetic data for simulations, and its generation procedure is described next.

The dataset generated has 20 job descriptions of 3 categories, from a professional network where all these job descriptions are related to J2EE domain. 1500 resume samples are generated, of which 1000 were chosen as candidates and the rest 500 as employees. The details are given in Table 2.

The structure of each resume is as follows:

1. Resume index
2. Education

   List of degrees (masters, bachelors), Degree name, Degree category (management or technology), Institute, Year of graduation, and grade obtained

3. Experience

   List of jobs, Position title, Organization name, Start year and End year

4. Educational skills
5. Experience skills (only for experienced candidates and employees)
6. Associated job description id (only for employees)

Table 2. Details of profile attributes of generated resumes

Candidate	Profile category	Position title	Resumes	Total
Experienced (60 %)	Manager/Lead (20 %)	Product manager (12 %)	180	300
		Technical lead (8 %)	120	
	Developer (20 %)	Software developer (12 %)	180	300
		Senior software engineer (8 %)	120	
	Tester (20 %)	Test engineer (12 %)	180	300
		Senior test engineer (8 %)	120	
Fresher (40 %)			600	600
Total number of Resumes				1500

Education: 60 % of the profiles have master's as their highest degree while rest have bachelor's as the highest degree. Educational degrees were divided into two categories: technology and management. All the degrees in technology category are assumed to be earned in Computer Science domain. Degrees which were considered include 4 types of bachelor's and 4 types of master's degrees in Computer Science, and 2 types of master's degrees in management. The schools and institutes are assigned by taking random samples from a list of 82 schools and 600 institutes, compiled from public sources. All the bachelor's degrees are assumed to have a span of 4 years, while masters and those in management are assumed to have a span of 2 years. Obtained grades follow a normal distribution with mean of 87 and standard deviation of 3.

Experience: Random samples were generated for each of the 6 job profiles from a list of 42 companies in IT domain. Profiles in management category are assigned job experiences with a minimum of 3 and a maximum of 7 years whereas those in development and testing category have job experiences with a minimum of 1 and a maximum of 3 years. For the candidate profiles generated, 60 % had existing work experience, and remaining 40 % were fresher.

Skills: Two kinds of skills were assigned to the profiles, viz., educational and industrial skills, from 16 product management related skills, 39 development related skills and 39 testing related skills. All the development and testing skills are in the domain of J2EE. These lists were compiled by referring to similar job profiles from social professional networks. Each resume has a minimum of 5 and a maximum of 10 skills in educational and/or experience category. Random samples of skills from each category, conforming to the position titles of profiles were created. Fresher resumes are assigned a mix of testing and development skills.

5 HR Graph Modelling Parameters

The graph modelling was achieved by inducing an undirected weighted graph among 1520 nodes representing job descriptions (20), employee resumes (500) and candidate resumes (1000). The edge weights were computed using the functions in Table 1. The features considered while calculating edge weights were: (1) education, (2) experience, and (3) skill. Thus, for both candidate-candidate and job description-candidate edges, the total affinity, i.e., edge weight was calculated as:

$$w_{e_1,e_2} = weight_{edu} * affinity_{edu}(e_1, e_2) + weight_{exp}$$
$$* affinity_{exp}(e_1, e_2) + weight_{skills} * affinity_{skills}(e_1, e_2)$$

where e_1 and e_2 were the two entities (either job description and candidate, or a pair of candidates). Each of these affinities was a weighted sum of sub-features, enumerated in subsequent sections. For JD-candidate edges, the feature weights were: $weight_{edu} = 0.2$, $weight_{exp} = 0.6, weight_{skills} = 0.2$. For candidate-candidate graph, the feature weights were: $weight_{edu} = 0.3, weight_{exp} = 0.4, weight_{skills} = 0.3$.

Education Affinity: For candidate-candidate edge weight, education affinity, $affinity_{edu}$, was calculated by finding match between degrees of the profiles in terms of degree category (technical or management), degree name, year of starting and graduation, and school/institute. Different levels of educational degrees were weighed differently. For JD-candidate graph, affinity was assigned the full value, i.e., 0.2, if the candidate's degree matched exactly to the required degree, 0.1 if it did not match but was under the same category (technology or management).

Experience Affinity: Experience affinity $affinity_{exp}$ was calculated by finding match between position titles, company names, start and end year of job and years of experience of the two profiles in candidate-candidate graph. For JD-candidate graph, highest affinity was assigned to the most recent job position if it matches the title of the given job description, and relatively lower to the earlier ones. Sub-features, viz., organization name, position title and minimum years of experience were weighted as: $weight_{organization} = 0.2, weight_{positiontitle} = 0.2, weight_{experience\_years} = 0.2$.

Skill Affinity: Skill affinity $affinity_{skills}$ was calculated as a weighted sum of matches for educational skills and experience skills. In the experiments, the weights were set as follows: $weight_{educational\_skills} = 0.4$, $weight_{experience\_skills} = 0.6$. The similarity over skill sets of the two profiles or a job description and profile was calculated using Sorenson Dice coefficient [12].

All the affinities for an edge in candidate-candidate graph are normalized over the set of all the candidates using feature scaling, before summing them up to calculate the total affinity.

6 Experimental Results

The spectral embedding of the induced HR graph was obtained by computing the eigen-decomposition of associated graph Laplacian matrix where only K = 304 (approximately 20 % of total number of eigenvectors, i.e., 1520) eigenvectors were computed.

Once the Laplacian embedding of the HR graph was computed, an example team configuration for a randomly selected company in the generated data was chosen with following details:

Job Profile	# of Positions
• Product manager	01
• Technical lead	01
• Senior software engineer	01
• Software developer	03
• Test engineer	02

For this specific team configuration, first relevance ranking of candidates for each job profile was computed by executing the candidate ranking query in TADSS using Laplacian embedding. Using this relevance ranking of candidates, 10 instances of team configuration were obtained, such that for the first team instance the top ranked candidates per job profile was chosen, and then the selection was shifted to one rank down for the next team instance. Next, team hiring query was executed to compute the team score for each of the 10 instances of team configuration and the obtained the respective score vector fields are listed in Table 3. It is interesting to note here that the score vector with the best value i.e., with minimum magnitude (highlighted in 3rd row) is actually

Table 3. Team score of difference team instances and respective overlap among academic background and past job experience of team members.

Team Instance	Score		#Unique Acad. Institutes/#Total Acad. Institutes	#Unique Companies/#Total Companies
	$sd(t_i)$	$avg\_dist(t_i)$		
t_1	0.018393	0.015963	10/15=0.67	7/8=0.87
t_2	0.026681	0.028860	09/13=0.69	5/7=0.71
t_3	**0.011318**	**0.014273**	**10/16=0.62**	**3/6=0.50**
t_4	0.013921	0.017169	11/16=0.68	5/8=0.62
t_5	0.017852	0.022248	11/14=0.78	6/10=0.60
t_6	0.015173	0.019246	13/14=0.92	4/8=0.50
t_7	0.016809	0.021587	10/16=0.62	4/7=0.57
t_8	0.017947	0.022839	10/14=0.71	3/5=0.60
t_9	0.011646	0.014761	10/13=0.76	5/6=0.83
t_{10}	0.011699	0.014563	10/14=0.71	2/4=0.50

the third team instance instead of the first team instance where top relevance ranked candidates were chosen.

In order to establish further confidence on the score value, an approximate measure of cohesiveness was computed among candidates (selected in each team instance) based on their academic background as well as past experience. In the former case, the fraction of unique academic institution divided by the total number of academic institutes where candidates pursued their higher education was computed. Similarly in latter case, the fraction of unique companies divided by the total number of companies to which candidates were affiliated was considered. These cohesiveness measures appropriately reflect the importance of respective score values. However, these are very coarse approximation of cohesiveness as the HR Graph is a multi-relations model and there are more relationships which need to be explored for getting a better estimate of cohesiveness (e.g., employee to candidate cohesiveness based on academic background or past job history).

As mentioned earlier, this simulation shows an example where the team which is staffed with the top ranked candidates from the individual relevance ranking list, need not to be the most cohesive team. Thus, TADSS can help the hiring manager to choose a team with better cohesiveness as reflected by its team score.

7 Preliminary User Evaluation and Discussions

The different team compositions for a given set of JDs given by TADSS were used for a qualitative feedback of the *team evaluation interface*. Users were given extended view of each suggested team in the interface. They were also given resume documents of top 5 candidates with respect to each JD for team creation. It was observed that hiring managers implicitly used the information related to HR entities (professional, educational and social) while coming up with team-member compositions. However, a team comparison view brings forth the importance of weightages provided by hiring managers. It was observed that users were referring the cohesiveness bar chart to understand the reasons for higher or lower affinity scores.

Converged teams require a lot of human decision making and TADSS aids HR practitioners and staffing specialists in making more informed decision in relatively less time. Such a system for creating team compositions can be a useful tool for hiring managers and project staffing experts. In case of hiring for a team, hiring managers may provide their own insights, based on past experiences, as user provided importance factor for different affinity factors. As part of future work, a larger and longitudinal user study of TADSS has been planned.

References

1. Aksin, Z., Armony, M., Mehrotra, V.: The modern call center: a multi-disciplinary perspective on operations management research. In: Production and Operations Management (2007)
2. Chung, F.R.K.: Spectral Graph Theory. American Mathematical Society, Providence (1997)
3. Qiu, H., Hancock, E.R.: Clustering and embedding using commute times. Pattern Anal. Mach. Intell. 29(11), 1873–1890 (2007)
4. Lehoucq, R.B., Sorensen, D.C., Yang, C.: ARPACK Users Guide: Solution of Large Scale Eigenvalue Problems by Implicitly Restarted Arnoldi Methods. Society for Industrial and Applied Mathematics, Philadelphia (1997)
5. Mehta, S., Pimplikar, R., Singh, A., Varshney, L., Visweswariah, K.: Efficient multifaceted screening of job applicants. In: EDBT (2013)
6. Hoye, G., Hooft, E.A.J., Lievens, F.: Networking as a job search behavior: a social network perspective. J. Occup. Organ. Psychol 82(3), 661–682 (2009)
7. https://www.linkedin.com/company/bright.com
8. Social networking job matching technology. United States Patent Application 20130013526
9. Method and apparatus for hiring using social networks. United States Patent Application 20110196802
10. Krauth, B.V.: A dynamic model of job networking and social influences on employment. J. Economic Dyn. & Control 28(6), 1185–1204 (2004)
11. Determination of a contractor team. WIPO Patent Application WO/2013/187866
12. Dice, L.R.: Measures of the amount of ecologic association between species. Ecology 26(3), 297–302 (1945)

Reading Through Graphics: Interactive Landscapes to Explore Dynamic Topic Spaces

Eva Ulbrich[1], Eduardo Veas[1(✉)], Santokh Singh[1], and Vedran Sabol[1,2]

[1] Know Center GmbH, Inffeldgasse 13, 8010 Graz, Austria
{eulbrich,eveas,ssingh,vsabol}@know-center.com
[2] University of Technology Graz, Graz, Austria

Abstract. An information landscape is commonly used to represent relatedness in large, high-dimensional datasets, such as text document collections. In this paper we present interactive metaphors, inspired in map reading and visual transitions, that enhance the landscape representation for the analysis of topical changes in dynamic text repositories. The goal of interactive visualizations is to elicit insight, to allow users to visually formulate hypotheses about the underlying data and to prove them. We present a user study that investigates how users can elicit information about topics in a large document set. Our study concentrated on building and testing hypotheses using the map reading metaphors. The results show that people indeed relate topics in the document set from spatial relationships shown in the landscape, and capture the changes to topics aided by map reading metaphors.

Keywords: Text visualisation · Dynamic information landscape · Interaction design · User study

1 Introduction

The already enormous amount of electronically available information keeps growing at ever faster rates. While retrieval tools excel at finding a single or a few relevant pieces of information, when a holistic view on large amount of complex data is needed, it becomes necessary to consider the entirety of the data set for analysis. Information Landscapes represent a powerful visualization technique for interactive analysis of complex topical relationships in large document repositories [7]. They convey topical similarity in a document set through spatial proximity [4,12]. However, we are not just confronted with large, but also with permanently growing and rapidly changing repositories. The concept of information landscapes has been adapted to addresses the visualisation of changes in the topical structure of a data set within a single, consistent visual metaphor - the dynamic topography information landscape [16]. Adding new documents to the set, shifts the position of topics in the dynamic landscape. But, representing temporal evolution in a comprehensive manner, although crucial for the analysis of large corpora, is not trivial. State-of-the-art research in the area identified caveats and pitfalls of representing change with information landscapes, particularly related to change blindness [11].

© Springer International Publishing Switzerland 2015
S. Yamamoto (Ed.): HIMI 2015, Part I, LNCS 9172, pp. 127–137, 2015.
DOI: 10.1007/978-3-319-20612-7_13

This paper presents an efficient web-based implementation of the dynamic information landscape. We introduce novel map-reading interactive metaphors for topic analysis including interactive morphological transitions, multiple views, trails and traces. In addition, a major contribution is a user study conducted with 18 test users to validate the map reading metaphors as analysis tools for information landscapes. In particular, we follow two goals: (i) to find out whether people can read information about topics and topical relationships out of spatial relationships shown in the landscape, and (ii) to discover if people can derive information about the evolution of topics in dynamically changing document collections. Our evaluations showed a relation between observations and assumptions elicited with aforementioned metaphors: participants built assumptions about the data that they could validate. Map reading metaphors, as applied here, are thus useful for topic analysis of a large body of documents. They give an overview of the distribution of concepts and topics. Transition techniques complemented with map reading metaphors were useful tools to analyse the evolution of topics, by visually comparing where new topics appeared, which topics moved closer together, and what new topics became important.

2   Related Work

The fundamental idea of information landscapes is to convey relatedness between data elements, in our case the topical similarity, through spatial proximity in the visualisation. The notion builds on the so-called "first law of cognitive geography", stating that people assume that close things are similar, validated in [9]. Reference [14] describes the research agenda for spatialisation methods, in particular the principles of the geographic metaphor for visualization of non-geographic information. Reference [5] describes a formalisation of spatialisation views and the theoretical foundations of the discipline. An interesting result is a discussion on visual features to better represent properties of the data, such as conveying similarity with spatial proximity, magnitude with height, and change with tectonic processes.

Information landscapes have been used to visualise topical distribution of document collections for more than 20 years, starting with Bead [4] in 1993 and SPIRE [17] in 1995. Using the VxInsight tool they have been successfully applied to the analysis of patent data bases [2] and of scientific and technological document sets [3]. InfoSky [1] demonstrated the applicability of the information landscape concept on hierarchically organised document collections, where the hierarchy is represented by nested Voronoi polygons.

The temporal behaviour in document sets is often represented by dedicated visualizations, such as the well-known ThemeRiver [6], which successfully conveys topical trends and correlations. To enable interactive visual analysis of both topical relationships and topical trends, an information landscape was combined with a ThemeRiver using a Multiple Coordinated Views interface [13]. The concept of a dynamic topography information landscape for visualisation of changes in document repositories was proposed in [12] and realised in [13] and [16].

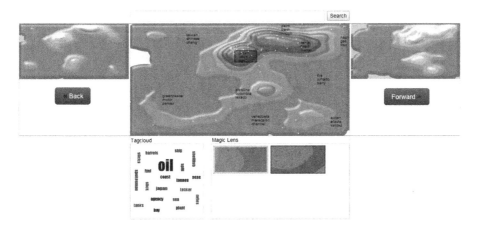

Fig. 1. The test UI: Multiple views metaphor shows previous and subsequent stages of the landscape. Back and Forward buttons will trigger the morphing process. A magic lense is used for selection whereby different selections can be saved (shown as thubmnails) and reapplied. Keywords from selected documents are shown in the tagcloud. Clicking on keywords triggers filtering of documents in the list (not shown).

These early versions lacked all but most basic interaction techniques, suffered from issues related to changes blindness and, most notably, their dynamic features were not evaluated in a user study. Issues related to change blindness in dynamic information landscapes were discussed in [11] with remedies proposed, but evaluated with a rather limited example, which solely changes height from appearing or disappearing documents. Documents positions were fixed, hence changes in document positions occurring due to the altered topical structure are not considered.

3   Dynamic Information Landscape

An information landscape conveys similarity of topics in a data set through spatial proximity and density of topics as elevation in the visualization. Hills represent groups (clusters) of topically related documents separated by areas represented as sea. Higher hills group more documents than lower ones. Landscape areas are labeled with descriptive terms extracted from the documents.

Besides topical relatedness, dynamic information landscapes represent changes to a document repository as changes in topography. As a repository evolves (e.g. documents are added) the collection of topics changes, new topics become important, documents move, attracted by new topical relationships. Hence the landscape topography is altered. A fading topic may cause islands and hills to disappear, while new hot topics cause new islands to arise from the seabed. Hills moving towards or apart from each other indicate topical convergence or divergence of the corresponding topical clusters, with merging (cluster fusion) and splitting (cluster break-up) of hills and islands occurring in extreme cases.

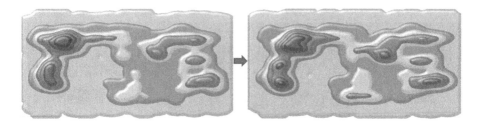

Fig. 2. Morphological changes after adding new documents.

To be comprehensible, transitions of the landscape topography from an old to a new temporal configuration must be incremental. The configuration of regions which are not (or are only little) affected by the modification of the data set must remain stable with respect to their relative positions and shapes. This enables users to immediately understand the altered landscape through the recognition and orientation provided by the already known, preserved (or scarcely modified) elements of the topography. A morphing procedure modifies the topography in smoothly animated transitions, that users can follow to understand the changes.

3.1   Computation Procedure

To compute the 2D similarity layout for the documents we use a fast, scalable, aggregation-based projection algorithm [10] which employs k-means clustering and cluster-oriented force-directed placement. The algorithm was modified to support incremental computation enabling seamless incorporation of changes into an existing similarity layout [15]. The landscape generation begins with the vectorisation of documents, and includes the above mentioned incremental clustering and projection, cluster labelling (using highest weight terms from the underlying documents), height matrix computation, and finally the extraction of contour lines (isohypses). As this process is computationally intensive it is performed on the server. The result of the computation is a JSON file defining the landscape geometry. The geometry is transferred to and displayed by the Web-Client built using the D3.js JavaScript library (http://d3js.org/). For pairs of consecutive landscapes we compute mappings between the corresponding contour lines and use morphing to smoothly visualise the transitions.

3.2   Map Reading Metaphors

Figuring out relations between documents in a large corpus is a cognitively demanding task. The algorithms proposed can establish a level of similarity between entities and documents. Metaphors based on map reading were introduced to foster the exploratory analytics workflow. The goals are to enable visual thinking in the exploratory phase, whereupon hypotheses are formulated, and to promote the explanatory role thereafter, whereby hypotheses are supported or revoked based on careful observation of data characteristics. Therefore metaphors for *map navigation*, *overview and details* and *temporal transitions* were introduced (Fig. 2).

Map Navigation and Selection. Map navigation can be broken down to a series of pan and and zoom operations. Special attention was put to enable incremental changes in information density with changing zoom levels, organizing labels and isohypses in respective level of detail hierarchies. *Search for terms* works as a keyword search on labels and feature vectors. It highlights documents and areas where the keyword occurs. *Area selection* highlights document points in a region. Selections can be stored to recover information after transitions.

Overview and Details. A multiple views metaphor was introduced to reveal details for areas of interest while maintaining overview (see Fig. 1). It consisted of a magic lens used for inspection and selection. The magic lens triggered miniature (zoomed) previews and a wordcloud view summarizing content. Selections can be stored to in a rectangular thumbnail to create a trail of selections of interest to allow tracking a chain of changes.

Temporal Transitions. The multiple views metaphor extends to temporal transitions. Mini landscapes show abstract views of preceding and subsequent stages in the progression. Upon selection and when using the magic lens, previews and wordclouds are added with for past and current temporal stages. Additionally, a *document trail* metaphor shows document flow between time stages. Additionally, new documents are highlighted in the landscape upon transition, for quick overview of the changes in density (see Fig. 3). The last two metaphors were particularly useful while fine-tuning the incremental layout algorithm: the developer could actually observe what similarities were enforced by it and adjust accordingly.

4   Evaluation

The motivation to enable interactive analysis on dynamic information landscapes stresses the analytic evolution of concepts and topics over time. A formative evaluation was carried out to establish that aided by map reading tools:

H1 people can elicit information about topics in documents out of spatial relationships shown in the landscape,
H2 people can derive information about the evolution of topics in a document set.

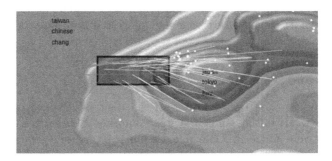

Fig. 3. Document trails show document movement between incremental stages.

The evaluation concentrates on the exploratory analytics workflow. It enforces the role of metaphors in an exploratory phase, whereupon facts are observed to formulate hypotheses. It then exploits tools for the explanatory phase of validating or discarding hypotheses.

4.1   Participants and Methodology

Eighteen participants took part in the experiment (14M, 4F, $X = 29$ years). Nine of them had corrected vision. Sixteen participants had experience in data analysis, fourteen used visual tools.

Following the aforementioned exploratory analytics workflow, the evaluation had iterative stages of exploration, hypotheses formulation, and hypotheses validation. To investigate the complexity of the hypotheses, we grouped them into:

Structural: only dealing with changes to geometry, without any association to topics.
N-entity: mentioning at most n entities.

Further, we analyzed the content of n-entity hypotheses to find out what kind of relations participants elicit between recovered entities.

The study consisted of a training phase and the proper evaluation. The training phase introduced the metaphors with a screen cast followed by hands-on practice. Thereafter, participants could freely use the tool until they felt confident with it. It took an average 15 min.

The proper evaluation consisted of three analytics phases based on three landscapes which were incremental progressions (see Sect. 4.2). In the exploration stage participants used tools to discover content. Participants were thus asked to identify areas, the number of documents in an area, a document with specific content, and an area with certain attributes. In the hypotheses formulation stage, participants were required to formulate 3 hypotheses based on changes introduced by adding new documents, by visually comparing the current landscape with the thumbnail of the subsequent one. The hypotheses validation stage followed by transitioning to the subsequent landscape. At this stage people used tools to validate their hypotheses.

The study closed with a subjective questionnaire whereby participants rated the usefulness on a 7-point-Likert scale and suggested improvements. The complete study took in average 52 min.

4.2   Stimuli and Apparatus

The stimuli were created from a subset of the Reuters Corpus Volume 1 documents, whereby an initial landscape was computed. Thereafter, incremental document sets were added in a controlled manner to create a sequence of landscapes. Hereby, Six incremental landscapes were obtained. The first three were used for the proper evaluation.

To obtain the training stimuli, the last two landscapes were relabelled with Christmas terms, to prevent familiarity with the concepts in the proper evaluation. Landscape 4 was left out to achieve aesthetic separation between training and evaluation stimuli. Additionally, the "sealevel" of the training data was placed a level higher, further altering the visual aspect of the landscapes.

The test was conducted in a calm, small room with a conventional screen connected to a notebook. Participants used mouse and keyboard to complete tasks. The visualization was running on Chrome Version 30.0.1599.101.

4.3   Results

Exploration Phase. Participants could identify regions of high density of documents by searching for high elevations. Thirteen participants found the seven high elevation regions (7/7), three miscounted and found eight (8/7), only two had trouble and counted more (11/7) or less (3/7). Participants identified real countries in labels. Ten of them found all six countries (6/6), six did not count Taiwan and found five (5/6), one counted four (4/6) and one counted eight (8/6). In the next task, participants had to find high density area with the terms ship and spill. All participants completed this task using search tools. When asked to identify important terms in a selected region, participants used the word cloud and identified Oil, Japan and tanker. One participant opted for using just labels (and not the word cloud) and chose Japan, Slicks, Reactors. Participants also had to identify topic mountains from abstract descriptions, namely they had to find a region about the oil price and one about a ship accident where neither oil price nor ship accident appear as labels. All participants chose a topic mountain solely containing information about money, market and cents to be the one about oil price and sixteen (16/18) chose the mountain with the labels Japan, Slicks, Reactors for the accident. One chose a region around the Exxon Valdez labels as he remembered it to be a tanker accident, another one chose a region around the label Greenpeace as he thought they might had caused a ship to sink. The latter two made their choice solely by interpreting labels, whereas the others used the search tool to find terms within documents related to accidents with ships, or selected areas and checked for significant terms in the word cloud.

Hypothesis Formulation. In this stage, participants had to visually compare the current landscape with the subsequent one and build three hypotheses. This lead to a total of 54 hypotheses in the first transition and 53 in the second (one participant only formulated two). Our intention here was to find out if participants could analyse the evolution of topics in a document set with the provided metaphors (Table 1).

In the first transition, we found 7 (0.13) purely structural hypotheses. Three of them from a single user who did not make any association of geometry to topics. 19 hypotheses (0.35) mention a single entity (1-entity), mostly observations about an increase or decrease of documents. 21 hypotheses (0.39) relate two entities (2-entity) in more complex relations. Finally we found 6 (0.11) 3-entity and 1 (0.02) 4-entity. Regarding the contents of hypotheses, 17 (0.31) and 9 (0.17) hypotheses predicted an increase or decrease of documents respectively in relation to a topic. 14 hypotheses predicted relocations of topics

Table 1. Classification of Hypotheses. Structural hypotheses only referred to changes in geometry, n-entity hypotheses established relations between n entities. For both transitions participants tended to build more hypotheses relating 2-entities.

Entity	Count (%) Transition 1	Count (%) Transition 2
Structural	7 (0.13)	3 (0.05)
1-Entity	19 (0.35)	8 (0.15)
2-Entity	21 (0.39)	23 (0.435)
3-Entity	6 (0.11)	13 (0.245)
4-Entity	1 (0.02)	5 (0.10)
5-Entity	0	1 (0.02)
Total	54	53

and 0.037 the appearance of new topics. Interestingly, 14 hypotheses stated complex relationships between entities, including 3 (0.055) similarity and 11 (0.203) varied complex ones, such as changes in oil-price due to accidents of tankers or delays with pipelines.

In the second transition, we found 3 (0.05) purely structural hypotheses all from the same user. 8 hypotheses (0.15) mention a single entity (1-entity). We also found 23 (0.43) 2-entity, 13 (0.24) 3-entity, 5 (0.1) 4-entity, and 1 (0.02) 5-entity hypotheses. Regarding contents, 19 (0.35) hypotheses predicted an increase in documents about a topic. Curiously no hypothesis mentioned decrease in a topic. 3 hypotheses predicted relocations of topics. Interestingly 29 hypotheses (0.54) reported complex relationships, including 10 (0.188) similarity and 19 (0.358) more complex assumptions (Table 2).

Hypothesis Validation. Building hypothesis was only a half of this test, after transitioning to the target landscape, participants had to validate or discard their hypotheses using the proposed tools. Results showed that people could actually analyse the evidence to (dis) prove hypotheses. In the first transition, 6 hypotheses could not be proved or rejected (score 3-4), 26 were proved (scored $<$ 3)

Table 2. Sample Hypotheses. Hypotheses were also classified regarding their contents, in whether they related an increase or decrease of importance of a topic or more complex assumptions.

Entity	Type	Hypothesis
structural	–	many new documents on one hill, rest remains similar
1-entity	increase	more news about Iraq
2-entity	decrease	Colombia and its pipeline lose importance as mountain shrinks
2-entity	assumption	a new development related to reactors in Japan
4-entity	similarity	more news relating Irak, Japan and Venezuela with gas

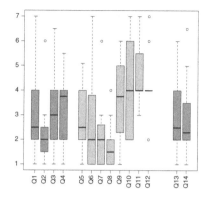

Fig. 4. Subjective ratings. Plots in blue rated overall usability while plots in yellow rated the metaphors. Refer to the text in Exit Questionnaire, Sect. 4.3

and 22 were disproved (scored > 4). In the second transition, 12 hypotheses could not be proved or rejected, 16 were proved and 24 were rejected. This shows that participants found evidence using the tools to either back or revoke the majority of hypotheses (Fig. 4).

Exit Questionnaire. Participants found that they could build useful hypothesis (Q1, Median = 2.5). They also found the landscape gives a solid overview about distribution of topics (Q2, M = 2), and that the thumbnail landscape helped to build hypotheses (Q3, M = 3). Participants were neutral about how exhausting it was to build hypotheses (Q4, M = 3.75). With regards to the tools used to prove hypotheses and how helpful they were, search for terms was helpful (Q5, M = 2.5), as well as the Word Cloud (Q6, M = 2) and the document flow (Q7, M = 2). The rectangle selection rated very well (Q8, M = 1.5). The magic lens was partially useful (Q9, M = 3.4), while the miniature preview borderline (Q10, M = 4), and saving labels positions was rated rather unuseful (Q11, M = 6). The list also scored poorly (Q12, M = 4). Finally, participants found that they could get information out of the data without having to read the documents themselves (Q13, M = 2.5). They also found the visualisation as a whole a useful tool to analyze data (Q14, M = 2.2).

4.4   Discussion

We can report that participants in general can relate changes in geometry to topical changes, as they formulated hypotheses majorly relating entities out of spatial relations in the visualization. Furthermore, participants formulated hypotheses relating two and up to four entities in complex relations. Although hypotheses were often invalid, the study showed that our metaphors aided participants to analyse the evidence, judge and retain or reject hypotheses. The fact that people could not decide about some hypotheses is not a limitation. These are the cases where they would have to find more evidence, e.g. by reading some of the documents. The proposed metaphors actually empower users to discriminate for which assumptions or hypotheses they would need more information.

The metaphors further direct users to the sources of that information, since the documents are actually linked and can be accessed from the tool.

The exit questionnaire validates our findings: participants found in general they could build useful hypotheses, although it was not trivial. In general participants found the interactive metaphors of dynamic information landscape are useful to analyze and obtain information from a large body of documents without having to read them all.

5   Conclusions

We built an HTML5-based information landscape using data from a text processing pipeline. The pipeline starts by gathering documents and clustering based on their content similarities. It then creates a three dimensional height matrix. Topic mountains are extracted by cutting these into isohypses.

Based on map analysis, a number of topic analysis metaphors were developed (e.g., focusing on a region to discover concepts, associating high density of topics/documents with elevation). Furthermore, we put special focus on interactive aspects of the map reading metaphors, to compare and obtain information from topic landscapes created incrementally. Our evaluations showed a correlation across observations and assumptions elicited with aforementioned metaphors: participants built assumptions about the data that they could validate. Map reading metaphors, as applied here, are thus useful for topic analysis of a large body of documents. They give an overview of the distribution of concepts and topics. Transition techniques complemented with map reading metaphors were useful tools to analyse the evolution of topics, by visually comparing where new documents appeared, where documents wandered to, and what new topics became important.

In the future, we plan to investigate the impact of individual tools. Additionally, we are currently investigating methods to tightly integrate the interactive metaphors with the algorithmic analytics methods.

Acknowledgement. This work was performed within the FIT-IT funded DIVINE and the EC FP7 EEXCESS (grant 600601) projects. The Know-Center is funded within the Austrian COMET Program – managed by the Austrian Research Promotion Agency (FFG) – under the auspices of BMVIT and BMWFW Austrian Federal Ministries and the state of Styria.

References

1. Andrews, K., Kienreich, W., Sabol, V., Becker, J., Kappe, F., Droschl, G., Granitzer, M., Auer, P., Tochtermann, K.: The infosky visual explorer: exploiting hierarchical structture and document similarities. J. Inf. Visulization **1**(3/4), 166–181 (2002). London, England
2. Boyack, K.W., Wylie, B.N., Davidson, G.S., Johnson, D.K.: Analysis of patent databases using VxInsight. In: Workshop on New Paradigms in Information Visualization and Manipulation (2000)

3. Boyack, K.W., Wylie, B.N., Davidson, G.S.: Domain visualization using VxInsight for science and technology management. J. Am. Soc. Inform. Sci. Technol. **53**, 764–774 (2002)
4. Chalmers, M.: Using a landscape metaphor to represent a corpus of documents. In: Campari, I., Frank, A.U. (eds.) COSIT 1993. LNCS, vol. 716, pp. 377–390. Springer, Heidelberg (1993)
5. Fabrikant, S.I., Buttenfield, B.P.: Formalizing semantic spaces for information access. Ann. Assoc. Am. Geogr. **91**(2), 263–280 (2001)
6. Havre, S., Hetzler, B., Nowell, L.: ThemeRiver: visualizing theme changes over time. In: Proceedings of the IEEE Symposium on Information Visualization 2000 (InfoVis 2000), pp. 115–123 (2000)
7. Krishnan, M., Bohn, S., Cowley, W., Crow, V., Nieplocha, J.: Scalable visual analytics of massive textual datasets. In: 21st IEEE International Parallel and Distributed Processing Symposium. Long Beach, USA, pp. 1–10 (2007)
8. Kroell, M., Sabol, V., Kern, R., Granitzer, M.: Integrating user preferences into distance metrics. In: Proceedings of the LWA 2013 Workshop on Knowledge Discovery, Data Mining and Machine Learning (2013)
9. Montello, D.R., Fabrikant, S.I., Ruocco, M., Middleton, R.S.: Testing the first law of cognitive geography on point-display spatializations. In: Kuhn, W., Worboys, M.F., Timpf, S. (eds.) COSIT 2003. LNCS, vol. 2825, pp. 316–331. Springer, Heidelberg (2003)
10. Muhr, M., Sabol, V., Granitzer, M.: Scalable recursive top-down hierarchical clustering approach with implicit model selection for textual data sets. In: Proceedings of the 2010 Workshop on Database and Expert Systems Applications (held at DEXA 2010), pp. 15–19 (2010)
11. Nowell, L., Hetzler, E., Tanasse, T.: Change blindness in information visualization: a case study. In: Proceedings of the IEEE Symposium on Information Visualization 2001 (INFOVIS 2001), pp. 15–22 (2001)
12. Sabol, V., Syed, K.A.A., Scharl, A., Muhr, M., Hubmann-Haidvogel, A.: Incremental computation of information landscapes for dynamic web interfaces. In: Proceedings of the 10th Brazilian Symposium on Human Factors in Computer Systems, pp. 205–208 (2010)
13. Sabol, V.: Visual analysis of relatedness and dynamics in complex, enterprise-scale repositories. Doctoral Dissertation, Graz University of Technology, May 2012
14. Skupin, A., Fabrikant, S.I.: Spatialization methods: a cartographic research agenda for non-geographic information visualization. Cartography Geogr. Inf. Sci. **30**(2), 99–119 (2003)
15. Syed, K.A.A., Kröll, M., Sabol, V., Gindl, S., Scharl, A.: Incremental and scalable computation of dynamic topography information landscapes. J. Multimedia Process. Technol. 3(1), Special Issue on the Theory and Application of Visual Analytics, 49–65 (2012)
16. Syed, K.A.A., Kröll, M., Sabol, V., Scharl, A., Gindl, S., Granitzer, M., Weichselbraun, A.: Dynamic topography information landscapes – an incremental approach to visual knowledge discovery. In: Cuzzocrea, A., Dayal, U. (eds.) DaWaK 2012. LNCS, vol. 7448, pp. 352–363. Springer, Heidelberg (2012)
17. Wise, J.A., Thomas, J.J., Pennock, K., Lantrip, D., Pottier, M., Schur, A., Crow, V.: Visualizing the non-visual: spatial analysis and interaction with information from text documents. In: Proceedings of the 1995 IEEE Symposium on Information Visualization, pp. 51–58 (1995)

Edge Bundling in Multi-attributed Graphs

Takafumi Yamashita and Ryosuke Saga[✉]

Department of Computer Science and Intelligent Systems,
Graduate School of Engineering, Osaka Prefecture University, Sakai, Japan
svl07041@edu.osakafu-u.ac.jp, saga@cs.osakafu-u.ac.jp

Abstract. Numerous information visualization techniques are available for utilizing and analyzing big data. Among which, network visualization that employs node-link diagrams can determine the relationship among multi-dimensional data. However, when data become extremely large, visualization becomes obscure because of visual clutter. To address this problem, many edge bundling techniques have been proposed. However, although graphs have several attributions, previous techniques do not reflect these attributions. In this paper, we propose a new edge bundling method for attributed co-occurrence graphs. Electrostatic forces work between each pair of edges; however, if the edges are under different attributions, then repulsion works between pairs. By bundling edges under the same attribution, a graph can more clearly show the relationships among data.

Keywords: Edge bundling · Network visualization · Attributed graph

1 Introduction

Information visualization is becoming increasingly important in improving the quality of service in various markets [1, 2]. Information visualization is a means of presenting data clearly to people by using diagrams, animations, and so on after performing preprocessing such as clustering. It enables observers to instinctively recognize the relationships among data that cannot be observed by looking at numerical data.

One technique in information visualization is node-link diagrams [3], which enable observers to recognize data by simply showing their relationships through connected links. However, as the number of nodes and links increases, graph visibility decreases because visual clutter forms as data become large.

To reduce visual clutter, the approach of changing the layout of graphs was first proposed in [4]. By correctly rearranging nodes, graph visibility increases to a certain degree. However, this approach cannot solve the problem when a graph has enormous edges. To address this issue, a new approach, called edge bundling [5], has been proposed. This method enables observers to recognize the main stream of edges through bundle edges based on certain rules. For example, several methods based on the hierarchical structure of nodes [6], parallel coordinates [7], mechanical models, and so on [8], have been proposed. The mechanical bundling method presented in related works has succeeded in improving graph visibility by making bundle of edges clear.

© Springer International Publishing Switzerland 2015
S. Yamamoto (Ed.): HIMI 2015, Part I, LNCS 9172, pp. 138–147, 2015.
DOI: 10.1007/978-3-319-20612-7_14

By contrast, some types of graph have invested in attributions. For example, for an air route diagram, in which the nodes are the airports and the links are the air routes, the differences in airline companies can be invested to edges as attributions. For another example, trend information can be attributions in FACT-Graph [9]. However, previous edge bundling methods do not consider such attributions, and thus, an assumption is drawn that previous methods do not represent all the information in a graph.

In this paper, we propose a new method for multi-attributed graphs, which bundles the edges of each attribution and increases graph visibility. We demonstrate the validity of our method by applying it to a co-occurrence graph of keywords from editorial articles.

2 Related Works

2.1 Force-Directed Edge Bundling (FDEB)

Holten et al. proposed FDEB [10]. In this method, edges are considered as a spring with several control points, and edges are bundled by an attractive force between the points based on Hooke's law. However, when the force is too strong, the edges are bundled excessively and node-link diagrams present incorrect relationships. To solve this problem, Holten at el. introduced a compatibility measure that works for the force between incorrect pairs of edges. This method has been applied to undirected and non-attributed graphs.

A spring force F_s that works at p_i is presented as follows:

$$F_s = k_p \cdot (\|p_{i-1} - p_i\| + \|p_i - p_{i+1}\|) + \sum_{Q \in E} \frac{C_e(P, Q)}{\|p_i - q_i\|} \tag{1}$$

where the control points are p_{i-1}, p_i, p_{i+1}, and q_i in edges P and Q; i is the index of the control point ($1 < i < n$); k_p is the spring constant; and $C_e(P, Q)$ is the compatibility between P and Q.

2.2 Divided Edge Bundling

Selassie et el. improved FDEB and proposed divided edge bundling [11]. The latter uses directed and non-attributed graphs as objects of bundling. In addition to spring force, Selassie at el. proposed Coulomb's force based on the potential in which the variable is the distance between control points p_i and q_j. Control point p_i is attracted to point m_j, which is the potential minimum point. When edges P and Q are going toward opposite directions, m_j moves to the right of edge Q. Hence, Coulomb's force changes according to the current pair of edge attributions.

Selassie at el. also introduced the parameter of compatibility, which depends on the number of edges in the minimum length path between edges P and Q. As a result of this parameter, bundling for graphs with several subgraphs is strictly limited.

The potential minimum m_j and Coulomb's force F_C that work at p_i are defined as follows:

$$m_j = \begin{cases} q_j & \text{if } P \cdot Q > 0 \\ q_j + lN_j & \text{if } P \cdot Q < 0 \end{cases} \tag{2}$$

$$F_C = \frac{-sk_C}{\pi C \left(s^2 + |p_i - m_j|^2 \right)^2} \tag{3}$$

where l, s, and k_c are the parameters; N_j is the vector which defines the direction of m_j; j is the index of the control point ($1 < j < C$); and C is the number of control points.

3   Edge Bundling Method for Attributed Graphs

3.1   Approach

In this paper, we assume that edges have attributions A, B, or C. Attributions A and B oppose one another. Attribution C can belong to both classes. Hooke's law and gravitational force work between all pairs of edges. In addition, Coulomb's force works between pairs of the same attribution as an attractive force and pairs of different attributions as a repulsive force. Based on these forces, edges are bundled by the same attribution.

3.2   Compatibility

Some pairs of edges are not suitable for bundling. To consider these pairs, we introduced compatibility measures that were proposed in related works. In Holten's method, compatibility is calculated by the angle, scale, position, and visibility of pairs. In Selassie's method, compatibility is measured by the shortest path of edges, which severely limits bundling in disjoint edges.

In the current study, we introduced Holten's compatibility measure because graph visibility is assumed to become clear when weights are added to improper pairs of edges. In the case, graph visibility becomes low when sparse parts of the graph are forcibly bundled. Furthermore, bundling disjoint edges in our data set is unnecessary. Therefore, we also introduced Selassie's compatibility measure.

3.3   Force of Control Point Based on a Potential Minimum

We note that the direction of edges can be translated into the attribution of edges; hence, Coulomb's force is customized in our method. To more clearly represent the difference of bundles in each attribution, we defined m_j and T_j as follows:

$$m_j = \begin{cases} q_j & \text{if } P \text{ and } Q \text{ are the same attribution} \\ q_j + lT_j & \text{else} \end{cases} \tag{4}$$

$$T_j = \begin{cases} p_i - q_j & \text{if } P \text{ and } Q \text{ are the same attribution} \\ q_j - p_i & \text{else} \end{cases} \tag{5}$$

where m_j is the potential minimum, and T_j is the direction of the force and m_j.

Handling edges as a spring is assumed to be practical. Hence, Hooke's law works in our method according to Eq. (1). Moreover, the customized Coulomb's force F'_C works. F'_C at p_i is defined as follows:

$$F'_C = f(J_P) \cdot \frac{T_j}{|T_j|} \cdot \frac{-C_e(P,Q)sk_C|p_i - m_j|}{\pi C\left(s^2 + |p_i - m_j|^2\right)^2} \tag{6}$$

$$f(J_P) = \alpha \cdot J_P + \beta \tag{7}$$

where s, l, α, and β are the parameters; k_p is the spring constant; k_C is the Coulombic constant; C is the number of control points; J_P is the weight of the current edge; and C_e is the compatibility between edges P and Q.

Considering the idea that an important edge should be the center of the bundle, we adopt edge weight into the force via $f(J_P)$. The total force F_C at point p_i is as follows:

$$F_C = \begin{cases} F_s & \text{if } P \text{ or } Q \text{ is attribution } C \\ F_s + F'_C & \text{else} \end{cases} \tag{8}$$

When the current pair of edges contains attribution C, the force only behaves as a spring force. When the pair consists of the same attributed edge, Coulomb's force works with an attractive force and the pair is bundled tightly. When the pair consists of different attributed edges, the force at work is repulsion.

4   Example

4.1   Preliminary Experiment

The result of the sample bundling is shown in Fig. 1. The sample graph has 11 parallel edges. The edges have individual attributions, which are depicted in red, blue, or green. The color green corresponds to attribution C, which can belong to both groups. As shown in Fig. 1, the mainstream of edges and the edges with the same attribution are bundled tightly. The parameters shown in Fig. 3, along with their values, are summarized in Table 1.

4.2   Effect of the Parameters

The effect of the parameters appears as a result of the sample bundling depicted in Table 2. The parameters in this method are as follows.

- k_p: The spring constant that defines the stiffness of the edges. The edges become stiff when k_p increases.

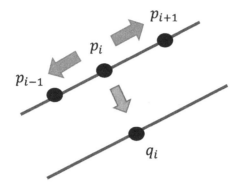

Fig. 1. A spring force works between p_{i-1} and p_i, as well as between p_i and p_{i+1}. An attractive force also works between p_i and q_i.

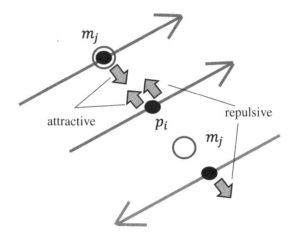

Fig. 2. Potential minimum m_j moves to the right side of edge Q when P and Q are going toward opposite directions. Coulomb's force is calculated based on m_j.

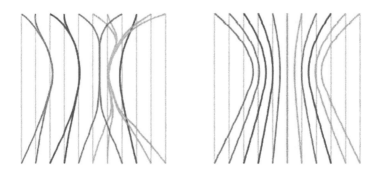

Fig. 3. Bundling for a sample graph. Left: Result of the proposed method. Right: Result of FDEB.

Table 1. Parameters and their default values

k_p	k_C	s	l	α	β
10.0	4.0×10^4	50.0	0.70	0.5	0.5

Table 2. Variation of the results with changing values

Parameters	High	Low
k_p		
k_C		
s		
l		
α		
β		

- k_C: The Coulombic constant that defines Coulomb's force. When k_C increases, Coulomb's force also increases regardless of which force is attractive or repulsive.
- s: This parameter also defines Coulomb's force. The force decreases when s increases.
- l: This parameter defines the moving distance of a potential minimum.
- α, β: These coefficients define the weight of Coulomb's force. Adopting the weight of the edge in the bundling method is assumed to be rational. However, weight can have different values. To properly adopt weight in the method, weight has to be normalized first.

The appropriate values of these parameters differ depending on the data set, the structure of the graph, and the node-link diagrams. The parameters have to be determined by comparing the changing values of the result.

5 Experiment

5.1 Data Set

In this paper, we choose editorial articles from two newspapers as the data set to draw an attributed graph. Given that similar topics are probably selected during the same period regardless of the newspaper, investing different attributions into a co-occurrence graph from different editorial articles of each newspaper is easy.

We draw co-occurrence graphs of keywords using data from the 2008 editorial articles of Asahi and Yomiuri newspapers, and then draw a compound graph from the two co-occurrence graphs. We apply our method to the compound graph. The total number of keywords is 200 for each newspaper. We use the Jaccard index as a co-occurrence degree, and its threshold is determined to be 0.25. When we draw the compound graph, we invest the attributions "Asahi," "Yomiuri," or "Both" into the edges. The attribution indicates in which graph does an edge appear on. "Asahi" and "Yomiuri" oppose each other, and "Both" can belong to both attributions. The total of the extracted keywords and edges is provided in Table 3.

Table 3. Total of the extracted keywords and edges

	Asahi	Yomiuri	Compound
Keywords	200	200	138
Edges	269	264	412

The coordinates of the nodes have to be determined arbitrarily because this data set does not include location information. Our method uses the force based on the law of dynamics. Consequently, we determine their coordinates by using the Kamada–Kawai algorithm [12]. This algorithm is also based on the law of dynamics.

5.2 Result

This section compares the result of our method with that of the other method. In all the results, the attribution of the red edges is "Asahi," the attribution of the blue edges is "Yomiuri," and the attribution of the green edges is "Both." The objective of this paper is edge bundling; hence, the following results do not show the keywords of the nodes (Fig. 4).

The diagrams before and after bundling are depicted in Fig. 4. In our method, the repulsion force between the red and blue edges works well, and thus, the edges are separated and bundled individually, as shown in the upper right area of Fig. 4(c). Therefore, compared with FDEB, our method can better represent graph attributions. In addition, a red node with numerous edges is observed in the upper right area. This node does not appear in the diagram before bundling. Accordingly, our method can reveal hidden nodes, that is, hidden knowledge and relationships (Fig. 5).

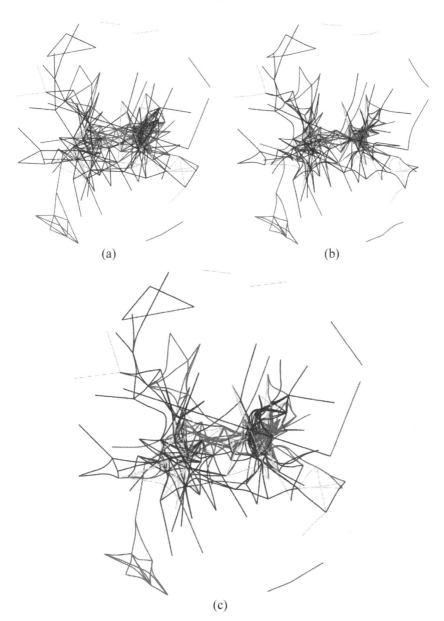

Fig. 4. Diagrams from the editorial data: (a) before bundling, (b) after FDEB is applied, and (c) after our method, which considers attributions, is applied.

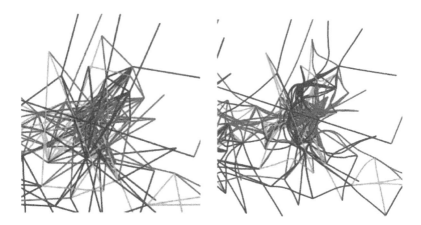

Fig. 5. Enlarged view of the upper right area. Left: Before bundling. Right: Result of the proposed method. The blue and red edges are obviously bundled individually.

6 Conclusion

In this paper, we proposed an edge bundling method for multi-attributed graphs to improve the visibility of diagrams. Our method combined and improved related works, and then bundled edges by individual attribution. Consequently, the diagram could represent attributions and its visibility was simultaneously improved.

Future works include the following.

Applying to other networks. In this paper, an object for bundling is denoted by the Kamada–Kawai algorithm; thus, nodes and edges are placed as symmetrically as possible. Applying our method to other networks, such as real networks or those with location information, is necessary.

Extending our method. Our method defines graph attributions as two attributions that oppose each other and another attribution that can belong to both groups. However, a graph with more than three attributions that oppose one another probably exists. Extending our method to such graphs is worthwhile.

Introducing the evaluation index. Several edge bundling techniques are available. However, an evaluation index for edge bundling remains lacking. Users have to decide which technique to apply by comparing results. By introducing an evaluation index, users can choose the correct method for each data set.

Acknowledgement. This research was supported by MEXT/JSPS KAKENHI 25420448.

References

1. Ward, M., Grinstein, G., Keim, D.: Interactive Data Visualization. A. K. Peters, Natick (2010)
2. Herman, I., Melançon, G., Marshall, M.S.: Graph visualization and navigation in information visualization: a survey. IEEE Trans. Vis. Comput. Graph. **6**(1), 24–43 (2000)

3. Gansner, E.R., Koutsofios, E.S., North, C., Vo, K.-P.: A technique for drawing directed graphs. IEEE Trans. Softw. Eng. **19**(3), 214–230 (1993)

4. Mueller, C., Gregor, D., Lumsdaine, A.: Distributed force-directed graph layout and visualization. In: Proceedings of the 6th Eurographics Conference on Parallel Graphics and Visualization, vol. 6, pp. 83–90. Lisbon (2006)

5. Zhou, H., Xu, P., Yuan, X., Qu, H.: Edge bundling in information visualization. Tsinghua Sci. Technol. **18**(2), 145–156 (2013)

6. Holten, D.: Hierarchical edge bundles: visualization of adjacency relations in hierarchical data. IEEE Trans. Visual Comput. Graph. **12**(5), 1077–2626 (2006)

7. Zhou, H., Yuan, X., Qu, H., Cui, W., Chen, B.: Visual clustering in parallel coordinates. Comput. Graph. Forum **27**(3), 1047–1054 (2008)

8. Telea, A., Ersoy, O.: Image-based edge bundles: simplified visualization of large graphs. In: Eurographics/ IEEE-VGTC Symposium on Visualization, vol. 29, issue no. 3, pp. 843–852, Bordeaux (2010)

9. Saga, R., Terachi, M., Tsuji, H.: FACT-Graph: trend visualization by frequency and co-occurrence. Electronic Commun. Japan **95**(2), 50–58 (2012)

10. Holten, D., van Wijk, J.J.: Force-directed edge bundling for graph visualization. Co-mput. Graph. Forum **28**(3), 983–990 (2009)

11. Selassie, D., Heller, B., Heer, J.: Divided edge bundling for directional network data. IEEE Trans. Vis. Comput. Graph. **17**(12), 2354–2363 (2011)

12. Kamada, T., Kawai, S.: An algorithm for drawing general undirected graphs. Inf. Process. Lett. **31**(1), 7–15 (1989)

Information Presentation

URU: A Platform for Prototyping and Testing Compatibility of Multifunction Interfaces with User Knowledge Schemata

Sandrine Fischer[1(✉)], Blaine Oelkers[1], Mitchell Fierro[1],
Makoto Itoh[2], and Eric White[3]

[1] Computer Science Department, California Polytechnic State University,
San Luis Obispo, USA
fischerw@calpoly.edu
[2] Risk Engineering Department, University of Tsukuba, Tsukuba, Japan
[3] Physics Department, California Polytechnic State University,
San Luis Obispo, USA

Abstract. We present a platform for prototyping and testing the information architecture of multifunctional products. A prototyping component supports the creation of feature outlines and their rendering into clickable prototypes. A user testing component implements an experimental method for characterizing the schemata operations involved during first use of multistate interfaces. Generation of the experimental material is automated via natural language processing techniques. The platform supports remote type of interface testing and fits well the needs for agile and data-informed user-centered design.

Keywords: User testing · Graphical user interface · Knowledge schemata · Quantitative evaluation · Prototyping · Design tool

1 Introduction

1.1 Context

Many software applications require users to navigate an interface comprising features (e.g., labels, icons) that are grouped into states (i.e., onscreen feature set). Innovative (or unfamiliar) features can challenge users' prior knowledge and undermine their experience, perceived usability [1, 2], and ability to use the application efficiently [3]. From a cognitive standpoint, navigation of user interfaces (UI) involves two broad knowledge schemata operations [4]: features compatible with prior knowledge are processed by transfer, while innovative features require users to induce (or abstract) new knowledge schemata.

While transfer is effortless and supports intuitive use, induction is demanding in cognitive resources and detrimental to both performance and assimilation. Provided they can be pinpointed, features whose function requires users to induce new schemata should either be explained in more detail or designed closer to what users are familiar with. In these cases, it is essential to refine and constrain feature appearance. In comparison, features that trigger the transfer of abstract knowledge (viz. schemata) are

© Springer International Publishing Switzerland 2015
S. Yamamoto (Ed.): HIMI 2015, Part I, LNCS 9172, pp. 151–160, 2015.
DOI: 10.1007/978-3-319-20612-7_15

processed at the level of their goal or meaning rather than appearance. Since such features are intuitive, their processing depends little upon surface detail and appearance, meaning intuitiveness of their use is robust to design change or innovation.

1.2   Schema-Based Screening

Schemata operations involved during first use of a UI can be simultaneously assessed through manipulation of schema induction (Fig. 1; for further details, see also [4–6].

Drawing upon Mayer [7], this method requires that participants study screenshots of the UI states, either through reading or induction conditions and then use the interface according to some "target task scenario". To elicit reading, participants match individual word clues to features in the screenshots. To elicit induction, participants match the screenshots with function clues, which are sentences describing screenshot feature(s) in terms of their function.

In both matching conditions, participants are shown a clue (word or function), followed by a screenshot of the UI, and respond "yes" or "no" depending on whether the clue matches the screenshot. Word and function clues elicit completely different types of encoding, though, and contrasting their matching amounts to manipulating schema induction. This manipulation is sensitive to participants' prior knowledge, and yields distinct experimental patterns such as [4]:

- a positive induction pattern: observed for features that are new, indicated by the reading group committing more first-use errors than the induction group,
- a transfer pattern: observed for features that are familiar, or compatible with prior knowledge, indicated by both groups performing equally well.

The method continues with screening patterns of transfer and induction at the level of the UI's states and features. For this purpose, effect sizes (e.g., Cohen's d, Cliff's Delta) are calculated from usage performances exhibited by the reading/induction groups and a control group, and examined at a desired granularity (state, feature, task). So far, such a screening has been considered for diagnosing the cognitive causes of usage errors and informing intuitive use design [5, 6].

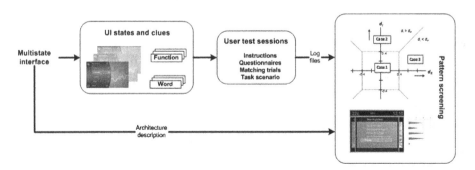

Fig. 1. Overview of the schema-based screening method

2 Transference to the Practice

2.1 Scope and Challenges

Since schema-based screening is based on experimental differences between groups, it is better suited for interfaces with a broad common-to-innovative spectrum compared to those with a narrow spectrum. Interfaces of multifunctional systems are thus prime targets for schema-based screening. As such systems typically provide a diverse selection of software functionality and service, they are more likely to blend basic functionalities (e.g., set an alarm) with advanced and potentially innovative ones (e.g., set an alarm for a different time zone). This applies to smart phones, infotainment services, and home automation applications (to name a few).

The main asset of schema-based screening is its programmatic. Being an experimental method, it does not rely on participant opinion – as would a questionnaire or Likert scale – nor does it require ad hoc judgments on behalf of the practitioners–as would any formal evaluation and coding approach. Instead, the method requires participants to conduct a series of cognitive tasks, including that of using an interface, and practitioners to perform quantitative analyses. A corollary of being experimental and quantitative is that schema-based screening is largely automatable. The challenge resides in its instrumentation. In particular, the experiment and resulting analytics should be seamless to deploy, especially for those practitioners (i.e., designers, user researchers, UX specialists) who are not familiar with the experimental principle underlying schema induction.

With the above considerations in mind, we next discuss existing tools relevant for reframing schema-based screening into a convenient instrument. Then, we present our prototype and discuss major components currently under development. After a section describing user workflow and ongoing evaluation, we conclude by outlining future developments for our tool.

2.2 Related Work

Various tools are available for design teams to create, analyze, and evaluate UI prototypes. At the very least, such tools offer libraries of graphical widgets that can be assembled into blueprints or wireframes. For some tools (e.g., Axure), widget behavior can be simulated by means of hyperlinks or connectors. The result is an interactive prototype that can be tested by users to determine which aspects would benefit from redesign in subsequent iterations. There exists a decade-old trend of deploying such tests online. Contrary to in-lab testing, online user testing is asynchronous and unmoderated, meaning test participants are not guided by a test moderator during a study–which saves a great deal of logistical effort. As to whether data collected in unmoderated conditions is comparable to data gathered in supervised experimental conditions, comparative studies show a positive cost-efficiency tradeoff in the advantages of unmoderated testing [8, 9].

Market leaders of remote testing, such as User-Zoom or UserTesting.com, perform a user evaluation that is mostly qualitative. Insight is taken from thinking-aloud protocols and questionnaires. Such an approach holds a number of issues. First, it relies on expert evaluators for analyzing verbatims and answers. Since video logs must be inspected frame by frame, a great deal of time is spent in analyzing each participant. For obvious time and budget reasons, remote user-testing services that adopt a qualitative approach scale down the extent to which prototypes can be tested (e.g., variety of features, number of participants). Second, qualitative testing introduces subjectivity biases and risks of *in fine* damage to the natural flow of thoughts. The interruptions caused by think-aloud protocols, as well as the additional cognitive effort they impose, can affect performance [10, 11]. Recently, Still et al. [12] found that simply asking participants to indicate how they would map buttons of a numeric keypad onto directions sufficed in changing how they used the buttons afterward (and vice versa). In other words, introspection can affect basic behaviors and may affect more complex activities as well.

An alternative approach is to automate the analysis of actions made by participants while using a prototype (for a review, see [13]). Nowadays, such tools better support agile and iterative development workflows. Data is not curated through someone's expertise or appraisal, and emphasis is placed on research-based methodology. The present work is an effort in this direction: inject an experimental paradigm, namely schema induction, into a remote user-testing platform. Expected application and plusvalue are the foundation of a design framework that is data-informed, largely automated, and does not rely on subjective judgments.

3   The URU Platform

URU (which stands for "Unsupervised and Remote User-testing") is a web-based platform we developed to:

- interactively create UI prototypes,
- test prototypes on participants, either on-site or remotely,
- automatically generate word and function clues in order to conduct a schema induction experiment,
- obtain usage metrics,
- screen experimental patterns corresponding to participants' schemata operations for any level of the UI.

URU is designed for two types of users: practitioners who prototype UIs, set up tests, and obtain results; and participants who use UI prototypes following a test procedure. We now describe the implementation of URU's main components and system architecture.

3.1   Implementation and Architecture

URU was developed in Python using the Django web framework, which follows a Model-View-Controller design pattern. Django handles both authentication and authorization consisting of users, permissions, participant groupings (e.g.,

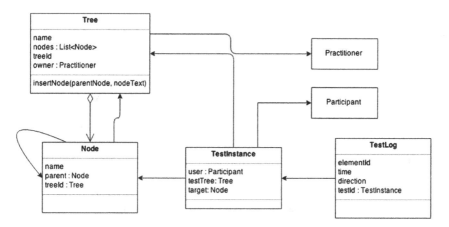

Fig. 2. Database schema employed by URU

experimental), and password hashing. An SQLite database is used to structure the data in a way that best reflects all possible queries made by the model. A schema of the URU data model is shown in Fig. 2.

URU implements Python controllers for converting user requests into proper database queries and for returning results in a format that can be used by HTML template files. Communication between server and clients is performed through Asynchronous Javascript and XML (AJAX) calls, which allow server requests to be made without refreshing the browser. Before being sent, data is wrapped using Java-Script Object Notation (JSON). User-friendly implementation of the interface is performed with Bootstrap, which is a mobile front-end framework for designing and styling websites through bundled HTML, CSS, and Javascript components. Finally, behavioral data collected among test participants are visualized in-browser using the Data Driven Documents (D3) library. D3 is a Javascript framework compliant with HTML, CSS, and SVG (Scalable Vector Graphics) that is used for rendering data in the form of scatter plots, networks diagrams, and other graphs.

3.2 Components Details

UI Prototyping. In URU, interface prototypes are specified as collections of features that are organized into a hierarchy of states. The django-mptt module [14] is used to maintain the prototype as a hierarchical tree data structure. This package employs a Modified Preorder Tree Traversal (MPTT) technique for storing hierarchical data in a relational database and efficiently retrieving sub-tree and node paths. AJAX calls handle and store changes to the MPTT as they are made by the practitioner. Individual features correspond to tree nodes that are specified by a label (string), unique identification number, parent (unique ID of another node), and optional comment (string). Commenting is not only a prescribed practice during development of software applications, but in this case practitioner comments provide additional context for generation of function clues (described in Sect. 3.3). The entire interface is specified as a tree with unique name, identifier, and root node (level 0). While this first node is not displayed, its children serve to define the uppermost menu (e.g., "home" menu) of the tree. Thus, each UI forms a separate data tree with its root node identified by the UI id.

When the practitioner selects a "skin" (a.k.a. look and feel), the data tree structure is passed to the browser in order to be rendered as a navigable, interactive prototype. For each element in the tree, jQuery is used to create an HTML DOM object with the appropriate feature label given at tree creation time. jQuery then inserts that object into the document with the appropriate children. Simple settings are used to control visibility of graphical elements at any given time, while appearance is determined through CSS styles applied to the elements. Hence, changing these CSS styles alters the look and feel, but neither the names of the features nor their relative positions in the hierarchy change. With this implementation, practitioners may easily create information architectures with a specific layout (e.g., website, mobile app, onboard computer) and fidelity (e.g., wireframe, hi-fi visual) of their choice.

Schema Induction Components. Schema induction consists in comparing usage performances for a group that studied each state under word-matching conditions, as well as under function-matching conditions, to the performances of a control group. For both conditions, state studying is administered by making each group compare every state in the prototype to either matching or mismatching clues. While word clues are merely words, function clues are sentences describing the relationship between two state features in terms of a concrete and familiar task. Thus, manipulation of schema induction requires four types of clues that can be derived from the prototype: word and function clues, either of which can match or mismatch the prototype's states. Although simple to do, the generation of word clues can be time-consuming, especially for prototypes having many states. In addition, function clues require an effort from the practitioner to explain and reformulate the features so as to prevent duplication of any word in the state from occurring. Since this endeavor would typically require the use of a thesaurus and/or technical dictionary, we propose a method (described below) for automating this process using Natural Language Processing techniques.

In URU, a clue-generating component is used to tokenize node labels and comments and tag them for part of speech (POS) using the Stanford POS-tagger [15]. Word clues are generated by first removing common words such as *the, a, to*, etc. Matching word clues are obtained by randomly selecting one remaining word per state. Mismatching word clues are obtained by first generating semantically proximate words for each feature label across the prototype. This is accomplished using WordNet [16], which is a lexical database that groups English words into "synsets," i.e., word relationships such as hyponym, hypernym, etc. Any word not matching a feature in the given state is selected at random from all synsets. Thus, URU randomly generates matching and non-matching word clues consistent with the prototype's domain for each participant.

Currently, our method for generating function clues draws upon an approach by Khosmood [17] for achieving natural-sounding paraphrasing. The method applies POS tags to each word in the comment in order to generate grammatically consistent synonyms. This is accomplished by selecting synonyms from WordNet and ConceptNet [18] with the smallest JCN distance [19], namely closest semantic distance according to information content of the Brown corpus. Word co-occurrences in each paraphrase are calculated using Microsoft's Web N-gram dataset of bi-grams and tri-grams [20]. Practitioners may then select the most convincing paraphrase or edit its formulation. While this process still requires some supervision, the burden of consulting dictionaries and creating alternate phrasings is greatly reduced for the practitioner.

After displaying an instruction page to the participant, a clue-matching component alternately displays each valid clue-state pair in random order. For each state, participants select a button labeled "Yes" or "No" to indicate whether the clue is matched. The clue generation and clue-matching components are still in the process of being integrated into URU's data model.

Data Collection and Analytics. To fully capture user performances with an interface prototype, URU records and stores each tree node that was clicked along with a corresponding timestamp. Essentially, each click on a feature creates a new object that stores the id of the node selected, as well as direction of navigation (to account for back clicks), and time between the last click. These objects are added to an array encapsulating the entire user interaction with the prototype. Click data is stored in the database and can be later be queried by node, feature, task, user, and experimental group. Raw click counts, timestamps, and basic statistical measures such as the mean, standard deviation, and pooled standard deviation between groups can be generated for any of these granularity levels. Results may also be sorted by demographic attributes of interest, and resulting patterns can be visualized with D3.

3.3   Workflow

Figure 3 illustrates the workflow for URU from the viewpoint of practitioners and test participants.

Upon account creation, a practitioner may either select an existing prototype or specify a new feature outline. In either case, features and menus are added/edited interactively in outline format through basic controls (Fig. 3.a):

- click a line to edit it,
- use right-click contextual buttons or keyboard shortcuts to add, modify, indent, or delete a line at any location,
- reorganize parts of the outline through drag-and-drop,
- select which features are targets of the task scenarios later completed by test participants.

The underlying data model is updated in real time, meaning that changes made to the feature outline are automatically stored. As illustrated in Fig. 3.b, once the menus and features of an interface have been defined, the practitioner selects a skin of choice. Should the practitioner intend to screen the interface in terms of schemata operation, URU automatically reads the data tree for label extraction and generates two lists of clues for the practitioner to check and edit. Once a prototype has been created and experimental details have been set, a test session URL can be sent to participants for logging in and performing the study. Since URU can be hosted online, test participants may log in at a time and location of their convenience and complete tests typically

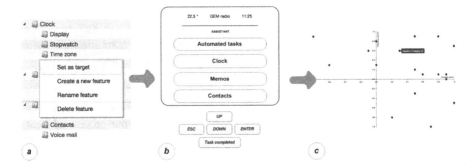

Fig. 3. The URU workflow. In (a), we show an example tree specification. In (b), this tree is rendered into an actionable prototype. Each feature of this prototype corresponds to the node of a tree, and an entire state (collection of child nodes) is labeled by its parent node (*Assistant*). In this case, the prototype is rendered as onboard computer wireframe. In (c), we show a scatter plot of effect sizes between a control, reading, and induction group for each feature of the tree. Contextual information, such as node statistics, label, and comment, are displayed upon mouseover.

consisting of instructions, questionnaires (e.g., demographics, opinion surveys), word/ function matching trials, and the interactive prototype to use following a predefined task scenario.

For word/function matching, which is the stage at which participants' schemata are manipulated, prototype states are paired with their corresponding word/function clues and displayed in random sequential order. Participants click on "Yes" or "No", depending whether the clue matches a feature on the screen, and the answer is recorded for later analysis. Assignment of experimental group is systematically rotated for each new participant in order to ensure equal subjects per group. At the time of using the UI prototype, participants read the goal of each target task and then attempt to perform them one after the other. Click data is stored and results may be analyzed afterward by group, task, demographics, etc.

URU currently provides effect size calculations so that practitioners may screen the experimental patterns discussed in Sect. 1.2 and shown Fig. 3.c. Screening may be made in an analytic fashion, *i.e.* at different granularities of an interface's states and features. States or features with large effect sizes indicate greater impact on participant performances from the experimental conditions relative to the control. A positive effect from the reading condition (viz. word matching) suggests that states/features required schema amendment, a moderately controlled and demanding cognitive operation. A positive effect from the induction condition indicates that states/features were processed by schema induction, an operation that is highly demanding in cognitive resources. The screening of states and features with small effect sizes is conditional upon overall performance. Equally good performances indicate that states/features yielded transfer (automatic), while equally poor performances indicate point states/ features that yield inoperative induction (highly demanding). The rationale and sensitivity of this screening requires additional research, which we plan to conduct with URU and translate into precise guidelines for practitioners that can be embedded directly into URU's analytics component.

4 Discussion and Outlook

In this paper, we propose a platform for screening schemata operations during the design cycle of innovative and multifunction interfaces. With URU, the prototyping and testing of complex information architectures is largely automated and easy to carry out. As it supports manipulation of participants' cognition in an experimental manner (viz. schema induction paradigm), URU goes beyond existing remote and/or unmoderated testing solutions. As discussed in Fischer et al. [4], HCI and UX practitioners have largely disregarded experimental paradigms from cognitive psychology for being time-consuming and difficult to transpose. On the contrary, we believe the mechanical manner in which many of these paradigms function make them readily automatable, and transposition is merely an issue of applied research. Hopefully, URU brings highlights the fact that experimental logic and quantitative analytics can supplant practitioner (or participant) subjectivity. In terms of man-hours, the workflow we propose is very effective and will lead design teams to test more participants than they could with qualitative user testing, all while working with data that is more quantitative and reliable.

Future developments for URU are three-fold: widened participant outreach, custom skinning capabilities, and improved analytics components. Participant outreach will consist in wiring URU to work marketplaces such as Amazon's Mechanical Turk service. While this grants access to a larger pool of participants and demographics [21], a proper means for controlling the quality of participants' contributions would be required. Custom skinning will be provided by a UI-rendering framework, allowing practitioners (e.g., graphic designers) to develop plug-ins and render their own skins through user-defined JavaScript and CSS files. A set of access methods would allow plug-ins to record participants' clicks as they navigate the custom interface and store the results for later analytics. Thus, developers will have more control in the way a given feature collection is prototyped. We also plan to improve URU's analytics through the addition of reporting and design recommendation capabilities. In the meantime, URU will serve research purposes, such as leveraging Natural Language Processing tasks for generation of material, and expanding the construct validity and sensitivity of schema induction as a means for schemata operations.

References

1. Kortum, P., Johnson, M.: The relationship between levels of user experience with a product and perceived system usability. Proc. Hum. Factors Ergon. Soc. Annu. Meet. **57**, 197 (2013)
2. McLellan, S., Muddimer, A., Peres, S.C.: The effect of experience on system usability scale ratings. J. Usability Stud. **7**(2), 56–67 (2012)
3. Langdon, P., Lewis, T., Clarkson, J.: The effects of prior experience on the use of consumer products. Univers. Access Inf. Soc. **6**, 179–191 (2007)
4. Fischer, S., Itoh, M., Inagaki, T.: Prior schemata transfer as an account for assessing the intuitive use of new technology. Appl. Ergon. **46**(A), 8–20 (2015)
5. Fischer, S., Itoh, M., Inagaki, T.: Identifying the cognitive causes of human error through experimentation. European J. Autom. **48**(4–6), 319–338 (2014)

6. Fischer, S., Itoh, M., Inagaki, T.: Screening prototype features in terms of intuitive use: design implications and proof of concept. Interacting with Computers (in press)

7. Mayer, R.E.: Elaboration techniques that increase the meaningfulness of technical text: an experimental test of the learning strategy hypothesis. J. Educ. Psychol. **72**, 770–784 (1980)

8. Tullis, T., Fleischman, S., McNulty, M., Cianchette, C., Bergel, M.: An empirical comparison of lab and remote usability testing of web sites. In: Proceedings of Usability Professional's Association (2002)

9. Thompson, K.E., Rozanski, E.P., Haake, A.R.: Here, there, anywhere: remote usability testing that works. In: Proceedings of SIGITE 2004, pp.132-137 (2004)

10. Preece, J., Rogers, Y., Sharp, H.: Interaction Design: Beyond Human-Computer Interaction. Wiley, New York (2002)

11. Holzinger, A.: Usability engineering methods for software developers. Commun. ACM **48** (1), 71 (2005)

12. Still, J. D., Still, M. L., and Grgic, J.: Designing intuitive interactions: exploring performance and reflection measures. Interact. Comput. (2014). doi:10.1093/iwc/iwu046

13. Ivory and Hearst: The state of the art in automating usability evaluation of user interfaces. ACM Comput. Surv. **33**(4), 470–516 (2001)

14. Django-MPTT: https://github.com/django-mptt/django-mptt/

15. Stanford POS-tagger: http://nlp.stanford.edu/software/tagger.shtml

16. WordNet: wordnet.princeton.edu

17. Khosmood, F.: Comparison of sentence-level paraphrasing approaches for statistical style transformation. In: Proceedings of the 2012 International Conference on Artificial Intelligence. CSREA Press, Las Vegas (2012)

18. ConceptNet: conceptnet5.media.mit.edu

19. Jiang, J., Conrath, D.: Semantic similarity based on corpus statistics and lexical taxonomy. In: Proceedings of International Conference Research on Computational Linguistics (ROCLING X), Taiwan (1997)

20. Microsoft Web N-gram services: http://weblm.research.microsoft.com/

21. Mason, W., Suri, S.: Conducting behavioral research on Amazon's Mechanical Turk. Behav. Res. **44**(1), 1–23 (2012)

An Exploration of the Effectiveness of Infographics in Contrast to Text Documents for Visualizing Census Data: What Works?

Marylisa Gareau[✉], Rebecca Keegan, and Lin Wang

U.S. Census Bureau, Suitland, MD, USA
{marylisa.gareau, rebecca.keegan, lin.wang}@census.gov

Abstract. The U.S. Census Bureau conducted a usability research study using 3 published Census infographics on different topics containing statistics produced from Census survey data. The study used a mixed-factorial design with repeated measures, comparing user performance (accuracy of information recall and accuracy of searching for information) and satisfaction after using either the 3 infographics, or 3 text documents containing the same information. 55 participants were randomly assigned to either the Infographics condition or the Documents condition, accordingly. Results revealed significant advantage in accuracy for participants with any amount of college education, and a significant interaction between the stimulus type (infographics compared to documents) and the condition (searching versus recall) with infographics being related to increased performance in the searching task and not the recall tasks. However, there were no significant memory-related advantages for infographics above documents, and no interaction between education and stimulus type.

Keywords: Usability · Infographics · Memory

1 Introduction

Infographics represent an emerging medium of information visualization and statistical communication. In an era of rapidly increasing availability of information, infographics can attenuate the effects of information inundation by presenting information in a way that is quickly and easily digestible, as well as engaging and attractive. Some studies show that the human visual system can process and assign meaning to imagery in less than a second, which can be much faster than reading through a text explanation [1, 2]. Other research suggests that for online content, people read less than 28 % of the words presented to them [3]. Thus, increasing imagery and using words sparingly, as in an infographic, seem like obvious choices.

At the Census Bureau, infographics are created with the intent to convey data about a topic or concept in a way that is appealing and easily interpreted by a wide, public audience, especially those who may not have a formal background in statistics, or high level of education. Dowse, R. & Ehlers, M. (2005) found that medicine labels containing text and visual representations were interpretable by 95 % of subjects as

S. Yamamoto (Ed.): HIMI 2015, Part I, LNCS 9172, pp. 161–171, 2015.
DOI: 10.1007/978-3-319-20612-7_16

opposed to labels with text alone for which the interpretability rate was much lower (70 % of subjects) [4].

There is a lack of published research pertaining to the effectiveness of infographics as an information visualization medium for complex statistics, and infographics can vary wildly in terms of composition, imagery, length, density, technical terms, use of traditional graphs, and content.

Currently, while Census data is available to the public, accessing these statistics requires querying complex data tables. If statistics on more than one aspect of a particular topic are desired, this can require multiple queries. This can be difficult and time-consuming for a member of the general public, who may have no knowledge of the structure of Census data. Census infographics allow for some comparison of multiple statistics on a particular topic to be presented without the need for querying or understanding the structure of Census data. Unlike data tables, infographics also allow visualization of the data (e.g. graphs) and imagery that may be engaging and related to the topic (iconic imagery). However, no research has yet been done to assess whether these presentations are effective and understandable for members of the general public.

The objective of the present research is to begin examining what makes an infographic effective at communicating statistical data and appealing to readers by measuring memorability, searchability, time required to read the infographic, understandability of language, use of imagery and graphs, user satisfaction data, and eye-tracking analyses. Results will be used to inform the development of future Census infographics and further research in the area of information visualization for a public audience.

2 Methods

A usability research study was conducted using 3 published infographics from the U.S. Census Bureau on different topics containing statistics produced from Census survey data. The study use a $2 \times 3 \times 3$ mixed factorial design, comparing user performance and satisfaction after using either the 3 infographics, or 3 text documents containing the same information.

Between-subjects variables are "Condition" (2 levels, Infographics and Text Documents) and "Education" (3 levels, Highschool, Some College, Bachelor's Degree).

Within-subjects (Repeated Measures) variables are "Stimulus" and "Response Condition." Stimulus has three levels: Memorial Day, Home Improvements, Child Care. Response Condition has three levels: Free-Recall, Multiple-Choice, Search.

Dependent Variables: Accuracy scores for each combination of the Within-Subjects factors (e.g. "Memorial Day Free-Recall Score" is one dependent variable). Accuracy was measured on a scale of 0 to 10 and was determined based on a pre-established rubric. Ranges of acceptable values for Free-Recall responses were established prior to the study, and partial credit was awarded in multi-part questions.

2.1   Participants

A total of 55 participants were randomly assigned to either the Infographics condition or the Documents condition, accordingly. Participants were recruited from a pool of volunteers maintained by the Human Factors and Usability Group at the U.S. Census Bureau. Participants were recruited based on the following criteria:

- Participant is 18 years of age or older.
- Participant has completed at least 3 years of high school.
- Participant has completed no more than a Bachelor's degree.
- Participant speaks English.

Sessions lasted one hour and participants were given a $40 dollar honorarium. Participant characteristics appear in Table 1 below.

Table 1. Participant Characteristics, $n = 55$

Total Participants	55
Gender	
Female	31
Male	24
Age (in years)	
Mean (SD)	42.5 (16.5)
Range	18 - 74
Education	
High school diploma or less	18
Some college	18
Bachelor's degree	19
Race	
White	13
Black	38
Hispanic	3
Asian	3
Other	1

2.2   Procedure

Participants were randomly assigned to either the infographics group ($n_i = 28$), or the text documents group ($n_t = 27$).

Three Census infographics and their corresponding text-documents were chosen based on length of the infographic, iconic value of imagery and density of information. Iconic value of imagery refers to the extent to which the imagery in the infographic was abstract (such as differently sized boxes representing varying statistical values) or iconic (imagery relates directly to the topic, e.g. drawings of people to represent quantities of people). The infographics chosen were of the following topics: Memorial Day (short length, low iconic value, high density), Home Improvements (short length, high iconic value, low density), and Child Care (longer length, moderate iconic value, moderate density).

Each participant was verbally introduced to the purpose of the study, signed a consent form, and was calibrated for eye-tracking.

For the text condition, the publicly available blind-accessible document version of each infographic was used. The text-only documents contained the same data and text descriptions of the data as their corresponding infographics, but contained no imagery or visualizations. An example of a Census infographic section with its associated text-document section appears in Figs. 1 and 2, respectively.

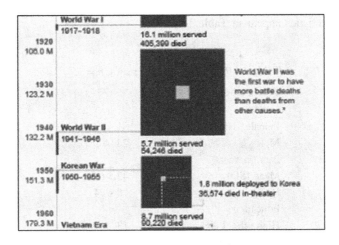

Fig. 1. Section from the Memorial Day infographic

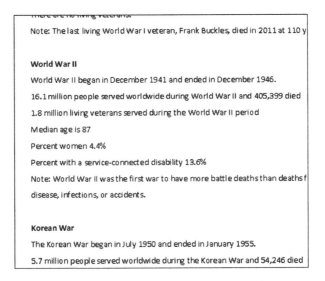

Fig. 2. Section from the Memorial Day infographic blind-accessible text-document

To examine possible effects of infographics on the memorability of the information, each participant was presented with a stimulus (either in infographic or text form) and instructed to read it. Then they responded to 10 factual questions about the content of the stimulus, first in open-format response (Free Recall condition), then the same 10 questions in multiple-choice format (Multiple Choice condition). This was repeated for each of 3 stimuli.

To examine searchability, each stimulus was then presented again simultaneously with the same 10 questions from the prior two conditions, but the participant was instructed to search the stimuli for the correct answers (Search condition). Finally, each participant was asked debriefing questions related to their satisfaction with different aspects of the stimuli.

2.3   Hypotheses

It was predicted that infographics would be associated with higher accuracy scores for both memorability (as measured by Free-Recall and Multiple-Choice accuracy scores) and searchability (as measured by accuracy scores in the Search condition) as compared with the text documents. Because participants were allowed as much time as they needed to examine the stimuli, it was predicted that the length of time spent examining the stimuli would be associated with higher accuracy scores.

Because Census infographics report statistical data, it was predicted that higher education level would be positively associated with overall accuracy scores. However, because of the presence of visualizations and imagery, it was predicted that infographics would be associated with higher accuracy scores for those with less education than the text documents, and that this effect would not be present for those with higher education level.

2.4   Apparatus

Tobii × 120 Monitor
Internet Explorer 10

3   Results

3.1   Time Spent on Stimuli

Contrary to predictions, time spent on stimuli was not found to be significantly correlated with accuracy scores ($r = .04$, $p = .52$).

3.2   Accuracy

A $2 \times 3 \times 3$ mixed ANOVA was performed to test the main effects and interactions of Condition, Education, Response Condition, and Stimulus on the accuracy scores for the recall question sets.

Mauchly's Test of Sphericity was not significant for the within-subject factor "Stimulus," but was significant for the within-subjects factor "Response Condition" $(X^2(2) = 21.10, p < .001)$, and for the interaction between Stimulus and Response condition $(X^2(9) = 29.03, p = .001)$. Therefore, the Greenhouse-Geisser correction was used to interpret significance for F values related to these factors ($\varepsilon = .73$, $\varepsilon = .77$, respectively).

ANOVA results revealed a main effect of Stimulus (topic) $(F(2, 96) = 38.23, p < .001)$. Furthermore these differences were significant, as indicated by repeated contrasts $(F(1,48) = 37.53, p < .001, F(1,48) = 9.65, p = .003)$. Regardless of experimental group, Response Condition or Education, accuracy scores for Child Care stimuli were the highest $(M = 6.25)$, followed by Home Improvements $(M = 5.61)$, followed by Memorial Day $(M = 4.50)$. In general, the Child Care topic appeared to be the easiest to interpret, despite it being the longest infographic/document (about 3 times as long as the other two). Therefore, it was inferred that length of the infographic is not necessarily a negative factor in the composition of an infographic.

There was a main effect for Response Condition $(F(1.47, 70.50) = 215.73, p < .001)$ as expected. This main effect indicates the overall difference in scores across groups and education level, with Search having the highest average score $(M = 7.24)$, followed by Multiple-Choice $(M = 5.37)$, followed by Free-Recall $(M = 3.75)$. Contrasts show that the differences between these means was significant $(F(1,48) = 200.22, p < .001, F (1,48) = 82.63, p < .001)$. Overall, Free-Recall was the most difficult condition, Multiple-Choice (a form of cued recall) was easier, and finding the answers by searching the stimulus was easiest, as expected.

There was also a main effect for the between-subjects factor of Education $(F (2,48) = 10.36, p < .001)$, with education level of Bachelor's degree being highest $(M = 6.10)$, followed by Some College $(M = 5.92)$, followed by High school or less $(M = 4.34)$. The Bonferroni post hoc test revealed that the difference in average scores was significant between Bachelor's and High school $(p < .001)$, and between Some College and High school or less $(p = .001)$, but it was not significant between Bachelor's degree and Some College. This overall effect shows the influence of even some college-level education on the interpretation of the stimuli, because the difference exists regardless of which stimulus was being viewed, which response condition was employed, or which type of stimulus (infographic or text document) was being viewed. Although this effect does not imply causality (i.e. college-level education cause these participants to perform better), it may be indicative of the difficulty level of the material being presented.

However, there was no significant interaction, as predicted, between Education and Condition. The information being presented in infographic form did not offer a distinct advantage to those of a lower education level in comparison to text documents. This could be due to the material being difficult enough to understand that imagery could not benefit the less-educated participants, or perhaps the imagery and visualizations that were chosen were not particularly effective.

There was a significant interaction between the between-subjects factor "Condition" (Infographics or Documents groups) and the repeated-measures factor Response Condition (Free-Recall, Multiple-Choice, Search) $(F(2,96) = 4.76, p = 0.02)$. Contrasts show that the interaction was significant between the Multiple-Choice and Search response conditions ($F(1,48) = 6.153$, $p = .017$). This interaction shows that Census infographics did not aid in accuracy for either of the memory conditions, but that they did improve accuracy for finding information compared to the text documents, regardless of the stimulus topic or the participant education level. The effect, although significant, represented an advantage of around 10 %, or 1 out of 10.

3.3   Eyetracking and Satisfaction

Eyetracking and item-by-item analysis of the recall questions for each stimulus, together with participant commentary during debriefing led to the identification of dimensions of each infographic that were both facilitative for finding information and detrimental to this task. Major areas of adjustment included size of font, spacing, use of plain language, and use of iconic imagery. Infographics with adequate spacing, font size, simple language, and iconic imagery were favored by participants and facilitated higher accuracy in recall and search task items, and those lacking in these dimensions were more difficult for participants to interpret. These results are not reported here.

4   Limitations

This study was partially exploratory in nature, and thus is subject to several limitations, including limitations in design and scope.

4.1   Scope

Perhaps the most obvious limitation of this study is that although we would like to address the potential benefits of infographics per se, we restricted our investigation to infographics published by the Census Bureau. Such infographics must necessarily conform to particular guidelines and are not representative of infographics in general, such as others that may be produced by other sources or concerning non-statistical topics.

4.2   Design

Participants in this study were asked the same set of 10 "factual" questions three separate times, and participants saw each stimulus twice. The second viewing of the stimulus, along with prior knowledge of the questions that would be asked could have influenced the accuracy scores for the "Search" condition. However it should be noted that despite having the stimuli present simultaneously with the recall questions in the "Search" condition (like an open-book test), few participants were able to achieve a full 10/10 score (8 for Memorial Day, 6 for Home Improvements, 12 for Child Care, out of 55 participants).

Another design limitation arose from usability. We intended to address regarding how long participants would spend on the infographics if given no specific direction.

Because we chose to allow participants to spend as much time as they needed to view the infographics and documents, this aspect of the study was not specifically controlled (i.e. we did not enforce a time limit). However, because education level may affect the amount of time needed to read the stimuli, and because we wanted to see possible differences in the behavior and performance of participants of different education levels, time was not enforced. In the end, the length of time spent reading the stimuli was not related to any of the measured factors, including education level, and is likely attributable to individual differences.

Text documents and infographics were not compared within subjects, so it cannot be assessed whether an infographic would be more effective than a text document at an individual level. Learning styles, reading ability, and spatial ability could all play a role in the interpretation of infographics and text documents.

Finally, the choice to use the blind-accessible documents as a control condition for the infographics was not truly representative of the differences that may be encountered when a person tries to extract statistics from Census data tables and compare them. A more true-to-experience control condition might have been to present participants with the data tables and require them to compare the data on their own. Providing the data in the form of blind-accessible text documents allowed us to examine the effect of the presence of imagery/visualizations, but this may have given the text condition an advantage over real-life data consumption processes.

5 Discussion

The present study did not provide overwhelming evidence that infographics in and of themselves increase memory for statistical information, but the results may suggest that they make information easier to locate when compared to finding the same information in text documents. This may be due to the imagery being used as a form of landmark or cue. While the results on accuracy scores may not be compelling on their own, other usability data was gathered which led to recommendations to the teams responsible for producing infographics. Thus, the present study combined of experimental and qualitative data to provide recommendations for the design of future Census infographics. We list only a few instances of these recommendations.

Some imagery which is very abstract was found to be difficult to interpret and actually become distracting and confusing to participants. The Memorial Day infographic was related to less accuracy for the infographics group than for the text-documents group, which was opposite of the data trend for the other two infographics. The Memorial Day infographic used abstract imagery (i.e. differently-sized boxes representing proportions of soldiers who served versus soldiers who died in each war (Fig. 3)) whereas the Child Care and Home Improvements infographics used iconic imagery and traditional graphs (e.g. a drawing of a house containing the data for each room (Fig. 4); bar graphs (Fig. 5), respectively). This accuracy data was supported by participants' verbal feedback that the "boxes" from the Memorial Day infographic were not understandable (only 3 of the 28 participants in the infographics group could identify the meaning of the boxes), so a recommendation to use more iconic imagery to represent data in future infographics was made.

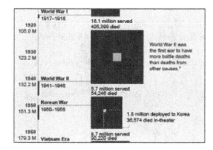

Fig. 3. Abstract "Boxes" from Memorial Day infographic

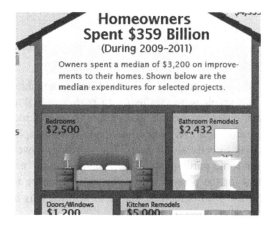

Fig. 4. Iconic "House Drawing" from Home Improvements infographic

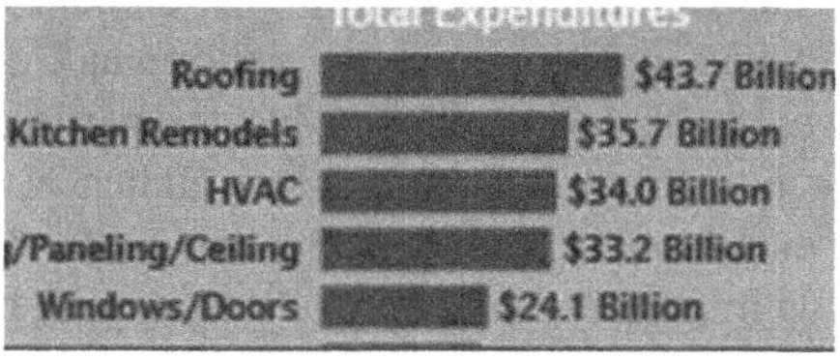

Fig. 5. Traditional bar graphs in Home Improvement infographic

Wording was found through debriefing questions to be an aspect of the infographics that could have been hindering performance and influencing the effectiveness of the imagery. Jargon words and complex sentence structure made some graphs difficult for participants to interpret. Despite the participants saying that they liked the imagery and layout of the data in the infographics, they pointed out areas in which the wording hindered their understanding of the graphs. Two small graphs had titles with wording that confused participants.

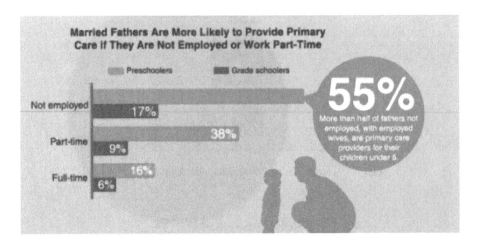

Fig. 6. Fathers section of the Child Care infographic, with difficult wording

For example, the title of one graph in the Child Care infographic and the text in the blue bubble next to the graph were confusing to participants due to the language/structure (Fig. 6). Participants had trouble interpreting these statements and answering the recall questionnaire question even when they had the infographic in front of them (and could therefore look directly at the data). The wording, however, made the data difficult to interpret for some participants. The repeated use of "employed" and "not employed" as modifiers for the parents within the same sentence made the sentences difficult to read. In the case of infographics, clarity in wording may be just as important as the imagery chosen to represent the data.

Interestingly, although Census infographics were created with the intention to convey statistical data to an audience with no statistical background, and to a broad range of education levels, results showed that those with a high school education or less responded much less accurately than those with any amount of college education. Furthermore, the infographics did not improve performance for the less educated participants to a greater extent than the college-educated participants (as compared to the text documents). To be consumable by a wider audience than just the college-educated, infographics may benefit from user testing research and reorganization. Accompanying the data with imagery may improve their appeal, but information clarity via reduction of jargon and simplification of wording may improve the understandability of the data.

Possible future studies could include investigations of infographics from sources and topics external to the Census Bureau, comparison of performance of infographics versus text-documents within subjects to explore individuals factors, comparison of infographics to text accompanied by varying levels of iconic imagery and traditional graphs, to address some of the topics that were not investigated in the present study.

References

1. Thorpe, S., Fize, D., Marlot, C.: Speed of processing in the human visual system. Nature **381**(6582), 520–522 (1996)
2. Holcomb, P., Grainger, J.: On the time course of visual word recognition: an event-related potential investigation using masked repetition priming. J. Cogn. Neurosci. **18**(10), 1631–1643 (2006)
3. Nielsen, J.: How Little Do Users Read? (2008) http://www.nngroup.com/articles/how-little-do-users-read/
4. Dowse, R., Ehlers, M.: Medicine labels incorporating pictograms: do they influence understanding and adherence? Patient Educ. Couns. **58**(1), 63–70 (2005)

Searching for Information: Comparing Text vs. Visual Search with Newspapers Websites

Victor M. González[1(✉)], Jesús García[1], and Bárbara Muro[2]

[1] Usability and Interactive Systems Lab, Department of Computer Science,
Instituto Tecnológico Autónomo de México, Mexico City, Mexico
{victor.gonzalez,jgarc293}@itam.mx
[2] School of Telematics, University of Colima,
Villa de Álvarez, Colima, Mexico
pao_muro@ucol.mx

Abstract. Different approaches used to define how a website shows information have an impact on how users evaluate its usability. As shown in the present study, how people accomplish a search of visual content in a newspaper website is an important factor to review while designing it. In this study, 47 participants were randomly assigned to evaluate one of two different newspaper websites and asked to do visual and written searches. The evaluation metrics were: task success and task time. Also the participants made an overall evaluation of the site, answering two Likert questions and an open-ended question to measure qualitative aspects. Finally, we measured the overall satisfaction with a SUS questionnaire. The results show that a poor performance in the search of visual content lead to lower usability perception, this might be a main aspect to improve when defining priorities to enhance overall usability.

Keywords: Data visualization · Information presentation

1 Introduction

In the past few years people have changed the way they read news, as they are moving from the traditional paper to online version of newspapers such as website or mobile apps; In 2011, surveys conducted by the Pew Project for Excellence in Journalism, showed that 34 % of respondents said they read news online within the past 24 h (as opposed to 31 % who favored physical newspapers); and a full 41 % said they get most of their news online, 10 % more than those who said they got most of their news from a physical newspaper [1, 2]. Therefore, the search of information in these sites becomes very important due to the amount of news that is posted everyday.

Good usability of the websites plays an important role because it can define if the user is going to develop fidelity to the site and use it often or, with new users, it determines whether they will ever use it again after a first try [3]. As with many other interactive products, with newspaper websites the evaluation of the user experience becomes necessary to find the characteristics that users seek.

Previous usability studies have been conducted to evaluate newspapers' sites from around the world. Among them, in the UK [4], "The Guardian" was evaluated as the

© Springer International Publishing Switzerland 2015
S. Yamamoto (Ed.): HIMI 2015, Part I, LNCS 9172, pp. 172–180, 2015.
DOI: 10.1007/978-3-319-20612-7_17

Fig. 1. "The Guardian" in the left and "La Crónica de Hoy" at the right

best among other major newspapers, and the same was for "La Crónica de Hoy" in a Mexican study conducted by a local usability consultancy [5].

To get in context, in Fig. 1 screenshots were taken from both websites. As seen, the general layouts are very similar and have similar information and options.

In this work, first, a general evaluation comparing these both sites ("The Guardian" and "La Crónica de Hoy") is reported to know and detect the usability differences and similarities between them. Then, an analysis was conducted to contrast the results of performing text vs. visual searches.

2 Method

This study follows a typical usability test approach where users were asked to do tasks for which standard metrics such as task success and duration were collected; after completing all of the tasks, users were asked some questions to evaluate qualitative aspects of the user experience. For the present study, the tasks were the following:

- Task 1 - Search for an image of the tennis player Novak Djokovic, winner of the 2010 Wimbledon tennis tournament.
- Task 2 - Search for information about the Strauss-Kahn's case.
  - In this task, the participant was asked to write the date of the article.
- Task 3 - Search for information in the "Business" section.
  - In this task, the participant was asked to write the title of the main article in the section.

In this study, 47 participants were randomly assigned to evaluate one of the previously mentioned websites. All the participants were bilingual with great experience reading and writing in both, English and Spanish. We did not detect any challenge related to interacting with an English-based web site despite the fact that all participants' mother tongue was Spanish.

Participants were asked to do two different types of search tasks, which are usually done while visiting this kind of sites. First, to perform a search of textual information and, second, a search of visual content (a photograph). The metrics of the evaluation were: task success and task time. The participants also made an overall evaluation of the site, answering two questions ("Ease of finding information" and "Visual appealing"), with a

7-point Likert scale [6], and an open-ended question to measure qualitative aspects. Finally, the overall satisfaction was measured with a SUS questionnaire.

The time elapsed from the presentation of the task to the click of the "Next" button that showed the selection of the answer was recorded automatically.

The metrics captured for each task were: on one hand, self-reported task success that is whether the participant reported if they had definitely found the answer, or not, and, on the other hand, task time.

In the post-study self-reported data, the captured metrics were: ease of finding information and visual appeal (with the 7-point scale), challenging or frustrating aspects (open-ended questions), effective or intuitive aspects (open-ended questions) and SUS scores.

3   Results

The results shown in this section are derived from using the geometrical means, and tests such as Chi Square test, t-test and the Mann-Whitney U test, which were used to calculate the statistical significance depending on the type of data, with an alpha of 0.05. In general, the differences between both sites were not significant; both sites were rated with similar scores. However, we found that, although both of them are well designed and have an overall good user experience, there are some differences that make one of the sites score better than the other. The rest of this section will describe some of these differences.

3.1   Comparison Between the Websites

Task Success. After completing every task, the participants were asked whether or not they believed they were able to finish the task successfully. This was a self-reported assessment. If the participant was sure that the task was done it was marked as a success. If the user was not sure the task did not count, and it was marked unsuccessful. "The Guardian" users reported 76.12 % of success vs. an overall 81.69 % of success reported by "La Crónica" users. These results are shown in Fig. 2.

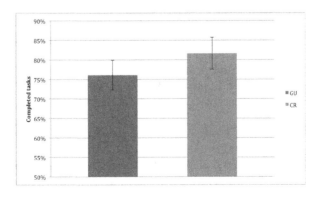

Fig. 2. Task Success

As seen in Fig. 2, the difference between both results is minimal. With the purpose of evaluating if the difference was statistically significant, the Chi-squared test was performed, as the data was dichotomous, i.e., accomplish or not the task. The result was not statistically significant between both sites, $c^2(1, N = 140) = 0.83$, $p > 0.05$.

Task Time. The second aspect evaluated was the time the participants had to take to finish a task. The geometrical mean of the "The Guardian" users was 55.7 s, while for "La Crónica" was 64.75 s. Despite that in Fig. 3 an apparent difference is noticeable it was not statistically significant, $t(136) = -1.35$, $p > 0.05$.

Satisfaction Assessment. Following the execution of all tasks, the participants were asked to express comments regarding any challenge or frustrating experience they had while using the site.

On one hand, for the site of "The Guardian" (GU), 13 out of 23 participants (56.5 %) commented that they had negative experiences; for the site of "La Crónica" (CR), 11 out of 24 participants (45.8 %) indicated finding this kind of aspects.

The negative comments about the GU site given by at least two participants were:

- Not being able to search for images (4)
- Too much information, bad distribution of the information (9)

The negative comments about the CR site given by at least two participants were:

- Color and content of the menu (2)
- Problems with the search of images (3)
- Presentation of the information, too much content (3)

On the other hand, for "The Guardian" site, 47.8 % of the participants (11 out of 23) indicated easy or intuitive aspects characterizing a good user experience; for "La Crónica" site, 62.5 % (15/24) indicated effective or intuitive aspects.

The effective or intuitive aspects about the GU site given by at least two participants were:

- Good, intuitive and helpful menu (4)
- Good headings that helps finding information (3)

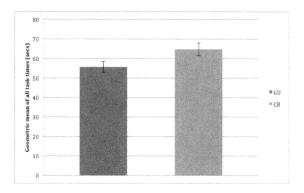

Fig. 3. Task Time

- The search tool is easy to use (2)
- Overall good design (2)

The effective or intuitive aspects about the CR site given by at least two participants were:

- Helpful and efficient search tool with good presentation of the results (9)
- Overall good design (6)

Overall Assessment. Among the collected comments concerning negative comments, on one hand, "The Guardian" had 13 negative ones, which are all related to the overload and bad distribution of the information, and the difficulty of finding an image. On the other hand, "La Crónica" had only six comments related to these aspects and two more negative ones about the color and content of the menus. As to positive comments, the same amount of users (nine) said that both sites have good and easy to use search tools. Nevertheless, the main difference in the comments is present in the ones related to the overall design, in which, nine came from users of "La Crónica" vs. two from "The Guardian" users. In this work, it is argued that the main reason of this difference may lie in the amount of negative comments that the "The Guardian" received.

Given that the qualitative assessment favors "La Crónica", it is worth to contrast this with the results of applying the SUS test. Following the open questions on the application, a SUS was asked to be completed and, as can be seen in Fig. 4, ten users rated with more than 60 points to "The Guardian" vs. 15 users to "La Crónica", making the last one 31.9 % easier to use as assessed by the participants. However, a significant difference was not found, t(45) = -1.14, p > 0.05.

Despite of this lack of significant difference, this leaded to the question of why there is a trend towards lower scores that the users give to "The Guardian" even when both are good sites, and from our results it was perceived that it seems that the main difference is between the visual and written search of content.

Consequently, a specific analysis to explore the differences between visual vs. written search was conducted. The aim was to find if the differences mentioned in the comments were visible in other tests and how they affected the general scores.

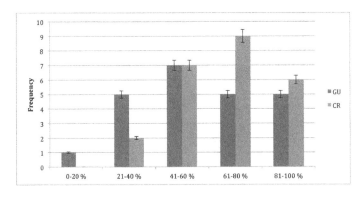

Fig. 4. SUS Scores

3.2   Comparison Between Visual and Written Search

Task Success. Figure 5 shows the task success by type of task. With a geometrical mean of 65.72 % for the visual task and 84.8 % for the written tasks, a statistical difference was found between both type of searches, $c^2(1, N = 140) = 4.62$, $p < 0.05$. This difference is mainly due to the lower rate of success of "The Guardian" which was significant too, $c^2(1, N = 69) = 6.59$, $p < 0.01$. These results show the first revealing finding, which leads to identify that the design of "The Guardian" makes it more difficult for the user to do the visual task.

Task Time. The same pattern is observed in the task time results as shown in Fig. 6. There was a significant difference between the two types of search, $U = 1,595$, $p < 0.05$. On one hand, the times from "La Crónica" users does not vary, but "The Guardian" users needed more time to complete the visual search than the written ones, which is a significant difference, $t(66) = 3.28$, $p < 0.05$. On the other hand, the difference between newspapers in the written tasks was significant, $U = 720.5$, $p < 0.01$.

As can be seen in the results of task success and task time, "The Guardian" shows results with significant differences between both types of tasks. This leads to the

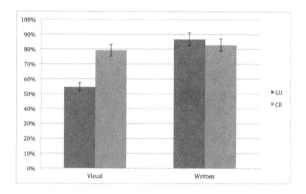

Fig. 5. Task Success by type of search

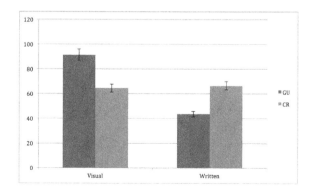

Fig. 6. Task Time by type of search

conclusion that this newspapers' website is good for written searches, but it is not as good in the visual content searches. This is observed in the lower rate of success in these tasks and the longer time required to complete the tasks compared to "La Crónica" users.

3.3   Post-Study Self-Reported Data

After finishing their three tasks, the participants were asked to rate the site they used on two 7-point scales (higher numbers better): Ease of finding information and Visual appeal.

Ease of Finding Information. The difference between both websites was not significant, $t(44) = -0.69$, $p > 0.05$. The geometric mean was 5.07 for the CR website and 4.58 for the GU site, as shown in Fig. 7.

Visual Appealing. As with the previous result, the difference between both websites was not significant, $t(44) = -0.66$, $p > 0.05$. The geometric mean was 4.55 for the CR website and 4.22 for the GU site, which can be seen in Fig. 8.

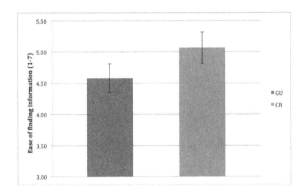

Fig. 7. Ease of Finding Information (Higher = Easier)

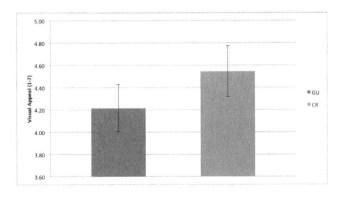

Fig. 8. Visual Appealing (Higher is better)

The results shown in this section, although they are not significant, showed that in general, "La Crónica" was rated with better scores than "The Guardian". These differences are important to understand the reason of the different results found in the SUS. This also shows the importance of how the information is presented to the users, in the main pages as well as the search tool results. A significant impact is seen in the general usability scores mainly because of a poor performance of this particular part of the interface.

4   Conclusions

The differences between the two search functions shows that, despite the fact that both sites were rated with good usability scores, slightly favoring "La Cronica", the design of the interface and the search tools were a significant factor to evaluate the usability of a newspapers' website. The finding is supported by the users' comments, which shows that the overload of information, the ease of use of the menus and the search tool were important aspects to define a website with better usability. As seen in the metrics, the difficulty to do the visual searches can lower the overall usability perception of the user, as seen in the SUS score, and in the perception of how easy is to find information and the general visual appealing.

This generates important information for future development of this kind of websites, finding new ways to make different kind of searches more intuitively and to pay attention in how they present visual content. This is because the users tend to evaluate the visual content first, and they will find difficult to understand the content or to find the needed information if they do not understand it. The information found in these results can lead to new studies to derive a deeper understanding of how to improve the usability of the search tools in the newspapers' websites.

Acknowledgements. This work has been supported by Asociación Mexicana de Cultura A.C. and the Consejo Nacional of Ciencia and Tecnología of México (CONACyT). We thank Frida Rojas for her help in the improvement of the quality of the text.

References

1. O'Dell, J.: For the First Time, More People Get News Online Than From Newspapers. Mashable. http://mashable.com/2011/03/15/online-versus-newspaper-news (Accessed on 20 September 2014)
2. Livemint: Internet is growing, but offline users are falling behind: McKinsey. http://www.livemint.com/Industry/XUNAjQbC0m8LbefgJMBKKL/Internet-is-growing-but-offline-users-are-falling-behind-M.html (Accessed on 20 October 2014)
3. Garrett, J.J.: The Elements of User Experience: User Centered Design of the Web. AIGA New Readers, New York (2003)
4. Webcredible, 360° news providers overview: An independent evaluation of the user experience across channels, London (2011)

5. UDEM, Study's result, Primer Estudio sobre la Experiencia del Usuario en Portales de Periódicos en Línea Mexicanos. http://www.webusability.com.mx/news/resultados.html (Accessed on 3 October 2014)
6. Tullis, T., Albert, B.: Measuring the User Experience Collecting, Analyzing, and Presenting Usability Metrics. Elsevier/Morgan Kaufmann, Amsterdam (2008)

The Usability of Magnification Methods: A Comparative Study Between Screen Magnifiers and Responsive Web Design

Elyse C. Hallett[1(⊠)], Blake Arnsdorff[1], John Sweet[1], Zach Roberts[1],
Wayne Dick[2], Tom Jewett[1], and Kim-Phuong L. Vu[1]

[1] California State University Long Beach, Long Beach, CA, USA
{elyse.hallett, thearnsdorff, johnsweethf,
zach.roberts100}@gmail.com,
{tom.jewett, kim.vu}@csulb.edu
[2] Knowbility, Austin, TX, USA
waynedick@knowbility.org

Abstract. Screen magnifiers, which often result in the need for horizontal scrolling, and enlarging content through the browser itself are two magnification methods used by computer-users with low vision. With responsive web design (RWD), the later can be done with word wrapping, thus eliminating the need to horizontally scroll. The present study compared the effectiveness of the two methods when participants performed two types of Web-based tasks: reading comprehension and data input. Results showed that when using RWD, participants completed the reading comprehension tasks more quickly and accurately compared to when using screen magnifiers. Participants were also able to complete data input more quickly with RWD than with the screen magnifier. Finally, participants rated RWD to be more usable than screen magnifiers. The results of this study have implications for further developments of web accessibility guidelines.

Keywords: Accessibility · Display · Screen magnifiers · Design · Responsive web design · Low vision · Usability

1 Introduction

Internet usage has increased rapidly in recent years. Only 37 % of Americans had access to the Internet in 2000; however by 2013, 72 % of Americans could claim the privilege [1]. As Internet-use becomes more common, the number of visually impaired people who want to use the web is growing steadily. Because electronic information is primarily conveyed through the visual modality, the low-vision population often runs into difficulties interacting with graphical user interfaces. In 2012, the population who reported experiencing vision loss included 20.6 million adult Americans aged 18 and over [2]. As visual problems tend to increase with age [3], difficulty in accessing online materials can deter older users from using the Internet.

Low vision has been defined as any visual impairment that cannot be corrected by eyewear, medication, or surgery [4]. Because these individuals must overcome

© Springer International Publishing Switzerland 2015
S. Yamamoto (Ed.): HIMI 2015, Part I, LNCS 9172, pp. 181–189, 2015.
DOI: 10.1007/978-3-319-20612-7_18

perceptual limitations, how information is displayed is of particular importance. Keeping users with visual impairments and other disabilities in mind, various groups have since come together to make the web more accessible. In 1997, the World Wide Web Consortium (W3C), an international standards organization for the Internet, launched the Web Accessibility Initiative (WAI), through which members of the W3C undertook the responsibility of improving the accessibility of the World Wide Web for people with disabilities. These guidelines support technical accessibility by ensuring a webpage is constructed in such a way to accommodate for assistive tools, two of which include screen magnifiers and responsive web design (RWD).

1.1 Screen Magnifiers

The most popular assistive technology used by people with low vision to interact with visual computer displays has traditionally been the screen magnifier [5]. Screen magnifiers essentially enlarge a portion of the application screen in the same way as an ordinary magnifying glass. The enlarged portion is typically the region around the cursor, since this is the user's point of focus. However screen magnifier users must contend with a number of trade-offs in the process.

One such trade-off is that as the magnification level increases, the amount of contained information on the viewing window decreases [6]. In other words, users with greater impairment and a need for more extreme magnification will see less content on the screen at once, thus forcing them to scroll back-and-forth much more frequently. Low vision computer-users report that following a cursor to read is a visually taxing task [7].

Another trade-off when using screen magnifiers arises from the loss of spatial orientation. The most commonly used magnification mode is full screen, which provides the user with the largest magnified visual field but sacrifices contextual awareness and spatial orientation [8]. As magnification increases in this mode, the amount of original content that fits on the page decreases, which results in a "lack of page context" [9] and inhibits access to global information. Such a trade-off decreases the user's effectiveness in skimming text to find information [10] and inputting information on an e-commerce website [7].

Additionally, people with low-vision should not be prevented from computer use by the high cost commonly associated with assistive technology. This comes as a problem considering that an estimated 90 % of the visually impaired population resides in low-income areas [11]. Despite the inherent issues faced by low-vision computer users when working with screen magnifiers, they must also face the huge price tag on these software packages.

1.2 Responsive Web Design (RWD)

In the past ten years, the booming smart phone industry has offered new platforms for Internet browsing. As a result, Ethan Marcotte [12] proposed RWD to accommodate for the number of platforms and to decrease the workload put out by web developers. Through web design, the content of application windows can wrap in such a way to present optimal presentation, regardless of the size of the device screen or magnification level.

Although not all responsive web sites are necessarily accessible, the principles of RWD promote accessibility. In a survey aimed to understand how people with low vision interact with computers to read content, 27 % of responders said they use the enlargement capabilities within the browser [13], a capability that RWD has direct implications for. Unfortunately many web developers have not adopted RWD. Integrating fluid layouts is an important consideration for professional designers who want their sites to be adaptive, accessible, and equally usable on a variety of platforms.

1.3   Present Study

The purpose of the present study is to compare the usability of a screen magnifier with RWD through efficiency and accuracy measures across different tasks web–based tasks. For one task, participants were asked to read a short or long passage and answer questions designed to assess their comprehension of the material. In another task, participants were asked to complete a data input form, simulating a payment screen on an e-commerce website. These tasks were chosen, as they simulate commonly performed web-based tasks. Participants completed these tasks using both a screen magnifier and RWD. Accuracy, time-on-task, and subjective usability assessments were measured from all tasks. Due to the increased action of scrolling horizontally, we predicted that participants would be less accurate and less efficient when using a screen magnifier for all tasks, as the additional action of scrolling will decrease the amount of resources normally used for comprehension. However similar performance measurements across conditions could indicate that the act of scrolling horizontally had no impact on comprehension thus demonstrating negligible differences in the two magnification methods.

2   Method

2.1   Participants

Sixteen California State University, Long Beach students (12 female, 4 male, Mage = 23.28 years, age range = 19–27 years) participated in the current study. They were compensated \$25 for their time (less than 2 h). All participants had normal or corrected-to-normal vision. To simulate a low-vision environment, a tablet was moved back to the participant's reported visual acuity limit (Macuity limit = 1322 mm, range = 920–1600 mm), so that content was barely discernable but not readable. The rationale behind testing participants with normal or corrected-to-normal vision was to test the study platform and demonstrate that good assistive technologies also benefit typical users under constrained situations (e.g., reading in low light conditions; viewing web content on a small device). All participants reported having experience with a smart phone or tablet, and 93.75 % reported using these devices to read.

2.2 Design

Participants performed a series of tasks using one of two magnification techniques. They were to use either RWD, in which the text wrapped to the size of the screen as magnification increased, or a screen magnifier, in which one portion of the screen magnified. The order of each magnification technique was counterbalanced across participants, and the tasks were counterbalanced within each condition block.

From each task, we measured accuracy by dividing the number of correct responses by the total number of possible responses. We also recorded the time it took for participants to work through the task (time-on-task) to measure task efficiency. At the end of each condition, participants completed a System Usability Scale (SUS) [14] to capture participants' subjective usability assessment. SUS is a brief questionnaire that asks responders to rate their level agreement to ten different statements. Responses fall in a range of 1–7, with 7 denoting a higher level of agreement with the statements. After calculation, final SUS scores fall between 0 and 100, with scores above 70 indicating acceptable usability. Scores between 50 and 70 indicate moderate usability, while scores below 50 indicate the system as unusable.

To further capture subjective user-experience, we also measured the expectancy of ease of task. Prior to each task, participants were asked to rate how easy they expected the task to be on a 1–7 point scale, with higher numbers denoting an easier expectation. After each task, participants were asked to rate how easy the task actually was, using the same rating scale. The expectancy of ease of task was calculated by subtracting the first rating score from the second. Negative numbers indicate that the task was harder than expected, while positive numbers indicate that the task was easier than expected.

2.3 Materials

All tasks were completed on a Dell Venue 8 tablet. For the testing station, the tablet was nested in a stand, with the display at eye-level. The stand started 457.2 mm from the table that the participant was seated at. To simulate mild low vision, the stand was moved back until the participant could no longer read the content on the page. This produced an average visual angle of 0.06 [15] for the original sized-content. An enlargement of 200 % produced a mean visual angle of 0.12, while an enlargement of 300 % produced an average visual angle of 0.17. The keyboard and mouse, which were connected to the tablet wirelessly, rested upon the table in front of the participant. A Cannon video camera recorded the screen of the tablet. This camera was positioned on a stand and was occluded from the participant's line of vision so as to not be a distraction.

Participants were given a total of six tasks to complete for each condition, but the present paper will only focus on three of them. Two tasks were reading comprehension passages from an SAT Practice Test book published by the College Board [16]. The passages differed in length, so that participants completed a short passage with questions and a long passage with questions. The third task was a data input task. Using a fictitious person's mailing address and billing information, participants were instructed to complete a page similar to an e-commerce website. The other tasks, which are not part of the present paper, were two math tasks and a proofing task.

The tasks were displayed in webpages that were presented through Mozilla web browser. The text was Verdana in 12-point font. RWD was programmed within the web browser to adjust according to the number of ems per line using media queries with relative units. For the screen magnification condition, we used Ai Squared's ZoomText, as that is one of the most popular screen magnifier currently used today. Participants were provided with a list of hotkeys for each magnification method at the beginning of each condition.

2.4 Procedure

After completing a consent form and demographics questionnaire, participants were asked to sit at the testing station. The tablet displayed an Orientation Page, which consisted of a passage from a short novel. A researcher moved the stand with the tablet away from the participant until the participant reported no longer being able to decipher the passage on the page. The researcher then provided a brief explanation of each hotkey required for the condition, while the participant followed along by using the keys. Once he or she felt comfortable with the hotkeys, the participant was handed instructions for the first task to read aloud. The participant then rated how difficult he or she expected the task to be. At this point, the participant pressed "Next" to begin the task, and the researcher stepped out of the room. Once the participant completed the task, he or she was instructed to turn over the instruction sheet and rate how difficult the task actually was. This process was repeated for each task. At the end of each condition, the participant completed a SUS for the magnification method. A break was given after the first condition. Upon completion of the second condition, the participant was asked for any longstanding reactions and was debriefed upon the purpose of the study.

3 Results

3.1 Reading Comprehension

Time-on-Task. A 2 (magnification technique: screen magnification /responsive design) × 2 (length: short /long) within-subjects ANOVA was conducted. Results indicated a significant main effect of magnification technique on time-on-task, $F(1, 15) = 9.35$, $p = .008$, $n^2 = .384$, such that when participants were performing the reading task, they were significantly quicker when using responsive design ($M = 344.55$, $SE = 24.10$) than a screen magnifier ($M = 435.67$, $SE = 28.42$). A significant main effect for length was also found, $F(1, 15) = 435.77$, $p < .001$, $n^2 = .967$, such that participants took less time completing the reading task with a short passage ($M = 185.48$, $SE = 140.50$) than a long passage ($M = 594.73$, $SE = 30.65$).

Accuracy. A 2 (magnification technique: screen magnification /responsive design) × 2 (type: short /long) within-subjects ANOVA was conducted. Results indicated a significant main effect of magnification technique on accuracy, $F(1, 15) = 5.58$, $p = .032$, $n^2 = .271$, such that participants answered a higher proportion of questions correctly when using responsive design ($M = .74$, $SE = .054$) than a screen magnifier ($M = .57$,

SE = .072). No difference in accuracy was found between the types of reading passages, *F* < 1.0 (Fig. 1).

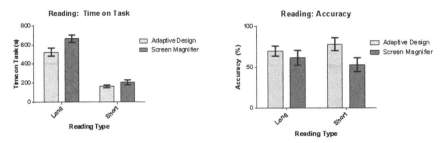

Fig. 1. Time-on-task (*left*) and accuracy (*right*) for reading comprehension. As shown in the figure, participants took longer to finish the task and were less accurate when using a screen magnifier.

Expectancy of Easy of Task. To investigate the difference in expectancy of ease of task ratings, a 2 (magnification technique: screen magnification /responsive design) × 2 (type: short /long) within-subjects ANOVA was conducted. Results indicated a significant main effect of magnification technique, $F(1, 15) = 13.97$, $p = .002$, $n^2 = .482$, such that participants rated the reading task to be significantly harder than originally expected when using a screen magnifier ($M = -1.06$, $SD = 1.08$) than responsive design ($M = -0.16$, $SD = 1.37$). No difference was found between the types of reading passages.

3.2   Data Input

Time-on-Task. A one-way ANOVA was conducted on time-on-task, with magnification technique as the within subjects variable. Results indicated that participants were significantly faster to complete the data input task when using responsive design ($M = 138.25$, $SD = 99.32$) than a screen magnifier ($M = 159.72$, $SE = 10.25$), $F(1, 15) = 5.27$, $p = .036$, $n^2 = .26$.

Accuracy. A one-way ANOVA was conducted on accuracy, with magnification technique as the within-subjects variable. No effects were significant, *F < 1.0* (Fig. 2).

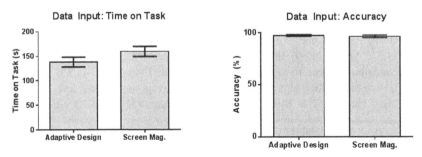

Fig. 2. Time-on-task (*left*) and accuracy (*right*) for the data input task. As shown in the figure, participants took longer to finish the task when using a screen magnifier. However accuracy was not affected by magnification method.

Expectancy of Easy of Task. A one-way ANOVA was conducted on expectancy of ease of task, with magnification technique as the within-subjects variable. A main effect of magnification type was found to be significant, $F = 4.84$, $p = .044$, $n^2 = .244$, such that participants rated data input as significantly easier than originally expected when using responsive design ($M = .50$, $SD = 0.97$) than when using a screen magnifier ($M = -0.19$, $SD = 1.05$).

3.3   SUS

Participants rated responsive design ($M = 92.81$, $SE = 2.16$) as significantly more usable than a screen magnifier ($M = 67.66$, $SE = 4.72$), $F(1, 15) = 25.81$, $p < .001$, $n^2 = .63$.

4   Discussion

The purpose of the present study was to investigate the usability of magnification methods through the comparison of a screen magnifier and RWD. There was a difference in performance between the two methods, thus indicating that the manner in which information is displayed for accessibility has an impact on comprehension tasks, even for participants with normal vision.

The results for the reading tasks showed that for both short and long passages, participants were not only slower but also less accurate while using a screen magnifier than RWD. According to the expectancy questionnaires, reading was much more difficult than originally expected while using a screen magnifier. During debriefing, many of the participants explained that the additional action of scrolling horizontally impeded upon comprehension. Participants were forced to reread lines and move back-and-forth repeatedly. This indicates that because less information could be displayed on the enlarged screen, participants were forced to rely more heavily on their working memory then when the information was displayed within the boundaries of the screen. Participants often reported feeling fatigued and complained of eyestrain, particularly after completing the long reading passage.

Results from the data input tasks did not show a difference in errors committed between the magnification techniques, thus indicating that participants were just as accurate when inputting information across both methods. However participants were slower to complete the task while using a screen magnifier compared to RWD. The increased time-on-task did not come from navigation style, as participants reported using the "tab" key to jump from one box to the next in both conditions. More likely, the efficiency of the participants' performance was degraded in the screen magnifier condition by the inability to predict what information would be needed next, as not all input boxes were visible, and participants would need to move their mouse back-and-forth to view all boxes and check that they were indeed filled in. Furthermore, participants needed to reorient themselves once the magnified portion switched locations after the "tab" key was used. Participants reported not feeling sure that all information had been inputted, an implication for e-commerce websites in general, especially with security measures like time limits.

Ultimately the results of this study have several implications for accessibility standards in web design. Screen magnifiers have inherent usability problems, such as horizontal scrolling, that impair efficient performance, and so should not be the sole assistive tool that low vision users rely on. Second, the findings suggest an error in the classification of accessibility levels in the WCAG 2.0 Guideline 1.4. In particular, success criterion (SC) 1.4.4, conformance level AA, requires that if text can be enlarged up to 200 %, but does not wrap to the size of the device screen, it still conforms to the WCAG 2.0 [17]. According to this criterion, if text does not fit within the device window, scrollbars should be provided. While this solution has been argued to be inferior to the ZoomText magnification provided in the current study, it is still considered sufficient to meet the criterion. Success Criteria 1.4.8, conformance Level AAA (part 5) however requires that text enlargement should be wrapped within the device window. This experience was provided by RWD within the current study. As it stands, level AA is legally binding, while Level AAA is voluntary. Thus WCAG 2.0 Level AA excludes enlargement with reflow as a legally binding accommodation for reading with low vision.

The decrease in efficiency and accuracy while using screen magnifiers indicate a cost in reading while scrolling back-and-forth. This cost was seen with a population that does not struggle with additional perceptual limitations, such as blurred vision, sensitivity to contrast or brightness, or loss of central vision. Horizontal scrolling has been deemed a "web design error" [18] and is one of the few features that users consistently report negatively to [19]. So the question remains why popular assistive technologies subject people with low vision to such demanding conditions. Should we not allow computer access to everyone, and make assistive technologies, which some rely on, as easy-to-use as possible?

To further provide support for changes in accessibility guidelines, this study must be done using the affected population, and indeed, follow-up studies are currently in place to investigate the effect of magnification methods on the performance of participants with low vision. While this study focuses on word-wrapping and horizontal scrolling, still much more should be done to fully understand how computer displays are accessed and perceived by individuals with visual impairments. We can no longer focus on the average, normal-sighted user but must also consider those with disabilities and not exclude the 6.6 million individuals with low vision [20].

Acknowledgments. We would like to extend a special thanks to Typometric Solutions, the CSULB Psychology Department, and the Center for Usability in Design and Accessibility for supporting this project.

References

1. Pew Research Center: Broadband Technology Fact Sheet, Pew Research Center, Washington, D.C. (2013). http://www.pewinternet.org/fact-sheets/broadband-technology-fact-sheet/
2. Blackwell, D.L., Lucas, J.W., Clarke, T.C.: Summary health statistics for U.S. adults: national health interview survey, 2012. National Center for Health Stat **10**(260), 1–161 (2014)

3. Fisk, A.D., Rogers, W.A.: Handbook of Human Factors and the Older Adult. Academic Press, San Diego (1997)
4. Legge, G.E., Rubin, G.S., Pelli, D.G., Schleske, M.M.: Psychophysics of Reading—II. Low Vision. In: Foster, D.H. (ed.). Vision Research, vol. 25, issue. 2, pp. 253–266. Elsevier, Amsterdam (1985)
5. Fraser, J., Gutwin, C.: A framework of Assistive Pointers for Low Vision Users. In: The Fourth International ACM Conference on Assistive Technologies, pp. 9–16. ACM Press (2000)
6. Beckmann, P.J., Legge, G.: Psychophysics of Reading-XIV: The Page Navigation Problem in Using Magnifiers. In: Foster, D.H. (ed.). Vision Research, vol. 36, issue. 2, pp. 3723–3733. Elsevier, Amsterdam (1996)
7. Murphy, E., Kuber, R., McAllister, G., Strain, P., Yu, W.: An empirical investigation into the difficulties experienced by visually impaired internet users. Univ. Access Inf. Soc. 7(1–2), 79–91 (2008)
8. Beckmann, P.J., Legge, G.: Psychophysics of Reading-XIV: The Page Navigation Problem in Using Magnifiers. In: Foster, D.H. (ed.). Vision Research, vol. 36, issue. 2, pp. 253–266. Elsevier, Amsterdam (1996)
9. Lerponini, B., Paterno, F.: Applying Web Usability Criteria for Vision-Impaired Users: Does It Really Improve Task Performance?. In: Motta. E. (ed.). International Journal of Human-Computer Interaction, vol. 24, issue. 1, pp. 17–47. Elsevier, Amsterdam (2008)
10. Bruggeman, H., Legge, G.E.: Psychophysics of Reading. XIX. Hypertext Search and Retrieval with Low Vision. In: Proceedings of the IEEE, vol. 90, issue. 1, pp. 94–103 (2002)
11. World Health Organization, http://www.who.int/mediacentre/factsheets/fs282/en
12. Marcotte, E.: Responsive Web Design. In: A List Apart, vol. 306 (2010, 2014)
13. Henry, S.L.: Understanding users' needs to customize text display (2013). http://www.tader.info/understanding.html
14. Albert, W., Tullis, T.: Measuring the User Experience: Collecting, Analyzing, and Presenting Usability Metrics, 2nd edn. Elsevier, Waltham Massachusetts (2013)
15. Legge, G.E.: Psychophysics of Reading in Normal and Low Vision. In OSA Noninvasive Assessment of the Visual System. Lawrence Erlbaum Associates Publishers, Monterey (2007)
16. The College Board, http://sat.collegeboard.org/practice (2014)
17. Techniques for WCAG 2.0: Technique G179. *W3C*. W3C, 2014. Web. 2014
18. Cappel, J.J., Huang, Z.: A Usability Analysis of Company Websites. In: Journal of Computer Information Systems, vol. 48, no. 1, pp. 117 (2007)
19. Nielsen, J.: Scrolling and scrollbars. In: Jakob Nielsen's Alertbox, Nielsen Norman Group (2005). http://www.nngroup.com/articles/scrolling-and-scrollbars/
20. Erickson, W., Lee, C., von Schrader, S.: 2011 Disability Status Report: United States. In Cornell University Employment and Disability Institute (EDI), Ithaca, NY (2012)

Generating Summary Videos Based on Visual and Sound Information from Movies

Yurina Imaji[✉] and Masaya Fujisawa

Tokyo University of Science, Tokyo, Japan
{yurina_imaji,fujisawa}@ms.kagu.tus.ac.jp

Abstract. Vast quantities of video data are now widely available and easily accessible; because of the many videos that users encounter, video summary technology is needed in order to help users find videos that match their preferences. This study focuses on movies to propose a method for extracting important scenes based on visual and sound information, and verifies the degree of harmony of the extracted scenes. The video segments thus characterized can be used to generate summary videos.

Keywords: Summary videos · Visual and sound information

1 Introduction

Thanks to faster video compression technologies, higher data transmission rates, and the widespread adoption of mobile devices, it is now possible to access vast quantities of video data, and there are ever more opportunities to use video media on the Internet. As a result, it can be difficult to quickly find videos that match one's preferences. Technologies that generate summary videos would be helpful for sifting through this vast quantity of videos to select which ones to watch. Summary videos would enable users to quickly understand the content and ambiance of the video and to decide whether to watch it, rather than simply fast-forwarding from the beginning to figure out what the video is about. Moreover, with the widespread adoption of tablets, users can now access videos from anywhere at any time, whether on a train or during breaks at work. In such situations, however, there is only a limited amount of time available for watching videos. Given a technology that generates summary videos, it would then become possible to specify how much time was available to watch a video and then watch the video within the specified time, skipping the parts that are relatively unimportant. For these reasons, technologies that generate summary videos are important.

This study considers methods for generating summary videos, targeting movies with long play times in particular. A number of studies on summary videos of movies have been reported to date, and methods have been proposed for extracting the segments that the filmmaker wishes to emphasize. One study [1] extracts four types of sensory information rendered in the movie by detecting seven types of camera work (such as pan, tilt, and zoom in) and the movie subject, and then provides the emphasized scenes as a summary video. Another study [2] generates summary videos by

© Springer International Publishing Switzerland 2015
S. Yamamoto (Ed.): HIMI 2015, Part I, LNCS 9172, pp. 190–203, 2015.
DOI: 10.1007/978-3-319-20612-7_19

detecting special events (close ups of key characters, gunshot or explosion sounds, onscreen text, etc.) and then linking these together. In "film grammar" [3], key scenes to be emphasized are described as belonging to one of four categories (action, calm, suspense, and release) based on dramatic effects resulting from shot-length transitions. Through experiments, another study [4] shows that each type of scene can in fact be distinguished based on shot length transitions. In an earlier study, we presented a method that builds on this method [4] by filtering candidates using color information, focusing on the "orange and teal" dramatic method that has been incorporated into numerous Hollywood movies. Unfortunately, using only color information and dramatic effects based on scene-length transitions resulted in the extraction of many locations unrelated to the four types of emphasized scenes.

In this study, we incorporated sound effects as extraction factors in addition to dramatic effects in order to isolate video segments more precisely. In previous studies, "sound effects" have been used to refer to background music, explosion sounds, and so forth, and segments found to contain sound effects have been regarded as having a high degree of importance. However, this method tends to extract only noisy action segments, and is unable to extract segments that are given dark and moody emphasis. This lead us to consider generating summary videos by focusing on the relationship between sound and video, rather than investigating sound and video separately. A study [5] has found that there is an interaction between visual and auditory senses so that resonant or competitive phenomena occur when sound and visual information are in harmony, and the scene becomes more emphasized. Accordingly, regarding the dramatic effects in the four types of scenes (action, calm, suspense, and release), we consider in more detail the features of the sounds for which resonant and competitive phenomena occur. This study focuses on frequency ranges and volume, the latter of which is likely to exhibit particularly intense modulations in representing the development of scenes or human emotions during the course of a movie. We accurately extract the four types of scenes (action, calm, suspense, and release) defined as points of emphasis according to the film grammar school, and we verify the degree of harmony between sound and visual information in each of these scenes.

2 Method for Identifying Scenes Within a Movie

2.1 Movie Structure

Movies are played back at either 24 or 48 frames per second, so the structure of a movie consists of the "film frame" as the smallest unit of visual information. This is followed in increasing order of size, by the "shot", the "scene", the "sequence", and finally the movie as a whole.

A "shot" refers to a single segment of visual information recorded without any discontinuities, and is defined in terms of this lack of discontinuities regardless of length. That is, a series of frames with no cuts makes a single shot. A "scene", then, is a series of several shots and refers to a block of action taking place at a certain location. A "sequence" is a combination of several shots or scenes, and is a situational unit that constitutes a single story.

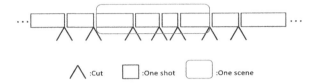

Fig. 1. Shots and scenes

According to the film grammar concept, the key scenes that the filmmaker wants to emphasize can be categorized into four types: action, calm, suspense, and release (Fig. 1).

2.2   Method for Identifying Scenes by Shot Length

In an earlier study, we attempted to identify the four types of scenes by focusing on changes in shot length intervals. As shown in the following figures, action scenes tend to consist of a series of short shots, calm scenes tend to consist of a series of long shots, ``suspense'' scenes have shot lengths that gradually become shorter and shorter, and shot lengths in release scenes gradually become longer and longer. However, when scenes were identified based on shot-length features alone, there were many misidentifications. Therefore, this study aims to improve precision by adding sound information (Figs. 2, 3, 4 and 5).

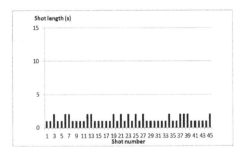

Fig. 2. Action scene

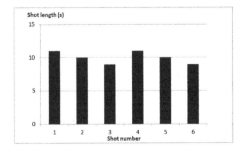

Fig. 3. Calm scene

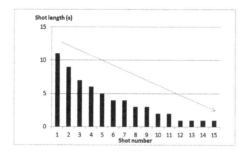

Fig. 4. Suspense scene

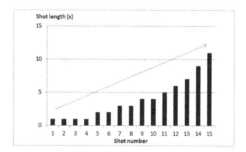

Fig. 5. Release scene

2.3   Method for Identifying Scenes, Focusing on Harmony Between Visual Information and Sound

Few movies consist of visual elements alone—the visual information is almost always accompanied by sound. Compared with other visual products, movies in particular incorporate numerous special effect sounds and music that match the situational or emotional content in order to increase the effect of the visual expression.

Taking into consideration that sound and visual information being in harmony gives a scene greater emphasis [5], this study looks at the dramatic effects of the four types of scene (action, calm, suspense, and release) and judges scenes where these dramatic effects occur as being important.

The frequency range of human hearing is from approximately 20 to 20,000 Hz. The frequencies that can be produced by human vocalizations is said to range from about 80 Hz at the low end to about 11,000 Hz at the high end, but generally the human voice ranges between 100 and 4000 Hz. Of this range, frequencies between 2000 and 4000 Hz are the easiest for humans to perceive audibly, and this range includes the sound of a baby crying, a woman screaming, and the warning alarm of an electrical appliance. After about 75 years of age, on average humans can only hear up to about 5000–6000 Hz, and so this study focuses on the frequency range from 0 to 4500 Hz, on the assumption that filmmakers produce movies aimed at people of all ages.

In each scene, we regard shot length (visual information) to be in harmony with the volume and frequency (sound information) when the following conditions are met.

- Action scenes
  Action scenes tend to be situations containing many sudden loud sounds, such as explosions, gunshots, yelling, screaming, and sounds of things breaking, and so we determine that a scene is an action scene with sound and visual information in harmony in sections where there are a series of loud sounds, with rapid and intense changes in volume, and there is a large low frequency components between 0 and 200 Hz.
- Calm scenes
  Calm scenes are regarded as unlikely to have abrupt loud sounds as these scenes tend to be relaxed situations, and so we determine that a scene is a calm scene when the volume remains low and constant, with the same large frequency components between 60 and 700 Hz lasting for a long time because of the long shot lengths.
- Suspense scenes
  Suspense scenes often immediately precede action scenes, or else the characters gradually become more and more psychologically strained, and so the volume increases gradually, reflecting the characters' pulses. The first half of a suspense scene has long shots, and so frequency components extend far horizontally, but in the second half of a suspense scene typically has a frequency distribution with many short bursts of low frequency components in the 0 to 200 Hz range, leading up to the action scene that follows. We determine that a section with this kind of pattern is a suspense scene, and that the sound and visual information are in harmony.
- Release scenes
  Release scenes are very often situations where the characters have become free after a tense situation has been resolved. Accordingly, these scenes tend to start with a loud volume that gradually decreases, reflecting the emotions of the characters. Also, the second half of a release scene has long shot intervals and so we determine that a section is a release scene, and that the sound and visual information are in harmony, if sounds with the same frequency components last for a long time.

Only when all three factors—shot interval, volume, and frequency—are as described above do we regard sound and visual information as being in harmony and then classify a segment as being a certain type of scene. We also verify the degree of harmony in each scene.

3   Evaluation Tests

3.1   Test Overview

We verify the discrimination precision of the proposed method (focusing on both visual information and sound information) for the four types of scenes. The distribution of scenes is likely to vary depending on the movie genre, and we therefore conduct the verification using three genres: action, drama, and fantasy. During the tests there were various different movie sound formats, but in this study we used two channels (left and right) with a quantization bit rate of 16 bits and a sampling rate of 44.1 kHz. For the evaluation scale, we made comparisons based on recall, precision, and F value.

	Relevant	Nonrelevant
Retrieved	tp	fp
Not retrieved	fn	tn

$$Precision = \frac{tp}{tp + fp} \quad Recall = \frac{tp}{tp + fn}$$

$$F - measure = \frac{2 * precision * recall}{precision + recall}$$

We determine the correct answer for each scene based on the following criteria:

Action: Scenes including chases, accidents, physical fighting, or fighting with machines
Calm: Scenes where the emotion and tone are calm and quiet
Suspense: Scenes with tension and a sense that something is about to happen
Release: Scenes where constraints and the like have been released and freedom has been achieved

Next, we verify the degree of harmony between the sound and visual information in each scene using the semantic differential method. The impression evaluation scale used in this test was a list of 22 adjective pairs (Table 1) considered likely to represent the impressions of both the sound and visual information. Each item is rated on a seven-point scale. To interpret the test results, we conducted factor analysis with the evaluation scale as the variable quantity.

For the target exhibitions of each of the four types of scenes (action, calm, suspense, and release), we prepared versions of the scene with sound only, visual information only, and both sound and visual information. In the test, we initially evaluated all scenes with sound only, followed by all scenes with visual information only, and finally all scenes with both sound and visual information. In each case, the scenes were all played in random order.

Table 1. Adjective pairs

Sloppy	— Well-formed	Sense of being there	—	No sense of being there
Erratic	— Precise	Expansive	—	Not expansive
Vague	— Clear	Orderly	—	Confused
Soft	— Hard	Dirty	—	Clean
Powerful	— Not powerful	Detached	—	Heated
Strong	— Frail	Gaudy	—	Plain
Fresh	— Stale	Cheerful	—	Sad
Like	— Hate	Light	—	Heavy
Interesting	— Uninteresting	Unique	—	Commonplace
Fun	— Boring	Fantastical	—	Realistic
Memorable	— Forgettable			

3.2   Results and Discussion

Precision of Scene Identification. The following tables show the results of comparing the scene discrimination precision using the previous method (visual information alone) and the proposed method (sound and visual information), for each of the three movie genres.

Tables 2, 3, and 4 shows that scene discrimination precision was improved in all three genres by additionally considering sound. The reduction in the misidentification rate meant that we succeeded in reducing incorrect extractions of sections that were not heavily emphasized or important with respect to the movie's editing. Conversations between characters are an example of scenes that were misidentified by the previous method. In conversational scenes, the camera typically faces the speaker, and the camera angle changes each time the speaker changes, meaning that a fast-paced conversation results in a series of short shots. When scenes are discriminated based on only shot intervals as in the earlier study, such sections are incorrectly identified as action scenes. However, by adding sound information we were able to correctly identify conversational scenes and avoid misidentifying them as action

Table 2. Precision for action movies

	Action		Calm		Suspense		Release	
	Vision	Vision + sound	Vision	Vision + sound	Vision	Vision + sound	Vision	Vision + sound
Number of scenes	8		17		22		7	
Accuracy	0.835	0.953	0.753	0.847	0.8	0.812	0.871	0.929
Misidentification rate	0.153	0.024	0.212	0.082	0.047	0.012	0.059	0.012
Precision	0.316	0.75	0.419	0.611	0.692	0.875	0.167	0.667
Recall	0.857	0.75	0.813	0.647	0.41	0.318	0.143	0.286
F-measure	0.462	0.75	0.553	0.628	0.515	0.466	0.154	0.4

Table 3. Precision for drama movies

	Action		Calm		Suspense		Release	
	Vision	Vision + sound	Vision	Vision + sound	Vision	Vision + sound	Vision	Vision + sound
Number of scenes	0		21		13		1	
Accuracy	0.831	1	0.718	0.761	0.873	0.887	0.887	0.972
Misidentification rate	0.169	0	0.197	0.169	0.042	0	0.113	0.028
Precision	0	0	0.517	0.571	0.667	1	0.111	0.333
Recall	0	0	0.714	0.762	0.5	0.333	1	1
F-measure	0	0	0.6	0.653	0.572	0.5	0.2	0.5

Table 4. Precision for fantasy movies

	Action		Calm		Suspense		Release	
	Vision	Vision + sound	Vision	Vision + sound	Vision	Vision + sound	Vision	Vision + sound
Number of scenes	10		14		23		3	
Accuracy	0.926	0.947	0.809	0.894	0.83	0.872	0.883	0.947
Misidentification rate	0.149	0.021	0.106	0.053	0.032	0	0.085	0.032
Precision	0.364	0.8	0.375	0.583	0.667	1	0	0
Recall	0.727	0.947	0.429	0.583	0.316	0.263	0	0
F-measure	0.485	0.762	0.4	0.583	0.429	0.417	0	0

scenes based on the fact that conversational scenes do not have a series of loud sounds and the frequency components tends to be concentrated in the 100–1000 Hz range of the human voice.

Degree of Harmony Between Sound and Visual Information. For each type of scene, we verified the impression of the sound and visuals using the impression evaluation scale. The following tables show the results for action scenes. Here, we used single scenes from movies, and for those cases where both sound and visual information are presented, the comparison is conducted on the assumption that they are in harmony.

Focusing on Factor 1 in Tables 5, 6, and 7, the impression results for sound alone or visual information alone include many impressions that could be applied to any scene, such as "fun", "interesting", and "like". However, when a section was played back with sound and visual information in harmony, there were many impressions unique to action scenes, such as "powerful", "well-formed", and "sense of being there".

Table 5. Impressions of action scenes with sound only.

	Factor 1	Factor 2
Fun – boring	0.978	0.299
Interesting – uninteresting	0.965	0.138
Unique – commonplace	0.834	0.233
Like – Hate	0.703	0.219
Expansive – not expansive	0.654	−0.157
Memorable – forgettable	0.536	−0.398
Sense of being there – no sense of being there	0.510	−0.251
Detached – heated	−0.679	0.223
Erratic – precise	0.191	0.777
Vague – clear	0.000	0.744
Sloppy – well-formed	−0.011	0.718
Powerful – not powerful	0.508	−0.527
Strong – frail	0.354	−0.614
Cheerful – sad	0.414	0.235
Light – heavy	−0.069	0.238
Fresh – stale	0.136	−0.002
Orderly – confused	0.260	0.442
Soft – hard	0.031	0.486
Dirty – clean	−0.200	−0.377
Gaudy – plain	0.490	−0.461
Fantastical – realistic	0.275	−0.384

Table 6. Impressions of action scenes with visual information only.

	Factor 1	Factor 2
Sense of being there – no sense of being there	0.899	−0.128
Memorable – forgettable	0.857	0.030
Fun – boring	0.845	0.030
Interesting – uninteresting	0.808	0.115
Expansive – not expansive	0.777	−0.261
Fresh – stale	0.748	0.005
Like – Hate	0.652	0.019
Detached – heated	−0.579	−0.411
Erratic – precise	−0.617	−0.169
Vague – clear	−0.653	−0.196
Strong – frail	0.012	0.833
Gaudy – plain	0.195	0.680
Orderly – confused	−0.314	−0.536
Sloppy – well-formed	0.126	−0.865
Soft – hard	0.426	−0.878
Dirty – clean	0.091	0.025
Cheerful – sad	0.471	−0.050
Light – heavy	−0.065	−0.019
Powerful – not powerful	0.205	0.373
Unique – commonplace	0.488	−0.172
Fantastical – realistic	−0.025	−0.260

Moreover, from Fig. 6 it is clear that the impressions likely to be emphasized by the dramatic effects unique to action scenes were most highly evaluated when sound and visual information were in harmony.

As shown in Tables 8, 9, and 10, no significant differences in Factor 1 were found between sound alone, visual information alone, and both sound and visual information for calm scenes. However, based on the result shown in Fig. 7, impressions likely to be emphasized by the dramatic effects specific to calm scenes (e.g., "erratic", "vague", and "no sense of being there") were more highly evaluated for a scene with sound and visual information in harmony than for the same scene with sound alone or visual information alone.

These results indicate that dramatic effects that cannot be obtained with visual features alone will have a stronger impression by incorporating audio features to harmonize sound and visual information and thereby creating an impression specific to each scene.

Table 7. Impressions of action scenes with both sound and visual information.

	Factor 1	Factor 2
Powerful – not powerful	0.964	−0.170
Memorable – forgettable	0.939	0.050
Strong – frail	0.818	0.029
Sense of being there – no sense of being there	0.690	−0.056
Fresh – stale	0.624	0.286
Unique – commonplace	0.592	0.130
Vague – clear	−0.736	−0.067
Sloppy – well-formed	−0.788	−0.197
Erratic – precise	−0.935	0.173
Interesting – uninteresting	−0.132	1.021
Fun – boring	−0.032	1.019
Like – Hate	0.044	0.863
Expansive – not expansive	−0.086	0.726
Orderly – confused	−0.004	0.512
Detached – heated	−0.098	0.080
Soft – hard	0.036	0.166
Cheerful – sad	−0.049	−0.020
Gaudy – plain	0.412	0.169
Dirty – clean	−0.124	−0.264
Light – heavy	0.114	0.382
Fantastical – realistic	0.249	0.384

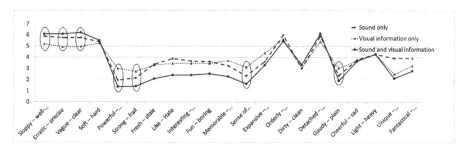

Fig. 6. Results for the semantic differential method

Table 8. Impressions of calm scenes with sound only.

	Factor 1	Factor 2
Detached – heated	0.983	–0.160
Erratic – precise	0.719	–0.113
Vague – clear	0.626	0.265
Sense of being there – no sense of being there	–0.583	–0.179
Strong – frail	–0.733	–0.163
Gaudy – plain	–0.886	–0.050
Dirty – clean	–0.158	0.960
Fun – boring	–0.349	–0.524
Interesting – uninteresting	–0.057	–0.556
Memorable – forgettable	–0.052	–0.670
Like – Hate	0.084	–0.687
Expansive – not expansive	–0.333	–0.695
Fresh – stale	–0.326	–0.699
Soft – hard	0.516	–0.804
Unique – commonplace	0.285	0.009
Sloppy – well-formed	0.496	–0.354
Cheerful – sad	–0.325	0.017
Light – heavy	0.038	–0.177
Powerful – not powerful	–0.415	–0.347
Orderly – confused	0.039	–0.401
Fantastical – realistic	–0.485	0.260

4   Conclusions

Focusing on the interplay between audio and visual senses to define emphasized sections as those where sound and visual information are in harmony, this paper has proposed a method for extracting the four types of scenes according to film grammar. The proposed method was compared with a previous method that extracted scenes using visual features alone. It was found that the proposed method was able to reduce the number of incorrect extractions relative to the previous method and to increase the overall precision. Although the precision has increased, some scenes corresponding to one of the four types of scenes were nonetheless overlooked using only the features of

Table 9. Impressions of calm scenes with visual information only.

	Factor 1	Factor 2
Sense of being there – no sense of being there	0.890	−0.177
Interesting – uninteresting	0.839	−0.115
Expansive – not expansive	0.750	0.163
Fresh – stale	0.742	0.121
Powerful – not powerful	0.702	−0.211
Fun – boring	0.640	0.164
Like – Hate	0.574	0.128
Detached – heated	−0.579	0.550
Vague – clear	−0.715	−0.118
Erratic – precise	−0.761	0.152
Orderly – confused	0.204	0.819
Light – heavy	−0.078	0.711
Cheerful – sad	−0.066	0.581
Dirty – clean	−0.237	−0.621
Gaudy – plain	0.276	−0.656
Memorable – forgettable	0.277	0.357
Strong – frail	0.076	−0.144
Unique – commonplace	−0.063	−0.163
Soft – hard	0.498	0.228
Sloppy – well-formed	−0.191	0.336
Fantastical – realistic	0.336	−0.046

sound and visual information as defined by the proposed method. As an issue for the future, we need to define scene features more precisely and also consider other features such as tone and camera work. We also performed impression rating tests using the semantic differential method for each scene. The results showed that the impressions of dramatic effects particular to each type of scene were not especially strong when viewing video alone or listening to sounds alone, whereas viewing video with the sound and visual information in harmony produced stronger impressions of the dramatic effects for each type of scene.

Table 10. Impressions of calm scenes with both sound and visual information.

	Factor 1	Factor 2
Orderly – confused	1.008	−0.211
Memorable – forgettable	0.556	−0.112
Fresh – stale	0.551	0.395
Expansive – not expansive	0.523	0.199
Erratic – precise	−0.519	−0.065
Dirty – clean	−0.710	−0.213
Vague – clear	−0.786	0.124
Gaudy – plain	−0.412	0.898
Like – Hate	0.161	0.820
Interesting – uninteresting	0.124	0.682
Fun – boring	0.352	0.578
Sense of being there – no sense of being there	0.181	0.564
Powerful – not powerful	−0.097	0.450
Light – heavy	−0.016	0.315
Sloppy – well-formed	−0.092	0.073
Soft – hard	0.121	0.344
Strong – frail	0.045	0.270
Detached – heated	0.025	−0.089
Cheerful – sad	0.204	0.378
Unique – commonplace	0.033	0.464
Fantastical – realistic	−0.160	0.327

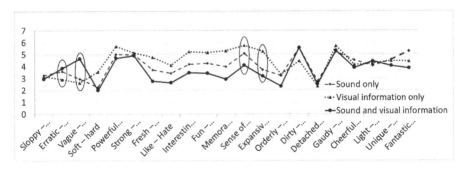

Fig. 7. Results for the semantic differential method

References

1. Yoshitaka, A., Matsui, R., Hirashima, T.: Extracting movie rendition based on camera work detection and classification. Trans. Inf. Process. Soc. Jpn. **47**(6), 1696–1707 (2006). (in Japanese)
2. Lienhart, R., Pfeiffer, S., Effelsberg, W.: Video abstracting. Commun. ACM **40**(12), 55–62 (1997)
3. Arijon, D.: Grammar of the Film Language. Focal Press, London (1976)
4. Takemoto, R., Yoshitaka, A., Hirashima, T.: Video editing based on movie effects by shot length transition. IEICE Technical report, PRMU-105-534, pp. 19–24, 2006 (in Japanese)
5. Iwamiya, S.: Audio-visual communication in visual media productions. IEICE Trans. Inf. Commun. Eng. 39–46 (2002) (in Japanese)

Narrower Conceptual Scope in the App Than the Web Store Interface – The Size Does It and the Ad Has It

Chien-Ling Kao and Man-Ying Wang$^{(\boxtimes)}$

Department of Psychology, Soochow University, Taipei, Taiwan
miaout@hotmail.com, mywang@scu.edu.tw

Abstract. How does screen size impact users in ways other than task performance or efficiency? The current study proposed and tested the hypothesis that a narrower conceptual scope was associated with the small/App than the large/web store interface leading to reduced ad relevance effect (i.e., evaluation of the ad and advertised products in high than low relevance ads was more positive). The hypothesis was supported. Implications for mobile shopping behavior and online ad placement were also discussed.

Keywords: Screen size · Online shopping · Conceptual scope · Eye tracking · Ad relevance

1 Introduction

Mobile sales by the leading 500 retailers grew 70 % in 2013 and are expected to grow another 80 % in 2014 in the Internet 500 mobile study. Global mobile data grew 81 % in 2013 and 45 % in 2014 [1]. The ardent expectation of the coming mobile commerce age spurred by these statistics, however, needs to consider a potentially limiting factor inherent in the mobile phone device, i.e., the small display size.

Small screen size is likely to reduce users' effectiveness on the task and increases the needed navigational activities [2, 3]. This unfavorable feature may interact with the multitasking and resource competition condition faced by mobile phone shoppers and deters them from shopping on the go (cf. [4]). Does the small screen size of mobile phones affect other dimensions of shopping related processing? The current study focused on one such possibility, i.e., the smaller spatial range of visual attentional processing due to the small screen size restricts the scope of conceptual processing [5]. It is hoped that the examination of this unexplored behavioral dimension of screen size and its consequence on shoppers' evaluation of products and advertisements may contribute to current knowledge of online store design.

2 Liturature Review

Earlier studies showed that the small display size of mobile phones adversely affects performance. Comparing PDAs and desktop computers, longer task completion times and lower task success rates in association with small than large screen sizes were

© Springer International Publishing Switzerland 2015
S. Yamamoto (Ed.): HIMI 2015, Part I, LNCS 9172, pp. 204–214, 2015.
DOI: 10.1007/978-3-319-20612-7_20

found by [6]. Reduced screen size (1.65 in. vs. 2.65/3.78 in.) impaired the effectiveness of video-based mobile learning [7]. The menu selection performance was compared between a large and a small screen (i.e., 800 × 600 vs. 240 × 320 pixels [8]. Task performance was more efficient (faster task completion time) and users' memory recognition (awareness) of the menu items was somewhat better for the large than the small screen.

Some recent studies found more limited effects of screen size on task performance. Reference [9] evaluated the effect of mobile phone screen size using three different sizes (i.e., 3.5, 4.3 and 5.3 in.) and information retrieval tasks. The screen size did not affect perceived usability (i.e., SUS scores), nor did it influence effectiveness (i.e., task completion rate). Larger screen size increased efficiency (i.e., task completion time) when the specific task required more interactions (more difficult). In a similar vein, J. Kim [10] found that it was more difficult for users of small than large screen sizes (i.e., phones vs. computers) to extract information from the search results page though the search performance of different screen sizes was equivalent. Whether screen size affects the success or efficiency dimension of task performance appeared to depend on the absolute level of sizes, nature and complexity of the task, among others.

Although the effect of screen size on task performance could be more subtle than expected, there could be other cognitive processing dimension that is impacted by size. The visual exploration on a small than a large screen spans lesser spatial extent and a narrower perceptual/attentional scope. Narrow attentional scope prompts the individual to maintain a conceptually limited array of information while wider scope enhance the allocation of resources to distal, less relevant information [11, 12]. Reference [5] provided experimental evidence supporting that the spatial extent of perceptual search affected one's conceptual scope. They asked participants to search for '3's in arrays of digits. When the digits spread out over a wider area, participants exhibited broad conceptual scopes enabling them to subsequently generate more original uses of a brick and more original category exemplars. The current study thus hypothesized that the small size of an App store interface on a phone engenders narrower perceptual and conceptual scope compared to the large interface of the Web store on a desktop computer (H_1, see Table 1).

Table 1. Hypotheses examined in the study

H_1	Conceptual scope of the small/App store interface is narrower than that of a large/web store interface
H_2	The total number of gazes and the total gaze duration on an small/App store interface are less than that of a large/web store interface
H_3	The total number of gazes and the total gaze duration on the ads of small/App store interfaces are less than those of large/web store interfaces
H_4	Size/interface type interacts with the effect of advertisement relevance
H_{4a}	Banner ads displaying highly relevant product category are more positively evaluated than those displaying low relevance products
H_{4b}	The ad relevance effect was more pronounced for the large/web store interface than the small/App store interface

Furthermore, as the user with a narrower processing scope devotes processing resources on the limited array of information [11, 13], he is expected to accomplish the task with less effort than when his processing scope is wide. Thus fewer gazes and less gaze duration are needed for the App store than the web store interface, given the equivalence in the processed products and user task demands for the two types of stores (H_2, see Table 1).

When the processing scope is wider than narrower, the user is likely to attend to information presented peripheral to the products such as advertisements. As a result, there is expected to be a greater number of gazes fallen on the ads and the total gaze duration on the ad is expected to be longer when the processing scope is wider than narrower (H_3, see Table 1).

Previous research on ad placement had found that advertisements displaying products related to the central context of the website were generally more effective than irrelevant ads. The click-through rate, ad attitude, ad memory, purchase intention were higher when the advertised products were related to displayed products [14–16]. Reference [14], for example, compared the evaluative responses towards the banner ad (e.g., student loan banner ad) that was highly relevant to the displayed website (e.g., online student financial loan service website) vs. low relevance banner ad (e.g., a computer branding ad), controlling familiarity of website and brand names as well as the locations of the ad. An ad relevance effect was found – high relevance ads were liked more and exhibited higher purchase intention over low relevance ads while memory of the ad was not affected by relevance. Relevant ads are perceived to be related to the current user goal in her interactions with the website and were thus more positively evaluated [17]. We expected similar ad relevance effects for banner ads in this study. However, the small display size of the App store interface is expected to narrow the conceptual scope of the participant making it more difficult for her to see the relevance or similarity between the advertised products and the website products. The ad relevance effect is thus smaller for the small/App than the large/web interface (H_4, H_{4a}, H_{4b}, see Table 1).

3 Method

3.1 Participants

Forty female undergraduates aged 19–24 participated to receive partial course credit. Half of them participated in the large/web and the other half in the small/App condition. Their online shopping experience was at least three years and they shopped online once every month on average.

3.2 Design and Materials

The study is an interface size/type (small/App vs. large/web) x ad relevance (low vs. high relevance) design with size/type as a between subject factor and relevance as a within subject factor. The product array was constituted by nine clothing presented in a 3 × 3 grid and the target product (a black jacket) randomly appeared at one location. These products were collected from the Internet controlling clothing prices US$12 ~ $30. Beneath the product array was a banner ad displaying either high relevance (i.e., clothing/accessary or shoes) or low relevance products (electronics/computer, food).

Forty different product arrays and forty different banner ads (ten for each of the four product categories) were generated. The combination of the specific target product and the banner ad category were counterbalanced so that each product appeared with the four different banner ad categories equivalently likely across participants in either the web or the app store condition. Each participant viewed a total of forty App or web store images, extended approximately 11 or 32° of visual angle in width each respectively. These two sizes are equivalent to the approximate screen visual angles of a 5-inch mobile phone viewed at the distance of 35 cm and a 17-inch monitor at 60 cm. A small/App interface image was constituted by the nine-product array and the banner ad while there was additional navigation bars and website ads placed to the left and right of the product array in the large/web interface image (see Fig. 1).

Participant responses were evaluated using the following items. The numbers in the brackets represent whether the response was taken during phase 1 or phase 2 of the experiment (see Procedure). Nine-point scales were used in all except for the manipulation check for the conceptual scope:

- Manipulation check for the conceptual scope (1): Items were selected from the Chinese Remote Association Test (CRAT) [18] – a Chinese version of the Remote Association Test [19]. Each item was comprised of three Chinese characters and the participants responded with one character that could constitute a two-character word with any of the two or three characters. Ten items were selected from the CRAT so that they were of the highest frequencies for the words constituted and of similar character locations in the words, i.e., the easier items in the CRAT to facilitate sensitivity to the manipulation.
- Manipulation check for ad relevance (2): *The banner ad is relevant to the webpage content, The banner ad is related to the features and functions of the webpage.*
- Product purchase intention: *I may purchase this product* (1), for the store products; *I may purchase the product in the banner ad* (2), for the ad products.
- Product attitude: *I like the product* (1), for the store products.
- Ad click intention: *I'd like to click on the ad* (1).
- Ad attitude: *I like the banner ad* (1), *The banner ad is pleasant* (2).

3.3   Procedure and Apparatus

The participant was seated 60 cm in front of the Tobii T60 (60 Hz) eye tracker in a quiet room when her eye position was tracked. The participant was asked to imagine that she was shopping online, looking for a black jacket. She was supposed to click on the black jacket in each product page and answer questions concerning the products and ads. The participant's eye position was calibrated using a five-point calibration procedure was repeated as needed according to Tobii's procedure.

Fig. 1. An example of the large/web store (top) and the small/app store (bottom) interface

The trials were then presented in random orders to the participant. In each trial, the App or web store image was presented as long as needed until the participant clicked on the target product (i.e., the black jacket) to terminate the presentation of the image. The webpage product purchase intention, webpage product attitude, ad attitude, ad click intention questions and rating scales were then presented consecutively on the screen for the participant to indicate her rated response with the mouse click. After they completed the forty trials, the participant responded to the manipulation checks for cognitive scope.

The forty app/web store images were presented again for rated purchase intention (advertised product), ad attitude, ad relevance manipulation checks. Participants then completed an online shopping experience questionnaire.

4 Results and Discussion

One participant was excluded from the analysis because of the partial loss of her data.

4.1 Manipulation Checks

The conceptual scope was measured by the numbers of associations generated on the CRAT. The mean number of associations was significantly more for the large/web interface than the small/App interface, $M = 8.15$ vs. 6.53, $t(37) = -4.92$, $p < .05$, suggesting larger conceptual scope for the large/web than the small/app interface, supporting H_1.

The two ad relevance ratings were averaged and submitted to a t-test, $M = 6.56$ vs. 3.38, $t(37) = 20.31$, $p < .05$, showing higher relevance ratings for high relevance (accessory and clothing) ads than low relevance (phones/computers and foods) ads.

4.2 Ad and Product Measures

The size x relevance mixed design two-way ANOVA was performed on the respective dependent measures and there was not any significant effect. The feedbacks from the participants suggested that food advertisements were strongly capturing their visual attention. Heat maps for the four categories of ad products show this difference (see Fig. 2). The mean total fixation times for the food ads was 2.73 s. while it was 1.6 s., 1.69 s., 1.55 s. for phones/computers, accessory, clothing ads respectively. As foods may have automatically captured attention that diminished the ad relevance effect, trials with food ads were excluded from the subsequent analysis.

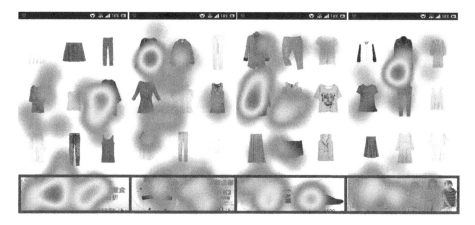

Fig. 2. Heat maps for the four types of banner ads in a small/App interface example: (from left to right) food, phones/computers, accessory, clothing.

The dependent measures were again submitted to the size/type x relevance ANOVAs. Ad relevance did not affect participants' attitudes and purchase intention for the webpage products. Significant effects of ad relevance were found for ads and advertised products: The willingness to click on the ad, $F(1,37) = 6.99$, $p < .05$,

η_p^2 = 0.16, purchase intention of advertised products, $F(1,37)$ = 45.41, $p < .05$, η_p^2 = 0.55, average ad attitude (the average of the two ad attitude questions), F $(1,37) = 5.23, p < .05$ $\eta_p^2 = 0.61$, ad attitude 1, $F(1,37) = 3.71, p < .05$, $\eta_p^2 = 0.46$, and ad attitude 2, $F(1,37) = 22.49, p < .05$, $\eta_p^2 = 0.38$) were all higher for high than low relevance ads. Participants were more willing to click on the ad and purchase the products in the ad and had better ad attitude toward the ad when the ad was of high than low relevance to the webpage products, supporting H_{4a}.

Ad relevance interacted with interface size/type for purchase intention of advertised products, $F(1,37) = 10.73, p < .05$, $\eta_p^2 = 0.23$, average ad attitude, $F(1,37) = 5.04$, $p < .05$ $\eta_p^2 = 0.59$. The simple main effect analysis showed that the purchase intention was higher for high than low relevance ads for the large/web store interface, $F(1,19) = 38.14, p < .05\eta_p^2 = 0.66$, while ad relevance did not affect purchase intention for the app store interface, $F(1,18) = 2.20, p > .05$. The simple main effect analysis for average ad attitude showed that ad attitude was higher for high than low relevance ad also for the large/web, $F(1,19) = 13.30, p > .05$, $\eta_p^2 = 0.93$, but not the small/App store interface, $F(1,18) = 0.001, p > .05$, (see Fig. 3). These findings supported H_{4b}. Interface size/type x ad relevance interaction was also significant for ad attitude 1, $F(1,37) = 7.62, p < .05$ $\eta_p^2 = 0.17$, but not for ad attitude 2, the willingness to click on the ad, attitude and purchase intention of webpage products.

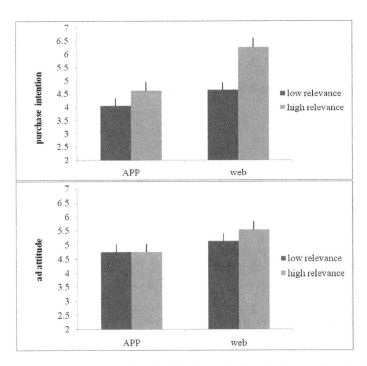

Fig. 3. Mean ratings of purchase intention (on the scale from 1 (not at all) to 9 (very)) for advertised products (top) and average ad attitude (bottom) as the function of ad relevance and interface size/type. The error bars were standard errors.

The main effect of interface size/type was significant for purchase intention of advertised products $F(1,37) = 6.73$, $p < .05$, $\eta_p^2 = 0.15$ and ad attitude 2, $F(1,37) = 4.98$, $p < .05$ $\eta_p^2 = 0.12$, but not for any other measures. Participants were more willing to purchase the advertised products and felt the banner ad was pleasant when the ad was displayed in the large/web than small/app interface.

4.3   Gaze Measures

The total gaze duration, total number of gazes, gaze duration on the banner ads and the number of gazes fallen on the banner ads were respectively analyzed using the interface size/type x ad relevance ANOVA. Total gaze duration: The duration was longer for high than low relevance ad, $F(1,37) = 14.22$, $p < .05$ $\eta_p^2 = 0.315$. The interaction effect $F(1,37) = 1.80$, $p > .05$, and the main effect of interface size/type, $F < 1$, was not significant. Total number of gazes: the main effect of ad relevance, $F(1,37) = 2.91$, $p > 0.05$) was not significant. The effect of interface size/type was marginally significant, $F(1,37) = 3.66$, $p = .06$, showing a greater number of gazes on the large/web than the small/App interface (see Fig. 4). Total gaze duration on banner ads: no significant effects. Number of gazes on the banner ads: no significant effects. To conduct the task of target product search, participants engaged fewer gazes when the store interface was

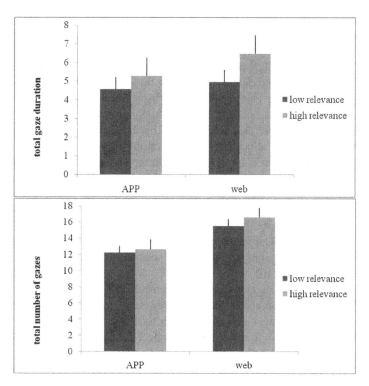

Fig. 4. Total gaze duration (top) and the number of gazes (bottom) as the function of ad relevance and interface size/type. The error bars were standard errors.

small/App than large/web but their gaze duration did not differ between two interface size/types, partially supported H_2. Neither the number of gazes nor the total gaze duration varied with the interface size/type. H_3 was not supported.

4.4   Discussion

The current findings showed that users' processing scope differs when they shop in a large/web compared to a small/App store interface due to the size difference between the devices. The narrow scope of processing due to the small spatial extent in the App store interface diminished the ad relevance effect and reduced the number of gazes deployed in the target product search task.

Such effects of display size contrast with previous effects of screen size on performance [6–10]. The viewing of the small/App interface was not more effortful than that of the large/web interface. In fact, our participants used fewer, not greater, numbers of gazes to locate the target products in the former than the latter. This is likely due to the fact that the visual angles of the product array and the banner ad were kept similar between the large/web and the small/App store interface in the current study. Both of them were approximately equivalent to that of a 5-inch phone at a hand-held distance. As such, the content and legibility of the critical product display and banner ads could be little disadvantaged toward the small than the large display. This situation is characteristic of the real world conditions considering the prevalence of phones such as iPhone 6 plus, Samsung Galaxy Note 3, 4, Sony Xperia Z Ultra, all of which have large screens well over five inches. The current practice of App design using large product images, limited texts as well as the hided/moved/reduced navigation scheme results in clear and clean App store interfaces. The current findings point out, however, that the narrower spatial processing extent of the small/App interface still cast an effect on users' processing scopes that, in turn, impacts shopping behavior.

As a result, the App store user characterized by the narrow scope of processing is more "focused" in terms of allocating resources on the current task than the web store user. Such a focused shopper is incompatible with the task of interacting with external environment, helping account for the limited shopping conducted on the go using mobile phones [4]. Our finding that the small/App interface was associated with fewer gazes thought not shorter gaze duration is consistent with this "narrow and focused" picture of the App store user. It is interesting to note that a study comparing search performance on small and large screens similarly found that eye movements on the small screen were more limited and the visual scanning patterns were narrower than those on the large screen [10].

Current findings also suggest that ad placement in an App store interface may require different considerations as that in a web store interface. On the one hand, context relevance is no longer a guideline as critical as in the web store interface. It awaits future study to clarify if an ad relevance effect defined in terms of self-relevance [17] will be less susceptible to the narrow processing scope of the App interface. On the other hand, participants actually had a lower purchase intention and attitude towards the advertised products and ads on average in the small/App than the large/web store interface even if the visual information in the two interface size/types was comparable.

The large/web interface allowing a wider processing scope may have enabled the viewer to assimilate both relevant and less relevant ad products with the product category in the product array, increasing the evaluation towards the ad and advertised products.

Current findings are limited in terms of the fixedness of banner ad location, the simulation of the mobile phone screen on a computer monitor as well as the interaction response with mouse clicks rather than touches and swipes. However, the consistent effects found suggest the needs for future studies to exemplify other dimensions of user behavior associated with display size.

References

1. Cisco: Cisco Visual Networking Index: Global Mobile Data Traffic Forecast Update 2014–2019 (2015). Retrieved from http://www.cisco.com/c/en/us/solutions/collateral/service-provider/visual-networking-index-vni/white_paper_c11-520862.html
2. Chae, M., Kim, J.: Do size and structure matter to mobile users? An empirical study of the effects of screen size, information structure, and task complexity on user activities with standard Web phones. Behav. Inf. Technol. **23**(3), 165–181 (2004)
3. Jones, M., Marsden, G., Mohd-Nasir, N., Boone, K., Buchanan, G.: Improving Web interaction on small displays. Comput. Netw. **31**(11), 1129–1137 (1999)
4. Google: The new multiscreen world: Understanding cross platform consumer behavior. Think Newsletter (2012). Retrieved from https://www.thinkwithgoogle.com/research-studies/the-new-multi-screen-world-study.html
5. Friedman, R.S., Fishbach, A., Förster, J., Werth, L.: Attentional priming effects on creativity. Creativity Res. J. **15**(2–3), 277–286 (2003)
6. Jones, M., Buchanan, G., Thimbleby, H.: Improving Web search on small screen devices. Interact. Comput. **15**(4), 479–495 (2003)
7. Maniar, N., Bennett, E., Hand, S., Allan, G.: The effect of mobile phone screen size on video based learning. J. Softw. **3**(4), 51–61 (2008)
8. Findlater, L., McGrenere, J.: Impact of screen size on performance, awareness, and user satisfaction with adaptive graphical user interfaces. Paper Presented at the Proceedings of the SIGCHI Conference on Human Factors in Computing Systems (2008)
9. Raptis, D., Tselios, N., Kjeldskov, J., Skov, M.B.: Does size matter? Investigating the impact of mobile phone screen size on users' perceived usability, effectiveness and efficiency. Paper Presented at the Proceedings of the 15th International Conference on Human-Computer Interaction with Mobile Devices and Services (2013)
10. Kim, J., Thomas, P., Sankaranarayana, R., Gedeon, T., Yoon, H.J.: Eye-tracking analysis of user behavior and performance in web search on large and small screens. J. Assoc. Inf. Sci. Technol. **66**(3), 526–544 (2015)
11. Friedman, R.S., Förster, J.: Implicit affective cues and attentional tuning: an integrative review. Psychol. Bull. **136**(5), 875–893 (2010). doi:10.1037/a0020495
12. Gable, P.A., Harmon-Jones, E.: Reducing attentional capture of emotion by broadening attention: increased global attention reduces early electrophysiological responses to negative stimuli. Biol. Psychol. **90**(2), 150–153 (2012)
13. Whitmer, A.J., Gotlib, I.H.: An attentional scope model of rumination. Psychol. Bull. **139**(5), 1036–1061 (2013). doi:10.1037/a0030923

14. Jeong, Y., King, C.M.: Impacts of website context relevance on banner advertisement effectiveness. J. Promot. Manage. **16**(3), 247–264 (2010)
15. Moore, R., Stammerjohan, C., Coulter, R.: Banner advertiser-Web site context congruity and color effects on attention and attitudes. J. Advertising **34**, 71–84 (2005)
16. Yaveroglu, I., Donthu, N.: Advertising repetition and placement issues in on-line environments. J. Advertising **37**(2), 31–44 (2008)
17. Kim, N.Y., Sundar, S.S.: Personal relevance versus contextual relevance: the role of relevant ads in personalized websites. J. Media Psychol. Theor. Methods Appl. **24**(3), 89–101 (2012). doi:10.1027/1864-1105/a000067
18. Jen, C.H., Chen, H.C., Lien, H.C., Cho, S.L.: The development of the Chinese remote association test. Res. Appl. Psychol. **21**, 195–217 (2004)
19. Mednick, S.: The associative basis of the creative process. Psychol. Rev. **69**(3), 220–232 (1962). http://dx.doi.org/10.1037/h0048850

Exploring Cultural Symbols in Nigeria for Contemporary Applications in Web Visual Design

Isah Bolaji Kashim[1], Oluwafemi S. Adelabu[2(✉)], and Sunday O. Ogunwole[3]

[1] Department of Industrial Design, Federal University of Technology,
Akure, Ondo State, Nigeria
ibykash@gmail.com
[2] Graduate School of Comprehensive Human Sciences,
University of Tsukuba, Tsukuba, Japan
femmysamuel@gmail.com
[3] Department of Industrial Design, Ahmadu Bello University,
Zaria, Kaduna State, Nigeria
soogunwole@abu.edu.ng

Abstract. The study aimed at exploring rich heritage of cultural symbols in Nigeria for meaningful and harmonious adaptations in web visual interface design. In this study, we focused on developing theme design for computer-based questionnaire form using selected cultural motifs from the Yoruba traditional textile tradition as a source of inspiration. Visual aesthetic evaluations were done by university students in south western Nigeria using semantic differential scales. We assessed the perceived aesthetic impression of the stimuli set through the main test procedure. The study reveals how the inflection and transfiguration of cultural symbols in web visual design can be visually appealing to the local computer users at a first glance and changes that might occur over extended exposure time. This paper underscores the relevance of cultural potentials from Nigerian heritage for modern day design application by using information technology as a platform towards adapting them.

Keywords: Arts and culture · Symbols · Culture-inspired aesthetic value and HCI

1 Introduction

The impact of human-computer interaction (HCI) has continued to grow over the decades, greatly enhancing interaction with products operating on information technologies. Following the remarkable influence of the HCI design methods and processes on human information processing and interaction with information systems, the understanding and consideration for culture-inspired aesthetic value can be essential towards creating a deeper layer of users' experience and fulfilling more users' affective needs. Today, the issue of cultural sensitivity in design especially for local designers has motivated the need for exploring a point of synergy between the forces of globalization and localization, modernization and traditional practices. In this case study,

© Springer International Publishing Switzerland 2015
S. Yamamoto (Ed.): HIMI 2015, Part I, LNCS 9172, pp. 215–225, 2015.
DOI: 10.1007/978-3-319-20612-7_21

we focus on Nigeria as a multi-cultural society and an emerging economy in Africa. Nigerian arts and culture embody both verbal and visual expressions that vary and represent different ethnic groups. With over 521 languages and a rich repertoire of values embedded in her visual and material culture, the diverse cultural manifestation highlight the vividness of Nigerian lifestyle in arts, music, literature, folklore, dance and architectural expressions, underlined by her glorious traditional heritage. In the pursuit for adapting to the current trend of global innovation design and new urban lifestyle aided by advanced information products and systems, local designers have been concerned with approach to evolve from traditional root into modern design expression.

Researchers have shown that users' perception of a visual appeal of webpage, particularly at first impression, can have a far-reaching effect on the attitude towards the use of the interface systems [1–3]. As the computer application for research purpose is gradually growing, we are concerned to know whether the adaptation of local design element can be a motivational drive for the attitude of local people towards response to online questionnaire form. Prior studies have suggested a clear relationship between user's previous experience and positive attitude induced by feeling of familiarity. A theoretical account by Zajonc [4] has suggested that familiar things tend to generate favorable affective responses. Also, Sanabria [5] reported a positive correlation between familiarity and pleasure in visual evaluation of familiar ad images and words combinations. Therefore, familiarity and congruity are considered to be contributing factors in testing user's implicit knowledge and triggering pleasurable emotions.

This study aimed at exploring rich heritage of cultural symbols in Nigeria for meaningful and harmonious adaptation in web visual interface design. Our supposition is that culture-inspired aesthetic values can also offer a platform to enrich users's experience in interaction with modern information system designed for local users. Based on this supposition, this study was developed involving student participants from South-western region in Nigeria. Using an evaluation tool of semantic differential, we assessed the visual appeal and motivational attitude towards the samples of theme design interface for an online questionnaire form. The study reveals how the inflection and transfiguration of cultural symbols in web visual design can impact on the impression and usability of the local design contents by local users.

1.1 Nigerian Cultural Heritage

Nigeria occupies a land mass of 923,766 sq. km and possesses lots of attributes. Apart from being an emerging economy in Africa, it is endowed with natural resources. The diversity of her cultural resources can be seen from the composition of her ethnic groups which is well over 521. These diversities can be seen in the arts, music, literature, folklore, dance and architecture among others. The Nigerian users need to be associated with their traditional heritage while interacting with contemporary technologies. Culture from Nigerian perspective is centred on the totality of ways and manner people live together and make some meaning out of their existence putting varying factor of cultural symbols which act as means of identity. The human expression finds their way through varied forms of art and cultural activities which represent the vividness of Nigerian lifestyle coupled together with glorious history of the past to rely upon. Nigerian art, culture and design symbols lie in the fact that they draw inspiration from the rural traditional folk heritage from different regions. These cultures that are demonstrated in Nigerians lifestyle will be translated in this paper using symbols form exhibited in visual art, dances, literature, folklores and different musics. The major forte of the Nok culture is the invention of terra cotta figurine and statues, the 10th century artistry of bronze work of Igbo Ukwu, terra cotta and metal works of Ife bronze decorated with ivory and precious stone, are major stake that earn them the popularity in other part of West Africa and beyond. Evolutional development of art and design saw the emergence of prominent crafts in the area of traditional architecture, pottery cloth weaving, wood carving mural design, body decorations and bronze casting which are popular, and peculiarities in concept influenced by cultural and religious beliefs.

Since culture is a set of distinctive spiritual material, intellectual and emotional feature of a society or social group encompassing (art, literature, value system, traditions and beliefs). They can be summed up to be either materialistic or non-materialistic. The emphasis of this paper will be placed on the materialistic aspect of human creation, which has to do with creativity in the use of talents that imbibes the symbolic expressions from various immediate environments. The diversity of Nigerian cultural symbols is exemplified in the following areas:

– The Nigerian clothing/embroidery
– The Nigerian architecture and surface treatment
– Leather work
– Body tattoo and decoration
– Music and instrumentation
– Dancing and costume
– Carving (wood, metal)

Today, there is a growing number of Nigerians who use computer interfaces to access data available on various information technologies. The issue of cultural sensitivity in design arose when users could not relate to their cultural experience with information technologies they interact. For example, when users want to customize their visual experience of a computer theme, they hardly can locate any indigenous resources to use. This gap creates the need to develop a platform that would support the exploration of cultural symbols for contemporary use. Through this cultural representation, a synergy between modernization and traditionalism can be explored within the framework of information and communication technology (ICT). This study draws experimental materials from the visual heritage of the Nigerian clothing/embroidery, focusing on the Yoruba sub-culture which is prominent in southwestern Nigeria.

1.2   The Yoruba *Adire* Textile Tradition

The Yoruba from the south western part of Nigeria are one of several sub-cultural groups with deep and vibrant design tradition. Among their creative and decorative products is the prominent hand crafted textile designs and materials used at different functions such as initiation ceremonies, marriage, passage of rite. The hand crafted woven textiles utilize traditional cloth for making *Aso-Ebi* which features in three different class referred to as *Etu*, *Alaari* and *sanyan*. This traditional hand-woven textile is long rooted in the Yoruba culture dating back to 18th century (Clark, 1998). The *Etu*, via blue and white stripes in the warp direction and dyed repeated in indigo blue dye, worn by important personality for social dress. *Alaari* is crimson in colour woven with silk yarn traditionally used for all events. *Sanyan* is very expensive hand-woven grayish in colour production from fibres made from cocoons. This popularity adds to the cultural image of Nigeria. Another prominent textile design tradition which was purposively chosen for this study is the tie and dye cloths or pattern cloth dyeing known as *Adire* (c.f. Fig. 1). While some scholars opined that the origin of pattern dyed cloths among the Yoruba people occurred by several dyeing accidents that happened centuries ago, the account according to the Yoruba philosophy and history relayed the origin to divine inspiration of Yoruba deity of wisdom – *Orunmila* [6]. The name *Adire*, coined from two Yoruba words *Adi* (tie) and *re* (dye), essentially indicates the making process of cloth dyeing and the product. Of great fascination are the designs and decorative patterns of the cloth which signify semiotic richness and visually communicative meanings that are relevant to the history and culture of the people. Based on the process of making, there are two kinds of *Adire* namely *Adire Eleko* and *Adire Eleso*. The *Aso oke* and *Adire* cloths are used for formal occasions. The men use them as three piece wrapper and loose blouse while the men uses then as three pieces suits and long gowns. The application of cultural symbols in the South-western part of Nigeria is noted prominently in their *Adire* textile designs. The designs on these materials reflect on cultural heritage using ethnic codes and symbols to create feeling of unity, patriotism and pride for which Yoruba culture is involved.

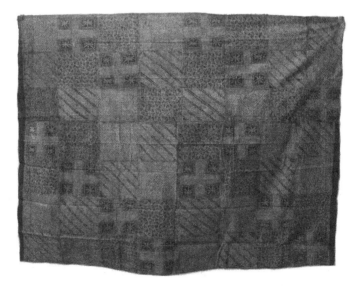

Fig. 1. A typical hand-painted adire eleko design *Adire* textile design called 'Ore merin' which means 'four friends'

2 Material and Method

2.1 Stimuli Development

In an attempt to evolve Nigeria's traditional root to modern design expression, her rich cultural heritage is explored. The exploration of the cultural heritage of Nigeria is through the selection of some cultural symbols from the Yoruba textile design tradition. For the initial selection of stimuli, we adopted 50 motifs from *Adire* textile designs which were previously studied and illustrated by Areo and Kalilu [6]. The motifs include faunal, floral and geometric symbols. These motifs bear names and they are connected with various meanings and stories which inspired them. The motifs are trans-generational and acceptable symbols which are creative and standardized elements related to the people's culture and are derived from history, proverbs, folklores, myth and everyday lives of the people [6]. For a screening purpose, a questionnaire containing the 50 adopted motifs was prepared for self-assessment through semantic differential method [7] using criteria such as familiarity, recognition of meaning and visual appeal. The screening evaluation was done by university students specialized in industrial design courses ($N = 8$, 33 % female, 18–25 age range). Before the participants' response to the main evaluation, they filled a set of evaluative scales which was set to explore their preferential tendency for foreign or local products. Figure 2 shows a sample of the motifs and a bipolar evaluation scale.

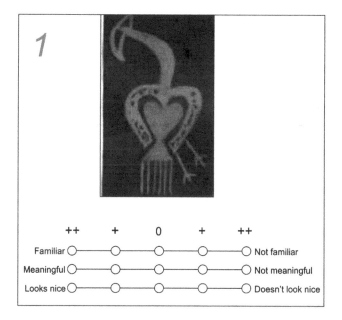

Fig. 2. An example of motifs and evaluation scales used for the screening process

2.2 Visual Semantic Evaluation Process

Following the screening evaluation, the adopted 50 motifs were sorted based on their average evaluation scores for familiarity, meaningfulness and visual appeal. A downsized number of 5 motifs set (M10, M24, M30, M29, M26) were selected for the design of the main test (this included 1 faunal, 3 geometric and 1 floral motifs). Using the 5 selected motifs, computer-generated design in form of repeated patterns were developed by two advanced graphic design students, into a standardized theme orientation that are suitable for building an online questionnaire form theme (see Fig. 3).

A visual semantic evaluation was set up for the main test. Six visual designs of an online questionnaire form were prepared using Google forms template. The themes of the forms were built using the computer-generated designs from the selected motifs and one form with a plain theme (Table 1).

Participants were 40 university students enrolled in industrial design courses (15 % female, $M_{age} = 21$, $SD_{age} = 2.3$). Using a projector and Microsoft PowerPoint program,

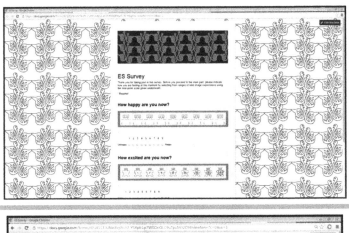

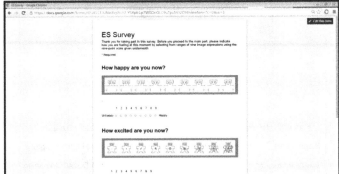

Fig. 3. Two samples of screen-shots of questionnaire form (the upper form template (M10) has motif pattern background/header design while the lower form template (MP) with a plain background/header design)

Table 1. Theme design template developed based on selected motifs

Sample Id/ Trad. name	Selected sample	Average rating scores (+2 to -2)	Computer-generated design (repeated patterns)
M10 Pepeye (Duck)		Familiar: 2.00 Meaningful: 1.63 Looks nice: 1.75	
M24 Agbo'le (Compound)		Familiar: 1.88 Meaningful: 1.63 Looks nice: 1.75	
M30 Igi Oye (Chieftaincy)		Familiar: 1.50 Meaningful: 1.75 Looks nice: 1.63	
M29 Waya (Wire)		Familiar: 1.50 Meaningful: 1.63 Looks nice: 1.63	
M26 Sekere (Gourd Rattle)		Familiar: 1.50 Meaningful: 1.50 Looks nice: 1.50	

the participants viewed and evaluated twice, 6 screenshots of on-line questionnaire forms with six thematic background layouts as earlier described. Screenshots of each form page were taken within a Google chrome browser at 1024*768 pixel resolution in 32-bit true color. The form page images were shown like they were being viewed in the Google chrome environment. The form header was made of a colored version of the motif pattern samples while the background was tiled with an outlined version of similar motif pattern (as shown in Fig. 3). The participants were allowed to view each screenshot twice under two exposure time conditions – 50 ms and 500 ms. In a fixed order, the first 6 six screenshots were displayed sequentially under 50 ms while the second 6 screenshots were viewed under the 500 ms in a random order. The purpose of varying the exposure time condition was to compare the effects of exposure time on the evaluation response. As shown in a study by Lindgaard et al. [3], visual appeal can be assessed within 50 ms and may not just be taken as a 'mere exposure effect'.

In addition to the main evaluation, participants responded to a set of two questions to evaluate their level of motivation at the beginning of the test and their preference towards computer-type or paper-type questionnaire forms. The evaluation scale used for the main evaluation is shown in Fig. 4 below.

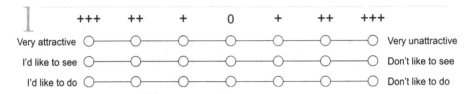

Fig. 4. Semantic differential scale for participants' evaluation for visual appeal and attitude of liking to respond to a displayed questionnaire form – participants ticked off one circle along each line to show their impression towards the projected screenshot

3   Analysis and Discussion

First, the average score of the participants' motivation prior to the main evaluation was almost 70 % high based on the self-report on the rating scale of 1 to 5. As can be seen in Fig. 5, the preference to answer a computer-type questionnaire over a paper-type questionnaire was almost equally divided among the participants (Paper-type 47.5 %, computer-type 52.5 %).

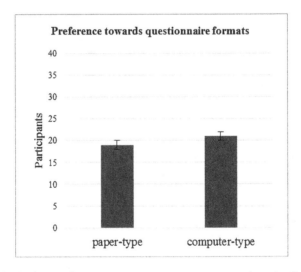

Fig. 5. Preference for paper-type vs computer-type questionnaire formats

For the analysis of the main evaluation, the average evaluation scores for each form design appearance for the first and second time conditions were calculated and compared. The summary is presented in Table 2. As can been seen, only 1 (M10) out of 6

Table 2. A summary of the evaluation six screenshots under two timing conditions

Screenshot Id	Evaluation factor	Mean rating First Phase (50ms)	Mean rating Second Phase (500ms)	Differential point of evaluation
M26	Visual appeal	-1.38	0.23	1.61
	Intend to see	-1.19	-0.41	0.78
	Intend to do	-1.42	-0.54	0.88
M30	Visual appeal	-1.15	0.90	2.05
	Intend to see	-1.05	0.89	1.94
	Intend to do	-1.30	0.57	1.87
MP	Visual appeal	-0.90	-1.63	-0.73
	Intend to see	-0.95	-1.41	-0.46
	Intend to do	-0.97	-1.62	-0.65
M10	Visual appeal	1.30	2.33	1.03
	Intend to see	1.00	2.17	1.17
	Intend to do	0.97	2.03	1.06
M24	Visual appeal	-0.23	0.58	0.81
	Intend to see	0.00	0.51	0.51
	Intend to do	-0.08	0.22	0.30
M29	Visual appeal	-0.25	-0.53	-0.28
	Intend to see	-0.49	-0.49	0.00
	Intend to do	-0.54	-0.65	-0.11

form templates had a positive rating based on the three evaluation factors for the first timing phase (50 ms) However, there seem to be a general improvement in the rating under the second timing phase (500 ms). In the latter, we found 4 (M26, M30, M10, M24) out the 6 templates gained a positive rating by the participants. The remaining two template (MP, M29) appear not be visually appealing to the participants even when the viewing time increased.

Overall, the results indicate a dissonance in the perception of the form samples under two timing conditions. While the initial impressions from the participants tend to indicate a less favorable visual appeal and attitudinal interest, the final appraisal showed a general improvement in the perceived quality and interest. At the initial rating stage, the form sample (M30) which is composed of a faunal motif, was most rated in both timing conditions.

This result suggests there could be other interacting factors which are responsible for the evaluation pattern. Apart from re-considering the physical condition of the test room such as the level of visibility of the projection and other participants-related factors, of further interest for the study will be an attempt to identify the graphical properties which triggered the visual appeal and attitudinal interest towards sample M30 over other samples. We suppose that a remarkable difference in the appreciation of the visual design could change over time as the participants assimilate other information contained in the form. Since answering a questionnaire could be seen as task, the study has observed the need for researchers using online survey instruments to pay more attention to the overall appeal of the form design. Perhaps, this might be a rewarding trigger that stirs the interest of the target respondents.

4 Concluding Remarks

In this study, we have attempted to use the Nigerian *Adire* traditional textile motifs as an adaptable element in building an attractive 'feel' to trigger respondent's interest towards on-line questionnaire forms. Following a test procedure of visual semantic evaluation, 6 samples of questionnaire theme design were prepared and evaluated under two exposure time conditions. Based on the evaluation response using three rating factors operationalizing visual appeal and intension of respondent's to like to see and answer to computer-based questionnaire form, the results indicate some positive attitudinal tendency towards local contents in computer interface designs. Possibly, this design adaptation might also be applicable for designing meaningful interactive and dynamic contents for webpage designs.

Cultural symbols are fascinating, but they represent concepts that are unique to traditions. They carry a wealth of associations and meanings. Iyang [8] noted that, "Continuous researches in the various culture of mankind have brought forth a large compendium of symbols and meanings that were once embedded in folklore". Iyang [8] added that "symbols may be anything: objects, words, colors, or patterns; their defining characteristic is that they stand for something other than their intrinsic property…" As the traditional arts and crafts of the pre-literate African society are fading gradually in the face of globalization, designers could stand for as preservers of this valuable cultural knowledge and creative visual expression by developing for them an adaptable modern platform. This paper underscores the relevance of cultural potentials from the landscape of Nigerian cultural heritage for modern day design application in information technology. With further advanced research on exploring means to integrating local designs and meanings into computer interface design, the study hopes for possibility of building a richer interactive experience and harmonious overlap between tradition and modern technology.

Conclusively, the study foresee that if the cultural symbols is offered a platform to enrich users' experience in interaction with modern information system, it can offer the advantage of enriching visual interface to make them more meaningful and rewarding to the local users while at the same time allowing intellectual cultural heritage go hand-in-hand with information technologies. Nevertheless, more questions remain to be addressed in order to promote an effective application of visual culture in HCI.

References

1. Tractinsky, N., Katz, A.S., Ikar, D.: What is beautiful is usable. Interact. Comput. **13**, 127–145 (2000)
2. Dahlen, M., Rasch, A., Rosengren, S.: Love at first site? A study of web site advertising effectiveness. J. Advertising Res. **43**, 25–33 (2003)

3. Lindgaard, G., Fernandes, G., Dudek, C., Brown, J.: Attention web designers: you have 50 milliseconds to make good first impression! Behav. Inf. Technol. **25**, 115–126 (2006)
4. Zajonc, R.B.: Feeling and thinking: preferences need no inferences. Am. Psychol. **35**(2), 151–175 (1980)
5. Sanabria, Z.J.C., Young, I.C., Toshimasa, Y.: The influence of familiarity on emotional responses to natural scene ads: a study of Kansei in Japanese advertising. Kansei Eng. Int. J. **11**(2), 81–89 (2012)
6. Areo, M.O., Kalilu, R.O.R.: Origin of and visual semiotics in Yoruba textile of adire. Art Des. Stud. **12**, 32–34 (2013)
7. Osgood, C.E., Suci, G.J., Tannenbaum, P.: The Measurement of Meaning. University of Illinois Press, Illinois (1967)
8. Iyang, E.: Logo for the Typical Client. Reflections on Theory and Practice of the Business Mark and Visual Identity, pp. 37–40. Awansca Books, Lagos (2005)

Generation of Infotips from Interface Labels

Eric White[1(✉)], Sandrine Fischer[2], and Foaad Khosmood[2]

[1] Physics Department, California Polytechnic State University (USA),
San Luis Obispo, USA
ewhite11@calpoly.edu
[2] Computer Science Department, California Polytechnic State University (USA),
San Luis Obispo, USA

Abstract. A method is presented for generating informative and natural-sounding infotips for graphical elements of a user interface. A domain-specific corpus is prepared using natural language processing techniques, and a term-frequency/inverse-document-frequency transform is used for vectorization of features. A k-means algorithm is then used to cluster the corpus by semantic similarity and retrieve the most similar infotips for any inputted interface label. We demonstrate the feasibility of this method and conclude by proposing several approaches to improve the selection of infotips by incorporating natural language processing and machine learning techniques.

Keywords: Natural language processing · Machine learning · Instructional design · Graphical user interfaces

1 Introduction

1.1 Context

Tooltips and infotips, collectively referred to as tips, are small pop-up windows that either label or explain, respectively, the function of elements found in a graphical user interface (GUI). They appear when a user hovers a cursor over GUI elements such as menu items, icons, and toolbar controls. This interaction principle, in which text does not need to be permanently displayed, constitutes a powerful way to un-clutter interfaces. Options and guidelines exist for customizing and optimizing tip appearance and behavior, notably their shape, position, discoverability, and duration. Several jQuery and Javascript web-based frameworks support developers in customizing the appearance and behavior of tips consistently throughout their application (e.g., Toolipster 3.0, qTip2, Tipso, Hovercard, Powertip, Darktooltip, see also WikiUp).

While the appearance and behavior of a tip are rendered consistently across the features in an interface, the textual content displayed in each tip must be written on a case-by-case basis. This requires further distinction between *tooltips*, which serve to simply label a feature (e.g., "share folder"), and *infotips*, which expand upon its role, meaning, or function (e.g., "Share the content of this folder with members of your network").

Infotips provide users with an on-demand benefit of learning more about features that are new or unfamiliar. Similarly, infotips can serve to extend the descriptiveness of

S. Yamamoto (Ed.): HIMI 2015, Part I, LNCS 9172, pp. 226–234, 2015.
DOI: 10.1007/978-3-319-20612-7_22

any interface so as to accommodate less knowledgeable users. Guidelines from Microsoft Developer Network [1] state that infotips should be informative (e.g., they supplement a given feature label with additional details) and supplemental (e.g., goes actually beyond common sense or self-descriptiveness). Judgment is required to determine if each feature is unknown, advanced, or innovative, and is thus in need of an infotip formulation that can be of service to users.

This reasoning is substantiated by instructional design studies concerning the learning benefits of added explanations. Such studies show that while less knowledgeable people do benefit from additional explanatory material, more knowledgeable people process the material better without the additions [2] (see also [3, 4]). This latter outcome, known as expertise reversal effect, comes from the fact that added information increases the cognitive load of knowledgeable people without being of any use to them (for a review, see [5]). These considerations transpose well to the addition of infotips to a GUI, in that a) infotips should target users in the need of a little more knowledge about the current features to progress in their activity, and b) since they appear only on demand, and not automatically, infotips minimize the risk of expertise reversal effect.

This suggests that designers should devote some effort to writing infotips. For interfaces having dozens (or even hundreds) of features, though, the task of creating meaningful infotips can be laborious. Indeed, none of the previously listed web-based frameworks address the generation of tip content. We explore an automatic generation of tip content using machine learning techniques and natural language processing. In this approach, labels from an interface are inputted, and descriptions are predicted from a domain-specific corpus. In addition, familiarity criteria and synonymy attributes are leveraged to determine the relevance of the infotip and expand its descriptiveness, respectively.

2   Methods

We gathered representative tip descriptions into a corpus. This data was collected from, an online database [6] of short, informative descriptions of keyboard shortcuts for various software applications. Nearly ten thousand shortcut descriptions are published under their parent menu, application name, and operating system (Mac, Windows, Linux, or web). Using the web crawler Scrapy [7], data for each shortcut was extracted and randomly ordered line-by-line into a comma-separated corpus. The data was preprocessed using standard NLP techniques (Sect. 2.1). A transformation related to term frequency was applied to convert each shortcut document (as a bag of words) into an n-dimensional vector (Sect. 2.2). Then, a k-means clustering algorithm was performed to find natural groupings in the data. Parameters were tuned to optimize performance, such as the cluster number, documents per cluster, and run number (Sect. 2.3).

2.1   Corpus Construction

Our corpus was constructed by converting rows of comma-separated shortcut descriptions and parent menus into "documents" with features. Features are informative yet non-redundant values –in this case word stems– that serve to potentiate our ability to cluster input labels by their linguistic regularity. To create our features, we selected words from both shortcut description and menu membership (*i.e.,* parent menu fields).

After stripping away special characters and numbers from the text, the Natural Language Toolkit (NLTK) was used to tokenize the words and remove English stop words [8], or frequently occurring function words that are not contextually relevant, such as *the, is, a, that,* etc. The remaining words are then stemmed, which is the process of normalizing all inflected or derived words to their stem. Stemming, and other normalization techniques such as lowercasing the words, helps the clustering algorithm capture semantic relationships between words by transforming seemingly different tokens, such as *editing, Edit,* and *editor,* into a single feature (*edit*).

Although not used by the clustering algorithm, additional pre-processing of the text was applied for post-analysis. Each document was tagged for its part of speech (POS) using the maximum-entropy-based Stanford POS tagger [9]. As most shortcut descriptions begin with a verb, which is not a common way to begin written sentences in English, the Stanford POS tagger outperforms NLTK's default Treebank POS tagger [10] in correctly identifying leading verbs. In addition, each word of the shortcut description was lemmatized. This is similar to stemming, except the word context and POS is taken into.

We leveraged the word labels associated with the category of each label by pre-pending the token *tip-* or *menu-* to each word stem, which identifies whether the stem belongs to the shortcut description (*tip-*) or to the parent menu (*menu-*). For example, the tip *Copy a selection of text,* located in the parent menu *Edit,* would result in the following bag of words for the features: *copy select text tip-copy tip-select tip-text edit menu-edit.*

2.2   Vectorization and Clustering

Vectorization of the documents and clustering was performed with scikit-learn [11], which is a Python module designed for machine learning. Features are prepared by transforming them based on term frequency–inverse document frequency (tf–idf), which is a numerical statistic reflecting the relative importance of a word to a corpus [12]. The tf–idf transformation is often used in information retrieval and text mining for weighting words based on their frequency in a document and inversely weighting the number of documents across the collection in which they appear. A collection of features in all documents was first converted into a matrix of token counts. For each token in the count matrix, a composite weight was then created to reduce the impact of tokens that occur very frequently across all the documents. Tokens appearing in less than two documents were not included in the vectorization process. The tf-idf transformation thus serves to transform each document into an n-dimensional vector having one component for each word in the corpus.

Documents were clustered into similar categories by subjecting the above vector space to a k-means algorithm [13]. With this algorithm, N observations are partitioned into subsets of mutually exclusive clusters $\{c_1, c_2, ..., c_k\}$ so that each observation belongs to the cluster with the nearest mean. This is achieved by randomly selecting

k centroid seeds, then varying their locations until the within-cluster sum of squares is minimized. Clustering is unsupervised, meaning no label for each cluster is considered. We employ a "hard" clustering, meaning shortcuts were grouped into one and only one cluster. Distances between points were calculated using a Euclidean metric.

2.3   Optimization of Clustering Performance

A series of validations was conducted to improve clustering performance. Corpus documents were randomly assigned to training (90%) and test sets (10%), so that the test set corresponded to 1000 labels that were not used in the clustering. In machine learning, validation typically involves varying key parameters until optimal criteria are reached. In this case, we examined the optimal number of clusters, number of documents per cluster, and number of runs.

First, we examined dissimilarity among clusters, as clusters should be well separated and non-overlapping, with lower values indicating too many or too few clusters. This was accomplished with a standard measure of cluster dissimilarity called the silhouette score [14]. Let a_k be the average distance of each data point to its cluster centroid c_k, and let b_k be the average distance of each point in c_k to all other centroids. The silhouette score is then defined to be $1 - a_k/b_k$ for $a_k < b_k$, 0 for $a_k = b_k$, and $b_k / a_k - 1$ for $a_k > b_k$. By its definition, silhouette scores are always between -1 and 1, with values less than zero indicating poor clustering. The left side of Fig. 1 shows the silhouette vs. number of clusters k. The significant increase in silhouette score suggests a k value of at least 350. The right side of Fig. 1 shows the inertia vs. the cluster number k. The inertia is defined to be the sum of squares from each point to its closest centroid.

While the inertia is expected to decrease linearly with increasing k, a rapid convergence is observed toward the value $k = 350$. Combined, these results suggest that at least 350 clusters should be used for the clustering process.

Second, in order to return a consistent number of shortcut descriptions per cluster, we require that the number per cluster does not vary wildly. The left side of Fig. 2

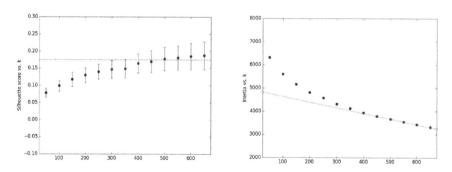

Fig. 1.   Silhouette scores vs. number of clusters k (left). No significant improvement above 0.17 is observed in the silhouette score beyond 350 clusters. While inertia is expected to decrease linearly with increasing numbers of clusters (right), a more rapid decrease is observed up to a cluster number of 350. When combined, these graphs suggest that a minimum value of $k = 350$ be used in our analysis.

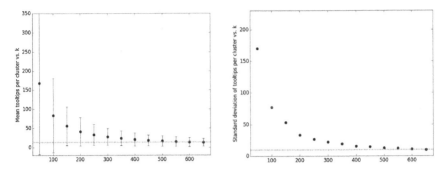

Fig. 2. Mean number of shortcuts per cluster vs. cluster number (left). In the right-hand figure, the standard deviation is plotted vs. cluster number. Stability in both distributions is achieved for values of k greater than 400.

shows the mean number of shortcuts per cluster vs. cluster number, along with standard deviation.

This data suggests that the mean number converges to a stable value for k > 400. The right side of Fig. 2 shows the size of the standard deviation vs. cluster number. No significant reduction in variation of number of shortcuts is achieved for k > 400. Thus, we select the value of k = 400 for our k-means clustering algorithm.

Third, we run the k-means algorithm multiple times with random starting centroids and keep the best result. While the k-means algorithm is one of the fastest clustering algorithms available, it is susceptible to falling into local minima. For each clustering, the algorithm is thus run five times with different centroid seeds, and the result with lowest inertia is kept. This ensures little-to-no variation in shortcut assignments when the algorithm is re-run in the future. In Fig. 3, we show the frequency distribution of shortcut descriptions by word length.

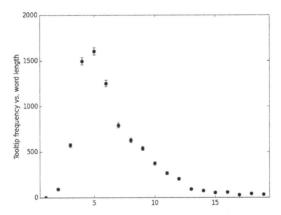

Fig. 3. Frequency of shortcuts by total number of words in their description. According to this graph, most shortcut descriptions in our corpus are five words in length, e.g., *Cancel command and close window*. Note: while stop words are counted in the above graph, non-alphanumeric characters and punctuation are not.

We found that the number of irrelevant candidates was lowered when the minimum number of shortcut descriptions in which a word must appear was set to two. In the following section, we discuss how candidate infotips are selected from the cluster that best matches a newly inputted label.

3   Results

3.1   Infotip Selection

Once the clustering has been performed, we inputted new labels from our test set and retrieved candidate shortcuts from the cluster with the highest degree of similarity. New labels were first preprocessed and vectorized in an identical manner as the shortcuts in the training set used by the k-means clustering algorithm. Once the best cluster had been found, the associated shortcut descriptions were extracted from this cluster. Stop words were removed and remaining words from the new label were compared against the candidate shortcuts. We calculated the percentage of normalized words from the new label that matched a word in the list of candidates. For example, consider the new label *Copy the text to clipboard*, which becomes *copy text clipboard* after normalization. If two of these words matched at least one word in the collection of candidate shortcut descriptions from the best cluster, the percentage for this new label would be 66.7%.

As we seek tips that are descriptive, we also considered candidate shortcut descriptions based on their word length. Synonyms for each word in the list of candidate were are also employed to improve the relevance of candidate shortcuts. This was accomplished with WordNet [15], a large lexical database of English nouns, verbs, adjectives, and adverbs that are grouped by their semantic relationship into *synsets*. We extracted word synonyms, hypernyms, hyponyms, and "similar" words from these synsets in order to both expand and refine the selection of shortcut candidates. If no word from the new label exactly matched a candidate shortcut description, the word was sought within a bag of "similar" words derived from the unmatched candidate. While no significant improvement was observed for "similar" words, the fraction of matches increased by about 10% when bags of synonym, hypernyms, and hyponyms were included. In Table 1, we list the percentages of new labels from the test set that were matched vs. the minimum word length for each shortcut candidate.

In the next section, we provide examples of candidate tips by our process for newly inputted labels chosen at random from our test set.

3.2   Examples

As GUI labels tend to be short in length, we skipped any labels from the test set greater than three words in length, after stop words had been removed. This served to remove shortcut descriptions that were wordier than a standard interface tooltip. We required that candidate infotips be at least three words long after stop-word removal. We thus differentiate between the length inputted labels and the resulting candidates of shortcut descriptions (infotips). This selection criterion guarantees that

Table 1. Fraction of words from new labels in test set that was matched to least one word from the candidate shortcut description in the best cluster. Minimum length is the minimum number of words required in the candidate shortcuts. Synonym, hypernyms, and hyponyms resulted in an increase of approximately 10%.

Min. length	Frac. of words matched in new label	Frac. with "similar" words	Frac. with synsets, hypo-/ hypernyms
1	0.62	0.63	0.74
2	0.60	0.60	0.71
3	0.52	0.53	0.63
4	0.45	0.45	0.55
5	0.36	0.37	0.46
6	0.29	0.29	0.38
7	0.22	0.23	0.29

the lengths of the infotip candidates are equal to or greater than those of the inputted labels. In this way, a label such as *Print all documents* would never return an uninformative infotip candidate such as *Print*. In Table 2, we show the result of several candidate infotips selected by our method, along with the corresponding label and parent menu inputted into our method.

Table 2. Example infotips generated from labels taken from the test set. Acceptable outcomes are listed for each label; those deemed unconvincing are listed in *italics*.

Menu / label	Infotip
Session / switch open window	- *Open new session*
	- *Open current session in PuTTY*
	- Cycle opened sessions
Image / file import	- Import multiple files or image sequences
	- Import one file or image sequence
Find / next in webpage	- Find next occurrence of search term
	- Find next find previous match
	- Find previous find next occurrence of search term
	- Find text on webpage
Compose message / paste without formatting	- *Paste as quotation*
Edit / deselect tracks	- Deselect all files
	- Deselect all the songs in the list
	- Select deselect file
Ribbon / expand ribbon	- Minimize or restore the ribbons
	- Show/hide the ribbon
	- Expand or minimize the ribbon
General / switch to debug mode	- Switch to Projects mode
	- Switch to Help mode
	- Switch to Edit mode

As Table 2 illustrates, several of the generated infotips match the inputted label rather well, such as *Cycle opened sessions* for the input label *switch open window*, and *Deselect all the songs in the list* for *deselect tracks*. As the sampling of infotips displayed in Table 2 was *ad hoc*, a more systematized rating scheme should be employed to determine the validity of our method in a more statistical way.

During the vectorization process, words occurring frequently throughout the training set receive less weight. This helps to offset the heavy weighting that ubiquitous words would receive otherwise. In our case, though, bias introduced by the tf-idf transform may not work as intended, as the impact of common interface labels, such as *paste and copy*, may be attenuated. However, common labels such as these correspond to basic functions that are familiar to most users. From the user-centered viewpoint advanced in introduction, this means that need for generating infotips is least justified for these labels. Conversely, the need for helpful infotips is greatest for interface labels that are less common or familiar, or too technical. Thus, the weighting scheme employed during vectorization may need to be tuned to match some predetermined threshold of familiarity established by corpus-based NLP techniques.

4 Perspectives

We envision several avenues along which the selection of infotips may be improved. For one, we could consider alternative vectorization transforms, such as a vector representation for words (VRW) model, which is an efficient implementation of the continuous bag-of-words and skip-gram architectures [16]. In the VRW model, a neural network is trained to generate a continuous vector representation of the words. While VRW models are known to suffer from their indifference to idiomatic phrases, they are particularly precise at capturing a large number of syntactic and semantic relationships among words. In the most general case, tf-idf and VRW transforms could be compared as components of a mixed model.

An altogether different clustering algorithm could be implemented, such as a Latent Semantic Indexing (LSI) model, which implements singular value decomposition in order to identify semantic patterns between terms and concepts in some reference corpus [17]. The LSI model is based on the idea that words used in the same context tend to have similar semantic relationships. This allows LSI models to accurately extract conceptual content of a text by establishing associations between terms that occur in similar contexts. Another refinement of our approach involves the expansion of the corpus used for the training process. For example, data dumps from technically relevant websites could be included, as well as help files and user documentation for various software applications. In addition, the method presented has potential for online learning, e.g., infotips may be hand-corrected by users and accepted back into the corpus for re-training. Finally, we are exploring several NLP techniques for improving infotip selection based on conditional word frequencies, named entity recognition, and grammatical features.

References

1. Microsoft Developer Network on Tooltips and Infotips. Accessed on January, 2015. http://msdn.microsoft.com/en-us/library/windows/desktop/dn742443%28v=vs.85%29.aspx
2. Yeung, A., Jin, P., Sweller, J.: Cognitive load and learner expertise: split-attention and redundancy effects in reading with explanatory notes. Contemp. Educ. Psychol. **23**, 1–21 (1998)
3. McNamara, D.S., Kintsch, W.: Are good texts always better? Interactions of text coherence, background knowledge and levels of understanding in learning from texts. Cogn. Instr. **14**, 1–43 (1996)
4. Mayer, R.E.: Research-based principles for the design of instructional messages. The case of multimedia explanations. Doc. Des. **1**, 7–20 (1999)
5. Sweller, J., Ayres, P.L., Kalyuga, S., Chandler, P.: The expertise reversal effect. Educ. Psychol. **28**(1), 23–31 (2003)
6. ShortcutWorld.com, a wiki-style reference database for keyboard shortcuts. http://www.shortcutworld.com
7. Hoffman, P.: Scrapy (2013). http://scrapy.org
8. Bird, S., Edwardd, L., Ewan, K.: Natural Language Processing with Python. O'Reilly Media Inc. (2009)
9. Toutanova, K., Klein, D., Manning, C., Singer, Y.: Feature-rich part-of-speech tagging with a cyclic dependency network. In: Proceedings of HLT-NAACL 2003, pp. 252–259 (2003)
10. Marcus, M.P., Santorini, B., Marcinkiewicz, M.A.: Building a large annotated corpus of english: the penn treebank. Comput. Linguist. **19**(2), 313–330 (1993)
11. Scikit-learn: Machine Learning in Python, Pedregosa et al., JMLR 12, p. 2825–2830 (2011)
12. Spärck Jones, K.: A statistical interpretation of term specificity and its application in retrieval. J. Documentation **28**, 11–21 (1972)
13. Lloyd, S.P.: Least squares quantization in PCM. IEEE Trans. Inf. Theor. **28**(2), 129–137 (1982)
14. Rousseeuw, P.J.: Silhouettes: a graphical aid to the interpretation and validation of cluster analysis. Comput. Appl. Math. **20**, 53–65 (1987)
15. Fellbaum, C. (ed.): WordNet: An Electronic Lexical Database. MIT Press, Cambridge, MA (1998)
16. Mikolov, T., Chen, K., Corrado, G., Dean, J.: Efficient estimation of word representations in vector space. In: Proceedings of Workshop at the International Conference on Learning Representations 2013 (2013)
17. Rehurik, R.: Scalability of Semantic Analysis in Natural Language Processing. Ph.D. thesis, Masaryk University, Brno, Czech Republic (2011)

Proposal of a Data Presentation Technique Using Four-Frame Cartoon Expression for a LifeLog System

Takashi Yoshino$^{(\boxtimes)}$ and Iori Osada

Faculty of Systems Engineering, Wakayama University, Wakayama, Japan
yoshino@center.wakayama-u.ac.jp, iori.osada@gmail.com

Abstract. In recent years, research on lifelogging has increased because of developments in information technology. However, few studies have dealt with communication with other people using lifelogging technology. Therefore, we have developed the BlogWear system, which automatically generates weblog entries using lifelog data. The results of our previous experiment showed that a large number of entries from lifelog data have few changes, and readers quickly tire of them. Therefore, this study proposes a method that generates a four-frame cartoon expression from lifelog data. The contribution of this study is to show that the use of four-frame cartoon expressions can make viewing lifelog data more enjoyable.

Keywords: Lifelog · Four-frame cartoon · Blog · Communication support

1 Introduction

Recent developments in information communication technology have led many researchers to become interested in lifelog support systems. Lifelogs store information about a human's daily life as digital data. There are two lifelog recording methods: automatic recording and manual recording by the user [1–3]. The recording equipment is small and increasingly sophisticated. Research into lifelogging is an active area of study, especially the applicability of lifelogs [1–3].

Few studies have examined the exchange of lifelog data. However, with the development of web services, Consumer Generated Media (CGM) are gaining popularity. In CGM, users contribute content to form part of the service, but CGM has poor collateral compared with the size of the cost to contribute contents in before. However, micro-blogging media such as Twitter represent a solution to this problem. Micro-blogging services allow users to contribute short sentences.

It is easy for users to contribute short sentences or photos. This is regarded as one of the reasons for the development of micro-blogs. Therefore, we have developed the BlogWear system, which automatically generates weblog entries using lifelog data [4,5]. The purpose of BlogWear is to promote communication

© Springer International Publishing Switzerland 2015
S. Yamamoto (Ed.): HIMI 2015, Part I, LNCS 9172, pp. 235–246, 2015.
DOI: 10.1007/978-3-319-20612-7_23

between the record person (logger) and the readers. BlogWear can automatically generate weblog entries using lifelog data, thus reducing the logger's burden of contribution. Experimental results indicated the following disadvantages of BlogWear: (1) BlogWear can create a lot of blog entries. (2) Minor differences in blog entries cause readers to become bored.

We found that these disadvantages decrease the logger's motivation. Thus, we propose a novel presentation method using four-frame cartoon expressions combining lifelog data. The purpose of this method is to summarize a lot of lifelog data and to add entertainment features to the content. We expect the method to motivate viewers' interest. Moreover, this should provide further motivation for the logger. The purpose of this research is to demonstrate the possibility of promoting communication by the automatic expression of lifelog data.

2 Related Work

The lifelog system is inspired by Vannevar Bush's concept of a memex [6]. A memex records everything that users see, hear, and read as digital data. This allows users to search a database for help in performing to their full potential. Microsoft developed MyLifeBits [7], which records everything that can be stored on a computer, such as images, music, e-mails, or the operational data of applications.

LifePod, which was developed by KDDI [8], combines a weblog and lifelog. This system uses a cellular phone and radio frequency identification (RFID). Users record their favorite things as lifelog data using a camera and the GPS of a cellular phone. By simply reading the RFID, LifePod users can record lifelog data. However, this system is less burdensome, because it does not involve amassing lifelog data; instead, it simply records a user's favorite activity. By nature, the lifelog system is mainly used by loggers. Our aim is to show a logger's lifelog data to a viewer with the aim of facilitating communication between the logger and the viewer.

Many researchers have focused on the effect of lifelogs. Sellen et al. conducted an experiment to investigate the effect that image data obtained through SenseCam [9] had on a viewer. Their results show that images automatically serve as long-term memory cues. Morishita et al. described the concept of the SpaceTag [10], in which the information provided varies with location and time. According to the results observed in an open experiment, SpaceTag benefits users who require location information, such as tourist information [11]. Kalnikaite et al. focused on the different effects of visual data and location data [12]. They confirmed that images promote a more genuine, detailed recall, whereas location data lead to inference.

Thus, many studies have reported the effects of lifelogs. However, these studies have focused on the effect of lifelog data on the loggers themselves. In contrast, in this study, we focus on the effect of lifelogs on both the loggers and their viewers. The purpose of this study is to investigate an approach for facilitating communication between loggers and viewers using lifelog data. We treat the

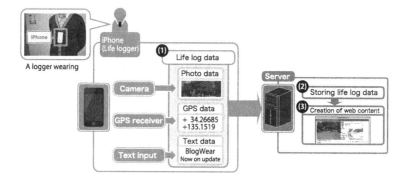

Fig. 1. System configuration of BlogWear.

behavior as a daily pattern. Our proposal uses a four-frame cartoon expression to produce a humorous impression of daily behavior.

3 BlogWear Overview

This chapter describes a BlogWear system that automatically generates weblog entries using lifelog data. BlogWear uses images and geographical locations (latitude and longitude) of various loggers as lifelog data.

3.1 System Configuration and Flow

Figure 1 shows the configuration of the BlogWear system. This system consists of an iPhone, a server, and a lifestreaming service. The iPhone records lifelog data and transmits them to the server. The server amasses lifelog data and generates and displays entries on BlogWear's webpage. The lifestreaming service provides information about a user's activities on the webpage. This study uses Twitter as the lifestreaming service.

The steps for recording lifelog data using an iPhone to generate entries are as follows.

1. Recording lifelog data
   The iPhone records lifelog data and generates information for entries.
2. Sending information for the entries to the server
   When the server receives information for the entries, it stores the information in its database.
3. Generating blog entries
   The server generates blog entries from its database, and automatically displays them on BlogWear's webpage.

3.2 Lifelog Application for iPhone

Our study used an iPhone as a tool for recording lifelog data. The iPhone can record image data and location data. The photo at the top-left of Fig. 1 shows an image of a logger wearing an iPhone.

Lifelog Recording Methods. We considered "automatic lifelog" and "manual lifelog" recording methods.

1. **Automatic lifelog.** The "automatic lifelog" records lifelog data automatically at preset intervals. We assume that this function is used when the logger wishes to record their daily life.
2. **Manual lifelog.** The "manual lifelog" records lifelog data at times determined by the logger. We assume that this function is used when the logger encounters a situation that they would like to record.

Recorded lifelog data are sent to the server at once.

Classification of Lifelog Data by an Event. BlogWear groups the activities, for example, meal times or going to school, that the logger encountered as "events."

This function improves the reading of a great deal of lifelog data. The logger determines each event. In other words, this research considers an event to be a record period set by the logger.

4   Presentation Method of the Lifelog Data

We discuss the following three methods of presenting lifelog data.

1. List expression
2. Separate expression
3. Four-frame cartoon expression

We call the presentations made with the above-mentioned expressions "content."

4.1   List Expression Method

The list expression shows lifelog data to a reader without processing. The left side of Fig. 2 shows an example of a list expression.

The list expression shows all photos recorded in the event in the photo space. The lower part of the screen displays routes on a map. The comments field shows a landmark at the recorded date and time, address and circumference. The address is shown to prefectural and city governments. This system uses reverse geocoding to find the address from the latitude and longitude.

4.2   Separate Expression Method

The separate expression separates content from communication services like weblogs and social network services (SNS). The left side of Fig. 2 shows an example of the separate expressions. A separate expression indicates each item recorded in the event separately. The content is shown in an article area. Each item of content has an address and a comment made by the logger. Articles generated automatically from lifelog data are indicated by a gray frame, and those formed manually are indicated by a blue frame. The left part of the separate expression screen displays routes on a small map.

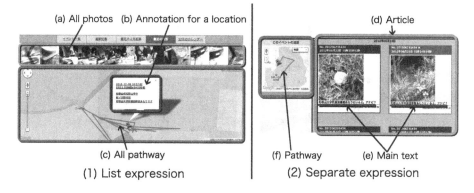

(a) All photos (b) Annotation for a location   (d) Article

(c) All pathway   (f) Pathway   (e) Main text

(1) List expression   (2) Separate expression

Fig. 2. Example of a list expression and separate expressions.

4.3 Four-Frame Cartoon Expression Method

The purpose of the four-frame cartoon expression is to summarize lifelog data and add an entertainment factor to the lifelog. We think this will arouse readers' interest. Moreover, we think that this will increase the number of readers, thus motivating the logger. Figure 3 shows an example of a four-frame cartoon expression on a screen. The four-frame cartoon expression creates one four-frame cartoon from each event.

5 Four-Frame Cartoon Generation Function Using Lifelog Data

We have developed a four-frame cartoon expression function for combining lifelog data.

5.1 Design Policy

The purpose of the four-frame cartoon expression is to encourage readers' interest, which will then motivate the logger.

1. Addition of an entertainment factor
   The results of previous experiments indicate that the lifelog of daily behavior patterns of a logger is tedious for readers. Therefore, we use four-frame cartoon expressions to add an entertainment factor to the content generated from lifelog data.
2. Maintaining motivation by a change in content
   Our experiments suggested that readers rapidly tire of the minor changes in presentation data. Therefore, the proposed method generates the content of lifelog data at random.

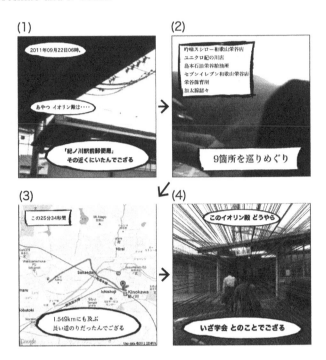

Fig. 3. Example of a four-frame cartoon expression.

3. Summary of lifelog data

The conventional BlogWear system showed all lifelog data as a separate expression. Our experimental results showed that these separate expressions are redundant for presenting all lifelog data to readers.

Therefore, our four-frame cartoon expression function generates a reduced amount of content, and generates four frames with a few story branches.

Thus, the method summarizes lifelog data from one event in one four-frame sequence, with the aim of reducing the readers' burden.

5.2   Processing of Each Frame

The four frames are created as follows.

First Frame. The background of the first frame is the most recent photo in each event. The words shown in the first frame present the BlogWear user's name and the most recently recorded landmark. The first frame is an introduction to each story. The purpose of the first frame is to arouse readers' interest. The first frame gives the latest information about a BlogWear user (logger) to a reader. The reader can easily grasp the logger's behavior from one event.

Second Frame. The background of the second frame is a randomly selected photo from each event. When the photo selected as the background has been recorded manually, the system draws "concentration lines" around the photo. A concentration line expresses the movement of a person or thing using additional lines peculiar to the cartoon. The system shows at most five landmarks from the event as words in a balloon. The total number of landmarks in the event is also indicated. This frame summarizes and presents information on all movement in the event. The randomly selected photo will unfold in a way that the reader cannot predict.

Third Frame. The third frame shows a map that has all the positional information recorded in the event. The words in a balloon state the time elapsed during the event, and the distance of the migration pathway. The words for its length are indicated according to the length of the displacement. We change how the story is unfolding by showing a map as the background. The background of the third frame is not a photo, but a map. This is the big difference from the other frames.

Fourth Frame. The background of the fourth frame is a randomly selected photo. When the photo selected as the background was recorded manually, the system draws concentration lines on the photo. This is like the processing of the second frame. The fourth frame displays a comment made by the logger. This comment, which is only shown in the last frame, is what the logger would most like to say about the event.

5.3   Changing the Function of Words

Our four-frame cartoon generation function can dynamically change the word style. The purpose of this function is to modify the content of the four frames. We have nine types of speaker, such as a normal Japanese person, provincial Japanese, samurai drama-inspired Japanese, a delinquent youngster, and so on.

6   Experiment

We carried out an experiment using the three lifelog presentation methods. We used pre-prepared log data. The experimental subjects were university students, graduate students, and staff at Wakayama University, Japan.

The experiments considered the following items.

1. How does each kind of presentation method stimulate readers' interest?
2. How does each kind of presentation method contribute to understanding the behavior of the logger?
3. How does each kind of presentation method influence the communication between logger and reader?

6.1   Experimental Lifelog Data

We used the lifelog data obtained from our past experiments. These lifelog data include both photos and positional information. The logger who generated the data is a graduate student of Wakayama University. These lifelog data gave a total of 36 events. Each event was used to generate the content for each of the presentation methods, giving a total of 108 content items.

6.2   Subjective Task

In the experiment, we showed 36 contents in each expression to all 18 subjects using the three presentation methods. The subjects then scored the content on four evaluation axes. The presentation order of the content was changed for each subject to remove order effects. Each subject answered a questionnaire after the task was completed. Each subject estimated while getting rest accordingly.

7   Results and Discussion

Figure 4 shows the evaluation results for each subject. Table 1 presents the questionnaire survey results. We used the following five-point Likert scale for the content evaluation and questionnaire survey—1: Strongly disagree, 2: Disagree, 3: Neutral, 4: Agree, and 5: Strongly Agree.

7.1   Amusement Value of the Content

The evaluation score for "I thought the content was amusing" in Fig. 4(1) shows that there is no significant difference in each presentation method. The four-frame cartoon expression scored more highly than the other presentation methods, as shown by the mode value of "I thought the content was amusing" in Table 1(1).

Some of the positive comments for our four-frame cartoon expression method were as follows.

– This expression relates a daily event humorously.
– This expression caught the eye with a unique expression.
– I think this expression has new value.

Some comments about the list expression were as follows.

– Positive comment: This expression is concise and easy to understand.
– Negative comment: When the situation is not readable from a photo, this expression is boring.

This expression is tired and a little monotonous. We found that the amusement of the list expression and separate expression methods depend directly on their own amusement value. Lifelogs deal with daily data, the nature of which often becomes mannerism. Therefore, we think that content presented by the list expression or separate expression methods also has a nature that often becomes mannerism. The four-frame cartoon method generates its own amusement in an expression. We think that the four-frame cartoon expression method may prevent content becoming tired.

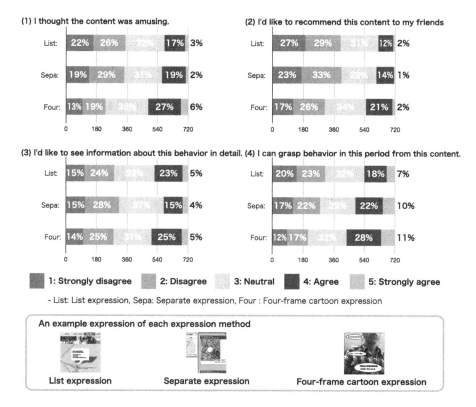

Fig. 4. Results of content evaluation by examinees.

7.2   Possibility of Communication

The results for "I'd like to recommend this content to my friends" in Fig. 4(2) shows that the four-frame cartoon expression method scores slightly higher than the other presentation methods. We found that the four-frame cartoon expression method is more attractive than the other techniques. However, "I'd like to give feedback (comment and evaluation) on the content" in Table 1(2) shows that there is no significant difference. Some positive comments on our four-frame cartoon expression method were as follows.

– I have something to say about the content (four-frame cartoon expression).
– I would like to comment or evaluate the content of the four-frame cartoon expression method.

About the list expression method, a subject commented that "I would like to comment if I want to know more detail." About the separate expression method, subjects commented that "The expression tends to make a comment like Facebook," and "I'd like to make a comment in each photo." Each presentation expression displays features of effective communication in the experimental results. The four-frame cartoon expression method triggers communication about the quality of the

Table 1. Results of questionnaire survey.

Question items	Method	Evaluation					Median value	Mode value
		1	2	3	4	5		
(1) I thought the content was amusing.	List	0	4	5	9	0	3.5	4
	Sepa.	0	2	6	9	1	4	4
	Four	0	1	3	6	8	4	5
(2) I'd like to give feedback (comment and evaluation) on the content.	List	2	2	5	6	3	3.5	4
	Sepa.	1	3	3	5	6	4	5
	Four	1	1	4	9	3	4	4
(3) The content was useful to grasp the behavior of a logger.	List	1	2	7	6	2	3	3
	Sepa.	0	2	6	6	4	4	3, 4
	Four	0	2	11	2	3	3	3
(4) I'd like to see content continually.	List	1	3	6	8	0	3	4
	Sepa.	1	4	5	8	0	3	4
	Four	1	0	4	8	5	4	4
(5) I'd like to make content with myself, too (I'd like to use this system.)	List	3	3	3	9	0	3.5	4
	Sepa.	1	5	6	5	1	3	3
	Four	0	3	4	6	5	4	4

four-frame cartoon expression. The list expression method provides communication by awakening interest in the behavior of the logger. The separate presentation method provides communication by making the photo a trigger.

7.3   Presented Information

The results for 'I'd like to see information about this behavior in detail" and "I can grasp behavior in this period from this content" in Fig. 4(3) and (4) shows that there is no significant difference between each presentation method.

Some of the positive comments on our four-frame cartoon expression method include:

- This expression provides a good volume of information for precisely grasping behavior.
- This expression is fascinating but incomprehensible.
- This expression was summarized too much, and a small part could not be grasped.
- This expression is more interested in amusement than the user's behavior.

The following positive comments were made about the list expression method.

- This expression is useful for grasping behavior across a big map.
- This expression transmits the user's rough behavior well.

The following negative comments were made about the list expression method.

– This expression could not grasp detailed behavior.
– I cannot understand the situation from a photo.

The separate expression method received the following comment.

– This expression can grasp the moment, but grasping the whole event is difficult.

Readers expect to be amused more than to grasp the logger's behavior from the four-frame cartoon expression method. The list expression helps give a rough grasp of behavior, and the separate expression method is helpful for obtaining small nuggets of information about behavior. We found that the four-frame cartoon expression method is less likely to give readers information about the logger's behavior than the other presentation methods.

7.4   Continuity of Use

There is no significant difference between the responses for "I'd like to see content continually" and "I'd like to make content myself, too (I'd like to use this system)" in Table 1(4) and (5). The following responses about the four-frame cartoon expression method were given in the questionnaire.

– This expression may be good for telling others that I have gone out in a funny way.
– This expression method can formulate an original story. Hence, it becomes pleasant.

The subjects considered the list expression to provide the clearest information. Of the separate expression method, subjects commented that "It does not change with other SNS," and "The function of Facebook and Twitter is enough." We think that the four-frame cartoon expression method can trigger continued use of lifelog systems.

8   Conclusion

We have developed an automatic blog article generation system called BlogWear. The results of previous experiments indicated that relatively few changes across a great many blog articles generated from lifelog data reduced users' motivation. Therefore, we proposed a novel lifelog presentation method using a four-frame cartoon expression. The contribution of this paper is to show that the four-frame cartoon expression method offers something novel to readers compared with other expression methods.

References

1. Shimura, S., Hirano, Y., Kajita, S., Mase, K.: Emotion recording interface using diary for experience recordings, IPSJ SIG Technical report, vol. 2005-HI-95, pp. 61–68 (2005) (in Japanese)
2. Sawahata, Y., Aizawa, K.: Wearable media for constant recording of daily life, Technical report of IEICE, vol. 102, No. 554, pp. 13–18 (2003) (in Japanese)
3. Tokunaga, S., Matsumoto, S., Nakamura, M.: Recording receipts for consumer-oriented lifelog services, Technical report of IEICE, vol. 110, No. 281, pp. 95–100 (2010) (in Japanese)
4. Kosuge, T., Yoshino, T.: Development and evaluation of blog entry auto-generation system using lifelog data, IPSJ SIG Technical report, vol. 2009, No. 10, pp. 1–8 (2009) (in Japanese)
5. Osada, I., Yoshino, T.: Evaluation of information provision methods for website audience on a life log collection system, Technical report of IEICE, vol. 110, No. 281, pp. 87–94 (2010) (in Japanese)
6. Bush, V.: As we may think. Proc. Atlantic Monthly **176**(1), 101–108 (1945)
7. Jim, G.: MyLifeBits: fulfilling the memex vision. In: Proceedings of the Tenth ACM International Conference on Multimedia, pp. 235–238 (2002)
8. Minamikawa, A., Kotsuka, N., Honjo, M., Morikawa, D., Nishiyama, S., Ohashi, M.: RFID supplement for mobile-based life log system, applications and the internet workshops. In: International Symposium on SAINT Workshops 2007, pp. 50. IEEE (2007)
9. Sellen, A., Fogg, A., Aitken, M., Hodges, S., Rother, C., Wood, K.: Do life-logging technologies support memory for the past?: an experimental study using sense-cam. In: Proceedings of the SIGCHI Conference on Human Factors in Computing Systems, pp. 81–90. ACM (2007)
10. Morishita, K., Nakao, M., Tarumi, H., Kambayashi, Y.: Design and implementation of the spacetag prototype system: an object system with spatio-temporarily limited access. Trans. Inf. Process. Soc. Jpn. **41**(10), 2689–2697 (2000)
11. Tarumi, H. et al.: Open experiments of mobile sightseeing support systems with shared virtual worlds. In: Proceedings of the 2006 ACM SIGCHI International Conference on Advances in Computer Entertainment Technology, No. 13. ACM (2010)
12. Kalnikaite, V., Sellen, A., Whittaker, S., Kirk, D.: Now let me see where I was: understanding how lifelogs mediate memory. In: Proceedings of the 28th International Conference on Human Factors in Computing Systems, pp. 2045–2054. ACM (2010)

Search in One's Hand: How Users Search a Mobile Library Catalog

Tao Zhang[1], Xi Niu[2(✉)], Liugen Zhu[2], and Hsin-liang Chen[3]

[1] Libraries, Purdue University, 504 West State Street, West Lafayette,
IN 47907, USA
zhanl022@purdue.edu
[2] School of Informatics and Computing, Indiana University,
535 West Michigan Street, Indianapolis, IN 46202, USA
{xiniu,louizhu}@iupui.edu
[3] Palmer School of Library and Information Science, Long Island University,
720 Northern Boulevard, Brookville, NY 11548, USA
hsin.chen@liu.edu

Abstract. With the rapid growth of mobile devices, mobile websites become an important channel of library resources and services. The mobile catalog is often significantly different from its desktop version in interface and features, but few studies of library catalog search behavior have been focused on mobile catalog searches. We present a study on user search behavior with a mobile library catalog based on transaction log analysis. We compared mobile and desktop catalog search behaviors and highlighted the similarities and differences, which could provide important evidence for improving mobile library catalogs' search performance and usability.

Keywords: Mobile search behavior · Library search · Search log analysis · Mobile application development

1 Introduction

With the rapid development of mobile technology, the amount of searches conducted on mobile devices has dramatically increased. A recent report by the Pew Internet and American Life Project showed that over one third of cell phone activities are looking for information online [1]. Particularly for libraries, recent surveys showed that a majority of users expect to use mobile devices to access library resources including the catalog, databases, and reference services [2, 3]. The number of libraries offering mobile sites and mobile catalogs is rapidly growing [4]. Thus mobile websites have become an important channel of library resources and services. The mobile catalog is the core of a library's mobile website, and it is often significantly different from its desktop counterpart in terms of interface and features. While previous researchers examined users' search behavior with desktop library catalogs, few studies were focused on mobile catalog searches. To fill this gap, we conducted a transaction log analysis of user search behavior with a mobile library catalog. In the study we compared mobile and desktop catalog search behaviors and identified the differences, which could be used as a basis for improving mobile catalog's search performance and usability.

© Springer International Publishing Switzerland 2015
S. Yamamoto (Ed.): HIMI 2015, Part I, LNCS 9172, pp. 247–257, 2015.
DOI: 10.1007/978-3-319-20612-7_24

2 Related Work

2.1 Mobile Websites and Libraries

Library websites provide users with access to the catalog, databases, online journals, as well as different types of information such as locations, hours, services, and events. Libraries have been attempting to implement these elements on their mobile websites along with the advancement of mobile web. As an early example, West et al. reported the development of a mobile website on small-screen devices (e.g., PDA) for Ball State University Libraries [5], which encompassed the library catalog, journal search, videos about the libraries, collection information, inter-library loan and course reserves. The UC San Diego Libraries developed a mobile website using rapid development and testing cycles and the mobile website included hours, catalog, ask a librarian, research tools and databases, maps and directions, contacts, and a link to the full desktop site [6]. Regarding the elements of mobile websites, Bridges et al. suggested that libraries should first focus on time-sensitive and location-based services [7]. It is also important to understand library users' likely goals and tasks in mobile use scenarios [8].

For library catalogs on the mobile websites, there have been several vendor-supplied solutions, such as the AirPAC by Innovative Interfaces and WorldCat Mobile by OCLC, although there was a lack of customization and feature enhancement among those solutions [7]. Libraries have also developed their own mobile catalogs, an example of which is the mobile catalog at Oregon State University Libraries [8]. The mobile catalog could be searched by keyword, title, subject, ISBN, and course reserves by instructor or subject. The search results include call numbers, availability, and physical locations; and each result (item record) includes title, author, description or table of contents, and a link to the item's shelf view. Users can email or text the item's call number from the mobile catalog. An emerging trend of mobile website and mobile catalog is the responsive design of interfaces to support a wide range of mobile devices with various screen sizes and resolutions [9, 10].

2.2 Mobile Search Behavior

With the increasing use of mobile devices as an essential platform for information access, it is important to understand the information access behaviors of mobile users, particularly on their use of mobile devices for query-based search and information browsing. A significant part of studies on mobile search behaviors are based on the analysis of transaction logs. Transaction logs are electronic records of user interactions (e.g., clicking on a link, entering search queries, selecting a search field, etc.) with information retrieval systems. Although the format of transaction logs may vary depending on specific server settings, most logs contain information elements such as the particular page (URL) requested by the user, the identity of the requesting user (IP address), the date and time of the request, and whether the request was successful [11]. Transaction logs capture users' behavior in natural settings and can accumulate to a large amount of data over time. Analysis of transaction logs can thus generate details of user behavior and interaction with the system at a large scale.

In general, previous studies have found that the diversity of mobile search queries was far lower than desktop searches, the length of mobile search queries was shorter, and users spend significantly more effort (time and key presses) to enter query terms [12, 13], possibly due to the physical constraints of mobile devices.

A seminal study by Church et al. analyzed the search behavior of more than 600,000 European mobile users in late 2005 [13]. They found that browsing dominated mobile information access in terms of traffic, but sessions involving search activities tended to be significantly longer and with more data usage than sessions without search. They compared a range of metrics of search and browsing behavior (e.g., query length, query reformulation, topic and interests) between mobile and desktop users. The results suggested that mobile search was in an early stage of development comparable to the desktop search in the mid 1990's. The majority of mobile users (76 %) used Google as their search engine, but the remaining 24 % of users used approximately 30 other search engines. Both mobile and desktop searches rarely used advanced search features. The average query length of mobile searches was shorter than desktop searches (2.06 vs. 2.3 query terms). Mobile searches had a high rate of query reformulation (23 %). The query substitution rate (i.e., replacing query terms without changing the query length) of mobile searches was 47 %, which was higher than the rate found in desktop search. Mobile searches contained a more limited set of query terms than desktop searches, probably because the content on the mobile Internet was relatively limited.

Users' search behavior with mobile devices is changing over time as users gain more experience. Kamvar and Baluja found that from 2005 to 2007 users typed faster (56.3 vs. 39.8 s) and increased their search query length (average 2.3 vs. 2.6 words). The queries were less homogeneous, as the top query in 2005 accounted for 1.2 % of all queries but that percentage decreased to 0.8 % in 2007.

There is an important distinction regarding the study of search behavior based on transaction logs between web search engines and digital library catalogs [14]. The goal of web search engine log analysis is to characterize users' information needs, such as how users make request by submitting queries; how users access and select search results; and how the search engine organizes and presents search results. Digital library catalogs usually have well-organized and explicitly described library collections (i.e., objects with much higher quality metadata than common web pages); and the goal of transaction log analysis is to study how users interact with the search interface in order to improve the effectiveness and efficiency of the search process.

Although a great deal of the literature was focused on users' search behavior with desktop library catalogs (more recently, discovery tools) [e.g., 15–17], little research has investigated how users search the mobile library catalogs. Extending previous studies that reported users' expectations and needs of libraries' mobile websites and catalogs, research on mobile catalog search behavior could reveal how the mobile interface supports information retrieval and how it should be better designed for the mobile context. Therefore, the goal of this study was to understand users' search behavior with a mobile library catalog. Particularly, we expected the study could help answer the following research questions: (1) who were the mobile users and what technologies mobile users used to access the mobile catalog; and (2) how users searched the mobile catalog and whether there was any difference between mobile and desktop catalog searches.

3 Research Method

3.1 Study Site

The mobile library catalog we studied was part of the University of North Carolina at Chapel Hill (UNC) Libraries' mobile website. The mobile website was launched in 2009 to support mobile users finding books and basic information such as library hours and branch locations. Users are automatically directed to the mobile website if they are using a mobile device. The mobile catalog interface was developed internally at UNC Libraries by accessing and reformatting the XML data into mobile-friendly representation from the desktop catalog (Endeca). The interface was implemented in PHP and iui web UI framework for mobile devices.

The mobile catalog was designed to support a primary use case: searching for a specific or known item by title or author. Thus it does not include most of the advanced search options in the desktop catalog. The item level display in the mobile catalog was designed to show essential item information, with clearly laid out physical location information and link for further actions. Figure 1 shows the homepage of the UNC Libraries mobile website and main interface of the mobile catalog. On the Catalog page, users enter search queries in the standard search box and the search fields include *Keyword, Title, ISBN, Journal Title, Author*, and

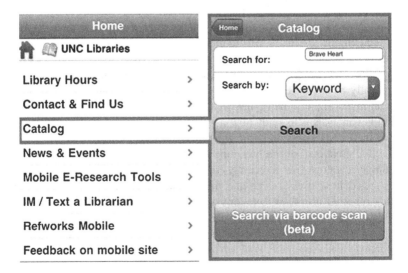

Fig. 1. The UNC Libraries' mobile website and mobile catalog

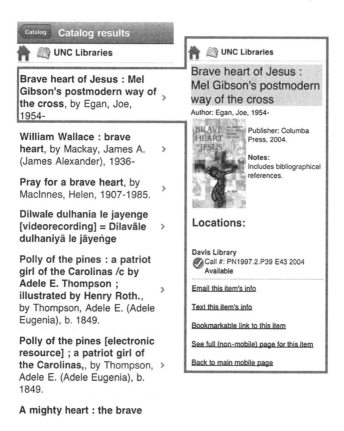

Fig. 2. The search results page and item page of the mobile catalog

Subject. Figure 2 shows the results list page and item page when users select a result from the list. Options on the item page include email, text, bookmark, and link to the full item page on the desktop catalog.

3.2 Data Collection

We used Google Analytics to understand basic user information and conducted deeper transaction logs of the mobile catalog for search behavior analysis. The time window for the analysis was one month, from March 1 to March 31, 2012, for which we collected 759 useful log records for 216 sessions from the mobile catalog server. In addition, we also analyzed the log data (21,685 records) from desktop search during the same time window. Information in each log record included IP address, date, time, URL requested, referrer URL, and user agent. The logs were parsed and imported into SAS 9.2 for statistical analysis. We also used a previously developed visualization application, VUTL [18], to visualize the log information and explore potential behavioral patterns.

Table 1. The top ten mobile devices used to access the mobile website

	Mobile device	Number of visits
1	Apple iPhone	357
2	Apple iPod Touch	63
3	Apple iPad	38
4	Not set	25
5	HTC ADR6300 Incredible	15
6	HTC EVO 4G	12
7	Samsung SC-02B Galaxy S	10
8	Sony Ericsson LT15i Xperia Arc	10
9	HTC Glacier	7
10	HTC ADR6350 Droid Incredible 2	5

4   Results

4.1   User Overview

Google Analytics data showed that visits to the mobile website were steadily increasing since its launch in 2009, from 1.14 % of overall traffic to the libraries' websites in spring 2011 to 3.45 % in spring 2012. During March 2012, the mobile website received 755 visits from 455 unique visitors. Among the 755 visits, 329 (43.6 %) were new visits and the rest 426 (56.4 %) were returning visits. The majority of the visits (692, 91.7 %) were from the U.S. Most of visitors were from North Carolina, especially the Research Triangle Area, where UNC is located. This suggests that the mobile website was primarily used by local users. Table 1 shows the top ten mobile devices used to access the mobile website (the No. 4 "Not set" means Google Analytics was not able to identify the mobile device for the visits). Most of the mobile devices were smartphones except for Apple iPod Touch and iPad.

4.2   Search Behavior

Action Distribution. The simple functionalities of the mobile catalog limited the types of user actions it could support. We identified three possible actions: *TypeQuery*, where the user typed search terms in the search box; *SwitchSearchField*, where the user switched between search fields for the inputted search query; and *ViewRecord*, where the user clicked an item on the search results page and opened the item page. The distribution of the three actions and its comparison with desktop searches are shown in Fig. 3. Note that the *TypeQuery* and *ViewRecord* actions were fairly evenly distributed for mobile searches and the *TypeQuery* action has a lower percentage than *ViewRecord*. On the contrary, the *TypeQuery* action in desktop searches had a higher percentage than *ViewRecord*. Switching search fields was uncommon for both mobile and desktop catalog searches.

The average time spent on each type of action was also calculated and shown in Table 2. The average time for typing a query was comparable between mobile and

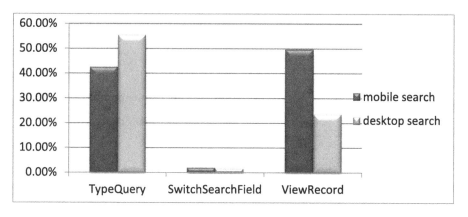

Fig. 3. Action distribution between mobile and desktop search

Table 2. Average time spent on actions

Action	Average time and standard deviation in mobile searches (seconds)	Average time and standard deviation in desktop searches (seconds)
Type query	44.8 (7.6)	43.7 (12.6)
Switch search field	95.8 (46.2)	81.7 (49.1)
View record	125.9 (100.4)	31.7 (20.8)

desktop searches. The relatively large standard deviation for typing queries in mobile searches suggests that mobile users had higher variations in formulating their queries than desktop users.

We defined session length as the number of actions within a particular session, and set boundaries between sessions if more than 30 min of inactivity occurred. Figure 4 shows the distribution of session lengths for mobile and desktop searches. Sessions longer than 30 actions were not displayed due to their low percentage (<the mobile website0.1 %). The session length distribution between mobile and desktop searches was roughly consistent with some differences at the lower end. Most search sessions were brief and the average number of actions per session was 3.5. The two-action session was the most common for mobile searches while the single-action session was the most frequent for desktop searches. Further visualization of sessions showed that the two-action pattern "*TypeQuery - ViewRecord*" was the most common action sequence among mobile searches.

Search Sessions. The average query length of mobile searches was 2.3 terms, comparable with the average of desktop search (2.7 terms). This similarity is in line with the comparable average time for typing queries in mobile and desktop searches. Two-term queries were the most frequent (32.5 %) among all queries and queries longer than six terms were very rare.

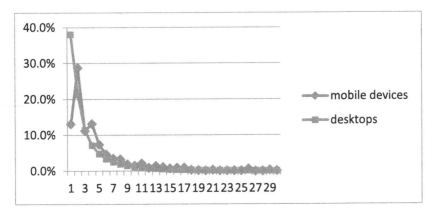

Fig. 4. The session length (number of actions) distribution for mobile and desktop searches

The most common search field among mobile searches was the default option *Keyword* (Fig. 5), similar to desktop searches and previous findings [13]. The *ISBN* search, usually a very specific and close-ended search, was much more common in mobile searches; while the exploratory and open-ended *Subject* search was less frequent in mobile searches than in desktop searches. These results suggest that users of the mobile catalog had a clearer goal of their searches and were looking for very specific information (e.g., a particular book).

Query Formulation and Reformulation. Approximate 48 % of mobile search sessions involved query reformulation, which is close to the percentage of desktop search sessions (50 %). The average number of clicks after each query formulation was 1.2, higher than the average number of 0.8 in desktop searches. This is possibly due to the fact that search results in the mobile catalog had limited information due to the screen display constraint and users had to view the item page to get more detailed information.

From the visualization of search logs of the mobile catalog, the most frequent queries were book title or author names, such as *From Darkness into Light, Principles*

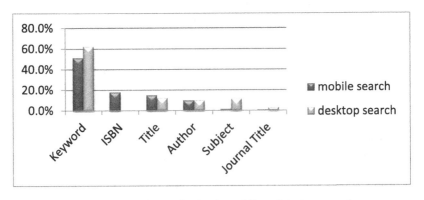

Fig. 5. Search field distribution in mobile and desktop searches

of Biochemistry, Hunger games, Nancy Bercaw, and *Lehringer*. Most of these book title and author name queries pointed to specific items in the catalog. Topic searches or open-ended searches were rarely seen. This is different from the desktop searches, where a considerable portion of searches were topical or open-ended.

Mobile searches had similar query reformulation patterns with desktop searches, as many reformulations involved subtle changes to or simple deviations from the original queries. This observation is consistent with White and Marchionini's finding that in desktop searches many further queries were simply "syntactic variants" of the initial queries [19].

Three reformulation strategies were identified from the log data: narrowing by adding query terms, broadening by removing query terms, and paralleling by changing query terms. Broadening was much less common than narrowing in mobile searches. There were no consecutive uses of broadening or narrowing in search sessions. Instead, the combination of adding, removing, and changing query terms was common. One example is: *botanical data* → *mods* → *mods metadata* → *darwincore* → *darwin core* → *Darwin core metadata*. A few users switched the search fields in order to change the search scope. Two examples are: *An American rhetoric* (keyword) → *Watt, w.w.* (author); and *Beyond post process* (keyword) → *Dobrin, Sidney* (Author). A possible reason for this switch is the original queries led to too many search results from the catalog, so that the user was trying to narrow down the search scope.

5 Discussion

In this study, we analyzed information from Google Analytics of the UNC Libraries mobile website and transaction logs from the mobile and desktop catalogs. The results showed that the mobile website was used mostly by local users with Apple mobile devices. Possible interactions with the mobile catalog were limited, due to the limited functionalities of the mobile catalog. Typing query and viewing item record were the dominant actions in mobile searches, while users rarely switched the search field. The query length and session length of mobile searches were comparable to desktop searches. Most mobile searches were about specific items; and exploratory searches were rare with the mobile catalog, different from the combined exploratory and known item searches with the desktop catalog.

There were differences of action distribution between mobile and desktop searches. Different from previous studies [12, 13], users spent less time on typing queries than viewing item records, possibly due to the mature input techniques on most current mobile devices. Users clicked more on the search results and spent more time viewing records than desktop searches, which is different from Church et al.'s finding [13]. This difference could be caused by the fact that the mobile catalog interface puts more emphasis on item level information than the search results list.

The percentage of queries reformulated in mobile searches was close to the percentage of desktop searches. While previous studies on general web searches [20] indicated that desktop searches had higher percentage of query reformulations than mobile searches, the recent development of smartphone interfaces has enabled users to overcome the usual input constraint and conduct more searches as they would with desktop catalogs. Similarly, the average query length of mobile searches was close to desktop searches and the longest mobile query we found was 14 terms. This suggests the traditional gap of query input between mobile and desktop searches is shrinking.

Our analysis of the query terms and search field distribution suggested that specific item (or known item) searches were common with mobile catalogs and the ability to locate the most relevant result is important. Thus the design of mobile catalogs need to well support this unique use scenario. For example, the relevance ranking could be adjusted to emphasize more on known items and the interface should allow easy change of the query and search field.

6 Conclusion

This study was an initial effort on investigating how users conduct searches in mobile library catalogs. The results revealed the similarities and differences of search behavior between mobile and desktop library catalog searches. The differences are partly due to the different motivations of mobile and desktop users, and partly caused by the simple mobile catalog interface with limited features for mobile users. Our findings could be used as a basis for further examination of mobile search behaviors with library catalogs and the improvement of mobile library catalogs.

References

1. Duggan, M., Smith, A.: Cell Internet Use 2013., Washington, D.C. (2013)
2. Caniano, W.T., Catalano, A.: Academic libraries and mobile devices: user and reader preferences. Ref. Libr. **55**, 298–317 (2014)
3. Seeholzer, J., Salem, J.A.: Library on the go: a focus group study of the mobile web and the academic library. Coll. Res. Libr. **72**, 9–20 (2010)
4. M-Libraries - Libraries offering mobile interfaces or applications. http://www.libsuccess.org/M-Libraries
5. Faust, B.D., Hafner, A.W., West, M.A.: Expanding access to library collections and services using small-screen devices. Inf. Technol. Libr. **25**, 103–107 (2006)
6. Critchlow, M., Friedman, L., Suchy, D.: Using an agile-based approach to develop a library mobile website. Code4Lib J. (12) (2010)
7. Bridges, L., Gascho Rempel, H., Griggs, K.: Making the case for a fully mobile library web site: from floor maps to the catalog. Ref. Serv. Rev. **38**, 309–320 (2010)
8. Griggs, K., Bridges, L.M., Rempel, H.G.: Library/mobile: tips on designing and developing mobile web sites. Code4Lib J. (8) (2009)
9. Gayhart, L., Khalid, B., Belray, G.: The Road to Responsive: University of Toronto Libraries' Journey to a New Library Catalogue Interface. Code4Lib J. **23**, 1–17 (2014)
10. Lynch, K.: Creating a seamless cross-platform online experience for mobile users. Code4Lib J. **26**(16), 1 (2012)
11. Jansen, B.J.: Search log analysis: what it is, what's been done, how to do it. Libr. Inf. Sci. Res. **28**, 407–432 (2006)
12. Baeza-Yates, R., Dupret, G., Velasco, J.: A study of mobile search queries in japan. Proc. Int. World Wide Web Conf. (2007)

13. Church, K., Smyth, B., Cotter, P., Bradley, K.: Mobile information access: a study of emerging search behavior on the mobile internet. ACM Trans. Web. **1**, 1–38 (2007)

14. Agosti, M., Crivellari, F., Di Nunzio, G.M.: Web log analysis: a review of a decade of studies about information acquisition, inspection and interpretation of user interaction. Data Min. Knowl. Disc. **24**, 663–696 (2011)

15. Lown, C., Sierra, T., Boyer, J.: How users search the library from a single search box. Coll. Res. Libr. **74**, 227–241 (2012)

16. Mischo, W.H., Schlembach, M.C., Bishoff, J., German, E.M.: User search activities within an academic library gateway: implications for web-scale discovery systems. In: Popp, M.P., Dallis, D. (eds.) Planning and Implementing Resource Discovery Tools in Academic Libraries, pp. 153–173. Information Science Reference, Hershey (2012)

17. Niu, X., Zhang, T., Chen, H.: Study of user search activities with two discovery tools at an academic library. Int. J. Hum. Comput. Interact. **30**, 422–433 (2014)

18. Niu, X., Hemminger, B.M.: A Method for Visualizing Transaction Logs of a Faceted OPAC. Code4Lib J. (12) (2010)

19. White, R.W., Marchionini, G.: Examining the effectiveness of real-time query expansion. Inf. Process. Manage. **43**, 685–704 (2007)

20. Kamvar, M., Kellar, M., Patel, R., Xu, Y.: Computers and iphones and mobile phones, oh my!: a logs-based comparison of search users on different devices. In: Proceedings of 18th International Conference on World Wide Web, pp. 801–810 (2009)

Knowledge Management

Fusing Text and Image Data with the Help of the OWLnotator

Giuseppe Abrami[1]([⊠]), Alexander Mehler[1], and Dietmar Pravida[2]

[1] Johann Wolfgang Goethe-Universität Frankfurt am Main, Frankfurt, Germany
`abrami@em.uni-frankfurt.de`
[2] Frankfurter Goethe-Museum/Freies Deutsches Hochstift, Frankfurt, Germany

Abstract. A central challenge for any approach to mining multimedia data concerns the availability of a *unified* semantics that allows for the *fusion* of multicodal information objects. To meet this challenge, a format is needed that enables the representation of multimedia data even across the border of different (e.g. iconic and symbolic) codes using the *same* ontology. In this paper, we introduce the *OWLnotator* as a first step to meeting this dual challenge by example of text-image relations. The *OWLnotator* is presented as part of the *eHumanities Desktop*, a browser-based, platform-independent environment for the support of collaborative research in the digital humanities. It focuses on modeling and analyzing multicodal, multimedia information objects as studied in the humanities. The eHumanities Desktop contains a wide range of tools for managing, analyzing and sharing resources based on a scalable concept of access permissions. Within this framework, we introduce the *OWLnotator* as a tool for annotating intra- and intermedia relations of artworks. The OWLnotator allows for modeling relations of symbolic and iconic signs of various levels of resolution: ranging from the level of elementary constituents to the one of complete texts and images. To this end, the *OWLnotator* integrates *TEILex* (a system for interrelating corpus and lexicon data as part of the eHumanities Desktop) with the expressiveness of *OWL*-based ontologies in order to meet the first part of our twofold challenge. As an evaluation, we illustrate the *OWLnotator* by means of *"Illustrations of Goethes Faust"*.

1 Introduction

At present, the field of digital humanities – and especially of digital art history – is still in its inception phase. Its main goals are to provide researchers access to large collections of images and to enable them to handle those materials. The first task is well understood and its importance is sufficiently appreciated. The digitizing of extensive bodies of images housed in archives and museums is under way all over the world, and it will continue to be a priority for most institutions for some time to come. There is an acute awareness of the necessity of standards for digitizing collections, some best practices have been established and are widely accepted. On the other side, the tools for exploring those research materials in-depth are still in need of being developed. For the descriptive metadata of images, museums have

© Springer International Publishing Switzerland 2015
S. Yamamoto (Ed.): HIMI 2015, Part I, LNCS 9172, pp. 261–272, 2015.
DOI: 10.1007/978-3-319-20612-7_25

generally adopted the CIDOC *Conceptual Reference Model* [5], which provides an extensible ontology for concepts and information in cultural heritage and museum documentation. However, the development of adequate content research tools for large volumes of digitized images is, owing to the inherent complexity of the task, not so far advanced. And yet, there is a need for devices that allow fine-grained searches in order to find similarities, non-obvious affiliations, patterns and connections between images and their relations to other media such as texts. At the present stage, one possible next step is to focus on single small- or mid-size corpora and develop viable solutions for some well-defined tasks of possibly general interest that allow further extension. A relatively coherent and thematically connected corpus of illustrations to a single literary work seems to be a good starting point for further explorations in digital art history and literary studies. Literary illustrations, by definition, stand in a relationship to the literary work they are supposed to illustrate. A vast part of the corpus will inevitably be of a conventional quality and thereby prevent that proposed solutions do not satisfy the requirements of extensibility and non-ad-hocness.

A written text presents a story world, whose inconspicuous conventional elements do not need to be explicitly described or can even dispense with any explicit mention, because the cognitive abilities of the reader will readily supply them. An illustrator cannot help but making such elements explicit and thereby supplementing and commenting on the text. The initiative is left to the artist, but at the same time there is a steady tradition of iconography that supports his endeavors and ensures that he will be understood. Thus, the relation between text and image and the devices of rendering complex narrative situations by a combination of typical pictorial elements is necessarily a complex one, and yet, the complexity should stay within the limits of a manageable one.

It will be an arduous task to develop the tools that help scholars accustomed to the highly developed and sophisticated methods and standards of the humanities in their daily work. Until that point will be reached, a large amount of elementary work needs to be done. But even on a much lower level, the digital exploration of images (such as literary illustrations) of a comparatively large corpus will offer possibilities that could not otherwise exist and allow scholars to ask and answer new questions. At the same time, the digital capturing of the contents of images by description, analysis and classification should allow a more intense and diverse use of image archives and collections in museums and for many educational purposes.

The present paper is about a tool in support of these goals. It concerns the mining of multimedia data based on a *unified* semantics that allows for the *fusion* of multicodal information objects. This is exemplified by text-image relations that are easily established by human beings to a degree still unequaled by any approach to automatic text or image understanding. To meet this and related challenges, a format is needed that enables the representation of multimedia data even across the border of different (e.g. iconic and symbolic) codes using the *same* ontology. In the line with previous work of the project "Illustrations of Goethes Faust"[1],

---

[1] https://www.goethehaus-frankfurt.de/sammlungen/digitaler-katalog.

images are the initial point for our paper. In the context of this project[2], we created a corpus of 2500 illustrations. The illustrations are segmented [1] in order to relate their subimages to segments of the "Faust" text corpus. In the present paper, we investigate the information content of images. To answer questions about this content by means of large corpora, a computer based solution is necessary. It has to face that based on ever changing research interests, the focus of information to be explored will vary. Therefore, flexibility is an indispensable requirement for the system to be developed. In this paper, we describe the so-called *OWLnotator*, a highly flexible system for the annotation of multimedia corpora of texts and images using OWL-based ontologies. The *OWLnotator* allows for modeling relations of symbolic and iconic signs of various levels of resolution: ranging from the level of elementary constituents to the one of complete texts and images. The *OWLnotator* integrates *TEILex* (a system for interrelating corpus and lexicon data as part of the eHumanities Desktop and based on the *Text Encoding Initiative*[3]) with the expressiveness of *OWL*[4]-based ontologies in order to meet the first part of our twofold challenge.

The paper is organized as follows: Sect. 1.1 briefly describes related work. Section 2 deals with the scope of the OWLnotator in terms of multimodal, multicodal and multimedia data. In Sect. 3, we describe the image and text corpus underlying the present paper. Section 4 is devoted to the technical description of the OWLnotator, while Sect. 5 contains a brief evaluation of this system. Finally, Sect. 6 gives a conclusion and a prospect on future work.

1.1 Related Work

There is a lot of previous work in the area of virtual research platforms. First of all, the digital image archive *Prometheus* [6], started in 2001, connects a lot of distributed image-databases for research. For the relation-based management and image segmentation, Prometheus uses the tool *Meta-Image* [7], which is based on one of the most used tools, that is, *HyperImage* [16]. *HyperImage* and its follower named *Yenda* [17] are used in the project *Hachiman Digital Handscrolls* [18]. The goal of the project is to present "monumental or moved imageformats" [18] to the research community. The project deals with seven illuminated Japanese cross-roles from the 14th to the 17th century. With the help of *Yenda*, all the functionality of *HyperImage* is included and extended with the possibility of semantic annotations for the content of the cross-roles. The tool is very promising and will be in the focus of further investigation as soon as being published in Summer 2015. Other research projects like *CLAROS*[5] and *The WissKI Project*[6] developed effective techniques for information integration and retrieval.

---

[2] Founded by LOEWE – *The State Offensive for the Development of Scientific and Economic Excellence* (https://www.proloewe.de/en).

[3] www.tei-c.org.

[4] *Web Ontology Language.*

[5] https://www.clarosnet.org/XDB/ASP/clarosHome.

[6] https://wiss-ki.eu/node/23.

2 Aspects of Fusing Multimodal and Multicodal Information Objects

In [10], we briefly described intra- and intermodal relations of textual and pictorial units. In this section, we extend this outline by additionally distinguishing multicodal relations and interpretation relations (see Table 1: from the point of view of the sender or receiver of a sign aggregate we speak of *multimodal* relations if producing/processing this aggregate involves different sensory channels (cf. Weidenmann [23]).

Table 1. Intra- and inter- as well as mono- and multimodal sign relations as object of interpretation processes using the OWLnotator.

$\longrightarrow$	text (Segment)	image (Segment)	code unit	interpretation unit
text (segment)	intratextual / intertextual relation	intermedial / multimodal relation	intracodal / intercodal abstraction	instantiation / fusion relation
image (segment)	intermedial / multimodal relation	intrapictural / interpictural relation	intracodal / intercodal abstraction	instantiation / fusion relation
code unit	intracodal / intercodal manifestation	intracodal / intercodal manifestation	intracodal / intercodal relation	instantiation / fusion relation
interpretation unit	abstraction / fision relation	abstraction / fision relation	abstraction / fision relation	ontological relation

From the point of view of the underlying sign systems we speak of *multicodal* relations if producing/processing the aggregate involves different (e.g., linguistic or pictorial) codes [23]. A linguistic example of multicodality is given by multilingual descriptions of the same image – making use of the code of different languages (e.g., terminological ontologies). From the point of view of the sign vehicles and media involved, we, finally, speak of *multimedia* relations if transferring the aggregate involves different (e.g., linguistic or pictorial) media or multicodal signs [23]. Generally speaking, we speak of multimedia, -modal or -codal signs when referring to one of these views. Whatever the complexity of a sign is along these distinctions, scholars need to present them in a simplified and unified manner that makes operations on the resulting representations manageable. An analog to this requirement comes from cognition in terms of *fusion*.

That is, we extend our triadic distinction in order to account for situated, cognitive processes of fusion that result in multicodal, multimodal sign representations.[7] The notion of information fusion is applied here to interpretation processes in the humanities where the same aggregate is object of ongoing interpretation processes contextualized by different goals, traditions, schools etc. Any such process involves a mapping of multimodal/multicodal signs onto the same (monocodal) interpretation language. The representational underpinning of this interpretation-related "interlingua" is the object of the OWLnotator: it maps from multiple codes and modes using the same unifying format. Its cognitive correlate guarantees the ease by which human beings can switch, for example, between images, diagrams, texts in multimodal documents [2,3,15] to manifest the same concepts. The distinction we make here is between long-term codes (distributed over a corresponding language community) and short-term interpretations based on these codes by means of fusing their manifestations.

What is at stake here is the possibility to account for a wide range of relations on the level of metadata-related descriptions as well as on the level of the form and meaning of signs [11]. Think, for example, of rhetorical relations interrelating images and texts on the level of their (pragmatic) meanings [21]. Whatever the signature of such a relation is (dyadic or polyadic, types of its arguments etc.), a tool like the OWLnotator has to face the openness of their inventory and of the structures being representable by means of them. That is, a kind of expressiveness is required that makes it prohibitive to pre-establish ontologies of text-image relations. Rather, this establishment has to be delegated to the interpreter (humanities scholar) in a way that the OWLnotator guarantees applicability of the resulting ontology for annotating any sign aggregate within the eHumanities Desktop by analogy to the openness and flexibility of processes of cognitive fusion. Moreover, by analogy to the hermeneutic circle [20] the OWLnotator has to additionally account for situations in which scholars repeatedly change their interpretation models in the light of ongoing interpretation processes. Meeting these two requirements (expressiveness and extensibility) is exactly the task of the OWLnotator to be described in the following sections.

3   Description of the Corpus

In this section, we briefly describe the corpus by means of which the OWLnotator is evaluated.

As argued in Sect. 1, literary illustrations are a worthwhile subject of research for digital art history on grounds of both their inherent art-historical interest and their suitability for digital exploration. The illustrations of Goethe's "Faust" drama are a case in point. The publication of the first part of Goethe's "Faust" in 1808 was a major event in the literary history of the 19th century. To be sure, his youthful "Sorrows of Young Werther" won him international fame and had a lasting impact on the sentimentalist and early romanticist tendencies at the end of the 18th and the beginning of the 19th centuries all over the continent (Fig. 1).

---

[7] Analogously, *fision* denotes the process of producing/manifesting such signs (cf. [19]).

Fig. 1. Eugène Delacroix, Gretchen in the Cathedral, scene from "Faust", 1827, Freies Deutsches Hochstift - Frankfurter Goethe Museum, Inv-Nr. III-13280/001c.

But only with "Faust" did Goethe emerge as a leading figure and universally recognized authority in the world of letters. With Goethe's drama, the "Faust" legend of the 16th century became one of the principal narratives of modernity, its possibilities and dangers. In particular, its Europe wide reception was an inspiration for artists to dedicate their work to the illustration of the "Faust" drama which thereby became the most frequently illustrated subject of Goethe's oeuvre and of world literature itself. The spectrum of artistic approaches that have been tried is very broad, ranging from a large amount of conventional illustrations of figures and objects mentioned in the drama, to many highly original interpretations that try to convey the somber and uncanny atmosphere of its scenes in another medium. The existing body of illustrations shows the different attitudes artists have had towards their subject: from renderings that try to keep as close to the text as possible to imaginative explorations of the possibilities of the pictorial medium which are barley hinted at in the corresponding text they are supposed to illustrate.

As a dramatic text necessarily lacks the wealth of descriptive detail other types of literary writing – especially narrative forms – have, there is ample latitude for individual solutions which might, in turn, be the starting point of pictorial traditions of their own.

Because of its wide variety of possibilities within a thematically defined corpus, the tradition of "Faust" illustrations is a rich source for the research into external and internal relations of images (relations between two or more images and relations between details within one image) and text-image-relations. The study of the diverse forms of artistic reception, appropriation and interpretation of Goethe's "Faust" has been the subject of numerous studies and research activities, mostly focused on individual artists or particular traditions; a new, comprehensive major treatment that follows earlier works such as Boehn 1924 [4], Wegner 1962 [22] or Giesen 1998 [8] is an important desideratum. The largest collection of illustrations to Goethe's "Faust" (of all type, especially drawings and prints) is held by the Goethe Museum in Frankfurt. The collection currently consists of about 2500 drawings and prints of "Faust" from the early 19th century to the present. The collection is completely digitized and fully accessible online. The images are provided with the necessary descriptive metadata which are represented on a first level in a metadata schema for museum objects (LIDO [12]) and on the second level in an ontology based on the CIDOC CRM.

Any form of in-depth research into the content of the corpus of "Faust" images will need a basis of systematically stored semantic information about the depicted objects and figures and their place within the dramatic action. Since there is no way of exhausting the material by some all-encompassing description, there has to be a decision of where to begin. First endeavors should start from elementary questions known to be of relevance to art historical and literary studies. One starting point might be the gestures in pictures, as they may relate as well to the stage directions in the dramatic text as to iconographic traditions of representing human conduct. At the same time, the descriptions of gestures are likely to be of interest to many other projects. For the semantic representation of gestures an ontology has to be devised that allows to capture the relevant information and complies both with the demands of precision, generalizability and of further extensibility to different corpora. This is a typical task to be performed with the help of the OWLnotator.

4   The OWLnotator

The OWLnotator is a highly flexible annotation system for annotating inter- and intramedial relations in multimedia corpora. As an annotation module it is part of the eHumanities Desktop [9], a browser-based, platform-independent research environment for the support of collaborative research in the digital humanities. The eHumanities Desktop contains a wide range of tools for managing, analyzing and sharing resources based on a scalable concept of access permissions. Based on ontologies, written in OWL[8], the *OWLnotator* is able to typecast elements with *OWL-Classes* and can annotate every resource of the eHumanities Desktop (words, texts and their segments as well as images and their segments). With the typecast, the elements become *OWL-Objects* with all the properties related to the base class. New properties can be added by means of drag and drop operations. While adding new properties, the *OWLnotator* assists researchers with an ontology-based pre-selection of available *OWL-properties* and the existing objects for selection (if there are no literals). Figure 2 shows the interface of the *OWLnotator*. In the center, the resource to be annotated is shown. Based on the media-type, the center-area is displayed appropriately. Pictures are presented as

---

[8] http://www.w3.org/TR/owl-features/.

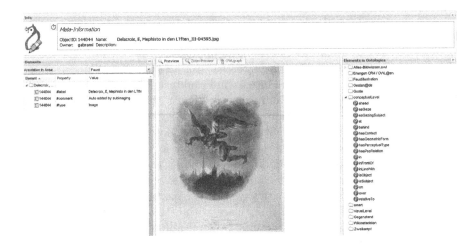

Fig. 2. The interface of the OWLnotator.

they are; text encoded in TEI P5 is displayed by means of its logical document structure and also in plain-text. The left side displays the current annotation of the element and on the right side the available ontologies are shown associated with their properties available for them.

As part of the eHumanities Desktop, which provides an environment for collaborative research, the *OWLnotator* can be used with a flexible system of access permissions. The *OWLnotator* is based on the free and open source Java framework of the Apache project for building Semantic Web and Linked Data applications, called *Jena*.[9] We use Jena because of its built-in reasoning-mechanisms and its flexible import and export features. Jena operates on a Quad-Store containing triples of subjects, predicates and objects embedded in the fourth dimension: *the Model*. Based on this, we create new resources within the eHumanities Desktop, *Annotation Locations* and *Annotation Areas*. *Annotation Locations* represent a Jena-TDB-Store[10] and contain the *Annotation Areas*. *Annotation Areas* are the representations of the *Model* mentioned above. Researchers can get access permissions on *Annotation Locations* as well as on *Annotation Areas*. The distinction of *Annotation Locations* and *Annotation Areas* allows for a detailed access management where the user can decide which other users or user groups[11] have access on *their Annotation Areas* within the eHumanities Desktop.

At the same time we can handle a clear division between *Annotation Areas* used for definitions and *Annotation Areas* used for annotations. Depending on the access permissions (see Fig. 3) they can add, modify or remove annotations in *Annotation Areas* or they can manage the access permissions directly. Every user, registered in the eHumanities Desktop, owns his own area, called

---

[9] https://www.jena.apache.org.
[10] TDB is a RDF-Store.
[11] To which users can belong.

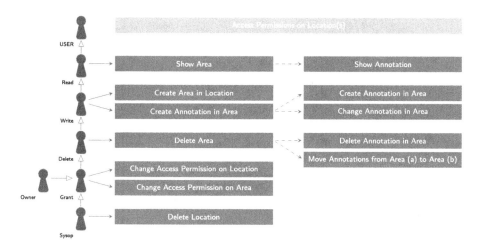

Fig. 3. Access Permissions on *Annotation Locations*.

Home Area. It is very easy to add new ontologies into the *OWLnotator*: Researchers only have to create a new *Annotation Area* and upload, from remote or local resources, the ontology into it. The ontology has to be valid. Its validity may be provided with the help of some open source tools like Protégé[12]. In the same way, it is possible to change views on annotations by uploading a new ontology which interprets the current annotations by means of other features, classes etc.

5 A Snapshot of Data Managed by the OWLnotator

The OWLnotator is used by several annotation projects in the digital humanities. This includes the *Illustrations of Goethe's Faust* and the Project on *Historical Knowledge of Pictures* [13,14]. Further, the OWLnotator contains several image and text-related ontologies as well as more than numprint758464[13] (See Fig. 4, left) annotations in 174 *Annotation Area*s of 7 *Annotation Location*s (see Fig. 4, right) – this amount of data increases every day. The time for creating one annotation is below one minute

Researchers can work independent of each other if their topics do not share any information objects. All the annotations are done based on the same software solution. Users can share there annotation results. With the help of a time measurement tool, which allows user-related measurements of annotation times, it is also possible to create annotations.

---

[12] https://www.protege.stanford.edu.
[13] Counted at 02/18/2015.

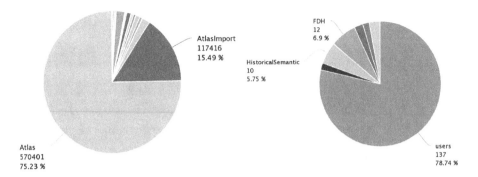

Fig. 4. Left: annotations in *Annotation Area*s. Right: *Annotation Area*s managed by the OWLnotator.

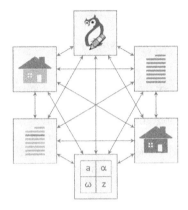

Fig. 5. The OWLnotator connects different types of media.

6   Conclusion and Future Work

With the *OWLnotator* we developed a tool fossr annotating multimedia resources as shown in Fig. 5. As part of the eHumanities Desktop, the OWL-notator allows for using all services of this platform for collaborative research, especially its tool for managing access permissions. After creating and upload-ing an ontology with the OWLnotatsor, the researchers can directly start with annotating art work.

The next development step is to make the OWLnotator a stand alone *web-service* to allow for adding it into other software projects in the digital humanities.

References

1. Abrami, G., Freiberg, M., Warner, P.: Managing and annotating historical multi-modal corpora with the eHumanities desktop - an outline of the current state of the LOEWE project illustrations of goethe's faust. In: Proceedings of the Historical Corpora Conference, 6–9 December 2012, Frankfurt (2012)

2. Bateman, J.A.: Text and Image: A Critical Introduction to the Visual/Verbal Divide. Taylor & Francis, NewYork (2014)
3. Bateman, J.A., Kamps, T., Kleinz, J., Reichenberger, K.: Towards constructive text, diagram, and layout generation for information presentation. Comput. Linguist. **27**(3), 409–449 (2001)
4. von Boehn, M.: Faust und die Kunst. In: Goethe, Johann Wolfgang: Faust. Hundertjahrs-Ausgabe, pp. 3–221. Askanischer Verlag, Berlin (1924)
5. CIDOC CRM Special Interest Group (SIG): Definition of the CIDOC Conceptual Reference Model, 5.0.4 edn. (2011). http://www.cidoc-crm.org/docs/cidoc_crm_version_5.0.4.pdf
6. Dieckmann, L.: Prometheus: the distributed digital image archive for research and education. In: L'Art et la Mesure: Histoire de l'art et méthodes quantitatives, sous la direction de Béatrice Joyeux-Prunel, avec la collaboration de Luc Sigalo Santos, pp. 141–151. Paris (2010)
7. Dieckmann, L., Kliemann, A., Warnke, M.: Meta-Image: forschungsumgebung für den bilddiskurs in der kunstgeschichte. cms-j. Comput.- und Medienservice **35**, 11–17 (2012)
8. Giesen, S.: Den Faust, dächt' ich, gäben wir ohne Holzschnitte und Bildwerke: Goethes "Faust" in der europäischen Kunst des 19. Jahrhunderts. Ph.D. thesis, Technische Hochschule Aachen, Aachen (1998)
9. Gleim, R., Mehler, A., Ernst, A.: SOA implementation of the eHumanities Desktop. In: Proceedings of the Workshop on Service-oriented Architectures (SOAs) for the Humanities: Solutions and Impacts, Digital Humanities 2012, Hamburg, Germany (2012)
10. Gleim, R., Warner, P., Mehler, A.: eHumanities Desktop - an architecture for flexible annotation in iconographic research. In: Proceedings of the 6th International Conference on Web Information Systems and Technologies (WEBIST 2010), Valencia, 7–10 April 2010
11. Hollink, L., Schreiber, A.T., Wielinga, B.J., Worring, M.: Classification of user image descriptions. Int. J. Hum.-Comput. Stud. **61**(5), 601–626 (2004)
12. ICOM-CIDOC Working Group Data Harvesting and Interchange: LIDO - Lightweight Information Describing Objects, 1.0 edn. (2010). http://www.lido-schema.org/schema/v1.0/lido-v1.0-specification.pdf
13. Jussen, B. (ed.): Atlas des Historischen Bildwissens 1: Liebig. Digitale Bibliothek, Berlin (2009)
14. Jussen, B. (ed.): Atlas des Historischen Bildwissens 2: Reklamesammelbilder. Digitale Bibliothek, Berlin (2009)
15. Kress, G., Leeuwen, T.: Multimodal Discourse. Arnold, London (2001)
16. Kuper, H.G., Loebel, J.M.: Hyperimage: of layers, labels and links. In: Proceedings of RENEW the 5th edition of the International Conference on the Histories of Media Art, Science and Technology. Riga (2014)
17. Kuper, H.G., Loebel, J.M.: Yenda - Picture Knowledge, Open-Source semantische virtuelle Forschungsumgebung (2015). http://yenda.tools
18. Loebel, J.M., Kuper, H.G., Arnold, M., Decker, E.: Hachiman digital handscrolls semantische annreicherung mit hyperimage und yenda. In: Bienert, A., Hemsley, J., Santos, P. (eds.) Elektronische Medien & Kunst, Kultur und Historie, pp. 262–267. Konferenzband, Berlin (2014)
19. Lücking, A., Pfeiffer, T.: Framing multimodal technical communication. with focal points in speech-gesture-integration and gaze recognition. In: Mehler, A., Romary, L. (eds.) Handbook of Technical Communication, Handbooks of Applied Linguistics, vol. 8, chap. 18, pp. 591–644. De Gruyter Mouton, Berlin and Boston (2012)

20. Poser, H.: Wissenschaftstheorie. Eine philosophosche Einführung, 2nd edn. Reclam, Stuttgart (2012)
21. Taboada, M., Habel, C.: Rhetorical relations in multimodal documents. Discourse Stud. **15**(1), 59–85 (2013)
22. Wegner, W.: Die Faustdarstellung vom 16. Jahrhundert bis zur Gegenwart. Erasmus Buchhandlung, Amsterdam (1962)
23. Weidenmann, B.: Multicodierung und Multimodalität im Lernprozess. In: Issing, L.J., Klimsa, P. (eds.) Information und Lernen mit Multimedia, pp. 45–62. Beltz, Weinheim (1997)

A Filtering System of Web History Using the Browsing Characteristic

Keita Arai[1]([✉]), Makoto Oka[2], and Hirohiko Mori[2]

[1] System Information Engineering, Tokyo City University, Tokyo, Japan
g1481802@tcu.ac.jp
[2] Department of Industrial and Management Systems Engineering,
Tokyo City University, Tokyo, Japan
{moka,hmori}@tcu.ac.jp

Abstract. Most Web browsers have a Web history function to support to go back to the pages which user use to watch. However, only few people use it to revisit Web pages. In this study, we suggest a filtering system of Web history that holds only the Web pages that is more likely to be revisited. Whether visited Web pages are more likely to be revisited or not is determined by the characteristics of user's browsing behaviors. Our results clarify users' browsing characteristics make a filtering system of Web history work well. This study shows a solution of revisit Web pages, using Web history function.

Keywords: Web history · Revisitation · Refinding · Browsing characteristic · Filtering

1 Introduction

Now, using the Internet for information gathering has become very common. In information retrieval using the Internet, user often wants to revisit the Web page that was viewed in the past. In these cases, most people try to trace similar or same routes in their previous visit (e.g., use a search engine, follow a link). However, when people don't remember the page title, the search query, or the route of the web surfing, they can't sometimes reach their previous visited pages. In such case, there is a way to use a Web history function. However, there are some problems in current Web histories and few people use it to revisit Web pages. For example, most Web histories are displayed in text format. As the visited Web pages increase, a lot of efforts are required to find target Web pages from a lot of list.

There are some sorts of situations when it is difficult for the user to revisit target Web page using Web history function. In one situation, there are many similar Web pages in the Web history because of visiting many Web pages to achieve an information retrieval task. In another situation, user cannot recall the pages because he/she does not visit them for a long time.

In this study, especially, to decrease useless information on the Web history, we propose a filtering system that holds only the Web pages that is more likely to be

S. Yamamoto (Ed.): HIMI 2015, Part I, LNCS 9172, pp. 273–279, 2015.
DOI: 10.1007/978-3-319-20612-7_26

revisited. Since the Web page that user felt interesting is more likely to be revisited, we proposed a filtering system that judge whether the visited Web pages are beneficial for users' tasks from their behaviors on the visited pages (we call this "browsing characteristics"), and hold only the pages that will seemingly revisited.

2 Related Work

A number of studies have been studied about Web browser so far.

Matsuo et al. [1] studied about browsing history. They proposed a keyword extraction method in consideration of the user's interested fields using browsing history. In this study, they tried to identify user's interest and focuses from individual browsing history. Hijikata et al. [2] studied about users' characteristics in browsing. They proposed a keyword extraction method to estimate the user's interests using mouse operations. Minami et al. [3] proposed a Web page filtering system in searching fit for the user's interests. They estimate user's search intention using his/her browsing characteristics and the natural language processing to the visited pages. We applied some parts of their methods to the Web history function. Sungjoon Won et al. [4] studied to improve usability of the Web history function. They improved it using visual and contextual cues. However, they didn't improve a fundamental factor of information overload. In our study, we approached this matter by a different way of removing the useless web pages from the history.

3 System

3.1 System Outline

Our proposed system filter out only the Web pages the user is not interested in from the Web history and holds only the pages that he/she visited and were interested in based on the collected behavior on each page in user's browsing. Detail of filtering module is described below.

3.2 Filtering Module

In filtering module, the system passes through only Web pages which users were interested in. Whether the visited Web pages are interesting or not for the user is determined by the browsing characteristic he/she behaves on each Web page he/she visited. Table 1 shows the browsing characteristics used for filtering.

Table 1. Recorded browsing characteristics.

Browsing characteristics	Details
Slight mouse movement	It count mouse moving; more than 10 pixel per 0.1 s
Sorjoum time (s)	Time between page visit and page leave
Page text	Text that deleted tag data from HTML

The filtering system we proposed consists of two steps. In the first step, the sojourn time on each visited page is used to filter. The purpose of first step is filtering the Web page whose contents the user is not interested in at all. The threshold of the sojourn time used in the first step will be determined in the experiment below. Here, when user visits the same page multiple times, the total sojourn time of each visit are used.

In the second step, whether the visited Web pages hold or not is decided by the frequency of the slight mouse movements or sojourn time per text. Frequency of mouse movement and sojourn time per text are defined as follows.

$$\text{frequency of slight mouse movement} = \frac{\text{amount of slight mouse movement}}{\text{amount of Web page text}} \quad (1)$$

$$\text{sojourn time per text} = \frac{\text{amount of the sojourn time}}{\text{amout of Web page text}} \quad (2)$$

The purpose of second step filters the Web page whose contents the user once feels interesting but does not judge beneficial. The frequency of slight mouse movement must be high when the user feels the page contents beneficial. Furthermore, the sojourn time per text can be considered to increase when the user feels it is beneficial for him/ herself he/she must read it carefully to understand it. The thresholds of the frequency of the slight mouse movement and the sojourn time per text also determined in the experiment below.

4 Experiment

4.1 Methods

We conducted the experiment to evaluate the filtering system.

The subject asked to perform three information retrieval tasks. Detail of each task is shown in Table 2. To simulate a realistic information gathering tasks, we made tasks by referring to the question that is really asked in the Japanese positing Q&A site (Yahoo! Chiebukuro [6]). We selected the tasks which the subjects should visit many pages to complete the task.

When the subjects completed each task, they were asked to make out a report about an approximately 1,500 Japanese characters, which is filled out about one page of A4 sheet with a word processor [7], during the experiment, the subjects prohibited taking notes not to memorize the Web page contents that visit in the past.

Table 2. Tasks.

Task number	Task details
Question 1	Gather information of japanese declining industry
Question 2	Gather information of life in medieval Europian
Question 3	Gather information of industry in Africa

After the completion of each task, the subjects were asked to evaluate all pages they visited whether they are useful or not to make out the report. This result is used to evaluate our system by comparing with the results of our filtering system as the following values:

Filter validity: percentage of correct answers of filtering.

$$\text{Filter validity} = \frac{\text{current classification of filtering}}{\text{amount of visited Web page}} \qquad (3)$$

Page recall ratio: ratio of the Web page that user may be re-display passes through the filter among the Web page that user may be re-display.

$$\text{Page recall ratio} = \frac{\text{current Web pages that pass through the filter}}{\text{amount of visited Web page}} \qquad (4)$$

Page precision ratio: ratio of the Web page that user may be re-display passes through the filter among the Web page that passes through the filter.

$$\text{page precision ratio} = \frac{\text{current Web pages that pass through the filter}}{\text{amount of beneficial web page}} \qquad (5)$$

F-measure: comprehensive measure in consideration of recall and precision.

$$\text{F} - \text{measure} = \frac{2 \times \text{recall} \times \text{precision}}{\text{recall} + \text{precision}} \qquad (6)$$

Ten people were involved in this experiment, and they were from 20 to 23 years old. Though we didn't instruct to use a specific search engine to do information retrieval tasks, all subjects use Google search engine [5]. In addition, after the experiment, they were asked to fill out the paper questionnaires which contain the questions about their daily use manner of Web browsing such as usage of Web history, and their impressions of the experiment, such as the difficulty of each task. Looking at this questionnaire, all of the subjects accessed the Internet in everyday life and there is no problem in operating the Web browser. Furthermore, no people usually use Web history function to revisit Web page, which we reconfirmed that there are usability problems with current browser history.

The questionnaire also says that seven subjects said there is no difference between the questions difficulty. Only two subjects said question 1 is a little more difficult than the other questions and only one subject said question 3 is more difficult than the other questions. Thus, we consider that three questions are no difference about the difficulties among the tasks.

The Web browser used in this experiment includes only the basic functions of popular Web browsers. For example, back button, forward button, URL bar, and display area (Fig. 1). This browser was built on C#.

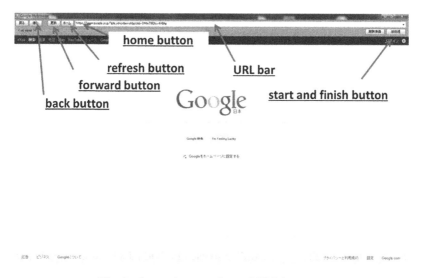

Fig. 1. Screenshot experimental Web browser.

5   The Results

5.1   Determination of the Thresholds of Each Filter

We determined the threshold of each filter by the result of this experiment.

In the experiment, amount of beneficial Web pages increased when their sojourn time was more than 10 s. Thus, we considered that threshold of sojourn time used in the first step should be set to 10 s. In the same way, frequency of slight mouse movement is set to 0.001 and sojourn time per text is set to 0.003 s.

5.2   Evaluation of the Filtering

In this experiment, the subjects visited 240 pages in total and felt 156 pages are interesting and 84 pages are not interesting among them. Our proposed filtering system filtered 47 pages, and 14 Web pages were mis-filtered among them.

Table 3 shows the result of each evaluation value.

In Table 3, the recall rate and F-measure were good. Therefore, it can be said that the filter works well overall.

However, several mis-filterings were occurred. In this experiment, 11 cases of 14 mis-filterings were occurred in the first step. Table 4 shows the number of mis-filterings in the first step for each subject

Looking at Table 4, most mis-filterings in the first step show a concentration in some subjects, such that 5 mis-filterings were occurred in one subject. In addition, the features of the sojourn time were also different by each subject ($M = 31.70$, $SD = 7.88$). This means that we must set up the thresholds considering the individual differences of browsing characteristic of each user.

Table 3. Result of evaluation value.

Validity	Recall	Precision	F-measure
0.729	0.910	0.740	0.814

Table 4. Relationship between the subject and mis-filtering of first step.

Subject	a	b	c	d	e	f	g	h	i	j
mis-filtering of first step	0	5	0	0	0	0	1	2	1	2

6 System Improvement

As explained above, we need to improve the first step filtering and to take individual differences of browsing characteristics in account. Therefore, to make the filter of the first step and to support the individual differences of browsing habits, we set the threshold dynamically changed according to each individual's browsing characteristics. We defined it as below:

$$\text{Individual variable threshold} = \frac{\text{individual average sojourn time}}{n} \qquad (7)$$

Here, "n" was a fixed number, and we set it 3.0 here.

Table 5 shows the result of the improved system and Table 6 shows the number of mis-filtering of first step in each subject.

Showing Tables 3 and 5, all evaluate values was improved. In comparison between Tables 4 and 6, total mis-filtering and the difference among the subjects were reduced. Therefore, it is effective to automatically adjust the values for filtering to individuals according to their browsing habits.

Table 7 shows a result of first step mis-filtering with improved system.

Table 5. Result of filter restricting.

Validity	Recall	Precision	F-measure
0.754	0.917	0.757	0.830

Table 6. Relationship between subject and mis-filtering of first step of restricted filter

Subject	a	b	c	d	e	f	g	h	i	j
mis-filtering	0	3	0	0	0	0	1	3	1	3

Table 7. First step mis-filtering with improved system.

Task	First step mis-filtering
Question 1	2
Question 2	0
Question 3	8

Table 8. Result of visited Web pages for each question.

Task	Visited Web pages (±s.d.)
Question 1	7.9 ± 3.2
Question 2	6.8 ± 2.3
Question 3	9.3 ± 4.9

From Table 7, most of mis-filterings in first step were happened in question 3 and Table 8 shows the result of the number of each subject's visited Web pages for each question.

From Tables 7 and 8, the mis-filtering in first step tend to increase as the standard deviation of the numbers of the visited Web pages increased. As we do not clarify the cause of this problem, to solve it is one of our future works.

7   Conclusion and Future Work

Since current Web history functions include much useless information, few people use it to revisit Web pages. In this study, we suggested filtering system of Web history that passes through only beneficial Web pages.

In conclusion, we suggested a filtering system of Web history function using users' browsing characteristics. This result showed a method that can decide the benefit of visited Web page from the browsing characteristic he/she behaves at the Web page and it is effective to automatically adjust the values for filtering to individuals according to their browsing habits.

However, the mis-filterings in the first step were happened when the numbers of the visited pages vary widely among the users. In the future, we should clarify the cause and overcome this problem.

References

1. Matsuo, M., Hayato, F., Mitsuru, I.: Browsing Suppot by Highlighting Keywords based on User's Browsing History, vol. 101, pp. 85–92. Technical Report, The Institute of Electronics, Information and Communication Engineers (IEICE) (2002)
2. Yoshinori, H., Yoshinori, A., Younosuke, F., Amane, N.: Text Part Extraction Based on Mouse Operations and Evaluation of Extracted Keywords, vol. 43, pp. 566–576. Information Processing Society of Japan (IPSJ) (2002)
3. Shoutarou, M., Makoto, O.: Extraction of Search Intention based on User Behavior and Classification of Search Result, vol. 8, pp. 1–6. Information Processing Society of Japan (IPSJ), HCI (2011)
4. Sungjoon, W., Jing, J., Jason, I.S.: Contextual web history: using visual and contextual cues to improve web browser history. ACM Conference on Human Factors in Computing Systems (CHI) (2009)
5. Google search engine. https://www.google.co.jp/
6. Yahoo! Chiebukuro. http://chiebukuro.yahoo.co.jp/
7. A document format of Electronic official document. http://www.soumu.go.jp/main_sosiki/gyoukan/kanri/dtd01.htm#04

Seed, a Natural Language Interface to Knowledge Bases

Bahaa Eldesouky$^{(\boxtimes)}$, Heiko Maus, Sven Schwarz, and Andreas Dengel

Knowledge Management Department, German Research Center for Artificial Intelligence (DFKI GmbH), Kaiserslautern, Germany
{bahaa.eldesouky,heiko.maus,sven.schwarz,andreas.dengel}@dfki.de

Abstract. The World Wide Web has been rapidly developing in the last decade. In recent years, the Semantic Web has gained a lot of traction. It is a vision of the Web where data is understandable by machines as well as humans. Developments in the Semantic Web made way for the creation of massive knowledge bases containing a wealth of structured information. However, allowing end-users to interact with and benefit from these knowledge bases remains a challenge.

In this paper, we present *Seed*, an extensible knowledge-supported natural language text composition tool, which provides a user-friendly way of interacting with complex knowledge systems. It is integrable not only with public knowledge bases on the Semantic Web, but also with private knowledge bases used in personal or enterprise contexts.

By means of a long-term formative user-study and a short-term user evaluation of a sizable population of test subjects, we show that *Seed* was successfully used in exploring, modifying and creating the content of complex knowledge bases. We show it enables end-users do so with nearly no domain knowledge while hiding the complexity of the underlying knowledge representation.

Keywords: Usability · Semantic Web · Natural language · Knowledge bases

1 Introduction and Related Work

The World Wide Web has seen rapid developments in the last decade. It is steadily transforming into the Semantic Web [6], a Web where data is understandable and consumable by machines as well as humans. Although the vision of the Semantic Web is making progress towards its realization, a gap between non-expert end-users and the content of the Semantic Web still exists. Tools for interacting with structured information on the Web remain directed almost entirely at highly trained individuals [5].

The progress of the Semantic Web vision can be observed in the field of modeling and structuring data, where huge knowledge bases such as DBPedia [7] and Freebase [8] contain millions of concepts and billions of facts about them. These huge knowledge bases comprise a web of Linked Open Data (LOD) [4].

© Springer International Publishing Switzerland 2015
S. Yamamoto (Ed.): HIMI 2015, Part I, LNCS 9172, pp. 280–290, 2015.
DOI: 10.1007/978-3-319-20612-7_27

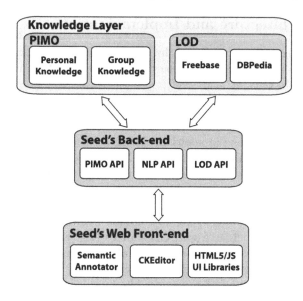

Fig. 1: *Seed* architecture diagram

In addition to public knowledge repositories, there are private ones, which focus on individual or group knowledge [15] (e.g. corporate knowledge repositories).

Development of user interfaces for non-experts that allow for user-friendly consumption and interaction with the existing knowledge on the Semantic Web is essential. In this paper, we present *Seed*, short for semantic editor. It is an extensible knowledge-supported web-based natural language text composition tool. We point out the structure of *Seed*, explain how it builds state-of-the-art developments in the fields of NLP, LOD and Semantic Web technologies to provide a user-friendly way of interacting with complex knowledge systems. By means of a long-term formative user-study and a short-term user evaluation of a sizable population of test subjects, we show that the use of *Seed* in exploring, modifying and creating semantic content reduces prerequisite domain knowledge and hides the complexity of the underlying knowledge representation.

Research on enabling end-users to interact with the Semantic Web in a friendly way is increasingly gaining interest. Examples include SemCards [17], which provides an intermediate ontological representational level that allows end-users to create rich semantic networks for their information sphere. OntoAnnotate [16] is an ontology-based annotation environment for web pages based on RDF [13] and RDFschema [9]. RDFaCE [11] provides an easy way for adding RDF-based annotations to text. RDFauthor [18] bases on making arbitrary XHTML views with integrated RDFa annotations editable. In [12] a WYSIWYG tool called Ontos-Feeder is proposed which annotates text for the news/journalism domain. In [3], Epiphany is used to get RDFa enhanced versions of their articles linking to underlying Linked Data models.

2   Seed Architecture and Implementation

As depicted in Fig. 1, Seed consists of three main logical parts: a knowledge layer, a back-end and a front-end. All three parts are loosely coupled and communicate via standard Web APIs.

2.1   Knowledge Layer

This logical part embodies the knowledge integrated with Seed. We distinguish between two scopes of knowledge: a personal and a world scope. With the personal knowledge scope, we refer to the knowledge model of the user(s) which contains things relevant to an individual or a group. Things present in the personal knowledge scope may not be relevant for many outside of the group. With the world knowledge scope, we refer to common knowledge publicly accessible on the Semantic Web such as from LOD sources (e.g. Freebase and DBPedia). It contains things common to a large group of people such as celebrities, companies, countries ... etc. This distinction gives priority to user knowledge and complements missing information using public knowledge.

PIMO. Personal/group knowledge refers to structured information about concepts from the point of view of an individual user or a specific group of users. The PIMO [15] is a personal and group knowledge base reflecting the mental models of the users with concepts such as persons, projects, tasks, topics, events and resources such as emails, files, webpages, notes, pictures. PIMO knowledge of the author and possibly that of the group to which the author may belong is integrable in *Seed*

LOD. General common knowledge on the other hand, refers to structured information available from public knowledge repositories such as DBPedia, Freebase and other LOD sources. The integration of common knowledge is important for complementing the user's knowledge. It also helps expand the context of knowledge in a text authored by the user.

2.2   Back-End

This component, physically realized on the server-side, consists of multiple APIs responsible for:

- Communication with integrated personal and public knowledge sources.
- Analyzing content authored by the user and enriching with information retrieved from knowledge sources.

NLP API. This component is implemented as a Java service which builds on two state-of-the-art NLP toolkits; Stanford CoreNLP [14] and Apache OpenNLP [1]. It can perform major NLP tasks such as named entity recognition, coreference resolution and relation extraction. The NLP API currently supports two languages; English and German.

LOD API. This component of the back-end communicates in real-time with live LOD sources to extract information about concepts mentioned in the text. This component can work independently or in combination with the NLP API. Following are example tasks where this component is involved:

- Entity disambiguation: By an entity we refer to a thing (e.g. person, city, event, organization ... etc.) that is mentioned in the text and is of interest to the user.
- Relation extraction: Finding relations between arbitrary entities.

PIMO API. This component interacts with personal and group knowledge from PIMO on behalf of the user. The interaction scenarios include but are not limited to:

- Identifying and disambiguating entities or suggesting related ones.
- Extracting information about recognized entities from the users's personal or group PIMO.
- Finding relations between entities mentioned in the text.
- Adding new entities from the text to the user knowledge in PIMO.

2.3 Web Front-End

The current prototype of *Seed's* front-end is meant to run in the browser. Therefore, it is written completely in HTML5 and JavaScript. However, it is also possible to embed it in graphical user interfaces (GUIs) built using other languages. The only prerequisite is the availability of an HTML capable user interface (UI) element to run the editor component.

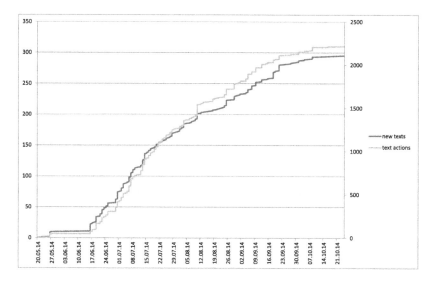

Fig. 2: Statistics about textual content created in *Seed* over a six-month period

CKEditor. At the core of the front-end, *Seed* builds upon CKEditor [2], the open source WYSIWYG HTML editor.

Semantic Annotator. The semantic annotator is a JS/HTML extension responsible for monitoring the HTML and continuously performing basic analysis of the content typed by the user. It also communicates with the back-end retrieving annotations and applying them to the text in a proactive way.

HTML/JS UI Libraries. Depending on the application scenario in which *Seed* is integrated, various HTML/JS libraries (e.g. jQuery, UI, Bootstrap ... etc.) are used to build the GUI.

2.4   Experimental Evaluation

In order to assess the value of *Seed* for end-users interacting with knowledge bases, we have performed two user-evaluations.

Long-Term Formative User-Study. This long term evaluation aimed at assessing the suitability of *Seed* as a natural language interface to PIMO. During the evaluation, we iteratively improved existing features of *Seed* or added new ones to it based on the feedback from our test subjects.

Demographics:

– Number of users: 4
– Occupation: Students of non-technical majors
– Duration: 6 months
– Languages: German, English

For the duration of six months between May and November 2014, four students extensively used a shared PIMO for personal and professional reasons. It allowed them to model things important to them such as places, events, companies, photos, files ... etc. The had the ability to share and collaborate on the information they increasingly accumulated throughout their use of PIMO. A lot of the PIMO things they modeled where composed of unstructured text. Examples included shopping lists, meeting notes, recipes ... etc.

We integrated *Seed* in Web-based and Java-based UIs of PIMO. The goal was to use it as the main interface for interacting with textual PIMO things or textual properties of many non-textual PIMO things. Before integrating *Seed*, tasks like annotating concepts, creating relations between them and adding new ones could be done only through interaction with menus, buttons and conventional UI elements. Using *Seed* in the case of textual PIMO things, users could perform the aforementioned tasks automatically or semi-automatically while composing natural language text. Users had access to *Seed* for the following purposes:

– Writing textual descriptions of existing PIMO entities, such as persons, photos, institutions, events or many other types.

- Composing free text documents, such as notes, meeting minutes, diary entries, shopping lists … etc.

While composing text, *Seed* identified mentioned entities and suggested related ones to the users. It helped them save time and effort of manually searching for and annotating entity with related ones.

During the six months, we met the students regularly on a weekly basis. In each meeting, they reported the types of activities they undertook using PIMO for the past week and highlighted success stories and fail stories. Their iterative feedback about interaction with textual PIMO things was used to guide the development of *Seed*. Figure 2 shows a plot of the number of texts created over the period of six month by the test subjects. It also shows the number editing actions performed on those texts. The so-called text actions refer to interactions with the content of the text through *Seed*.

During the first month, *Seed* was being integrated in various GUIs of PIMO. Test subjects got introduced to it and provided preliminary feedback about their most frequent text composition needs. As seen during the first month, users created few texts and rarely interacted with them once created. They mostly interacted with PIMO through non-textual interfaces. As can be seen in Fig. 2, by the end of the first month, the students had become more familiar with *Seed* and started using it more frequently for creating new texts. They increasingly adopted it for interacting with textual PIMO things. However, during most of the second month, test subjects tended to rarely edit texts once they were created. Using their feedback we iteratively improved interaction possibilities with annotations to address the problem. Towards the end of the third month, test subjects edited documents they had created substantially more often. As seen in Fig. 2, from the fourth month onwards, multiple edits per document became more often resulting in a considerable increase over the number of documents created.

Short-Term User-Study. In this evaluation, we assessed the usability of *Seed* in annotating texts with semantic information from public knowledge source, namely Freebase and DBPedia.

Demographics:

- Number of users: 115
- Language: English

Figure 4 shows statistics about the population of test subjects who participated in our evaluation experiment. As can be seen, the diversity of profiles of the participants as well as the number of participants are high enough to guarantee representative results.

Procedure: We have set up an evaluation website where test subjects, performed the experiment which proceeded as follows:

1. Registration, where participants provided demographic information about themselves.

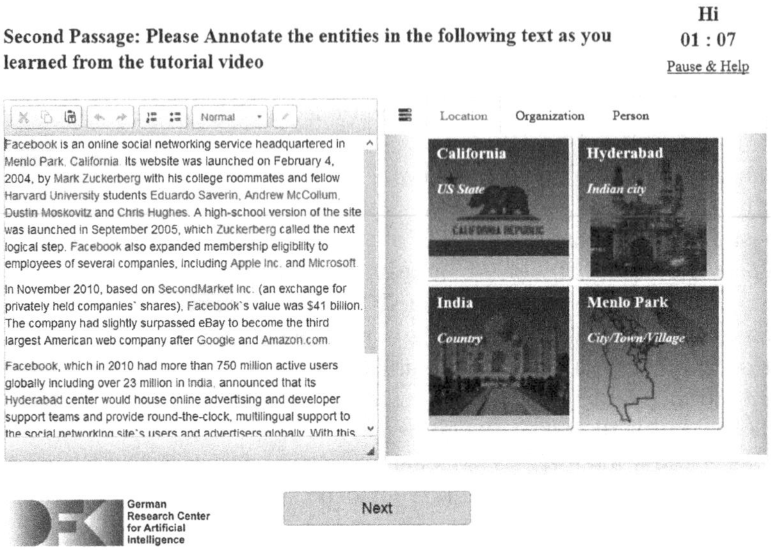

Fig. 3: Sample snapshot of the evaluation interface

2. Then, participants watched a short non-technical tutorial video [1] explaining the concept and use of *Seed*. We avoided technical aspects in the video in order to safely assume no technical domain knowledge.
3. Participants were asked to annotate 3 text passages from various domains using *Seed*. They reviewed automatic annotations by *Seed* and suggestions for annotations that they could confirm or reject.
4. Afterwards, participants were asked to type in a given text passage, which *Seed* proactively annotated as it got written.
5. Finally, participants were asked questions including but not confined to a Standard Usability Score (SUS) [10] questionnaire.

Standard Usability Score. After the end of the evaluation, users filled in a SUS questionnaire. Figure 5 shows the aggregated results of the questionnaire. Across the population of test subjects, *Seed* scored an overall mean SUS of 73.56 with standard deviation equal to 13.71. According to [10], this means *Seed* has above average usability.

Knowledge Exploration. As seen in Fig. 3, *Seed*'s front-end contains a faceted browsable view of the things mentioned in the text. It provides a user friendly way of interacting with the knowledge present in the text. The content of the faceted view is automatically extracted from PIMO, DBPedia and Freebase by *Seed*. In order to evaluate the faceted view, we asked users after the evaluation two questions whose answers are not mentioned the in text passages, but are available through the faceted view as well as through the interactive annotation

---

[1] Seed, the Semantic Editor - https://www.youtube.com/watch?v=CSFS4sxWm0w.

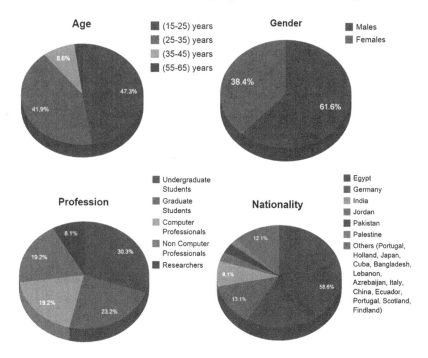

Fig. 4: Age, gender, background and nationalities of participants

information pane which shows up when users inspect the annotations in the text. Our hypothesis was that users would discover the information in the UI easily. The results of users answers were as follows:

- For the first question, 94.9 % of the participants managed to find the correct answer.
- For the second question, 51.5 % of the participants managed to find the correct answer.

To avoid the participants looking up the answer elsewhere outside of *Seed*, we explicitly asked them how they found it. For those who could answer at least one question, 93.9 % did so using *Seed*'s UI elements. This shows how *Seed* managed to relieve the majority of the users from the manual effort of browsing the knowledge base to search for the answers.

Learnability. To quantitatively evaluate how fast users learned to use *Seed*, we measured the time required to annotate each of the text passages. After cleaning up the data and normalizing it with respect to length, we got the values shown in Fig. 6. We can see an overall trend of decrease in the time required for interaction with the text using *Seed*. Although the number of the text passages was limited due to practical reasons, it can be seen that the time required to read and annotate passages decreased with progress in the experiment. It is worth noting that the number of annotations increased with the progress in the experiment,

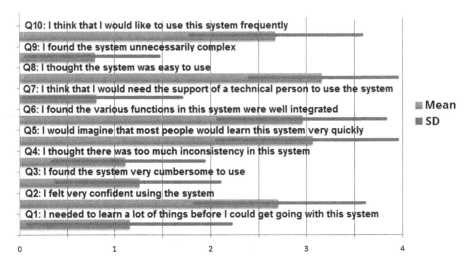

Fig. 5: Aggregated results of the SUS questionnaire. (Strongly Disagree: 0, Disagree: 1, Neutral: 2, Agree: 3, Strongly Agree 4)

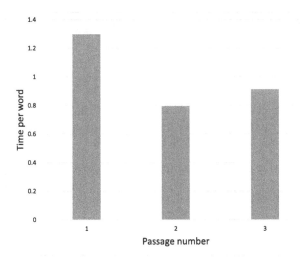

Fig. 6: Mean annotation time in seconds for all participants

which implies increased user familiarity with the system. This can also explain the slight increase in the time of the third passage 3 in comparison to the second passage.

3   Conclusion

In this paper, we presented *Seed*, a user-friendly natural language interface to complex knowledge bases. We explained its architecture and pointed out how it aims to enable user-friendly interaction with knowledge bases through natural language text composition. We put the system to a long-term formative user-study and a short-term usability evaluation involving a large group of test subjects. The results of the experiments show how *Seed* enabled non-expert end-users to interact with personal as well as common public knowledge bases.

For future work we plan to add more interaction possibilities with the text beyond annotation and knowledge browsing. We also plan to investigate other aspects related to collaborative interaction with the knowledge through the text.

Acknowledgments. The work presented was partially funded by the European Commission in the context of the FP7 ICT project ForgetIT (under grant no: 600826).

References

1. Apache opennlp, October 2014. URL: http://opennlp.apache.org/index.html
2. CKEditor Website, October 2014. URL: http://ckeditor.com
3. Adrian, B., Hees, J., Herman, I., Sintek, M., Dengel, A.: Epiphany: adaptable RDFa generation linking the web of documents to the web of data. In: Cimiano, P., Pinto, H.S. (eds.) EKAW 2010. LNCS, vol. 6317, pp. 178–192. Springer, Heidelberg (2010)
4. Auer, S., Bryl, V., Tramp, S.: Linked Open Data-Creating Knowledge Out of Interlinked Data: Results of the LOD2 Project. LNCS, vol. 8661. Springer, Heidelberg (2014)
5. Benson, E., Karger, D.R.: End-users publishing structured information on the web: an observational study of what, why, and how. In: Proceedings of the 32nd annual ACM Conference on Human Factors in Computing Systems, pp. 1265–1274. ACM (2014)
6. Berners-Lee, T., Hendler, J., Lassila, O., et al.: The semantic web. Sci. Am. **284**(5), 28–37 (2001)
7. Bizer, C., Lehmann, J., Kobilarov, G., Auer, S., Becker, C., Cyganiak, R., Hellmann, S.: Dbpedia-a crystallization point for the web of data. Web Semant: Sci. Serv. Agents World Wide Web **7**(3), 154–165 (2009)
8. Bollacker, K., Evans, C., Paritosh, P., Sturge, T., Taylor, J.: Freebase: a collaboratively created graph database for structuring human knowledge. In: Proceedings of the 2008 ACM SIGMOD International Conference on Management of Data, pp. 1247–1250. ACM (2008)
9. Brickley, D., Guha, R.V.: Resource description framework (rdf) schema specification 1.0: W3c candidate recommendation, 27 March 2000 (2000)
10. Brooke, J.: SUS: a quick and dirty usability scale. In: Jordan, P.W., Thomas, A., Weerdmeester, B.A., McClelland, I.L. (eds.) Usability Evaluation in Industry. Taylor and Francis, London (1996)
11. Khalili, A., Auer, S., Hladky, D.: The RDFa content editor - from WYSIWYG to WYSIWYM. In: 2012 IEEE 36th Annual Computer Software and Applications Conference (COMPSAC), pp. 531–540. IEEE (2012)
12. Klebeck, A., Hellmann, S., Ehrlich, C., Auer, S.: OntosFeeder – a versatile semantic context provider for web content authoring. In: Antoniou, G., Grobelnik, M., Simperl, E., Parsia, B., Plexousakis, D., De Leenheer, P., Pan, J. (eds.) ESWC 2011, Part II. LNCS, vol. 6644, pp. 456–460. Springer, Heidelberg (2011)

13. Lassila, O., Swick, R.R., et al.: Resource description framework (rdf) model and syntax specification (1998)
14. Manning, C.D., Surdeanu, M., Bauer, J., Finkel, J., Bethard, S.J., McClosky, D.: The stanford coreNLP natural language processing toolkit. In: Proceedings of 52nd Annual Meeting of the Association for Computational Linguistics: System Demonstrations, pp. 55–60 (2014)
15. Sauermann, L., van Elst, L., Dengel, A.: PIMO - a framework for representing personal information models. In: Pellegrini, T., Schaffert, S. (eds.) I-SEMANTICS Conference, pp. 270–277. J.UCS, Know-Center, Graz, 5–7 September 2007
16. Staab, S., Maedche, A., Handschuh, S.: Creating metadata for the semantic web - an annotation environment and the human factor. In: Institute AIFB (2000)
17. Thórisson, K.R., Spivack, N., Wissner, J.M.: Semcards: a new representation for realizing the semantic web. In: Nguyen, N.T., Kowalczyk, R., Chen, S.-M. (eds.) ICCCI 2009. LNCS, vol. 5796, pp. 425–436. Springer, Heidelberg (2009)
18. Tramp, S., Heino, N., Auer, S., Frischmuth, P.: RDFauthor: employing RDFa for collaborative knowledge engineering. In: Cimiano, P., Pinto, H.S. (eds.) EKAW 2010. LNCS, vol. 6317, pp. 90–104. Springer, Heidelberg (2010)

Managing References by Filing and Tagging

An Exploratory Study of Personal Information Management by Social Scientists

Pierre Fastrez[(✉)] and Jerry Jacques

Center for Research in Communication, Université catholique de Louvain,
Louvain-la-Neuve, Belgium
{pierre.fastrez,jerry.jacques}@uclouvain.be

Abstract. This paper presents the preliminary results of a cognitive ethnography of the personal information management (PIM) practices of five social science researchers. Based on video-recorded interviews involving guided tours of our informants' personal digital spaces of information, we study how they create digital workspaces that support their informational activity. We introduce a semio-cognitive theoretical framework to elucidate the relationships between the users' informational activity, the technical and semiotic properties of the software tools they use, and their conceptual models of these tools. Based on this framework, our analyses of PIM practices highlight how conceptual models play a mediation role between the affordances of the tools and the activities that they support.

Keywords: Personal information management · Folders · Tags · Cognitive semiotics · Conceptual models · Conceptual metaphors

1 Introduction

Contemporary information workers face the challenge of managing personal and shared information collections (documents, emails, bookmarks, pictures, videos) that constantly grow in size. These collections can be accessed through a multiplicity of devices and services, in an increasing number of mobile and sedentary contexts. When they are shared, they often support complex collaborative activities. This paper presents the theoretical framework and methodological protocol, as well as the preliminary results, of an ongoing research program focused on the personal information management (or PIM) practices of scientific researchers.

2 Personal Information Management (PIM)

PIM can be defined as "the practice and the study of activities a person performs in order to acquire or create, store, organize, maintain, retrieve, use and distribute the information needed to meet life's many goals (everyday and long-term, work-related

S. Yamamoto (Ed.): HIMI 2015, Part I, LNCS 9172, pp. 291–300, 2015.
DOI: 10.1007/978-3-319-20612-7_28

and not) and to fulfill life's many roles and responsibilities (as parent, spouse, friend, employee, member of community, etc.)" [1].

PIM research has dedicated a fair amount of effort to documenting the practices of individuals organizing digital collections of information, in the prospect of formulating recommendations for the design of future PIM software applications. These studies have generally focused on how individuals organize a specific type of digital resources, such as files [2–5], emails [6–9], photographs [10], web bookmarks [11], or, in a minority of cases, several types of resources [12]. Twenty years ago, initial studies in this field have highlighted how users sorted their digital information based on a limited number of categories, organized at the same level (e.g. a distinction between ephemeral, working and archived files, with no or few sub-categories) [2]. More recent studies have shown a greater variety in the organizations produced by users, especially regarding the number of folders or the complexity of folder hierarchies they created [4, 12], in a context where information workers have to deal with increasing loads of information to be processed [3, 8].

Several studies have described the different types of strategies adopted by users to organize their personal information. These strategies differ in terms of the nature of the categories used to group resources (e.g. by level of priority in their expected processing, or by subject [6]), or based on the frequency of sorting, or the proportion of sorted resources [4, 8, 9, 12]. Some of these studies have shown that the same users can adopt different strategies both within the same application and between different applications (file managers vs. email clients vs. bookmark managers) [12].

As of today, the description of the cognitive functions fulfilled by the personal organization of information collections is still shaped by the seminal distinction introduced by Malone [13], deriving from his observation of desk organization practices, between *filing* documents into named folders (within cabinets), which affords *(re) finding* them later, and *piling* documents in sight, which *reminds* the office occupant what needs to be done.

In the context of the descriptive studies of PIM practices presented above, the research presented in this paper focuses on a specific set of practices: the categorization of digital resources using either folders or tags. Our perspective is a comprehensive one: we examine how the kinds of organization produced by users with these two types of functionalities support their activities as they are situated in their natural contexts of use.

3   Cognitive Semiotics of PIM

We consider PIM practices as a semio-cognitive activity. PIM tools can be viewed as cognitive artifacts "designed to maintain, display, or operate upon information in order to serve a representational function" [14]. We use the concept of *techno-semiotic affordances* to describe how each tool offers specific means of action on ("techno-") and representation of ("semiotic") the information items it helps organize.

With these tools, users construct actionable representations (folder hierarchical trees, item lists, collections of dynamic tags, etc.) which make the conceptual categories underlying their activity perceptible and manipulable.

Our analyses of PIM practices emphasize the role of conceptual models of technology constructed by users. A conceptual model corresponds to the representation a given user holds of the functioning of a tool or system, and of how to interact with it [15]. When constructing a conceptual model for a system, users rely on the system image [16], i.e. the way it presents itself through its interface, its documentation, etc. We study how conceptual models can play a mediating role between the actual affordances and constraints of the tool for the user, and the user's activity it is meant to support.

These models can be described in terms of the conceptual metaphors they involve. Conceptual metaphor theory [17] considers metaphors as cognitive tools that are essential and ubiquitous to the way humans understand their experiences. As human beings, we understand most of our abstract concepts (time, love, causality, money, the self, etc.) by using what we know of more concrete conceptual domains (space, heat, physical forces, inanimate objects, etc.). A conceptual metaphor is the cognitive operation through which the conceptual structure of a source domain (e.g. heat) is projected onto a target domain (e.g. love) to provide an understanding of the target in terms of the source (e.g. yielding linguistic expressions such as "he was in a *heated* relationship").

In this theoretical perspective, the conceptual model of an interactive system (as constructed by its user) is structured by multiple layers of conceptual metaphors [18] that call upon the user's knowledge and experience in various (source) conceptual domains. Higher-level metaphorical projections inherit and build upon the conceptual structure established by lower-level projections [19]. In the case of PIM software applications, folders and tags share the low-level metaphor of DIRECT MANIPULATION [20], in which a system corresponds to a model-world composed of objects the user can act on "directly" [21]. The user' bodily experience of objects in physical space are projected onto their experience of the system, so that they understand it in terms of direct manipulation of computer objects [22] (see top portion of Fig. 1). Although computer folders and tags fulfil a common categorization function, they correspond to two distinct conceptual models, relying on different metaphors that build upon the common primary metaphor of object manipulation. Folders rely on the CONTAINER metaphor, in which the act of categorizing an item corresponds to the act of placing it into a folder that contains it (see middle portion of Fig. 1, left). Tags rely on the TAGGING metaphor, in which the act of categorizing an item corresponds to the act of attaching a descriptive label to this item (see middle portion of Fig. 1, right).

The implementation of folders and tags into a particular software application further specifies these metaphors, each application adding its own conceptual structure to the conceptual model (see bottom portion of Fig. 1). In some cases, these specifications can contradict the lower-level metaphors that underlie them. For instance, folders can, depending on their implementation in different applications, contain only categorized items (in conformity with the source domain of physical folders), or contain an undetermined number of levels of subfolders (in contradiction with the source). Similarly, a folder can be the exclusive storage location of the items it contains (conformity), or contain items that also reside in other folders (contradiction). The techno-semiotic affordances of each application act as material anchors [23] for the user's conceptual model of the system and its functionalities: the material structure of

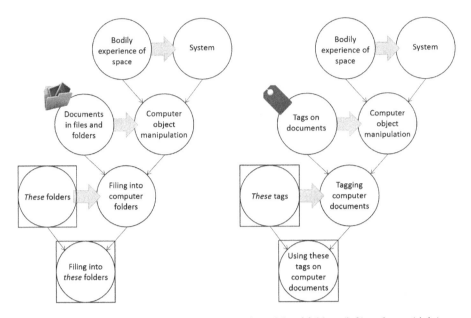

Fig. 1. Layers of metaphors in the conceptual models of folders (left) and tags (right)

the system's interface is mapped onto the conceptual structure of the model, thereby providing stability to the conceptual model (the material structure of each application is represented as a square around the source domain in Fig. 1).

Our analyses also rely on the tenets of distributed cognition theory [24], which defines cognitive activity as the creation, transformation and propagation of representational states through (internal or external) representational media brought into coordination. We examine how the conceptual structure of the informational activity is brought into coordination with the techno-semiotic structure of the technological tool used to support it, through the mediation of the user's conceptual model of this tool.

4   Method

We conducted a series of ten semi-structured interviews with five social science researchers active in the same scientific domain, representing a variety of profiles in the advancement of the academic career. Each informant was interviewed twice, three years apart. At the time of the second interviews, Laurent was halfway through his PhD thesis, Thomas was finishing writing his Ph.D. dissertation, Benoît had recently defended it, Patrick had been an Associate Professor for five years, and Michel was a Full Professor, three years away from retirement.[1] The interviews were video-recorded, and took the form of a guided tour of their personal digital workspaces.

---

[1] The informants' names were modified.

5   Preliminary Results

The preliminary results presented in this section focus on the analysis of the PIM practices of our five informants involving the use of their bibliographical reference manager of choice (Zotero[2] or Mendeley[3]), which affords the categorization of references and texts both with folders and with tags. Despite the limited number of informants, our observations reveal an important variety in the practices involving these functionalities, as well as in the practices dedicated to coordinating the resources contained in the reference managers with those stored in the folders of their operating system (Windows or MacOS). In this paper, we will focus on the practices developed within the reference managers, as well as on their diachronic evolution.

5.1   Folders and Tags in Zotero and Mendeley

Categorizing Texts... The folders and tags of reference managers are used by our informants to map sets of conceptual categories related to their professional activities onto a representational structure, and to determine which texts[4] are part of which categories. Three types of categories are reified by folders or tags: (1) categories related to the subjects or concepts detailed in the categorized texts, (2) categories related to the user's projects (or, more generally, their activity domains) involving the sorted texts (e.g. the user's Ph.D. thesis, an article he wrote, a class he is in charge of, etc.), and (3) categories related to the processing of the texts (e.g. "need to borrow", "need to read", "can be read in the evening", etc.).

In Zotero as in Medeley, the same document can be placed into multiple folders, and the same tag can be applied to multiple documents. Folders and tags act as filters on the complete list of texts encoded by the user: selecting a folder and/or one or several tags limits the list of displayed texts to those corresponding to the cumulated selection criteria.

Among the five researchers we interviewed, all use folders, but only the two youngest (Laurent and Thomas) use tags. All of them make use of the possibility of placing texts in multiple folders, but neither Laurent nor Thomas filters his bibliographic list by selecting multiple tags. Therefore, folders and tags are put to use by our informants in functionally equivalent ways, despite their different affordances. They are used to sort texts into multiple categories (i.e. placing one text into multiple folders, applying multiple tags to one text), and to generate text lists based on their belonging to a single category (i.e. selecting a single folder or tag, whereas tags afford to generate lists from the selection of multiple tags).

---

[2] http://www.zotero.org/.

[3] http://www.mendeley.com/.

[4] Even though one could argue that the records in a reference manager are *references*, we will refer to them as *texts*, and consider that each encoded reference ultimately refers to a text (book, article, book chapter, etc.).

Nevertheless, the ways in which our informants categorize texts using folders and tags differ, both between informants and within the practices of a given informant. For example, Michel only creates folders that correspond to his research projects and classes. Patrick and Benoît's folders include all three types of categories described above (subjects, projects, and work management). Laurent creates subject-based tags, and folders for projects and work management categories. Thomas assigns subject-based tags to the notes he writes in Zotero (which are all attached to a text, and related to one of its sections), which allows him to create ties between fragments of texts he read. He also created folders for each part of his Ph.D. dissertation, as he progressed through its writing. Hence, when tags are used by our informants, their use is exclusively associated to the contents of the texts: the distinction between the texts' subjects and the categories related to the user's activity (projects and work management) corresponds to the distinction between tags as properties of texts-objects and folders containing these texts.

Additionally, we identified two other techno-semiotic affordances of folders and tags in Zotero and Mendeley that may explain their respective adoption in a given context, although we cannot fully articulate them to the observed practices of our informants yet. On the one hand, folders (not tags) in both applications afford to be organized into hierarchical levels, without these hierarchical relationships having any incidence on the categorization of the texts contained in the folders: for example, selecting a first-level folder only makes the texts contained in that folder appear in the active list, not the texts contained in the subfolders. On the other hand, in addition to being displayed in a general list of all used tags, the tags applied to a text (contrary to the folders containing them) appear and can be edited on the text's details panel (which includes a "tags" tab).

… In Order to Produce Relevant Lists. Our informants mainly categorize texts using folders or tags to be able produce a limited list of texts corresponding to a given criterion, through the selection of a folder or a tag, or by using the search function with specific keywords (Zotero and Mendeley's search index includes tags, but also all the encoded references' metadata as well as the full-text contents of the pdf files stored inside the software database and their associated notes).

The production of such a list is essentially used as a means to two different ends by our informants: (1) re-finding a specific text (generating the list is the first step of a search task, before sorting it and identifying the searched text) or (2) "seeing what one has" on a given subject, project or domain. These two uses are reminiscent of the distinction between finding and reminding introduced by Malone [13]. The second type of use actually corresponds to two distinct contexts of use in our informants practices. In some cases, the informant "reviews" the list to improve his knowledge of the literature on the selected topic, which may lead him to further search for additional bibliographic resources (outside of the reference manager) to complement his collection. In other cases, the informant generates and goes through the list as part of the writing process of a text, typically to see what research works could or should be cited in the section being written. Between these two contexts, Thomas is the only one to adopt different practices: whereas he uses tags to "review" the contents of his collection on a specific topic, he uses folders when checking what texts to cite in his writing.

5.2   The Diachronic Dimension of PIM

Incremental Constructions. Our observations of the PIM practices of scientific researchers make the temporal distribution of the cognitive activity they involve apparent [25]. One the one hand, the products of past organization practices support future organization practices. For example, Thomas explained how he broke down the work of organizing his references into folders in Zotero, by importing the contents of each subfolder of his "sources" folder (located on his hard drive) at a time, and by frequently checking the tags he assigned to the notes associated with the references he is organizing. Both the hard drive subfolders and the note tags that were created previously act as guides for the creation of new reference manager folders.

On the other hand, the organization process itself is an activity that yields benefits for the user: Laurent and Thomas justified the utility of creating folders and tags both by mentioning the possibility they created to select relevant sets of texts for their current activity (cf. supra) and by emphasizing the better knowledge of their bibliography which resulted from the act of organizing.

The Weight of History. However, the observed PIM practices do not always evolve for the better over time. Our informants' digital workspaces are cluttered with residues of past practices. For example, Laurent pointed us to a series of subject-based folders he created in Mendeley, for which he now has equivalent tags that replace them. During our second interview, Patrick found a forgotten folder named "unread pdf files" on his hard drive. In both cases, these abandoned structures are ignored by the user, and do not seem to get in the way of their current practices. Both informants claim they could delete them, or convert them into the structures they now use.

In other cases, the products of the informant's past practices hinder his current practices. When he first started using Zotero, Patrick used its import function to recover the 560 references he had encoded in a homemade database, which he previously used as a reference manager. The import process converted the hundreds of keywords he had assigned to the encoded references into tags. The automated coordination between this set of keywords, which were initially created to be used with a search engine, and the tagging function of Zotero, generated a list of hundreds of tags, most of which were assigned to only one text. Not only were these keywords useless as tags from Patrick's standpoint, but their number made any newly created tag automatically lost among them. The impossibility to delete several tags at a time, or to merge them, prevents him from using tags altogether to organize his bibliography.

6   Discussion

We study the PIM practices of scientific researchers by studying them as the coordination (or disjunction) of three types of structure: the conceptual structure of an informational activity (e.g. managing scientific references), the techno-semiotic structure of the tools (including their affordances) that support this activity, and the structure of the conceptual models of the tools held by their users (including the conceptual metaphors they involve).

As the research presented in this paper is work in progress, the first observations we presented can only be considered as the basis for hypotheses to be validated by future analyses. For instance, we observed differences in the uses of folders *vs.* tags that correspond to conceptual distinctions related to the user's activity. Our current hypothesis is that this correspondence could be best explained by differences in the user's respective conceptual models of folders and tags, not by their respective affordances: if our informants use folders and tags differently, it is because they understand them differently, not because they function differently. Indeed, when they use either folders or tags, our informants exploit the same basic affordances: multiple categorization of texts, and selection of one unique category at a time to generate a limited list of texts. By contrast, the exclusive use of tags to categorize texts by subject (not by project) could indicate a privileged correspondence between a conceptual model relying on the LABELING metaphor and a topical categorization of texts.

Our observations also define several research directions regarding the collaboration practices anchored by shared document collections.

First, the semio-cognitive conceptual framework introduced in Sect. 3 allows for a fine-grained analysis of the coordination between internal (mental) representations and external (semiotic) representations within PIM practices. Such analyses make it possible to answer the question of what is explicitly encoded in the external representations (as opposed to being located in the user's internal representations), and hence can be shared, when these representations are resources for the coordination between individuals.

Second, taking the diachronic dimension of PIM practices into account sheds light on the benefit of organization both as a process and as a product of this process. By reifying the conceptual categories of the user's activity (subjects, projects, etc.), the work of tagging items and placing them into folders affects the way the user understands these very categories, by providing them with a deeper knowledge of their collection (in our observations: their bibliography). In the context of shared collections, this finding emphasizes the necessity of making the organization process itself visible, and in particular the part of this process operated by other users of the shared collection. Making the process of organizing a collection visible would place it in the common conceptual ground [26] of the users sharing the collection, which would support the development of a shared understanding of the organization of the knowledge domain covered by the collection. This shared understanding could, in turn, support further activities, such as the collective writing of a publication or a research proposal.

Third, in terms of recommendations for the design of PIM tools, our observations on the diachronic dimension of PIM practices also highlight the issue of transitions between successively adopted PIM tools. These observations suggest the possibility of including "negotiated" import procedures into PIM tools. Such procedures would allow the user to accommodate previous organization structures with the specific affordances of the system in which they are imported.

Finally, our analyses show how our informants explore the contents of their (folder-based or tag-based) categories in the context of a variety of activities (e.g. searching, reviewing, and writing). As such, they raise the question of the desirability of seeing PIM tools generate multiple representations of the same organizations, each tailored to a specific context of use.

Acknowledgements. Pierre Fastrez is a Research Associate at the Belgian *Fonds de la Recherche Scientifique* (F.R.S.-FNRS). Jerry Jacques is a Research Fellow at the Belgian *Fonds de la Recherche Scientifique* (F.R.S.-FNRS).

References

1. Jones, W.: Keeping Found Things Found: The Study and Practice of Personal Information Management. Morgan Kaufmann, Burlington (2008)
2. Barreau, D., Nardi, B.A.: Finding and reminding: file organization from the desktop. SIGCHI Bull. **27**, 39–43 (1995)
3. Barreau, D.: The persistence of behavior and form in the organization of personal information. J. Am. Soc. Inf. Sci. Technol. **59**, 307–317 (2008)
4. Hardof-Jaffe, S., Hershkovitz, A., Abu-Kishk, H., Bergman, O., Nachmias, R.: How do students organize personal information spaces? Educational Data Mining, pp. 250–258 (2009)
5. Zhang, H., Twidale, M.: Mine, yours and ours: using shared folders in personal information management. In: Proceedings of the PIM 2012 Workshop. ACM Press, Seattle, WA (2012)
6. Mackay, W.E.: Diversity in the use of electronic mail: a preliminary inquiry. ACM Trans. Inf. Syst. **6**, 380–397 (1988)
7. Civan, A., Jones, W., Klasnja, P., Bruce, H.: Better to organize personal information by folders or by tags?: the devil is in the details. In: Proceedings of ASIST 2008. American Society for Information Science and Technology, Columbus, OH (2008)
8. Fisher, D., Brush, A.J., Gleave, E., Smith, M.A.: Revisiting Whittaker & Sidner's "email overload" ten years later. In: Proceedings of CSCW 2006, pp. 309–312. ACM, New York, NY (2006)
9. Whittaker, S., Sidner, C.: Email overload: exploring personal information management of email. In: Proceedings of the SIGCHI Conference on Human Factors in Computing Systems, pp. 276–283. ACM, New York, NY, USA (1996)
10. Rodden, K., Wood, K.R.: How do people manage their digital photographs? In: Proceedings of the SIGCHI Conference on Human factors in Computing Systems, pp. 409–416. ACM, New York, NY, USA (2003)
11. Jones, W., Dumais, S., Bruce, H.: Once found, what then? A study of "keeping" behaviors in the personal use of web information. In: Proceedings of ASIST 2002, pp. 391–402 (2002)
12. Boardman, R., Sasse, M.A.: "Stuff goes into the computer and doesn't come out": a cross-tool study of personal information management. In: Proceedings of the SIGCHI Conference on Human Factors in Computing Systems, pp. 583–590. ACM, New York, NY, USA (2004)
13. Malone, T.W.: How do people organize their desks?: implications for the design of office information systems. ACM Trans. Inf. Syst. **1**, 99–112 (1983)
14. Norman, D.A.: Cognitive artifacts. In: Carroll, J.M. (ed.) Designing Interaction: Psychology at the Human-Computer Interface, pp. 17–38. Cambridge University Press, Cambridge (1991)
15. Jonassen, D.H.: Operationalizing mental models: strategies for assessing mental models to support meaningful learning and design-supportive learning environments. In: The First International Conference on Computer Support for Collaborative Learning, pp. 182–186. L. Erlbaum Associates Inc., Hillsdale, NJ, USA (1995)
16. Norman, D.A.: The Design of Everyday Things. Basic Books, New York (1988)
17. Lakoff, G., Johnson, M.: Metaphors We Live By. University of Chicago Press, Chicago (1980)

18. Collard, A.-S., Fastrez, P.: A model of the role of conceptual metaphors in hypermedia comprehension. In: Proceedings of CICOM 2009, pp. 241–255. Aletheia, Braga, Portugal (2010)
19. Lakoff, G.: The contemporary theory of metaphor. In: Ortony, A. (ed.) Metaphor and Thought, 2nd edn, pp. 202–251. Cambridge University Press, Cambridge (1993)
20. Frohlich, D.M.: The history and future of direct manipulation. Behav. Inf. Technol. **12**, 315–329 (1993)
21. Hutchins, E.L., Hollan, J.D., Norman, D.A.: Direct manipulation interfaces. Hum.-Comput. Interact. **1**, 311–338 (1985)
22. Fauconnier, G.: Conceptual blending and analogy. In: Gentner, D., Holyoak, K., Kokinov, B. (eds.) The Analogical Mind: Perspectives from Cognitive Science, pp. 255–286. MIT Press, Cambridge (2001)
23. Hutchins, E.L.: Material anchors for conceptual blends. J. Pragmat. **37**, 1555–1577 (2005)
24. Hutchins, E.L.: Cognition in the Wild. The MIT Press, Cambridge (1995)
25. Hutchins, E.L.: Distributed cognition. In: Smelser, N.J., Baltes, P.B. (eds.) International Encyclopedia of the Social and Behavioral Sciences, pp. 2068–2072. Elsevier Press, Amsterdam (2001)
26. Tomasello, M.: Origins of Human Communication. MIT Press, Cambridge (2008)

Towards a Class-Based Model of Information Organization in Wikipedia

Michael Gilbert[(⊠)] and Mark Zachry

Human Centered Design and Engineering, University of Washington,
Box 352315, Seattle, WA 98195, USA
{mdg, zachry}@uw.edu

Abstract. As complexity increases in commons-based peer production communities, the means of organizing and facilitating collective action must also mature to ensure the ongoing health and active maintenance of those communities [1]. This study examines the types of structured data that exist in Wikipedia, introduces an argument for an extension to the types of structured and semi-structured data within Wikipedia supported by that descriptive analysis; and presents an implementation of that extension that supports instantiations of semi-structured content that facilitate both human and tool-mediated interactions with Wikipedia data. This extension offers a novel means of structuring data to support the ongoing health and maintenance of online communities like the community of editors that maintain and develop Wikipedia.

Keywords: Information organization · Information design · Tool-mediated interaction · Wikis · Templates

1 Introduction

As a world-class online encyclopedia written by volunteers, Wikipedia is driven by the Quixotic goal of creating an online resource representing the "sum of all human knowledge". Because the system has grown for more than a decade, supporting this goal requires an increasingly complex ecosystem of tools and processes to ensure that community members can effectively create, update, and maintain quality content across the myriad categories of knowledge now encompassed in the encyclopedia. These tools range from the simple to the complex, from built-in templates and modules that form part of the core of the MediaWiki platform, to sophisticated agents such as ClueBot NG, an autonomous bot user that utilizes advanced machine learning to identify and automatically revert vandalism in the encyclopedia. And while the user experience for most visitors to the encyclopedia is limited to a rather seamless display of encyclopedic content, that content and the community responsible for its creation rely on many tools, a web of functionality that fundamentally facilitates and alters both how users experience Wikipedia and how editors contribute to it. For example, one of the most frequently used tools, the Yesno template, is responsible for normalizing an input to be a yes/no output, and has been used on over 6.7 million pages.[1] ClueBot NG, a

---

[1] All data from this and the following figures was fetched from the Wikimedia Tool Labs databases, http://tools.wmflabs.org/, containing the complete metadata history for all edits to Wikipedia.

© Springer International Publishing Switzerland 2015
S. Yamamoto (Ed.): HIMI 2015, Part I, LNCS 9172, pp. 301–309, 2015.
DOI: 10.1007/978-3-319-20612-7_29

vandalism-fighting bot, made over 600,000 edits to the English language Wikipedia in 2013 alone. Further, of the ten most active accounts on Wikipedia during 2013, eight were bot accounts and the remaining two were primarily tool-mediated edits – namely, edits made with the ProveIt[2] and HotCat[3] tools, neither of which are part of the MediaWiki platform, but which facilitate and simplify interactions with the content stored within it.

Clearly, our interactions within Wikipedia are increasingly affected by the tools available to the community, both those that are enabled by default such as the templates and modules so frequently used and the many other tools that exist outside the platform to aid in editing efforts. While such tools enable many varied interactions with the Wikipedia content and community, significant opportunities to improve information organization and presentation within the encyclopedia are numerous. For example, the system would benefit from an improved, robust means of organizing information. Such an enhancement could provide a powerful and extensible way to extend the efforts of individual editors. This paper presents a principled approach to the design of such a tool, using an analysis of existing tools and solving for a problem that has not yet been addressed by a system tool.

Our new approach introduces a tool capable of storing and presenting tabular lists of arbitrary data in a way that is resilient to both human and non-human edits in the encyclopedia. Our approach allows for storing information about an arbitrary object (the data) as well as for defining relevant behavior for the validation and presentation of that object (the code). By adopting an object-oriented language to define and present this work, our tool-based approach is distinctly different from existing mechanisms in Wikipedia.

The goals of this paper are three-fold. First, we conduct a quantitative analysis of existing uses of templates and modules in Wikipedia, concluding with a brief descriptive analysis of those most frequently in use. Second, we discuss the benefits and shortcomings of current approaches, highlighting a direction to move forward with more resilient strategies. And, finally, we introduce a new method of data storage that allows for a robust and stable means of defining object information in Wikipedia. Our tool, employing this method, will allow editors to gain more control over tabular data and its presentation within the system. Our approach emphasizes the need for the data to be fault tolerant, to avoid breaks by human edits, as well as to be flexible, facilitating multiple methods of presentation between multiple destinations. Our new data structure thus utilizes existing potential in the MediaWiki platform to allow more nuanced control of information storage and presentation within Wikipedia.

2 Related Work

To guide our work, we sought to first understand the potential behind structured and semi-structured data in Wikipedia. Additionally, we considered the use of automated and semi-automated tools to mediate the ongoing health and operation of Wikipedia.

---

[2] https://en.wikipedia.org/wiki/User:ProveIt_GT, allowing editors to more easily "find, edit, add, and cite references in Wikipedia articles".

[3] https://en.wikipedia.org/wiki/Wikipedia:HotCat, allowing editors to easily add or remove categories from individual or groups of articles with a single click.

As we discovered, the intersection between these two classes of related work indicates the need for a novel approach to supporting human efforts and tool-mediated interactions.

In several studies, researchers have considered different means of both structuring semantic data in Wikipedia as well as means of mining that data for external use. Bizer, et al. [2], explore how the DBpedia project extracts information for *infoboxes* in Wikipedia, archives them locally, and makes these data pairs accessible to third party applications via a public API on the World Wide Web. These infoboxes represent a common means of data re-use in Wikipedia. Using these infoboxes, editors have a simple and straightforward means of defining any number of attribute-value pairs and the presentation of that information can be delegated to a specialized *Template*. See Fig. 1 below for an example of both the declaration and instantiation of one such infobox for the chemical element Oxygen. Beyond the simple instantiation, presentation, and extraction of attribute-value pairs present in these infobox templates (e.g., [3]), another project [4] explores means of automatically populating empty attribute pairs in Wikipedia articles, building on prior work by Wu and Weld [5].

Related to these examinations of semi-structured data as information object is prior research on mediating tools in Wikipedia. This "bespoke code" that supports the

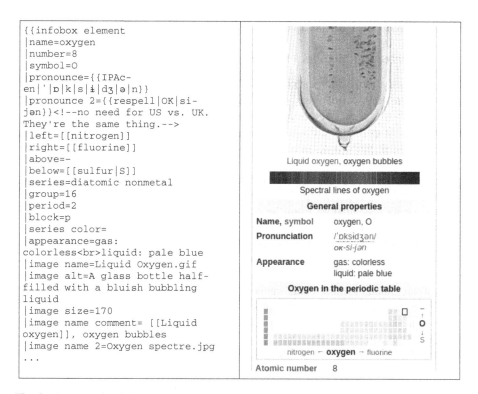

Fig. 1. An example of the instantiation and presentation of the infobox template for the element Oxygen. The cell on the left contains the text used to define the template attributes, the image on the right is part of the resulting presentation.

ongoing operation of the encyclopedia makes up an estimated six million lines of code, an order of magnitude greater than the about 600,000 lines of code that represent the core MediaWiki platform [6]. These tools are crucial for the ongoing health of the encyclopedia, providing editors with the means to patrol and revert vandalism, monitor edits, and increase the visibility of information intended to aid editors in their ongoing efforts, mediating the work that occurs between the "social" and the "technical" [7].

Our contribution presents a variation of bespoke code that allows editors to interact with the system in ways that have thus far not been possible. Beyond that, by creating a novel means of structuring tabular data in Wikipedia we provide a new avenue for research on semantic data extraction and re-use to progress (such as [2, 3, 5]) providing a vast amount of contextual data that can be mined and interpreted, with the potential to inform the design and implementation of new tools in the future.

In the next section we lay out a more detailed description of the templates and modules used within Wikipedia, including their construction, prevalence and utility, as well as potential shortcomings with regard to managing more complex data types requiring greater flexibility in both presentation and behavior. Following, we introduce a novel approach to utilizing these existing affordances to resolve these shortcomings and to better support complex cooperative work.

3   The Current Landscape

3.1   Templates and Modules - Introduction

There are many tools built directly into the MediaWiki platform that simplify the process of creating, formatting, and maintaining different types of information. As introduced above, primary among these are templates and modules. The idea behind these tools is simple: once created, both templates and modules allow editors to define simple key value pairs, and once instantiated the template or module will handle the presentation of that data. As shown in Fig. 1 above, these template instantiations can be arbitrarily complex, allowing the template designer to craft complicated visualizations from the information passed in by the template caller (separating the instance of the template, or its instantiation, from the class, its definition), although more frequently templates are used for "boilerplate messages, standard warnings or notices, infoboxes, navigational boxes, and similar purposes," [8]. An instance of a template can be created on any Wikipedia page by simply including the template name in braces. For example, a simple template transclusion may be to include "{(lambda)}" on a page, which would result in the lambda symbol being included in the resulting text, "λ".

Modules are similar to templates in both their instantiation and capacity to simplify the structure and presentation of data – many modules have actually been created to replace existing templates. However, while templates define their presentation through standard Wiki markup, modules allow users to define custom Lua scripts that are run when the module is transcluded on the target page. This allows users a more powerful means to "analyze data, calculate expressions, and format results using functions or object-oriented programming," [9]. The ability to run these Lua scripts on the MediaWiki platform was added through the Scribunto interface, originally installed on the English language Wikipedia in February, 2013.

3.2   Templates and Modules in Use

The first template was checked into the English language Wikipedia on September 30, 2002. Since that time, templates have become one of the most ubiquitous and frequently used tools available to Wikipedians, with over 605,000 templates created, transcluded over 312 million times on pages within the English Wikipedia. Modules, with their more recent release date, currently only number just over 2,100. However, despite their more modest number, modules have currently been transcluded over 179 million times on pages. As the total number of pages across all namespaces[4] (including the template and module namespaces) is just over 35 million, it is evident that many of these transclusions are occurring multiple times per page, highlighting a pattern of usage verifying the central role that these tools play in the presentation of standard information within Wikipedia. For a more detailed view of the distribution of pages over namespaces, as well as the distribution of template and module transclusions over namespaces, see Figs. 2 and 3 below.

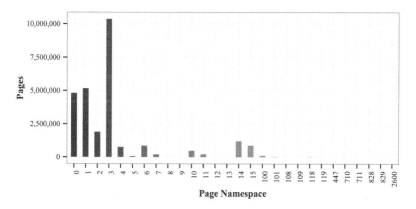

Fig. 2. Distribution of pages across namespaces

The ubiquity of these tools is clear, but what are they most often being used for? The single most used Template is the Yesno Template referred to above, which is currently transcluded over 6.7 million times. Following that is the Transclude Template, with over 6.1 million transclusions, which handles resolving page names to clarify Wikipedia links. Top among Modules is Arguments, with over 15 million transclusions, a meta-module which enables other Modules to process arguments passed in when they are invoked. Following that is the Module version of the Yesno Template, with over 11 million transclusions. The top templates and modules that are currently in use in the English Wikipedia, along with the number of transclusions for each, is included in Table 1 below.

---

[4] Namespaces are how the MediaWiki software categorizes pages of distinct type, for instance allowing the clear separation between Article pages and User pages. See https://en.wikipedia.org/wiki/Wikipedia:Namespace for more detail.

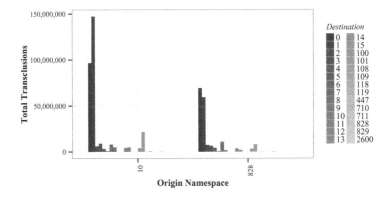

Fig. 3. Template and module transclusions on all pages, split by destination namespace

Table 1. The most frequently transcluded templates and modules in the English language Wikipedia.

Template	Transclusions	Module	Transclusions
Yesno	6,763,997	Arguments	15,526,763
Transclude	6,197,441	Yesno	11,481,409
Navbar	6,182,642	No_globals	7.192,709
Pagetype	6,107,802	Namespace_detect	6,230,069
WPBannerMeta	6,049,255	Pagetype	6,107,727
Class_mask	6,003,990	Category_handler	5,759,067

3.3 Existing Shortcomings

While these templates and modules exist for a wide array of purposes, addressing both simple and complex needs, there are several shortcomings of existing approaches. First, our primary motivator to embark upon this analysis was driven by a need to have a means of modifying semi-structured text by both human and non-human agents to more effectively support tool-mediated modifications of tabular data within Wikipedia. In this context, semi-structured text must be machine parsable in a predictable format, allow for any amount of attribute-value pairs within that format, and finally, support values that can be an open text string of any length. This flexibility was required to ensure that a single class of module could be instantiated with multiple data sets, facilitating a broad set of data manipulation and presentation possibilities. Second, our use case required granular control of error handling, so that if human agents entered malformed or unexpected data in the instantiation of the module that it could attempt to correct or properly display the remaining data. And third, we desired a solution that had the capacity to normalize input data, as well as providing a mechanism for Wikipedians to have a broad range of control over the style of presentation of that data.

Finally, while solutions like infobox templates work adequately for defining more complex information about individual items, such as the Oxygen molecule in Fig. 1 above, we required a solution that would provide a means of defining lists of arbitrary semi-structured data. While it is trivial to instantiate a table using Wiki markup, if that table does not contain predictable data encoded in a predictable fashion it becomes a far more non-trivial task to utilize a tool-mediated approach to interacting with that data. Consider for instance Wikipedia's "List of astronauts by name,"[5] presented as a simple bullet-point list of astronauts, sorted alphabetically, including various additional information about each one such as former names, birth and death dates, and the shuttles each astronaut went up on. Creating a tool that could read this list, parse it, and update it would be fairly simple. However, attempting to utilize that same tool to update the many other lists on the English Wikipedia,[6] as well as the many other task lists, member lists, and list of lists present on WikiProject pages, would likely fail. Without a structured way of storing and presenting this vast assortment of semi-structured text, the number of tools required to support tool-mediated edits to that text could conceivably approach the total number of lists in Wikipedia. Accordingly, a more flexible approach is needed to ensure that this data can be accurately parsed by both human and non-human agents, to more effectively support both the individuals who create and consume that content, as well as the researchers who could far more easily mine the semantic data present in such lists if it were accessible in a more viable format.

No such structure currently exists. In the sections that follow, we lay out the strategies we adopted to create this data structure, and introduce our initial implementation of that approach.

4 Implications for Information Designers

In defining our implementation of the data structure defined above we had two primary goals. First, we wanted to address the shortcomings identified to ensure that our approach would be resilient to potentially incomplete or malformed data, enabling both tool-mediated and manual modifications. And second, we wanted our solution to utilize an approach that is already highly accepted and widely adopted by the Wikipedia community; namely, we wanted to adopt the module as the primary means of storing and presenting data. This implementation allowed us to increase the usability of our approach by reducing the complexity of adoption, as well as ensured that we could take advantage of the expanded functionality offered by the Lua scripting language compared to existing templates.

4.1 Templates and Modules Expanded

In object-oriented programming, an object can have both a state (the data) and behavior (the code). For our implementation, we created two separate modules. The first is a parent module which manages parsing the arguments list, determining the style of the

---

[5] https://en.wikipedia.org/wiki/List_of_astronauts_by_name.

[6] According to the Wikimedia Tools database, there are 187,959 pages in the Article namespace in the English Wikipedia with a title starting "List of," indicating that this could be a wide-reaching solution.

resulting presentation, and handling errors or malformed data. The primary argument to this parent module will be a series of calls to a child module, which will be treated as the data items that should be presented as the output of module instantiation. Specifically, when instantiating our implementation of a list module, four steps are taken. First, the parent module determines the style of presentation. This could take the form of a standard table, a page section, or any repeatable form of presentation that MediaWiki is capable of displaying. Second, the parent module determines the elements that should be displayed in Wiki markup, required to ensure that parameters passed as individual data items are correctly normalized and accounted for before calling the child module. This includes ensuring that the data items that are defined within the parent module invocation have the required values to be displayed properly defined in their sub-module invocation or that a suitable default exists, as well as ensuring that malformed data passed to the parent module is ignored so that the remaining data can be properly parsed and displayed. The actual data in the child module inclusions does not matter – the parent module can determine the greatest common set of identical attributes and present the data as requested. And fourth, the child module invocation strings are created and processed, returning Wiki markup for the desired format for each data item presented to the parent module. An initial implementation of these modules is available from Wikipedia under Module:ListMaster and Module:ListItem.

To take a more specific example, recall the list "List of astronauts by name" article mentioned above, which included alphabetized bullet points for each astronaut, potentially but not always including additional information such alternate names, birth and death dates, and the name of the shuttles the astronauts were on. Utilizing the approach described above, this list could be implemented similar to the following (this example was broken across multiple lines to increase readability, although this is not required):

```
{{#invoke:ListMaster|printTable|style=bullet|
  display=name,lifespan,shuttle#|
    {{#name=[[Joseph M. Acaba]]|
      shuttle0=[[STS-119]]|shuttle1=[[Soyuz TMA-04M]]
    }}
    {{#name=[[Loren Acton]]|
      shuttle0=[[STS-51-F]]
    }}
    {{#name=[[Mike Adams]]|
      lifespan=(1930-1967)|shuttle0=[[X-15]]
    }}
    {{#name=[[James Adamson]]|
      shuttle0=[[STS-28]]|shuttle1=[[STS-43]]
    }}
}}
```

By providing a simple, fault tolerant way to structure arbitrary semi-structured data, editors have the capacity to flexibly control the style and structure of their data. For example, by modifying the invocation above from *style* = *bullet* to *style* = *table*, each astronaut would be represented as a row on a table, sortable by any column, with the built-in ability to provide reasonable defaults for missing values and to skip or attempt to correct malformed data items, here defined as the sub-module invocations inside the #invoke statement. Further, due to the structured nature of the semi-structured data, it becomes a trivial matter to parse attribute value pairs from any arbitrary list defined in Wikipedia, providing a unique means to collate and analyze data as well as to create novel tool-mediated interactions that have the capacity to further shape and improve the way that we interact within that online community.

5   Conclusion

The approach presented in this paper is not meant to be a monolithic solution to replace module usage, but as a means to improve editors' abilities to manage their own content in a manner that is both human editable and machine parsable, extending the research listed above by allowing simple constructs to inform the display of arbitrary objects within the community. By defining an extensible solution for storing, validating, and displaying data within Wikipedia, we hope to facilitate a more flexible means of information presentation than is now possible, as well as providing new means for researchers to parse and utilize an identifiable instantiation of the wide array of semi-structured text present within Wikipedia.

Acknowledgements. This research is supported by a National Science Foundation (NSF) grant, Enhancing Social Translucence in Systems to Support Virtual Teaming (#1162114).

References

1. Marwell, G., Oliver, P.: The Critical Mass in Collective Action. Cambridge University Press, Cambridge (1993)
2. Bizer, C., Lehmann, J., Kobilarov, G., Auer, S., Becker, C., Cyganiak, R., Hellmann, S.: DBpedia - a crystallization point for the web of data. J. Web Semant. **7**, 154–165 (2009). doi:10.1016/j.websem.2009.07.002
3. Wu, F., Weld, D.S.: Open information extraction using Wikipedia. In: Proceedings of the 48th Annual Meeting of the Association for Computational Linguistics (ACL 2010), pp. 118–127 (2007). http://dl.acm.org/citation.cfm?id=1858681.1858694
4. Lange, D., Böhm, C., Naumann, F.: Extracting structured information from Wikipedia articles to populate infoboxes. In: Proceedings of the 19th ACM International Conference on Information and Knowledge Management (CIKM 2010), pp. 1661–1664 (2010). doi:10.1145/1871437.1871698
5. Wu, F., Weld, D.S.: Automatically refining the wikipedia infobox ontology. In: Proceeding of the 17th International Conference on World Wide Web WWW 08, pp. 635–644 (2008). doi:10.1145/1367497.1367583
6. Geiger, R.S.: Bots, bespoke, code and the materiality of software platforms. Inf. Commun. Soc. 1–15 (2014). doi:10.1080/1369118X.2013.873069
7. Ribes, D., Jackson, S., Geiger, S., Burton, M., Finholt, T.: Artifacts that organize: delegation in the distributed organization. Inf. Organ. **23**(1), 1–14 (2013). doi:10.1016/j.infoandorg.2012.08.001
8. Help:Template. https://en.wikipedia.org/wiki/Help:Template
9. Wikipedia:Lua. https://en.wikipedia.org/wiki/Wikipedia:Lua

A General Framework for Text Document Classification Using SEMCON and ACVSR

Zenun Kastrati$^{(\boxtimes)}$, Ali Shariq Imran, and Sule Yildirim Yayilgan

Faculty of Computer Science and Media Technology,
Gjøvik University College, Gjøvik, Norway
{zenun.kastrati,ali.imran,sule.yayilgan}@hig.no

Abstract. The text document classification employs either text based approach or semantic based approach to index and retrieve text documents. The former uses keywords and therefore provides limited capabilities to capture and exploit the conceptualization involved in user information needs and content meanings. The latter aims to solve these limitations using content meanings, rather than keywords. More formally, the semantic based approach uses the domain ontology to exploit the content meanings of a particular domain. This approach however has some drawbacks. It lacks enrichment of ontology concepts with new lexical resources and evaluation of the importance indicated by weights of those concepts. Therefore to address these issues, this paper proposes a new ontology based text document classification framework. The proposed framework incorporates a newly developed objective metric called SEMCON to enrich the domain ontology with new concepts by combining contextual as well as semantic information of a term within a text document. The framework also introduces a new approach to automatically estimate the importance of ontology concepts which is indicated by the weights of these concepts, and to enhance the concept vector space model using automatically estimated weights.

Keywords: Ontology · Classification · Text document · SEMCON

1 Introduction

Web is the main source of information with large number of documents rapidly increasing every passing day. The information is usually kept in unstructured and semi-structured formats - be it text (e.g. word, pdf), images, video or audio. More than 80 % of the information produced by an organization is stored in unstructured textual format in the form of reports, email, views, news, etc [1]. Discovering and extracting useful information from these resources is therefore difficult without the organization and summarization of the document content. This is both an extremely vital and a tedious process in today's digital world [2]. Automatic classification in this respect plays a key role in organizing these massive sources of unstructured textual information into a structured format. Automatic text document classification (categorization) is the process of automatically assigning a

© Springer International Publishing Switzerland 2015
S. Yamamoto (Ed.): HIMI 2015, Part I, LNCS 9172, pp. 310–319, 2015.
DOI: 10.1007/978-3-319-20612-7_30

text document from a given domain to one or more class labels from a finite set of predefined categories.

Classification process has been tackled in two ways in literature: text based and semantic based. In the text based approach, the classification uses extraction of tokens and keywords thereby providing limited capabilities to capture and exploit the conceptualization involved in user information needs and content meanings. Aiming to solve these limitations, the semantic based approach follows the idea of using the content meaning rather than literal strings. It uses domain ontologies to exploit the content meanings of a particular domain.

Most of the indexing techniques used in the ontology based classification approach relies on the statistical vector space model, which represents text documents and categories as term vectors. The components of these term vectors are domain ontology concepts and their relevance represented by the frequency of concepts' occurrence.

Although the existing approaches use the domain ontology to index and retrieve text documents, they lack two important issues regarding the domain ontology (1) enrichment of ontology concept (2) importance of ontology concept.

Concept enrichment means linking new available lexical resources from a particular domain to the existing ontology concept and this is a crucial step for a domain ontology to be actually usable in real applications.

Importance of ontology concept defines the contribution of this concept in the classification process. This contribution depends on the position of concept where it is depicted in the ontology hierarchy, e.g. the higher the concept in the ontology hierarchy, the less the contribution in the classification and vice versa.

To address these issues, in this paper we propose a new ontology based text document classification framework. The proposed framework uses a new objective metric called SEMCON [9] developed at our laboratory to enrich the domain ontology with new concepts by combining contextual as well as semantic information of a term within a text document. In addition, the framework introduces a new approach to automatically estimate the importance of ontology concepts which is indicated by the weights of these concepts, and to enhance the concept vector space model using automatically estimated weights [10].

The reminder of this paper is organised as follows. Section 2 describes related work while Sect. 3 presents a detailed description of our proposed framework. In Sect. 4, we describe the process of labelling of unclassified document into appropriate category. Lastly, Sect. 5 makes some conclusions and gives some directions for future work.

2   Related Work

An increasing number of recent information retrieval systems make use of ontologies to help the users clarify and categorize their information needs and move towards semantic representations of documents. Many ontology based classification systems and models have been proposed in the last decade and all these follow the idea of considering the semantic relations between the terminology information extracted from the text documents and the terminology information extracted from the domain ontology. An in depth review of ontology based classification approach is presented in [3,4]. The authors built an ontology in the economy domain for document classification. They indexed a corpus of economy related documents using the domain ontology by comparing the terminology extracted from the documents and the terminology extracted from the domain ontology.

The semantic indexing of documents using the domain ontology was also used later by researchers in [5]. They performed the semantic indexing and retrieval of biomedical documents through the process of identifying domain concepts extracted from the Medical Subject Headings (MeSH) thesaurus. The authors used a content-based cosine similarity measure. The semantic indexing of documents in domain of biomedicine was also subject of research in [6]. The authors established an ontology based information retrieval system (OBIRS) which uses a domain ontology and documents that are indexed using its ontology concepts e.g. genes annotated by concepts of the Gene Ontology or PubMed articles annotated using the Medical Subject Headings (MeSH). OBIRS system, through a user friendly interface, provides query formulation assistance through auto-completion and ontology browsing. The interface estimates the overall relevance of each document with respect to a given query. The relevance is obtained by aggregating the partial similarity measurements between each concept of the query and measurements indexing the documents. Finally the retrieved documents are ordered according to their overall scores, so that the most relevant documents are ranked higher than the least relevant ones. Furthermore, the scores are summarized in a small explanatory pictogram and an interactive semantic map is used to display top ranked documents.

In contrast to the above methods which use all concepts of a domain ontology to calculate similarity score between the ontology and documents, research in [7] presents a novel ontology-based automatic classification method which uses only a small number of ontology concepts. More precisely, the paper proposed using only the lowest level concepts (instances) of a ontology and this can be achieved thanks to the technique of ontology reasoning. In other words, the approach initially represents documents by a set of weighted terms and categories by ontologies. Then, ontology reasoning is performed to obtain the instances of an ontology. Finally, Google Distance is used to calculate similarity score between these instances and the set of weighted terms for each document. Documents are then classified into different categories according to the computed scores.

3   Proposed Model and Methodology

This section describes the proposed framework for automatic text document classification using the objective metric SEMCON and an adaptive concept vector space representation (ACVSR) model. The proposed framework, inspired by [12], is illustrated in Fig. 2. Our framework consists of four main components detailed below: (1) Domain Ontology, (2) Categories, (3) Building the semantics of the categories and (4) Unlabelled documents.

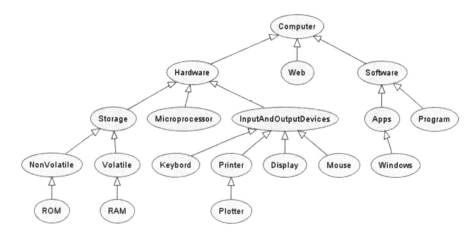

Fig. 1. Ontology sample of the computer domain

3.1 Domain Ontology

The work presented in this paper is in line with the ontology based approach and takes as a starting point the existence of a domain ontology. Domain ontologies are used to model in a formal way the basic vocabulary - concepts for describing a domain and interpreting a description of a problem in that domain.

A 5-tuple based structure [8] is a commonly used formal description to describe the concepts and their relationships in a domain. The 5-tuple core ontology structure is defined as:

$$O = (C, R, H, rel, A) \tag{1}$$

where:

- C is a non-empty set of concepts
- R is a set of relation types
- H is a set of taxonomy relation of C
- rel is a set relationship of C with relation type R, where $rel \subseteq C \times C$
- A is a set of description of logic sentences

Figure 1 shows an ontology tree specified for the concept computer, a part of computer domain.

The main purpose of introducing domain ontologies is to move from a document evaluation based on terms to an evaluation based on concepts, thus moving from lexical to semantic interpretation. The goal is to use the knowledge in domain ontologies to match categories and documents on a semantic level.

3.2 Categories

The second module represents the predefined categories *cat* such as *software*, *hardware*, *web* etc., and the documents *doc* within these categories *cat* for a

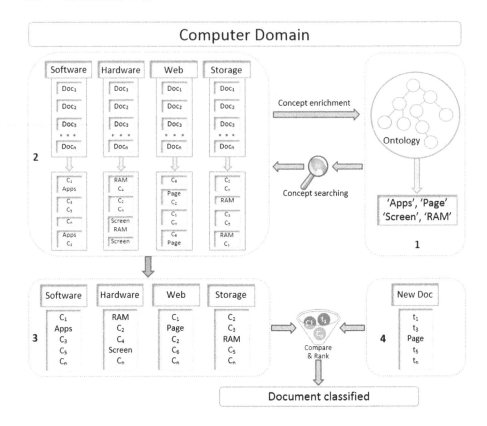

Fig. 2. The architecture of proposed model

certain domain (*Doc*). The documents are organized into appropriate categories manually by an expert from that domain. The documents are represented as plain texts without any semantics associated with them at this point. The semantic aspect is built in using the predefined domain ontology defined in Sect. 3.1. In other words, the semantic for each document (doc_1, doc_2,..., doc_n) is built by matching the terms t in the document *doc* with relevant concepts c in the domain ontology. This is achievable thanks to the presence/availability of at least one of concept labels within documents and/or through identification of associated terms.

The former is a straightforward process. There maybe single label concepts (*Windows*, *RAM*, etc.) in a domain ontology as well as compound label concepts (*InputAndOutputDevices*), as indicated in Fig. 1. For single label concepts, we use only those terms from the document for which an exact term exists in the domain ontology. For example, for concepts in the domain ontology such as *Windows*, *Printer*, *RAM*, etc., there exists exactly the same term extracted from the document. For compound label concepts, we use those terms from the document which are present as part of a concept in the domain ontology. For example, consider *InputAndOutputDevices* as one of the compound ontology concept. In this case the ontology concept *InputAndOutputDevices* is matched if either term, *Input, Output* or *Device* is present in the document.

The latter is a more complex process. Rather than simply looking for an ontology concept, it looks for new terms within documents which are associated semantically with those concepts. To find these associated terms of a particular ontology concept within documents, the proposed framework employs the SEM-CON model [9]. The SEMCON model is an objective metric which combines the contextual and semantic information of the given terms through its learning process. More formally, the SEMCON initially computes an observation matrix by exploiting the statistical features such as frequency of the occurrence of a term, term's font type and term's font size. The context is then defined by using the cosine measure where the dot product between two vectors of the observation matrix reflects the extent to which two terms have a similar occurrence pattern in the vector space. In addition to the context information, the SEMCON incorporates the semantics by computing a semantic similarity score between two terms - term that is extracted from a document and term that already exists in the ontology as a concept.

3.3   Building the Semantics of the Categories

The third module deals with incorporating the semantics to the categories. By incorporating the semantics into categories, the overall classification system can replicate the way an expert organizes/categorizes the documents into each category.

The category semantics is built by aggregating the semantics of all documents which belong to the same category, i.e. each category is represented as a vector whose components are concepts of a domain ontology. The relevance of a concept is defined by a weight computed based on the frequency of occurrence of the concept in a document.

The quantity of information given by the presence of concept c in a document depends on (1) the importance of concept c which is defined by the depth of c in the ontology graph and the number of concepts which subsume or are subsumed by c and (2) Relevance of concept c defined by the frequency of occurring of c in the document.

It is a well established fact that some concepts are better at discriminating between documents than others, in the classification process. In other words, concepts of a domain ontology do not contribute all equally. The contribution depends on the position of concepts where they are depicted in the ontology hierarchy and a concept's contribution is indicated by its corresponding weight. For example, if a concept is positioned in a lower level in the hierarchy tree this means that it is more abstract and it hardly belongs to other domain ontology. On the other side a more general concept is positioned in a higher level in hierarchy tree and it may exists in much ontology.

The ontology hierarchy consists of classes, subclasses and instances that may have different weights to reflect the concepts' importance. The concept's importance is calculated automatically using the model described in [10]. To show

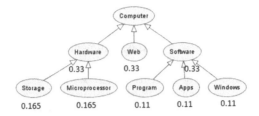

Fig. 3. Ontology representation for concept "Computer"

how the model computes the concept's importance, we have illustrated a simple example which can be explained starting from the lightweight ontology indicated in Fig. 3.

Let us consider concept *Program* which is a descendant of another concept *Software* which has m children including *Program*. Concept *Software* is a descendant of a concept *Computer* which has k children including *Software*. Concept *Program* is a leaf of the graph representing the computer domain ontology. For instance, considering a document containing only *Program* and *Software* concepts, the importance of concept *Program* in the document is $1 + \frac{1}{m}$. In the document containing *Program*, *Software*, *Computer* concepts, the importance of concept *Program* is $1 + \frac{1}{m(1+\frac{1}{k})}$.

Aggregating the relevance and the importance of concept c, we obtain the overall weight given by the presence of concept c in a document and mathematically, it is formulated in Eq. 2.

$$w(c) = Freq(c) + \sum_{Path(c,...,H) \in t_n} \sum_{m=2}^{depth(c)} \left(\frac{Freq(c_m)}{\prod_{k=2}^{m} |children(c_k)|} \right) \tag{2}$$

where $w(c)$ is the overall weight of concept c and $Freq(c)$ is the frequency of occurring of concept c in the document. The first part of sum given in Eq. 2 represents the relevance of concept c while the right part indicates the importance of concept c.

Finally, categories of a given domain are represented by the following tuple:

$$cat_i = \{(c_1, w_1), (c_2, w_2), (c_3, w_3), \dots, (c_n, w_n)\} \tag{3}$$

where c_i is concept in domain ontology and w_i is its weight which is calculated using Eq. 2.

3.4   Unlabelled Documents

The last module encompasses a corpus of new documents which have to be classified. This module performs following preprocessing steps to represent and bring the new and unclassified documents into an appropriate form for further processing:

1. The text is cleaned by removing all punctuation and capitalization,
2. A tokenizer is used to separate the text into individual terms (words),
3. Passing all terms through the term stemmer to convert them in their base or root form to develop a list of potential terms which are a noun, a verb, an adverb or an adjective,
4. Remove all the stop words, words which do not contain important significance to be used,
5. Normalizing the texts using one of the techniques from the Information Retrieval such as Term frequency tf or Term Frequency Inverse Document Frequency $tf \times idf$.

From the list of potential terms, we extract only the nouns as part-of-speech (POS) of a language, since they represent the most meaningful terms in a document [11].

Finally, an unlabelled document to be classified is represented by a finite set of weighted terms as described by the following tuple:

$$doc_j = \{(t_1, w_1), (t_2, w_2), (t_3, w_3), \ldots, (t_n, w_n)\} \tag{4}$$

where t_i is term occurring in document and w_i is its weight which is calculated using the Term Frequency Inverse Document Frequency $tf \times idf$ model.

4   Assigning Documents to Categories

Consequently, the main goal of the above proposed model is to classify every new unclassified text document to its appropriate category automatically. Automatic text classification is the process of automatically assigning a text document from a given domain to one or more class labels from a finite set of predefined categories. For instance, for a binary text classification, it is the task of assigning a single binary value to each pair $(doc_j, cat_i) \in Doc \times Cat$, where Doc is a domain of documents and $Cat = (cat_1, cat_2, cat_3, cat_i)$ is a set of predefined categories. A threshold value T is assigned to (doc_j, cat_i) that denotes a decision to file doc_j under cat_i, on the contrary a value of F denotes a decision not to file doc_j under cat_i. The task is to approximate the unknown target function $\phi : Doc \times Cat \prec (T, F)$ by means of a function $\phi' : Doc \times Cat \prec (T, F)$ called the classifier, rule or model such that ϕ and ϕ' coincide as much as possible [13].

In our ontology-based classification framework, the assigning of an unlabelled document to a given category depends on the similarity score between them. The higher the score, the closer the relations between the document and the category. In other words, the document is more likely belongs to this category.

Once the category and document vectors given in Eqs. 3 and 4 are constructed, the similarity measure between a document doc_j and the category cat_i is computed as:

$$Similarity(doc_j, cat_i) = \frac{\overrightarrow{doc_j} \times \overrightarrow{cat_i}}{\| \overrightarrow{doc_j} \| \cdot \| \overrightarrow{cat_i} \|} \tag{5}$$

Finally, we will use a threshold λ to determine which category to assign the document. After doing the same treatment for all documents and ontologies by using above method, documents are assigned to their respective categories.

5 Conclusion and Future Work

In this paper we proposed a new framework for automatic text document classification. The proposed framework is ontology based utilizing concepts of a domain ontology rather than keywords, to capture and exploit the conceptualization involved in user information needs and content meanings.

The indexing technique used in this framework relies on the statistical vector space model, which represents text documents and categories as term vectors. The components of the term vectors are domain ontology concepts and their weights. The ontology concepts have to be supplemented with new lexical resources of this particular domain in order to capture better the content meanings. To achieve this, the paper introduced the SEMCON model which combines the semantic and contextual information.

The paper also proposed to use the importance of the concept in addition to the concept's relevance defined by the frequency of occurring. The importance is defined by the depth of concept in the ontology graph and the number of concepts which subsume or are subsumed by this concept. Thus, the overall weight of a concept in the term vectors is defined by aggregating the importance and the relevance of the concept.

In the future work, we plan to implement this framework in a real application domain and to evaluate and compare the performance of this approach with existing ontology based classification approaches.

References

1. Raghavan, P.: Extracting and exploiting structure in text search. In: SIGMOD Conference, pp. 635 (2003)
2. Al-Azmi, A.-A. R.: Data, Text, and web mining for business intelligence: a survey. Int. J. Data Min. Knowl. Manag. Process (IJDKP), 3(2) (2013)
3. Song, M.-H., Lim, S.Y., Kang, D.-J., Lee, S.-J.: Ontology-based automatic classification of web documents. In: Huang, D.-S., Li, K., Irwin, G.W. (eds.) ICIC 2006. LNCS (LNAI), vol. 4114, pp. 690–700. Springer, Heidelberg (2006)
4. Song, M., Lim, S., Kang, D., Lee, S.: Automatic classification of web pages based on the concept of domain ontology. In: Proceedings of the 12th Asia-Pacific Software Engineering Conference (2005)
5. Dinh, D., Tamine, L.: Biomedical concept extraction based on combining the content-based and word order similarities. In: Proceedings of the ACM Symposium on Applied Computing, SAC Q1, pp. 1159–1163, NY, USA (2011)

6. Sy, M.-F., Ranwez, S., Montmain, J., Regnault, A., Crampes, M., Ranwez, V.: User centered and ontology based information retrieval system for life sciences. BMC Bioinform. **13**(Suppl 1), S4 (2012). doi:10.1186/1471-2105-13-S1-S4

7. Fang, J., Guo, L., Niu, Y.: Documents classification by using ontology reasoning and similarity measure. In: Proceedings of the 7th International Conference on Fuzzy Systems and Knowledge Discovery (2010)

8. Maedche, A.: Ontology Learning for the Semantic Web. Kluwer Academic Publishers, Norwell (2002)

9. Kastrati, Z., Imran, A.S., Yayilgan, S.Y.: SEMCON: semantic and contextual objective metric. In: Proceedings of the 9th IEEE International Conference on Semantic Computing, Anaheim, California, USA (2015)

10. Kastrati, Z., Imran, A.S.: Adaptive concept vector space representation using Markov chain model. In: Janowicz, K., Schlobach, S., Lambrix, P., Hyvönen, E. (eds.) EKAW 2014. LNCS, vol. 8876, pp. 203–208. Springer, Heidelberg (2014)

11. Liu, J.N.K., He, Y.-L., Lim, E.H.Y., Wang, X.-Z.: A new method for knowledge and information management domain ontology graph model. IEEE Trans. Syst. Man Cybern. Syst. **43**, 115–127 (2013)

12. Calvier, F.-E., Plantié, M., Dray, G., Ranwez, S.: Ontology Based Machine Learning for Semantic Multiclass Classification. In: TOTH- Terminologie & Ontologie: Théories et Applications, Chambéry, France (2013)

13. Sebastiani, F.: Machine learning in automated text categorization. ACM Comput. Surv. (CSUR) **34**(1), 1–47 (2002)

A New Information Architecture: A Synthesis of Structure, Flow, and Dialectic

Rico A.R. Picone[1,2]([✉]) and Bryan Powell[1]

[1] Dialectica, LLC, Olympia, USA
rpicone@stmartin.edu
[2] Department of Mechanical Engineering,
Saint Martin's University, Lacey, USA

Abstract. We introduce a new information architecture that is a synthesis of an information structure, information flow (e.g. narrative), and information dialectic (its evolution). Insights from the memory mnemonic the *method of loci* and the philosophical process of *dialectic* are introduced. Three cumulative syntheses are presented: the organic architecture with (1) the hierarchical architecture with (2) the sequential architecture with (3) the dialectical method.

1 Background

Since the conception of personal computing, it has been the goal of various researchers and designers to create a computing system that can be a medium for human thought [3]. Certainly, we have come a long way toward realizing this; but we remain encumbered by the standard information architectures. We will examine each of the common information architectures and find their strengths and weaknesses, before synthesizing them into a new information architecture.

1.1 Information Architecture

Information architecture [1, p. 88] is the manner in which pieces of information are interrelated. The basic unit of an information architecture is the *atom* (e.g. file, paragraph, etc.). Atoms are logically related via *categories* (e.g. directory, tag, etc.). Categories can be considered as *sets* of atoms.

Hierarchical Architecture. The *hierarchical architecture* is an architecture in which atoms and categories are organized with parent-child relationships in a *tree*-structure. The categories are arranged to encompass one-another, as in the case of a computer file-system. Then atoms populate the structure at various levels (see Fig. 1).

The advantages of this architecture include that it gives an intuitive structure to the information (with its spatial analogies like "up" and "in"), that it can be easily instantiated in a computing device, and that — in many instantiations — it can be navigated with minimal atoms and categories displayed at each level.

© Springer International Publishing Switzerland 2015
S. Yamamoto (Ed.): HIMI 2015, Part I, LNCS 9172, pp. 320–331, 2015.
DOI: 10.1007/978-3-319-20612-7_31

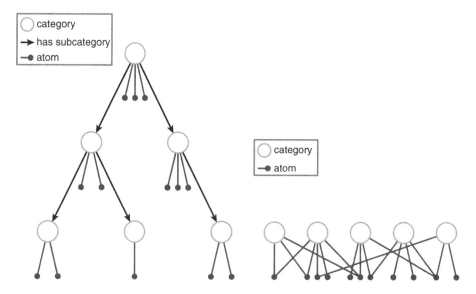

Fig. 1. A graph of the hierarchical architecture in terms of parent-child relations.

Fig. 2. A graph of the organic architecture. Its "flat" structure allows all categorizations.

The hierarchical architecture has limitations, however. It cannot allow certain categorizations of atoms. For instance, if an atom is associated with categories that lie in different "branches" of the tree, this cannot be properly expressed. Another limitation is that there is only a single path to each atom. We will address the concept of path in Sect. 3.3, but for now we can think of it as being like a file-path in a standard computing system. With only a single path to it, a browser of the architecture must know all the "right" moves in order to arrive at the atom.

Organic Architecture. The *organic architecture* is one which allows atoms to be categorized with any combination of categories, but does not directly relate the categories to each other. This architecture is instantiated in "tagging" systems, for instance, in which a tag can be considered a category.

The lack of explicitly defined relations among the categories gives this architecture its characteristic "flat" structure (see Fig. 2). It is a significant improvement (over the hierarchical architecture) in connectivity, allowing all possible relationships to be expressed, but the structure among the categories is opaque, and, in fact, undefined.

This is problematic when the architecture is instantiated into a computing system that is to be navigated (i.e. browsed). Where does one begin to navigate? What should be displayed at a given state of navigation? In Sect. 2.1, we will continue to discuss these issues.

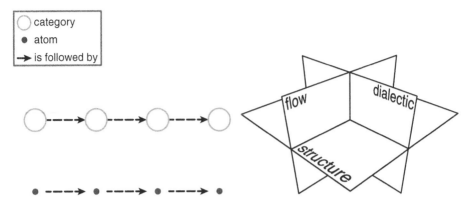

Fig. 3. A graph of the sequential architecture.

Fig. 4. Three planes of information architecture.

Sequential Architecture. The *sequential architecture* is one which arranges atoms or categories in sequences with the relation "is followed by" (see Fig. 3). This architecture is that of narrative, film, and music — and is generally the architecture of the human experience of events in time. For this reason it is ubiquitous, although it is very limited, structurally. The categorization of atoms, for instance, is not defined in this architecture.

It is common to create a synthesis of the sequential and hierarchical architectures, as in a document, such as this, with sections. Nominally, each subsection is related only to its (parent) section, although this is rarely actual. This synthesis is obviously fruitful, but inherits the limitations of the hierarchical architecture. We use this as an example of a successful synthesis of information architectures. What follows is a series of three cumulative syntheses that sublates the standard architectures in an attempt to capture the structure of human thinking. The primary objective of this work is to enable a computer — instantiating an information architecture — to be used as a better medium for human thinking.

2   Structure

We will distinguish among three planes of information architecture: the *structure plane*, the *flow plane*, and the *dialectic plane* (see Fig. 4).

Definition 1 (Structure Plane). The structure plane of an information architecture is the set of logical relations among the categories and atoms.   □

The structure plane is often the focus of an information architecture, but it can take different forms. The hierarchical architecture has structure in its category-category and atom-category relations, whereas the organic architecture has structure only in its atom-category relations.

2.1   Synthesis I: Organic and Hierarchical Architectures

The first synthesis is of the organic and hierarchical architectures. We begin with the cornerstone of the organic hierarchy: *each atom may be associated with any categories.* Beginning here ensures that the architecture will preserve the capacity for completely general categorization of information.

However, category-category relations are undefined. This is a limitation, especially for navigation and discovery.[1] The synthesis of the organic and hierarchical architectures hinges on this precept: *a hierarchical architecture can be defined as implicit in an organic architecture.*

We call this synthesis an *organic hierarchy.* It stands alone as an information architecture, but two more cumulative syntheses will include it in the following sections. The organic hierarchy is described in the following series of mathematical definitions. The definitions need not be a hurdle to the understanding of the architecture. On the first reading, it is sufficient to skip them and proceed to Sect. 3.

Definition 2 (Subcategory). Given a collection of categories $\mathcal{C}$, let $X \in \mathcal{C}$ be a nonempty proper subset of $Y \in \mathcal{C}$. We call X a *subcategory* of Y. □

Definition 3 (Graph Nodes). Let $\mathcal{C}$ be a collection of categories; let $\mathcal{U}$ be the union of all categories in $\mathcal{C}$; and let $\mathcal{I}$ be the set of all possible nonempty recursive intersections of the elements of $\mathcal{C}$. Let *graph nodes* be defined as

$$\mathcal{N} = \mathcal{U} \cup \mathcal{C} \cup \mathcal{I}. \qquad \qquad \square \qquad (1)$$

Definition 4 (Graph Level Function). The *graph level function* $L : \mathcal{N} \to \mathbb{Z}$ is defined to be equal to 0 if the node $n \in \mathcal{U}$, equal to 1 if the node $n \in \mathcal{C}$, and equal to the number of categories $C \in \mathcal{C}$ for which the node n was the intersection, otherwise. Therefore, $0 < L(n) \leq \mathbf{card}(\mathcal{C})$ for $n \in \mathcal{N}$. Let $\mathcal{L}_i$ be the collection of sets for which $L(n) = i$ for $n \in \mathcal{N}$, and let $\mathcal{L}_i$ be indexed such that we can denote a relation $\mathbf{r}_i^{jk}$ to be that from element j of $\mathcal{L}_i$ to element k of $\mathcal{L}_{i+1}$.[2] □

Definition 5 (Metacategories). Given a set of nodes $N \subseteq \mathcal{L}_i$, we can construct a collection $\mathcal{M}$ of all recursive unions of the elements of N. We call the elements of $\mathcal{M}$ *metacategories* of N.[3] Furthermore, let the map **meta** be defined as $\mathbf{meta}(N) = \mathcal{M}$. Finally, let $\mathcal{M}^d$ be the set containing the elements of $\mathbf{meta}(N)$ that were constructed from the unions of d nodes; we call d the *metacategory depth.* □

Example 1 (Nodes, Levels, and Metacategories). Given a collection of categories $\mathcal{C} = \{X, Y, Z\}$, the union of all categories is $\mathcal{U} = \{X \cup Y \cup Z\}$. The set of all recursive intersections of the categories is

---

[1] Discovery is the activity of learning something new about an information system.

[2] In order to minimize notation, at times we refer to a node by its index.

[3] All original nodes in N are also metacategories because the empty set $\emptyset$ is a subset of every set, and the union of any set with $\emptyset$ is just that set. Given ν nodes, the total number of metacategories is $\sum_i^\nu \binom{\nu}{i}$.

$$\mathcal{I} = \{X, Y, Z, X \cap Y, Y \cap Z, X \cap Z, X \cap Y \cap Z\}. \tag{2}$$

Therefore, assuming all intersections are nonempty, the set of nodes is

$$\mathcal{N} = \{X \cup Y \cup Z, X, Y, Z, X \cap Y, Y \cap Z, X \cap Z, X \cap Y \cap Z\}. \tag{3}$$

The collections of graph nodes at each level are

$$\mathcal{L}_0 = \{X \cup Y \cup Z\}, \tag{4a}$$
$$\mathcal{L}_1 = \{X, Y, Z\}, \tag{4b}$$
$$\mathcal{L}_2 = \{X \cap Y, Y \cap Z, X \cap Z\}, \text{ and} \tag{4c}$$
$$\mathcal{L}_3 = \{X \cap Y \cap Z\}. \tag{4d}$$

If we give **meta** the set of nodes $N = \{X, Y, Z\} \subseteq \mathcal{L}_1$, we get the collections of metacategories of N at each depth:

$$\mathcal{M}^1 = \{X, Y, Z\}, \tag{5a}$$
$$\mathcal{M}^2 = \{X \cup Y, X \cup Z, Y \cup Z\}, \text{ and} \tag{5b}$$
$$\mathcal{M}^3 = \{X \cup Y \cup Z\}. \quad \Box \tag{5c}$$

We define three types of *graph relation* (or graph edge).

Definition 6 (s-relation). The relation s is *has a priori subcategory*. An *a priori* subcategory is a subcategory that is required by construction, and is independent of the contents of the categories. For instance, $A \cap B$ is an *a priori* subcategory of A, assuming it is not the empty set. An s-relation s_i^{jk} is defined from tail-node j of $\mathcal{L}_i$ to head-node k of $\mathcal{L}_{i+1}$ if node k is an *a priori* subcategory of j. $\quad \Box$

Definition 7 (vs-relation). Consider a node j of $\mathcal{L}_i$. Let N be the set of (s-relation) head-nodes in $\mathcal{L}_{i+1}$ for which j is the common tail-node. Let $\mathcal{M}_{ij}$ be the set of metacategories of N, $\mathcal{M}_{ij} = \mathbf{meta}(N)$. A *has visible subcategory* **vs**-relation with tail-node j is an s-relation with head-node an element of the set of nodes used to construct $\mathcal{M}_{ij}$ that have the minimum depth $d_{\min}$ and that equal j': the tail-node j intersected with the union of the elements of N. $\quad \Box$

Definition 8 (hs-relation). An s-relation that is not a **vs**-relation is defined as a *has hidden subcategory* **hs**-relation. $\quad \Box$

Definition 9 (Visible Atom). For a node $j \in \mathcal{L}_i$, a *visible atom* is an atom that is in the set $j \setminus j'$, where j' is the (s-relation) tail-node j intersected with the union of all head-nodes with tail-node j. $\quad \Box$

Definition 10 (Graph of Categories). Together, the set of nodes $\mathcal{N}$ and **hs**- and **vs**-relations define a *graph of categories*. The graph can be *navigated* by beginning at any node and following an edge to an adjacent level ($\mathcal{L}_i$ to $\mathcal{L}_{i+1}$ or to $\mathcal{L}_{i-1}$). When the level increases, the edge represents the intersection of the current node with a single category, and can therefore be represented as

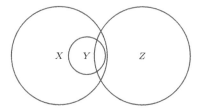

Fig. 5. Venn diagram for the categories of Example 2.

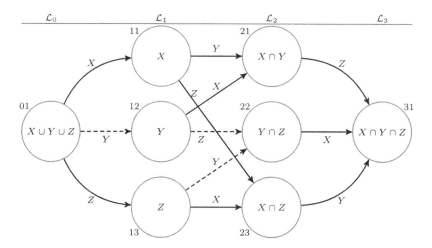

Fig. 6. Graph of categories for Example 2. Dashed lines are **hs**-relations and solid lines are **vs**-relations.

"selecting" an additional category. When the level decreases, the edge represents the union of the current node with a single category, and can therefore be represented as "deselecting" that category. At a given node, visible atoms and **vs**-relations should be displayed; **hs**-relations should be somehow accessible, but not displayed.   □

Example 2 (Graph of Categories). Given a collection of categories $\mathcal{C} = \{X, Y, Z\}$, and the set relations defined by the Venn diagram Fig. 5, we can construct the graph shown in Fig. 6 using Definition 10 as follows. The graph nodes were already discussed in Example 1.

The *has subcategory* graph relations **s** are determined by construction, as long as they are nonempty. The *has visible subcategory* **vs**-relations for a given node can be determined by examining the **s**-relations with the node as its tail. The heads of these **s**-relations can be constructed into a set of metacategories, from which we can determine visibility. See Table 1, which lists the metacategories for each node. Let's examine Node 01 ($X \cup Y \cup Z$), for instance. It is the tail for three **s**-relations because X, Y, and Z are all subcategories. Then the metacategories, divided into sets of depth 1–3, are

$$\mathcal{M}_{01}^1 = \{X, Y, Z\}, \tag{6a}$$

$$\mathcal{M}_{01}^2 = \{X \cup Y, Y \cup Z, X \cup Z\}, \text{ and} \tag{6b}$$

$$\mathcal{M}_{01}^3 = \{X \cup Y \cup Z\}. \tag{6c}$$

Table 1. Metacategories used to determine **hs**- and **vs**-relations for Example 2. Nodes are referred to by Level i and index j.

Node ij	$\mathcal{M}_{ij}^1$	$\mathcal{M}_{ij}^2$	$\mathcal{M}_{ij}^3$
01	$\{X, Y, Z\}$	$\{X \cup Y, Y \cup Z, X \cup Z\}$	$\{X \cup Y \cup Z\}$
11	$\{X \cap Y, X \cap Z\}$	$\{X \cap (Y \cup Z)\}$	-
12	$\{X \cap Y, Y \cap Z\}$	$\{Y \cap (X \cup Z)\}$	-
13	$\{X \cap Z, Y \cap Z\}$	$\{Z \cap (X \cup Y)\}$	-
21, 22, 23	$\{X \cap Y \cap Z\}$	-	-

Let us consider those metacategories of depth $d = 1$. Evaluating the metacategories shows that no single category equals $j' = (X \cup Y \cup Z) \cap (X \cup Y \cup Z) = X \cup Y \cup Z$. Now consider those metacategories of depth $d = 2$. Only $X \cup Z = j'$; therefore, the **s**-relations from Node 01 to 11 (X) and 13 (Z) are **vs**-relations. The only visible atoms at $\mathcal{L}_0$ are those that are uncategorized. Similarly, for Node 11 (X), which is at Level 1,

$$\mathcal{M}_{11}^1 = \{X \cap Y, X \cap Z\} \text{ and} \tag{7a}$$

$$\mathcal{M}_{11}^2 = \{(X \cap Y) \cup (X \cap Z)\} = \{X \cap (Y \cup Z)\}. \tag{7b}$$

Let us consider those metacategories of depth $d = 1$. Evaluating the metacategories shows that no single category equals $j' = X \cap ((X \cap Y) \cup (X \cap Z))$. Considering the single metacategory at the maximum depth $d = 2$, we can see that, by definition, it evaluates to j', and it requires all metacategories for construction. Therefore, all **s**-relations with tail-node X are **vs**-relations. This is why we gray-out the maximum-depth metacategories in the table; they needn't be evaluated in order to know the result. The visible atoms at this node are $X \setminus (Y \cup Z)$.

Proceeding in a similar manner for each node, we define all **s**-relations as either **vs**- or **hs**-relations, and define the visible atoms for each node. □

3   Flow

The *method of loci* is an ancient memory mnemonic still in use by most memory champions [2]. The technique requires a subject to "place" memories in an imaginary world familiar to the subject. It turns out that the technique is not then used as random-access memory in which the user can access any memory at will; rather, each memory-location is accessed *in series* by "journeying" through the imaginary world [2, p. 93].

This architecture is already expressed in the standard sequential information architecture. This architecture is fundamentally different than the other information architectures mentioned, which express the logical relations among sequences and atoms (i.e. they are *structural*). The sequential architecture has little structure itself; rather, *it expresses the movement of thinking through information structure*. It moves in another dimension, which we call the *flow plane* of information architecture.

Definition 11 (flow plane). The flow plane of an information architecture is the sequential presentation of atoms or categories.   □

3.1 Flow and Structure in Standard Information Architectures

As in the method of loci, thinking flows from one idea to the next, not necessarily in some order prescribed by the structure, but through the structure, which provides context for each idea. This is what separates the concept of flow from that of *path*. A path is the logical categorization of an idea, whereas flow is a sequential presentation of ideas.

The quintessential example of a flow is a narrative, which is often presented in terms of chapters, sections, and subsections. This is a synthesis of the sequential and hierarchical architectures. Its utility is undeniable; it is the structure of nearly all scientific and technical literature. However, it inherits the limitations of the hierarchical architecture in that a flow cannot move freely through the structure due to its restrictions on logical categorizations.

3.2 Synthesis II: Flow and Structure

The second synthesis is the sublation of the organic hierarchy proposed in Sect. 2.1 and the sequential architecture. Therefore, it is the synthesis of structure and flow. This synthesis revolves around two insights, one presented in each of the following examples.

Example 3 (flow not limited by structure). The first insight is that flows should not be limited by structure. Consider the simple example of a chapter that compares the works of Søren Kierkegaard and Friedrich Nietzsche. In a hierarchical architecture, the dilemma is whether this belongs in `Kierkegaard/Nietzsche` or `Nietzsche/Kierkegaard`. It imposes a structure on the flow that does not exist.

In an organic hierarchy, however, a flow has no such limitations. The cornerstone of the organic hierarchy is that each atom — the `Kierkegaard-Nietzsche` chapter, in this case — may be associated with any category. Therefore, in any instantiation of this architecture, it will be available to a user under *both* `Kierkegaard/Nietzsche` and `Nietzsche/Kierkegaard`. And yet, the structure among the categories is not lost, as in a purely organic architecture. It still may be the case that in a given information system every atom associated with `Nietzsche` is also associated with `Kierkegaard`, but some atoms associated with `Kierkegaard`

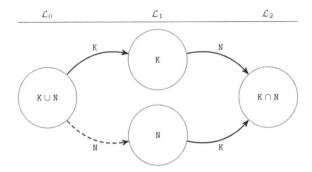

Fig. 7. Graph of categories for Example 3. Dashed lines are **hs**-relations and solid lines are **vs**-relations. K is the category `Kierkegaard` and N is the category `Nietzsche`.

are not associated with `Nietzsche`. Therefore `Nietzsche` $\subset$ `Kierkegaard`, and `Nietzsche` would be hidden within `Kierkegaard` in graph navigation, as illustrated in Fig. 7.

This would look identical to a user browsing the structure as a hierarchy with `Nietzsche` a subcategory of `Kierkegaard`, *but it does not restrict future categorizations*, unlike the hierarchy. Moreover, unlike in a hierarchy, there is nothing prohibiting a user from navigating to `Nietzsche` immediately (by manual input). It is an allowed, but not a visible (displayed to the user), navigation.   □

Example 4 (travel journal). The second insight that defines the synthesis of flow and structure is that the structuring of a flow must be highly granular. Categorizing a flow or even, say, a chapter, as a single atom is typically not sufficiently granular to capture the movement of the flow through the structure. Consider a travel journal as a flow with contents structured in an organic hierarchy, as illustrated in Fig. 8.

We will consider the first five paragraphs of the journal in question, *Journal 12*. Let all paragraphs be atoms associated with the categories `Journal`, `Travel`, and `Italy`. Furthermore, let paragraphs 1, 2, and 3 be associated with `Mosaics`; paragraphs 1–3 be associated with `Mausoleums`; paragraphs 3 and 4 associated with `Justinian I`; paragraphs 3–5 associated with `Byzantine Empire`; and paragraphs 4 and 5 associated with `Byzantine Artwork`. The flow side of the figure shows these categorizations.

If we assume that this journal lies in a broader structure of categories and atoms, we can construct a possible structural view, as shown at right. The graph has been navigated along one of many possible paths. (The order of the categories selected is irrelevant to a given node, so the user may have come along many paths to that node.) The node shown appears to be simply `Byzantine Artwork`, but it is, in fact

$$\texttt{Journal} \cap \texttt{Travel} \cap \texttt{Italy} \cap \texttt{Byzantine Empire} \cap \texttt{Byzantine Artwork}. \quad (8)$$

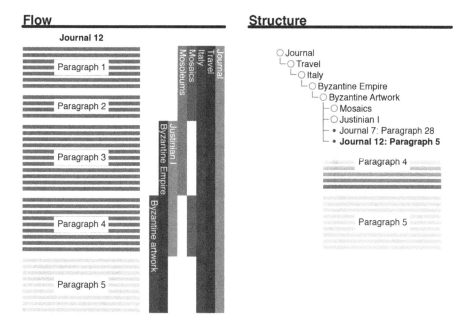

Fig. 8. Illustration of a travel journal for Example 4. *Paragraph 5* is shown in both a flow (*Journal 12*) and a structure.

The intersection operator commutes, so any order is equivalent, and therefore any path including the same categories is as well. The further intersection with the categories Mosaics and Justinian I is possible, which would reveal the atom paragraph 4. At the node shown, however, there are two visible atoms: *Journal 7: Paragraph 28* and *Journal 12: Paragraph 5*. *Paragraph 5* are associated with all the categories in the path, but no others. Therefore they are visible, and can (depending on the instantiation) be previewed in context, as shown.

This shows the possibility of discovery in this architecture. Let us imagine that the journaler reviews the journal later and is struck by something about *Paragraph 5*. Now interested to know if any related information in her broader information system, she views the structure and discovers that *Journal 7: Paragraph 28* was also associated with the same categories, and that other information that is related is associated with categories Mosaics and Justinian I.   □

3.3   Path

Path is the description of the logical place of a node in a structure, and of how a user navigated to that node. In a hierarchy, there is only one path to each node. For instance, consider categories X and Y, and path X/Y. There is only one path X/Y to reach that node. In an organic hierarchy, however, many paths are possible because the order is inconsequential. In our example, X/Y and Y/X are equivalent because each path represents the intersection $X \cap Y = Y \cap X$. This

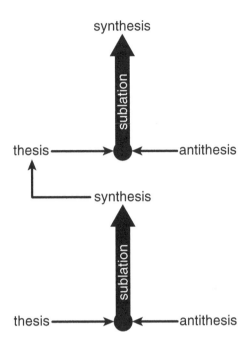

Fig. 9. A formulation of the dialectical process.

flexibility of path is especially important for information discovery. It allows a user to navigate "up" along a different path than they navigated "down," for instance.

4   Dialectic

The Fichtean/Hegelian *dialectic* provides a framework for the evolution of thinking. One formulation of this process is shown in Fig. 9. It begins with a *thesis*, which gives a perspective on a topic. If a new perspective is introduced, it is called an *antithesis*. Antitheses can be contradictory to the thesis, but often they are not. Rather, they reveal something previously unknown about the topic, and the relationship between the thesis and antithesis is unresolved. The process of *sublation* forms a *synthesis*, which includes both the thesis and antithesis. This synthesis is considered a new thesis. *Et cetera.*

4.1   Synthesis III: Structure, Flow, and Dialectic

In this final synthesis with that of Sect. 3.2, the dialectical framework can be used to express the evolution of thought. Each category may be assigned a *thesis flow* that is a definition or description of the category.[4] It will certainly

---

[4] Each node may also be assigned a thesis flow. For instance, a thesis flow for category X ∩ Y might be *the relation of X and Y.*

intersect a number of other categories, but it is specifically used to define its *thesis category*. Similarly, any flow can be considered the thesis flow for a thesis category it generates.

When a flow is newly associated with a category, it becomes an *antithesis flow* of the category's thesis flow. It may contradict, supplement, or be redundant with the thesis flow. In any case, when a user sublates these flows, they become a *synthesis flow*, which is the new thesis flow for the category.

This third synthesis is called the *dialectical architecture*. It allows information to be structured as in the organic hierarchy (first synthesis), incorporates free-ranging flows (second synthesis), and systematically structures the evolution of thinking (third synthesis). This captures a third plane of information architecture.

Definition 12 (dialectic plane). The dialectic plane of information architecture is the evolution of the structures and flows within the architecture.   □

This plane is often ignored in information architecture and its instantiations. Attempts to incorporate it include *backup software*, *wiki* revision histories, and *version control*. Framing it with the dialectical method allows the user to focus on the evolution of the *ideas* and not a specific flow. It also allows the user to discover new antitheses that arise in connection with other work in the information system.

5   Conclusion and Prospects

We have presented a new information architecture, the dialectical architecture. It enables thinking to be structured in a general manner, flow through that structure, and evolve through dialectic — all in a computing medium.

As with other information architectures, there are many viable instantiations. One instantiation, a note-taking system, is currently in development. Much work remains to determine how successful the architecture is at providing a medium for human thinking. Its basis in the standard architectures, the method of loci, and the dialectical method is a reason for optimism.

References

1. Garrett, J.: Elements of User Experience, The: User-Centered Design for the Web and Beyond. Voices That Matter. Pearson Education, Boston (2010)
2. Maguire, E.A., Valentine, E.R., Wilding, J.M., Kapur, N.: Routes to remembering: the brains behind superior memory. Nat. Neurosci. **6**(1), 90 (2003)
3. Markoff, J.: What the Dormouse Said: How the Sixties Counterculture Shaped the Personal Computer Industry. Penguin Group, Newyork (2005)

Haptic, Tactile and Multimodal Interaction

Effects of Tacton Names and Learnability

Daniel Barber[✉] and Christopher Beck

Institute for Simulation and Training, University of Central Florida,
Orlando, FL, USA
{dbarber, cbeck}@ist.ucf.edu

Abstract. Increasing robotic capabilities and a strong impetus for mixed-initiative Soldier-Robot teaming is pushing the boundaries of current communication paradigms. These future teams are expected to perform along a continuum of operating environments, in which traditional auditory and visual modalities may be hindered or unavailable. The tactile modality offers an alternative means for a robot to communicate words, phrases, or cues to a Soldier, providing an additional channel to facilitate more robust multimodal communications. However, fundamental research is still needed to understand how to design tactile icons called "tactons." In order to better understand the relationship of a tacton and their assigned names, this paper presents results from an experiment comparing the ability of participants to classify existing tactons from the literature using original versus nonsense-syllable labels.

Keywords: Tactile displays · Tactons · Tacton names · Tactile belt · Human robot interaction · Nonsense syllables

1 Introduction

With continued increases in robotic capabilities, future unmanned systems will have the necessary intelligence move beyond their current role as tools. In order to collaborate effectively in mixed-initiative teams, robots must also advance the methods in which they communicate with their human counterparts. When working in highly dynamic and kinetic environments typical of military operations, it is critical that communications robots employ are natural and intuitive such that they are quickly and accurately understood by human teammates. The use of the auditory channel through speech is a logical choice for human robot interaction. Speech commands are shown to reduce operation time for discrete tasks, with natural language processing systems demonstrating the ability of robots to execute navigation and mobile manipulation tasks successfully [1, 2]. Visual signaling is another modality regularly used in the military. The Army Field Manual for Visual Signals defines many arm and hand signals for ground forces to use when interacting with each other and vehicles [3]. Although highly effective standalone, the combination of auditory and visual signals via multimodal communication impacts the effectiveness (how well) and efficiency (how fast) of interfaces [4–6]. Multimodal communications takes

© Springer International Publishing Switzerland 2015
S. Yamamoto (Ed.): HIMI 2015, Part I, LNCS 9172, pp. 335–344, 2015.
DOI: 10.1007/978-3-319-20612-7_32

advantage of multiple channels to convey more complex information over single modes, with ideas conveyed redundantly (back up signals), [7, 8]. The ability of multimodal communication to facilitate back up signals is especially critical for teammates working with robots in environments where one or more modality may be impaired due to noise, visual occlusion, or unavailability (e.g. underwater, darkness).

As an alternative speech and gestures, the tactile modality offers a previously untapped channel for robots and others to use for communication. Tactile displays, typically in the form of belts, deliver messages via electromechanical stimulation of the skin in the form of tactile icons, called "tactons," [9]. These structured messages are defined using multiple parameters including: frequency, amplitude and duration of pulse, rhythm, and location [9]. Tactile belts incorporating linear actuators at eight cardinal and inter-cardinal zones (e.g. north, northeast, east) surrounding the abdomen are oriented to the wearer, providing egocentric directions particularly effective in hands-free navigation tasks [10, 11]. Gilson, Redden and Elliott developed tactons matched to visual signals from the Army Field Manual, with participants demonstrating an ability to learn the signals with minimal training time of 5 min [12]. These and other tactons are a starting point in the creation of tactile lexicon, with "words" having a matching counterpart in the visual modality ideal for experiments in multimodal communication with complex messages. Barber, Reinerman-Jones, and Matthews further evaluated these and other tactons from the literature within three category types: static, directional, and dynamic [13]. Static tactons are presented as a constant pattern, with directional and dynamic tactons using motion within the sequence through activation of different actuators at each time increment. Directional tactons represent some type of navigational context (e.g. north, east), where static and dynamic tactons describe a word or symbol without any directional component (e.g. danger). Through the pairing of dynamic and directional tactons it was further shown participants are able to accurately interpret two-word tacton "phrases" with accuracy greater than 92 % with less than an hour of training [13]. Although promising, a limiting factor in the use of tactile displays for transmission of complex multi-part messages similar to speech is the lack of a standard tacton lexicon. Furthermore, it is still unclear what the best practices in the design of tactons should be.

Currently, the primary method employed in the design of tactons is to match the physical pattern to a visual signal or egocentric location with a known semantic label. This encoding paradigm attempts to approximate visual patterns to leverage a wearer's prior knowledge to aid teaching [14]. To further aid in the design of tactons it is helpful to understand the semantic relationship of tactons and their names. Nonsense syllables are any combination of letters to create labels that have no associated meaning often used in learning tasks [15, 16]. Due to their lack of meaningful association, nonsense syllables are ideal for understanding participants' ability to learn tactons without the use of a semantic name. The purpose for the present effort is to evaluate the classification accuracy of tactons paired with semantic and nonsense syllable labels to understand the effects of tacton labels on learnability.

2 Method

2.1 Participants

A total of 72 (29 male, 43 female) between the ages of 18 and 40 ($M = 20.31$, $SD = 4.00$) participated in the study, with 38 (15 male, 23 female) in the Named Tactons (NT) group and 34 (14 male, 20 female) in the Nonsense Syllables (NS) group. All participants received credit for their psychology courses for completing the study. Participants were required to be right handed with a waistline between 34 and 50 inches to accommodate the Tactor Belt used. Additionally, participants were asked not to consume alcohol or any sedative medication for 24 h or caffeine for 2 h prior to the study. Data from four participants, two from each group, was excluded due to participant failure to achieve a score of 90 % or better during the tactile sensitivity test. A description of the sensitivity test is described in the procedure.

2.2 Design

A 2 × 3 (Tacton Name × Tacton Category) between groups measure design was employed with the use of nonsense syllable names as grouping variable. The tacton name groups were defined as NT and NS, and categories of tactons included: Directional, Dynamic, and Static. Each tacton category contained eight (8) tactons as detailed in [13]. Nonsense syllable names were selected from [16], with names selected having the lowest equivalent level of reported meaning.

Performance Measures. Classification accuracy was recorded using a graphical dialog with a drop-down menu from which participants selected the label of the tacton presented. If the participant was unsure they could select "I don't know" as a response option. Accuracy was then calculated as a percentage of tactons correctly classified. Reaction time (RT) was record from the end of tacton presentation to when participants pressed the spacebar on a keyboard. Participants were instructed to press the spacebar when the recognized the tacton presented, not when they perceived the stimulus. The median RT in milliseconds was calculated for all tactons classified correctly. Workload was measured using the NASA TLX [17].

2.3 Equipment and Stimuli

Participants were required to perceive and classify tactons leveraged from the existing literature as described in [13]. The tactons were presented using the C-2 Tactor Belt with ATC 3.0 Controller from Engineering Acoustics, Inc. and a custom software application developed at the University of Central Florida called Tacton Presenter. The Tacton Presenter application is able to shown a graphical representation of the eight tactor locations on the tactor belt and shows which tactors are currently activated at each time step on the belt while also presenting the name for the sequence, Fig. 1.

The ability to visually show the sequence and the tacton name was used in training conditions only and disabled for experimental conditions where only the

Fig. 1. Tacton presenter application showing a visual representation of a tacton with name (left) and without (right). The 1 position indicates the front of the body (naval) and 5 the middle of the back, with 7 and 3 left and right respectively.

tactor belt was used. In addition to the Tacton Presenter application, a visualization of a robot driving through a geo-typical Middle Eastern environment was also used during the experiment to represent the view from a robot team member sending while communicating to the participant through the tactor belt. For all tactons, the duration of vibrotactile stimulation was 250 ms at a sinusoid frequency of 230 Hz, gain level 4 (24 dB), and inter-tactor interval of 100 ms. These parameters were chosen to allow participants to accurately perceive and distinguish individual tactors [18]. Additionally, white noise was also used to prevent audio interference from the tactor belt [13].

2.4   Procedure

Upon arrival, participants were assigned to either the SN or NS group. After completing an informed consent document, they were equipped with the tactor belt around the abdomen with the belt buckle on the naval. Next, participants were presented with a consecutive sequence of tactor activations started at position 1, traveling clockwise to position 8, and then again counter clockwise ending at 1. This step was taken to introduce them to the sensation of the individual tactors. Following this step, participants performed a sensitivity test where they classified ten (10) activations of each tactor presented at random for a total of eighty (80) classifications. This test verified equal sensitivity to all eight tactor locations across participants, with a required percent accuracy of 90 % or greater for individual data to be included in data analyses. After the sensitivity test, participants completed each category of tactons. Presentation order of tacton category was counter balanced across participants, and presentation order of individual tactons was also randomized within each classification task of a given category.

For each tacton category, participants completed two training and one experimental task. The first training task presented each tacton twice at random paired with the visual animation and name using an inter-stimulus interval of one second. For the first training task participants were not required to classify the tactons, only experience them. For the second training task, participants were presented each tacton four times, but without the name. In addition to the visual and tactile presentation, participants were required to indicate when the recognized the tacton using the keyboard and classify the tacton from a drop-down list. After classifying the tacton, participants were given auditory and visual feedback indicating correct/incorrect classification, and if incorrect, what the correct tacton name was. Next, after completing both training tasks, participants performed the experimental task, classifying each of the eight tactons ten times, in random order, without any visual animation or feedback. The inter-stimulus interval for tactons was one second after classification of the tacton using the drop-down list. After completion of all tasks, participants completed the NASA TLX test. This process was repeated two more times for the remaining tacton categories, and participants were not required to recall tactons from previous categories. Further detail regarding the procedure used can be found in [13].

3   Results

3.1   Classification Accuracy

A 2 (Tacton Name: NT and NS) × 3 (Tacton Category: Directional, Dynamic, and Static) mixed ANOVA was performed to compare classification accuracy between NT and NS groups. A significant main effect for tacton name was revealed between NT and NS, ($F(1, 62) = 16.31$, $p < .001$, $\eta^2 = .208$), such that NT ($M = 77.66$, $SD = 16.33$) showed better performance than TS ($M = 61.14$, $SD = 16.33$) for overall classification accuracy, Fig. 2.

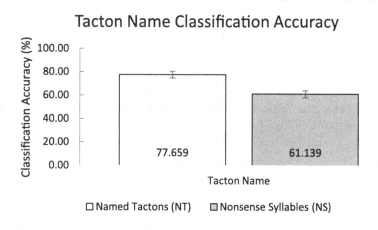

Fig. 2. Classification accuracy between tacton name groups

Tacton Category Classification Accuracy

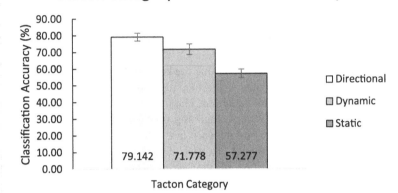

Fig. 3. Classification accuracy by tacton category across both NT and NS groups

A significant main effect for tacton category was also revealed, ($F(2, 124) = 25.76$, $p < .001$, $\eta^2 = .294$), such that Directional ($M = 79.14$, $SD = 18.94$) showed better performance than both Dynamic ($M = 71.78$, $SD = 25.41$) and Static ($M = 57.28$, $SD = 20.35$), and Dynamic better than Static tactons for overall classification accuracy, Fig. 3.

Furthermore, a significant interaction was shown between tacton name and tacton category, $F(1, 62) = 8.93$, $p = .004$, $\eta^2 = .126$. To further understand this interaction, independent sample t-tests were performed to compare tacton categories between tacton name groups. Results showed a significant difference between groups for Directional tactons, ($t(63) = 7.00$, $p < .001$), such that NT ($M = 95.37$, $SD = 8.22$) showed better performance than NS ($M = 62.74$, $SD = 25.78$). No significant difference was shown for Dynamic tactons between tacton name groups. For Static tactons a significant difference was shown, ($t(63) = 2.702$, $p = .009$), such that NT ($M = 63.97$, $SD = 17.19$) showed better performance than NS ($M = 50.44$, $SD = 22.99$).

A repeated measures ANOVA was performed and revealed a significant main effect for classification accuracy, ($F(2, 58) = 6.35$, $p = .003$, $\eta^2 = .180$), within the NS tacton name group, such that Dynamic ($M = 69.92$, $SD = 26.57$) showed better classification accuracy than Directional ($M = 62.92$, $SD = 26.21$) and Static ($M = 50.58$, $SD = 23.37$), and Directional better than Static. Overall classification accuracy results for all groups and categories is shown in Fig. 4.

3.2   Reaction Time

A 2 (Tacton Name: NT and NS) × 3 (Tacton Category: Directional, Dynamic, and Static) mixed ANOVA, with Box correction due to violation of sphericity, was performed to compare reaction time between NT and NS groups. No significant main

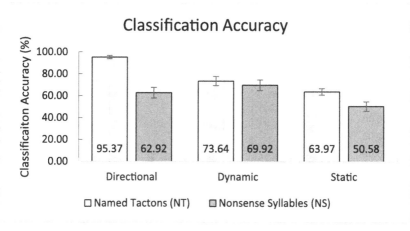

Fig. 4. Classification accuracy for NT and NS groups and tacton categories

effect for tacton name was shown between NT and NS. A significant main effect for tacton category was revealed, $(F(1.75, 123.70) = 8.40, p < .001, \eta^2 = .119)$, such that Dynamic ($M = 663.65$, $SD = 1321.41$) showed faster responses than both Directional ($M = 925.72$, $SD = 1025.08$) and Static ($M = 1125.31$, $SD = 997.92$), and Directional faster than Static tactons for overall reaction time. Overall reaction time values are shown in Fig. 5.

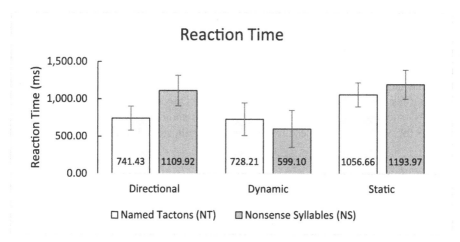

Fig. 5. Reaction time in milliseconds for tacton name groups (NT and NS) and tacton categories (Directional, Dynamic, and Static).

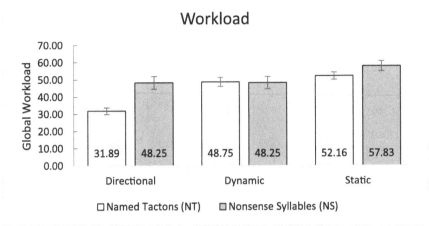

Fig. 6. Global (mean) workload levels from the NASA-TLX for tacton name groups (NT and NS) and tacton category (Directional, Dynamic, and Static).

3.3   Workload

A 2 (Tacton Name: NT and NS) × 3 (Tacton Category: Directional, Dynamic, and Static) mixed ANOVA was performed to compare global workload between NT and NS groups. A significant main effect for tacton name, ($F(2, 62) = 4.74$, $p = 0.033$, $\eta^2 = .071$), such that NT ($M = 44.27$, $SD = 13.16$) was lower than NS ($M = 51.44$, $SD = 13.16$). A significant main effect for tacton category was also revealed, (F(2, 124) = 29.73, $p < .001$, $\eta^2 = .324$), such that Directional ($M = 40.07$, $SD = 16.10$) showed lower workload than both Dynamic ($M = 48.50$, $SD = 17.44$) and Static ($M = 54.99$, $SD = 14.10$), and Dynamic lower workload than Static tactons across tacton name groups. Moreover, a significant interaction was also shown between tacton name and tacton category, $F(2, 124) = 9.66$, $p < 0.991$, $\eta^2 = .135$. An independent samples t-test showed a significant difference for Directional tactons ($t(63) = 0.09$, $p < .001$) such that NT ($M = 31.89$, $SD = 11.37$) showed lower workload than NS ($M = 48.09$, $SD = 19.81$). These results are further illustrated in Fig. 6.

4   Conclusion

The study presented was designed to investigate tacton name effects on a participant's ability to learn and classify tactons from the literature. Results for classification accuracy clearly show participants were less likely to accurately classify tactons when nonsense syllables were used for names. This effect is most clearly demonstrated when comparing directional tactons, with a drop in accuracy of 32.45 %. This decrement in performance is further highlighted in that unlike results previously published by Barber et al. [13], overall Directional tactons did not show the highest classification accuracy when nonsense syllables were used. Overall, it appears as though tactons designed with some motion or alternating tactors within the sequence (e.g. Directional and Dynamic categories) will demonstrate better classification accuracy than static tactons. Both of these findings are further supported from workload scores, which shown lower perceived workload in when the original tacton names were used and for dynamic/motion-based tactons.

Overall, the results presented from this effort support previous tacton design strategies which attempt to encode visual patterns and names that leverage a wearer's prior knowledge. However, further research is needed to confirm this. Specifically, follow on efforts should compare other named labels that are not nonsense syllables with the same tactons to determine if this paradigm holds true. One likely explanation for the current findings could be the difficulty of remembering the nonsense syllables themselves, where participants may have been able to distinguish between patterns but could not accurately recall the nonsense syllables. Therefore, a comparison of the current tacton names with simple nouns of equal complexity across tactons (e.g. apple, peach) may show equal performance. With this and future follow on efforts, a better understanding of how to design tactons will aid in the creation of tactile lexicons. With this solid foundation, developers will be able to increase the current number of tactons while ensuring patterns have the highest saliency, lowest reaction times, and least mental demand making it possible to include tactile displays within a large variety of applications beyond human robot teams.

Acknowledgements. The authors would like to thank Dr. Florian Jentsch at the University of Central Florida for his support in having participants receive course credit for participation in this experiment.

References

1. Redden, E., Elliott, L.: Robotic control systems for dismounted soldiers. In: Jentsch, F.G., Barnes, M.J. (eds.) Human-Robot Interactions in Future Military Operations, pp. 335–352. Ashgate, Farnham (2010)
2. Tellex, S., Kollar, T., Dickerson, S., Walter, M.R., Banerjee, A.G., Teller, S., Roy, N.: Understanding natural language commands for robotic navigation and mobile manipulation. In: Proceedings of the National Conference on Artificial Intelligence (AAAI 2011) (2011)
3. U.S. Army: Visual signals. U.S. Army, Washington, D.C. (1987)
4. Oviatt, S.: Breaking the robustness barrier: recent progress on the design of robust multimodal systems. Adv. Comput. **56**, 305–341 (2002)
5. Haas, E.C.: Integrating auditory warnings with tactile cues in multimodal displays for challenging environments. In: 13th International Conference on Auditory Displays, Montreal (2007)
6. Haas, E.C., Van Erp, J.B.: Multimodal research for human-robot interactions. In: Jentsch, F., Barnes, M. (eds.) Human-Robot Interactions in Future Military Operations, pp. 271–292. Ashgate, Farnham (2010)
7. Bischoff, R., Graefe, V.: Dependable multimodal communication and interaction with robotic assistants. In: 11th IEEE International Workshop on Robot and Human Interactive Communication (2002)

8. Partan, S., Marler, P.: Communication goes multimodal. Science **283**(5406), 1272–1273 (1999)
9. Brewster, B., Brown, L.M.: Tactons: structured tactile messages for non-visual information display. In: Austrailian User Interface Conference, Dunedin, New Zealand (2004)
10. Elliot, L.R., Duistermaat, M., Redden, E., Van Erp, J.: Multimodal guidance for land navigation. U.S. Army Research Laboratory, Aberdeen Proving Ground (2007)
11. Elliott, L.R., van Erp, J., Redden, E.S., Duistermaat, M.: Field-based validation of a tactile navigation device. IEEE Trans. Haptics **3**(2), 78–87 (2010)
12. Gilson, R.D., Redden, E.S., Elliott, L.R.: Remote tactile displays for future soldiers. U.S. Army Research Laboratory, Aberdeen Proving Ground, MD (2007)
13. Barber, D.J., Reinerman-Jones, L.E., Matthews, G.: Towards a tactile language for human-robot interaction: two studies of tacton learning and performances. J. Hum. Factors Ergon. Soc. (2014)
14. Brill, C.J., Gilson, R.D.: Tactile technology for covert communications. In: Proceedings of the Human Factors and Ergonomics Society Annual Meeting (2006)
15. Dictionary.com, LLC., Nonsense Syllable. http://dictionary.reference.com/browse/nonsense+syllable. Accessed 19 Feb 2015
16. Hull, C.L.: The meaningfulness of 320 selected nonsense syllables. Am. J. Psychol. 730–734 (1933)
17. Hart, S.G., Staveland, L.E.: Development of NASA-TLX (task load index): results of empirical and theoretical research. Hum. Ment. Workload **1**(3), 139–184 (1988)
18. White, T.: Suitable body locations and vibrotactile cueing types for dismounted soldiers. U.S. Army Research Laboratory, Aberdeen Proving Grounds, MD (2010)

Augmenting Soldier Situation Awareness and Navigation Through Tactile Cueing

Linda R. Elliott[1]([⊠]), Bruce Mortimer[3], Gina Hartnett-Pomranky[2],
Gary Zets[3], and Greg Mort[3]

[1] Army Research Laboratory, Fort Benning, GA, USA
linda.r.elliott.civ@mail.mil
[2] Army Research Laboratory, Fort Rucker, AL, USA
regina.a.hartnett.civ@mail.mil
[3] Engineering Acoustics, Castleberry, FL, USA
{bmort,zets,gmort}@eaiinfo.com

Abstract. The objective of this study was to evaluate the effectiveness of a dual-row tactile belt comprising two different types of advanced tactors to communicate both navigation information and incoming alerts, during a waypoint navigation night operations scenario. Navigation information was provided to the Soldier by providing a pulse pattern on the torso corresponding to the direction towards the next waypoint. At the same time, the Soldier received incoming situation awareness alerts regarding threat and robot status indicators. Each Soldier participated in two comparable navigation scenarios, where the task performance with a front-mounted visual map display was used. A tactile assisted interface was also part of the Soldier ensemble, such that the tactile system was turned on during one navigation scenario, and turned off for the other. When using the tactile system, Soldiers reported being more situationally aware of their surroundings and having better control of their weapon. They also navigated more quickly, and very rarely consulted their visual dispay, when the tactile system was turned on.

Keywords: Soldier performance · Navigation performance · Tactile cueing tactile display · Tactile communication

1 Introduction

It has been established that dismounted Soldiers consistently experience heavy cognitive and visual workload, not only during combat operations, but also during navigation and patrol [1–3]. At the same time, the Soldier must master new technology that have high demand for visual focal attention, such as smart phone/tablet map displays and various controller and communication devices. Emerging technologies assessed for Infantry Soldier combat teams during the Army Expeditionary Warrior Experiment (AEWE) included a variety of sensor-based information from aerial and ground vehicles, all which must be integrated in comprehensible fashion [4].

While these advanced technology devices are meant to assist the Soldier, care must be taken not to further overload him or her with additional demands or distracters.

© Springer International Publishing Switzerland 2015
S. Yamamoto (Ed.): HIMI 2015, Part I, LNCS 9172, pp. 345–353, 2015.
DOI: 10.1007/978-3-319-20612-7_33

Given the high demands for visual attention, consideration turned towards off-loading attentional demands to other sensory channels, as this has been demonstrated to ease workload [5, 6]. Tactile displays present an opportunity to provide direction and alerting cues that are both intuitive and covert [7, 8]. Studies have showed the effectiveness of tactors and recent research has proposed combinations of different types of tactors to provide a wide range of perceivable features [9, 10]. In this paper, we summarize findings of a user-based evaluation of a dual-row tactile belt comprising two different types of advanced tactors, to communicate both navigation information and incoming alerts. The system was integrated with a chest-mounted tablet display similar to NettWarrior concepts for the future Soldier.

2 Equipment

The NavCom user hardware comprises a smart phone with integral visual display and touch screen interface, a dual row tactor belt array, and a commercial off the shelf (COTS) GPS/inertial sensor (INS). The smart phone was mounted in a MOLLE (Modular Lightweight Load-carrying Equipment) vest. Soldiers could flip down the display to check their visual map display or read incoming text alerts (Fig. 1).

This experiment used commercially-available tactors which are relatively small, light, salient, sturdy and bio-isolated available from Engineering Acoustics, Inc. (EAI). Figure 2 shows the EAI C-2 tactor that has been proven effective in previous experiments, along with the newer, and smaller, C-3 tactor, and a low frequency motor based tactor, the EMR tactor. These tactors are based on a linear actuator design that is more resistant to loading effects typical of more widely used eccentric mass motors [13]. The C-2 and C-3 are almost equivalent in vibratory output and believed to be equivalent in sensation. The C-3 (6 g) is substantially lighter than the C-2 (18 g).

In this experiment, the EMR tactor was used primarily for navigation signals. For incoming alerts, C-3 tactors were used, programmed at the frequency that is optimal for

Fig. 1. NavCom tactile belt showing tactor placement (left) and chest-mounted visual display (right).

Fig. 2. The EAI EMR, C-2, and C-3 tactor transducers (left to right respectively)

Table 1. Characteristics of C-3 and EMR tactors

Characteristic	C-3 tactors	EMR tactors
Mechanism	Moving magnet linear actuator	Motor-based actuator
Diameter	0.8″	1.00″
Thickness	0.25″	0.4″
Main frequency	200–300 Hz (but can operate at lower frequencies)	50–140 Hz,
Peak displacement	0.016″	0.03″
Material	Anodized aluminum, polyurethane	Polycarbonate and ABS plastic

human perception (250 Hz). The C-3 produces a highly salient, "sharp" sensation. Both types of tactors create a strong localized sensation on the body by utilizing a moving contactor that is located within the tactor housing and works like a plunger. Table 1 provides a description of characteristics of each type of tactor.

3 Taction Patterns

The navigation information was provided to the Soldier during navigation legs by providing a pulse pattern on the tactor sector corresponding to the direction towards the next waypoint. As the Soldier moved closer to the waypoint, the tactor pulse repetition rate increased until the waypoint was reached, upon which the Soldier was notified with a tactor message pattern.

Soldiers also received incoming alerts ("threat ahead"; "NBC threat") and status updates ("robot wheels are spinning", "robot battery low"). In the Visual-only condition, the alerts were communicated through text messages accompanied by an audio alert. In the Tactile-visual condition, they were communicated by tactile patterns based on the C-3 tactors.

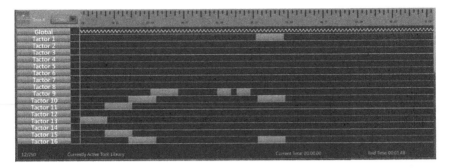

Fig. 3. "Threat ahead" taction: 100–200 ms pulses moving form the back and ending on a large area on the front torso, activating one EMR (tactor 1) and several C-3 tactors.

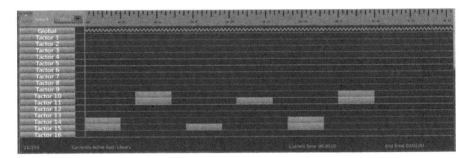

Fig. 4. "NBC detected" taction: 250 ms pulses on diagonal C-3 tactors emulating the hand signal for this command.

Tactile patterns have been developed and validated, using Soldiers in static postures and dynamic movements [11, 12]. These patterns were intended to be salient (e.g., easy to perceive and interpret). Figures 3 and 4 shows how characteristics of two tactions, "threat ahead" and "NBC detected", were programmed, using the EAI taction Creator editor. Tactors 1-8 were EMR while tactors 9-16 were C-3.

4   Experiment Design

Two equivalent 900 m routes were developed, comprising 3 major waypoints, each indicating the end of a navigation leg. Each Soldier navigated these routes twice: once with the tactile system turned off (i.e., Visual condition) and once with the tactile system turn on (i.e., Tactile/Visual condition). Experiment conditions were counter-balanced for order and for navigation course.

During the first navigation leg, each Soldier navigated while also receiving incoming alerts. During the second leg, each Soldier navigated while avoiding exclusion areas. During the third leg, each Soldier navigated while receiving incoming alerts and searching for silhouette targets (Fig. 5).

Fig. 5. Photograph of course A with navigation path and exclusion zones (shaded red area) (Color figure online).

5   Results

Data were collected on thirty-six Soldiers who volunteered to perform in this experiment-based evaluation during night operations.

Results showed that missions performed with the tactile system turned on were associated with significant ($p < 0.05$) differences with regard to reduced mission times (35.61 min tactors off vs. 28.05 min tactors on) (Fig. 6).

Table 2 provides the means and SD for the times (min) associated with each leg, by condition. The Visual condition was associated with slower times, for each leg.

Differences in navigation times were more pronounced for leg 2 (navigation with exclusion area) and leg 3 (navigation with alerts and target detection), indicating that the contribution of the tactile system was more pronounced when attention demands on

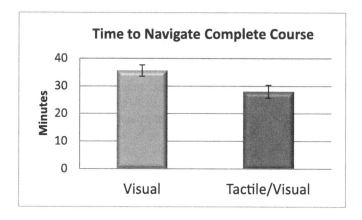

Fig. 6. Mean time to navigate complete course. Error bars represent 95 % confidence interval

Table 2. Mean time and standard deviation to complete each leg by condition

	Means and SD for time to navigate (min)			
	Leg 1	Leg 2	Leg 3	N
Visual	8.504 (2.303)	11.896 (2.879)	15.212 (2.766)	36
Tactile/visual	7.029 (1.986)	8.578 (2.765)	12.447 (3.759)	36

the Soldier are higher. In leg 1, the route was more linear and the terrain not as challenging; thus, the need for rerouting was potentially lower.

The total distance walked by each Soldier was significantly shorter when Soldiers used the tactile system, indicating that the use of the Tactile/Visual system decreased the navigation path each Soldier walked to complete the course. The navigational cues felt by the Soldier around their torso allowed Soldiers to route plan and move more directly to the next waypoint leading to shorter distances between waypoints. Results by leg were similar to that of navigation time: Soldiers were significantly aided by the tactile system for legs two and three, where there were greater demands for attention (e.g., rerouting, target detection).

Results also showed that the tactile capability was associated with significantly increased navigation accuracy (1.40 vs. 1.65 path ratio), and significantly lower reported experience of cognitive workload, effort, and frustration using the NASA TLX scale (see Table 3).

Table 3. Comparison of NASA-TLX means and standard deviations for visual and tactile/visual conditions.

	Mental	Physical	Temporal	Effort	Frustration
Visual	4.50 (2.42)	3.17 (1.97)	3.17 (1.98)	4.03 (2.26)	3.44 (2.67)
Tactile/visual	3.00 (2.03)	2.67 (1.80)	2.78 (2.17)	2.75 (1.98)	2.06 (1.69)

Results also showed that Soldiers were able to perceive and correctly interpret tactile patterns representing incoming alerts and status reports, with high (i.e., 92.7 %) accuracy, while on the move. This is impressive given that each signal was presented only once; there were no repetitions. Ratings regarding the ease of feeling the tactors showed that Soldiers found the tactors to be easy to feel, with means ranging from 6.33 to 6.69 (7 pt scale). The NBC signal was most frequently reported as being more easily felt. Soldiers did suggest adding a "please repeat" button as an improvement.

Soldiers provided feedback on many aspects of equipment use. They rated both systems highly for characteristics related to comfort and fit, with ratings ranging from 6.08 to 6.57 based on a 7.0 semantic differential scale, with 7 = extremely comfortable/ effective. Soldiers also provided many comments regarding the system. Typical positive statements include:

- "It has the ability to send signals quickly and silently. You can do land navigation with no thought involved."
- "A faster way to get to one point to another and it's a lot quieter than a radio."

- "It is way more effective and faster than conventional land nav. It allows the Soldiers to stay more effective towards threats."
- "Using the belt required less screen use. This prevented my eyes having to readjust to the night."
- It takes a lot less time; you can pay more attention to your surroundings and be more aware of your surroundings.

At the same time, Soldiers provided insightful comments with regard to how to make the system more combat-ready. The system must be durable, weatherproof and reliable. Battery and power usage will also be important. Soldiers suggested that the tactors should be adjustable, such that tactor intensity and noise levels can be changed to fit situation demands. Soldiers also suggested that tactile messages should be repeated until the Soldier acknowledges understanding (e.g., push a button, etc.). Some Soldiers tended to stop in order to better interpret the tactile signal. Repeated signaling would reduce the need to stop.

When using the tactile system, Soldiers reported being more situationally aware of their surroundings and having better control of their weapon. Soldiers reported that they were able to keep their hands on their weapons instead of a display resulting in hands free aspect. They also reported that not having to look down at a display screen to navigate or receive incoming alerts resulted in increased situation awareness and an eyes free aspect to their mission. Additionally, Soldiers reported not having to be concerned with tasks such as pace count or declination resulting in mind free task requirements.

The most compelling finding between groups was the number of visual display checks (17.7 tactile off vs. 1.3 tactile on). When the tactile capability was "on", the Soldiers predominantly used the tactile information resulting in low rates for visual display use. This in turn, is associated with greater light security (e.g., threat from enemy observations), higher preservation of night vision (e.g., glancing at a lighted display degrades night vision), and more attention available to attend to surroundings.

6   Conclusions

This experiment-based evaluation of tactile display technology compared the efficacy of a chest-mounted visual display, when used with, and without, an integrated tactile display. Core conclusions include:

User preference. When Soldiers had the tactile system available for use, they used it almost exclusively. They assigned the tactile capability high ratings for effectiveness and operational relevance.

Enhanced performance. The tactile system improved navigation performance, with regard to distance and time.

Hands-free performance. The tactile system allowed interpretation of both navigation information and incoming alerts without having to consult a visual display. When the tactile capability was on, Soldiers consulted the visual display an average of 1.3 times, compared to an average of 18.2 times when the tactile capability was not available.

<u>Lower workload</u>. Soldiers also reported less workload when using the tactile system. Mean ratings were significantly lower for frustration, effort, and mental workload.

<u>Increased safety</u>. Use of the visual display breaks light security, revealing Soldier position (e.g., to the enemy). It also disrupts night vision. Soldiers rarely consulted the visual display when the tactile capability was on.

In summary, these results augment collected findings with regard to development of tactile displays for dismount Soldier performance. Further research is planned to investigate issues affecting the salience (i.e., ease of perception) of tactile cues, following up on recent data collection (Elliott et al. in review). Further investigations are also warranted with regard to ease of learning and recognition, as moderated by tactile characteristics.

References

1. Mitchell, D.K., Samms, C., Glumm, M., Krausman, A., Brelsford, M., Garrett, L.: Improved performance research integration tool (IMPRINT) model analyses in support of the situational understanding as an enabler for unit of action maneuver team soldiers science and technology objective (STO) in support of future combat systems (FCS); ARL-TR-3405. U.S. Army Research Laboratory, Aberdeen Proving Ground, MD (2004)
2. Mitchell, D.K., Brennan, G.: Infantry squad using the common controller to control an ARV-A (L) soldier workload analysis (Technical Report, ARL-TR-5029). US Army Research Laboratory, Aberdeen Proving Ground, MD (2009)
3. Elliott, L., Redden, E.: Reducing workload: a multisensory approach. In: Savage-Knepshield, P. (ed.) Designing Soldier Systems: Current Issues in Human Factors. Ashgate, Farnham (2013)
4. U.S. Army Evaluation Center: Army Expeditionary Warrior Experiment (AEWE) Spiral H Final Report. Request from Commander, U.S. Army Test and Evaluation Command (CSTE-AEC-FFE), 2202 Aberdeen Boulevard, Third Floor, Aberdeen Proving Ground, MD 21005-5001 (2013)
5. Wickens, C.: Multiple resources and mental workload. Hum. Factors **50**(3), 449–454 (2008)
6. van Erp, J.: Tactile Displays for Navigation and Orientation: Perception and Behavior. Mostert and van Onderen, Leiden, The Netherlands (2007)
7. Elliott, L., van Erp, J.B.F., Redden, E., Duistermaat, M.: Field-based validation of a tactile navigation device. IEEE Trans. Haptics **3**(2), 78–87 (2010)
8. Elliott, L., Schmeisser, E., Redden, E.: Development of tactile and haptic systems for U.S. Infantry Navigation and communication. In: Proceedings of the 14th International conference of Human Computer Interaction, Orlando, FL, July 2011
9. Elliott, L., Mortimer, B., Cholewiak, R., Mort, G., Zets, G., Pittman, R.: Development of dual tactor capability for a soldier multisensory navigation and communication system. In: Proceedings of the International Conference of Human Computer Interaction, Las Vegas, NV, July 2013
10. Harnett-Pomranky, R., Elliott, L., Mortimer, B., Mort, G., Pettitt, R.: Soldier-based evaluation of dual-row tactor displays during simultaneous navigational and robot-monitoring tasks (Technical Report, ARL-TR-xx). US Army Research Laboratory, Aberdeen Proving Ground, MD (in review)

11. Stafford, S., Gunzelman, K., Terrence, P., Brill, C., Gilson, R.: Constructing tactile messages. In: Gilson, R., Redden, E., Elliott, L. (eds.) Remote Tactile Displays for the Contemporary Soldier (Technical Report No. ARL-SR-0152). Army Research Laboratory, Human Research and Engineering Directorate, Aberdeen Proving Ground, MD (2007)

12. Merlo, J., Stafford, S., Gilson, R., Hancock, P.: Physiological stress messaging studies. In: Gilson, R., Redden, E., Elliott, L. (eds.) Remote Tactile Displays for the Contemporary Soldier (Technical Report No. ARL-SR-0152). Army Research Laboratory, Human Research and Engineering Directorate, Aberdeen Proving Ground, MD (2007)

13. Mortimer, B., Zets, G., Cholewiak, R.: Vibrotactile transduction and transducers. J. Acous. Soc. Am. **121**(5), 2970–2977 (2007)

Multisensory Information Processing for Enhanced Human-Machine Symbiosis

Frederick D. Gregory[✉] and Liyi Dai

U.S. Army Research Office, Durham, NC, USA
{frederick.d.gregory5.civ,liyi.dai.civ}@mail.mil

Abstract. Multisensory information processing is a basic feature of neural systems and has been exploited to facilitate development of Army systems that augment Soldier performance through multisensory displays. However, the full potential of these systems has yet to be determined and will require understanding fundamental features of the underlying neurophysiology of multisensory processing, the neuroergonomics of multisensory machine interface and analytical methods for neural signal analysis, dimensionality reduction and pattern recognition. Here, findings from basic and applied research efforts will be presented that have focused on various aspects of human (brain)-computer interfaces to uncover understanding in these areas and mediate recent technological developments in multisensory display technology, passive mental state detection, attention/orientation detection, and human activities recognition from video in general. Based on the knowledge of multisensory processes acquired from these efforts there are emerging opportunities for creating new human gesture-controlled recognition systems based upon multimodal data analysis which will allow for unprecedented human-machine symbiosis.

Keywords: Human-machine interfaces · Brain-computer interface · Data analysis · Human activity monitoring · Multisensory cueing

1 Introduction

The modern Army is quickly transforming into a highly networked force with integrated platforms that will enable vast amounts of on-demand multimodal data. Individual soldiers will be responsible for unprecedented information management duties while ensuring personal and team situational awareness, decision-making and overall mission effectiveness. Strategies that mitigate the impact of information overload on the soldier are vital and must inform future system designs. Head mounted displays for the dismounted soldier [1], unmanned autonomous aerial and ground sensors [2–5] and communication platforms [6] could all simultaneously push information to the soldier through smaller and lighter displays. Therefore, strategies for ideal presentation of information to a user must continue to be an area of active research. Symbiosis of the soldier with machines is envisioned as a mutually-interdependent, tightly-coupled relationship that maximally exploits human and machine strengths in a seamless interface. Research communities have shown growing interest in this symbiosis due in part to recent progress in modern computing capabilities combined with the availability

© Springer International Publishing Switzerland 2015
S. Yamamoto (Ed.): HIMI 2015, Part I, LNCS 9172, pp. 354–365, 2015.
DOI: 10.1007/978-3-319-20612-7_34

of ubiquitous sensing modalities for capturing information about the human user in non-laboratory conditions [7, 8]. In this paper, we highlight a few technologies that have potential to be important components of human-machine interfaces and present new scientific opportunities.

2 Multisensory Information Processing

Our brains generate a unified percept of the world through partially redundant sensory information about an object or event. We watch movies and derive enjoyment even though we are aware that the sounds from people and objects on-screen originate from television or movie theater speakers. We readily perceive that voices in the movie are coming from the actor's lips. This sensory illusion, the ventriloquist effect, is a result of our innate ability to integrate auditory and visual information which results in the perceptual alteration of speech sound location [9]. The McGurk effect [10], another audio-visual illusion, occurs when lip movements alter the phoneme that is perceived. Sensory illusions are important tools for elucidating the neural processes underlying multisensory integration. Behavioral studies have suggested that when two sensory cues are separated by even 200 ms, the advantage of multisensory integration and perceptual consequences of ventriloquism are greatly reduced [11]. However, multisensory cells such as those recorded in the superior colliculus [12] and cortex [13] still show integrative responses to sensory cue separation of 600 ms and longer. The relationship between the temporal dynamics of single unit responses in the brain to behavior must be linked with multisensory neural network activity to inform multisensory information presentation and display technology.

2.1 Multisensory Displays

Dynamic and highly adverse operational environments often present scenarios where sensory information is degraded or obstructed. Multisensory cueing has been demonstrated as an effective strategy for orienting attention under non-ideal conditions [14, 15]. Multisensory cueing has also shown to be an effective strategy for offsetting performance decrements due to stress [16]. Delivery of temporally congruent information is being actively explored for multisensory displays with combined audio-visual and other multisensory interactions for augmenting human performance [17–19]. While some studies have reported less effective impacts of combined sensory cues for specific tasks [20], the emerging and unified view is that cueing underused sensory streams provides an overall performance advantage [20, 21]. Human multisensory integration is suggested to rely upon correlations between converging sensory signals that result in statistically optimal input to the nervous system and behavioral outputs [22]. However, the manner in which congruent multisensory information impacts a user's nervous system in real world situations has yet to be fully exploited. Emerging applications for navigation, covert communication and robotic control will benefit by further understanding how the underlying neurophysiological mechanisms of multisensory processing relate to the statistics of behavior.

2.2 Multisensory Information Processing in the Brain

The integration of information from multiple senses was originally thought to occur in high level processing areas in the frontal, temporal or parietal lobes [23–25]. More recent anatomical, neurophysiological and neuroimaging studies in non-human primates and functional brain studies in humans lead to the emerging view that multisensory processing involves a diversity of cortical and sub-cortical neural networks [26–28]. Based on behavioral studies with multisensory cueing, the neural coding strategy within multisensory integrative neural networks must be biased by the extent of spatial and temporal congruency of incoming sensory information [29]. Preliminary findings suggest that converging synaptic signaling by pre-cortical sensory integrating neurons of the thalamus show augmented output to the primary auditory cortex [30]. Both excitatory and inhibitory signals are strengthened by these congruent sensory inputs and highlight the diversity of computational modifications occurring within multisensory integrating networks [31]. Decoding multisensory neural network activities could potentially serve as feedback commands for closing the human-machine interaction loop.

The underlying neural codes of multisensory processes must be considered within the context of mathematical and theoretical models in order to best define pathways for improving multisensory interfaces. Feed-forward convergence of information from simultaneous senses (sensory organ to cortex) is accompanied by feed-back input from unisensory processing cortical areas onto lower-level multisensory integrating sites [32]. This view of multisensory processing builds upon the modality appropriateness hypothesis which offers the proposal that the greater acuity sensory modality for a particular discrimination task, ultimately dominates perception in a winner-take-all competition [33]. A similar, and complementary, view is that multisensory integration obeys Bayesian probability statistics [34, 35] and most closely resembles the properties of a maximum likelihood integrator [22, 36, 37]. An alternative view is that multisensory enhancement of information processing is a result of temporal or spectral multiplexing, where, for example, spike timing information from single neurons and activity from network oscillations interact in time and lead to an enhanced multiplexed code [38]. The complexity of multisensory integration-induced modifications of the neural code require improved signal processing approaches for decoding multiscale neural activity combined with appropriate theoretic frameworks and mathematical modeling to fully realize the potential of multisensory information processing for informing advanced display technologies.

3 Complementary Approaches

Three areas of active research are utilizing methods and creating technologies that can support multisensory information display technologies.

- Brain State Awareness
- Human Activity Monitoring
- Direct Brain-Computer Interfaces

Together, these areas lay foundations for next-generation systems that exploit principles of human cognition to mediate ergonomically enhanced human-system interfaces that maximally augment performance. Here we review example technologies by superficially highlighting potential opportunities.

3.1   Brain State Awareness

Performing tasks under complex, dynamic, and time-pressured conditions is troublesome for maintenance of operational tempo. Mental workload is a topic of increasing importance to human factors and significant effort has been devoted to developing innovative approaches to objectively assessing cognitive load in real-time. Stress is another topic of significant importance for the deleterious impact on performance of the user of any display technology [14]. Strategies are sought to offer fatigue offsetting interventions like selecting the best information content and format for presentation of information to the human operator. Data relevant for mental state detection include facial features, involuntary gestures, tactile signals, brain neural signals, and physiological signals (e.g., speech, heart rate, respiration rate, skin temperature, and perspiration). Mental states such as anxiety or fatigue often lead to temporal changes in biophysiological signals that might be classified by machine learning algorithms. For example, anxiety may result in increased rate of heartbeat and increased blood pressure relative to physiological signals of an individual's "normal" mental state. A major challenge is the lack of precise quantitative metrics that define mental states and the difficulty for cross-subject validation.

Stress, Anxiety, Uncertainty and Fatigue (SAUF). Recent attempts have been made to detect stress, anxiety, uncertainty and fatigue from visual and infrared images of a human face [39, 40]. An infrared image, either long wave or mid wave IR, captures the thermal signatures of the skin. Mental states, like stress or anxiety, generate subtle changes in local blood flow beneath the skin, reflected as changes in skin temperature. Thermal imagery is rather sensitive to such physiological changes although the changes may be invisible to the naked eye in certain groups of individuals [39, 41]. Non-invasive detection methods are highly desirable and offer a simple and affordable computer interface solution. State detection from imaging modalities allow for a passive means of detection without interfering with the operator's normal activities or requiring operator cooperation, which could be amenable to real-world applications.

For visual/thermal video based SAUF detection, the first step is to determine facial landmarks such as mouth corners, eye inner and outer corners, nasal tip, eyebrow start and end points. These landmark points are algorithmically tracked so that spatial and temporal information, called features, can be extracted from both the visual and thermal videos and subsequently used in pattern classification. Features include eye and/or mouth movement and physiological features such as the temperatures of these facial points. The data size is typically huge: Frame rates for visual and thermal videos can be 30 fps or higher. Recording from hours of thermal and visible videos are needed for algorithm training. In [40], the authors described the development of a computer system for SAUF detection using both visual and thermal videos in real-time. The system achieved detection errors in the range of 3.84 %–8.45 % for anxiety detection. In addition to algorithmic accuracy, errors may also be due to view changes (resulting in face deformation), full or partial occlusion, or individual variation. While this approach may not serve as a single source solution, non-invasive imaging provides an alternative and complementary approach for brain state detection that can accompany brain signal-based detection of mental states [42].

3.2 Human Activity Analysis and Prediction

The objective of human activity analysis and prediction is to understand the physical behavior of a human operator. Near term activity analysis focuses on understanding what the operator is doing and predicting the operator's intention for imminent action. Long term activity analysis aims at recognizing an operator's habits and personality such as right-handed person or left-handed person, or patterns of keyboard strokes for identity confirmation. Intention recognition and high level activity recognition are active research areas in artificial intelligence [43–49]. The methods for visual data analysis are general and applicable to a wide range of applications including human-machine interfaces as well as surveillance across a wide-span geographical region.

Visual data contains rich information for activity analysis and understanding. An adult can recognize activities from an image or a video segment with little effort. However, visual activity analysis and understanding by a computer has proven extremely difficult. The key challenges are that spatiotemporal features in imagery or video are typically high dimensional, noisy, ambiguous, and lie on (unknown) non-linear manifolds. There is a lack of robust methods for detecting the underlying patterns. Human activities occur in a wide variety of contexts and at wide range of scales. In many cases, contextual information is essential for understanding human activities but often unavailable. Conceptually, vision based human activity analysis and understanding consists of several components: action representation, action recognition, activity recognition and prediction although the boundary between action and activity may not be analytically definable.

Action Representation. Activity analysis and understanding is typically carried out in a general hierarchical framework. The low-level, atomic components are "actions" or "actionlets", i.e. primitive motion patterns typically lasting for a short duration of time, such as turning of the head or lifting the left arm. An activity is a temporal, typically complex composition of multiple actions. For example, "making a phone call" can be decomposed into four actions. At the low signal level, actions are characterized by spatiotemporal features and potentially distinguishable through pattern classification of the features. A component based hierarchical model was proposed to account for articulation and deformation of the human body due to factors such as view change or partial occlusion [48, 50, 51].

Action Recognition. Motion is a critical attribute for action recognition and spatio-temporal features can be extracted from multiple sequential frames in a video. Examples of spatial features include Scale-Invariant Feature Transform points,

Histograms of Oriented Gradients and Histograms of Optical Flow. Algorithms are used for frame registration and landmark or object tracking in video to extract temporal motion information. The spatial features and temporal information are combined to feed into pattern analysis and classification algorithms for action recognition.

Activity Recognition and Prediction. Activity recognition typically requires behavior modeling and high level reasoning, which is essential for activity or near real-time intention prediction. Parametric models like Hidden Markov Model or Petri Nets and non-parametric models such as Bayesian methods for inference require the incorporation of prior knowledge learned from past data or to be manually coded. Such frameworks are flexible to allow the incorporation of novel action dependencies for human activities. A general framework for human activity analysis and prediction has been developed [49, 52, 53] and supplemented by a hierarchical framework that can automatically detect contextual information and incorporate it in activity understanding [54].

3.3   Direct Brain-Computer Interface

Machines and humans, unfortunately, do not have an inherent common language for engaging in the human-computer interaction loop. In order for the human in the loop to derive maximal benefit from the interface the computational framework on the other end must be able to accurately determine user intent in real-world settings. This includes when the user is under duress and is placed into a dynamic physiological and/or neural state. Software specifications like those used in Controlled Natural Languages may provide a possible solution [55, 56]. However, these methods have mainly been tested for simple interfaces. Complex operational environments will require other complementary solutions.

Brain-Computer Interface Methods. Brain-computer interfaces permit direct communication of user intent to machine interfaces. The general framework for open-loop brain-computer interface system control originates from the detection of brain activity related to user intent. Electroencephalography (EEG), electrocorticography (ECoG) and intracortical (single unit) recording configurations are some of the technologies currently in use for brain-computer interfaces. Other sensing modalities include magnetoencephalography (MEG), Positron Emission Tomography (PET), functional magnetic resonance imaging (fMRI) and functional near-infrared spectroscopy (fNIRS). These imaging modalities together are complementary in information attributes, spatial-temporal resolution and degree of invasiveness. For example, EEG provides high temporal but low spatial resolution while fMRI provides low temporal but high spatial resolution. ECoG is a semi-invasive technique and intracortical recordings are invasive. Following analog to digital conversion, advanced signal processing and machine learning algorithms can then be deployed to classify neural activity information and derive user intent or state.

Detection of Silent Speech. A recent effort attempted to develop a brain-based communication and orientation system using EEG and ECoG signals [57, 58]. The objective was to create signal processing methods that allow detection of imagined speech for communication and determining directional attention for orientation from brain signals. One key challenge was a lack of understanding how imagined speech related to overt speech brain function. In order to be successful this study also had to overcome the limited understanding about the interaction among networked neurons in speech processing pathways, the difficulty of determining a baseline for imagined speech and the existence of noise in the neural recording. Based upon the existing real-time software system BCI2000, algorithms were generated that are capable of extracting electrophysiological features on a single-trial basis. Based on chance accuracy of 25 %, ECoG-based decoding showed overall ∼40 % performance levels for detection of vowels and consonants during both overt and covert speech [57, 58]. The results indicate higher than chance likelihood of correctly decoding imagined consonants and vowels.

For detecting attention and orientation, the setup is similar to that for imagined speech detection. Each subject was presented with visual cues and stimuli on a computer screen with built-in eye tracker, which verified ocular fixation on the central cross during data acquisition. The system achieved average detection accuracy of 84.5 % for attention engagement and 48.0 % for attention locus [59, 60] from ECoG data. While this line of work has only been able to achieve recognition of phonemes, a multisensory information processing approach may be taken to improve algorithm performance. Communication inherently involves multisensory processes which may be exploited to elucidate a new regime of neural network activity that might drive classification schemes of future brain-computer interfaces. Exploration of this idea may offer an opportunity to advance research in fundamental mechanisms of the neural processing of speech and close the loop in brain-computer interface design to facilitate performance for applications like covert communication and device control.

4   Vision for Future Multisensory Information Displays

Advances in functional neuroimaging combined with signal processing capabilities have led to new opportunities to identify spatial and temporal features of neural processing during real world experimentation [7, 8]. Research on human-machine interfaces has also considered methods for combining physiological data (e.g., respiration rate, heart rate, blood pressure and temperature) and behavioral information (e.g., posture, eye movements, gesture, and visual/thermal facial expression). The larger neural real estate devoted to multisensory processes and the diversity of signaling mechanisms available open new opportunities for human machine interfaces. Signal processing and data analytic advances can be devoted to decoding information related to this complex signaling and modification as a result of presentation of sensory information through multisensory displays. Brain-computer interface research has largely focused on the presentation of information to one of a user's senses while decoding brain activity with open-loop pattern classification, i.e. using electroencephalography while watching a visual display. The research has demonstrated utility in direct brain-computer communications for simple choices like user control of a cursor on a screen but state-of-the-art pattern classification algorithms only show limited performance for complex tasks such as decoding intended speech. Recent advances point to an emerging opportunity for a paradigm shift. To understand how simultaneous information presentation modifies behavioral response we need to determine where and how information from different senses is combined in the brain and what are the neural computational advantages rendered by these processes.

4.1 A Lesson from Sensory Deprivation

Sensory deprivation can lead to improvements in perceptual abilities in the intact senses for the blind or deaf. For example, individuals with early onset blindness show improved temporal and spectral frequency discrimination when compared to those with late-onset blindness or those who are sighted [61]. The early-blind have also been demonstrated to show enhanced sound localization ability relative to sighted individuals [62]. Surprisingly, in the study of Lessard et al., a group of blind subjects that had maintained some level of residual peripheral vision showed degraded sound localization ability relative to the completely blind. These observations together highlight the complicated mechanisms mediating multisensory processing when information is missing or corrupted in one sensory stream. This may be relevant to situations when only degraded sensory information is available in a high attentional load operational environment to a person with full sensory capabilities. A more recent study showed that by depriving normal sighted mice of light for as little as two days was enough to elicit potentiation of specific pre-cortical inputs from the thalamus into the auditory [30] or somatosensory cortices [63]. More work is needed in this area but the underlying neurophysiological mechanisms that mediate responses to sensory deprivation, not from disease or injury, may be relevant and provide inspiration for novel neuroplasticity-based approaches to advanced human-machine interfaces capabilities and augmented cognition.

5   Conclusion

The state-of-the-art view of multisensory displays has shown advantages of multi-sensory stimulation and has highlighted the need to understand the underlying neural bases mediating cueing-induced behavioral improvements. New approaches leading to higher resolution multimodal data as a result of developments in sensor technologies are an enabling tool but pose significant computational challenges. However, statistical modeling approaches and advancing computational analysis capabilities are providing new methodologies to facilitate the availability of neural information for direct human-computer interaction. There is a fundamental need to study human cognitive behavior under real-world conditions and multisensory information displays offer a unique capability to engage humans while they perform outside the laboratory.

State-of-the-art advances have not completely approached the vision of closed-loop human-machine symbiosis, but have paved the way for more sophisticated theories and technologies that will enable the attainment of this vision. Here we have described example technologies that provide emerging opportunities to exploit advances in understanding the underlying principles governing neural processing of information from simultaneous sensory streams to create systems that interface with the human in intuitive and, potentially, seamless ways. Multisensory displays show great potential to support future soldier-machine technologies and future designs should be created based on principles grounded in data and theory from basic cognitive neuroscience and neurophysiology. The future military operational environment will be more complex and require more from the human operator as she interacts with soldier systems. In order to take full advantage of scientific opportunities presented by multisensory information processing, a deep understanding of how the human brain, body, and sensory systems work in concert to accomplish tasks is required in order to close the loop in human-systems interactions.

6 Disclaimer

The views and opinions contained in this paper are those of the authors and should not be construed as an official Department of the Army position, policy, or decision.

References

1. Rash, C.E., Russo, M.B., Letowski, T.R., Schmeisser, E.T.: Helmet-Mounted Displays: Sensation, Perception and Cognition Issues. Army Aeromedical Research Laboratory, Fort Rucker (2009)
2. Murphy, D.W., Gage, D.W., Bott, J.P., Marsh, W.C., Cycon, J.P.: Air-Mobile Ground Security and Surveillance System (AMGSSS) Project Summary Report. NRAD-TD-2914. Naval Command Control and Ocean Surveillance Center RDT&E Div, San Diego (1996)
3. Wargo, C.A., Church, G.C., Glaneueski, J., Strout, M.: Unmanned Aircraft Systems (UAS) research and future analysis. In: 2014 IEEE Aerospace Conference, pp. 1–16 (2014)
4. Mitchell, D.K., Brennan, G.: Infantry Squad Using the Common Controller to Control a Class 1 Unmanned Aerial Vehicle System (UAVS) Soldier Workload Analysis. ARL-TR-5012. U.S. Army Research Laboratory, Aberdeen Proving Ground (2009)
5. Mitchell, D.: Soldier Workload Analysis of the Mounted Combat System (MCS) Platoon's Use of Unmanned Assets. ARL-TR-3476. U.S. Army Research Laboratory, Aberdeen Proving Ground (2005)
6. Goldberg, D.H., Vogelstein, R.J., Socolinsky, D.A., Wolff, L.B.: Toward a wearable, neurally-enhanced augmented reality system. In: Schmorrow, D.D., Fidopiastis, C.M. (eds.) FAC 2011. LNCS, vol. 6780, pp. 493–499. Springer, Heidelberg (2011)
7. Liao, L.D., Lin, C.T., McDowell, K., Wickenden, A.E., Gramann, K., Jung, T.P., Chang, J.Y.: Biosensor technologies for augmented brain–computer interfaces in the next decades. Proc. IEEE 100, 1553–1566 (2012)
8. McDowell, K., Lin, C.T., Oie, K.S., Jung, T.P., Gordon, S., Whitaker, K.W., Hairston, W.D.: Real-world neuroimaging technologies. IEEE Access 1, 131–149 (2013)
9. Howard, I.P., Templeton, W.B.: Human Spatial Orientation. Wiley, Oxford (1966)
10. McGurk, H., MacDonald, J.: Hearing lips and seeing voices. Nature 264, 746–748 (1976)
11. Jack, C.E., Thurlow, W.R.: Effects of degree of visual association and angle of displacement on the "ventriloquism" effect. Percept. Mot. Skills 37(3), 967–979 (1973)

12. Meredith, M.A., Nemitz, J.W., Stein, B.E.: Determinants of multisensory integration in superior colliculus neurons. I. Temporal factors. J. Neurosci. **7**(10), 3215–3229 (1987)
13. Wallace, M.T., Meredith, M.A., Stein, B.E.: Integration of multiple sensory modalities in cat cortex. Exp. Brain Res. **91**(3), 484–488 (1992)
14. Hancock, P.A., Szalma, J.L. (eds.): Performance Under Stress. Ashgate Publishing, Burlington (2008)
15. Merlo, J.L., Duley, A.R., Hancock, P.A.: Cross-modal congruency benefits for combined tactile and visual signaling. Am. J. Psychol. **123**(4), 413–424 (2010)
16. Hancock, P.A., Warm, J.S.: A dynamic model of stress and sustained attention. Hum. Factors J. Hum. Factors Ergon. Soc. **31**(5), 519–537 (1989)
17. Oron-Gilad, T., Downs, J.L., Gilson, R.D., Hancock, P.A.: Vibrotactile guidance cues for target acquisition. IEEE Trans. Syst. Man Cybern. Part C Appl. Rev. **37**(5), 993–1004 (2007)
18. Myles, K., Kalb, J.T.: Guidelines for Head Tactile Communication. ARL-TR-5116. U.S. Army Research Laboratory, Aberdeen Proving Ground (2010)
19. Hancock, P.A., Mercado, J.E., Merlo, J., Van Erp, J.B.: Improving target detection in visual search through the augmenting multi-sensory cues. Ergonomics **56**(5), 729–738 (2013)
20. Santangelo, V., Spence, C.: Assessing the automaticity of the exogenous orienting of tactile attention. Percept. London **36**(10), 1497–1506 (2007)
21. Prewett, M.S., Elliott, L.R., Walvoord, A.G., Coovert, M.D.: A meta-analysis of vibrotactile and visual information displays for improving task performance. IEEE Trans. Syst. Man Cybern. Part C Appl. Rev. **42**(1), 123–132 (2012)
22. Parise, C.V., Spence, C., Ernst, M.O.: When correlation implies causation in multisensory integration. Curr. Biol. **22**(1), 46–49 (2012)
23. Jones, E.G., Powell, T.P.S.: An anatomical study of converging sensory pathways within the cerebral cortex of the monkey. Brain **93**(4), 793–820 (1970)
24. Schroeder, C.E., Foxe, J.: Multisensory contributions to low-level, 'unisensory' processing. Curr. Opin. Neurobiol. **15**(4), 454–458 (2005)
25. Schroeder, C.E., Foxe, J.J.: Multisensory Convergence in Early Cortical Processing. The Handbook of Multisensory Processes, pp. 295–309. MIT Press, Cambridge (2004)
26. Ghazanfar, A.A., Schroeder, C.E.: Is neocortex essentially multisensory? Trends Cogn. Sci. **10**(6), 278–285 (2006)
27. Driver, J., Noesselt, T.: Multisensory interplay reveals crossmodal influences on 'sensory-specific' brain regions, neural responses, and judgments. Neuron **57**(1), 11–23 (2008)
28. Cappe, C., Rouiller, E.M., Barone, P.: Multisensory anatomical pathways. Hear. Res. **258**(1), 28–36 (2009)
29. Calvert, G.A., Thesen, T.: Multisensory integration: methodological approaches and emerging principles in the human brain. J Physiol. Paris **98**(1), 191–205 (2004)
30. Petrus, E., Isaiah, A., Jones, A.P., Li, D., Wang, H., Lee, H.K., Kanold, P.O.: Crossmodal induction of thalamocortical potentiation leads to enhanced information processing in the auditory cortex. Neuron **81**(3), 664–673 (2014)
31. Stein, B.E., Stanford, T.R.: Multisensory integration: current issues from the perspective of the single neuron. Nat. Rev. Neurosci. **9**(4), 255–266 (2008)
32. Driver, J., Spence, C.: Multisensory perception: beyond modularity and convergence. Curr. Biol. **10**(20), R731–R735 (2000)
33. Welch, R.B., Warren, D.H.: Immediate perceptual response to intersensory discrepancy. Psychol. Bull. **88**(3), 638–667 (1980)
34. Battaglia, P.W., Jacobs, R.A., Aslin, R.N.: Bayesian integration of visual and auditory signals for spatial localization. JOSA A **20**(7), 1391–1397 (2003)

35. Sato, Y., Toyoizumi, T., Aihara, K.: Bayesian inference explains perception of unity and ventriloquism aftereffect: identification of common sources of audiovisual stimuli. Neural Comput. **19**(12), 3335–3355 (2007)
36. Alais, D., Burr, D.: The ventriloquist effect results from near-optimal bimodal integration. Curr. Biol. **14**(3), 257–262 (2004)
37. Ernst, M.O., Banks, M.S.: Humans integrate visual and haptic information in a statistically optimal fashion. Nature **415**(6870), 429–433 (2002)
38. King, A.J., Walker, K.M.: Integrating information from different senses in the auditory cortex. Biol. Cybern. **106**(11–12), 617–625 (2012)
39. Puri, C., Olson, L., Pavlidis, I., Levine J., Starren, J.: Stress cam: non-contact measurement of users' emotional state through thermal imaging. In: Proceedings of the 2005 ACM Conference on Human Factors in Computing Systems (CHI), pp. 1725–1728 (2005)
40. Zhu, M., Wu, Y., Li, Q., Contrada, R., Ji, Q.: Non-intrusive Stress and Anxiety Detection by Thermal Video Analysis. U.S. Army Research Office Final Report (2014)
41. O'Kane, B.L., Sandick, P., Shaw, T., Cook, M.: Dynamics of human thermal signatures. In: Proceedings of the InfraMation Conference (2004)
42. Haynes, J.D., Rees, G.: Decoding mental states from brain activity in humans. Nat. Rev. Neurosci. **7**, 523–534 (2006)
43. Huang, T., Koller, D., Malik, J., Ogasawara, G.H., Rao, B., Russell, S.J., Weber, J.: Automatic symbolic traffic scene analysis using belief networks. In: AAAI-94, pp. 966–972 (1994)
44. Jaimes, A., Sebe, N.: Multimodal human–computer interaction: a survey. Comput. Vis. Image Underst. **108**(1), 116–134 (2007)
45. Ryoo, M.S., Aggarwal, J.K.: Recognition of composite human activities through context free grammar based representation. In: Proceedings of IEEE Conference on Computer Vision and Pattern Recognition, pp. 1709–1718 (2006)
46. Schmidt, C., Sridharan, N., Goodson, J.: The plan recognition problem: an intersection of psychology and artificial intelligence. Artif. Intell. **11**, 45–83 (1978)
47. Turaga, P., Chellappa, R., Subrahmanian, V.S., Udrea, O.: Machine recognition of human activities: a survey. IEEE Trans. Circuits Syst. Video Technol. **18**(11), 1473–1488 (2008)
48. Wang, C., Wang, Y., Yuille, L.: An approach to pose based action recognition. In: IEEE Conference on Computer Vision and Pattern Recognition, pp. 915–922 (2013)
49. Wu, Y., Huang, T.S.: Vision-based gesture recognition: a review. In: Braffort, A., Gibet, S., Teil, D., Gherbi, R., Richardson, J. (eds.) GW 1999. LNCS (LNAI), vol. 1739, pp. 103–116. Springer, Heidelberg (2000)
50. Chen, X., Yuille, A.L.: Articulated pose estimation with image-dependent preference on pairwise relations. In: Advances in Neural Information Processing Systems 27 (NIPS 2014) (2014)
51. Fidler, S., Mottaghi, R., Yuille, A.L., Urtasun, R.: Bottom-up segmentation for top-down detection. In: IEEE Conference on Computer Vision and Pattern Recognition, pp. 3294–3301 (2013)
52. Li, K., Fu, Y.: Prediction of human activity by discovering temporal sequence patterns. IEEE Trans. Pattern Anal. Mach. Intell. (T-PAMI) **36**(8), 1644–1657 (2014)
53. Yao, Y., Zhang, F., Fu, Y.: Real-time hand gesture recognition using RGB-D sensor. In: Shao, L., Han, J., Kohli, P., Zhang, Z. (eds.) Computer Vision and Machine Learning with RGB-D Sensors, pp. 289–313. Springer, Cham (2014)
54. Ma, Z., Yang, Y., Li, X., Pang, C., Hauptmann, A.G., Wang, S.: Semi-supervised multiple feature analysis for action recognition. IEEE Trans. Multimedia **16**(2), 289–298 (2014)

55. Fuchs, N.E., Schwitter, R.: Specifying logic programs in controlled natural language. In: Proceedings on Computational Logic for Natural Language Processing, vol. 95, pp. 1–16 (1995)

56. Kuhn, T.: A survey and classification of controlled natural languages. Comput. Linguist. **40** (1), 121–170 (2014)

57. Pei, X., Barbour, D.L., Leuthardt, E.C., Schalk, G.: Decoding vowels and consonants in spoken and imagined words using electrocorticographic signals in humans. J. Neural Eng. **8** (4), 046028 (2011)

58. Pei, X., Hill, J., Schalk, G.: Silent communication: toward using brain signals. IEEE Pulse Mag. **3**(1), 43–46 (2012)

59. Gunduz, A., Brunner, P., Daitch, A., Leuthardt, E.C., Ritaccio, A.L., Pesaran, B., Schalk, G.: Neural correlates of visual–spatial attention in electrocorticographic signals in humans. Front. Hum. Neurosci. **5**, 89 (2011)

60. Gunduz, A., Brunner, P., Daitch, A., Leuthardt, E.C., Ritaccio, A.L., Pesaran, B., Schalk, G.: Decoding covert spatial attention using electrocorticographic (ECoG) signals in humans. Neuroimage **60**(4), 2285–2293 (2012)

61. Gougoux, F., Lepore, F., Lassonde, M., Voss, P., Zatorre, R.J., Belin, P.: Neuropsychology: pitch discrimination in the early blind. Nature **430**(6997), 309 (2004)

62. Lessard, N., Pare, M., Lepore, F., Lassonde, M.: Early-blind human subjects localize sound sources better than sighted subjects. Nature **395**(6699), 278–280 (1998)

63. Jitsuki, S., Takemoto, K., Kawasaki, T., Tada, H., Takahashi, A., Becamel, C., Takahashi, T.: Serotonin mediates cross-modal reorganization of cortical circuits. Neuron **69**(4), 780–792 (2011)

Increase and Decrease of Optical Illusion Strength By Vibration

Teluhiko Hilano[✉] and Kazuhisa Yanaka

Kanagawa Institute of Technology, 1030 Shimo-ogino, Atsugi, Japan
{hilano,yanaka}@ic.kanagawa-it.ac.jp

Abstract. Optical illusions, such as the optimized FraserWilcox figures, are perceived to be moving although they are perfectly still. Optical illusion intensity substantially increases in a color-dependent FraserWilcox figure vibrated at several Hz. By contrast, the intensity decreases in other types of optical illusion subjected to vibration. It is difficult to control the frequency and amplitude of vibration made by hand precisely. Vibrating a figure on the PC display by software may be affected by the response time and limited refresh rate of the PC display. Therefore, we developed a vibration equipment by using a positive mechanical constraint cam. Various optical illusion figures were vibrated using the equipment to determine the relationship of optical illusion strength to the amplitude and frequency of vibration. Results showed that the proposed equipment can effectively determine the vibration frequency and stroke in which optical illusions can be recognized.

Keywords: Optical illusion · Fraser-Wilcox · Vibration

1 Introduction

1.1 Moving Optical Illusions

An optical illusion is visual trick in which the shape, size, length, and color of an object is perceived differently from its actual condition. Optical illusions, such as the Ouchi illusion (Fig. 1), Pinna illusion, and FraserWilcox illusion, appear as moving although they are perfectly still.

The center part of the Ouchi illusion is perceived as floating, which intensifies when the figure is moved or vibrated. Similarly, Ninio established a pattern, which appears as floating when moved [[5], p. 81].

1.2 Fraser-Wilcox Illusion

Fraser-Wilcox illusion is perceived to be moving although they are perfectly still. Kitaoka produced many optical illusion figures with enhanced illusion strength compared with the original FraserWilcox illusion; these figures are called "optimized FraserWilcox illusion".

© Springer International Publishing Switzerland 2015
S. Yamamoto (Ed.): HIMI 2015, Part I, LNCS 9172, pp. 366–373, 2015.
DOI: 10.1007/978-3-319-20612-7_35

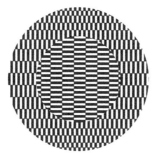

Fig. 1. Ouchi illusion, reproduced by Hilano

Kitaoka further categorized these illusions into five types (Types I, II, and so on) according to brightness and color gradients. Types I, II, III, and IV do not necessary need colors and can be perceived even in monochrome. By contrast, red and blue colors are essential in Type V. Other color combinations can also produce similar illusions but with low intensity. Generally, these optical illusion types are collectively called as color-dependent FraserWilcox illusion.

As example is shown Fig. 2.

Fig. 2. Color-dependent Fraser-Wilcox illusion, reproduced by Yanaka Color figure online

As this type of illusion is observed in peripheral vision, some people unfamiliar to it cannot perceive it. When this figure is displayed on the PC display and vibrated with software at several Hz, the illusion becomes strong that most people can perceive it [8]. This phenomenon is also perceived in the case using a manually or mechanically vibrated printed figure [9]; in this technique, stroke and frequency cannot be accurately controlled.

Previous studies showed that the optimized FraserWilcox illusion intensifies when the figure is viewed under bright condition. However, recent studies revealed that the color-dependent FraserWilcox illusion becomes strong when visualized under dark illumination, such as under a desk [6].

Kitaoka [2] reported that color-dependent FraserWilcox optical illusion discs appear rotating clockwise when visualized in peripheral vision under light. Conversely, they seem to rotate counterclockwise when observed under dark. Kitaoka suggested that this phenomenon could be related to the Purkinije effect [1].

Reverse illusion phenomenon is dependent on how the image is presented. According to Kitaoka, a positive optical illusion could occur when an optical illusion figure is shown on an liquid crystal display(LCD) but the reverse phenomenon would not occur. By contrast, opposite results are obtained when the same figure is printed on a paper.

As these characteristics remain unchanged even if the color of the display and the printed matter is similar, spectral constitution could be more important than the perceived color in these two optical illusions [1].

1.3   Other Examples of Illusions of Which the Optical Illusion Strength Become Strong by Vibration

The drifting triangle illusion (Fig. 3) becomes stronger when vibrated perpendicular to the moving direction of the original illusion [7].

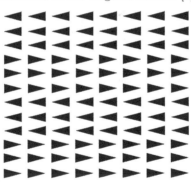

Fig. 3. Drifting triangle illusion

1.4   Random Dot Figures that We Perceived Some Message in It When It Vibrate

Some optical illusions, such as that presented Figure 7-2 in the book [[5], p. 73], can be perceived only when they are vibrated.

Hilano et al. [4] fabricated a figure that reveals messages when vibrated (Fig. 4).

We perceive the message HCII in this figure when it is vibrated. This image is prepared using the following:

1. construct a black and white bitmap image of a hidden message,
2. create two groups of figures with a fixed size and two types of randomly arranged blocks to satisfy the some conditions chosen by the user. In Figure 4, blocks belonging to the first group are shown in the first column consisting of 4 × 4 pixels. Five out of 16 blocks are painted black (#000000), with the remaining painted dark gray (#404040). In the second group, the blocks are painted dark gray and darker gray (#101010) (Fig. 5).
3. create the final image by randomly selecting the image in the group corresponding to the color of each pixel of the bitmap image created at step 1.

The difference of the mean brightness of two groups allow us perceive the image.

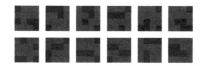

Fig. 4. A figure which we perceive some message when it is vibrated

Fig. 5. Random dot images used in Fig. 4

1.5 Purpose of Our Research

As the optical illusion strength varies when optical illusion figures are vibrated, a consistent vibration is needed. In this regard, we developed an equipment with controllable stroke and frequency of vibration. This equipment was used to determine the condition under which various optical illusions can be perceived.

2 System to Make Vibration

Figure 6 shows our proposed vibration system used in the experiment.

A stand made of aluminum alloy with a size of 210 mm × 300 mm (approximately equal to A4 paper size) is used to maintain the sample in the upper part of the equipment. The stand is inclined from zero to 90 °. The object beside the stand is a counter weight, which keeps the equipment stable when it is operated.

Reciprocation is generated by changing the revolution of the electric motor to direct advance movement at the ditch cut into a disk. The vibration stroke

Fig. 6. The whole view and side of the equipment

can be modified by shifting the revolving center from the center of the disk. The stroke is manually set every 0.5 cm from 5 cm to 1 cm.

Revolution speed is changed by rotating the dial of the controller on the side and checked with the digital speed indicator above the dial, as shown in the right part of Fig. 6, where the speed is set at 240 rpm. The designed maximum speed is 420 rpm.

An iPad mini is set on the stand (Fig. 7) and allows to vibrate to remove the after-image effect of the display on the optical illusion strength.

3   Experiments and Results

We evaluated several optical illusion figures by using the stand inclined to about 45 °. Figures were placed sideway, and iPad was mounted on the stand. The figures were observed at a distance higher than 30 cm.

3.1   Color-Dependent Fraser-Wilcox Illusion

Figure 2 was printed on a horizontal A4 paper and vibrated at a frequency of 7 Hz, with a stroke of 1 cm. A weak clockwise rotation was perceived in the light, and a counter-clockwise rotation was observed in the dark. At a frequency of 6 Hz or lower, some people could not perceive this illusion. Optical illusion and its reverse phenomenon were perceived by changing the brightness of the environment. These results are consistent with previous research [2], but the present experiment can be repeated under the same condition.

3.2   Moving Snakes Illusion

Figure 8 is an example of moving optical illusions (Kitaoka [3]) and its monochrome version. These figures were reproduced by Hilano, which are a little diffrent from the original.

Fig. 7. iPad mini on the stand

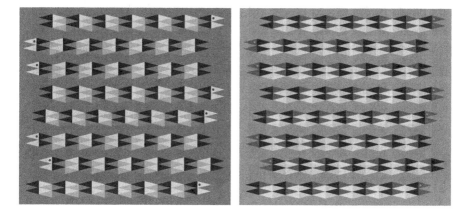

Fig. 8. Moving Snakes by Kitaoka and mono-chrome version Color figure online

These figures were printed with about 19 cm width and then observed in the peripheral view. The snakes around the middle part do not move, whereas the other snakes move to their heads (violet triangles). The monochrome version exhibited a lower optical illusion intensity than Fig. 8 (left) [3]. These figures were vibrated using the equipment set with 1 cm stroke at 2–3 Hz. In the light, the snakes move faster, except the one placed at the center. In the dark, the snakes move slowly first and then suddenly move to their first position.

3.3 Random Dot Figures

This illusion is dependent on the patterns of random dots and displays used and cannot be easily perceived when printed on a paper. The figure displayed on the iPad mini was vibrated at 3 Hz, with a stroke of 1 cm. The displayed message appeared as moving to the left and right direction of the stand.

3.4 Hermann's Grid

Figure 9 are Herman's grid(left) and scintillating Hermann's grid(right) [[5], pp. 64–65].

In these figures, dark spots appeared in the intersections of the vertical and horizontal lines or in the white discs when we move our gaze. When these figures were vibrated at 3 Hz, the illusion disappeared. Hence, it takes a short time to perceive the illusion. The illusion does not occur if the figure moves to a different location before the brain perceives it.

We also found that the Hermanns grid illusion disappeared when observed in the dark. These phenomena could be used to elucidate the mechanism of this illusion.

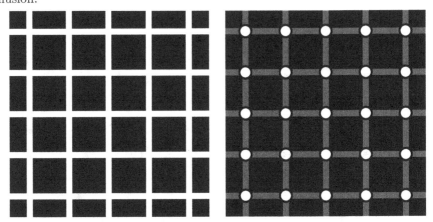

Fig. 9. Hermann'grid and scintillating Hermann's grid

4   Conclusion

In this research, we established an equipment that generates steady stroke and frequency to determine the conditions resulting in strong optical illusion strength. The proposed equipment can effectively specify the vibration frequency and stroke, in which optical illusions can be recognized. The intensity of some of the optimized FraserWilcox optical illusion, in addition to Type V, becomes strong when they are vibrated. Furthermore, when the Hermann grid was vibrated, the intensity of the optical illusion decreases. Thus, this can be used for optical illusion studies.

References

1. Kitaoka, A.: Color-dependent motion illusion in a stationary image and rods [in Japanese]. J. Color Sci. Assoc. Jpn. **37**(4), 400–401 (2013)
2. Kitaoka, A., Yanaka, K.: Reversal of the color-dependent Fraser-Wilcox illusion under a dark condition. In: Perception 42 ECVP Abstract Supplement, p. 97 (2013)

3. Kitaoka, A.: Moving Snakes. http://www.psy.ritsumei.ac.jp/akitaoka/motion18. html
4. Hilano, T., Kageyama T., Yanaka K.: Pseudo-random pattern image with an embedded hidden message perceived when vibrated. In: Perception 42 ECVP Abstract Supplement, p. 98 (2013)
5. Ninio, J.: Science of Illusions. Cornell Universiaty Press, New York (2001)
6. Yanaka, K.: Enhancement of the optimized Fraser-Wilcox illusion type V by swinging the image. In: Talk in the 5th Illusion Workshop, Meiji University, Tokyo (2012)
7. Yanaka K., Hilano T., Kitaoka A.: Drifting triangles illusion and its enhancement by shaking or blinking. In: Perception 42 ECVP Abstract Supplement, p. 96 (2013)
8. Yanaka, K., Mitsuhashi, R., Hilano, T.: Automatic shake to enhance Fraser-Wilcox illusions. In: VISAPP 2011, pp. 405–408 (2011)
9. Yanaka K., Hilano T.: Mechanical shaking system to enhance Optimized Fraser-Wilcox Illusion Type V. In: Perception 40 ECVP Abstract Supplement, p. 171 (2011)

Presentation Method of Walking Sensation Based on Walking Behavior Measurement with Inertial Sensors and Pressure Sensors

Kohei Ichihara[1(✉)], Koichi Hirota[2], Yasushi Ikei[2],
and Michiteru Kitazaki[3]

[1] The University of Tokyo,
7-3-1 Hongo, Bunkyo-Ku, Tokyo 113-8656, Japan
qql46303@iii.u-tokyo.ac.jp
[2] The University of Electro-Communications,
1-5-1 Chofugaoka, Chofu-city, Tokyo 182-8585, Japan
hirota@vogue.is.uec.ac.jp, ikei@computer.org
[3] Toyohashi University of Technology, 1-1 Hibarigaoka, Tenpakucho,
Toyohashi-City, Aichi 441-8580, Japan
mich@tut.ac.jp

Abstract. In this paper, we give the way to make the sitting user feel the walking sensation, by using the walking sensation presenting device in which we put the data we got from measuring walking behavior. We measured walking behavior from the inertial sensors which we put on the insteps and waist of the pedestrian and pressure sensors on the bottoms of their feet. We get the data of back-&-forth movements of feet from the data of acceleration and directions from inertial sensors on insteps. In the same way, we get back-&-forth and left-and-right movements of the whole body from the sensor on back. Walking sensation presenting device has a chair for user to ride, which moves back-&-forth and right-&-left to presents walking body's swing to user and the device which presents walking sensation to user's lower limb. The device which presents walking sensation to user's lower limb consists two parts. One part are the lower limb movement presenting board that moves back-&-forth to make user's lower limbs do the same movement as the real walking. The other is the landing vibration presenting device. About 10 % of amount of the whole body movement in real walking presents the best walking sensation to the user. About 20 % of amount of the lower limb movement in real walking presents the best walking sensation to the user.

Keywords: Walking behavior measurement · Lower limb movement · Sole vibration · Walking sensation · Physical exercise

1 Introduction

In these days, with the development of information and communication technology, it is expected to construct display about five senses and give new space experiences. In this research, we tried to show users' physical feeling of walking by precise control of information through five senses. When we succeed in presenting users quasi-real

© Springer International Publishing Switzerland 2015
S. Yamamoto (Ed.): HIMI 2015, Part I, LNCS 9172, pp. 374–385, 2015.
DOI: 10.1007/978-3-319-20612-7_36

walking sensation, they can experience travels and sports in the system. This is useful in study through experience, entertainment industry, and enhancing the QOL of the people who have trouble moving their limbs freely.

In early study, Helig gave the users the senses other than visual and auditory in *The Sensorama Machine* [1]. This presented users the wind, smell and vibrations experienced through riding a motorcycle.

Recently *Five Senses Theater* [2] by Ikei et al. is well known. In this research, they experimentally made smell and wind-touch displays and got knowledge and methods about how to mix smelling ingredients and control wind in the space. They researched presentation of human walking sensation, too. In their research, they collected various patterns of walking data through the measurement of real walking behaviors using motion-tracking markers. Based on these data, they studied vertical movements of lower limb. They said about 10 % of lower limbs' movement in real walking fits best walking sensation by passive movement [3].

Figure 1 shows the outline of the system we made. In our research, we think main body movements in walking consist of back-&-forth and right-&-left slow movement of whole body and back-&-forth movements of lower limbs. And then we have constructed the system to show them to the users. Currently wearable computing has become more feasible due to technological progress that has enabled us to produce compact and light weight computers and sensors with lower battery consumption. Considering these situations, we have also constructed the walking movement measuring system that can process and present the walking data of a distant user wearing compact sensors and computers in real time.

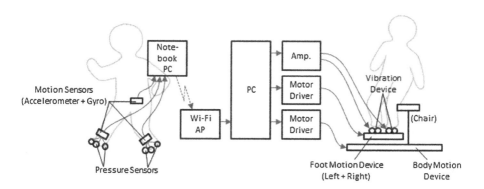

Fig. 1. Outline of the system

2 Walking Behavior Measurement with Inertial Sensors and Pressure Sensors

In this section we discuss the walking behavior measuring system that we've constructed in this research.

2.1   Constitution of the Walking Behavior Measuring System

In the measuring system, we attached inertial sensors to the user's waist and insteps of both feet to detect and measure walking behavior. Figure 2 shows the footwear equipped with the inertial sensor units.

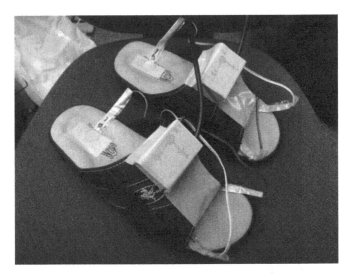

Fig. 2. Appearance of the footwear with the sensor units

We used IMU (Inertial Measurement Unit) chip (MPU-9150 by InvenSense). This is composed of 3 axis accelerometer, gyroscope, and compass. We connect this to the lap-top computer using I2C communication through microcontroller (H8 by Renesas Electronics). When we put the microcontroller to the lap-top computer to measure walking behavior, we did USB converting and communicated through USB port. We set all the accelerometers so that their x axis plus shows forward, y axis plus shows right and z axis plus shows upward. The user walks in the footwear with the sensor units, a belt with the sensor unit around his/her waist and a lap-top computer on his back to get the walking behavior data. Figure 3 shows the user with these sensor units. In this research, we got the data every 1/200 s from the sensor units.

In the sensor units for the feet, we attached pressure sensors (FSR402 by Interlink Electronics Inc.) to the feet to detect the landing timing and amount of the shock. We connected them to the measuring lap-top computer through the microcontroller, too. We attached these pressure sensors to the inside and outside of the bottom of user's feet near his toes, and to the heels.

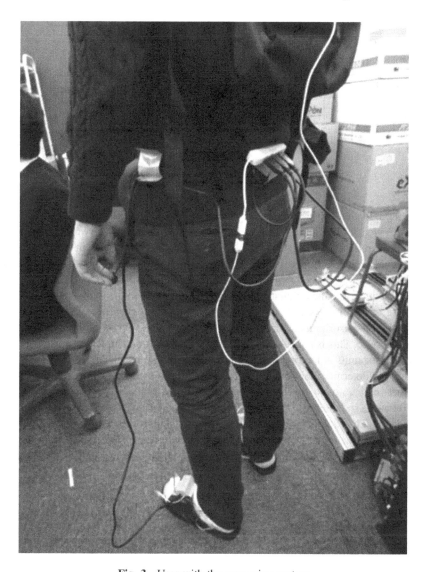

Fig. 3. User with the measuring system

2.2 Estimate of the Forward Vector and the Integration Calculation of Walking Behavior

In this section, we describe the method to estimate the forward acceleration vector which we need to drive the walking sensation presenting device by analyzing the data from inertial sensor units. Also, we describe the method to integrate the forward vector of the lower limbs and the waist of the pedestrian and calculate the coordinates which we finally put into the device. Figure 4 shows the outline of the calculation steps.

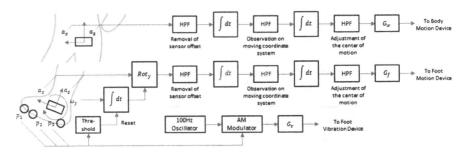

Fig. 4. Outline of the calculation steps

We thought that lower limb mainly move back-&-forth and vertically in walking, and we divided legs' walking motion into two direction levels, forward and vertical. So we measured how much x axis and z axis turn around y axis in horizontal and vertical level and determined each axis' forward acceleration vectors. Then we estimated the acceleration vector of lower limb by summing them up.

First, we integrate the angular velocity vector gotten from the gyroscope to estimate the turning angle of the sensor units around y axis (θ_y) at each time. At this time, we set the angle of sensor units at landing at 0 degree to correct errors brought by the drifts of the gyroscope. This is because by adjusting the sensor units on feet, we can make the angle of sensor units at landing at 0 degree. We use pressure sensors to know when the feet land. We determine feet landing time when all the pressure sensors on the bottom of the feet indicate over the threshold. We confirmed that we properly set the sensor unit at 0 degree in landing. Figure 5a shows θ_y at each time. θ_y reduces to 0 smoothly, not suddenly. That demonstrated that our process is appropriate.

Then we estimate feet's forward acceleration vector a'_f, using sensor units' turning angle around y axis(θ_y) at each time. That is to say, adding forward acceleration vector on x axis a_x and that on z axis a_z, we get feet's forward acceleration vector a'_f.

$$a'_f = a_x \cos \theta_y + a_z \sin \theta_y$$

Apropos, we ignored the rotation of the sensor unit of the waist, because it is very small.

The back-&-forth acceleration vector that we got above (a'_f) include the offset of the accelerometer. We use a high-pass filter to remove this offset. Figure 5b shows the back-&-forth acceleration vector of right foot (a_f) at each time that we got through this process.

Then we get the velocity of the foot by integrate a_f. We use a high-pass filter again to remove the constant body movement in walking behavior. Figure 5c shows the back-&-forth velocity of right foot (v_f) at each time that we got through this process.

Then we get the coordinate of the foot by integrate v_f. We use a high-pass filter again to set the center of the locomotion on the origin of the walking sensation presenting device. Figure 5d shows the back-&-forth coordinate of both feet at each time that we got through this process.

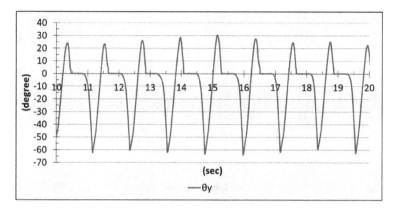

Fig. 5a. θ_y at each time

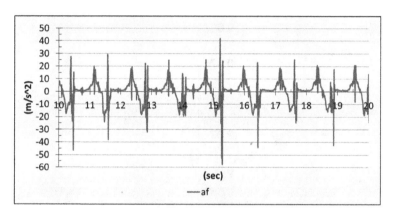

Fig. 5b. a_f at each time

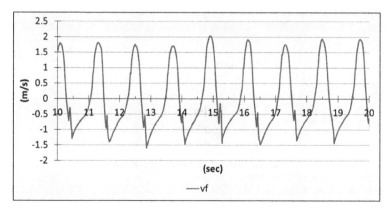

Fig. 5c. v_f at each time

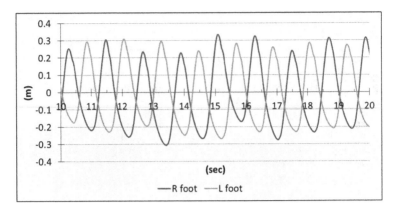

Fig. 5d. Waveform of the feet locomotion

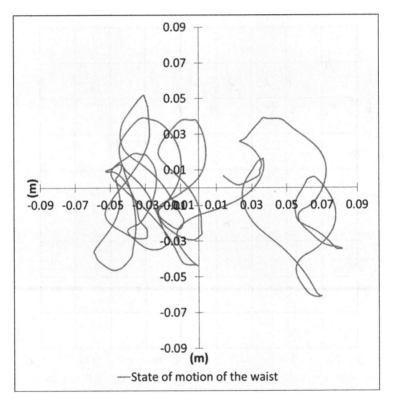

Fig. 6. State of motion of the waist

Also, Fig. 6 illustrates the movements of the waist.

3   Walking Sensation Presenting Device

In this section, we describe the device which works based on the measured walking locomotion data and presents users walking sensation. First in 3.1 we explain the structure of it and then in 3.2 we state its operation.

3.1   Constitution of the Device

Figure 7 shows the appearance of the walking sensation presenting device. Walking sensation presenting device has a chair for user to ride, which moves back-&-forth and right-&-left to presents walking body's swing to user and the device which presents walking sensation to user's lower limb. The device which presents walking sensation to user's lower limb consists two parts. One part are the lower limb movement presenting board that moves back-&-forth to make user's lower limbs do the same movement as the real walking. The other is the landing vibration presenting device. Next we describe them in detail.

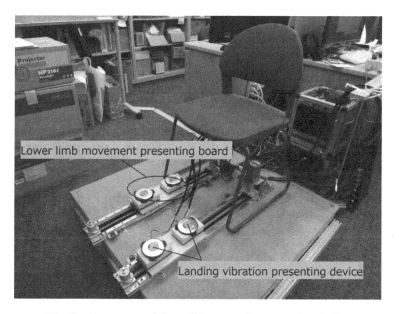

Fig. 7.   Appearance of the walking sensation presenting device

3.1.1   Walking Sensation Presenting Moving Floor

The walking sensation presenting moving floor presents users back-&-forth and right-&-left body movements. This system works corresponding to the coordinate measured by the accelerometers on the pedestrian's waist. The floor can move both back or forth and right or left by 15 cm. We used a pulse motion controller (PEX-H741444V by

Interface Co.). We attached this to the walking sensation presenting device and controlled the 2-axis motors' drive.

3.1.2   Lower Limb Movement Presenting Boards

The lower limb movement boards presents users back-&-forth movement of lower limbs while walking. This system works corresponding to the coordinates measured by the inertial sensors on the pedestrian's insteps. The boards can move back-&-forth by 15 cm. As is mentioned above, we used a pulse motion controller (PEX-H741444V by Interface Co.).

3.1.3   Landing Vibration Presenting Device

The landing vibration presenting device presents users the vibrations to the bottoms of the feet when the feet touch down the ground. This system presents users vibrations according to the timing and pressure of feet landing measured by pressure sensors on the pedestrian's feet. We used an analogue output interface (PCI-3329 by Interface Co.). We attached this to the walking sensation presentation device and controlled vibrator at four points of the front and back of both feet. We used vibrators (vibro-transducer Vp604 by Acouve Laboratory, Inc.). We amplified the analogue signals output with a power amp (EPQ304 by Behringer) and input them into vibrators to produce vibrations.

3.2   Operation of the Device

Then we checked the operation of the walking sensation presenting device to know whether or not we can control it precisely. We compared the coordinate calculated through the data from accelerometers with that of motors' indicating. We used the function included in the driver of the pulse motion controller PEX-H741444V to know

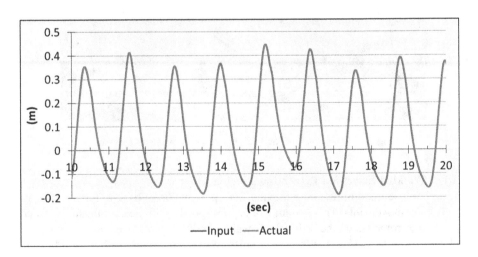

Fig. 8. Input position & actual position

the coordinate that the motor actually worked and indicated. In the actual control, measured amount are multiplied by the gain to reduce the amount of the movement, so that the amount of the movement is within the limits of the device. Figure 8 plots motors indicating coordinates divided by this gain and the coordinates calculated from the accelerometers' data. Both coordinates corresponded and it was confirmed that the device operates accurately. Figure 8 illustrates the right foot's lower limb movement presenting board. The same was confirmed with the left foot and with and the walking sensation presenting moving floor. And the gap between moving sensors and the device operation is 1 s.

4 Experiment

In this section, we describe the experiments, using the walking behavior measuring system and walking sensation presenting device we made.

4.1 Purpose of the Experiment

In the research of Ikei et al., they said that about 10 % of lower limbs movement in real walking presents the best walking sensation to the user. We made experiments to know what presents the best walking sensation to the user with our device.

4.2 Method of the Experiment

First, we took the subject's walking data for 30 min through our walking behavior measuring system. We measured 60BPM (60Beat Per Minute 60 steps in 60 s), 86BPM and 100BPM. Ikei et al. experimented with 86BPM. To compare with this experiment, we did with a little faster beat and a little slower beat. Walking sensation presenting device worked on this data.

Second, we made the subject operate the walking sensation presenting device to match the best his/her real walking sensation and recorded it. It was recorded as the gain to the actual walking movement. To be specific, the subject operated the device by pressing the key of the wireless keyboard. Every time the subject presses the "↑" key, the gain of the walking sensation presenting moving floor(GainW) increases by 0.1 %, and the "↓" key, decreases by 0.1 %. And every time the subject presses the ";" key, the gain of the lower limb movement presenting boards(GainF) increases by 0.1 %, and the "-" key, decreases by 0.1 %. We presented the subject 60BPM, 86BPM, 100BP at random. Each subject operates on each BPM 6 times, so he/she operates 18 times in all. We repeated the date while the subject operated the device. Subjects are 5 men and 1 woman who have proper walking functions.

4.3   Result of the Experiment

Table 1 below shows the results of the experiment. The average of the gain of the walking sensation presenting moving floor (GainW) is about 10 % of all walking speed. Also, the average of the gain of the lower limb movement presenting boards (GainF) is about 20 % of all walking speed. And particularly in GainF, it seems that as the walking speed become faster, the gain become smaller.

Table 1. Results of the experiment

(a) GainW   (b) GainF

GainW	Walking Pitch (BPM)			
Subject	60	86	100	Ave.
a	4.15%	3.23%	3.83%	
b	8.32%	6.97%	7.52%	
c	19.15%	16.23%	14.45%	
d	10.48%	10.50%	11.75%	
e	15.55%	13.57%	11.17%	
f	12.10%	10.43%	6.67%	
Ave.	11.63%	10.16%	9.23%	10.34%

GainF	Walking Pitch (BPM)			
Subject	60	86	100	Ave.
a	30.48%	26.88%	23.80%	
b	19.13%	14.65%	17.13%	
c	24.45%	16.48%	16.10%	
d	33.53%	21.88%	19.10%	
e	24.88%	17.98%	13.70%	
f	20.80%	22.42%	11.32%	
Ave.	25.55%	20.05%	16.86%	20.82%

4.4   Experience of the Real-Time Transmission of the Walking Behavior

To investigate how much fine the walking behavior measuring system and the walking sensation presenting device we made can present the walking sensation, we tried to do different patterns of walking behavior and present them to users by using the real-time transmission of the walking behavior. As a result, we found that users can know how they walk to some extent in some patterns, for example turn 90 degree, back, and who are walking actually with the measuring system.

5   Conclusion

In this paper we discussed the walking behavior measuring system and the walking sensation presenting device that we've constructed. We proposed a method of measuring the human walking locomotion by using inertial sensors and pressure sensors. Also, it was confirmed that the walking sensation presenting device operates accurately, based on the measured walking locomotion data. About 10 % of amount of the whole body movement in real walking presents the best walking sensation to the user. About 20 % of amount of the lower limb movement in real walking presents the best walking sensation to the user. We will research the factors which influence the walking sensation user feels in more detail through more experiments.

Acknowledgements. This study was carried out under support of Ministry of Internal Affairs and Communications' SCOPE (Strategic Information and Communications R&D Promotion Programme).

References

1. The Sensorama Machine. http://www.mortonheilig.com/InventorVR.html
2. FY2012 Research and development goals and achievements and future research plans of "The ultra-realistic communication technology research and development by innovative three-dimensional imaging technology". http://www2.nict.go.jp/collabo/commission/seika/h24/143u1_gaiyo_g.pdf
3. Generation method of walking sensation by the presentation of proprioception at the lower limb. http://mgikta.sd.tmu.ac.jp/2012J/masuda.pdf

Induction of a Relaxed State Using a Vibration Stimulus Based on the Respiratory Cycle

Naoto Iwamoto[1](✉) and Hiroshi Hagiwara[2]

[1] Graduate School of Information Science and Engineering,
Ritsumeikan University, 1-1-1 Noji Higashi, Kusatsu Shiga 525-8577, Japan
is0102sv@ed.ritsumei.ac.jp
[2] College of Information Science and Engineering,
Ritsumeikan University, Shiga, Japan
hagiwara@ci.ritsumei.ac.jp

Abstract. The purpose of this study was to induce different states using a vibration stimulus based on an individual's breathing cycle. Based on the results of Lorenz plot area S (LP-area-S), breathing control with the long-period breathing pattern was able to induce a state of increased parasympathetic activity. Parasympathetic activity was greatly reduced during the task with the short-period breathing pattern. The results of LP-area-S and the AAC (alpha attenuation coefficient) showed that LP-area-S was increased with the short- and long-period breathing patterns when AAC was decreasing. Given the results of this experiment, it appears that breathing control using a vibration stimulus based on individual breathing cycles can lead to a relaxed state in terms of the physiological and psychological changes.

Keywords: Breathing control · Autonomic nervous system · Central nervous system · Lorenz plot · Vibration stimulus

1 Introduction

Effective rest is needed more today than ever before because stress and a shortage of sleep caused by various societal factors adversely affect health and work efficiency.

In addition, wearable terminals have emerged as the next generation of portable devices that can be easily worn that measure biological information such as the breathing cycle and heart rate. We think that wearable terminals will be easily used to provide biofeedback of personal biometric information in the near future.

The respiratory cycle is one of the important factors for biomedical signals. It has been reported that the respiratory cycle can affect the autonomic nervous system and brain activity in research that has involved respiratory control using vibratory stimulation derived from the respiratory cycle in test subjects that induced rest states [1]. However, respiratory control was performed using vibration changes based on the respiratory cycle of the same cycle. Thus, this does not provide accurate biofeedback of personal biometric information.

The purpose of this study was to induce a relaxed state using a vibration stimulus based on an individual's breathing cycle. The physiological changes were evaluated by

© Springer International Publishing Switzerland 2015
S. Yamamoto (Ed.): HIMI 2015, Part I, LNCS 9172, pp. 386–395, 2015.
DOI: 10.1007/978-3-319-20612-7_37

EEG (electroencephalography), ECG (electrocardiogram), and respiratory cycle measurements. Changes in vigilance and autonomic nervous system activity were then monitored.

2   Experimental Methods

2.1   Subjects and Experimental Instruments

Thirteen healthy, non-medicated men (21–22 years old) participated in the experiment. All subjects provided written informed consent prior to participation. An EEG1100 (Nihonkoden, Tokyo, Japan) and a 45360 (GE Health Care Japan, Tokyo, Japan) were used for EEG, ECG, and respiratory cycle measurements.

2.2   Experimental Methods

The experimental protocol was performed using alpha attenuation test (AAT) specific activity (eyes closed (30 s), eyes opened (30 s) × 3) for 3 min, followed by a 5-minute task (breathing control), and a final AAT of 3 min. One cycle was a total of 11 min. The roken arousal scale (RAS) was evaluated before and after measurement. Subjects were given 10-minute breaks between each cycle. EEG and ECG findings and respiration were evaluated. Details of the experimental protocol are shown in Fig. 1. The task (breathing control) was randomized for every experiment to exclude an order effect.

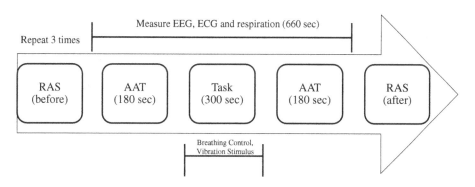

Fig. 1. Experimental protocol

2.3   Breathing Control

A vibration generator (Nihon Suribi Scientific, Tokyo, Japan) was used for breathing control. Breathing control was performed according to the strength of the vibration. A hand (finger-tip) vibration stimulus was given. When vibration was strengthened, the subjects breathed in and then breathed out when the vibration was weakened. The vibration frequency of the vibration generator in this experiment was 60 Hz.

Prior to this experiment, the subjects were seated with closed eyes for 5 min, followed by bicycle exercise (load: 40 W, speed: 45–50 rpm) for 5 min as a preliminary experiment to measure the breathing cycle. Then, three breathing patterns were created from the average period during activity breathing and resting breathing: short-period (activity breathing cycle), middle-period (resting breathing cycle), and long-period (middle-period × 1.5). The respiratory cycles of the subjects are shown in Table 1.

Table 1. Respiratory cycles of the subjects

Subject number	Short-period (s)	Middle-period (s)	Long-period (s)	Subject number	Short-period (s)	Middle-period (s)	Long-period (s)
No. 1	2.656	4.082	6.124	No. 8	2.464	5.448	8.172
No. 2	2.248	5.541	8.312	No. 9	2.68	3.452	5.18
No. 3	2.258	3.47	5.206	No. 10	1.678	4.104	6.156
No. 4	2.204	3.618	5.428	No. 11	2.476	3.418	5.128
No. 5	1.632	2.908	4.364	No. 12	2.522	3.46	5.19
No. 6	2.632	5.97	8.954	No. 13	2.666	3.924	5.888
No. 7	2.428	3.878	5.816	Average	2.349	4.097	6.147

2.4   Electrode Fixation Points

EEGs were taken using the international 10–20 system. Electrodes were attached to the heads of the subjects, and measurements were taken from electrodes C3, C4, O1, O2, A1, and A2. To reduce electric resistance, cutaneous sebum was removed using a polisher before electrode application. The EEG was continuously recorded during the experimental period. The EEG signals obtained from O2–A1 were analyzed since alpha waves appear mainly from the back of the head under the conditions of wakefulness, rest, and closed eyes. An ECG was taken using the 3-point lead system. The difference in the electrodes was measured between the right clavicle and the left ribs. A respiratory sensor wrapped around the thoracoabdominal region measured the respiratory rate.

3   Analytical Method

3.1   Roken Arousal Scale (RAS)

The roken arousal scale (RAS) is a psychological evaluation method to quantify the psychological rating values of fatigue and alertness. The RAS provides a quantitative index of the following six states: sleepiness; activation; relaxation; strain (tension); difficulty of attention and concentration; and lack of motivation. The six states consisted of two similar questions. The average of the two similar questions was defined as the state value.

3.2   Alpha Attenuation Coefficient (AAC)

The awakening degree was evaluated using the alpha attenuation coefficient (AAC). Alpha waves appear mainly from the back of the head under the conditions of wakefulness, rest, and closed eyes. The alpha waves decrease when the eyes are opened and with sleepiness. In addition, there is a large difference in the times when the eyes are opened and when they are closed. In contrast, the difference is small in the sleeping state. The power spectrum of the alpha-wave spectrum (8–13 Hz) was calculated by fast Fourier transform (FFT) after noise was suppressed from the measured EEG with a high-pass filter (0.1 Hz), a low-pass filter (120 Hz), and a band-stop filter (57–63 Hz). Then, the ratio of the average power with the eyes closed (30 s × 3) and the average power with the eyes opened (30 s × 3) of the alpha wave was defined as AAC. The AAC was analyzed using EEG signals obtained from O1–A2. A high AAC value indicates a high degree of awakening. A low AAC value indicates a low degree of awakening [2, 3].

$$AAC = Average\ power\ eyes\ closed / Average\ power\ eyes\ opened \qquad (1)$$

3.3   Lorenz Plot (LP)

The ECG RR interval change was evaluated by Lorenz plot (LP) analysis. LP-area-S was calculated by Lorenz plot analysis as an index of parasympathetic activity (Fig. 2).

The LP was prepared with the nth RRI (RRI n) on the horizontal axis and the $n + 1^{th}$ RRI (RRI n + 1) on the vertical axis. The LP was divided into RRIs using the evaluation index area S. From the y = x axis, the standard deviation (σ (x)) of the distance from the coordinate origin was calculated. Similarly, from the y = −x axis, the standard deviation (σ (−x)) of the distance from the coordinate origin was calculated. Area S, the area of the ellipse showing variations in the LP, is S = π × σ (x) × σ (−x). A high LP-area-S value indicates a high level of parasympathetic activity [4, 5].

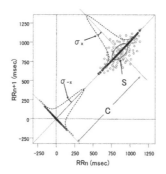

Fig. 2. Lorenz plot of RR intervals

3.4   Statistical Analysis

The values of RAS obtained before and after the task were compared using Wilcoxon's signed rank test as a non-parametric method. The values of AAC obtained before and after the task were compared using the paired *t*-test. The values of LP-area-S obtained before, after, and during the task were compared using the Tukey multiple comparison procedure. A p value of less than 0.05 was accepted as indicating a significant difference between the compared values [6]. Statistical analysis was performed using a statistical software package (IBM SPSS Statistics version 20, Tokyo, Japan).

4   Results

4.1   RAS

From the results of the RAS, the average value of the six states was calculated. Comparing the differences between before and after states, there was a tendency for psychological change in every breathing period. The result is shown in Fig. 3. The RAS results for sleepiness, relaxation, difficulty of attention and concentration, and lack of motivation increased in all periods. In addition, activation and strain decreased in the long-period breathing pattern. This showed a rest tendency. The RAS results for sleepiness and activation were significantly different (p < 0.05), while difficulty of attention and concentration showed a tendency to be significantly different (p < 0.10) in the long-period breathing pattern.

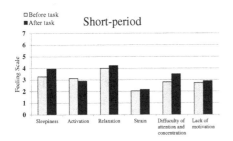

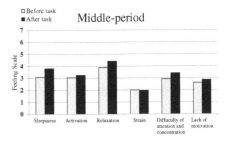

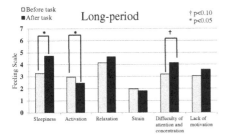

Fig. 3. Variation of RAS in each task

4.2   AAC

The AAC was normalized and compared before and after a task. The result is shown in Fig. 4. The AAC decreased with the short- and long-period breathing patterns and was slightly increased with the middle-period breathing pattern after the task. In addition, the amount of change in the AAC increased in the following order: short-period > long-period > middle-period. The AAC before and after a task was significantly different ($p < 0.05$) in the short-period breathing pattern.

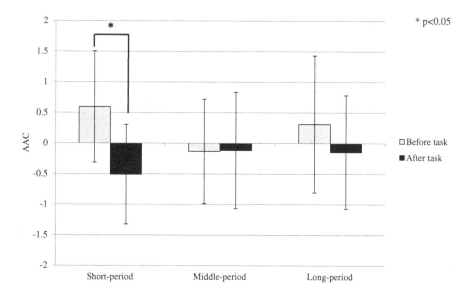

Fig. 4.   Variation of AAC

4.3   LP-area-S

The LP-area-S was normalized and compared before, after, and during the task. The result is shown in Fig. 5.

Comparing LP-area-S before and after the task, LP-area-S increased with all breathing patterns. In addition, LP-area-S showed large changes in parasympathetic activity in the following order: long-period > middle-period > short-period. LP-area-S decreased with the short- and middle-period breathing patterns and increased with the long-period breathing pattern from before the task through during the task. LP-area-S increased with the short-, middle-, and long-period breathing patterns from during the task through after the task.

LP-area-S during the task was significantly different ($p < 0.01$) between the short-period and long-period breathing patterns. Similarly, LP-area-S during the task was significantly different ($p < 0.01$) between the middle-period and long-period breathing patterns.

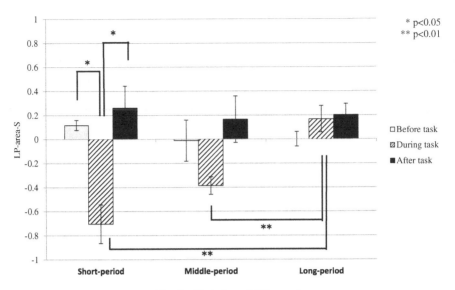

Fig. 5. Variation of LP-area-S

4.4   Relationships

Table 2 shows the correlation coefficients as a measure of the linear correlations among physiological variables (AAC, LP-area-S, respiratory cycle) for each breathing pattern. Table 3 shows the correlation coefficients as a measure of the linear correlations between the psychological (RAS) and physiological (AAC, LP-area-S, respiratory cycle) parameters for each breathing pattern. Table 3 shows (a) the short-period, (b) middle-period, and (c) long-period results. The correlation coefficients ranged between +1 and −1 inclusive, where 1 is total positive correlation, 0 is no correlation, and −1 is total negative correlation.

Examining the relationships between psychological evaluation (RAS) and physiological evaluation (AAC) parameters, a correlation was observed with activation in the short period breathing pattern. A strong correlation was also observed with sleepiness, activation, and relaxation, difficulty of attention and concentration, and lack of motivation in the long-period breathing pattern. In addition, examining the relationships between psychological evaluation (RAS) and physiological evaluation (LP-area-S) parameters, a strong correlation was observed with strain in the long-period breathing pattern and difficulty of attention and concentration in the short-period breathing pattern. When examining the relationships between psychological evaluation (RAS) and physiological evaluation (respiratory cycle) parameters, a strong correlation was observed with Activation in the middle-period breathing pattern. However, there were no correlations among the physiological evaluation parameters (AAC, LP-area-S, respiratory cycle).

Table 2. Relationships among physiological evaluation parameters

Relationship	Short-period		Middle-period		Long-period	
	LP-area-S	Respiratory cycle	LP-area-S	Respiratory cycle	LP-area-S	Respiratory cycle
AAC	−.052	−.009	−.301	−.053	−.056	−.436
LP-area-S		−.329		−.076		−.066

Table 3. Relationships between psychological and physiological evaluation parameters

(a) Short-period

Relationship (Short-period)	AAC	LP-area-S	Respiratory cycle
Sleepiness	-.146	.286	.019
Activation	.565*	-.186	.017
Relaxation	.093	.276	.217
Strain	-.155	-.117	-.043
Difficulty of attention and concentration	.038	.567*	.178
Lack of motivation	-.284	.511†	.207

(b) Middle-period

Relationship (Middle-period)	AAC	LP-area-S	Respiratory cycle
Sleepiness	.058	-.373	-.402
Activation	-.279	.347	.579*
Relaxation	-.123	-.062	-.171
Strain	.425	-.069	-.185
Difficulty of attention and concentration	.146	-.412	-.311
Lack of motivation	.284	-.403	-.144

(c) Long-period

Relationship (Long-period)	AAC	LP-area-S	Respiratory cycle
Sleepiness	-.705**	.081	-.091
Activation	.603*	.136	.251
Relaxation	-.638*	.328	-.194
Strain	-.251	.609*	.219
Difficulty of attention and concentration	-.761**	.244	-.450
Lack of motivation	-.739**	.483	-.156

4.5   Breathing Control Rate

The breathing control rate was calculated to reflect the degree to which the subjects were able to breathe at the target rate in response to the vibration stimulus for the different breathing patterns. The task (300 s) was divided into 60-sec intervals, and the average breathing period was calculated for every 60 s to determine the breathing control rate. The breathing control rate is shown in Table 4 for the (a) short-period, (b) middle-period, and (c) long-period breathing patterns.

From the average (5 min) of Table 4, the average breathing control rate for many subjects for the 5-minute period was greater than 98 %, and it is thought that many subjects were able to breathe at a rate that was very close to the target rate in all periods. On the other hand, a few subjects had a low breathing control rate.

Table 4. Breathing control rate (%)

(a) Short-period

Subject Number	0-60 (sec)	60-120 (sec)	120-180 (sec)	180-240 (sec)	240-300 (sec)	Average (5 min)
No.1	98.772	98.527	96.874	98.393	99.264	98.366
No.2	99.808	99.567	98.980	99.698	98.884	99.388
No.3	99.795	99.574	99.526	97.897	95.992	98.557
No.4	95.811	98.021	95.679	99.723	92.913	96.430
No.5	97.050	99.605	99.839	99.993	99.981	99.294
No.6	99.733	99.292	96.059	99.965	99.174	98.845
No.7	99.808	99.938	99.896	97.914	99.808	99.473
No.8	99.873	99.198	98.268	95.713	96.879	97.986
No.9	99.449	99.988	95.543	99.888	99.922	98.958
No.10	99.437	99.479	99.101	99.076	99.816	99.382
No.11	99.818	99.892	99.533	99.582	99.085	99.582
No.12	99.986	99.297	99.734	99.925	99.286	99.646
No.13	99.175	99.889	99.881	95.506	98.101	98.510
Average	99.117	99.405	98.378	98.713	98.393	98.801

(b) Middle-period

Subject Number	0-60 (sec)	60-120 (sec)	120-180 (sec)	180-240 (sec)	240-300 (sec)	Average (5 min)
No.1	98.926	97.644	99.073	99.269	98.594	98.701
No.2	91.378	91.286	92.118	91.393	91.001	91.435
No.3	99.362	99.597	97.376	99.123	98.878	98.867
No.4	99.602	86.911	93.941	96.716	94.757	94.385
No.5	99.808	99.704	99.508	99.779	99.897	99.739
No.6	98.620	98.598	99.272	99.427	99.345	99.052
No.7	99.341	99.595	99.202	93.715	99.031	98.177
No.8	99.585	98.634	99.493	99.554	91.473	97.748
No.9	99.891	99.783	99.406	99.714	99.532	99.665
No.10	99.741	99.663	98.792	97.944	98.827	98.993
No.11	99.442	99.824	99.633	99.574	99.997	99.694
No.12	99.819	99.619	97.093	99.693	99.854	99.216
No.13	99.862	99.814	99.825	94.574	97.554	98.326
Average	98.875	97.744	98.056	97.729	97.595	98.000

(c) Long-period

Subject Number	0-60 (sec)	60-120 (sec)	120-180 (sec)	180-240 (sec)	240-300 (sec)	Average (5 min)
No.1	99.452	99.013	99.592	97.003	98.952	98.802
No.2	99.768	97.842	98.057	98.155	99.224	98.609
No.3	98.798	98.806	98.696	99.021	98.457	98.755
No.4	99.591	99.952	98.225	99.959	99.959	99.537
No.5	98.784	99.736	99.725	99.905	99.993	99.629
No.6	93.195	98.979	99.202	100.000	98.641	98.004
No.7	99.818	99.736	99.499	97.708	99.438	99.240
No.8	99.168	99.580	99.451	98.406	97.553	98.831
No.9	99.596	98.863	98.979	99.792	99.021	99.250
No.10	97.278	99.479	99.572	99.640	97.859	98.766
No.11	98.011	94.856	95.152	99.869	98.511	97.280
No.12	99.468	99.986	99.559	99.668	99.304	99.597
No.13	99.566	99.415	98.094	99.180	97.985	98.848
Average	98.653	98.942	98.754	99.101	98.838	98.858

5   Discussion

Based on the results of LP-area-S, breathing control with the long-period breathing pattern was able to induce a state of increased parasympathetic activity. Parasympathetic activity was greatly reduced during the task with the short-period breathing pattern. This result is presumably the result of the fact that the short-period breathing pattern was created based on the activity breathing cycle. Furthermore, LP-area-S increased with the short- and long-period breathing patterns when AAC was decreasing.

From the results of the breathing control rate, it appears that the breathing control rate of some subjects decreased temporarily in the middle of the time period. For example, the breathing control rate in (a) short-period No. 4 120–180 (sec) of Table 4 decreased temporarily compared to before and after the breathing control rate. Thus, it is thought that it is necessary to judge the relationship between the diachronic physiological change and the breathing control rate changes of every subject.

Based on the correlation coefficients between the psychological (RAS) and physiological (AAC, LP-area-S) parameters, it appears that the central nervous system

(EEG) and psychological changes were strongly correlated, while heartbeat (autonomic nervous system) and psychological changes were weakly correlated.

In this experiment, the results were significantly different, and short-period breathing control decreased the degree of awakening from before to after the task, decreased parasympathetic activity from before to during the task, and increased parasympathetic activity from during the task to after. On the other hand, middle-period breathing control was not significantly different. However, the middle-period breathing pattern showed increased parasympathetic activity from during the task through after the task. Long-period breathing control increased sleepiness and difficulty of attention and concentration and reduced activation. Only long-period breathing control affected the psychological state.

Short-, middle-, and long-period breathing control showed differences in the psychological and physiological evaluation parameters. Depending on the purpose and circumstances, it is necessary to use the breathing pattern appropriately.

From the results of this experiment, it appears that breathing control using a vibration stimulus based on individual breathing cycles can lead to a relaxed state in terms of the physiological and psychological changes.

Based on the different results with different breathing patterns, a breathing pattern can be put together, e.g., we change breathing control into the middle-period pattern on the way from the long-period pattern to increase parasympathetic activity from before the task through after the task. It is thought that this may provide a way to produce physiological changes, such as inducing a more effective relaxation state.

References

1. Inoue, H., Hagiwara, H.: Feature extraction of physiological changes in breathing control of different cycles using a vibration stimulus. In: Proceedings of the Human Interface Symposium, pp. 755–758 (2013)
2. Hagiwara, H., Araki, K., Michimori, A., Saito, M.: A study on the quantitative evaluation method of human alertness and its application. Psychiatr. Neurol. Jpn. **99**(1), 23–24 (1997)
3. Inamoto, T., Kanakura, T., Hagiwara, H.: Relationship between changes of alpha wave components and arousal level. Japan. J. Ergon. Soc. **45**, 478–479 (2009)
4. Toyofuku, F., Yamaguchi, K., Hagiwara, H.: Simplified method for estimating parasympathetic nervous activity by Lorenz plot of ECG RR intervals. Jpn. J. Ergon. **43**(4), 185–192 (2007)
5. Toichi, M., Sugiura, T., Murai, T., Sengoku, A.: A new method of assessing cardiac autonomic function and its comparison with spectral analysis and coefficient of variation of R-R interval. J. Auton. Nerv. Syst. **62**(1), 79–84 (1997)
6. Ichihara, K.: Statistics for Bioscience, pp. 28–69. Nankodo, Tokyo (1990)

Designing Memorable Tactile Patterns

Daiji Kobayashi[✉] and Hiroyasu Mitani

Chitose Institute of Science and Technology, Hokkaido, Japan
{d-kobaya,b2112010}@photon.chitose.ac.jp

Abstract. In our previous study, the requirements for designing memorable vibration patterns such as a rhythmical vibration pattern called "vibration rhythm" were proposed. However, almost all participants, regardless of their age, could only recognize a few vibration patterns. Therefore, we attempted to determine a method to create memorable vibration patterns that enabled the users to understand the meaning of the many vibration patterns presented. In this study, a method, designing the vibration patterns with language rhythms implied the Japanese pronunciation of the corresponding message, were tried. The method was evaluated through experiments, and its validity was verified by comparing its results with a working memory system proposed by Baddeley. From the results, we concluded that the method can help the user improve his learning skills and memory. Consequently, our proposed new method is a better option to create memorable vibration patterns.

Keywords: Tactile interface · Vibration perception · Memorable · Vibration pattern · Working memory

1 Introduction

Recently, vibratory tactile interfaces such as pagers and mobile phones, which inform their users about incoming messages or calls, have been widely used. The vibration stimuli of the tactile interfaces can convey messages confidentially and silently. Users who suffer from auditory dysfunction can perceive the information from the vibrating communication devices. Although tactile stimuli as a communication medium was considered in the 1950 s, many recent vibratory devices would rather send a simple message than multiple messages. For example, Geldard's fundamental article about the perceptual characteristics of vibration stimuli [4] referred to vibratory intensity discrimination, temporal discrimination, and learning curves for communication using "vibratese language." The letters or some prepositions of the "vibratese language" were represented by five thoracic buzzes representing vibration stimuli composed of two dimensions such as intensity and duration. There are some researches that focus on improving the efficiency of communication through tactile and haptic sensory modalities [10, 11].

In practice, almost all mobile devices, including an actuator such as a vibrating motor with eccentric mass, and the sensation of the oscillatory vibration presented by the mobile devices, are at a constant intensity. Thus, the vibration pattern presenting messages should be composed of constant intensity durations as it is in Morse code.

© Springer International Publishing Switzerland 2015
S. Yamamoto (Ed.): HIMI 2015, Part I, LNCS 9172, pp. 396–404, 2015.
DOI: 10.1007/978-3-319-20612-7_38

However, it is not feasible to make mobile device users learn Morse code in order to gain a wider range of capabilities from the viewpoint of accessibility. The concept of representing messages by vibration patterns requires not only spelling alphabets such as Morse code but also a method of imaging the message.

The Japanese use phonograms, in which the pronunciation and the letter coincide, and they also use ideographs, i.e., Kanji characters of Chinese origin. To learn many ideographic Kanji characters is difficult for children; however, the ideographs represent their own definitions. In other words, the form of an ideogram that suggests the meaning is a key to an understanding the letter's message.

In this regard, the feasibility of "tactons" or "tactile icons" are part of the concept of an ideograph. The tacton is a type of vibration stimuli made from audial rhythms, and has been researched from the physiological and sensory viewpoints [2, 3]. However, almost all researchers evaluated the vibration stimuli by attaching a linear tactile actuator or "tactor" to a young subject's skin. These tactile actuators generate vibration with a simple waveform and stimulate the skin. However, the represented waveform of the vibration by the devices, including a vibrating motor, depends on the device chassis. Rough waveforms are observed at the surface of the devices.

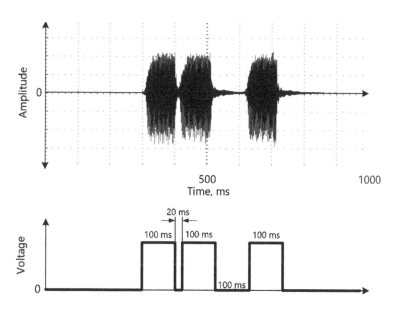

Fig. 1. Represented vibration waveform on surface of vibration mouse with (top) vibrating motor and (bottom) voltage powering the vibrating motor [9]

The upper portion of Fig. 1 shows an example of a waveform observed at the surface of a computer mouse that included a vibrating motor. Although the vibrating motor was rotated at approximately 65 rpm at 0.7 V, the frequency of the vibration during acceleration was approximately 116 Hz according to a digital oscilloscope (Tektronix DPO2024B) via the vibration sensor of a vibrometer (MotherTool VB-

8205SD). Further, the amplitude changed according to the voltage level, with a delay. These results suggested that not much was known about the perceptual characteristics of such rough vibration stimuli. Investigation of the perceptual characteristics of devices that included a vibrating motor was required. We took up the challenge of researching the perceptual characteristics of young as well as older adults.

In this regard, ISO 9241-910 [6], a framework for tactile and haptic interaction, pointed out that it is important to consider the age of potential users of tactile/haptic devices, because there is a considerable decline in haptic sensitivity with age. In this regard, the relation between vibration perception threshold and age and height has been investigated using a biothesiometer [12]. The biothesiometer, which measures the large nerve fiber function of patients, produces vibrations with varied amplitudes. As a result, the significant factor for the vibration perception threshold was age rather than sex; therefore, it is assumed that a higher amplitude of vibration, or a higher vibration velocity, is perceptible in other parts of an older person's body such as the palms.

In our previous study [8, 9], the factors of appropriate vibration patterns for the older person were determined from the perceptual and cognitive viewpoints, to some extent. For example, the minimum perceptible gap and the minimum vibration duration were studied through experiments with young and older adults. We determined that the minimum vibration duration included in the vibration pattern of a vibration mouse is 50 ms in round figures, and that the minimum gap between vibration durations was determined to be 20 ms. Further, we found that higher amplitudes of vibration were useful for older persons to recognize the vibration patterns. Thus, we designed vibration patterns based on the results of this study.

We are yet to find an effective method of designing vibration patterns reminding the representing message. Although we attempted to create distinguishable vibration patterns that had musical rhythm characteristics, almost all participants were able to identify only two vibration patterns, regardless of the participant's age. The participants said that they had difficulty with learning the messages corresponding to the respective vibration patterns. Thus, it was assumed that vibration patterns with musical rhythm characteristics are not effective in reminding the representing message. Therefore, owing to the abovementioned reasons, in this study, we search for an alternate method to design vibration patterns.

2   Method

To develop a method to design vibration patterns that represent messages from an information technology device such as a vibrating mobile phone, we conducted experiments under three conditions using our custom-built vibration mouse (see Fig. 2). The three conditions were defined by using vibration patterns characterized by different cues implying a corresponding message, and included our previous method of using vibration patterns that had characteristics of musical rhythms.

2.1   Vibration Mouse

The vibration mouse can present vibration stimuli with an average vibrational wave velocity of 2.3 mm/s. The power voltage for activating the vibration motor was controlled using a high-precision analog I/O terminal (CONTEC AIO-160802AY-USB) and a personal computer (DELL XPS 8300) running Windows 8 Pro Japanese edition. The voltage applied to the vibration motor was controlled by the I/O terminal with our custom software. In addition, the vibration mouse also functioned as a computer mouse, with two buttons and a scroll wheel.

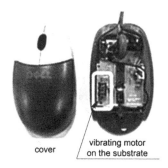

cover   vibrating motor on the substrate

Fig. 2.   Vibration mouse used in this study

2.2   Participants

Considering the intended use of information technology devices, vibration patterns are for young as well as aged users. Thus, the participants should have been selected from the young and elderly age groups. However, our previous study suggested that the cognitive characteristics of elderly groups were as strong as the younger group's cognitive characteristics, although the sensitivity was different between the groups. Therefore, we randomly chose 21 students, including 16 males ranging from 20 to 23 years of age (mean = 21.9, SD = 0.5) and 5 females ranging from 21 to 28 years of age (mean = 22.8, SD = 2.9). All participants were physically unimpaired, could perceive the vibration stimuli from the vibration mouse, and could feel the vibration patterns.

2.3   Experimental Conditions and Procedure

The experiment was conducted under three conditions (A, B, and C) using a within-participants design. Condition-A was identical to the condition of our previous study as described later [9]; therefore, we considered condition-A as the control condition in this study. In condition-A, seven vibration patterns with a musical rhythm characteristic were created, and they corresponded to a message randomly for respective vibration patterns. The messages were, for example, "The battery has run out," and "You have a call." The participants had to learn seven messages related to respective vibration patterns using the learning software. The software featured a window for the participants on the screen and included seven buttons, each with a message. The corresponding vibration patterns were indicated by the vibration mouse when the participant pressed a button.

The participants learned the messages of the seven vibration patterns using the learning software repeatedly. Next, the seven vibration patterns were randomly presented to the participants one by one, and the participants attempted to identify the vibration pattern's message by answering orally. Each of the participants' answers were verified by an observer.

After taking enough break at the participant's request, the participants learned another set of seven messages using vibration patterns, this time under condition-B. However, the vibration patterns with language rhythms were created. In this regard, the vibration pattern implied the Japanese pronunciation of the corresponding message. After learning seven vibration patterns, the subject attempted to identify the randomly presented vibration rhythms and answered orally. The participant's answers were verified by the observer.

In condition-C, taking enough break at the participant's request, every participant created vibration patterns using the software under the requirements of condition-B. Every participant created the seven vibration patterns by clicking the button on the vibration mouse. The duration of the respective vibration patterns was 2 s each. Further, we allowed the subjects to redesign the patterns as per their comfort. After the subjects made the vibration patterns, the observer questioned the respective subjects how to characterize the vibration patterns in order to easily remember the corresponding message. Then, we randomly presented the seven vibration patterns, which the participants made sequentially, and the participants attempted to identify and orally answered the corresponding message. The observer checked their answers.

The goal of the experiment was to research a method to design vibration patterns for sending messages to the users of a vibrating device. Therefore, we investigated how to create vibration patterns based on the rhythm of the language, and examined better ways to create these patterns. After we completed the trials under condition-C, we interviewed the participants about the method for making vibration patterns and gathered their opinions about the experiment.

3   Result

To measure the memorability of a vibration pattern's meaning, we counted the number of correct answers by the participants under all three conditions and compared the results. The number of the participants' correct answers were averaged and statistically compared. The averaged numbers of correct answers and two-sided 95 % confidence intervals under the three conditions are shown in Fig. 3.

Figure 3 indicates that the differences between the number of correct answers among the three conditions were statistically significant. Therefore, the vibration patterns, which were characterized by rhythms implying the pronunciation of messages or the other way the participant thought of, affected the learning of the vibrating messages instead of the vibration patterns that had characteristics of musical rhythms. In addition, the number of correct answers under condition-A was approximately two. This was approximately the same as the result of our previous research [9] described above. Therefore, we can say that a more effective method of designing vibration patterns was developed in this study. In this regard, the number of correct answers under condition-C was the highest; however, the method of designing vibration patterns by the participants varied.

From the interviews with the participants, we found that 13 of the 21 participants adopted the method for creating vibration patterns utilizing the Japanese pronunciation of the message. On the other hand, 5 of 21 participants utilized the pronunciation and the sound associated with the message. The other two participants ranked the message according to importance and created vibration patterns based on that importance of the message for them. One participant utilized vibration patterns in his smartphone. However, this strategy may not be effective regardless of the messages. In addition, the number of correct answers was not different between the strategies regardless of the strategies used in condition-C.

Therefore, it is assumed that the method to utilize a speech message in Japanese and/or the sound associated with the message could be effective for Japanese participants in any case. Meanwhile, the appropriate method to create vibration patterns could depend on the person. Therefore, the vibration patterns for sending messages should be created by the user of the vibrating device.

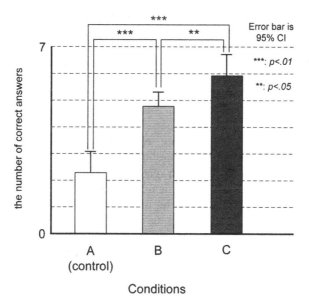

Fig. 3. Comparison of the number of collect answers (n = 21) between the following three conditions: Condition-A is the case of learning vibration patterns that have musical rhythm characteristics. Condition-B is the case of learning vibration patterns that have rhythms implying the Japanese pronunciation of the corresponding message. Condition-C is the case of using vibration patterns that were created by each participant.

4 Discussion

Although it is not clear that creating vibration patterns based on pronunciation in other languages such as English is appropriate, the experimental results show that creating the vibration pattern based on the pronunciation of the message in Japanese is more appropriate than utilizing musical rhythms. However, the results under condition-B were significantly less accurate than those under condition-C. According to the participants who were unable to correctly answer the meaning of some vibration patterns, the vibration pattern under condition-B was created based on Japanese pronunciation by a young Japanese but the participant's; therefore, it was difficult to infer the messages from some vibration patterns. This could be relevant to our working memory.

The model of a working memory system proposed by Baddeley includes a "visuospatial scratch pad" and "articulatory loop" or "phonological loop" [1]. In addition, it was suggested that there are similarities in the manner in which speech and rhythms are processed that appear to extend beyond reliance on temporal coding mechanisms [5]. With regard to tactual information processing, Kass et al. suggested that many working memory tasks with tactual input might draw on more general supramodal spatial or verbal working memory processes, either primary or along with tactual coding. Further, the tasks with tactual input are especially relevant if a task can be solved on the basis of high-order "non-tactual" information rather than based on the original tactual characteristics [7].

As can be inferred from the above knowledge, if there is an association between a vibration pattern and its meanings (such as the case under condition-A), both the vibration pattern's meaning and musical rhythm represented by the vibration pattern must be processed by working memory. In particular, a message with a vibration pattern's meaning is considered to be processed by a phonological loop for maintenance rehearsal. On the other hand, musical rhythms are also processed by the phonological loop for maintenance rehearsal. Therefore, these two processes are related to the phonological process of working memory. According to the knowledge about working memory proposed by Baddeley, respective capacities of the visuospatial scratch pad and the phonological loop are limited. Hence, two processes of the phonological loop could interfere with each other, and then the meaning of a vibration pattern characterized by musical rhythm is difficult to memory.

In creating vibration patterns based on one's own pronunciation of the message (such as participants under condition-C), the characteristics of vibration patterns represent the pronunciations of the messages. Thus, it is required to learn either the vibration pattern or the pronunciation of the message. Therefore, it could be easy to learn the vibration pattern's meaning, and then this memory strategy can encourage the participants to understand more messages under condition-C. However, if the vibration patterns are created from pronunciations by anyone else (such as the case under condition-B), some participants may find it difficult to extract the phonological characteristics from the vibration patterns, especially if the participant's pronunciation is different from the pronunciation of the person who created the vibration patterns. Therefore, it is assumed that the number of correct answers under condition-C was higher than those under condition-B.

5 Conclusion

In this study, we researched a method of designing memorable vibration patterns. It is expected that memorable vibration patterns enable users to understand the meanings of many vibration patterns presented, so that the users can easily understand the messages conveyed by the vibrating device. Thus, we proposed a method for designing vibration patterns that are characterized by the message's pronunciation, and we evaluated the method in an experiment. Further, other strategies were attempted in the experiment.

From the results, we found that our method affected the number of recognized vibration patterns, although we did not find another effective method through the experiment. In addition, we found that it is crucial for the users to be able to create memorable vibration patterns by using their own pronunciations of the messages corresponding to the vibration pattern.

Considering the above results, we assumed that, from the viewpoint of Baddeley's working memory system, vibration patterns based on the message pronunciation are easy to obtain through the working memory. Considering the process of the phono-logical loop of working memory, it could be difficult for the users to learn the vibration patterns based on musical rhythm.

Consequently, we found that our new method for making memorable vibration patterns was more effective than the method using musical rhythm.

References

1. Baddeley, A.D., Logie, R.H.: Working memory–the multiple-component model. In: Miyake, A., Shah, P. (eds.) Models of Working Memory: Mechanisms of Active Maintenance and Executive Control, pp. 28–61. Cambridge University Press, New York (1999)
2. Brewster, S., King, A.: An investigation into the use of tactons to present progress information. In: Costabile, M.F., Paternó, F. (eds.) INTERACT 2005. LNCS, vol. 3585, pp. 6–17. Springer, Heidelberg (2005)
3. Brown, L.M., Brewster, S.A., Purchase, H.C.: Multidimensional tactons for non-visual information presentation in mobile devices. ACM Int. Conf. Proc. Ser. **159**, 231–238 (2006)
4. Geldard, F.A.: Adventures in tactile literacy. Am. Psychol. **12**, 115–124 (1957)
5. Hall, D., Gathercole, S.E.: Serial recall of rhythms and verbal sequences: impact of concurrent tasks and irrelevant sound. Q. J. Exp. Psychol. **64**(8), 1580–1592 (2011). Psychology Press, Hove
6. ISO 9241–910: Framework for Tactile and Haptic Interaction (2011)
7. Kaas, A.L., Stoeckel, M.C., Gorbrl, R.: The neural bases of haptic working memory. In: Grunwald, M. (ed.) Human Haptic Perception-Basics and Applications. Birkhäuser, Basel (2008)
8. Kobayashi, D.: Study on perception of vibration rhythms. In: Yamamoto, S. (ed.) HCI 2014, Part I. LNCS, vol. 8521, pp. 208–216. Springer, Heidelberg (2014)
9. Kobayashi, D., Takahashi, K.: Designing understandable vibration patterns for tactile interface. In: Yamamoto, S. (ed.) New Ergonomics Perspective, pp. 259–266. CRC Press, London (2015)
10. Rinker, M.A., Craig, J.C., Bernstein, L.E.: Amplitude and period discrimination of haptic stimuli. J. Acoust. Soc. Am. **104**(1), 453–463 (1998)

11. Tan, H.Z., Reed, C.M., Duriach, N.I.: Optimum information transfer rates for communication through haptic and other sensory modalities. IEEE Trans. Haptics **3**(2), 98–108 (2010)
12. Wiles, P.G., Pearce, S.M., Rice, P.J.S., Mitchell, J.M.O.: Vibration perception threshold: influence of age, height, sex, and smoking, and calculation of accurate centile values. Diabet. Med. **8**, 157–161 (1991)

Changes in Heart Rate Variability by Using Tactile Thermal Interface Device

Kentaro Kotani[1,2(✉)], Shigeyoshi Iizuka[1,2], Takafumi Asao[1,2], and Satoshi Suzuki[1,2]

[1] Kansai University, 3-3-35, Yamate-Cho, Suita, Osaka 564-8680, Japan
kotani@kansai-u.ac.jp
[2] Kanagawa University, Tsuchiya 2946, Hiratsuka, Kanagawa 259-1293, Japan

Abstract. As an interface for calling attention without noticing others, presentation of tactile thermal information, equipped with an input device was evaluated. The thermal presentation device was designed such that emotional changes were generated after the exposure of the warm and cold stimuli, which may lead to the alarm effect. The experiment was conducted to examine physiological and behavioral responses for the thermal stimuli by measuring reaction time to the stimuli with heart rate variability. The results revealed that the reaction times given by cold stimuli were shorter than those by warm stimuli although the changes in R-R interval of heart rate decreased significantly only by the presentation of warm stimuli. Further evaluation included the usability for the effects associated with alarm and recovery of drowsy situations.

Keywords: Thermal information · HRV · Tactile interaction

1 Introduction

There have been introduced numbers of new communication medium through computers by using presentation of sensory stimuli such as visual, auditory and tactile stimuli. Such medium has been applied to diverse communication devices including the system for preventing dozing while driving a car. Compared with visual and auditory stimuli, communication medium using tactile stimuli can deliver apparent perception without focusing exclusively on the stimuli. This advantage accelerates the research and development opportunities for using tactile information transmission technique.

Thermal stimulus, a type of tactile stimuli, has been studied for supporting tangible communication technology. Their study demonstrated dynamic characteristics of impression by perceiving information consisted of thermal stimuli. These studies however only confirmed their effectiveness subjectively by questionnaire [1], objective evaluation needs to be conducted. When emotional responses were given to the human, it is imaginable that changes in autonomic nervous system were occurred with emotional responses.

The objective of this study is to monitor the changes in autonomic nervous system along with the changes in emotional reactions caused by thermal tactile stimuli given to the participants. We developed a thermal presentation device equipped with a computer mouse, which can be operated to induce thermal stimuli on the users' hand [2].

© Springer International Publishing Switzerland 2015
S. Yamamoto (Ed.): HIMI 2015, Part I, LNCS 9172, pp. 405–411, 2015.
DOI: 10.1007/978-3-319-20612-7_39

The objective of this paper is to show such changes by monitoring electrocardiograms when thermal stimuli were abruptly given at their hands during concentrating on the computer tasks.

2 Methods

A total of 10 male university students (mean = 21.5, s.d. = 0.5) participated in this study. They reported that they regularly use computer mouse with their right hand. Each participant had informed consent prior to beginning the experiment.

Two tasks were given to the participants.

The primary task was set to the computer jigsaw puzzle game where participants constructed a pictured puzzle from scattered pieces. The pictured puzzle at primary level (63 pieces in total) was selected not to put an excessive mental workload by playing the game.

The secondary task was a simple reaction task, where they were instructed to show verbal reaction as soon as they noticed the thermal stimulus. In this experiment, two computer mice were used. One on their right hand side was for playing the puzzle game and the other on their left hand side was used for presenting thermal stimuli, thus their left palm was located gently on the mouse. Figure 1 shows the environment for the experiment.

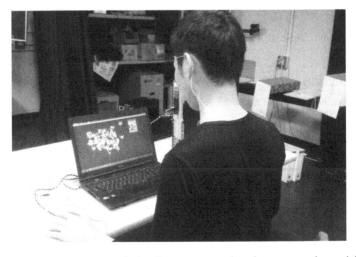

Fig. 1. Experimental setup. Thermal stimuli were presented on the mouse at the participant's left hand while the participant performed computer puzzle game.

Three levels of thermal stimuli for each of warm and cold stimulus conditions, i.e., ±1 °C, ±5 °C, and ±10 °C from the skin temperature at the finger, were tested in this study. These temperature changes were generated by the thermal presentation device using a Peltier device. In order to set particular temperature, the skin surface temperature of the finger was monitored and the Peltier device generated the designated warm and cold stimuli with reference to the skin surface temperature. The Peltier device was attached on the top surface of the computer mouse on the left hand side. Figure 2 shows the mouse with thermal presentation device and its specifications are summarized in Table 1.

Fig. 2. Thermal presentation device based on a computer mouse where a Peltier device was appeared on the top left corner of computer mouse. Participants placed their index finger. Size of the Peltier device was 1 cm by 1 cm.

A total of three trials were given. Each trial consisted of two states, that is, three minutes of resting state and eight minutes of task state. Two sets of thermal stimuli were given during the task state, and taken all together, six thermal stimuli were given to the participants. ECG measurement and subjective evaluation of the emotional conditions were obtained for each trial. Reaction times for the given thermal stimuli were recorded as well.

A typical ECG monitoring setup was applied in this study. Active electrodes (NM-512G, NIHON KODEN) were used for the ECG signal measurement as bipolar lead CM5. Reference electrode was attached to the forehead of the participant. EMG signals were recorded during the performance. The sampling frequency was set to 1000 Hz. Amplifier (AP1132, NIHONSANTEKU) and data sampling software (AP Monitor, NIHONSANTEKU) were used for the ECG recording as well. Figure 3 illustrates ECG measurement system in this experiment.

From the taken ECG waveforms, peak values of R waves were extracted and the time intervals between peak values, defined as R-R intervals, were computed. Time-series signal analysis package (MEMCALC, GMS, Inc) was used for extraction of R-R intervals. Changes in R-R interval have been reported as a typical index of heart rate variability for both sympathetic- and parasympathetic-mediated responses, that is, decrement of R-R interval was induced by activations of sympathetic nerves and increment of R-R interval was induced by activations of parasympathetic nerves [3].

Table 1. Specification of the thermal presentation device

Item	Value
Maximum voltage [V]	2.3
Maximum current [A]	4.0
Power of heat absorption [W]	5.1
Maximum steady state temperature [°C]	40
Minimum steady state temperature [°C]	15
Thermal gradient for 1°C [deg/sec]	0.11
Thermal gradient for 5°C [deg/sec]	0.56
Thermal gradient for 10°C [deg/sec]	1.11

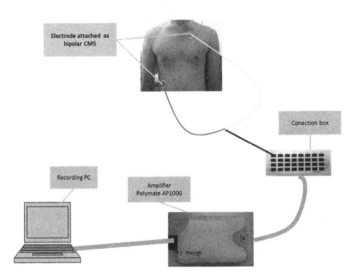

Fig. 3. Apparatus of ECG measurement in the experiment

3   Results and Discussion

Figure 4 shows the relationship between the temperature of the stimuli and number of participants responded by the stimuli. When the thermal stimuli were 1 °C higher than the skin temperature, all participants reported that no temperature changes were noticed; hence they showed no reaction to the stimuli. Two participants reacted when 1 degree lower than the skin temperature.

The results appeared different from previous findings, where the perceived temperature was less than 1 degree when the temperature varied at the rate of 2.1°C/s for heating condition [4]. Our results implied that the participants spent substantial amount of attention resources towards the primary task, thus available resource was not enough for perceiving such a small change of temperature. Based on the results of number of perceptions made, we further analyzed behavioral and physiological changes comparing 10°C of heat stimuli and -10°C of cold stimuli (Table 2).

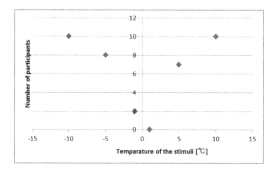

Fig. 4. Differences in temperature obtained from finger skin surface and number of participants responded to the stimuli.

Table 2. Reaction time for each participant and thermal stimuli

Participants	Reaction time [sec]					
	Warm stimuli [deg]			Cold stimuli [deg]		
	+10	+5	+1	-1	-5	-10
A	2.31	4.42	–	–	2.84	2.02
B	3.95	2.45	–	–	2.40	2.97
C	3.93	3.64	–	–	–	–
D	0.48	3.02	–	2.45	2.09	1.84
E	3.09	2.31	–	–	2.57	1.91
F	5.22	–	–	–	2.38	3.67
G	2.75	0.96	–	2.16	1.70	0.81
H	2.18	2.63	–	9.81	3.18	1.82
I	2.99	–	–	–	2.56	3.72
J	2.92	2.60	–	–	2.24	1.24

Average reaction time between warm and cold stimuli showed that the participants tended to respond quicker when cold stimuli were given ($F(1,9) = 3.79$, $p < .1$). This may be due to the difference of thresholds between warm and cold stimuli, where the threshold was lower when cold stimuli were applied at the finger and hand area [4].

Changes in R-R interval as a typical example are depicted in Fig. 5. As it can be seen in the figure, R-R interval was decreased when thermal stimuli were given whereas relatively fewer changes seemed to be occurred when thermal stimuli were not given to the participants. The change in R-R intervals by the thermal stimuli was occurred after 10 s from the onset of temperature changes. Average R-R intervals before and after the stimulus presentation were compared, shown in Fig. 6. ANOVA on R-R intervals revealed that there was a significant difference of R-R intervals between before and after the presentation of warm stimuli ($10°C$)(($F(1,9) = 6.56$, $p < .05$)), whereas no significant differences were found between before and after the presentation of cold stimuli($-10°C$) (($F(1,9) = 0.40$, $p > .1$)).

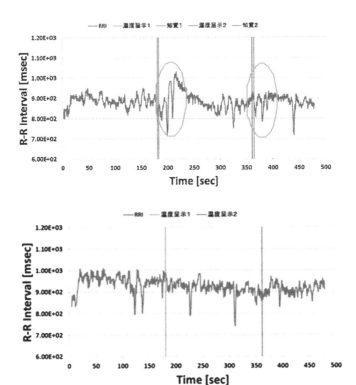

Fig. 5. Changes in R-R intervals when thermal stimuli were given (10°C, top) and not given as much as sensory threshold (-1°C, bottom). Circled areas on the figure above show changes in R-R intervals after the stimuli are given. The onset of the stimuli was shown as vertical lines on the figure.

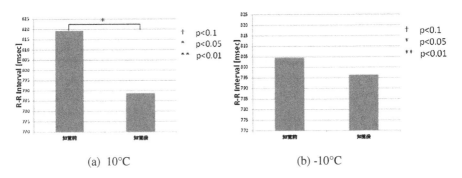

Fig. 6. Comparison of R-R intervals between before and after the stimulus. In each figure, the left bar shows R-R interval before the stimulus presentation, and the right bar shows R-R interval after the stimulus presentation.

The results seemed contradicted from the previous physiological findings in which the density of cold spots on the surface of the skin was 5 to 10 times more than that of warm spots, hence the sensitivity to the cold stimuli were rather higher than that to the warm stimuli [5]. In this experiment we gave warm stimuli ranging from 33 to 45°C and cold stimuli ranging from 15 to 25°C, which facilitated effective warm stimulus perception, yielding decrement of R-R intervals when warm stimuli were given to the participants.

Whether or not the thermal stimuli were perceived affected the presence of emotional changes. According to the results from subjective responses, participants reported emotional changes triggered by thermal stimuli. Typical responses included 'warm' and 'cold', as well as 'surprised' and 'painful'. These emotional responses affected changes in R-R intervals. In order to verify the influence of autonomic nervous activity induced by thermal stimuli, heart rate variability such as HF and LF components should be considered as further analysis.

It was also a big concern that how much physical transfer of the heat was controlled to the participants. In this experiment the temperature of the Peltier device was assumed to be the temperature of the skin surface which was contacted with the Peltier device. It was difficult to conclude that the completion of thermal equilibrium was confirmed. We would construct an experimental protocol, in which heat flow ratio would be controlled for further experiment.

Acknowledgment. Part of the present study was funded by Advanced-biomedical sensing technology research group Kansai University and Kakenhi of the Japan Society for the Promotion of Science (24370143, 24657182).

References

1. Miura, T., Yai, T., Masuda, S., Suzuki, M.: A study of prevention of drowsy driving by using arousal level. In: Proceedings of JSCE Annual Meeting, CD-ROM (2008)
2. Iizuka, S., Yamamoto, S.: The effect of presenting thermal information on the computer mouse during viewing images on the display. J. Hum. Syst. **14**(1), 1–8 (2012). (In Japanese)
3. Fujisawa, S., Kakigi, S., Yamazaki, K.: New Psychophysiology Part 1. Fundamentals of Psychophysiology, Kitaoji Shobo, Tokyo (1998). (In Japanese)
4. Stevens, J.C., Choo, K.K.: Temperature sensitivity of the body surface over the life span. Somatosen. Mot. Res. **15**(1), 13–28 (1998)
5. Stevens, J.C., Stevens, S.S.: Warmth and cold: dynamics of sensory intensity. J. Exp. Psychol. **60**, 183–192 (1960)

Human Factors to Consider During the Early Development and Dissemination of New Displays to Improve Spatial Orientation and Situation Awareness

Ben D. Lawson[1]([⊠]), John Christopher Brill[2],
Linda-Brooke I. Thompson[1], Amanda M. Kelley[3], Casey R. Harris[1],
and Angus H. Rupert[1]

[1] U.S. Army Aeromedical Research Laboratory, Fort Rucker, USA
{benton.d.lawson.civ, linda-brooke.i.thompson.ctr,
casey.r.harris.ctr, angus.h.rupert.civ}@mail.mil
[2] Old Dominion University, Norfolk, USA
jcbrill@odu.edu
[3] National Highway Transportation Safety Administration,
Washington, DC., USA
amanda.kelley@dot.gov

Abstract. When a new technology is contemplated to enhance situation awareness (SA), thought must be given to designing, prototyping, and demonstrating it to enhance usability and acceptance. The focus during this process is typically upon the end-user. We introduce three SA-enhancing displays (designed to avoid spatial disorientation (SD), falling, and collisions, respectively) and describe the typical end-users of such displays. We then argue for a wider consideration of human factors (HF) that includes the needs of those in the entire human chain of technology development before the final end-users. We intend to show how solving problems associated with the early development and refinement of new technologies requires a consideration of multiple types of "users". Consideration of only the end-user is not sufficient to ensure technology acceptance in any of the three case studies described in this report. Everyone in the chain of technology development must be considered a user.

Keywords: Orientation · Usability · Tactile · Vestibular · Balance · Collision · Display

1 Introduction to the Technologies

Three display technology efforts are described that shared HF-related "growing pains" during development. These technologies benefit distinct aviation, medical, or transportation end-user communities, but common HF principles apply to their preparation for transition. We start with an introduction to the three technology end-users:

1. The first example we discuss derives from the military aviation setting. When a new display is developed to decrease the incidence of SD episodes, most of the focus of

© Springer International Publishing Switzerland 2015
S. Yamamoto (Ed.): HIMI 2015, Part I, LNCS 9172, pp. 412–424, 2015.
DOI: 10.1007/978-3-319-20612-7_40

the scientists, engineers, and software developers is placed upon whether an aviator will be able to readily learn to use the new display and will find it helpful.

2. A second example derives from the health care setting: when a display is developed to assist balance patients with their rehabilitation, emphasis must be placed upon whether the patients can rapidly and intuitively use the enhanced sway cues.

3. The third example applies (but is not limited) to automobile traffic. When a collision avoidance display is developed to warn automobile operators, pedestrians, or police officers (making a traffic stop) concerning approaching vehicles, careful thought must be devoted to whether end-users can easily employ the display.

These are important considerations that have instigated HF development practices to ensure the satisfaction of such end-users, including subject-matter-expert evaluations, job/task analyses, and usability evaluations. Nevertheless, in order to be widely accepted and disseminated, a new display must be readily usable by many persons *in addition* to the final user, including members of the original development team (e.g., the engineer or programmer), display demonstration spokespersons, and funding sponsors or decision-leaders receiving demonstrations. If any of the people in this human chain leading to the end-user cannot understand the product easily, technology development may break down and the product may not reach fruition. Therefore, we recommend technology developers broaden the saying "know thy user" beyond a consideration of the end-user. While the end-user's satisfaction with the final product is necessary, there are several reasons why it is not sufficient and designing for usability must extend to other people dealing with product prototypes and demonstrations:

1. The end-user's knowledge, skills, and abilities may differ from the other persons in the chain of technology development. For example, in the military aviation setting, it would be inappropriate to demonstrate to a funding sponsor (who may lack advanced knowledge or currency concerning the piloting of aircraft) the full set of product features one may show to a rated instructor pilot. Conversely, pilots may be less receptive to a "lite" system, which rapidly demonstrates a "proof of concept" to a decision-maker but lacks the features and feel pilots expect. In fact, several of the authors have demonstrated the Tactile Situation Awareness System (TSAS) [2] to pilots who initially resisted the idea when they experienced the TSAS in a primitive part-task flight simulator, only to endorse it once experienced in a fully-featured Army flight simulator or helicopter. Unfortunately, the converse problem arises when demonstrating the display to key decision-makers, i.e., it is possible to design a sophisticated flight system that interests pilots while not convincing a decision leader to recommend the system for transition to the cockpit. Clearly, the development team must balance the needs of these different users and cannot assume that a satisfied end-user ensures acceptance by other people in the human chain of technology development and transition.

2. Conversely, even when the end-users do have reduced needs or knowledge relative to others in the chain of product development, the technology will never be adopted for use solely by considering end-users' needs. For example, in the health care setting, the visible software features and demonstration modes for a device meant to aid balance and prevent falls must be different for physical therapists, patients, or hospital administrators. There are two main system "users" whose needs differ: the

patient and the patient's physical therapist. Any system that is too time-consuming for a physical therapist to learn or use will end up collecting dust, even if the system may have benefitted the patient had it been designed appropriately. Also, a physical therapist or clinician needs to access advanced features that would exceed the understanding of a patient. It is common practice to create alternative interfaces for users with differing expertise or roles [1], e.g., "wizards" for beginners and expert modes for advanced users. This is one approach to designing for multiple users that can be of benefit to the aviation, health care, and transportation display development efforts discussed in this report.

3. Even in the seemingly simple case of a display system to warn of impending vehicle collision (where an expert is not required to grasp the problem), usability will mean different things to different people within the original development team. For example, the best collision warning display will not be adopted by end-users or customers if its features cannot be readily explained and reliably demonstrated without error by key demonstrators (e.g., the team scientists or leaders who often serve also as spokespersons for the product during presentations where technical support personnel may not be onsite). A new display may save lives that would have been lost due to vehicle collisions, but it will garner no interest if it takes longer to prepare or demonstrate than the amount of time the team was permitted by a key decision leader (e.g., 5 min to set-up and 5 min to demonstrate). In any of the three technology cases studied in this report, the systems must be optimized for satisfactory use by *all* potential users.[1]

2   Case Study 1: HF Challenges During the Development of Display Technology to Improve Aviation Safety

The first case study evaluates a demonstration system for a TSAS for pilots [2, 3], wherein users operate a simulated helicopter while receiving vibratory navigation cues in order to understand how a touch cue can aid with SA. The vibrotactile display is integrated with a semi-portable, part-task flight simulator, but it is driven by its own native hardware, which was developed independently. The original version of the simulation was fairly user-friendly and satisfactorily integrated with the hardware. The system required an upgrade to make the graphics modern, add more demonstrations, and permit the user and demonstrator to sit side-by-side in the cockpit and easily transfer control to one another. Unfortunately, the upgrade introduced usability issues due to a failure to properly consider several HF principles of display design. First, the interface lacked *flexibility* and *efficiency of use* [4], as evidenced by the fact that it was more difficult to demonstrate the same scenarios as had been shown in the past. When sponsors or decision-leaders see a demonstrator restart a simulation or fruitlessly search through menus, this may cause them to conclude that the underlying display concept is

---

[1] Satisfactory simplification will be limited by the degree of irreducible complexity in the task, but even complicated surgical procedures previously thought not amenable are benefiting from HF (see *The Checklist Manifesto* by Gawande, 2010).

unreliable or unrefined. Such was the case with the new TSAS flight simulator. The demonstrator had to compensate for numerous software idiosyncrasies that increased setup time and the likelihood of human error. Indeed, demonstrators had to receive significant training to effectively cope with poor system design and prevent failed demonstrations to influential persons. This runs contrary to Mayhew's [5] admonition that *ease-of-use* should be emphasized when designing systems with high frequency of mandatory usage. This sentiment is echoed by Shneiderman [1], who emphasizes the importance of ease-of-use, particularly for non-technical "users" (adopting our wide usage of the word being advocated in this report). If key technical personnel are not available for demonstrations, other team spokespersons must serve as demonstrators, making ease-of-use essential.

The simulation also failed to design for *control stability*, an HF principle of control design [6]. To initiate motion of the simulated helicopter, the user was required to maximally displace the joystick/cyclic. This change was implemented to simplify demonstrations, but it introduced an inordinately large dead space² in the joystick, creating an inappropriately low gain (i.e., ratio between change in outputs as a function of change in inputs, [6]), which forced the user to "max out" the controls to resume even slow forward flight. *Moderate gain levels* are usually considered more desirable for balancing responsiveness and stability [7].

Another problem with the upgraded simulator is that once motion had been achieved, if the joystick was moved near the center/neutral position (even momentarily), the simulated aircraft motion stopped. This was not desirable because the TSAS only activates when one is moving and the point of the demonstration is to feel and understand the functioning of the TSAS display.

In combination, the need to move the joystick all the way over to move the aircraft and the cessation of aircraft motion when the joystick was near center left the end-user feeling as if he/she must "fight" the controls. This reaction was consistent with past research suggesting increased dead space decreases user control accuracy during tracking tasks [8]. Such problems could decrease the interest of a decision-leader from whom one is seeking endorsement of the underlying display concept being conveyed by the prototype. Even when a technical member of the original development team learned to compensate for this problem rapidly during situations where the "demonstratee" was merely in the role of a passenger, the problem was still obvious to the demonstratee, due to the repeated starting and stopping of the simulated motion.

Control instability also contributed to the time-consuming and error-prone nature of the altitude control lock. Altitude control is a feature of flight simulators that allows the current altitude to be locked into place. This is helpful to demonstrators (spokespersons or members of the development team) when presenting the TSAS, e.g., it alleviates the need for a spokesperson to focus on altitude control while explaining other capabilities of the TSAS. In the previous version of TSAS, when altitude lock was deactivated, approximately 30 % of the simulated helicopter's available lifting power was required when manipulating the collective. Unfortunately, deactivating altitude lock in the upgraded version of the simulator initiated a rapid freefall that could only be

---

² Dead space represents an area of non-responsiveness near a control's null position.

counteracted with approximately 90 % of the simulated lifting power, requiring extreme excursion of the collective. Crash recovery thus became more difficult, which led to frequent system resets and unimpressed observers.

In the situation described above, the new system neglected design principles such as *flexibility, efficiency of use*, and *error tolerance* [1]. The control scheme was unforgiving to novices, yet also lacking in realism experienced pilots appreciate. A better design strategy is to implement realistic controls and flight dynamics for experts, but have the option for an easier "arcade mode" for demonstration to non-pilots. The users also should be able to adjust the collective easily. This can be done by modifying flight control to produce a more responsive system with moderate gain [7].

A problem presented by the updated software occurred during a tank-hunting scenario. TSAS can guide the pilot to target locations (via tactile cues on the body corresponding to the direction the pilot should head). Initially, the first target (a tank) was located in a sandy area. When the helicopter flew over this area, a dust storm was created to demonstrate the usefulness of TSAS upon inadvertent entry into a degraded visual environment (DVE). Unfortunately, the dust storm overloaded the computer's processor, causing system lag. *Time lags* greatly degrad a user's ability to control a system and increase user errors [6]. Another related issue was that the "sand pit" from which the dust storm originated was surrounded by green grass, trees, lakes, and small, grass-covered rolling hills. Therefore, this aspect of the system failed to be consistent with the user's *mental model* [9] of likely environmental features. Design constraints should be implemented to make the simulation more natural and prevent users from performing actions that exceed system capabilities. A principle of HF design is the use of *constraints*, i.e., design elements that limit the ways in which users can interact with systems [10].

Another problem with the new software was the misleading display of system status, which violated design principles of *visibility, feedback*, and *consistency* [5]. The user was always shown a visual indicator of the current "mode". The user could choose to work in "advanced mode" or "easy mode". This was a good feature, but upon initialization, when the simulator was in "advanced mode", it was incorrectly labeled as "easy mode". If the user then chose to switch into "easy mode", the display changed to "advanced mode". A similar feedback problem arose whenever the software began to experience lag (as in the "sand pit" problem in the previous paragraph). Under normal circumstances, highlighted buttons indicated activation (e.g., when altitude control was activated, its corresponding button stayed highlighted until deactivated). Unfortunately, if a button was selected just before a system slow-down, then after the system recovered that button remained highlighted, despite the fact that the command was never executed. This lack of *consistency* and accurate *feedback* for user inputs and status displays led to frequent *mode errors,* wherein the users interacted with the system inappropriately for the active mode [10, 11], typically because of ignorance or memory lapses regarding which mode is presently active. In our simulation, mode errors occurred because the design induced them. A principle of display design is to provide *visibility regarding system status* [4]. Users should be kept informed of which mode is active. Furthermore, the principle of *feedback* mandates that users be provided with information regarding the effectiveness of their inputs [4, 5].

The new software violated these design principles: first, by providing unreliable information regarding the current active mode, and second, by providing feedback to users that failed to reflect actual mode changes. This placed a greater memory burden on demonstrators to remember the idiosyncrasies of the simulator. Good HF design requires reducing memory load and instead placing *knowledge in the world* [12].

A final problem was the placement of the crosshairs for aiming missiles (during the shooting portion of the simulation), which violated the principle of *consistency* and use of *real world conventions* [4, 5]. The new version of the simulator software relocated the crosshairs to the bottom left quadrant of the screen, which failed to match users' expectations based upon experience with other systems, including previous versions of the TSAS. Crosshairs for simulations emulating a first-person, egocentric perspective are usually centered. Crosshairs not only represent a tool for "sighting" weapons, but also provide the primary anchor for a user to orient his or her personal perspective. By decentering the crosshairs, a perceived misalignment between a user's ego-center and the simulation can arise, resulting in inaccurate targeting, adoption of unintuitive compensatory aiming strategies, and awkward flight patterns. In the new version, weapons fire still tracked centrally, as though the crosshairs were located in the center of the screen. These design flaws failed to conform to platform interface or *real-world conventions* [4]. The new system was awkward for demonstration participants to use because they could neither use it in the same manner as other fixed-reticle flight simulators, nor could they hit targets despite aiming perfectly.

3   Case Study 2: HF Challenges During the Development of Medical Technology to Aid with Balance

Our second case study involves a tactile balance assistance display [13, 14] designed to help orient and rehabilitate people with balance disorders. The technology integrated a balance platform with a wearable vibrotactile belt. The original technology was represented visually on a computer screen from an allocentric top-down perspective and was easy to demonstrate. The user's center of pressure (represented by a dot) was surrounded by a virtual ring that contracted slowly, requiring the user to maintain balance to keep from colliding with virtual walls through postural tilt and sway. Swaying forward would cause a tactile collision with a virtual wall, intuitively triggering vibrotactile feedback from that direction. The user then compensated by moving in the opposite direction, typically to a more upright posture. By the point at which the shrinking circle had reached its smallest size, the user was required to maintain a consistent upright posture to keep the dot centered and avoid receiving tactile cues. If the user could not avoid hitting the edges of the circle, the ring would expand slightly to adapt to the user's ability to maintain balance. The original system was well-designed and facilitated demonstration to groups of people, who could easily view its utility without wearing the tactile display.

A revised version of the balance test software was developed to integrate with the second generation of the balance-sensing and feedback hardware. Unfortunately, user-centered design for optimal demonstration was not considered as carefully. The new software eliminated the adaptive shrinking function of the circular visual feedback during the balance test and, in fact, provided a screen where no circle of stability was visible during the balance testing part of the demonstration. The user could still see his/her center-of-pressure represented as a dot moving across the screen but could not see where the limit, which triggered the tactile cue, had been set. In other words, the user had no way to know he/she had reached the static virtual circle visually, but only could do so tactually. At the end of the test, the software indicated the user's degree of postural sway via a percentage presented via text (e.g., "You scored a 30 %"). This new design limited the potential for effective demonstrations, particularly to more than a single person at a time. Real-time visual *feedback* was an essential element of the original software, not only to assist the participant in learning to use the system and providing confirmation to the demonstrator that the system was operating correctly, but also to demonstrate the system to groups of observers. The new design violated the aforementioned principle of *visibility* by failing to provide feedback to users, irrespective of their role in the demonstration. Some people attending the demonstration may not have had time to try the system themselves, or they may have been shy or self-conscious (e.g., wondering if the tactile belt would fit around their waist), so it was important for everyone to understand what was happening to the person experiencing the tactile cues. Moreover, the test feedback provided to the user was cryptic, since users could not readily interpret the results. The display of cryptic messages violates one of Nielsen's [4] usability design guidelines: providing a *match between the system and the real world*. One aspect of this guideline is to convey information through familiar conceptual models and metaphors. In the present case study, the use of a percentage can be viewed as a metaphor for a test grade, which *can* be consistent with users' mental models [9], provided they also know the grading scale. A possibly superior approach is to provide test feedback using conceptual metaphors to which users can relate readily [4], such as *unstable, slightly unstable, stable,* or *very stable.*

A new mobile tablet version of the system was developed for demonstrations where a spokesperson may require a portable system that is immediately usable (e.g., for unscheduled demonstrations). This system required the user to hold the tablet against his/her chest so that the accelerometers in the tablet could detect its orientation and activate vibrations when postural sway exceeded a set threshold. The user responded by moving in the opposite direction of the vibration (e.g., vibration on the abdomen indicated to the user that he/she was leaning too far forward). The tablet also depicted the balance test visually for demonstration to observers who were not wearing the tactile display. It showed a dot, representing the user, inside two concentric circles. The dot moved in response to postural tilt, and when its movements breached the confines of the innermost circle, tactile feedback was presented in the appropriate direction and a blinking light activated on the tablet screen to convey the pulse rate. Exceeding the confines of the outermost concentric circle resulted in a faster tactile pulse rate. The size of the concentric circles was scalable via a gain control to adjust the difficulty of the balance task to each patient.

The tablet-based demonstration system enhanced portability, but its initial implementation had flaws from a human-use perspective. First, the visual *feedback* provided to the audience viewing the tablet screen indicated postural feedback was being provided to the front of the torso, when it was actually presented to the back. The same was true for lateral tactile cues (i.e., there was a left-right reversal). This violated the design principle of *stimulus-response compatibility* [15] and the *principle of the moving part* [16]. In this case, there was a spatial mismatch between the tactile display and visual feedback, which confused the user or people observing the demonstration. Secondly, manipulating the gain control not only changed the system's sensitivity to postural change, but it also reversed the direction of tactile cues without providing feedback regarding this reversal. Rather than providing repellent/avoidance cues, (i.e., move away from the tactile cue), the system began to provide attractive/guidance cues. (i.e., move towards the tactile cue). The lack of visual confirmation of the mode change violated the principle of feedback [5]. Without such feedback, mode errors and confusion were commonplace, causing demonstration failures.

Many of the flaws above were corrected in the latest version of the tablet-based balance demonstrator. However, the text labels for the controls remained too small. Based upon an average viewing distance of 40 cm (as estimated in the laboratory) and an average character height of 0.013 cm, a typical lowercase letter in the tablet display subtended a visual angle of only 0.21×0.18 degrees (vertically and horizontally, respectively). The low-contrast display text was the equivalent of a 6-point font, violating the principle of *legibility* [6], and requiring demonstrators/spokespersons to memorize each button. When designing displays for dynamic environments (e.g., during locomotion or vehicular transportation) or for persons over age 65, then sans serif fonts greater than 12-point should be adopted to improve visibility [17, 18].

4   Case Study 3: HF Challenges During the Development of a Vehicle Collision Avoidance Display[3]

There are a variety of circumstances where a vehicle collision warning may be useful. One circumstance is when a police officer conducts a road-side traffic stop. In this event, the officer exits his/her vehicle and approaches the stopped vehicle on foot. Often, the officer will approach the driver-side of the vehicle. This exposes the officer to risk of collision by an approaching vehicle on the roadway. Avoiding this hazard requires the officer to divide his/her attention between the motorist and the roadway, which could slow the officer's reactions if the motorist intends to harm the officer. All states have adopted a "move-over" law, mandating that drivers must slow down and change lanes if possible when approaching a police vehicle that is pulled to the side of the road. However, police officers are still injured (some fatally) each year by approaching vehicles. Vehicle collision warning systems have yet to be leveraged to prevent these events. To customize existing technologies to accommodate this application, the optimal sensory modality and stimulus presentation must be considered. The roadside environment can be very noisy, implying that an auditory stimulus may not be optimal. A possible solution is to create a multi-modal display that includes a tactile cue to ensure a more salient stimulus. However, such a system will never be adopted if it is difficult to use or provides unhelpful or false alerts. The team designing and testing such a device should consider practical HF limitations during development to maximize the potential for utility. When developing software, utility is usually enhanced by

---

[3] Traffic collisions are discussed, but the technology also has a cueing mode to alert a pilot concerning collision with the ground.

building upon existing formats and layouts that have been proven to be efficient and intuitive, thus reducing the recurrence of poor system design. Moreover, leveraging preexisting user knowledge by retaining similarities between versions can facilitate transfer of training [19]. If reprogramming is necessary, it should incorporate HF principles such as those described in the example below.

A simple proof-of-concept tactile array was created in an effort to demonstrate a tactile cueing concept that could reduce vehicle collisions in various settings. The seat display contained a 32-tactor grid that could signal the approach of an object (via radial expansion of concentric rings of tactor activation on the surface of one's body, e.g., the back). The formation of the prototype necessitated that a new version of the underlying tactile display software must be written to allow the system to control 32 tactors without causing the tactor controller (signal amplification and selection hardware) to fail. The new cue was well-liked by demonstration participants, but the system presented many usability problems to the demonstrator. The most outstanding software issue was one of *conveyance*. Ideally, instructions for using the software should be conveyed in an easily comprehensible manner, in language the user can readily comprehend [4]. This was not the case for the tactile warning system. An example of poor conveyance was the task of loading a saved file that had been created by a technical member of the development team. This task required the user to click the "menu" tab in the center of the screen, which led to another "menu" tab on the right side of the screen, which led to yet another "menu" tab to the left. This complex menu hierarchy confused users and taxed their memory unnecessarily.

A similar usability problem arose with the simple act of booting up the program for demonstration. The new version of the program required at least twice as many steps to be completed before the demonstration could begin, some of which were not intuitive. As a result, one group demonstration failed despite the fact that the spokesperson had 30 min to set-up the system and ensure the software was working. A principle of HF design is to minimize demands on long-term memory through standardization and visibility [6]. Placing regularly used functions in locations consistent with users' mental models [9] (e.g., due to past experience), and making them quickly accessible and visible eliminates frustration and confusion caused by navigation through embedded menus. This is important because the spokesperson may not have even 30 min to get a demonstration ready for a decision-leader or group.

Another problem related to context. The user should be able to clearly and quickly understand the function of all of the software "tools". Typically, tools are represented by icons that cue the user on what the tool does. The match between the pictorial representation and a "real world" object should be close and make use of familiar metaphors. Certain aspects of the new software, however, violated these design principles. For example, the tactile seat warning system featured a "Database" tool, which allowed the user to access the computer's stored files. The icon for this tool was an envelope, which connoted sending or receiving files. The mismatch between the icon and associated function confused users. A better icon in this situation would be that of a vault, floppy disk, or hard drive, which would additionally conform to the principle of *mental models* [9] by using a common iconic representation.

Table 1. HF Recommendations for People in the Chain of Technology Development *Prior* to the End-User, and Problems that Arise from Not Following Recommendations (see Conclusion).

Personnel	Case 1: Aviation display	2: Balance display	3: Collision display
1. Engineer or Technician (hardware)	*-Recommendation:* Hardware should support software demands.		
	-Problems with device that could arise, as discussed in this paper:		
	Demonstration failure due to control problems (pp. 4-5).	Demo. failure due to misleading feedback (pp. 7-8).	__ __ __
2. Programmer (e.g., software expert on the development team)	*-Recommendations:* (1) Software instructions should be clear & (2) according with HF principles.		
	-General problems due to ignoring HF principles include: (1) Loss of time; (2) Confusion or memory overload; (3) Avoidable user error; (4) misinformation.		
	-Examples of *specific problems* from this report, organized by HF principle violated:		
	-Problems Caused by Violating Principle of Mental Models:		
	__ __ __	Unclear feedback (p. 7).	Using an envelope icon to indicate file storage (p. 9).
	-Problems Caused by Violating Principle of Feedback:		
	Inaccurate display of mode status (pp. 5-6).	Tactile cues changing direction without visual confirmation (pp. 7-8).	__ __ __
	-Problems Caused by Violating Principles of Consistency & Real-World Conventions:		
	Not placing crosshairs where expected (p. 6).	__ __ __	Inconsistent "Ctrl-Z" outcome (p. 11).
	-Problems Caused by Violating Principle of Visibility:		
	__ __ __	Providing no info. to audience (p. 7).	__ __ __
3. Spokesperson (e.g., people not expert in hardware or software; such as the team leader or public relations rep.)	*-Recommendations:* (1) Must be able to demonstrate the product easily & quickly, & (2) must be able to do so without being a system expert.		
	-Problems that could arise from not following recommendations:		
	Faulty hard/software causes system restarts/failures, costing demo. time (pp. 4-8) & convincing participants the system is flawed.		Inconsistency with mental models (p. 9) increases memory load, delay, & error.

(*Continued*)

Table 1. (*Continued*)

Personnel	Case 1: Aviation display	2: Balance display	3: Collision display
	Inaccurate feedback (pp. 5-6) confuses demonstrator; audience unimpressed.	Non-intuitive info. (p. 7) burdens spokesperson; confuses audience.	Inconsistent controls (p. 11) burden memory; cause mistakes/lost time.
	Unusually-placed crosshairs (p. 6) cause spokesperson to suspect system malfunction.	Demonstrator unaware of system changes (pp. 7-8) misleads audience.	— — —
	— — —	Audience lacks visual info. (pp. 6-7) to grasp demo.	— — —
4. Decision Leader or Sponsor	-*Recommendations*: (1) Seldom should be given a full demo.; rather, needs general understanding of the product, problems it solves, its maturity, & its potential.		
	-*Problems* that could arise from not following recommendations:		
	Simulation problems (pp. 4-5) cost time & are interpreted as flaws in the concept.	Cryptic feedback (p. 7) causes poor decisions.	Problems with bootup/files (p. 9) cause leader/sponsor to deem product immature.
	Inaccurate/absent feedback (pp. 5-6) harms endorsement.	If system is confusing (pp. 6-7), leaders & sponsors will not be interested.	Inconsistent controls (p. 11) lead to lost time, poor demo., & withheld support.
	Poor crosshairs (p. 6) raises suspicion of larger problems.	Explaining idiosyncrasies (pp. 7-8) costs demo time.	— — —

A final problem encountered by users of the tactile seat warning system who wished to develop new tactor firing sequences was an absence of consistency. In one section of the software, using the keyboard shortcut "Ctrl-Z" (undo) cancelled only the previous step. In another section of the software, using the same keyboard shortcut cancelled all previous steps, violating the design principle of *consistency* [5] and leading to confusion and lost progress.

5 Conclusion

This report describes case studies of HF problems we have encountered during the development of several prototype display technologies, emphasizing the problems and needs specific not only to the end-user, but also to technology developers, spokespersons, decision-makers, and others in the human chain of technology development. HF practitioners will not be surprised to learn that when these problems were initially described to the programmer who had made the modifications, he felt that most of the problems simply required more training and practice on the part of the other personnel in the technology development chain. This common and understandable reaction is nevertheless a violation of the HF principle that *the fault is never with the user* [20]. Fortunately, this and other problems were overcome by discussion and trouble-shooting among all team members. HF professionals know that it is important to involve the end-user in the development process [20], but in all three cases studies in this report there were several people *prior* to the end-user who needed to be engaged in communication and pre-testing in order to make the technology successful. In Table 1, recommendations are offered for four of the people (viz., the engineer/technician, the programmer, the spokesperson, and the decision leader or sponsor) in the chain of technology development leading to the end-user. Examples are provided of problems that can arise for due to a failure to consider HF principles. The three display technologies are shown in three vertical columns, with the horizontal rows representing some of the people in the development chain.[4] A review of the table should give the reader ideas for how the challenges encountered with these applications can foster innovations in his/her own field of technology development.

References

1. Shneiderman, B.: Designing The User Interface: Strategies for Effective Human-Computer Interaction, 2nd edn. Addison-Wesley Publishing Co., Reading (1992)
2. Kelley, A.M., Cheung, R., Lawson, B.D., Rath, E., Chiasson, C., Ramiccio, J.G., Rupert, A. H.: Efficacy of tactile cues in orienting pilots during helicopter extractions over moving targets. Aviat. Space Environ. Med. **84**(12), 55–61 (2013)
3. Kelley, A.M., Newman, R.L., Lawson, B.D., Rupert, A.H.: A materiel solution to aircraft upset. In: Proceedings of AIAA Guidance, Navigation & Control, p. 9 National Harbor, MD (2014)
4. Nielsen, J.: Enhancing the explanatory power of usability heuristics. In: Proceedings of the SIGCHI Conference on Human Factors in Computing Systems, pp. 152–158. ACM, New York (1994)
5. Mayhew, D.J.: Principles and Guidelines in Software User Interface Design. Prentice Hall, Englewood Cliffs (1992)
6. Wickens, C.D., Lee, J.D., Liu, Y., Becker, S.E.: An Introduction to Human Factors engineering, 2nd edn. Pearson, Upper Saddle River (2004)

---

[4] We demonstrated the prototype technologies to attendees of the panel session, soliciting further ideas.

7. Wickens, C.D.: The effects of control dynamics on performance. In: Boff, K.R., Kauffman, L., Thomas, J.P. (eds.) Handbook of Perception and Performance, vol. 2, pp. 39-1–39-60. Wiley-Interscience, New York (1986)

8. Rockway, M.R. Effects of variations in control dead space and gain on tracking performance. Technical report WADC-TR-57-326, Wright Air Development Center

9. Mania, K., Robinson, A., Brandt, K.R.: The effect of memory schemas on object recognition in virtual environments. Presence-Teleoperator. Virtual **14**(5), 606–615 (2005)

10. Norman, D.A.: The Design of Everyday Things. Basic Books, New York (2002)

11. Lewis, C., Norman, D.A.: Designing the user interface: strategies for effective error. In: Norman, D.A., Draper, S.W. (eds.) User-Centered System Design: New Perspectives of Human-Computer Interaction, pp. 411–432. Lawrence Erlbaum Associates, Hillsdale (1986)

12. Wickens, C.D., Gordon, S.E., Liu, Y.: An Introduction to Human Factors Engineering, 1st edn. Longman, New York (1998)

13. Lawson, B.D., Rupert, A.H., Legan, S.: Vestibular balance deficits following head injury: Recommendations concerning evaluation and rehabilitation in the military setting. Technical report 2012–10, Fort Rucker, AL: US Army Aeromedical Research Laboratory (2012)

14. Lawson B.D., Rupert, A.H., Raj A., Parker J., Greskovich, C. Invited lectures from a spatial orientation symposium in honor of Frederick Guedry, Day 1. Technical report 2014–2010, Fort Rucker, AL: US Army Aeromedical Research Laboratory (2014)

15. Fitts, P.M., Seeger, C.M.: SR compatibility: spatial characteristics of stimulus and response codes. J. Exp. Psychol. **46**(3), 199 (1953)

16. Roscoe, S.N.: Airborne displays for flight and navigation. Hum. Factors **10**, 321–332 (1968)

17. Sanders, M.S., McCormick, E.J.: Human Factors in Engineering and Design, 7th edn. McGraw-Hill, New York (1993)

18. Leavitt, M.O., Shneiderman, B.: Research-Based Web Design & Usability Guidelines. US Department of Health and Human Services, Washington, DC. (2006)

19. Holding, D.H.: Concepts of training. In: Salvendy, G. (ed.) Handbook of Human Factors, pp. 939–962. Wiley, New York (1987)

20. Mejdal, S., McCauley, M.E.: Human factors design guidelines for multifunction displays. Technical report DOT/FAA/AM-01/17. Office of Aerospace Medicine, Washington (2001)

Computer Input System Using Eye Glances

Shogo Matsuno$^{(\boxtimes)}$, Kota Akehi, Naoaki Itakura, Tota Mizuno,
and Kazuyuki Mito

Graduate School of Informatics and Engineering, The University of
Electro-Communications, 1-5-1 Chofugaoka, Chofu, Tokyo 182-8585, Japan
ml440004@edu.cc.uec.ac.jp

Abstract. We have developed a real-time Eye Glance input interface using a
Web camera to capture eye gaze inputs. In previous studies, an eye control input
interface was developed using an electro-oculograph (EOG) amplified by AC
coupling. Our proposed Eye Gesture input interface used a combination of eye
movements and did not require the restriction of head movement, unlike conventional eye gaze input methods. However, this method required an input start
operation before capturing could commence. This led us to propose the Eye
Glance input method that uses a combination of contradirectional eye movements as inputs and avoids the need for start operations. This method required
the use of electrodes, which were uncomfortable to attach. The interface was
therefore changed to a camera that used facial pictures to record eye movements
to realize an improved noncontact and low-restraint interface. The Eye Glance
input method measures the directional movement and time required by the eye
to move a specified distance using optical flow with OpenCV from Intel. In this
study, we analyzed the waveform obtained from eye movements using a pur-
pose-built detection algorithm. In addition, we examined the reasons for
detecting a waveform when eye movements failed.

Keywords: Eye glance · Eye input · Optical flow · Input interface

1 Introduction

Eye movements are the quickest among face movements. In this study, we developed a
new method for automatically detecting eye glances by analyzing video images captured using a Web camera. We aimed to develop a multichannel computer system
incorporating an eye movement input technique based on the eye-glance detection
method. Improvements in computing performance have led to the downsizing and
widespread use of wearable devices. However, these wearable devices are difficult for
users to control because they are small, have many functions, and are complicated. To
solve this problem, several methods involving eye movements have been attempted
[1, 2], and eye-movement input has attracted attention as a hands-free input system.
However, information devices need to become smaller and easier to control to develop
an eye-movement input system.

A study of conventional eye-gaze input interfaces revealed that the most popular
type of gaze input interface uses the gaze position to input characters. However, if the
subject's head moves, it is not possible to identify the gaze position precisely by only

© Springer International Publishing Switzerland 2015
S. Yamamoto (Ed.): HIMI 2015, Part I, LNCS 9172, pp. 425–432, 2015.
DOI: 10.1007/978-3-319-20612-7_41

detecting the eye movement. Even if there is no eye movement, the gaze position changes unless the head is immobilized. Special equipment is required to identify the gaze position with high accuracy without fixing the head; therefore, the equipment becomes more expensive.

Thus, we devised an input method capable of accepting gaze inputs [3]. A previous study [4] of ours suggested the use of Eye Gesture inputs in combination with the directional movement of the eye instead of gaze inputs and realized a simple eye-gaze input method using the AC-EOG (Alternating Current-Electro-oculogram). Furthermore, we proposed that the only input that the Eye Glance input method should require should be the characteristic eye movement in combination with the direction of the eye movement as used by the Eye Gesture input. To summarize, we demonstrated the possibility of realizing a simple eye-gaze input that, unlike Eye Gesture inputs, does not require an input start operation. In the case of Eye Glance inputs, it is only necessary to detect the direction of the eye movement, which does not require a high degree of accuracy. The Eye Glance input is therefore a facile method for obtaining inputs. To date, Eye Glance input has been realized using the AC amplification EOG; however, its use of an electrode patch required effort to apply and caused discomfort.

In this study, we proposed a new method for automatically detecting eye glances by using a Web camera. We show the experimental results of this system using this method.

2 Eye Glance Input

The eye-gaze input method is popular among systems that use eye information [5, 6]. In a previous study [7], we reviewed existing input methods with the aim of reducing system costs and the restrictions placed on the user. The result was a novel Eye Gesture input interface that did not require a HMD. Instead, directional combinations for eye-gaze displacement were used as the selection method. We found that eye gaze displacements could be determined precisely using a derivative EOG signal amplified via AC coupling. A desktop display design created for use with the Eye Gesture input interface is shown in Fig. 1. In that study, it was assumed that Eye Gesture movements followed oblique patterns (upper left, lower left, upper right, lower right) and that each pattern consisted of a combination of two movements.

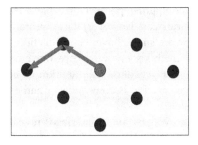

Fig. 1. Eye gesture input model

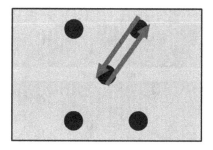

Fig. 2. Eye glance input model

However, in this study, we used eye glances (eye movements) because they are relatively fast and easy to input. Using an eye glance has two advantages over the eye-gaze input method: the wait time of the input is short, and the eye movement is a very quick and unique motion that leads to relatively light processing load. As the first step, we examined a four-channel input method that can be applied to the operation of various devices such as smartphones [3]. Figure 2 shows an example of the eye-glance model. The input trigger is the coming-and-going movement of the eyes in the slant direction.

Eye Glance input is a technique that uses eye movements that occur when someone only looks at something for a moment as inputs. Previous studies have used the AC EOG method, in which an electrode patch must be placed on the face. New methods use video cameras instead.

3 Eye Glance Detection Method

Incorporating eye movement detection equipment in commonly used devices such as tablets would necessitate the use of inexpensive equipment such as the device's built-in camera or a USB camera, rather than using expensive equipment such as a high-speed camera. Therefore, we used an inexpensive USB Web camera in this experiment. The camera has a resolution of 1.3 million pixels and can obtain images at 30 fps. Figure 3 shows the measurement range, the size of which is 200 × 60 pixels.

Fig. 3. Measurement range

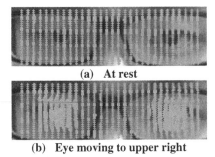

(a)   At rest

(b)   Eye moving to upper right

Fig. 4. Measurement of optical flow

This method uses the optical flow to detect eye movements. The optical flow was measured using a library based on that of Gunnar Farneback in OpenCV. To calculate the vector, 200 points are considered in the measurement range. Figure 4 shows facial images that were obtained by measuring the optical flow. Any eye movement has the result of changing the vector of every point around the eye. This value is used to calculate the optical flow between the two images. By repeating this from the first frame to the last frame, the amount of movement of the eye in the area is recorded as the amount of change in the optical flow. The frame rate of the camera was 30 fps.

Figure 5 shows the waveform obtained during eye glance movements (upper right). If we can automatically detect ocular movements in each direction, we can use a multichannel input system that has different commands for each direction. An input is recorded when the waveform exceeds the threshold set for the horizontal direction and when this occurs continuously within the stationary time. The stationary time is the time between two peaks of a round-trip waveform. We calculated the optical flow and determined the threshold required to detect eye glances automatically. The threshold of the speed vector was assumed to be 70 % of the average of the data obtained by each

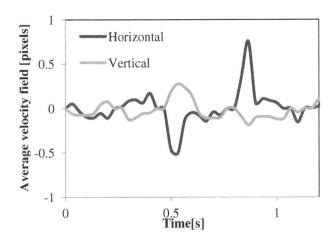

Fig. 5. Waveform of eye glance moving to upper right

subject. Further, thresholds were determined using a separate waveform for the positive and the negative directions.

4 Experiment

We investigated the process to determine the threshold to detect eye movements automatically by experimenting with five subjects. Figure 6 shows an overview of the experimental system. The subjects were shown video images of the eye captured using a Web camera. First, the subjects performed a calibration to determine the threshold to remove artifacts. They watched the index at the center of the screen for 5 s so that they would not move their face; we measured the optical flow and determined the threshold. We then displayed the experimental image that set the photographed image of the eye at the center and the indexes at the four corners. The view angle between the middle indicator and the corner indicators in the experimental image was 15 × 7. The subjects gazed at the indexes once each in the following order: center, one of the four corners, and center clockwise from the upper right. The obtained data were treated as one set. The subjects performed 10 trials and took a break between these trials. They adjusted the face position by looking at the image photographed by the camera and displayed before each set.

4.1 Non-Real-Time Measurement Experiment (Experiment 1)

Table 1 presents the experimental results. The pre-evaluation (non-real-time measurement) experiments indicated that the average detection rate of the proposed method

camera→

Fig. 6. Overview of experimental system

Table 1. Results of experiment 1

Subjects	Upper right [%]	Lower right [%]	Lower left [%]	Upper left [%]	Average [%]
A	80.0	80.0	90.0	80.0	82.5
B	70.0	60.0	50.0	60.0	60.0
C	100.0	60.0	100.0	60.0	77.5
D	90.0	80.0	70.0	60.0	75.0
E	90.0	60.0	90.0	70.0	75.0
Average	86.0	68.0	80.0	66.0	74.0

was 74 %. In this experiment, 900 points are considered in the measurement range to calculate the vector.

4.2 Real-Time Measurement Experiment (Experiment 2)

In this experiment, the system, method, and environment are the same as those in experiment 1. However, four different subjects are used. These subjects performed 30 trials and took a break between these trials. In addition, this system sends feedback signals to the subject about when to input an eye glance. Figure 7 shows the experimental screen. The feedback signal is shown after 0.8 s (Fig. 8).

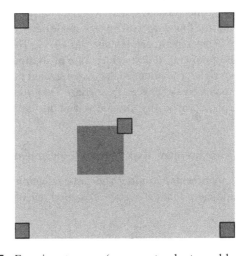

Fig. 7. Experiment screen (movement order toward lower left)

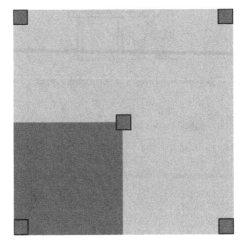

Fig. 8. Feedback signal (to input eye glance)

Table 2. Results of experiment 2

Subjects	Upper right [%]	Lower right [%]	Lower left [%]	Upper left [%]	Average [%]
A	83.3	70.0	86.7	83.3	80.8
B	80.0	66.7	63.3	73.3	70.8
C	93.3	90.0	83.3	93.3	90.0
D	93.3	86.7	66.7	83.3	82.5
Average	87.5	78.4	75.0	83.3	81.0

Table 2 presents the experimental results. The evaluation experiments indicated that the average detection rate of the proposed method was 81 %.

5 Discussion

Overall, the real-time measurement (experiment 2) showed a higher successful detection rate than the non-real-time measurement (experiment 1) despite lesser vector points being calculated in experiment 2 than in experiment 1. We attribute this to the presence of feedback signals in experiment 2. The average input success rate will increase if the feedback signal contributes to successful input and habituation of the subjects because subjects use this system for the first time during this experiment.

By using our proposed method, the average rate of successful eye glance input is ~80 % for the experimental sample of four subjects (Table 2). We think this rate is sufficient for device control if the system can tolerate some missing inputs. However, subject B's average rate was comparatively low because of the noise of waiting time. Some subjects move their eye frequently and do not perform eye glances in order. We attribute this to unconscious movements by the subjects. This movement destabilizes the vector of the near-eye area. We consider changing the measurement area of the vector to the black eye area from the near eye area to solve this problem.

6 Conclusion

We proposed a real-time eye glance input method that detects eye glances using a Web camera. This method realizes easy noncontact inputs to a computer to detect eye movements using image analysis. We experimentally tested the system implemented using this method. In our experiments with four different subjects, the average successful input rate was 81 %.

In the future, we plan to conduct additional experiment with more subjects. We also plan to improve this method to increase the detection accuracy. In addition, we will investigate the incorporation of this method into mobile devices.

References

1. Miluzzo, E., Wang, T., Campbell, A.T.: Eye gesture recognition: eyephone: activating mobile phones with your eyes. In: Proceedings of the Second ACM SIGCOMM Workshop on Networking, Systems and Applications on mobile handhelds, pp. 15–20 (2010)
2. Mayberry, A., Hu, P., Marlin, B., Salthouse, C., Ganesan, D.: iShadow: design of a wearable, real-time mobile gaze tracker. In: Proceedings of the 12th Annual International Conference on Mobile Systems, Applications, and Services, pp. 82–94. ACM (2014)
3. Naoaki, I., Takumi, O., Kazutaka, S.: Investigation for calculation method of eye-gaze shift from electro-oculograph amplified by ac coupling with using eye-gaze input interface. IEICE Trans. Inf. Syst. **J90-D**(10), 2903–2913 (2007)
4. Dekun, G., Naoaki, I., Tota, M., Kazuyuki, M.: Improvement of eye gesture interface system. In: Proceedings of the 16th Asia Pacific Symposium of Intelligent and Evolutionary Systems, No. 3, pp. 1–3 (2012)
5. Abe, K., Ohi, S., Ohyama, M.: An eye-gaze input system using information on eye movement history. In: Stephanidis, C. (ed.) UAHCI 2007 (Part II). LNCS, vol. 4555, pp. 721–729. Springer, Heidelberg (2007)
6. Majaranta, P., Raiha, K.-J.: Twenty years of eye typing: systems and design issues. In: Proceedings of the Symposium on ETRA 2002, pp. 15–22. ACM (2002)
7. Gao, D., Itakura, N., Mizuno, T., Mito, K.: Study of eye-glance input interface. In: Kurosu, M. (ed.) HCII/HCI 2013, Part IV. LNCS, vol. 8007, pp. 225–234. Springer, Heidelberg (2013)

Basic Study of Evoking Emotion Through Extending One's Body Image by Integration of Internal Sense and External Sense

Sho Sakurai[✉], Takuji Narumi, Toki Katsumura,
Tomohiro Tanikawa, and Michitaka Hirose

The Graduate School of Information Science and Technology,
The University of Tokyo, 7-3-1 Hongo, Bunkyo-Ku, Tokyo, Japan
{sho,narumi,katsumura,tani,
hirose}@cyber.t.u-tokyo.ac.jp

Abstract. Emotion has closely relationship with one's body image. In some cases, external object that physically separates from body is recognized as one's body image. In other words, the body image extends to the external object. This phenomenon happens by integration of internal sense that perceives one's body and external sense that perceives the outside of the body. On the other hand, the type of evoked emotion is decided from cognizing not only body image but also attribution of causality. General approaches to evoke emotion in recent have not discussed the causal attribution in depth. This study has proposed a new method for evoking emotions through touching upon the discussion of causal attribution. To investigate the feasibility of our approach, we made "Interactonia Balloon" that lets users evoke a tense feeling by coupling and decoupling a change in respiratory condition and a movement of a balloon. In this paper, we report on the feedback and implications obtained through the exhibition of this work.

Keywords: Interaction design · Multimodal interaction · Evoking emotion · Body image · Somatopsychology

1 Introduction

Emotion has a closely relationship with body perception. In the field of psychology and cognitive science, there have been discussed that either emotion or physiological changes in earlier. Generally, it is considered that emotion evokes by recognizing outside world and physiological changes occurs as the result of the change in the emotion, such as heart rate and facial expression. However, theories that claim body perception changes prior to change in emotion are met with acceptance recently [1, 2]. Besides, it is clarified that an awareness of physiological changes evokes emotion even if real physiological changes does not occur [3]. In other words, emotion evokes depending on not real bodily condition but an imaginary one's body condition.

In recent years, there have been some studies to evoke a specific emotion by presenting external stimuli that is felt as if own body changes based on the above-mentioned findings [4–7]. These methods can evoke emotion without interpreting meaning of presented stimuli. Nevertheless, these have a problem that it is difficult to evoke emotion when the presented stimuli are not felt like own physiological changes.

S. Yamamoto (Ed.): HIMI 2015, Part I, LNCS 9172, pp. 433–444, 2015.
DOI: 10.1007/978-3-319-20612-7_42

Moreover, it is required to be recognized not only physiological changes but also the reason why the physiological changes occur [2]. The recognized the reason is called "attribution of causality," which determines the type of emotion experienced. Many of existing studies for evoking emotion try to evoke emotion by changing presented stimulation depending on the context of surrounding environment. However, it is difficult to evoke specific emotion at aimed timing when the change of the recognized stimuli is not attributed to aimed emotion.

On the other hand, emotion changes by through volantary activity. This reason is considered that the attribution of causality of the physiologial changes switchs from individual own will to other factors when human move own body intentionally. We hypothesis that emotion also evokes by leading a person to move his/her body actively in a specific way, and swich the recognized attribution of causality of tha change in the body from his/her will to other elements in midstream.

The authors focus on a phenomenon that an external object is recognized as a part of body through intentional controlling of the object. The phenomenon happens when the internal sense that perceives a own body and the external sense that perceives the controlled object are perceived as synchronized temporally and spatially. The external object recognized as a part of body is described as "extended body" in other words.

In this study, we propose a method for evoking emotion by giving recognition to the external object as the extended body through intentional controlling the object using their body in a specific way, and swithcing the attribution of cousality of the extended body's change from the volantary activity to other outside factor.

To investigating the feasibility of such an approach, the current study focused on using respiration as a physical response that relates to emotion. For instance, respiration is closely related to a tense feeling, and respiration can be changed both automatically and intentionally. The current study also proposes an interactive apparatus named "Interactonia Balloon", which evokes and enhances tense feelings by switching an attribution of causality of the choking feeling. In this paper, we first explain the concept and design of the Interactonia balloon. We also describe participants' reactions and feedback on using the apparatus.

2   Emotion and Body Image

2.1   Emotion

Emotion is used as a term for relational mental phenomenon. What is the emotion called differs depending on the mental condition. Sometimes, "affect" and "mood" are used as equivalent terms with "emotion." "Affect" refers to externally displaying of emotion, such as facial, vocal, or gestural means [8]. "Mood," as represented along a "positive/negative" or "pleasant/unpleasant" dimension, refers to a more long-term mind-set that changes gradually [8]. Furthermore, mood responses are not as strong as would be expected when referring.

For the current study, we treated "emotion" as comprising three psychological states: "emotion," "affect," and "mood." We defined emotion as, "subjective experiences and actions, which are caused by changes in bodily responses, including facial expressions and physiological reactions."

2.2   Emotion and Body Perception

In the field of cognitive science, numerous researchers argue that changes in bodily and physiological responses can unconsciously evoke an emotion. The basis for these theories is the James-Lange theory [1]. James aptly expressed this phenomenon: "We don't laugh because we're happy - we're happy because we laugh." Many studies verify the theory. For example, the facial feedback hypothesis indicates that changes in facial expressions affect emotional experience: smiling enhances pleasant feelings while diminishing unpleasant feelings [9]. Many works based on the James-Lange theory demonstrate that changes in physiological states affect feelings. For example, a pleasant feeling is evoked by smiling and by only seeing smiley faces [10]. Facial expression has greatly effect on what emotion evokes regardless of the facial expression is created consciously or unconsciously [11]. This indicates that the unconscious physiological change in the motion of muscles evokes a specific emotion. As other example, Valins et al. shows that cognition of false heart rate affects how participants are attracted to a woman in a picture [12].

There are some engineering studies for evoking emotion by making a user feel like own body changes. For instance, Fukushima et al. proposed an interface that tries to enhance a "chilly" feeling by reproducing a feeling that raises body hair while watching a movie that induces surprise [4]. Yoshida et al. showed that having to recognize minute computer-generated facial changes could evoke pleasant or unpleasant feelings and suggests the possibility that evoked feelings influences a user's preferences [5]. Sakurai et al. propose methods to evoke plural emotions using some tactile stimuli that have a huge similarity to various physiological changes [6, 7].

On the other hand, the two-factor theory of emotion, advocated by Schachter et al., states that changes in bodily responses can be related to several emotions; thus, discreet emotions cannot be completely determined by changes in bodily responses [2]. Recognizing changes in bodily responses, such as nervousness, sedation, raised heart rate, elevated blood pressure, or tremors, referred to as the "attribution of causality," determines the type of emotion experienced. Therefore, different emotions would evoked according to how people interpret their own environments, including situations when similar circumstances and bodily responses arise [13].

General approaches used in previous studies mainly try to evoke emotion by changing body image through generating and regulating virtual physiological changes. Using these methods, it is required to provide extraneous sensory stimuli that resemble bodily responses without discomfort. It would be a problem if these stimuli do not mimic changes that would occur in one's body, as the aimed emotions will not be evoked. In addition, when trying to evoke the aimed emotion by varying the presented stimulus, there are two key issues: the change in physiological state is not recognized, or the change in state is recognized, but is not attributed to the target emotion. This can make it difficult to definitively evoke an emotion.

In response to previous studies, our approach lets the cause of a physiological change attribute in intentional movement (arising of a sense of ownership) firstly. This has persons clearly perceive that the attribution of causality of the physiological change shifts from the intentional movement to aimed emotion as a side effect of unconscious change of external situation that is not intended (switching attribution of causality). Our approach addresses the ambiguity of the causal attribution by replacing the attribution.

2.3   Body Image Construction via Integration of Internal and External Senses

What an emotion evokes is determined based on perceived body image, which is not necessarily the same as real bodily condition. The body image is constructed depending on how various senses integrate. The internal senses are to know own body. These include visceral and somatic sensations (i.e. deep and cutaneous senses.) The body that is perceived through the internal senses based on somatic sensory is the representation of the physical position that is referred to as "body schema" [14, 15]. On the other hand, the representation of the body is not always perceived based on only body schema. For example, to grasp the position or movement of viscera and muscles is very difficult even if we know these organs exist inside own body. In order to infer such physical condition, external senses complements the internal senses. The external senses are specific senses to perceive outside of body, which includes visual and auditory sensations. For instance, although we cannot grasp own face or back directly, we can grasp these body sites. The representation of own body, which is perceived subjectively, is termed "body image" by combination of internal and external senses [15].

The body image is free from physically restriction. What is not actual body is sometimes contained in the body image [16, 17]. Conversely, actual body is not perceived as own body in some cases [18]. The scope that is perceived as own body is determined depending on senses of ownership and agency [19]. The sense of ownership is a feeling that the thing belongs own body, for example "This is my body." The sense of agency is a feeling that the agent of action is one's owns self, for example "I manipulate this." The thing that is not actual body is perceived as a part of own body when these senses arise in the thing. It is clarified that synchronization of the internal senses that perceive own physiological changes and external senses that perceive the changes of outside of body arise senses of ownership and agency in the external thing temporally and spatially without a feeling of strangeness [16].

Using the finding, we propose a method for evoking a specific emotion by giving recognition of a change in an extended body as the causal attribution of actual specific physiological change after giving perception of the external object as a part of own body. Our approach utilizes bodily responses that change both passively and actively. In our approach, firstly, a system constructed that actual physiological condition fed back to the situation of outside of body. This system makes a person understand intentional controlling the physiological condition alter the outside of body. At this time, the physiological change is attributed to one's intentional action, and senses of ownership and agency arise in the outside of body. After this, the correspondence between the physiological condition and the situation of the outside of body is altered at aimed timing for evoking the emotion. This alternation of the correspondence makes the person feel like controlling the situation of outside of body is difficult though s/he has controlled the outside of body. When the emotion is to be evoked, this feedback system variegates the correspondence between the physiological change and the situation of outside of body. This change in the correspondence makes it hard to control one's own bodily response (in this case, respiration), even if the individual feels s/he can control respiration at will. Since this cognitive change gives rise to a recognition that the physiological change occurs due to active or passive action, the feedback system makes the user aware of the possibility that the cause for the change in bodily response was altered (replacing the causal attribution) (Fig. 1).

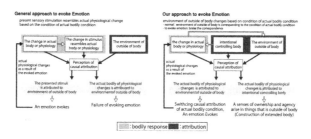

Fig. 1 General approach of previous studies and our approach (created based on [2])

The main difference between previous studies and our approach is whether causal attribution is considered. A sense of discomfort within a sensory stimuli resemble physiological changes have become a problem, since approaches from previous studies needed to provide sensory stimuli passively to evoke changes in actual physiological changes. However, our approach can solve problem of such an uncomfortable feeling, since our approach forms a process of inferring the conscious control of a physiological change. A loss of a sense of ownership and agency creates an unconscious change in physiological changes both actively and passively.

Considering causal attribution in this process for evoking emotion, our approach also could the target emotion at specify timing. This is because the time needed to replace the causal attribution can adapt to the adjustment of the time required to alter the correspondence between the bodily condition and the situation of outside of body.

In this paper, we focused on respiration as a consciously controllable physiological changes and a tense feeling as the emotional response related to respiration. This method evokes a tense feeling by alternating the correspondence between the intentionally controlled respiratory phase and changes in the external condition associated with respiration.

3   Evoking Emotion by Extending Body Image

In order to investigate feasibility of a method for evoking emotion by switching causal attribution, we make an interactive device named "Interactonia Balloon." This apparatus evokes and enhances the tense feeling by shift the perceived causal attribution of respiratory phase using a balloon (Fig. 2). In this section, we describe the Interactonia Balloon's design.

Fig. 2 Interactonia balloon

3.1 Definition of the Feeling of Tension from Respiratory Condition

A tense feeling is an emotion defined as a psychological state that braces for a motivated action [20]. The tense feeling results in some physiological changes such as sudation, dry throat, elevated heart rate, and changes in respiration [21]. Sudation, dry throat, heart rate cannot be consciously controlled, since they are automatic physiological response. Conversely, respiration can be both an automatic and volitional physiological reaction. Respiration is also interrelated mutually with psychological and physiological phenomenon. Some emotions can be elicited by changes in breathing rate, and certain emotions can influence the rate of respiration.

The tense feelings have a close relationship with respiration [22, 23]. Tense feelings can cause shallow and rapid breathing or the cessation of breathing in extreme circumstances. Thus, unconscious breathing can evoke tense feelings depending on how an individual evaluates the situation they find themselves in.

3.2 System Design

Evoking a Tense Feeling by Controlling Respiration. Since a tense feeling tension can be rephrased as a smothering feeling, having trouble breathing could easily become a way to evoke tension. The Interactonia Balloon lets a person recognized a balloon as his/her own extended body through consciously controlling respiration firstly. Next, the apparatus alter the movement of a balloon in midstream for leading a tense feeling to evoke when suffocation feeling is brought to the person due to the controlling breathing. Following through with these steps, the attribution of causality of the smothering feeling switches from consciously controlling respiration to unconscious change of the extended body and a tense feeling evokes.

Interaction Design for Evoking a Tense Feeling. This apparatus utilizes a balloon in order to interact in order to evoke a tense feeling. The balloon has two functions: One of the functions is inducing consciousness of controlling respiration actively. The first thought that comes to mind for inflating a balloon is to breathe into the balloon. Based on this expectation, the balloon acts as a reminder that respiration is actively involved in the process.

Another function is an extended body of the user for evoking a tense feeling by creating a sense of ownership in the balloon. The action of the balloon corresponding to respiration is paradoxical. The user can inflate the balloon by intentionally controlling his/her own respiration, if this correspondence is understood. In this situation, labored breathing attributed to the user's conscious. Besides, the senses of ownership and agency arise in the balloon, if the user understands the correspondence between respiration condition and the movement of the balloon and how control the balloon as intended. Conversely, when the balloon keeps inflating, the correspondence changes because it becomes difficult to get air out of the balloon if the user holds his/her breath. This change in the correspondence switches the perception that the user is controlling the balloon, producing the perception that the balloon controls the user. Then, there is paradoxical movement of the balloon resulting in impatience about not being able to inflate the balloon, and the potential for breaking the balloon. This obscures the correspondence between the respiratory phase and the balloon. This leads to an increased feeling that the user cannot control the balloon. This change in causal attribution is recognized, and the balloon evokes and enhances a tense feeling (Fig. 3).

Fig. 3 Interaction design of interactonia balloon for evoking tense feeling

3.3 System Configuration

Figure 4 shows the system configuration of the interactonia balloon. This system of consists of a respiration detection unit, an air control unit, and an output unit. The respiratory detection unit (Fig. 5) put under the nose detects a user's respiration. To detect respiration, we use a method that employs a temperature sensor in reference [24] to the system used in. When a user exhales through the nose, temperature increases because the air heated by the body that is blown out through the nose flows into the detection unit. In contrast, when the user inhales through the nose, the temperature in the detection unit decreases because the air within the room is cool as it flows into the detection unit. However, holding one's breath keeps the temperature within the device constant since the air in the detection unit does not transfer.

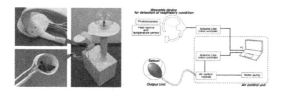

Fig. 4 System configuration

In order to amplify the change in temperature around the temperature sensor within this unit, resistors are placed on the device between the temperature sensor and the user's nose. The heat created by electric current from the resistors is utilized as a heater. If temperature change in a given period is greater than a certain level, the system deems

Fig. 5 Respiration detection method and obtained respirogram using the method

that a person is either exhaling or inhaling. In contrast, if the change is less than a certain level, the system deems that the person is holding their breath. Figure 5 shows the respiration curve that illustrates the above-mentioned method for detecting respiration.

A photo-interrupter is attached to the internal left temporal region of the wearable device in order to detect whether the device is actually being worn. When the device is being worn, a motor pump in the air control unit turns on. Conversely, when the device is not being worn, the motor pump turns off, and the air comes out of the balloon. The output unit consists of a balloon and a plastic capsule covering the balloon. The air control unit controls an air pump to inflate or deflate a balloon within an output unit based on the respiratory condition. A pump forces air into the balloon within an output unit and lets the balloon grow bigger when the wearable device is worn, detecting that breath is being held. In contrast, when the pump stops, the air flows back into the air tube, and the balloon deflates when inhalation is detected.

4 Investigation of a Method for Evoking Emotion by Switching an Attribution of Causality of Changing in Extended Body

4.1 Feedback Given Regarding Interactonia Balloon at an Exhibition

We exhibited the Interactonia Balloon at Siggraph Asia 2012, held in Singapore, from November 28 to December 1 2012 (Fig. 6.) During the exhibition, over 100 people visited the exhibit.

Fig. 6 Exhibiting the interactonia balloon at siggraph Asia 2012

Most visitors were told how to inflate the balloon before the exhibition. We had visitors wear the device and breathe normally. After visitors verified whether breathing was detected in a normal way, we had them play with the balloon. After a visitor was done with the demonstration, we explained the concept of this apparatus, regardless of whether they could inflate the balloon or not. If we did not explain how to play with the balloon, several people tried to inflate the balloon by exhaling.

Feedback about the apparatus can be classified into three major categories: (1) visitors felt tension, (2) visitors did not feel the tension, and (3) visitors could not work the balloon. Detailed feedback is mentioned below.

Group 1: Visitors Who Could Feel Tension. We obtained the following feedback from participants who said they felt tension.

- I surely felt tension when I kept holding my breath and the balloon kept inflating.
- It was a little bit scary, since I could not understand why the balloon inflated when I held my breath, even though this was explained to me beforehand.
- When the capsule was filled with the balloon, I felt tense and impatient, and my breathing was disordered.
- I was relieved when the balloon deflated.
- We control our own breathing to be released from a tense feeling, in most cases. However, the balloon requires that we breathe to bring about a tense feeling. This is interesting.

There were several cases where other visitors watched a person playing with the balloon. The onlookers remarked as follows:

- I felt tension, too.
- Watching others play made me feel tense.
- I could not understand what was happening by just observing.

Thus, the visitors felt tension and made remarks related to the paradoxical action of the balloon becoming the cause for evoking a tense feeling.
These visitors also laughed after playing with the balloon, regardless of whether they played or watched and whether they were acquainted or not.

Group 2: Visitors Who Did Not Feel Tense. We obtained the following feedback from visitors who said they did not feel tense.

- The inflation of the balloon did not cause me to feel any tension.
- Just merely controlling my breathing did not cause me to feel tension.
- I felt tension not by operating the balloon but by watching others playing with the balloon.
- There was a lack of tension because the exhibition hall was noisy.
- I did not feel that the balloon synchronized with my respiration.

Based on this feedback, the inflation of the balloon did not appear to facilitate tense feelings among these individuals.

Group 3: Visitors Who Could Not Operate the System. Some visitors could not inflate the balloon. They made the following remarks:

- I thought that the balloon was not working because my respiration decreased.
- I regret that the balloon did not work as I expected.

There were special cases were people gave up if they could not understand the timing of changes to the balloon and respiration after several seconds.

4.2   Discussion

Participants belonging to Group 1 remarked that tense feelings were evoked by a synergistic influence of intentionally controlling their breathing and changes to the balloon. In contrast, participants belonging to Group 2 remarked that they did not understand that their respiration and changes to the balloon were related. Additionally, their feedback suggested that the surrounding environment influenced their causal attribution to a greater degree than changes to the balloon. It appears that tense feelings were evoked by activity from the balloon "controlling" their own breathing.

As concerns the laughing of all participants belonging to Group 1 persons watched the experience of the participants after playing with the balloon, we postulated that their laughter was a way to relax the tension Thus, it is possible that laughter was brought about once the evoked physical tension had been reduced. Kant said, "laughter is an affection arising from a strained expectation being suddenly reduced to nothing" [25]. Based on this theory, we hypothesized that an evoked tense feeling due to actively controlling respiration reaches a certain threshold, and laughter is brought about once an individual is free from that evoked tense feeling.

We observed that holding one's breath and inflating the balloon caused visitors in Group 1 to feel tension, even if they knew that the apparatus worked in this way. This indicates that inflation of the balloon fulfilled its function of replacing the causal attribution related to evoking a tense feeling. The balloon facilitated a paradoxical outcome whereby the balloon performed a certain function that caused visitors to feel a loss of autonomous control.

Some participants could not manipulate the balloon as we intended. It is possible that these individuals had a problem in accurately detecting their own respiration. The temperature of the air conditioner in the exhibition venue was very low, and air current within the venue was variable. Therefore, even though these individuals held their own breath, it was difficult to detect changes in airflow. Besides, there were some cases where the variation of an individual's breathing habits prevented detection of respiration (e.g., breathing stops for a second when switching between inhalation and exhalation). In these cases, the respiratory phase was not correctly detected. It is possible that such false detections made it difficult for some participants to correctly experience the apparatus. One way to solve this issue would be to assess any potential technical problems. However, it could just be the case that these individuals did not find value in the demonstration. Participants belonging to Group 3 finished playing with the balloon in less than a minute, whereas people from Groups 1 and 2 played with the balloon for at least 5-10 min. These results suggest that in order to maintain a participant's attention with this demonstration, synchronization needs to happen rapidly (i.e., in first several seconds).

Based on the aforementioned results, we suggest that a tense feeling was evoked among participants due to the following: (1) a loss of a sense of belonging to one's own self, (2) the cause of changes to one's own bodily response was attributed to changes in the external environment, and (3) after being able to control their own bodily response, the participants felt that they could manipulate the external situation. However, the paradoxical actions of the balloon made participants lose a sense of belonging to their own self, and differences in individual recognition were not presently investigated. Therefore, further studies are needed to validate this measure in a more experimental setting, in order to examine how changing the external condition is associated with changes in bodily responses.

5   Conclusion

In this paper, we proposed a method for evoking and enhanced emotion by switching attribution of causality of a specific physiological change through giving perception of extended body. Concretely, we made an apparatus that evokes a tense feeling by shift causal attribution of respiratory condition from conscious controlling to movement of balloon. Feedback from participants who played with the apparatus suggested a need to create a training regimen that allows a user to feel like they are manipulating the external situation by controlling their own bodily reactions. For this, a feeling of loss of control and attribution of changes to bodily responses to external conditions for emotion evocation is warranted.

Based on these results, we will examine how changing an external condition associated with changing a bodily response replaces a sense of actions belonging to one's own self to influence emotion evocation in a more controlled experimental setting. To better explain the process of evoking emotions through the validation of our proposed method, we need to understand the interactive components of the apparatus and the types of bodily responses elicited. The results of the current paper suggest a feasible way for switching causal attributions by altering the correspondence between variability in physiological changes and a condition of outside of body. Conversely, understanding how to alter causal attributions is not yet fully understood. Future studies will need to better assess methods for evoking emotion aimed at the timing needed to replace causal attributions.

References

1. Schachter, S., Singer, J.: Cognitive, social and physiological determinants of emotional state. Psychol. Rev. **69**(5), 379–399 (1962)
2. James, W.: The Principles of Psychology, vol. 2. Dover Publications, New York (1950)
3. Valins, S.: Cognitive effects of false heart-rate feedback. J. Pers. Soc. Psychol. **4**(4), 400–408 (1966)
4. Fukushima, S., Kajimoto, H.: Chilly chair: facilitating an emotional feeling with artificial piloerection. In: SIGGRAPH 2012, p. 1 (2012). Article 5
5. Yoshida, S., Sakurai, S., Narumi, T., Tanikawa, T., Hirose, M.: Manipulation of an emotional experience by real-time deformed facial feedback, In: AH2013, pp.35–42 (2013)

6. Sakurai, S., Katsumura, T., Narumi, T., Tanikawa, T., Hirose, M.: Evoking emotions in a story using tactile sensations as pseudo-body responses with contextual cues. In: Yamamoto, S. (ed.) HCI 2014, Part I. LNCS, vol. 8521, pp. 241–250. Springer, Heidelberg (2014)

7. Sakurai, S., Ban, Y., Katsumura, T., Narumi, T., Tanikawa, T. and Hirose, M.: Communious Mouse: A Mouse Interface to Experience Emotions in Remarks on the Web by Extending and Modulating One's Body Image. SA 2014 E-Tech, Article 4, 3 pages (2014)

8. Batson, C.D., Shaw, L.L., Oleson, K.C.: Differentiating affect, mood and emotion: toward functionally based conceptual distinctions. Rev. Pers. soc. psychol. 13, 294–326 (1992)

9. Tomkins, S.: Affect, imagery and consciousness: the Positive affects, vol. 1. Tavistock, London (1962)

10. Strack, F., Martin, F., Stepper, S.: Inhibiting and facilitating conditions of the human smile: a non-obtrusive test of the facial feedback hypothesis. J. Pers. Soc. Psychol. 54(5), 768–777 (1998)

11. Kleinke, C.K., et al.: Effects of self-generated facial expressions on mood. J. Pers. Soc. Psychol. 74(1), 272–279 (1998)

12. Valins, S.: Cognitive effects of false heart-rate feedback. J. Pers. Soc. Psychol. 4(4), 400–408 (1996)

13. Dutton, D., Aron, A.: Some evidence for heightened sexual attraction under conditions of high anxiety. J. Pers. Soc. Psychol. 30(4), 510–517 (1974)

14. Head, H., Holmes, G.: Sensory disturbances from cerebral lesions. Brain 34(2–3), 102 (1911)

15. Schwoebel, J.: Coslett: H.B: Evidence for Multiple, Distinct Representations of the Human Body. J. Cogn. Neurosci. 4(17), 543–553 (2005)

16. Botvinick, M., Cohen, J.: Rubber hands 'feel' touch that eyes see. Nature 391, 756 (1998)

17. Armel, K.C., Ramachandran, V.: S: Projecting sensations to external objects: evidence from skin conductance response. Proc. Roy. Soc. B Biol. Sci. 270, 1499–1506 (2003)

18. Holmes, E.A., Brown, R.J., Mansell, W., Fearon, R.P., Hunter, E.C.M., Frasquilho, F., Oakley, D.A.: Are there two qualitatively distinct forms of dissociation? Rev. Some Clin. Implications Clin. Psychol. Rev. 25(1), 1–23 (2005)

19. Jeannerod, M.: The mechanism of self-recognition in humans. Behav. Brain Res. 142, 1–15 (2003)

20. Longman English Dictionary Online. http://www.ldoceonline.com/dictionary/tense_1. Accessed 28 February 2015

21. Hubert, W., de Jong-Meyer, R.: Psychophysiological response patterns to positive and negative film stimuli. Journal of Biological Psychology 31(1), 73–93 (1990)

22. Yu, M.C., Ko, J.C., Lin, C.Y., Chang, C.H., Yang, Y.H., Lin, S.C., Chen, J.S., Chang, K.J., Kuo, S.W., Hsu, S.C., Hung, Y.P.: Multimedia feedback for improving breathing habit. Proc. Ubi-Media Comput. 2008, 267–272 (2008)

23. Fried, R., Grimaldi, J.: The Psychology And Physiology Of Breathing In Behavioral Medicine, Clinical Psychology And Psychiatry. Plenum Press, New York (1993)

24. Yamada, T., Yokoyama, S., Tanikawa, T., Hirota, K., Hirose, M.: Wearable olfactory display: using odor in outdoor environment. In Proc. the IEEE VR 119–106, 2006 (2006)

25. Kant, I.: The Critique of Judgement (Bernard, J.H.), 2nd edn. Macmillan & Co, London (1914)

Development of Tactile and Gestural Displays
for Navigation, Communication,
and Robotic Control

Anna Skinner[⊠], Jack Vice, and Lisa Baraniecki

AnthroTronix, Inc., Silver Spring, MD, USA
{anna.skinner,jack.vice,lisa.baraniecki}@atinc.com

Abstract. Cognitive demands on dismounted Soldiers are ever increasing. This is an investigation into using gestural controls and a tactile display vest to reduce cognitive, physical, and temporal demands as relevant to covert communications and robot control. Data was collected on 31 Soldiers for this experiment-based evaluation consisting of task demands of a typical rural reconnaissance patrol deconstructed into specific tasks involving a platoon leader role, a squad leader role, and a robot controller role. Results found that use of an instrumented glove and a tactile display vest was associated with a higher average percentage and faster average speed of signal detections when compared to traditional hand and arm signals. Glove-based robot control was also compared with traditional methods and evaluated.

Keywords: Human interface · Information management · Robotic control

1 Introduction

1.1 Background

Soldier Visual and Cognitive Workload. Dismounted soldiers are constantly exposed to heavy cognitive and visual workloads, especially during navigation and patrol, and under conditions of high stress and time pressure. (Mitchell et al., 2004; Mitchell, 2009; Mitchell and Brennan, 2009a, 2009b; Pomranky and Wojciechowski, 2007). Additionally, a review of emerging technologies for infantry Soldier combat teams during the Army Expeditionary Warrior Experiment included aerial and ground vehicles with sensor arrays, small stationary sensors, more robust communication capabilities, and improved visual capabilities encompassing weapon sights, binoculars, night vision, and targeting aids (Scalsky et al., 2009; U.S. Army Evaluation Center, 2013). This provides evidence that cognitive task demands on dismounted Soldiers are increasing.

There are also increased physical and temporal demands placed on the Soldiers as the complexity of team communications increases. As Soldiers gain and control additional assets (command and control, robotic, etc.), the issue of weight and bulk presents itself as the additional assets must be carried. Current control interfaces for unmanned vehicles will often significantly increase the weight and quantity of equipment carried by the dismounted Soldier. Additionally, the controls and displays

© Springer International Publishing Switzerland 2015
S. Yamamoto (Ed.): HIMI 2015, Part I, LNCS 9172, pp. 445–457, 2015.
DOI: 10.1007/978-3-319-20612-7_43

must be easy to understand and use. The following is an exploration of incorporating advanced concepts into smaller lightweight wearable displays and controls that reduce cognitive, physical, and temporal demands as they relate to dismounted Soldier performance.

Hands-Free Covert Communications. In order for Soldier teams to work effectively, Soldier communication is essential. Communications should be rapid, concise, and immediately understood within and across teams. However, using handheld communication devices presents some challenges. They often distract a leader's visual attention away from the tactical battlefield environment and can sometimes hinder their ability to use their weapons or increase their response time to target engagement when transitioning from the device to the weapon. If the communication is speech-based, it is no longer functional in noisy environments. These constraints show that there are many scenarios in which hand-held devices for communication are less than optimal, however Soldier communication will always be necessary.

The use of hand and arm signals has served as a fundamental form of communication among Soldiers. Dismounted Soldiers in the field will utilize an established set of hand and arm signals to communicate with others in order to maintain noise discipline (e.g., when approaching an objective) or when noise levels are elevated to a point where radio or voice communication is not possible. These hand signals are standard practice and most military personnel are familiar with them. They can be found in documented sources such as the U.S. Army Field Manual No. 21-60 and U.S. Marine Corps Rifle Squad Manual (FMFM 6-5). Additionally, mission scenarios might dictate further requirements, such as a need for covert operations (e.g., low noise and/or electronic transmissions) or combat operations may be characterized by high stress, high time pressure, high noise, low visibility, and/or night operations. Such commands will typically be relayed from one team member to the next, not via direct communication from the Soldier initiating the command to the Soldier who is the intended recipient. This is typically due to the communication recipient being positioned outside of the line of sight of the initiating Soldier. Relaying the commands from one team member to another requires aural and visual attention to receive the commands as well as excess time. This point highlights a need for a technology-based alternative to traditional hand and arm signals.

Glove-Based Gestures. Wearable instrumented gloves present an effective solution for a technology-based solution for effective hand and arm signal communication. This approach is the most commonly used approach for wearable instrumented systems for robotic control. The glove concept is most congruent for many work situations where operators may already have to wear gloves.

Tactile Display Technology. The reception of signals by individuals beyond the LOS has been proven effective via a torso-mounted vest containing an array of vibrating tactors. This tactile modality has been proven to be a reliable and covert means of conveying critical information during infantry tactical operations (Van Erp 2005). When directly compared with visual displays, tactile displays have been identified to increase performance in select circumstances (Elliot et al., 2009). Tactile display is also effective under conditions of high cognitive workload. For navigation in field evaluations, torso-mounted tactile displays have been proven effective (Pettitt et al., 2006). When integrated with GPS, these displays enable Soldiers to navigate in low visibility conditions, hands-free (allowing the Soldier to hold his/her weapon) and eyes-free (i.e., allowing focused attention to surroundings rather than a visual display) (Elliot et al., 2011; Elliot and Redden, 2013).

1.2   Research Objectives

This evaluation serves to assess concepts and capabilities related to the use of an integrated gestural glove and a tactile vest for Soldier communications. The system, Communication-based Operational Multi-Modal Automated Navigation Device (COMMAND), integrates an instrumented glove for automated gesture-based communication and control, a tactile display vest, and a GPS-enabled ruggedized handheld computer. The study objectives are to (a) identify issues pertaining to Solder use (e.g., operational relevance) and (b) evaluate usability (human factors assessment) of system components and the system as a whole. This evaluation was situated around task demands characteristics of a rural reconnaissance mission scenario requiring inter-Soldier communications and robot control.

2   COMMAND Communication System

The COMMAND system components include a ruggedized instrumented glove, GPS-enabled ruggedized handheld computer, and tactile display vest.

2.1   Instrumented Gloves for Hand and Arm Gestures

The gesture recognition gloves used for signal communication among Soldiers consisted of a standard tactical glove with accelerometers embedded within each fingers, as well as an accelerometer, gyroscope, and digital compass embedded in the back of the hand.

2.2   Handheld Computer

Data processing and signal communication were performed by two TDS Nomad GPS-enabled ruggedized handheld computers (one carried by the individual generating hand signals and the other carried by the individual receiving communications via the haptic vest). The handheld computers included touchscreen and visual displays, and Android operating system, custom gesture recognition software and tactor controller software, as well as embedded GPS and wireless communication capabilities.

2.3   Tactile Vest

The tactile vest worn by the individual receiving communications consisted of a cus-tom-made, ruggedized, adjustable harness with six embedded vibrotactile actuators (tactors) on the front interface, six tactors on the back, and eight tactors spaced evenly around the waist.

The vest design was previously developed under an Office of Naval Research (ONR)-funded effort, and consisted of a custom tactor solution, using original manufacturer tactor motors and a custom electronics board. It was found that the Precision MicroDrive 310-101 provided optimal performance within a small form factor and provided a cost-effective price point. The board configuration allowed for the tactor system to operate for approximately 3–5 h.

2.4 Gestural and Tactile Cues for Covert Communication

Four hand and arm signals were used to test the COMMAND system. One of the four signals ("freeze") followed standard Army guidelines while the other three ("rally", "double time", "danger area") were created to demonstrate the generative capability of the signals used in the COMMAND system.

3 Robot Control System

3.1 Robot Control Glove and Gestures

The robot control system used an instrumented glove for gestural control. The glove selected was the AcceleGlove, a commercial off-the-shelf (COTS) instrumented glove developed by AnthroTronix (ATinc). The glove was used within the robotic control tasks and was compared with a traditional gamepad controller.

The AcceleGlove consists of a nylon glove with the finger tips exposed, with accelerometers embedded within each finger and on the back of the hand. The robot control tasks consisted of maneuvering the robot through a series of paths and obstacles, driving both forward and backward, as well as approaching an object, coming as close to it as possible without coming in contact. Therefore, the necessary controls included forward, reverse, left, right, and stop. Forward control was achieved by angling the hand downward; reverse control was achieved by angling the hand upward; left turning was achieved by flexing the index finger; and right turning was achieved by flexing the middle finger. Since the robot was within view of the participants at all times during task completion, visual feedback was provided by observing the robot directly, rather than via a visual or haptic feedback display.

3.2 Baseline Robot Controller

The traditional controller used for comparison with the AcceleGlove during the robot control tasks was a COTS gamepad with thumb joysticks and binary buttons.

3.3 Robot

The robot used for the experiment was a dual tracked, skid steer mobile robot developed as a precursor to the Packbot® series of robots manufactured by iRobot®. The robot contains motorized "flipper style" arms that can be used to navigate the robot over uneven terrain that other robots might find difficult. Movement is provided by three 90-W direct current motors, which independently power the robot's tracks, allowing for zero-point turning. For this experiment, the robot was fitted with a class 1 Bluetooth® module to allow for wireless communication with the operator control unit (OCU).

4 Experiment Method

4.1 Participants

Participants were recruited from the 11 Bravo (Infantry) or similar military occupational specialty (MOS). Initially, 36 Soldiers voluntarily and fully consented to participation as required by Code of Federal Regulations (CFR) 219 (1991) and Army Regulation (AR) 70-25 (1990). The investigators adhered to the policies for the protection of human subjects as prescribed in AR 70-25. All participants signed a Volunteer Agreement Informed Consent Form. Participants did not receive any compensation for participating in this investigation.

Data was collected on 31 of the originally consenting 36 Soldiers due to attrition from external factors (i.e. weather, equipment). Twelve Soldiers were from an Explosive Ordnance Disposal (EOD) MOS and had extensive experience with robot control. Six Soldiers were from an active Infantry unit (3rd Infantry Division). The remaining Soldiers were form the Officer Candidate School; some had previous military experience while some did not. Participants included 25 males and 6 females. Twenty-eight were right-handed or ambidextrous.

4.2 Experiment Scenario Tasks

For this experiment-based evaluation, the task demands of a typical rural reconnaissance patrol were deconstructed into specific tasks in order to better structure the data collection and performance measurement process. Task demands were separated into two data collection stations, one that included a platoon leader (PL) role and a squad leader (SL) role, and another that focused on a robot controller (RC) role.

The PL role was relatively passive but enabled the participant to use the COMMAND communications unit. The PL walked behind the SL and used the instrumented glove to send communications to the SL, who in turn received the signals via the tactile vest array. In the baseline manipulation, the PL performed traditional hand and arm signals, and the SL would perceive and recognize them visually (e.g., by turning and looking).

The RC role had the participant wear the instrumented gesture recognition glove to control robot movement and performance through four robot control courses to assess different robot control maneuvers.

Prior to each station event, participant trained with the equipment. Each Soldier was introduced to the equipment and demonstrated understanding and use of the equipment prior to the experiment session. Training evaluation information was collected during data feedback sessions.

Station 1: Covert Communication During IMT and Tactical Movement. Station 1 compared the glove/tactile system to traditional hand and arm signals during tasks associated with Soldier movement. Data collected at this station included (a) whether the Soldier perceived a signal, (b) the time taken to notice a signal, and (c) accuracy of signal interpretation. Additionally, during the tactical movement phase, the number of flags noticed by the Soldiers was also collected.

Individual Movement Technique (IMT) Phase. Soldiers used the two systems to communicate while performing standard IMT maneuvers, such as walking, climbing, and crawling. The Soldier acting in the SL role would perform the movements as the PL Soldier would follow behind the SL and provide either glove-based tactile or traditional hand and arm signals. When the traditional hand and arm signals were administered, the SL Soldiers were required to visually scan for the hand and arm signals given by the PL. It is obvious that many hand signals generated by the assigned leader can easily be missed by the designated point man. However, for the glove-based condition for IMT maneuvers, signals given by the assigned leader were able to be perceived by the designated point man immediately and without turning around.

Tactical Movement. During the tactical movement phase, one experienced data collector guided the SL Soldier through 400 m of wooded terrain. The data collector provided the glove-based signals while another recorded performance data. Each SL traversed 200 m using the glove system, and 200 m with traditional hand and arm signals. The SL walked ahead of the person generating the signals. As with the IMT Phase, using the instrumented glove and vest enabled the hand signals generated by the PL to be perceived by the SL immediately and without turning around whilst navigating in the wooded terrain and looking for hidden flag markers. Without the glove and vest, the SL was required to turn around while navigating and searching for flags in order to detect the hand signals.

Station 2: Robot Control. Station 2 was used to evaluate robot control performance using the instrumented glove against a more traditional handheld baseline controller. Collected data included (a) time and (b) driving errors. Participants were asked to navigate through each of the following robot control tasks:

1. Zigzag course. The robot was maneuvered between two engineering tapes outlining a zigzag pattern. The operator was required to keep the robot within the tape while accomplishing the course.
2. Narrow gap course. The robot was maneuvered through a gap created by engineering tape, while avoiding small flags that were situated on and around the direct route. The robot was maneuvered from start to finish, going forward, then from the finish point back to the beginning, by going backwards.
3. Figure-8 course. The robot was maneuvered around logs situated in a figure-8 pattern. The robot had to move around the left of one log, then the right of the next log, and so on, turning around the last one, and continuing the pattern back, going backwards.
4. Movement to contact. The robot was maneuvered forward towards a pole and would stop as close as possible. It was then directed backwards, to another pole, also to stop as close as possible.

4.3   Experiment Design

Orientation. Each Soldier participant was briefed on the purpose, procedures, and any risks involved in their participation. They were provided with copies of the Informed Consent Form to ensure the voluntary nature of their participation. Participants were given an opportunity to review the experiment objectives, have any of their questions answered by the investigators, and were then asked to sign he consent form indicating their informed voluntary consent to participate. All Soldiers agreed to participate. A demographic questionnaire was then administered to obtain pertinent information on his/her background.

Each of the Soldiers was assigned a unique roster number based on groups of 6 participants per day. It was ensured that each Solider would participate at each station, for each role, in a counterbalanced order.

Post-Session Evaluations. In order to obtain Soldier feedback, participants filled out feedback questionnaires after performing each station role. The questions asked the ease of use, perception, and interpretation of the COMMAND system components. Soldiers were also asked to provide ratings of workload using the National Aeronautics and Space Administration task load index (NASA TLX), ratings of operational utility for various combat missions, and additional open-ended comments, suggestions, and issues relevant to performance of the system in the field.

5   Results

5.1   Covert Communications

Detection of the four communication signals provided by the glove to a tactile vest was compared to visual recognition of the signals administered via traditional hand and arm signals. Soldiers used both system types during two performance scenarios, IMT maneuvers and tactical movement. These scenarios are described in more detail in the Experiment Method section.

Detection Rate, Accuracy, and Time (N = 31). Table 1 shows mean signal detection rate, time (seconds), and accuracy rate for the glove/tactile vest and the hand and arm signal conditions, by course type (IMT versus tactical movement). The detection rate represents the percentage of commands recognized by the Soldier, time represents the time to detect the command, and the accuracy rate represents the percentage of detected signals that were correctly identified. In some runs, only two of four signals were working (problems were associated with the 'danger' and 'double-time' signals for five of the first ten Soldiers).

Using the repeated-measures analysis of variance (ANOVA) program by Statistical Package for the Social Sciences, specific comparisons within the IMT and tactical movement task demands were analyzed. The F statistic associated with degrees of free-dom (df), the p-value, and the partial eta square measure of effect size (ηp^2) are reported.

Table 1 Mean values for detection rate, time to detect, and accuracy for the glove/tactile vest and the hand-arm condition, during IMT maneuvers and tactical movement.

Course	Glove/Tactile Vest			Hand and Arm		
	Mean Detect (Std. Dev.)	Mean Time (Std. Dev.)	Mean Correct (Std. Dev.)	Mean Detect (Std. Dev.)	Mean Time (Std. Dev.)	Mean Correct (Std. Dev.)
IMT	1.00^a	2.01^a	0.87	0.88^a	3.70^a	0.95
	(0.0)	(0.38)	(0.16)	(0.15)	(0.57)	(0.12)
Tactical Movement	1.00^a	1.89^a	0.95	0.84^a	4.26^a	0.87
	(0.00)	(0.64)	(0.20)	(0.15)	(0.50)	(0.16)

[a]p less than 0.01.

A significant difference was found between glove and hand-arm means for both the IMT condition (F 1, 30 = 20.13, p = 0.00, $\eta\rho^2$ = 0.40) as well as the tactical movement (F 1, 30 = 36.25, p = 0.00, $\eta\rho^2$ = 0.547), where detection rates were higher for the glove/tactile system. There was also a significant difference between the systems in time for detection for IMT maneuvers (F 1, 30 = 214.84, p = 0.00, $\eta\rho^2$ = 0.877) and tactical movement (F 1, 30 = 455.479, p = 0.00, $\eta\rho^2$ = 0.938). However, the differences in accuracy rate were not significant for IMT tasks (F 1, 30 = 3.95, p = 0.056, $\eta\rho^2$ = 0.116) or for tactical movement (F 1, 30 = 0.616, p = 0.439, $\eta\rho^2$ = 0.02).

Breakdowns by Type of IMT Maneuvers. Signals were presented to the Soldiers both during obstacle events (e.g., climbing, crawling, combat roll, running) and between obstacles. Table 2 shows the descriptive statistics for the glove/tactile vest system versus hand-arm signals, for the IMT task and tactical movement demands. There was no difference between the mean detection rate (both 100 %) or mean time for the glove/tactile vest system due to type of task event (i.e., walking versus obstacle events). The percentage of correct identifications was somewhat lower with obstacle events, while with the hand and arm condition, the effect was that of lower detection rates associated with obstacle events.

Differences between the glove/tactile vest system and the hand-arm signals are similar to overall results, in that the glove/tactile vest system was associated with

Table 2 Mean performance measures by system and type of movement

Course	Glove/Tactile Vest			Hand and Arm		
	Mean Detect% (Std.Dev.)	Mean Time (Std. Dev.)	Mean Correct% (Std. Dev.)	Mean Detect% (Std. Dev.)	Mean Time (Std. Dev.)	Mean Correct% (Std. Dev.)
Walking	100	2.03	0.92	0.94	3.46	0.96
	(0.0)	(0.60)	(0.27)	(0.23)	(1.08)	(0.20)
Obstacle	100	1.92	0.85	0.82	3.82	0.94
	(0.0)	(0.60)	(0.36)	(0.39)	(1.19)	(0.23)
Tactical Movement	1.00	1.89	0.95	0.84	4.26	0.87
	(0.00)	(0.64)	(0.20)	(0.15)	(0.50)	(0.16)

higher detection rates and faster times. This breakdown examines the effect of task demand on glove/tactile system.

Effects of Task Demand on Performance Measures.

Time to detect signal. There were no significant differences for the glove system throughout task demand (F 2, 60 = 2.379, p = 0.101, $\eta\rho^2$ = 0.07). The differences between the glove/tactile vest system and the hand-arm signals reflect the same trends found between the IMT and tactical movement tasks.

Effect of task demand on detection rate when using the glove/tactile vest system. There was no difference in detection rate for the glove/tactile vest system. All conditions were associated with 100 % detection.

Accuracy. The differences in time due to task demands were not significant (F 2, 60 = 1.74, p = 0.185, $\eta\rho^2$ = 0.06). The same trends found between the IMT and tactical movement tasks reflect the differences between the glove/tactile vest system and the hand-arm signals (F 3, 66 = 1.18, p = 0.32, $\eta\rho^2$ = 0.05).

Performance by Tactile Signal.

Differences in glove/tactile signal detection due to signal. Signal detection using the glove/tactile vest system was 100 %, regardless of signal, across all task demands.

Differences in glove/tactile signal time to detect, due to signal. Repeated measures ANOVA showed overall significant differences in time to detect due to signal (F 3, 66 = 14.55, p = 0.00, $\eta\rho^2$ = 0.40). Using the Holm's Bonferronni correction for multiple comparisons, all paired comparisons were significantly different, except for the difference between "freeze" and "double-time."

Differences in glove/tactile signal accuracy rate, due to signal. Repeated ANOVA measures showed no overall significant differences in time to detect due to signal.
Impact of task demand on correct identifications of glove/tactile system signals. The detection rates and accuracy rate of each signal were associated by task demand. Accuracy rates remained high regardless of task demand, though rates were somewhat lower when negotiating IMT obstacles.

Number of flags detected. Soldiers detected an average of 10.61 flags with the glove/tactile system (standard deviation = 2.70) and 9.71 flags with the hand-arm signals (standard deviation = 2.77). While the mean number was higher with the glove system, the difference did not meet significance criteria, though it did come close (F 1, 30 = 3.64, p = 0.07, $\eta\rho^2$ = 0.11). There was considerable variance among the Soldiers with regard to this performance.

Perceptions of Workload and Self-Efficacy. Soldiers provided self-reported ratings of workload and self-efficacy for using the glove to send signals and the tactile vest to receive signals. These were provided using the NASA-TLX rating scales. Each scale ranged from 1 (extremely low) to 10 (extremely high). Workload ratings were relatively low for both components, while performance ratings were relatively high. Direct ratings were used as they have been demonstrated as valid when compared to weighted ratings (Hart and Staveland, 1988; Hart, 2006). Soldiers tended to report confusion with the weighted process, which also confounded measures of workload with a measure of self efficacy (i.e., performance scale). For this reason, we kept these constructs separate.

5.2   Robot Control: OCU and Glove-Based Control

Performance of the robot control tasks using the OCU was compared to the Glove-Based Control. Additionally, participants were asked to provide workload ratings using the NASA TLX and their spatial ability scores were compared with their robot controller performance.

Performance Measures. Performance of the tasks was recorded through the mean and standard deviations for time to complete task (in seconds), number of minor errors, and number of major errors. There was no significant difference between the two control methods for time taken to complete the task (F 1, 27 = 1.39, p = 0.25, $\eta\rho^2$ = 0.05). This could be due to the high variance around OCU time (SD = 19.30 for OCU versus 7.82 for glove control). The difference in minor errors was also not significant (F 1, 27 = 2.49, p = 0.13, $\eta\rho^2$ = 0.08). However, the number of major errors associated with the glove system was significantly higher (F 1, 27 = 6.31, p = 0.02, $\eta\rho^2$ = 0.19).

Perceptions of Workload and Performance. Overall, the mean values and standard deviations for NASA-TLX constructs were higher for the glove controller with regard to workload. The differences were significant for mental workload (F 1, 27 = 16.98, p = 0.00, $\eta\rho^2$ = 0.39), physical workload (F 1, 27 = 7.90, p = 0.01, $\eta\rho^2$ = 0.23), time pressure (F 1, 27 = 6.82, p = 0.01, $\eta\rho^2$ = 0.20), effort (F 1, 27 = 15.43, p = 0.00, $\eta\rho^2$ = 0.36), and frustration (F 1, 27 = 16.43, p = 0.00, $\eta\rho^2$ = 0.38). Self-ratings of how well each Soldier thought they performed were also significantly different (F 1, 27 = 8.79, p = 0.01, $\eta\rho^2$ = 0.25), with higher performance ratings associated with the OCU.

Spatial Ability: Robot Control. Participant spatial ability scores did not correlate significantly with any robot controller performance measure. These scores were also analyzed as a covariate in analyses regarding robot controller performance. This factor was not significant for most of the criterion performance values; however, it approached significance for forward movement distance.

6   Discussion

6.1   Glove/Tactile Vest System for Covert Communications

In comparison to traditional hand and arm signals (84 %–88 %), average percentage of signal detections of Soldiers using the instrumented glove with a tactile display was significantly higher. The glove-based signals were also detected significantly faster. This finding was not unexpected, as traditional hand and arm signals presented from behind depend upon the Soldier's ability to periodically look at other team members while also maneuvering through the woods and visually monitoring his surroundings. This situation is common when platoon leaders or point persons are placed between two squads in formation. The differences between the glove-based systems and the hand-arm signals are more pronounced during tactical movement and IMT objectives, in comparison to signals presented during walking. Soldiers were also able to interpret the received tactile signals with similar accuracy (87 %–95 %, across task conditions) to that of hand and arm signals. The data also suggested that Soldiers were able to pay more attention to their surrounds while using the glove and tactile vest system. Cognitive workload ratings provided by the soldiers were relatively low for the glove/tactile vest system, ranging from 1.79 to 3.40 on a 10-pt scale.

We are able to assume that the strength of the presented signals was sufficient for percentage, given the high percentage of detected glove-based signals. Interpretation is also dependent on other characteristics of the tactile patterns regarding tactile salience (Hancock et al., in press; Mortimer et al., 2011). It is worth noting that only two to four signals were used; however operator accuracy of tactile signal interpretation was high. This evaluation is a preliminary effort to inform the development of the system during the course of the funded project. Suggested research would include an examination of the characteristics of tactile patterns that would make the signals more easily and correctly interpreted. Additionally, research regarding the number of tactile signals that can be easily training and discriminated is recommended for the effort.

The glove-based system demonstrated performance-based results, however it also demonstrated some limitations. Some of the glove-based cues experienced functionality failures, resulting in Soldiers only experiencing two or three of the four signals. Technical refinement of the system is necessary in order to extend capabilities to provide a greater range of signals with more reliable signaling. Additionally, some soldiers experienced difficulty performing particular gesture(s). This highlights a need for modification of the gestures for ease of execution.

6.2   Gesture-Based Robot Control

Using the glove-based robot control system and a traditional handheld robot controller, Soldiers performed several robot maneuver tasks. The task demands were designed to be difficult and challenging. Although the handheld controller was associated with lower average number of driving errors, the overall glove-based robot control concept was demonstrated as effective. While the handheld controller and glove-based controller were associated with similar times to perform the robot maneuver tasks, the handheld controller displayed greater variability in times across Soldiers; some Soldiers performed much faster while others performed much slower. In contrast, the glove-based controller was associated with less variance in timed performance, even after a short training session. These findings may reflect differences in Soldier experience with handheld controllers. They also suggest that novice operators may more easily learn the glove-based approach, as it is associated with a shorter training time. Further investigation would be necessary in regards to training content, training time, and individual differences.

Soldier perceptions of workload using the NASA-TLX were higher for the glove than the handheld system. These differences were significant for mental, physical, time pressure, effort, and frustration. Self-ratings of performance were also significantly different, with higher ratings for the handheld OCU.

Soldiers with higher spatial ability were associated with somewhat faster times for the handheld controller. In contrast, there was no association between spatial ability and difference in performance times for the glove condition. This suggests that the glove-based approach may be less difficult overall, with regard to spatial skill demand, particularly when one controls for experience with robot controllers. These results also suggest a need for further investigation regarding training content, training time, and individual differences.

References

Army Regulation 70–25. Use of Volunteers as Subjects of Research (1990)

Elliott, L., Redden, E.: Reducing Workload: A Multisensory Approach. In: Savage-Knepshield, P. (ed.) Designing Soldier Systems: Current Issues in Human Factors. Ashgate, U.S. Army Research Laboratory, Aberdeen Proving Ground, MD (2013)

Elliott, L.R., Coovert, M.D., Redden, E.S.: Overview of meta-analyses investigating vibrotactile versus visual display options. In: Jacko, J.A. (ed.) HCI International 2009, Part II. LNCS, vol. 5611, pp. 435–443. Springer, Heidelberg (2009)

Elliott, L.R., Schmeisser, E.T., Redden, E.S.: Development of Tactile and Haptic Systems for U. S. Infantry Navigation and Communication. In: Smith, M.J., Salvendy, G. (eds.) HCII 2011, Part I. LNCS, vol. 6771, pp. 399–407. Springer, Heidelberg (2011)

Hancock, P.; Elliott, L.; Cholewiak, R.; Lawson, B.; van Erp, J.B.F.; Mortimer, B.; Rupert, A.; Redden, E.; Schmeisser, E. Tactile Cueing to Augment Multisensory Human-Machine Interaction. Ergonomics in Design (in press)

Hart, S.: Nasa-Task Load Index (Nasa-TLX); 20 Years Later. Human Factors Ergon. Soc. Annu. Meet. Proc. **50**, 904–908 (2006)

Mitchell, D.K.: Workload Analysis of the Crew of the Abrams V2 SEP: Phase I Baseline IMPRINT Model, ARL-TR-502. U.S. Army Research Laboratory, Aberdeen Proving Ground, MD (2009)

Mitchell, D.K., Brennan, G.: Infantry Squad Using the Common Controller to Control an ARV A (L) Soldier Workload Analysis, ARL-TR-5029. U.S. Army Research Laboratory, Aberdeen Proving Ground, MD (2009)

Mitchell, D. K., Brennan, G.: Infantry Squad Using the Common Controller to Control a Class 1 Unmanned Aerial Vehicle System (UAVS) Soldier Workload Analysis, ARL-TR-5012. U.S. Army Research Laboratory: Aberdeen Proving Ground, MD (2009)

Mitchell, D. K., Samms, C., Glumm, M., Krausman, A., Brelsford, M., Garrett, L.: Improved Performance Research Integration Tool (IMPRINT) Model Analyses in Support of the Situational Understanding as an Enabler for Unit of Action Maneuver Team Soldiers Science and Technology Objective (STO) in support of future combat systems (FCS), ARL-TR-3405. U.S. Army Research Laboratory, Aberdeen Proving Ground, MD (2004)

Mortimer, B., Zets, G., Mort, G., Shovan, C.: Implementing effective tactile symbology for orientation and navigation. In: Jacko, J.A. (ed.) Human-Computer Interaction, Part III, HCII 2011. LNCS, vol. 6763, pp. 321–328. Springer, Heidelberg (2011)

Pettitt, R., Redden, E.: Carstens, C.: Comparison of Army Hand and Arm Signals to a Covert Tactile Communication System in a Dynamic Environment. ARL-TR-3838. U.S. Army Research Laboratory, Aberdeen Proving Ground, MD (2006)

Pomranky, R., Wojciechowski, J.: Determination of Mental Workload During Operation of Multiple Unmanned Systems; ARL-TR-4309; U.S. Army Research Laboratory: Aberdeen Proving Ground, MD (2007)

Protection of Human Subjects. Code of Federal Regulations, Part 219, Title 32 (1991)

Scalsky, D., Meshesha, D., Struken, S.: Army Expeditionary Warrior Experiment (AEWE) Spiral E Final Report. U.S. Army Test and Evaluation Command, Alexandria (2009)

U.S. Army Evaluation Center U.S. Army Expeditionary Warrior Experiment (AEWE) Spiral H Final Report; Request from Commander, U.S. Army Test and Evaluation Command (CSTE-AEC-FFE); Aberdeen Proving Ground, MD (2013)

U.S. Marine Corps Rifle Squad Manual (FMFM 6-5). http://www.amazon.com/Century-Marine-Marines-Training-Manuals/dp/1422052672/ref=sr_1_1?ie=UTF8&qid=1387307357&sr=8-1&keywords=fmfm6-5. Accessed September 2013

Van Erp, J.: Tactile Displays for Navigation and Orientation: Perception and Behavior. Mostert & Van Onderen, Leiden (2005)

Human Characteristics of Figure Recognition in Tactile Feedback

Motoki Tanuma[1(✉)], Makoto Oka[2], and Hirohiko Mori[2]

[1] System Information Engineering, Tokyo City University, Setagaya, Japan
g1481814@tcu.ac.jp
[2] Department of Industrial and Management Systems Engineering,
Tokyo City University, Setagaya, Japan
{moka,hmori}@tcu.ac.jp

Abstract. In car, information presented to drivers is increasing and most of information is done using the visual and auditory displays. Presenting the information only to visual and auditory modes must cause drivers' cognitive overloads in the near future and it is necessary to find the way using other modes to reduce them. In this study, we especially focus on human tactile figure recognition of the train of sticking stimuli and examine the human characteristics of what kinds of figures people can recognize as the tactile feedback. We developed tactile device that expresses four figures. We found there are interactions between the interval time of each sticking and the figures and human has quite different mechanisms between the cases of the simultaneous sticking and the consecutive sticking in recognizing the figures.

Keywords: Tactile · Feedback

1 Introduction

Recently, in car, there is a lot of information presentation using vision, such as car navigation systems. The visual information is effective to transfer information fast and effectively. However, too much information in sight cause information overload, information is not transmitted well, and consequently, many traffic accidents must be caused by failing to transfer correct information. Presenting the information only to visual and auditory modes must cause the cognitive overloads in the near future and it is necessary to find the way using other modes to reduce them. In this paper, therefore, we focused on the tactile feedback. In this study, we especially focus on human figure recognition of the train of sticking stimuli and examine the human characteristics of what kinds of figures people can recognize as the tactile feedback. Assuming a car-driving environment, we give sticking stimuli to a calf not to disturb driving.

2 Related Works

Muhammad et al. [1] explored the impulsion and vibration properties of different tactile patterns. They prepared for 8 Braille-like patterns by 8 vibrating pins and investigated how many patterns people can identify each other. This experiment showed that

© Springer International Publishing Switzerland 2015
S. Yamamoto (Ed.): HIMI 2015, Part I, LNCS 9172, pp. 458–465, 2015.
DOI: 10.1007/978-3-319-20612-7_44

identification rate among 4 patterns is better than the one among 8 patterns, because the subjects could not memorized the 8 patterns. Shintani et al. [2] developed a tactile display to use small-sized solenoid that drives with low voltage and is mobile. However, in their research, the subjects only count the number of pins and do not examine the recognition of complicated figures.

3 The Device

We developed a device to give sticking stimuli (Fig. 1) to convey four kinds of figures by 9 solenoids: circle, cross, square, and triangle. The reason why we selected these figures is that those are used in most cultures and can be expressed with few pins. Furthermore, each figure mostly shares the common meaning with most cultures. The cross and triangle have a diagonal line, the square and triangle have the bottom. We don't adapt more complex figures than the circle, because the people must not be able to recognize them with tactile. We also do not prepare more than four patterns to reduce the loads by subjects' memorizing a lot of figures. The number of the pins used to draw each figure is 8pins, 5pins, 4pins, 3pins respectively. This device is attached on the calf of the subject.

Fig. 1. The prototype device

4 Experiment Environment

During all experiments we conducted in this study, the subjects were listening to music with a headset not to hear the sound of moving the solenoids and we also installed a curtain between the face and the foot to hides the device. The subjects put a foot on the stand and we put the device under a foot (Fig. 2).

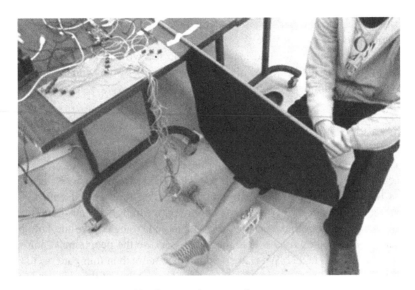

Fig. 2. Experiment environment

5 Experiment I

5.1 Aims and Methods

Before investigating the human capability of figure recognition in drawing a figure one sticking after another, we should clarify how long the interval time between one sticking and the next one people can discriminate between them. It will be better if the interval time is shorter, because the information can be conveyed rapidly. Prior to the detail experiment, we conducted the subjective experiment to reduce the number of the interval range factors. The interval time we prepared is 0.05, 0.1, 0.2, 0.3, 0.4, and 0.5 s and asked the subjects whether they could discriminate two consecutive sticking. 10 subjects (9 men and 1 woman) were involved in this experiment. Their ages ranged from 20 to 23 years old. We attach the device to subject's calf directly. The drawn figure is only the circle here. In order to avoid habituation, we change the position of the initial point each pattern.

5.2 Results

Table 1 indicates each subject's answer whether he/she is able to discriminate two train of the sticking. It shows that in the interval time of 0.1 s and 0.05 s were too short. In the interviews after the experiment, some subjects claimed that too long intervals cause the difficulty to understand the figure while they could discriminate the movements. As a few subjects also claimed that 0.1 s was too fast. We, therefore, decided to investigate the time around 0.1 s and 0.2 s more detail in Experiment II.

Table 1. The result of experiment I

Second/Subjects	Subject1	Subject2	Subject3	Subject4	Subject5	Subject6	Subject7	Subject8	Subject9	Subject10	Average	
0.05	2	1	2	2	1	2	2	2	2	1	1.7	1.recognizable
0.1	1	1	1	1	1	1	2	1	2	1	1.2	2.not recognizable
0.2	1	1	1	1	1	1	1	1	1	1	1.0	
0.3	1	2	1	1	1	1	1	2	1	1	1.2	
0.4	1	1	1	1	1	1	1	1	1	1	1.0	
0.5	1	1	1	1	2	1	1	2	1	1	1.2	

6 Experiment II

6.1 Aims and Methods

In the Experiment I, we found that the interval time longer than 0.3 s is too slow to convey information. The aim of Experiment II is to determine which duration is appropriate in giving sticking stimuli in more detail. In this experiment, we asked the subjects how many train of the pin hit consecutively. The interval time investigated here is 0.04, 0.05, 0.07, 0.1, 0.15, 0.2, 0.25 s and the number of hitting is 2, 3, 4, 5 times. So, 84 trials of 7(seconds) × 4(hit times) × 3(times) were presented to each subject in random order. Subjects (9 men and 1 woman) were involved in this experiment. Their ages ranged from 20 to 24 years old.

6.2 Results

Table 2. Percentages of the correct answers

Second/Times	2	3	4	5
0.04	86.7	26.7	6.7	3.3
0.05	73.3	33.3	16.7	0.0
0.07	76.7	43.3	10.0	13.3
0.10	80.0	70.0	33.3	13.3
0.15	80.0	56.7	66.7	36.7
0.20	60.0	36.7	66.7	46.7
0.25	50.0	36.7	70.0	53.3

Table 2 shows that, all correct rates in train of two stimuli were high in all interval time and the correct rate in train of 3 sticking was especially high in the only case of 0.1 s. When interval time is 0.25 s, the correct rate was the best in 4 and 5 times. These results indicate the appropriate interval time depends on how many pins are used to draw a figure and it is necessary to change the interval time by the number of a pin. Table 2 shows that a percent of correct answers is not high, because there are individual differences. We conduct third experiment based on the result.

7   Experiment III

7.1   Aims and Methods

The third experiment was conducted to investigate the human tactile characteristics of figure recognition. The figures used in this experiment are a circle, a square, a triangle and a cross. The pins were activated one by one to the counterclockwise direction in the circle, the square, the triangle (Fig. 3). The conditions for the interval time were 0 s (simultaneous), 0.1 s, and 0.25 s. So, 36 trials of 3(seconds) × 4(shapes) × 3(times) were presented the subjects in random order and 15 subjects were involved. The subjects were asked kind of figure was presented.

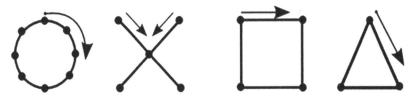

Fig. 3. How to move the pin each figures

7.2   Results and Considerations of the Correct Rates

Table 3 shows the results of the correct rates of each figure in each interval time. We analyzed the data by ANOVA to examine about the relationships between the interval time and the figure recognition ($p < 0.05$). The results showed that there are interactions between the interval time and the figures and it is consistent with the results in the second experiment.

Table 3. The correct rate of each figure

Second /Figure	○	✕	□	△
0s	11.1	24.4	24.4	40.0
0.1 s	71.1	24.4	26.7	42.2
0.25s	88.9	17.8	40.0	24.4

Before the experiment, we assumed that cross must be the most recognizable figure and its correct rate must be the highest among the figures, because the cross is only the figure which the center pin is used to draw. However, the correct rate of cross is the lowest in all figures. The most of subjects claimed that it was difficult to recognize the stick of the center pin. We must investigate this reason in the future. Table 3 also shows that the correct rate of the circle is especially high when it is drawn sequentially while the one is especially lowest in case of simultaneous sticking. Moreover, the correct rate of square is high when interval time is 0.25 s and triangle is high when interval times are 0 s and 0.1 s. These results mean that each figure has each appropriate interval time to make people recognize it and, to convey a figure by tactile, easy an appropriate interval time should be set up for each figure.

7.3   The Way of Mistakes of Each Figure for the Other Figures

The correct rates of all figures were not better than we had expected. To investigate the reason and what sorts of misrecognition happened, we consider about which figures the subjects mistook each figure for.

Case of Interval Time 0 s

Table 4. The rates of mistakes of each figure when interval time is 0 s

	◯	✕	☐	△
◯		22.50	35.00	42.50
✕	17.65		29.41	52.94
☐	5.88	20.59		73.53
△	7.41	29.63	62.96	

In Table 4 vertical rows mean the figures that we presented and each lateral column means the error rates the subjects answered by misrecognizing the figure presented in the case of simultaneous sticking. It shows that all figures were recognized as the triangle by mistake most frequently, the square in the second, the cross in the third, and the circle in the least. This means all figures tend to be mistaken for the figure using fewer pins than the presented. It is known that the threshold of the human ability of the discrimination of two-point stimuli on the calf is 3-4 cm. As the distance among the pins on our devise is a little closer than the two-point threshold, the subjects might not be able to discriminate the adjoining stimuli of the pins and recognize two stimuli as one. We will discuss about this matter in the Considerations.

Case of Interval Time 0.1 s

Table 5. The rates of mistake of each figure when interval time is 0.1 s

	◯	✕	☐	△
◯		38.46	46.15	15.38
✕	52.94		35.29	11.76
☐	18.18	27.27		54.55
△	19.23	57.69	23.08	

Table 5 indicates that the tendency shown in the case of simultaneous sticking is disappeared and the subjects often mistook the cross for the circle and the square for the triangle in the case of interval time 0.1 s.

Case of Interval Time 0.25 s

Table 6. The rates of mistakes of each figure when interval time is 0.25 s

	○	×	□	△
○		40.00	40.00	20.00
×	62.16		27.03	10.81
□	40.76	25.93		33.33
△	11.76	35.29	52.94	

Table 6 shows the results of case 0.25. This result is similar to the case of 0.1. The subjects often mistook the cross for the circle and the square for the triangle. This means the mechanisms of human tactile recognition are quite different between the simultaneous and the sequential drawings.

8   Considerations

First of all, we got s quite different the results between the cases of the simultaneous sticking and successive sticking in recognizing the figures. While, in the case of simultaneous sticking, the subjects tended to mistake a figure for the figures which are drawn with fewer pins than the ones actually presented, this phenomena were disappeared in the case of the successive sticking. If our device is too small and the pin is arranged too close to each other beyond the two-point discrimination threshold, the same phenomena must be observed. This means that human has quite different mechanisms between the cases of the simultaneous sticking and the successive sticking in recognizing the figures. As, in the experiment III, the figures has the different number of sticking to draw and the subjects might judge the figures simply by counting the number of sticking. Actually some subjects said that they did so. To investigate this issue, we examine that the relationship between the correct rate and the time to draw one figure. The presentation time is calculated by multiply interval time and the number of pins (Fig. 4).

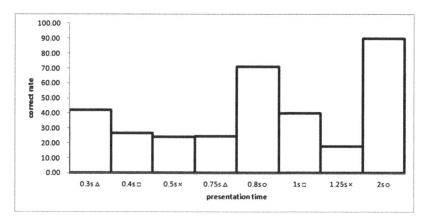

Fig. 4. The correct rate of each presentation time

If they count the number of sticking, longer interval time would be easier for them to count. However, Fig. 4 shows that both correct rates of the circle are high and the interval time doesn't affect the results. This means the subjects did not count the number of sticking and the total presentation time, but discriminated the characteristic of each figure.

9   Conclusion and Future Work

In this study, we examined the human abilities and characteristics of the tactile figure recognition. In the experiments, we found that each figure has each suitable duration time to draw. This means each figure has each appropriate interval time to make people recognize it and, to convey a figure by tactile, easy an appropriate interval time should be set up for each figure. Furthermore, we also found that human has quite different mechanisms between the cases of the simultaneous sticking and successive sticking in recognizing the figures. At this moment, however, we do not clarify the detail mechanisms about it. So, we should try to do it in the near future.

References

1. Tahir, M., Bailly, G., Lecolinet, E.: Exploring the impulsion and vibration effects of tactile patterns. In: BCS-HCI 2008. British Computer Society, Swinton, pp. 237–240 (2008)
2. Shintani, K., Yukino, R., Tange, Y., Mihara, K.: Trial production of braille display for the visually impaired using small solenoids. J. JACT **17**(3), 35–38 (2012)

Recognition of Written Cues System for Users of General Paper Media

Daiki Yamaji$^{(\boxtimes)}$ and Jiro Tanaka

University of Tsukuba, Tsukuba, Japan
{yamaji,jiro}@iplab.cs.tsukuba.ac.jp

Abstract. This paper proposes a system for users of "general paper media (newspaper, books, publications, etc.)" using recognition of written cues (made by handwritten entries) and performing digital processing. Users are able to use this system by a smartphone and on paper-media to save a favorite paragraph or image on the paper, illustrate data associations, and search for English translations, all the while being able to use the paper-media in a natural way. Moreover, users are able to browse the interaction logs from both the paper-media and smartphone. Experiments to evaluate the performance of this system shows the high recognition accuracy, and high discrimination accuracy depending on written cues.

Keywords: Document recognition · Handwriting · Image processing · Image recognition · Data management · Smartphone

1 Introduction

Due to recent development in digital technology, there has been much research going on to improve usability by connecting digital technology with the real world. For instance, in the field of NUI and TUI, it is possible to capture real-world actions and perform feedback based on those actions. However, considering our daily activities, there have not been many cases of smoothly transitioning our real-world actions into digital processing. In such cases, we focus on using the general paper medium (newspaper, books and publications), and consider the following scenarios. (1) when discovering a content, figure or photo that you like, putting a sign around it and capturing by a camera or scanning it, (2) classifying paper media including various writing and related articles and storing them in files together, (3) when trying to check the meaning of a word, putting a sign around it and searching the word by using a computer or smartphone, etc. Based on these cases, in this paper we propose a system of applying digital processing by using the natural human action of "writing something on a paper medium" as a trigger to smoothly realize transitioning our real-world actions into digital processing. Basically, a pen is used on a paper medium to (1) draw "⌈⌉" at diagonal ends of the desired region to save it, (2) draw the same characters on the upper-left side of the "⌈⌉" to associate that regions, (3) enclose "▢" the

© Springer International Publishing Switzerland 2015
S. Yamamoto (Ed.): HIMI 2015, Part I, LNCS 9172, pp. 466–476, 2015.
DOI: 10.1007/978-3-319-20612-7_45

Fig. 1. (Left) Favorite figures, pictures or paragraphs enclosed by "⌈⌋", (middle) English word enclosed by "□" to search for its translated meaning, (right) similar characters ("1" is written in this case) written on the upper-left side of the regions enclosed by "⌈⌋" to associate the regions.

English word user does not understand the Japanese meaning. Using analog actions on the paper medium as input allows users to enjoy the benefits of the digital platform during casual use of the paper medium (Fig. 1).

2   Related Work

2.1   Link Between Paper Medium and Digital Data

Among the field of seamless integration of digital and analog media, there have been a number of research focussing on the link between paper medium and digital data. Koike et al. [1] and Do-Lenh et al. [2] have developed a system that links the real world with digital data, where, upon placing something like a book with a marker pasted on it on a table, the system can project digital information related to the book in the vicinity. Although these systems are similar to our research in terms of connecting paper medium with digital data, the aforementioned systems require markers to be pasted and digital data prepared beforehand for the systems to work. These are not required for our system. Sangsubhan and Tanaka [8] have developed an idea generation support system by automatically digitizing data written using a digital pen on a paper medium. This research also focused on the uses of the digital data after digitizing analog data, and depending on written cues, digitized English words can be looked up for meanings and kept for later study, or multiple data can be grouped together for combined browsing.

2.2   Extracting Written Cues

Nakai et al. [4] have proposed a method of extracting written cues on a paper medium by comparing the image of the paper with an original digital version and detecting the position of the cues made. Iwata et al. [5], by attaching a miniature camera on the tip of a pen, have managed to detect the position of the written cues made without scanning, and by using subtraction technique were able to extract written cues. However, the aforementioned systems require a digitized version of the data present on the paper medium, which is not required for our system. Moreover, the recognition process is huge and time consuming. Stevens et al. [12]. have developed a high performance system for extraction of written cues by restricting the color used for the written cue. Guo and Ma [10] and Zheng et al. [11] have developed a system that can extract written cues only from paper medium where written cues have been made. However, the system is only capable of extracting handwritten letters but unable to do so for handwritten lines or figures. In our system, we have used color information of written cues for detection, in order to be able to use the system on smartphones which have significantly lower specs compared to PCs. Here, high precision extraction of written cues has been achieved. In addition, by allowing users to choose the color used for extraction, the system provides flexibility.

3   Data and Commands Arrangement Design

In this section, we will introduce the method of use and application processing. There are two modes in this system.

– Recognition mode
– View mode

In use of recognition mode, system applies digital processing by recognizing cues written by the user. In use of view mode, the user are able to browse digital datas stored by recognition mode.

3.1   Recognition Mode

To use this system, users hold a pen and use a smartphone. The user holds the phone up over the paper while writing or after he finished writing. There are three types of written cues (made by handwritten entries) recognized by this system.

(1). Enclosure by "⌈⌋". The user likes an image or paragraph on the paper, and would like to save it. By drawing "⌈⌋" at the diagonal ends of the desired region with a pen, "⌈" is enclosed by red square and "⌋" is enclosed by green square on smartphone, the user is able to confirm that this system recognizes "⌈⌋" (Fig. 2(a)). By touching the region, the rectangular area enclosed by "⌈⌋" will be saved on the smartphone as digital data (Fig. 2(b)).

(2). Drawing the same character. By writing a character with a pen on the upper-left side of the "⌈⌋" used in (1)., associations can be made in between regions designated by the same character. The character is enclosed by a yellow square on the smartphone, and the user is able to confirm that this system recognizes it. In Fig. 3(a) the character "1" is written; the corresponding region and the other region where the same character (i.e. "1") is written are automatically associated by touching the region (Fig. 3(b), (c)). This function can be useful in

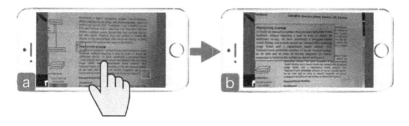

Fig. 2. (a) By drawing "⌈⌋" and touching the region the user would like to save, (b) the region will be saved as digital data.

scenarios where the user wants to save an figure and the description associated with it as a set. The user can read the description while looking at the figure on the smartphone.

(3). Enclosure by "□". The user does not understand the meaning of an English word on the paper. By enclosing the word with "□" with a pen, the word is enclosed by a blue rectangle on the smartphone; the user is able to confirm that this system recognizes "□" (Fig. 4(a)). Touching the region prompts the system to show the translated (Japanese) meaning on the upper left side of the display (Fig. 4(b)). In addition, the word enclosed by "□" and the corresponding translation will be saved on the smartphone.

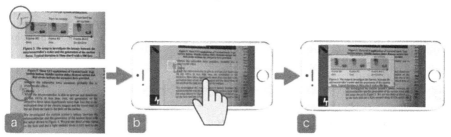

Fig. 3. (a) By writing "1" on the upper-left side of the "⌈⌋" and (b) touching one of the region (the lower figure of (a) in this case), (c) the other region associated with the region will be displayed.

Selection of region by touching on screen. The regions saved using the above methods can be selected by touching them on the smartphone. With the selection of a region, if created with (1)., the digital image of that region will be displayed on the screen. If created with (2)., the digital images associated with the region will be displayed, then one of the digital images will be displayed larger. If created with (3)., the translated meaning of the word within the region will be displayed on the top-left side of the screen.

Registration of the pen. Due to different pens being used by users, the system allows for any pen to be used for making cues. The process for registering a pen for making cues is as follows. While the system is running, the user scribbles something on a scrap of paper with the desired marker pen (Fig. 5(a)).

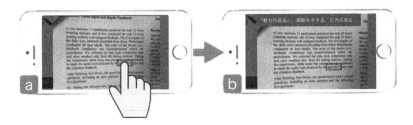

Fig. 4. (a) By drawing "□" and touching the word, (b) display the translated (Japanese) meaning on the upper left side of the display

By touching the pen icon on the upper left corner of the screen, the pen icon turns yellow and the system goes to pen registration state. Then, by touching the scribbled region on the smartphone screen (Fig. 5(b)), the system extracts the color of the ink (Fig. 5(c)), and the color is registered as the default color for future recognition and extraction.

Fig. 5. (a) Scribbling something on a scrap of paper with the desired marker pen, (b) by touching the pen icon and the scribbled region, (c) the system extracts the color of the ink

3.2   View Mode

Since the data extracted using the written cue are saved on the smartphone, the data can be accessed and browsed anytime. The data may consist of figures, pictures, images of paragraphs, English words and their translations, and are divided into two categories: "IMAGE" and "WORD". The "IMAGE" category allows users to collectively browse extracted figures, pictures or paragraphs (Fig. 6(a)). In addition, image data that have been grouped together using the same letter show a yellow triangle mark on the upper right corner and the letter used for grouping on the upper left corner, and can be browsed as a set of grouped images (Fig. 6(b)). By selecting the "WORD" category, English words previously extracted and looked up for meanings can be rechecked (Fig. 6(c)) and their meanings rechecked as well.

4   Implementation

This system has been implemented as an application running on iOS. In this chapter, we will explain the implementation method used for the "recognition mode" described in the previous chapter.

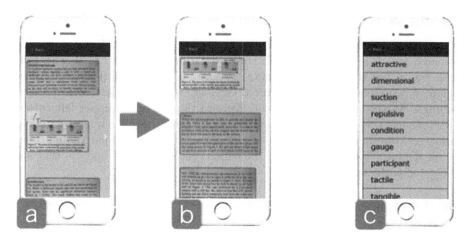

Fig. 6. (a) "IMAGE" category shows images list saved by recognition mode, (b) images list grouped by "1", (c) "WORD" category shows words list saved by recognition mode

4.1   Recognition of Written Cues

In this mode, simple shapes such as "⌈⌋" or "□", as well as letters used for grouping can be extracted. In addition, by taking into account the processing power of smartphones, we have used extraction of specific colors to detect written cues; thus reducing the processing load and improving accuracy.

4.2   Color Extraction

The robust HSV color space has been used for color extraction. The written cues extracted with regard to the specific color are distinguished as a separate region from the main text, and then binarized for the shape recognition process explained in the following.

4.3   Shape Recognition

After detection of written cues, recognition is performed. To recognize the written shape in the image obtained from the smartphone camera, "template matching" has been used as the recognition algorithm. In this mode, the digital processing performed differs depending on the detected shape.

4.4   Processing for the Shape "⌈⌋"

Using template matching, the coordinates of the upper left positions of "⌈" and "⌋" are obtained. A rectangular region is determined using these coordinates, and then cut out from the RGB image obtained from the camera.

4.5   Processing for Written Letters

In order to recognize letters, the region containing the written letter is cut out as image data. The method used for this is described as follows. First, a rectangular region has to be obtained using "⌈" and "⌋". Then, another rectangular region of 30 px containing the letter is cut out, with upper left corner of the rectangle starting at 15 px above and 20 px to the left of the upper left corner of "⌈". Using this image as a template and by performing template matching on images containing letters obtained later, the letters are compared, and upon finding similar letters, would group the regions enclosed by "⌈" and "⌋" that are associated with the letters.

4.6   Processing for the Shape "☐"

Using template matching, the coordinates for the upper left corner of "☐" can be obtained, and by applying these coordinates on the RGB image obtained from the camera, the English word enclosed within the "☐" can be cut out. Then, from the image data obtained, the text can be extracted from the image file using OCR.

4.7   Text Extraction Using OCR

In this mode, OCR (optical character recognition) has been used for text extraction from image data (using "tesseract-ios" from OCR libraries). However, in case of noise in the image backdrop or blur in the image, the accuracy tends to drop significantly. Therefore, the images used in the system are magnified, converted to grayscale, sharpened and the contrast increased in order to improve the accuracy.

4.8   Translation of English Words

To look up the word extracted using OCR for its meaning, an English-Japanese dictionary web service called "Dejizo" has been used. By including the English word in the request URL while accessing Dejizo, the corresponding translation can be obtained included in an XML file.

4.9   Data Processing

The figures, pictures, paragraphs, English words and the corresponding meanings obtained from the recognition mode are then stored on the iPhone storage. Figures, pictures and paragraphs are stored as image files; the metadata of the image files and English words extracted for translation, and the corresponding translations are stored as XML files. While using the recognition mode, the data stored in the storage is imported into the application memory. This is to reduce the processing time for the application. When saving data, the data present on the application memory is compared to the one in the storage in order to determine if the data is the same or not. In addition, the data is also used when viewing the data in the "view mode".

5   Evaluation

A preliminary experiment has been performed for performance evaluation of the recognition accuracy of the recognition mode and the discrimination accuracy for the generated data.

5.1   Experiment Outline

We evaluated the following: the recognition and discrimination accuracy for "⌈" and "⌋", the discrimination accuracy for the letters written to the upper left corner of "⌈", the recognition accuracy for "□" and the discrimination accuracy for the enclosed region (English word). In addition, three types of marker pens have been used to evaluate difference of recognition by color of pen. A thesis paper written in English has been used as the paper medium for the experiments. Three university students of age 21–22 have been chosen as participants for the experiments.

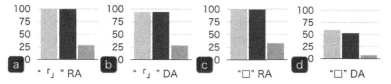

Fig. 7. (a) "IMAGE" category shows images list saved by recognition mode, (b) images list grouped by "1", (c) "WORD" category shows words list saved by recognition mode

The color of the graph represents the color of the ink of the marker pen used. "⌈⌋ recognition accuracy" represents the recognition accuracy for "⌈" and "⌋", and "⌈⌋ discrimination accuracy" represents the discrimination accuracy for the data obtained (such as paragraphs, figures, etc.). Similarly, "□ recognition accuracy" represents the recognition accuracy for "□", and "□ discrimination accuracy" represents the discrimination accuracy for the data obtained (English word).

The color of the graph represents the color of the ink of the marker pen used. Each graph represents the discrimination accuracy for the letter written on the upper left corner of "⌈".

5.2   Considerations

From the graphs it can be seen that, while using the red and blue pen, the results for the recognition and discrimination accuracies were similar, while the recognition and discrimination accuracy for the yellow pen was lower. The reason for this can be assumed to be the low contrast created by yellow ink on a white paper. From this it can be inferred that, for the system to work properly, the color of the ink used for writing cues needs to have high contrast with regards to the color of the paper used as the medium. However, when using red and blue pens, the recognition for "⌈⌋" and "□" tend to be accurate (Fig. 7(a), (c)). In addition,

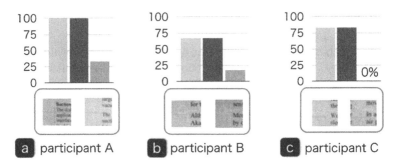

Fig. 8. The discrimination accuracy for the letter written by (a) participant A, (b) participant B, (c) participant C

data such as paragraphs and figures obtained using "⌈⌋" also have high discrimination accuracy (Fig. 7(b)). On the other hand, the English word obtained from "□" appears to have a discrimination accuracy of about 60 % (Fig. 7(d)). This result is seemingly affected by the accuracy of the text extraction of OCR. In this system, to increase the discrimination accuracy, several image processing have been applied on the image files of the data. For implementation of this system in the real world, the discrimination accuracy for "□" needs to be further increased by using improved processes. However, the ability to extract an English word enclosed within "□", with an accuracy of 60 %, might become the foundation of a real-world implemented version of a system based on paper medium. On the matter of discrimination accuracy for letters, for participant A, 100 % accuracy was obtained. However, for participants B and C, the accuracy turned out to be lower (Fig. 8). The decrease in accuracy for participant C might have been caused due to the inability of the participant to recreate the subtle intricacies of a star symbol (Fig. 8(c)), and for participant B, the similarity between the two symbols (Fig. 8(b)) might have caused confusion in the recognition process thus reducing accuracy. Although using simple letters and symbols gave accurate results, the system needs to be further improved to accommodate complex symbols, and the ability to differentiate between similar-looking but different symbols.

6   Discussion and Conclusion

In this research, we have developed a system for performing digital processing on data obtained through written cues on the "general paper medium" such as books, newspaper, publications, etc. Users are able to use the system with a smartphone, and by writing cues on a paper medium, the system can be used to save desired figures, pictures or paragraphs from the physical paper, associate aforementioned figures, pictures and paragraphs with each other, or show meanings of English words chosen by the user. In addition, the saved data and associated data can be browsed anytime on the smartphone, and since the written cues persist on the paper medium, they can also be browsed on the physical paper. Moreover, since the system only requires a smartphone and pen in addition to the paper medium, and the digital processing requiring the natural process of writing something on paper, the system is very accessible and easy to use for the general people. From the preliminary experiments conducted, we have obtained high accuracy for recognition and discrimination depending on the pen used and written cues. However, on the matter of extraction of English words, we have deduced the need of further study to improve processing method to increase accuracy. In addition, to give accurate results, we have inferred the need of thick marker pens with the color of the ink having high contrast with regards to the color of the paper, which gives rise to some inflexibility for the system. Furthermore, while this system requires the source text material to be in English, we want to further improve the system to accommodate for other languages such as Japanese.

References

1. Koike, H., Sato, Y., Kobayashi, Y.: Integrating paper and digital information on enhanceddesk: a method for realtime finger tracking on an augmented desk system. ACM Trans. Comput. Hum. Interact. **8**(4), 307–322 (2001)
2. Do-Lenh, S., Kaplan, F., Sharma, A., Dillenbourg, P.: MultiFinger interactions with papers on augmented tabletops. In: Proceedings of the 3rd International Conference on Tangible and Embedded Interaction, pp. 267–274 (2009)
3. Brandl, P., Richter, C., Haller, M.: NiCEBook: supporting natural note taking. In: CHI 2010: Proceedings of the 28th International Conference on Human Factors in Computing Systems, pp. 599–608 (2010)
4. Nakai, T., Kise, K., Iwamura, M.: A method of annotation extraction from paper documents using alignment based on local arrangements of feature points. In: Ninth International Conference on Document Analysis and Recognition, ICDAR 2007, vol. 1, pp. 23–27 (2007)
5. Iwata, K., Kise, K., Iwamura, M., Uchida, S., Omachi, S.: Tracking and retrieval of pen tip positions for an intelligent camera pen. In: Proceedings of ICFR 2010, pp. 277–282 (2010)
6. Yoon, D., Chen, N., Guimbretire, F.: TextTearing: expanding whitespace for digital ink annotation. In: Proceedings of UIST 2013, pp. 107–112 (2013)
7. Harrison, C., Xiao, R., Iwamura, M., Schwarz, J., Hudson, S.E.: TouchTools: leveraging familiarity and skill with physical tools to augment touch interaction. In: Proceedings of CHI 2014, pp. 2913–2916 (2014)
8. Sangsubhan, P., Tanaka, J.: Idea generation support system utilizing digital pen and paper. Master Thesis, University of Tsukuba (2013)
9. Mazzei, A.: Extraction and classification of handwritten annotations for pedagogical use. In: Proceedings of EDIC 2009 (2009)
10. Guo, J.K., Ma, J.K.: Separating handwritten material from machine printed text using hidden markov models. In: Proceedings of 6th international Conference on Document Analysis and Recognition, pp. 436–443 (2001)
11. Zheng, Y., Li, H., Doermann, D.: The segmentation and identification of handwriting in noisy document images. In: Lopresti, D.P., Hu, J., Kashi, R.S. (eds.) DAS 2002. LNCS, vol. 2423, p. 95. Springer, Heidelberg (2002)

12. Stevens, J., Gee, A., Dance, C.: Automatic proceessing of document annotations. In: Proceedings of 1998 British Machine Vision Conference, vol. 2, pp. 438–448 (1998)
13. Yi, C., Tian, Y.: Text extraction from scene images by character appearance and structure modeling. In: Proceedings of CVIU 2013, pp. 182–194 (2013)
14. Huang, R., Shivakumara, P., Uchida, S.: Scene character detection by an edge-ray filter. In: Proceedings of ICDAR 2013, pp. 462–466 (2013)
15. Jain, A., Sharma, J.: Classification and interpretation of characters in multi-application OCR system. In: Proceedings of ICDMIC 2013, pp. 1–6 (2013)

Study of Haptics and Tactile Sense
of the Direction of Movement

Sakae Yamamoto[1(✉)], Yukiko Yokomizo[2], and Daiji Kobayashi[3]

[1] Tokyo University of Science, Tokyo, Japan
sakae@ms.kagu.tus.ac.jp
[2] Tokyo Metropolitan University, Tokyo, Japan
mogeta3159@gmail.com
[3] Citose Institute of Technology, Chitose, Hokkaido, Japan
daiji.kobayashi@dream.com

Abstract. The operating tool is not mentioned for the case of a location cannot be directly confirmed visually. In above cases, by that people touch the operation tools at our fingertips, its direction can be confirmed. This paper was focused onto the touch, in other words, tactile and haptic. When the operator touches the operation device, for example, button, switch, etc. It is possible to understand of the direction of its movement of machine (equipment) from texture information of device obtained from the operation of the tactile device. From this, when performing multiple operations at the same time, and also the working conditions it is difficult to be confirmed an operation device in the eye, it is to aim to reduce operation errors. The experimental study was done. Tow impression are found as follows; the raise-get down and positive rotation – negative rotation. It has been proven that there is an association between directionality and textural sense of materials.

Keywords: Haptics · Tactile · Direction of operation · Direction of movement

1 Introduction

In recent years, users have been required to perform multiple tasks simultaneously when operating a machine or system. For example, some drivers may be required to shift gears using a button located on the back side of the steering wheel to operate a car navigation system while driving. In such situations, it is difficult or impossible to confirm every single operating device visually.

Hence, for the purpose of such confirmation, touch sense support may be incorporated into the machine. In this case, it is necessary to work on the design of buttons and device surfaces. In other words, touch support is a means of providing a different type of information. In the operation of a machine or system, the functions that this information represents, and, in particular, to which direction of movement such functions lead is important. However, it is often dangerous when driving a car to confirm the functions of various operational devices by checking what results they cause.

© Springer International Publishing Switzerland 2015
S. Yamamoto (Ed.): HIMI 2015, Part I, LNCS 9172, pp. 477–487, 2015.
DOI: 10.1007/978-3-319-20612-7_46

For direction of movement, an international standard is provided by ISO1503: Spatial orientation and direction of movement-Ergonomic requirements. Therefore, industrial operating tool products have to be manufactured in compliance with this standard in relation to the direction of movement. Operating tools that do not comply with the standard are difficult to operate and even can lead to dangerous situations in some cases.

The objective of this study is to clarify how the texture of a button may convey the resulting direction of movement of a machine or system just by touching it. It is desirable to convey such information to the operator. In particular, touching an operating tool with a finger may be contribute an important interface.

It may result in activating touch sense among the five human senses. Studies on touch sense have been performed for centuries but many of them have been physiological such as those by Katz (1925) and Iwamura (2001). Furthermore, there have been applicative studies relating to braille and tactual mapping as well. It is believed that even sighted people may be able to enhance their certainty while simplifying operation through use of the tactile sense. In this study, we performed basic research toward the development of operational interfaces based on touch. Specifically, we examined whether operational or movement direction of a machine or system may be properly extracted from the textural information conveyed by touching operating tools with a finger.

Therefore, we considered sense of direction according to pairs of antonymic directional adjectives to indicate directionality as shown in ISO1503. In addition, we examined how kinetic sensation is felt by the tactile sense.

As a preliminary experiment, we prepared buttons whose surfaces were coated with plain rubber (n = 10), felt (n = 5), silicon rubber (n = 22 ± 0.4), stockings (n = 5), polyurethane (n = 24.6 ± 4.72). Test subjects were made to operate each button, and their tactile sensation was examined. As a result, six types of subjective reactions regarding directionality were extracted:

Clockwise/Counterclockwise
Upward/Downward
Forward/Backward
Forward/Backward tilting
Straight line/Diagonal
Advance/Retreat (Progress/Regress)

In addition, nine pairs of words were obtained regarding the feeling of pressing on the button:
Detectable by pressing once/Detectable by pressing repeatedly.

Fast/Slow
Warm/Cold
Strong /Weak
Low/High
Automated/ Manual
Frozen /Chilled
Soft/Hard
Clear/Confused

We believe that on the basis of our results, it may be possible to provide information to enhance operational support and safety by examining the association between the textural sense of the button and directionality.

2 Purpose

In this study, we clarify the association between the functions of a button and the sensations evoked by difference in textures of button material. In particular, we would like to clarify the association between directionality and impressions from haptic sense.

3 Experiments

The touch senses are divided into Tactile and Haptics at the described above.

In Experiment 1, we examined whether touching way of both tactile and haptic is good. In Experiment 2, using a good touch way, to examine the relationship between the movement direction and material.

3.1 Experiment 1: Experimental Test of Detectability of Differences in Texture Using Different Ways of Tactile and Haptics

In general, the touching motion is roughly divided into two actions: pressing (tactile) and rubbing (haptic) by a finger. In the experiment 1, we determine whether "pressing" or "rubbing" allows greater detectability of differences in texture in the case where the evaluation target is a button.

3.2 Experiment Methods

The test subjects were 21 students (male 16 and female 5) with a mean age of 21.7 and a standard deviation of 0.82. They were asked to press or rub reference button and stimulus buttons on which different materials coated without looking at them. The reference button was placed on the left and the stimulus buttons were placed on the right. Subjects were instructed to touch the buttons with the index finger of their dominant hand, allowing repeated touch during the experiment. After touching the reference button and each of the stimulus buttons once, they were asked to respond which way of touching –pressing or rubbing– was more effective for detecting the differences of materials on a 5-point scale, as shown in Fig. 1. The case where pressing was more detectable was defined as "+ and that where rubbing was more detectable was defined as –". Every experiment was performed with two buttons made of polyurethane, felt, and plain rubber; so six patterns of experiment were performed in total. The combinations of the materials in these experiments are listed in Table 1.

Fig. 1. Example of questionnaire

Table 1. Combinations of materials

Combination No.	Reference switch	Stimulus switch
1	Polyurethane	Felt
2	Polyurethane	Plain rubber
3	Felt	Polyurethane
4	Felt	Plain rubber
5	Plain rubber	Polyurethane
6	Plain rubber	Felt

3.3   Materials Used in the Experiments

Three types of materials – polyurethane (Exseal, Pit Cushion PC-16), felt (Ambic, Feltace, K-7 301) and plain rubber (Matech, 123-41) – were affixed to push buttons (Miyama Electric, DS660R-C(R)). Buttons with polyurethane, felt, and plain rubber applied are shown in Figs. 2, 3, 4 applied.

Fig. 2. Button with polyurethane

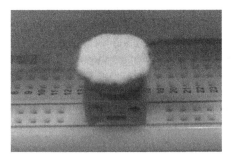

Fig. 3. Button with felt applied

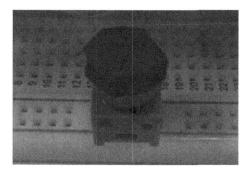

Fig. 4. Button with plain rubber applied

3.4   Experimental Device

An experimental device that incorporated the buttons was prepared using polystyrene boards (85 × 90 × 70) as the outer frame, and the inside of the device was hidden with a cloth curtain (Fig. 5). Furthermore, by combining breadboard (CIXI WANJIE ELEC-TRONICS, 0BB-801), jumper cord (CIXI WANJIE ELECTRONICS, BBJ-20), cord with a compact chip (AVVICON ELECTRONIC CORPORATION, MC-761), a AAAA×3 battery holder with lead wire (TAKACHI, MP- 4-3), and 5 mm red LED for 5 V with a built-in resistor (OptoSupply, OSR6LU5B64A-5 V), the LED was set to flash with the pressing of a button. Figure 6 shows inside of the experimental device.

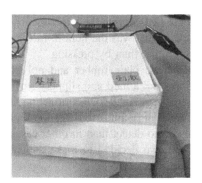

Fig. 5. Experimental device

3.5   Results

The sum of the evaluation points for all subjects is shown in Table 2.

3.6   Discussion

As Table 2 shows, the values of subjective reaction are negative under all combinations, suggesting that difference in materials is more detectable by rubbing rather than

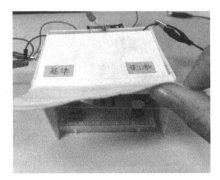

Fig. 6. Inside of the experimental device

Table 2. Evaluation by all subjects

Combination No.	Evaluation points
1	-33
2	-3
3	-35
4	-16
5	-8
6	-27
Sum	-122

pressing. We also observed the LED during the experiments, and it did not flash, even though the object of the experiments was the button. In other words, the results were obtained simply by touching, rather than by pressing.

Combinations 2 and 5 include plain rubber and polyurethane. In a comparison between softness (plain rubber) and a hard and slippery surface (polyurethane), it was proved that the sensory difference is smaller when touching than it is when rubbing. It is understood that the difference in textural sense at the time of touching the surface before pressing is more difficult to detect than in other cases.

On the basis of this result, we decided to make subjects identify differences in button surface through a haptics motion.

4   Experiment 2: Experimental Test of the Association Between Different Textures and Impressions of Directionality and Function

In response to the result of experiment 1 (described in Sect. 3), another experiment was performed to clarify what impressions the different textures conveyed regarding function and directionality of motion.

4.1 Experimental Method

Subjects were 30 students (male 25 and female 5) with a mean age of 22.4 and a standard deviation of 2.33. Using buttons covered with three types of materials as described above, the experiment was performed using pair comparison method (revised Scheffe's method). Methods of switch layout and the like were the same as those in the experiment 1, described in Sect. 3.

Subjects, for the same items as in Experiment 1, have been asked to answer their impression by the comparing with two buttons. In this experiment, subjects were touched button by using a repeatedly haptics to compare. A major factor estimation was obtained by analysis of the variance of resulted the questionnaire.

4.2 Pairs of Question Items

In the questionnaire, subjects were asked to rate stimulus switches on scales pertaining to six directional impressions.:

Clockwise /Counterclockwise, Upward/Downward, Forward/Backward,
Forward/Backward tilting, Straight line/Diagonal,
Advance/Retreat (Progress/Regress)

In addition, pair words regarding material characteristics were also provided, including the following nine items of paired questions:

Detectable by pressing once/Detectable by pressing repeatedly,
Fast/Slow, Warm/Cold, Strong/ Weak, High/Low, Automated/Manual
Frozen/Chilled, Soft/Hard, Clear/Confused

4.3 Results

From analysis of variance on the reaction results, significant differences were observed in major effects, and the number of question items that could be ignored was 11 in total. Of those 11 items, two were about directionality, seven were about the impression of the function, and two were about the switch itself. The results of the variance analysis are shown in Tables 3, 4, 5.

Table 3. The table of analysis of variance for Positive rotation-Negative rotation

Factor	Sum of Squares	Degree of freedom	Mean Squares	F0	Test result
α	16.411	2	8.206	9.95	***
α (k)	103.589	58	1.786	2.166	***
β	0.272	1	0.272	0.33	ns
σ	0.05	1	0.05	0.061	ns
o (k)	28.283	29	0.975	1.183	ns
ε	73.394	89	0.825		
τ	222	180		*** : p < 0.01	

Table 4. Directional property estimated value of each item

Combination of directionality/motion	Plain rubber	Felt	Poly-urethane	Test result
Clockwise/ Counterclockwise	–0.094	–0.150	0.244	***
Upward/Downward	–0.033	–0.172	0.206	**
Forward/Backward	0.033	–0.172	0.206	**
Forward/Backward tilting	–0.028	–0.122	0.150	Interaction
Diagonal/Straight line	0.078	0.424	–0.267	***
Advance/Return (Progress/Reverse)	–0.078	–0.167	0.222	*** (Interaction)

***: p < 0.01, **: p < 0.05

Table 5. Estimated value of textural sense

Combination of directionality/motion	Plain rubber	Felt	Poly-urethane	Test result
Press repeatedly/ Press once	0.36	–0.16	–0.19	***
Fast/Slow	–0.16	–0.16	0.32	***
Warm/Cold	0.08	0.40	–0.48	***
Strong/Weak	–0.01	–0.24	0.24	***
High/Low	–0.01	–0.19	0.21	***
Automated/Manual	–0.01	–0.25	0.26	***
Frozen/Chilled	–0.17	–0.07	0.23	***
Soft/Hard	0.47	0.24	-0.71	***
Clear/Confused	–0.12	–0.32	0.44	***

***: p < 0.01

4.4   Discussion

As these results were obtained by performing separate pair comparisons, we attempted to obtain their correlation by combining directionality and textural sense. The results are shown as follows: (Tables 6, 7, 8, 9, 10).

Here, directionality was examined for just five items, excluding the "forward/backward tilting" pair because this pair resulted in a strong interaction between the major effects and the individual. Those items with higher negative correlation were also omitted because we considered distinguishability as well as operability. Therefore, the examination was limited to the same directionality of the impression, leaving negative correlations as a problem to be considered in the future.

Since materials are considered to be suitable if they provide a sense of fast or slow for rotation and a sense of clear or confused from these results, we determined that the combination of polyurethane and plain rubber is excellent from the perspectives of directionality and textural sense. We concluded that polyurethane is suitable for use in a positive direction (in this case clockwise) and plain rubber is suitable for use in moving in a negative direction (in this case counterclockwise).

Table 6. Major factors, test results and coefficient of rotation and textural sense of each material.

Major factor estimate value of each material				
Directionality/Motion type	Plain rubber	Felt	Polyurethane	Test result
Rotation (Clockwise/ Counterclockwise)	-0.09	-0.15	0.24	***

Major factor estimate value of each material					
Pair of quality	Plain rubber	Felt	Polyurethane	Test result	Correlation coefficient
Fast/Slow	-0.16	-0.16	0.32	***	0.991
Clear/Confused	-0.12	-0.32	0.44	***	0.993

***: $p<0.01$

Table 7. Major Factors, test results, and correlation coefficient of upward/downward and textural sense of each material.

Major factor estimate value of each material				
Directionality/Motion type	Plain rubber	Felt	Poly-urethane	Test result
Upward/ Downward	-0.03	-0.17	0.21	**

Major factor estimate value of each material					
Pair of quality	Plain rubber	Felt	Polyurethan	Test result	Correlation coefficient
Strong/Weak	-0.006	-0.239	0.244	***	0.991
High/Low	-0.011	-0.194	0.206	***	0.995
Automated/ Manual	-0.006	-0.25	0.256	***	0.991
Clear/Confused	-0.122	-0.317	0.439	***	0.993

**: $p<0/05$, ***: $p<0.01$

Table 8. Major factors, test results, and correlation coefficient of forward/backward and textural sense of each material.

Major factor estimate value of each material				
Directionality/Motion type	Plain rubber	Felt	Poly-urethane	Test result
Forward/ Backward	0.03	-0.17	0.21	**

Major factor estimate value of each material					
Pair of quality	Plain rubber	Felt	Poly-urethane	Test result	Correlation coefficient
Strong/Weak	-0.01	-0.24	0.24	***	0.998
High/Low	-0.01	-0.19	0.21	***	0.995
Automated/ Manual	-0.01	-0.25	0.26	***	0.998

In case of other directions, the result was the same as that for rotation. However, in the case of diagonal or straight lines, we showed that it is effective to assign felt to the positive direction (in this case clockwise) and polyurethane to the negative direction (in this case counterclockwise) to provide a sense of warmth or coldness.

Table 9. Major factors, test results and correlation coefficients of diagonal/straight line and textural sense of each material.

Major factor estimate value of each material					
Directionality/ Motion type	Plain rubber	Felt	Poly-urethane	Test result	
Diagonal/ Straight line	0.078	0.424	-0.267	***	
Major factor estimate value of each material					
Pair of quality	Plain rubber	Felt	Poly-urethane	Test result	Correlation coefficient
Warm/Cold	0.078	0.400	-0.478	***	0.988

Table 10. Major factors, test results, and correlation coefficients of advancing/retreating direction and textural sense of each material.

Major factor estimate value of each material					
Directionality/ Motion type	Plain rubber	Felt	Poly-urethane	Test result	
Advance/ Return (Progress/ Reverse)	-0.078	-0.167	0.222	*** (Interaction)	
Major factor estimate value of each material					
Directionality/ Motion type	Plain rubber	Felt	Poly-urethane	Test result	
Fast/Slow	-0.161	-0.161	0.322	* * *	0.976
Clear/ Confused	-0.122	-0.317	0.439	* * *	1.000

This result may be considered reliable because the material is easy for humans to accept. It is necessary to incorporate such considerations into designs.

Furthermore, in the context of virtual reality (VR), it is necessary to consider what types of sensations should be given to humans to suggest directions of movement. Some may be of the opinion that just considering the asperity of a surface is enough; however, humans must accept certain stimulation to perform operations. Therefore, the textural sense of a material becomes a crucial factor. In ISO 1503, directionality in human motion management is standardized for use in product design. Nevertheless, some products do not comply with this standard. Since certain directions tend to be accepted by humans on the basis of certain textures, operating tools that that imply such directions are demanded. However, it is important to select materials carefully in such cases.

From 30 types (30 pairs) of textural sense of materials selected at an early phase depending on personal experiences, we narrowed to six types (six pairs) by directionality. Moreover, textural senses were also narrowed down to nine items (nine pairs). In consideration of diverse reactions in humans, we do not believe that what we have done is sufficient. It is necessary to undertake further examination by increasing the number of items. However, whether these same reactions are also observed in people other than the Japanese has not been examined, and will be considered later. In addition, even though quantification of stimulation is necessary, we believe it is necessary to perform basic research to determine whether there is any association between directional sense and textural sense.

5 Summary

It has been proven that there is an association between directionality and textural sense of materials. From these findings, it is believed that such an association may be applied to directionality in the design of new switches and the VR world.

References

Katz, D.: Der Aufbau der Tastwelt. Verlag von Johann Ambrosius Barth, Leipzig (1925). translated Japanese by Higashiyama, A., Iwakiri, K., Shinyousha, Tokyo, Japan (2003)

Iwamura, Y.: Touch (Japanese). Igakushoin, Tokyo, Japan (2001)

Service Design and Management

Proposal of New Lighting Which Combined Functionality of Street Light and Outdoor Light

Takeo Ainoya[1(✉)], Keiko Kasamatsu[2], and Akio Tomita[3]

[1] Consultant & Design Director, Misawa Homes Institute of Research
and Development Co., Ltd, Tokyo, Japan
kasamatu@tmu.ac.jp
[2] Tokyo Metropolitan University, Tokyo, Japan
kasamatu@tmu.ac.jp
[3] Misawa Homes Institute of Research and Development Co., Ltd, Tokyo, Japan
akio_tomita@home.misawa.co.jp

Abstract. The two types of illuminations were developed as security sensing with motion sensor instead of the image. We focused on the lights in outdoor in this study. As the role of outdoor lights, the proposed light has a function that feels natural presence of residents and pedestrian light as illumination. We examined about a new style of lighting and proposed the lighting which combined functionality of street light and outdoor light. We conducted concept planning, prototyping, experiments for determining flash lighting and evaluation, and proposed two design models. The proposed lightings in this study were able to provide a solution by data and sensing, and to achieve safety and security.

Keywords: Lighting for safety and security · Sensing · Light-emitting pattern · Street light · Outdoor light

1 Introduction

Lighting has not only a role that illuminate objects but also a psychological effect. For example, Lighting gives comfort and relief to people. As the light of outdoor, there is the role of the security and psychological to ease the fear of not visible in the dark or at night. In this way, lighting is an important element in our life.

Therefore, we focused on the lights in outdoor in this study. As the role of outdoor lights, the proposed light has a function that feels natural presence of residents and pedestrian light as illumination. We examined about a new style of lighting and proposed the lighting which combined functionality of street light and outdoor light.

2 The Lighting for Safety and Security

The brightness of the outdoor lights at night in Japan show the development of civilization and culture, and it is believed to symbolize the modern life. In particular, such as convenience stores and signs not only outdoor lights illuminate brightly the town in

S. Yamamoto (Ed.): HIMI 2015, Part I, LNCS 9172, pp. 491–499, 2015.
DOI: 10.1007/978-3-319-20612-7_47

urban areas. People are able to live without being aware anxiety coming from the night darkness. However, such brightness is inhibited that feel the original of calm on the town and natural signs. This is different from the Japanese seems sensibility.

In "In Praise of Shadows", Junichiro Tanizaki, one of the most eloquent Japanese novelist described essential difference between Japan and the West, was pursuing the essence of Japanese beauty within the shadows and dark circles. In this way the shadows not only the brightness are present Japanese beauty.

The illumination products, not only light up at all times illumination for safety and security features. This utilizes the sensing technology, has the light-emitting pattern and a motion in the equipment, and is fused features on street lights and outdoor lights. This report proposed new lighting with a fusion of these features.

The concept of safety and security was provided in two axes. The first axis was ordinary and extraordinary. The second axis was reassurance and anxiety. We investigated the safety by superimposing level of feeling for these axes. As a result of examination, we had defined two types, type A and B.

- Type A: Lighting that provides the comfort and reassurance in daily life.
- Type B: Lighting that possess the function of the alarm in order to reduce anxiety in a non-daily state.

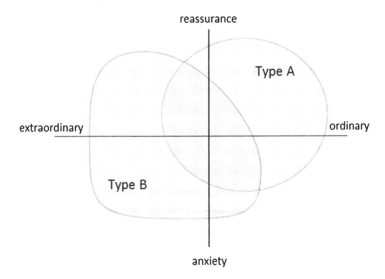

Fig. 1. Concept of illumination

These have the function to react to the movement as a sensor technology and represent a comfort or dangerous condition by way of the reaction. Moreover, these incorporate the weather data like temperature, humidity, rain, and wind, as an environmental sensor technology. These lighting have the role of information presentation tool.

3   Concept

The concept of developed illumination product is to respond the human motion by sensing technology and to have the watching illumination as function.

This lighting has the functions which feel reassurance like illumination, sensing the strange motion and intruder by motion sensors and do emission in accordance with the abnormal state of the attention to the warning (Fig. 1).

4   System Concept

The system concepts are the following two points.

- Light-emitting pattern and the illumination equipment by sensing device are operating, lighting range is changed.
- Provide information to the town security system, and operate to have a function as a security sensor in the street.

5   Sensing and Feedback Pattern

The proposed product is to apply the sensing technology, in cooperation with big data and home energy management system (HEMS), can provide information as Fig. 2. In addition, the feedback, including the cooperation with the community as illumination was defined as Fig. 3.

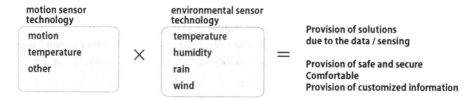

Fig. 2.   Sensing

6   Lighting-Emitting Patterns and Impression Evaluation

6.1   Purpose

There are two purposes for evaluation. At first, the purpose was to determine the threshold on the flashing frequency value for reassurance/danger (Exp. 1). The next purpose was to examine the physiological response and impression evaluation for comfortable, attention, and warning conditions (Exp. 2).

Fig. 3. Feedback and feeling

6.2   Methods

6.2.1   Presentation Conditions

Exp. 1: The flashing frequency value for reassurance/danger determined the threshold by up-down method.

Exp. 2: The presentation conditions were 9; 3 comfortable conditions (C1-C3), 3 attention conditions (A1-A3), and 3warning conditions (W1-W3). Presentation time was 1 min for comfortable conditions, 30 s for attention conditions, and 15 s for warning conditions. However, experimenter informed consent to the participants. The experimenter told the participants to close eyes when the participant feel "feel bad" or "eye hurts", and decided to interrupt the experiment.

6.2.2   Measurement Indices

The measurement indices on Exp. 2 were galvanic skin response (GSR) and electro-cardiogram (ECG) as physiological responses. The integral value of every second was calculated for GSR, and LF/HF was calculated by frequency analysis for ECG. Impression was evaluated using 8 items by visual analog scale (VAS) (Table 1).

Table 1.

warm	feel relief
strong	bright
humaneness	natural
scary	feel danger

6.2.3   Experimental Procedure

The experimental procedure was rest for 1 min, presentation of a condition and evaluation. This procedure was repeated for 9 conditions. At last, the experimenter interviewed to participants (Fig. 4).

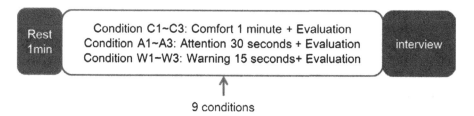

9 conditions

Fig. 4. Experimental procedure

6.2.4 Participants

The participants were ten person (7 males and 3 females). The average age were 22.4.

6.3 Results

6.3.1 The threshold on Exp. 1

The threshold for reassurance/danger on flashing of light was examined by up-down method. As the result, frequency of threshold was 1.21 ± 0.135 Hz. This value was with reference, presentation conditions of Exp. 2 were created.

6.3.2 GSR

The presentation time for warning conditions was 15 s, therefore the first 15 s for comfortable and attention conditions were analyzed.

The ANOVA for conditions was performed to examine the difference between conditions. There was no significant difference on 9 conditions, however integral value for GSR was high on attention conditions and the sympathetic nerve tended to activate (Fig. 5).

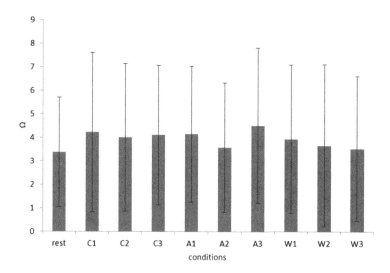

Fig. 5. Result on GSR

6.3.3   LF/HF

The presentation time for warning conditions was 15 s, therefore the first 15 s for comfortable and attention conditions were analyzed similar to GSR.

The ANOVA for conditions was performed to examine the difference between conditions. There was no significant difference on 9 conditions, however LF/HF on C2 of comfortable condition was low, in other words, the parasympathetic nervous was activated. On the other hand, LF/HF on A3 of attention condition was high, sympathetic nervous was activated (Fig. 6).

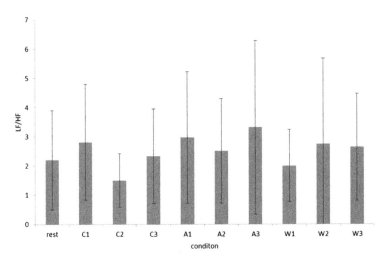

Fig. 6. Result on LF/HF

6.3.4   Impression Evaluation

Figure 7 shows the results of VAS evaluation on 8 items. As the results of ANOVA for conditions, there were significant differences on conditions with the exception of "humaneness". Therefore, multiple comparison was occured to examine the differences between conditions. There were significant differences between comfortable and warning conditions.

6.4   Discussion

The threshold which felt safe and dangerous revealed to flash illumination from this experiment, and obvious differences were observed in the impression evaluation of flashing pattern which presented comfortable, attention and warning. Moreover, it was possible to find the potential effects on the autonomic nervous activity appeared.

In presentation conditions of this experiment, same condition, i.e., comfortable condition had C1-C3, 3 kinds of patterns were presented. The impression changed by not only flashing frequency but also patterns and the effects of physiological response were recognized. Therefore, these proposal products have possibility to apply the

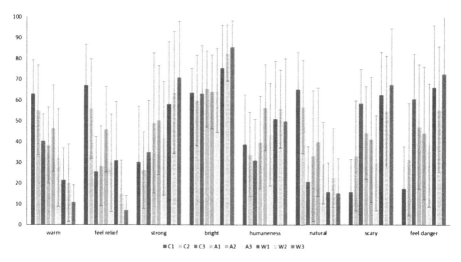

Fig. 7. Impression evaluation on 9 presentation conditions

environment and situation as illumination equipment and the concept of illumination need to be clarified.

In this study, we applied the 9 conditions, and designed lighting of two types of following.

7 The Two Design Models

7.1 Design Model A

The design model A is the lighting equipment with the function as fence and with light-emitting pattern for security with motion (the left on Fig. 8).

7.2 Design Model B

The design model B is the lighting equipment with the function as foot light and with light-emitting pattern for security (the right on Fig. 8).

8 Conclusion and Future Works

The two types of illuminations were developed as security sensing with motion sensor instead of the image. We conducted concept planning, prototyping, experiments for determining flash lighting and evaluation, and proposed two design models.

The proposed lightings in this study were able to provide a solution by data and sensing, and to achieve safety and security. It is possible to provide customized information, they can be expected to be deployed in public spaces as well as residential area. As the application of these lights, they will have a function as a watch and protect

A type   **B type**

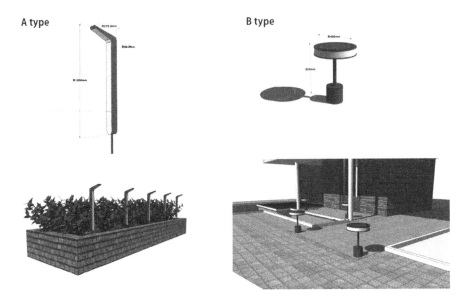

Fig. 8. Design model A and B

device that can accommodate a variety of situations by taking advantage of other sensor technology.

These will be not only a function of the light that lighting, these lead to visualization of safety and security in cooperation with the sound and HEMS. Moreover, in future possibility, it can be performed to improve the energy efficiency in the home by considering the external situation in cooperation with HEMS (Fig. 9). In addition, it is possible to check the status of HEMS using smartphone and to grasp the situation around the house even from a remote location. It is possible to measure the environment in the area by combining the city of sensing data (Fig. 10) and to provide services such as pinpoint weather forecast (Fig. 11).

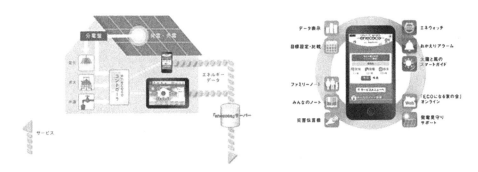

Fig. 9. Example of HEMS Service

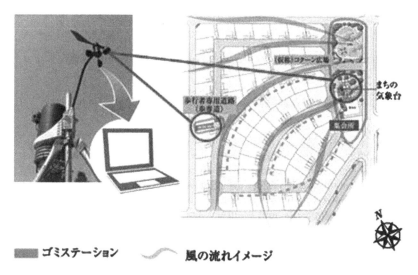

Fig. 10. Sensing for weather information

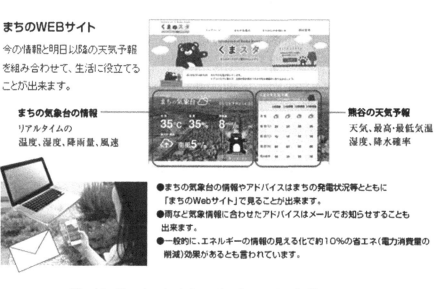

Fig. 11. The pinpoint information for weather in Kumagaya

References

1. Tanizaki, J.: In Praise of Shadows. Vintage Classics, Poland (2001)
2. http://www.330navi.com/kumagaya/community/index.html

A Multi-agent Based System for Route Planning

Eugene Belyi$^{(\boxtimes)}$, Indravan Patel, Anusha Reddy, and Vijay Mago

Troy University, Troy Al 36081, USA
{ebelyi,ipatel132433,ayarava,vmago}@troy.edu

Abstract. Route-planning is a perplexing problem in the field of computer science. Finding computationally viable solutions to route-planning
is a challenging task. Various techniques have been devised to solve this
problem; however, there is a trade-off in these techniques between computational complexity and accuracy. One paradigm defined in artificial
intelligence which can contribute to this problem's solution is a multi-
agent system, in which a group of agents work together to achieve a
common goal. These agents require a robust mechanism for coordination
and information exchange in order to achieve this goal. When applied
to route-planning, these agents interact to compute the optimal path
based on distance, speed, and a variety of environmental factors that
may impact travelling time. The consideration of these factors allows a
solution generated by the system to be applicable to real world sitations.
In this work, a hybrid model is proposed which utilizes a multi-agent system to compute travelling time for a given route. This system utilizes a
Bayesian network to model interdependencies which exist between environmental factors. In order to illustrate the potential effectiveness of
the proposed model, several case studies from the state of Alabama are
presented.

Keywords: Route planning · Road transportation network · Bayesian
network · Intelligent transportation system · Multi-agent system

1 Introduction

Over the last few years, several systems have been developed that provide solutions for route-planning. One recent work has emphasized the development of a
route planning system which allows for the creation of custom routes through
user created trip criteria (Zolfpour-Arokhlo et al. 2013). The focus of this work
is route planning in city-trip planning systems, and route-planning algorithms
are used to take into account underlying dynamic conditions such as weather
forecast and traffic conditions.

The majority of proposed solutions to route-planning take into account
factors which affect travel time and allow for the use of user-defined criteria. It
is crucial to consider factors affecting the selection of an optimal route in a route-
planning system. However, maximizing the accuracy of a route-planning system
in choosing an optimal route requires the consideration interdependencies which

© Springer International Publishing Switzerland 2015
S. Yamamoto (Ed.): HIMI 2015, Part I, LNCS 9172, pp. 500–512, 2015.
DOI: 10.1007/978-3-319-20612-7_48

may exist between any of these factors. In the solution proposed by this article, the factors affecting route-planning are modelled after agents in an agent-based model (ABM). The representation of each factor using its own agent allows for the model to display atomicity. This allows the structure of the system to be modified easily. In this ABM, interdependencies between the agents are modelled using a Bayesian network (BN).

A variety of other machine-learning techniques can be applied to create such a model. However, the main advantage of using a Bayesian network as opposed to fuzzy logic, artificial neural network, support vector machine, or other algorithms is that it is a significantly less computationally expensive technique than its alternatives (Mago et al. 2014). Setting node evidences in and computing node values in a BN allows for far greater efficiency and scalability.

1.1 Contribution of This Work

The primary contribution of this work is to propose and illustrate the structure of a configurable and scalable hybrid model by using multi-agent system which implements a BN. The intended goal of the proposed design is to provide a computationally light and simple solution to the route-planning problem. Simplicity is emphasized with the intention of making model configuration as well as the addition or subtraction of new components a straight-forward and intuitive task. The remainder of this paper is structured as follows: a brief overview of related works in Sect. 2, an explanation of the methodology in Sect. 3, an illustration of the usability of the model through case studies in Sect. 4, a discussion of the the model and possible future directions in Sect. 5, and a conclusion for the work in Sect. 6.

2 Related Work

A web-based tourist expert system for planning custom city-trips are described in (Zolfpour-Arokhlo et al. 2013). This worzk uses heuristic procedures where user-defined criteria facilitates trip customiztion to build travel itineraries. Algorithms extending route planning are used to take into account environmental conditions such as the weather, traffic, and road conditions. The methodology described in this work serves as an inspiration for the route planning system described in our work. However, the system described in our work seeks to further increase accuracy by modeling interdependencies between environmental conditions.

Ant colony optimization is a swarm based algorithm that has been successfully used for optimization problems. Ants find minimum-distance routes from the nest to food sources by using swarm behavior (Gajpal and Abad 2009). The use of a simulated ant colony system for route planning and optimization proved to be efficient and robust for large and complex environments. One key disadvantage to using ant-colony optimization however is the difficulty in conducting theoretical analysis. This is because the algorithm is iterative by nature and based on a sequence of random decisions which are dependent upon each other.

As such, the probability distribution changes for each iteration of the algorithm (Umarani and Selvi 2010). The difficulty in conducting theoretical analysis makes this approach infeasible for our model because it lessens both the scalability and configurability of the model.

Another related work concerning personalized route guidance systems describes obtaining a proper route based on minimizing a combination of user defined criteria. This minimization is performed using a weighted linear aggregation rule and navigation algorithm (Nadi and Delavar 2011). The method extends personalization in route planning by incorporating user preferences along with their relative importance into the routing process. A decision strategy is then created to select the portion of the important criteria which defines the level of satisfaction necessary for an acceptable solution. This method however, fails to incorporate the interdepencies between user preferences.

Route planning optimizaiton utilizing a multi agent system often employs a hybrid architecture. One work utilizing this approach incorporates real time learning using the A* and compares it with the A* searching algorithm (Zafar and Baig 2012). This shows better results for multi-agent environments and proves to be an efficient and robust algorithm. This research concludes by providing a statistical comparison of results, namely the exploration time for different environmental conditions. In a route guidance system however, the real time routing problem is substantially different from classical network routing problems. The work concerning this guidance system proposes multi-agent based negotiation between agents that represent network managers, information service providers, and drivers equipped with route guidance systems (Adler and Blue 2002).

In an intelligent tourism recommender system (Borràs et al. 2014), a different optimization technique is used. This system employs machine-learning techniques such as an artificial neural network, fuzzy logic, or artificial potential field to assess the relevance of each context component for each user. It then uses a genetic algorithm to plan a route that goes through different points of interest around the city. Most of the tourism recommended systems that build personalized routes or itineraries implement an ad-hoc planning mechanism, but some of them apply more classical domain independent AI planning techniques (Garcia et al. 2010,Vansteenwegen 2009, Yu and Chang 2013). The drawback to many of these methods is that they use machine-learning algorithms which perform complex calculations in multi-dimensions, and thererefore these algorithms are very difficult to visualize. In order to be able to intelligently adjust the parameters of a model for increased accuracy, it is important to understand and follow how the model produces its output.

3   Methodology

The proposed methodology attempts to establish a cohesive multi-agent system through the use of a hybrid model. A primary component of this model is a BN. Each node in the network represents an agent which models an environmental

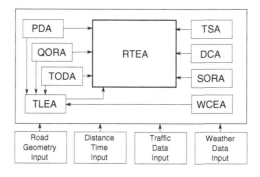

Fig. 1. Route-planning system model

factor affecting the time needed to traverse a given route. We will describe the input used by the model, the functions of each of the agents, and the general structure of the hybrid model. The general structure of the model is shown in Fig. 1.

3.1 Input

The inputs for our route-planning model is as follows:

- *Road Network Geometry*: Extracted from Google Maps using their native API. Routes are stored as *.kml* files, and the contents of these files are used as an input for the model.
- *Current Time*: Obtained using a synchronized clock and used as an input for the model.
- *Route Distance*: Calculated using an agent defined in the system. This agent extracts a route from the *.kml* file obtained from Google Maps. This route is stored in the file as a list of latitude-longitude coordinates. The agent calculates the distances of the route segments using the Haversine distance formula over pairs of coordinates. The route distance is obtained by summing the distances of these segments.
- *Travelling Speed*: For each route segment, there is an associated speed limit. This limit assumed by the model to be the ideal travelling speed over the segment. This data may accompany the road-network geometry. If it does not, then it is either obtained through public access data or generated using probability distributions.

3.2 A Generic Overview

The system is modeled using nodes, of which a subset belong to a BN, and is illustrated in Fig. 2.

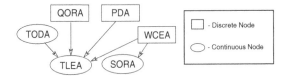

Fig. 2. A Bayesian network of different agents

Time of Day Agent (TODA). The function of the TODA is to act as a synchronized clock in order to provide input data for the TLEA. This allows the system to model how traffic congestion varies throughout the course of the day.

Quality of Road Agent (QORA). This agent categorizes roads by quality in order to report which roads should be avoided when an alternative is available. Namely, this includes old or not-well maintained roads but also takes into consideration roads on which construction is an impediment to travel time.

Population Density Agent (PDA). The PDA's function is to take into consideration the population density of a given area. This allows the system to model the effects that population density have on traffic congestion. The data produced by this agent acts as a direct input to the TLEA.

Weather Control Estimation Agent (WCEA). The WCEA accounts for the effects of weather conditions on both the travel time and the safety of the road. The function of this agent is to approximate the weather's effects on roads. Additionally, it works to factor in weather related road hazards such as ice patches or conditions which may cause hydroplaning. Ideally, the data used for this agent would be obtained from local weather stations or live online sources. However, when such resources are not available, probabilistic forecasting or statistical approximation may also be used.

Safety of Road Agent (SORA). This agent represents the current safety of the road being travelled upon. It is assumed by our model that the weather has a direct impact on road safety, and because of this, the agent takes a direct input from the WCEA in order to calculate its own output.

Distance Calcualtion Agent (DCA). The DCA takes map data as an input, deconstructs the data as set of points, and calculates the distance between the points using the Haversine formula.

Travelling Speed Agent (TSA). The TSA is the agent responsible for obtaining the speed limits of a given route in order to calculate the ideal travelling time. Ideally, this data is taken from public access data, if however this data is

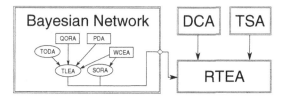

Fig. 3. Structure of hybrid model

unavailable it can be statistically approximated using average or standard speeds associated with the classification of a road.

Traffic Load Estimation Agent (TLEA). The TLEA will update the traffic status of each route. Its output is computed from environmental information such as traffic conditions and historical information of each route. Also, since part of its input comes from the traffic input data, it is possible for new information about the route, such as an incident on the road, to be passed to the TLEA. This could trigger a recalculation of the route based on the newly available data. Along with this input, the estimation details of this agent are dependent on the PDA, WCEA, QORA and TODA. The results of this estimation will be used by the RTEA.

Route Time Estimation Agent (RTEA). The RTEA acts as a decision maker in the proposed model. It evaluates the route distance and vehicle speed in each route by using a road network map and specific input data. This agent takes input from all other agents and its calculated output is used for determining the optimal route.

3.3 Route Weight Formulation

In order to calculate accurate travel time while taking into account environmental factors, it is imperative to formulate a process which takes these factors into account. By developing a hybrid model, all factors impacting travel time are considered. The inclusion of a BN into the hybrid model allows for the accounting of interdependencies which exist between factors. Figure 3 shows the BN used for this hybrid model. When used in conjunction with statistical techniques, the graphical model has several advantages for data analysis. Firstly, because the model encodes dependencies among all variables, it readily handles situations where some data entries are missing. Secondly, the BN implemented by the model can be used to learn causal relationships, and hence it can be used to gain understanding about a problem domain and to predict the consequences of intervention. Thirdly, because the model has both a causal and probabilistic semantics, it is an ideal representation for combining prior knowledge and data. Additionally, Bayesian statistical methods in conjunction with the proposed hybrid model offer an efficient and principled approach for avoiding the overfitting of data. In this paper, the model is used to account for the effects of environmental factors and their interdependencies as relationships between different agents.

Several of the agents defined in the previous section actively function as nodes in this network, and each node has a unique role and is individually defined.

Time of Day Agent (TODA). The output of this agent is drawn from a uniform distribution as shown below where each value in this distribution represents an hour of the day:

$$unif(a, b) : where\ a = 0,\ b = 23 \tag{1}$$

The distribution is normalized to the range [0,1]. It is imperative to model this node in order to model how traffic congestion changes throughout the day.

Quality of Road Agent (QORA). The Quality or Road Agent is modeled as a three-state categorical distribution, the categorization of which is as follows:

$$P(PDEA = High\text{-}Quality\ Road) = 0.7$$
$$P(PDEA = Moderate\text{-}Quality\ Road) = 0.2 \tag{2}$$
$$P(PDEA = Poor\text{-}Quality\ Road) = 0.1$$

Population Density Agent (PDA). This agent is modeled using a binary categorical distribution. The two states of this distribution signify the percentage of the population living in rural and urban areas as taken from 2010 US Census data (United States Census Bureau 2010).

$$P(PDEA = Rural) = 0.75$$
$$P(PDEA = Urban) = 0.25 \tag{3}$$

Weather Condition Estimation Agent (WCEA). This agent is modeled using a three-state categorical distribution. The values given in the states are based on an averaging of dates during which winter storm and hurricane (Midwest Regional Climate Center 2013, National Hurricane Center 2014) seasons occur in United States during a given year. The percentage of dates classified as *Good* are those excluded from the seasons, *Moderate* dates are months which are in the the left and right tails of a normal distribution of storms during the seasons, and the *Bad* dates are the months during which the majority of storms occur during the seasons.

$$P(WCEA = Good) = 0.53$$
$$P(WCEA = Moderate) = 0.31 \tag{4}$$
$$P(WCEA = Bad) = 0.16$$

Safety of Road Agent (SORA). The Safety of Road Agent is modeled using a Gaussian normal distribution as shown in Eq. 5. Due to the existence of a dependency between the SORA and the WCEA, the input parameters of the SORA change based on the output produced by the WCEA. The WCEA?s output affects not only the mean value and standard deviation of the SORA, but also affects the skewness of the distribution as illustrated by Table 1.

$$N(\mu, \sigma) = f(x, \mu, \sigma) = \frac{1}{\sigma\sqrt{2\pi}} e^{-\frac{(x-\mu)^2}{2\sigma^2}}$$

$$where \; \mu = mean \; and \; \sigma = standard \; deviation$$

(5)

Traffic Load Estimation Agent (TLEA). The Traffic Load Estimation Agent is defined by taking into account the TODA, PDA, WCEA, and the QORA. Each of the nodes affects the output of the TLEA in a distinct way. The value of the TLEA given the TODA can be illustrated using a bimodal distribution, where the modal values in the distribution correspond to the times of the day during which rush hour occurs. The values of the TLEA given either the PDA or the WCEA produce skewed normal distributions. For the TLEA given the PDA, this value is skewed positively for urban areas and skewed negatively for rural areas. This is because the impact of traffic congestion is more severe on urban areas. For the TLEA given the WCEA, the values are skewed positively, neutrally or negatively for good, moderate, and bad weather conditions respectively. The values of the TLEA given the QORA can be illustrated using a normal distribution where a higher quality of road is correlated with a larger mean value and smaller standard deviation. The collective effect of these nodes on the TLEA is given in the equation below. The format of the BN allows for such a definition, and it is given as follows:

$$P(TLEA) = P(TODA) * P(QORA)$$
$$* P(PDA) * P(WCEA)$$

(6)

The formulation of the entire BN is given to the Route Time Estimation Agent. The network itself, based on the agents, can be defined as follows:

$$\beta = P(TLEA|QORA, TODA, PDA, WCEA)$$
$$* P(SORA|WCEA) * P(TODA)$$
$$* P(PDA) * P(QORA) * P(WCEA)$$

(7)

Table 1. SORA distribution parameters

Parameter	Good condition	Moderate condition	Bad condition
mean	0.75	0.55	0.40
standard deviation	0.20	0.25	0.15
skewness	positive	neutral	negative

3.4   Route Time Calculation

The *DCA* and the *TSA* are used to obtain the route distance and maximum legal travelling speed respectively, and the the output value of the BN is used as a weight in the final calculation of the travel time of a given route. The routes used as input for the model are exported from a road netowrk in Google Maps in the form of a *.kml* file. From this file, a list of latitude-longitude coordinates are extracted. Sequential pairs of coordinates are treated as segments of the route.

Distance Calculation Agent. This agent takes the latitudal and longitudnal coordinates from the *.kml* file as direct input. The pairing of two sequential sets of these coordinates represents a segment of the route in the form of a vector. The length of one of these vectors, which is the distance between one of these pairs or coordiniates, is calculated using the Haversine formula. The sum of these vector lengths can be used to calculate the total distance.

Travelling Speed Agent. The travelling speeds are sampled for each segment of the route using a random number generator which draws from a uniform distribution. A sample is drawn for each segment, and this sample determines what travelling speed to associate with the segment. Due to a lack of data with regards to the speed limits associated with non-highway roads, the assumption made by this model is that there is a standard speed associated with each class of road. The classes of road used in the model and their related speeds are listed in the table below.

Route Time Estimation Agent. This agent takes input from all other agents in order to calculate travelling speed. For each route segment in a given route, the ideal travelling time T_i is computed using the output values of the *DCA* and the *TSA* as the input values for D_i and S_i respectively. The output values of the BN is used as a weight for each route segment in order to account for environmental conditions. The product of the weight and the ideal travelling time gives the actual travel time as estimated by the model.

$$RTEA = \sum_{i=1}^{n}[\beta_i * T_i] = \sum_{i=1}^{n}[\beta_i * (\frac{D_i}{S_i})] \tag{8}$$

$\beta_i = weight\ computed\ in\ Eqn(7)\ for\ route\ segment\ i$
$T_i = ideal\ travel\ time\ on\ route\ segment\ i$
$D_i = distance\ of\ route\ segment\ i$
$S_i = maximum\ legal\ speed\ on\ route\ segment\ i$

The output for the RTEA serves as the output of the model for a given set of input values. Output values for different routes are compared in order to determine which route is preferable.

Table 2. Speeds by road classification

Road classification	Travelling speed
Highway	70 mph
County	55 mph
City	30 mph

4   Example Scenarios

In order to illustrate the intended usage and functionality of the model, this section will outline several use cases. A detailed version of the experimentation over the case studies will be presented in the journal version of this article Table 2.

4.1   Case 1: Traffic Congestion and Road Safety

Figure 4 shows three feasible routes between Atlanta, Georgia and Tallahassee, Florida. Let us consider a scenario where traffic is congested in Atlanta at the time of departure and weather conditions are bad. Routes 2 and 3 are the shortest and second-shortest distance routes respectively; however, route's 1 and 3 have the fastest ideal travel time due to their routes being mostly on highways. While the traffic may be bad due to the time of departure, particularly if this time is during rush hour, the weather conditions can also factor into the congestion. In this given scenario, Route 2 would be the preferable Route. This is because there is less use of major freeways in this route, making it less affected by the traffic congestion. The travel time would be less than the alternatives, even though the average speed limit on the roads on Route 2 would be smaller.

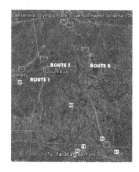
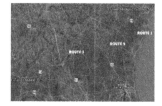
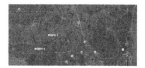

Fig. 4. Case 1   **Fig. 5.** Case 2   **Fig. 6.** Case 3

4.2   Case 2: Approaching Storm

Figure 5 shows three feasible routes between Savannah and Tallahassee. Without taking environmental factors into account, Route 1 provides the fastest travel time. Let us assume that after the user's departure from Savannah, weather conditions become bad due to an incoming storm from the Eastern coast. If the storm were taken into account at the time of departure, Route 1 would have been deemed a less preferable route to take than the Route 3. Since the user has already departed, they cannot travel down Route 3. However, using the model, another route can be calculated from the current point to Tallahassee, FL through Route 2.

4.3   Case 3: Road Construction

Figure 6 illustrates two routes from Troy, AL to Jacksonville, FL. Both paths are routed down mostly the same road apart from a divergence, as can be seen on Fig. 6. Both routes run approximately the same average speed limits, but Route 1 is the shorter path. Let one consider a scenario where there was construction being done on Route 1. If the quality of the road is taken into consideration, the model will indicate that Route 2 is the preferable route.

5   Discussion and Future Work

In real world situations, there are many environmental factors which impact travel time. While this work focuses on major factors of travel time, the addition of nodes to the model's BN could serve to further improve the accuracy of the model. Though the functionality of the system's components is primarily modelled around static data, any or all of the agents in the system could be configured to take live data as input. The use of live data would facilitate the model's ability to dynamically alter the route given changes in the environment, thus improving its usability. The model presented in this work shows a capacity for scalability and configurability. This scalability is facilitated through the atomicity of the model's components. The ability to add or subtract agents and modify settings of existing agents gives the model the potential for a wide range of specific uses. A modified version of this model could be applied to large-scale supply logistics, or even naval and aerial logistics. This can be done by adding nodes dealing with the alternative applications' factors and modifying existing nodes to accomodate new nodes. Using our hybrid model, it is possible to extrapolate an optimal path given environmental factors. It is equally important, however, to facilitate a user-friendly interaction between the application using the model and the individual. One way to accomplish this is to allow the application to have both a video output for a route and a voice-based audio output for directions. Since the model takes a road network as part of the input, it is possible to recalculate the route from any point during travel. If an incident which affects travel time, such as an accident, is detected on the road it would be possible to recalculate the route. The interface would issue a request to the user for recalculation using the voice-based audio output to which the user could reply using his or her device's native input.

6 Conclusions

This study has presented a multi-agent system for finding an optimal path between origin and destination points given different environment factors. When the different environmental factors considered for available routes between origin and destination, the hybrid model in this work allows for a fine-tuned approximation of the travel time. The accuracy of the approximation can be attributed to the modelling of interdependencies between environmental factors. This model has the capacity for user interactivity as well as reactivity with regards to changing conditions. This facilitates the model's applicability in solving the complex problem of route-planning in a dynamic setting. Agents within the model implement methods which allow them to calculate estimates given statistical data and predict the effects of a set of interdependent factors. This set of factors is modeled in the multi-agent system by using a BN. Due to the scalability and atomicity of the systems components, the model presented in the paper has the capacity for a wide range of applications when configured properly.

7 Author Contributions

- Eugene Belyi - Implementation, Formulation of Solution, Design of System, Discussion, Research
- Indravan Patel - Design of System, Discussion, Research
- Anusha Reddy - Discussion, Research
- Vijay Mago - Introduction of Problem, Project Guidance, Discussion

References

Adler, J.L., Blue, V.J.: A cooperative multi-agent transportation management and route guidance system. Transp. Res. Part C: Emerg. Technol. **10**(5), 433–454 (2002)

Borràs, J., Moreno, A., Valls, A.: Intelligent tourism recommender systems a survey. Expert Syst. Appl. **41**, 7370–7389 (2014). Please check the edit made in Ref. [2]

Gajpal, Y., Abad, P.: An ant colony system (acs) for vehicle routing problem with simultaneous delivery and pickup. Comput. Oper. Res. **36**(12), 3215–3223 (2009)

Garcia, A., Arbelaitz, O., Linaza, M.T., Vansteenwegen, P., Souffriau, W.: Personalized tourist route generation. In: Daniel, F., Facca, F.M. (eds.) ICWE 2010. LNCS, vol. 6385, pp. 486–497. Springer, Heidelberg (2010)

Mago, V.K., Woolrych, R., Dabbaghian, V., Sixsmith, A.: Artificial intelligence: a tool for better understanding complex problems in long-term care, Chapter 23. In: Israr, N., Issac, B. (eds.) Case Studies in Intelligent Computing, pp. 500–520. Auerbach Publications, Boston (2014)

Midwest Regional Climate Center, Winter storms (2013)

Nadi, S., Delavar, M.R.: Multi-criteria, personalized route planning using quantifier-guided ordered weighted averaging operators. Int. J. Appl. Earth Obs. Geoinf. **13**(3), 322–335 (2011)

National Hurricane Center, Hurricane season dates (2014). http://www.nhc.noaa.gov/

Umarani, R., Selvi, V.: Comparative analysis of ant colony and particle swarm optimization techniques. Int. J. Comput. Appl. 5(4), 1–6 (2010). Published By Foundation of Computer Science

United States Census Bureau, 2010 census urban and rural classification and urban area criteria (2010). http://www.census.gov/geo/reference/ua/urban-rural-2010.html

Vansteenwegen, P.: Planning in tourism and public transportation. 4OR **7**(3), 293–296 (2009)

Yu, C.-C., Chang, H.: Towards context-aware recommendation for personalized mobile travel planning. In: Vinh, P.C., Hung, N.M., Tung, N.T., Suzuki, J. (eds.) ICCASA 2012. LNICST, vol. 109, pp. 121–130. Springer, Heidelberg (2013)

Zafar, K., Baig, A.R.: Optimization of route planning and exploration using multi agent system. Multimedia Tools Appl. **56**(2), 245–265 (2012)

Zolfpour-Arokhlo, M., Selamat, A., Hashim, S.Z.M.: Route planning model of multi-agent system for a supply chain management. Expert Syst. Appl. **40**(5), 1505–1518 (2013)

Improving Service Quality by Prioritizing Service Attributes Using SERVQUAL and Kano Model

A Case Study of Nursing Home in Taiwan

Chin-Mei Chou[✉], Cindy Sutanto, and Shu-Kai Wu

Department of Industrial Engineering, Yuan Ze University,
Zhongli District, Taiwan R.O.C.
kinmei@saturn.yzu.edu.tw

Abstract. The purpose of this study is to improve the healthcare service in nursing home base on customer desire. Previous studies found that Taiwan nowadays is facing the rapid growth of the ageing population and lack of resources for taking care of elderly. Nursing home has become one of solutions to overcome these issues. However the current condition indicates that some nursing homes can not satisfy the customer desires, especially for elderly who are more sensitive. SERVQUAL model is used to measure the service quality base on the gap score between customer expectation and perception. Kano model is used to categorized and prioritize each service attributes according the degree of influence toward customer satisfaction. The findings of a case study are presented.

Keywords: Service quality · SERVQUAL · Kano · Nursing home · Elderly

1 Introduction

Recent studies show Taiwan is one of country that encounters ageing population issue (Hsu, et al. 2004, Chen, et al. 2010). The Council for Economic Planning and Development (CEPD) had predicted that the rapid growth of elderly population would change Taiwan from ageing society to aged society in 2017 (Bartlett and Shwu-Chong 2000, Kang 2012). In consequence, the rising of many healthcare issues included the long term care for disabled people are unavoidable (Chang, et al. 2010). The global economy changing also would have affected the family structure changing (Kang 2012) and declined birth rates (Tien and Tsai 2013). Every couple in Taiwan nowadays only gives birth to an average of 1.1 children (C.-Y. Chen 2010). As the result, the available resources for taking care of elderly at home are gradually reduced and these changes present considerable challenges to meet the needs of Taiwan's ageing society (Phillips 2002).

Nursing home has become one of solutions to overcome this problem. Nursing home is a multi-residence housing facility that provides service package to elderly. Nursing home plays important role in a long-term care service system which related with people's live (Zinn, Aaronson and Rosko 1993). Elderly feeling and experiences should be involved in the service process because these are important for the life's

© Springer International Publishing Switzerland 2015
S. Yamamoto (Ed.): HIMI 2015, Part I, LNCS 9172, pp. 513–525, 2015.
DOI: 10.1007/978-3-319-20612-7_49

meaning in nursing home (Anderberg and Berglund, Elderly persons' experiences of striving to receive care on their own terms in nursing homes 2010). Customer desire is an important component for new product or service development and the innovation process (Hartono and Chuan 2011). An assessment of service quality based on customer desire can give valuable information to improve the service quality in health service (Mostyn, et al. 2000). SERVQUAL (Parasuraman, Zeithaml and Berry 1988) model has been widely used in health care service area. It was designed to measure the service quality as customer perceived by analyzing the gap between customer expectation and perception. This model provides 22 basic service attributes as analyzing factor with five basic dimensions, (1) Tangible (the appearance of physical facilities, equipment, personnel, and communication materials) (2) Reliability (the ability to perform the promised service dependably and accurately) (3) Responsiveness (the willingness to help customers and to provide prompt service) (4) Assurance (the knowledge and courtesy of employees and their ability to convey trust and confidence) (5) Empathy (the provision of caring, individualized attention to customers). However, even though SERVQUAL provides the gap as the analysis result, it was not designed to address the element of innovation and how the gap can be closed (Tan and Pawitra 2001). Furthermore, it was found that there were nonlinear and nonsymmetrical relationship between service quality and customer satisfaction (Kano, et al. 1984, Baki, et al. 2009). Therefore, it is needed to integrate SERVQUAL model with other service quality tools which more focus on analyzing the relationship between service quality and customer satisfaction.

Nowadays, the use of Kano model (as shown in Fig. 1) has been barely presented into healthcare service business. The Kano model has ability to take out unspoken customer desires (Hartono and Chuan 2011) and to identify attributes which have greatest influence on customer satisfaction (Matzler and Hinterhuber 1998). Kano model provides the categorization of service attributes into three major groups, M-must be, O-one dimensional, and A-attractive (Kano, et al. 1984). Categorizing the service attributes makes the prioritization for services easier because it can be seen clearly which service attributes give greatest effect to increase customer satisfaction.

In addition, the use of Kano model should be initiated by developing questionnaires and SERVQUAL has the ability to develop the questionnaires base on five dimensions to cope all of the service aspects. The purpose of this study is to improve the health care service in nursing home base on customer desires. Servqual and Kano model will be integrated to investigate and to prioritize the service attributes which have greatest impact to the elderly through customer expectation-perception relationship and Kano categories (availability-unavailability relationship of service attributes).

2   Methodology

2.1   Setting

This study was conducted in 4 nursing homes in Taoyuan County. To accomplish the purpose of this study, a quantitative research approach was adopted and the integration method between SERVQUAL and Kano model was used to develop research instruments and to analyze the result. The research framework is shown in Fig. 2.

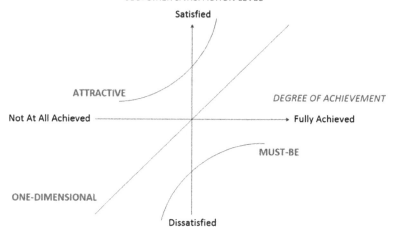

Fig. 1. Kano model (Kano, et al. 1984)

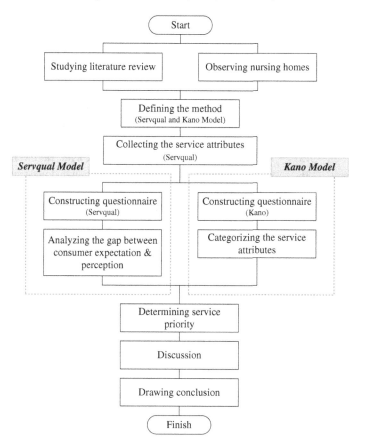

Fig. 2. Research framework

2.2   Collecting Service Attributes

The service attributes were collected base on 22 items basic service attributes of SERVQUAL model and therefore were adjusted to be used in nursing home according to observation results. A total of 24 services attributes (as shown in Table 1) were categorized into 5 basic dimensions of SERVQUAL.

Table 1. List of service attributes

Dimension	No.	Code	Service Attributes
Tangible	1	T1.	Medical instrument and physical facilities are visually appealing
	2	T2.	Employees uniform are clean, nice, and neat
	3	T3.	Clean, adequate supplies, and well maintained for every rooms
	4	T4.	Well lighted for every rooms
	5	T5.	Suitable temperature at patient rooms
	6	T6.	Meals served are clean and hygiene
	7	T7.	Meals served are delicious
	8	T8.	The atmosphere for every rooms are cozy
	9	T9.	The scent for every rooms are refreshing
Reliability	10	RL1.	Appropriate employees response
	11	RL2.	Medical treatment and doctor visiting are well scheduled
	12	RL3.	Available and adequate patient family visiting time
	13	RL4.	All patient activities are well scheduled
	14	RL5.	The employees solve the patient's problem sincerely
	15	RL6.	All equipment (AC, TV, radio, light, etc.) work properly
Responsiveness	16	R1.	Employees give clear information and understandable
	17	R2.	Appropriate and prompt services
	18	R3.	Quick medical treatment response when patient need it
Assurance	19	A1.	Feel safe and feel at home
	20	A2.	Employees behavior instills confidence in patients
Empathy	21	E1.	Good communication among employees and patients
	22	E2.	Employees are helpful, careful, and friendly
	23	E3.	Nurses understands patient's needs
	24	E4.	No discrimination to the patients

2.3   Constructing Questionnaire

SERVQUAL Questionnaire. To evaluate the service quality, customers will compare the service they expected/expectation and perceived/perception (Lewis and Booms 1983, Parasuraman et al. 1985). Two types of questionnaires were first developed to identify customer expectation and perception. The question to identify consumer expectation is how important these services attribute, with 5-point Likert scale method ranging from not important at all (1) to very important (5). The question to identify consumer perception is how do you feel about these services attributes provided, also with 5-point Likert scale method ranging from very bad (1) to very good (5).

Kano Questionnaire. A pair of question was formulated and the elderly were asked to answer in one of five different ways, ranging from 'I like it very much' (1) to 'I do not like it' (5). The first question (functional questionnaire) concerns with the response of the elderly due to the availability of services (how do you feel if these service attributes are well provided) and the second question (dysfunctional questionnaire) concerns with elderly response to the unavailability of services (how do you feel if these service attributes are NOT provided).

2.4 Pilot Study

The result of pilot study showed, since there were 4 types of questionnaires (expectation, perception, and a pair of Kano questionnaire), the elderly could reply to a maximum 3 questionnaires before losing patient and interest. Hence, the interviewer asked those four questions in once for each service attributes. Some service attributes were also modified by adjusting to the elderly viewpoint. For instance, the speed of the employees' service will not affect the elderly response since they are old and do every activity slowly, but what the elderly need is the appropriate service and the employees' understanding to their needs.

2.5 Data Collection

After the final questionnaires was constructed, the data collection was proceed. A total of 42 elderly which selected randomly were participated in this study. Firstly, the interviewers explained the study objective to elderly. Secondly, the elderly were asked for responses base on service attributes in 4 questionnaires (expectation, perception, functional, dysfunctional). The process of interviewing an elderly took around 30 min.

3 Result

3.1 Participants

The elderly gender was split into 67 % (28) males and 33 % (14) females. The average age was 76 years old (at range 71–80) and the average length of staying in the nursing homes was 5 years (at range 1–5). The average age when the elderly started to live in nursing home was 71 years old.

3.2 Questionnaure Validity and Reliability Test

Validity and reliability test was conducted using SPSS 16.0 to evaluate the adequacy of relationship model between constructs and the measurement items of the research instrument. Validity refers to the degree to which evidence and theoretical support the interpretations of test scores entailed by proposed uses of test (Messick 1995). Reliability refers to the internal consistency of construct variable by using Cronbach's Alpha coefficient (Osburn 2000, Streiner 2003).

In this study, criterion-related validity was evaluated using Pearson correlation coefficient to examine the relationship between the score of each attribute and the total score. The results showed the item code RL2 (medical treatment and doctor visiting are well scheduled) from expectation questionnaire and A1 (feel safe and feel at home) from perception questionnaire were not valid because the coefficient r (RL2 = 0.193; A1 = 0.258) < 0.304 (for n = 42). For Kano questionnaires, all of the service attributes were valid (r > 0.304).

For reliability test, the value of 0.7 of Cronbach's Alpha was suggested as a standard (Nunnally 1994). The result showed the coefficient for all questionnaires were reliable (expectation = 0.884, perception = 0.900, Kano = 0.891 and 0.944).

Some of variables did not reach the standard of validity test. However, based on some literature review and peer evaluation, it was decided to keep those invalid variables on the next analysis in order to have better comprehension of the study.

3.3   Data Analysis

SERVQUAL. The service quality evaluation process generated the mean score of expectation and perception for each service attributes based on total score from each elderly divided by the number of the elderly. The result showed the elderly have high expectation where all the mean of each service attribute reached score above 4. The highest mean score was 4.69 for item code T3 (clean, adequate supplies, and well maintained for every rooms) and the lowest mean score was 4.19 for item code RL4 (all patient activities are well scheduled). The result also showed the elderly have high expectation on the 'empathy' category. For the customer perception, the highest mean score was 3.98 for item code T9 (the scent for every rooms are refreshing) and RL6 (all equipment such as AC, TV, radio, light work properly), and the lowest mean score was 3.14 for item code A1 (feel safe and feel at home). The result also showed that the elderly had high perception on the 'reliability' category.

The gap score which is the difference value between perception and expectation score showed the range of difference between how the services were experienced and expected by the elderly. The lower of the gap value, the wider the range of difference between the services are experienced and expected. The result showed the item code T5 (suitable temperature at patient rooms) and A1 (feel safe and feel at home) had the lowest gap scores (−1.26 and −1.19).

Kano. The elderly responses for each service attribute from functional and dysfunctional questionnaire were combined and categorized based on Kano evaluation table (shown in Table 2). Frequency analysis was applied as shown in Table 3 to evaluate and to define Kano category for each service attributes regarding the highest frequency they had (Sauerwein, et al. 1996, Bayraktaroglu and Özgen 2008).

Table 2. Kano evaluation table (Kano, et al. 1984)

		Dysfunctional				
		1	2	3	4	5
Functional	1	Q	A	A	A	O
	2	R	I	I	I	M
	3	R	I	I	I	M
	4	R	I	I	I	M
	5	R	R	R	R	Q

Table 3. Frequency analysis

Service Attributes	A	O	M	I	R	Q	Total	Category
Medical instrument and physical facilities are visually appealing	15	12	5	10	0	0	42	A
Employees uniform are clean, nice, and neat	10	14	4	13	1	0	42	O
Clean, adequate supplies, and well maintained for every rooms	14	16	3	9	0	0	42	O
Well lighted for every rooms	12	11	5	13	1	0	42	I
Suitable temperature at patient rooms	15	11	4	12	0	0	42	A
Meals served are clean and hygiene	7	16	3	14	2	0	42	O
Meals served are delicious	9	15	6	10	2	0	42	O
The atmosphere for every rooms are cozy	15	12	4	8	3	0	42	A
The scent for every rooms are refreshing	16	12	5	9	0	0	42	A
Appropriate employees response	14	7	8	12	1	0	42	A
Medical treatment and doctor visiting are well scheduled	18	8	4	12	0	0	42	A
Available and adequate patient family visiting time	18	6	5	11	2	0	42	A
All patient activities are well scheduled	11	11	4	15	1	0	42	I
The employees solve the patient's problem sincerely	20	11	5	6	0	0	42	A
All equipment (AC, TV, radio, light, etc.) work properly	17	8	7	10	0	0	42	A
Employees give clear information and understandable	19	9	8	6	0	0	42	A
Appropriate and prompt services	12	12	3	14	0	1	42	I
	16	12	4	10	0	0	42	A

(*Continued*)

Table 3. (*Continued*)

Service Attributes	A	O	M	I	R	Q	Total	Category
Quick medical treatment response when patient need it								
Feel safe and feel at home	17	9	4	11	1	0	42	A
Employees behavior instills confidence in patients	11	11	6	12	1	1	42	I
Service Attributes	A	O	M	I	R	Q	Total	Category
Good communication among employees and patients	15	12	6	9	0	0	42	A
Employees are helpful, careful, and friendly	14	15	6	5	2	0	42	O
Nurses understands patient's needs	18	13	3	8	0	0	42	A
No discrimination to the patients	15	16	5	6	0	0	42	O

According to Kano (1984), there are 6 Kano model categories: (1) Attractive/A, the increase of service attributes quality will increase the consumer satisfaction, but the decrease of service attributes quality will not decrease the consumer satisfaction (2) One-dimensional/O, the service attributes quality is proportional to the customer satisfaction (3) Must-be/M, the increase of service attributes quality will not increase the consumer satisfaction, but the decrease of service attributes quality will decrease the consumer satisfaction (4) Indifferent/I, whether the service attributes quality increase or decrease will not affect to consumer satisfaction (5) Reverse/R, the service attributes quality is not linear to the customer satisfaction (6) Questionable/Q, whether the service attributes quality increase or decrease, it has possibility to satisfy and/or to disappoint the consumer.

The result of Kano categorization showed 14 items were on Attractive category, 6 items on One-dimensional category, 4 items on Indifferent category. Five of six service attributes in 'reliability' dimension had attractive (A) quality, which were appropriate employees response, medical treatment and doctor visiting are well scheduled, available and adequate patient family visiting time, the employees solve the elderly problem sincerely, all equipment (AC, TV, radio, light, etc.) work properly, and the rest was indifferent (I) quality which is all patient activities are well scheduled. This showed that the elderly expected the ability of employees to perform the promised service dependably, consistently, and accurately. The elderly did not expect their activities are well scheduled (this had the lowest score of expectation questionnaire, 4.19), therefore whether this attribute quality increase or decrease will not affect the elderly satisfaction (Indifferent category). This was understandable since the average age of the elderly was 76 years old, thus they are not able to do a lot of activities and they had a lot of free times. What the elderly needed was empathy or the provision of caring and individualized attention.

Integration of SERVQUAL and Kano. Offering consumers the expected service attributes (must-be) will not meet customer satisfaction in few next day because of the temporary world and the environment changing (Shen, Tan and Xie 2000, Pawitra and Tan 2003). Thus, instead focusing on Must-be or One-dimensional attributes, the nursing homes should focus on Attractive attributes (please refer to Fig. 1) in order to get higher elderly satisfaction (Chen and Su 2006, Hartono and Chuan 2011). The statistic data of combination of SERVQUAL (gap score) and Kano model (categorization) is shown in Table 4.

The result of this study showed the service attributes provided had not achieved the elderly desires since all the gap had negative scores with average score $= -0.83$. The 5 service attributes with lowest of gap scores were suitable temperature at patient rooms (-1.26), feel safe and feel at home (-1.19), medical treatment and doctor visiting are well scheduled (-1.10), meals served are clean and hygiene (-1.05), appropriate and prompt service (-1.05).

Refining to Kano model, improving the service attributes with Attractive quality would give more impact to elderly satisfaction, thus the attributes 'meals served are clean and hygiene' and 'appropriate and prompt service' were eliminated because they were on one-dimensional and indifferent category. As the final result, the first priority of service attributes need to be improved was 'the adjustment of the temperature of patients' rooms'. The second and the third priority would be 'feel safe and feel at home' and 'medical treatment and doctor visiting are well scheduled'.

The results of this study were based on the elderly desires through the questionnaire responses. Based on gap score analysis, 24 items of service attributes had not satisfy the elderly needs since all items had negative gap score. During the service encounters, customers compare the services provided with their expectation and evaluate the service quality based on that comparison. The negative gap scores indicated the services provided were less than customer expectation. It was naturally understandable that the elderly had higher expectation to the suitability of the temperature of patients' rooms since the weather is unstable recently. Thus, it is important for nursing homes to adjust the temperature carefully in order to enhance the elderly comfort.

4   Discussion

The prioritization of service attributes based on Kano and SERVQUAL in nursing homes has significant implications for improving service quality. Both Kano and SERVQUAL model collect and analyze data base on customer desire. Customer desire is important to be involved in service process, specifically for elderly who are more sensitive and easily to get hurt. The elderly were active in receiving care on their own terms and demands. The elderly also tried to manage and maintain their own abilities to have a sense of control for their life (Anderberg and Berglund 2010).

SERVQUAL model emphasized the analysis based on the gap score between perception and expectation, while Kano emphasized the analysis based on categorization.

Table 4. Statistic data of SERVQUAL and Kano model combination

No.	Code	Service Attributes	Expectation	Perception	Gap	Kano Category
Tangible			*4.42*	*3.62*	*-0.80*	
1	T1.	Medical instrument and physical facilities are visually appealing	4.26	3.74	-0.52	A
2	T2.	Employees uniform are clean, nice, and neat	4.24	3.83	-0.40	O
3	T3.	Clean, adequate supplies, and well maintained for every rooms	**4.69**	3.88	-0.81	O
4	T4.	Well lighted for every rooms	4.33	3.69	-0.64	I
5	T5.	Suitable temperature at patient rooms	4.57	3.31	**-1.26**	A
6	T6.	Meals served are clean and hygiene	4.29	3.24	**-1.05**	O
7	T7.	Meals served are delicious	4.29	3.36	-0.93	O
8	T8.	The atmosphere for every rooms are cozy	4.43	3.55	-0.88	A
9	T9.	The scent for every rooms are refreshing	4.64	**3.98**	-0.67	A
Reliability			*4.39*	*3.73*	*-0.67*	
10	RL1.	Appropriate employees response	4.43	3.74	-0.69	A
11	RL2.	Medical treatment and doctor visiting are well scheduled	4.48	3.38	**-1.10**	A
12	RL3.	Available and adequate patient family visiting time	4.33	3.71	-0.62	A
13	RL4.	All patient activities are well scheduled	**4.19**	3.88	-0.31	I
14	RL5.	The employees solve the patient's problem sincerely	4.62	3.67	-0.95	A
15	RL6.	All equipment (AC, TV, radio, light, etc.) work properly	4.31	**3.98**	-0.33	A
Responsiveness			*4.41*	*3.38*	*-1.03*	
16	R1.	Employees give clear information and understandable	4.52	3.57	-0.95	A

(*Continued*)

Table 4. (*Continued*)

No.	Code	Service Attributes	Expectation	Perception	Gap	Kano Category
17	R2.	Appropriate and prompt services	4.50	3.45	**-1.05**	I
18	R3.	Quick medical treatment response when patient need it	4.33	3.38	-0.95	A
Assurance			*4.37*	*3.30*	*-1.07*	
19	A1.	Feel safe and feel at home	4.33	**3.14**	**-1.19**	A
20	A2.	Employees behavior instills confidence in patients	4.40	3.45	-0.95	I
Empathy			*4.46*	*3.60*	*-0.86*	
21	E1.	Good communication among employees and patients	4.43	3.48	-0.95	A
22	E2.	Employees are helpful, careful, and friendly	4.40	3.81	-0.60	O
23	E3.	Nurses understands patient's needs	4.52	3.50	-1.02	A
24	E4.	No discrimination to the patients	4.50	3.62	-0.88	O
Grand Mean			*4.42*	*3.58*	*-0.83*	

*Notes: Gap = Perception − Expectation; A : attractive; O : one-dimensional; I : indifferent

By using SERVQUAL only, even though the difference between customer perception and expectation can be identified, it still cannot identify whether the improvement of those service attributes with lowest gap score can give significant improvement to increase customer satisfaction. In this case, further analysis of customer expectation to see how attractive those service attributes targeted are needed. Thus, the measurement based on the gap score is confused by customer expectation level which is necessary to be analyzed.

Kano has ability to categorize how attractive the service attributes toward customer by analyzing customer responses for its availability and unavailability. As mentioned before that the relationship between customer response and service quality is not always linear and SERVQUAL model cannot overcome this issue, therefore Kano model can be used to measure customer expectation by categorizing the service attributes into Attractive/One-dimensional/Must-be/Indifferent/Reverse/Questionable.

The result showed some service attributes which have low gap scores were not categorized in Attractive category. This means improvisation to those service attributes can make the gap between customer perception and expectation closer, but it does not give significant effect to improve customer satisfaction, because those service attributes are not attractive for the elderly. Since the goal of nursing homes is to improve service quality base on elderly desire, therefore the combination of SERVQUAL gap score and Kano categorization method is appropriate to be used.

5 Conclusion

This present study has proposed the application of SERVQUAL and Kano model with the object of determining the service improvement priority in which consumer perception and expectation influences the service attributes. The results had showed the SERVQUAL and Kano model were useful as tools to measure the service quality and to define the prioritization of which service attributes need to be improved according to elderly desires. This study conclude there were 3 service attributes (in sequence) need to be improved which had the lowest gap score and were categorized in Attractive (A) quality. They were 'the adjustment of the temperature of patients', 'feel safe and feel at home' and 'medical treatment and doctor visiting are well scheduled'. In addition, the improvement of service should be performed across all the dimensions with higher emphasis on Reliability dimension in order to enhance the elderly satisfaction.

References

Anderberg, P., Berglund, A.-L.: Elderly persons' experiences of striving to receive care on their own terms in nursing homes. Int. J. Nurs. Pract. **16**(1), 64–68 (2010)

Baki, B., Basfirinci, C.S., Ilker Murat, A.R., Cilingir, Z.: An application of integrating SERVQUAL and Kano's model into QFD for logistics services: a case study from Turkey. Asia Pacific J. Mark. Logistics **21**(1), 106–126 (2009)

Bartlett, H.P., Shwu-Chong, W.: 11 Ageing and aged care in Taiwan. Ageing in the Asia-Pacific Region: Issues, Policies and Future Trends **2**, 210 (2000)

Bayraktaroglu, G., Özgen, Ö.: Integrating the Kano model, AHP and planning matrix: QFD application in library services. Libr. Manage. **28**(4/5), 327–351 (2008)

Chang, H.-T., Lai, H.-Y., Hwang, I.-H., Ho, M.-M., Hwang, S.-J.: Home healthcare services in Taiwan: a nationwide study among the older population. BMC Health Serv. Res. **10**(1), 274 (2010)

Chen, C.-R., Lydia Hsu, W.-H., Tsai, H.-L., Lu, C.-W., A study of employer background in care demand in southern Taiwan. In: Proceedings of the 11th WSEAS international conference on Applied Computer and Applied Computational Science, pp.134–138 (2012)

Chen, C.-Y.: Meeting the challenges of eldercare in Taiwan's aging society. J. Clin. Gerontol. Geriatr. **1**(1), 2–4 (2010)

Chen, Y.-H., Chao-Ton, S.: A Kano-CKM model for customer knowledge discovery. Total Qual. Manage. Bus. Excellence **17**(5), 589–608 (2006)

Hartono, M., Chuan, T.K.: How the Kano model contributes to Kansei engineering in services. Ergon. **54**(11), 987–1004 (2011)

Hsu, W.-M., Cheng, C.-Y., Liu, J.-H., Tsai, S.-Y.: Prevalence and causes of visual impairment in an elderly Chinese population in Taiwan: the Shihpai Eye Study. Ophthalmology **111**(1), 62–69 (2004)

Kang, S.-C.: Initiation of the Suan-Lien Living Lab–a Living Lab with an Elderly Welfare Focus. Int. J. Autom. Smart Technol. **2**(3), 189–199 (2012)

Kano, N., Seraku, N., Takahashi, F., Tsuji, S.: Attractive quality and must-be quality. J. Japan. Soc. Qual. Control **14**(2), 147–156 (1984)

Lewis, R.C., Booms, B.H.: The marketing aspects of service quality. Emerging Perspect. Serv. Mark. **65**(4), 99–107 (1983)

Matzler, K., Hinterhuber, H.H.: How to make product development projects more successful by integrating Kano's model of customer satisfaction into quality function deployment. Technovation **18**(1), 25–38 (1998)

Messick, S.: Validity of psychological assessment: validation of inferences from persons' responses and performances as scientific inquiry into score meaning. Am. Psychol. **50**(9), 741 (1995)

Mostyn, M.M., Race, K.E., Seibert, J.H., Johnson, M.: Quality assessment in nursing home facilities: Measuring customer satisfaction. Am. J. Med. Qual. **15**(2), 54–61 (2000)

Nunnally, J.C.: Psychometric Theory, 3rd edn. McGraw-Hill, New York (1994)

Osburn, H.G.: Coefficient alpha and related internal consistency reliability coefficients. Psychol. Methods **5**(3), 343–355 (2000)

Parasuraman, A., Zeithaml, V.A., Berry, L.L.: Servqual. J. Retail. **64**(1), 12–40 (1988)

Parasuraman, A., Zeithaml, V.A., Berry, L.L.: A conceptual model of service quality and its implications for future research. J. Mark. **49**(4), 41–50 (1985)

Pawitra, T.A., Tan, K.C.: Tourist satisfaction in Singapore–a perspective from Indonesian tourists. Managing Serv. Qual. **13**(5), 399–411 (2003)

Phillips, D.R.: Ageing in the Asia-Pacific region: Issues, policies and future trends. Routledge, London (2002)

Sauerwein, E., Bailom, F., Matzler, K., Hinterhuber, H.H.: The kano model: how to delight your customers. Int. Working Sem. Prod. Econ. **1**, 313–327 (1996)

Shen, X.-X., Tan, K.C., Xie, M.: An integrated approach to innovative product development using Kano's model and QFD. Eur. J. Innov. Manage. **3**(2), 91–99 (2000)

Streiner, D.L.: Starting at the beginning: an introduction to coefficient alpha and internal consistency. J. Pers. Assess. **80**(1), 99–103 (2003)

Tan, K.C., Pawitra, T.A.: Integrating SERVQUAL and Kano's model into QFD for service excellence development. Managing Serv. Qual. **11**(6), 418–430 (2001)

Tien, C.H., Tsai, W.C.: Resource Integration Strategies for Elder Education Organizations: A Case Study in Taichung, Taiwan. US-China Education Review, pp. 459–469 (2013)

Zinn, J.S., Aaronson, W.E., Rosko, M.D.: Variations in the outcomes of care provided in Pennsylvania nursing homes: Facility and environmental correlates. Medical Care, pp. 475–487 (1993)

Travel-Information Sharing System Using Tweets with Location Information

Junko Itou$^{(\boxtimes)}$, Keiichiro Nakamura, and Jun Munemori

Faculty of Systems Engineering, Wakayama University, 930 Sakaedani,
Wakayama 640-8510, Japan
{itou,munemori}@sys.wakayama-u.ac.jp

1 Introduction

In this article, we propose a travel-information sharing system. Internet-based travel-advisory services have been widely used, and these sites allow users to search and garner information regarding tourist destinations more easily. However, with such services it is difficult to find live information about a particular location, including route information, owing to the quantity of information posted on the Web.

In this study, we focus on tweets containing location information from online posts on Twitter. Twitter users often post tweets that include travel information, such as information concerning traffic, stores, and accommodation. The proposed system automatically places these tweets on a map as a pictorial symbol. The symbols represent categories of information. Users who search for travel information will easily obtain live information by filtering the information according to the category or location, and by replying to the tweet to ask for additional details.

This paper is organized as follows: in Sect. 2, we describe the related service for sharing travel information. In Sect. 3, we explain our proposed system, which supports sharing travel information using tweets. A validation test for our system will be given in Sect. 4. Finally, we discuss conclusions and future work in Sect. 5.

2 Related Works

Google Places is one information-sharing service that uses a map [1]. Users share information such as addresses, photographs, and comments about popular locations. Most of the information relates to shops, and especially to restaurants, and users can evaluate the shops on five levels. In some cases, a lot of information may overlap so users cannot easily locate the information they are trying to seeking.

In existing systems or services that offer a shared digital-travel diary [2,3], users post reports about their experiences at a tourist destination in a shared diary. In general, the diaries are collections of multiple postings based on the respective viewpoints of various writers. Therefore, these include information

© Springer International Publishing Switzerland 2015
S. Yamamoto (Ed.): HIMI 2015, Part I, LNCS 9172, pp. 526–534, 2015.
DOI: 10.1007/978-3-319-20612-7_50

that is unnecessary and descriptions that are redundant to users seeking pertinent travel information. Searchers must read through all of the postings, making it difficult to obtain travel information in a short period of time.

Approaches using geotagged photo data posted to a photo-sharing service are proposed [4,5]. They analyzed large quantities of photograph and extracted travel information such as activities or typical patterns of sightseeing. These systems provide users visual analysis result about attractive areas or example itineraries. Tiwari and Kaushik [6] proposed a tourist spot recommender system using enrichment information including weather conditions and traffic conditions. They assemble a database that contains location data and contextual information registered by users. Users could obtain detailed graphical information about a tourist area using these systems; however, users could not ask a question to investigate the location in more detail or to know the conditions under which the information was posted.

In order to solve these problems, we propose a system that can communicate information with a poster and a visitor using twitter. In Sect. 3, we describe the system's details.

3   System Framework

3.1   Goal

The kind of Information that tourists require differs according to the purpose, means of transportation, and the time during which they intend to visit. Our goal is to realize a system for both prospective tourists and those who have visited the destination so that they can share well-organized visual information about the location and routes. In this study, we focus on Twitter because tweets well reflect the situation at the time of posting.

Our system is an application that runs on an Android phone. Users can post a tweet, browse others' tweets, and use a map with the system. Users who post travel information can choose a category that corresponds to the content of their post. The tweets are plotted on a map based on position information. Users who are seeking travel information can view the contents of these tweets on the timeline and on the map.

3.2   Pictorial Symbols

Tweets are displayed as pictorial symbols on the map. Figure 1 provides an illustration of the map with some pictorial symbols. The pictorial symbols represent different selected categories. Figure 2 is a list of the available pictorial symbols. The pictorial symbols in this list denote (i) chances, (ii) road signs, (iii) events, (iv) accidents, (v) accommodations, (vi) landscape, (vii) souvenirs, (viii) stores (including restaurants), (ix) traffic information, and (x) other.

These ten categories were adopted based on the results of preliminary research that involved college students who use Twitter every day. The preliminary research was carried out in two steps.

Fig. 1. Pictorial symbols on the map.

Fig. 2. List of the pictorial symbols.

As the first step, we asked the eight participants to answer the question, "When you post a tweet about tourism on Twitter, what content do you post?". They answered questions about twenty kinds of content including landscape, festival, impressions of food, unexpected encounters with friends, unidentifiable things, and so on. We classified these answers into the ten categories.

Second, we investigated whether these ten categories were appropriate and could be chosen when users posted a tourist tweet. We collected actual tweets posted in tourist areas, and asked seven participants to classify them into the ten categories. The participants checked forty tweets, and multiple answers were allowed. The results of this classification are shown at Table 1. The values in Table 1 are the numbers of tweets.

Eight of the ten categories were selected more than three times. Some participants responded that sometimes it was difficult to distinguish (vii) and (viii) and (ii) and (ix). Category (ii) was not selected even once. We applied these ten categories, including the two less-used categories, to our system, and we considered the need for the categories through an experiment.

Table 1. Result of classification of tweets.

Subjects	Categories										Total
	(i)	(ii)	(iii)	(iv)	(v)	(vi)	(vii)	(viii)	(ix)	(x)	
A	4	0	2	0	3	7	5	4	0	15	40
B	5	0	7	0	3	13	7	7	5	3	50
C	3	0	8	0	4	18	6	4	6	1	50
D	5	0	3	1	2	19	6	6	6	15	63
E	6	0	4	0	3	16	7	1	8	1	46
F	7	0	6	0	3	5	8	3	4	4	40
G	6	0	7	2	3	13	9	7	5	0	52
Avge.	5.1	0.0	5.3	0.4	3.0	13.0	6.9	4.6	4.9	5.6	48.7

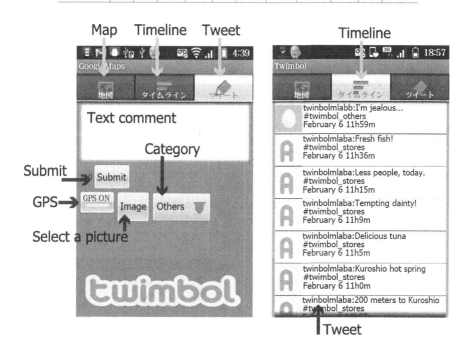

Fig. 3. Overview of the proposed system.

3.3 Post Screen and Browsing Screen

The overview for our system is shown in Fig. 3. Our system consists of two parts. One part is the post screen, and the other part is the browsing screen. An example of the post screen is in the left image in Fig. 3, and the browsing screen is in the right image in Fig. 3. The browsing screen is further divided into two parts. Users operate each function by switching tabs.

Users enter text in the text box in the posting screen and post a tweet by tapping the submit button. Users select a category to suit the content of the tweet using the category button. The category 'others' is selected by default. When the GPS button is turned ON, the system adds location information to the tweet. The image selection button is used when users attach an image to the tweet. Users can select an image from the image data stored in the Android device. They can also use image data captured by the Android device's camera. When users tap the category button, the list of categories is shown. The category name that users tap is automatically added to the tweet as a hash tag.

The right image in Fig. 3 is an example of the browsing screen that consists of a user's timeline. In its initial state, the most recent twenty tweets are displayed. When users scroll to the bottom, the next twenty tweets are shown. In this screen, users can logout of their twitter account, search tweets, update the timeline and run a category search. Furthermore, users can reply in order to ask a question about a place or a situation and they can retweet a tweet to share the information.

3.4   Search Function

Users have three ways to search for travel information using the search function. One of the ways is a timeline search as described above. The second way is to search on the map of tweets represented as pictorial symbols. The third way is to refine a search by using categories. In each search function, it is possible to narrow down the search by entering a radius starting from the current location. Figure 4 provides an example of a tweet search with the category search function. Users select a category in the left image in Fig. 4, and users enter the search range in kilometers from the current position in the right image. The search results

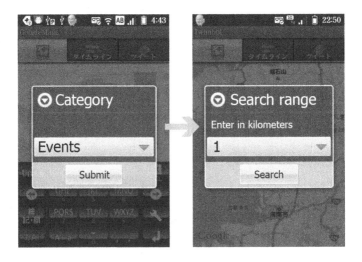

Fig. 4. Example of tweet search.

Fig. 5. Example of search result.

are shown as pictorial symbols on the map. Figure 5 provides an example of a search result. Users tap a pictorial symbol on the map, and then the detail of the tweet is displayed as shown in Fig. 5. Users can obtain detailed information by replying and retweeting this screen.

4   Experimental Results

4.1   Experimental Outline

We conducted two experiments to evaluate the interface of the proposed system from both perspectives - posting and browsing - and to investigate the effect of sharing travel information using categories and a map.

The experimental subjects consisted of nine college students - seven males and two females. They were divided into three groups.

In the first experiment, each group visited a tourist location. We asked the participants to act on the assumption that they were tourists and instructed them to tweet in the area. They were free to post impressions, messages, photographs, and information for one hour. The tourist destinations were a shopping mall along the beach, a Japanese castle, and an amusement park. At the shopping mall, people enjoy shopping and walking beside the sea, the Japanese castle provides some events, and in the amusement park, people can ride some attractions and enjoy the streetscapes.

Table 2. Average values from the posting questionnaire.

Questionnaire item	Avge.
(1-i) I could easily operate this system using an Android phone	3.3
(1-ii) I could easily select an appropriate category for each tweet	3.3
(1-iii) It was easy to reply to a posted tweet	3.4
(1-iv) It was easy to post a photograph	4.7
(1-v) I could feel the presence of other members' actions from the map	4.2
(1-vi) Post motivation increased by browsing from others	3.7

Table 3. Average values from the browsing questionnaire.

Questionnaire item	(a)	(b)
(2-i) I could easily search for travel information	4.2	2.6
(2-ii) I could easily browse the photographs	3.3	3.6
(2-iii) I could obtain the information that I wanted	3.8	2.9
(2-iv) I could easily understand the meaning of the pictorial symbols	3.8	-
(2-vi) I required the search function for the categories	4.6	-

In the second experiment, the same nine subjects browsed travel information indoors for ten minutes. Under condition (a), the participants only used the proposed system. The travel information they browsed was the data posted by a different group from the first experiment. Under condition (b), the data was not categorized, and tweets were placed using a simple marker on the map.

4.2 Experimental Results

We asked the participants to complete a questionnaire at the end of each experiment. The results from the questionnaires are provided in Tables 2 and 3. The values listed are the mean values on a five-point scale. The number of tweets at each tourist destination from the posting experiment is shown in Table 4.

Based on comments written in the free description field in the posting questionnaire, users felt the need to categorize tweets, and they enjoyed the symbols that appeared one after another in the map in real time. On the other hand, as

Table 4. Number of tweets at each destination.

Tourist destination	Tweets
Shopping mall along the beach	46
Japanese castle	35
Amusement park	35

Table 5. Average values from the questionnaire concerning the proposed system.

Questionnaire item	Avge.
(3-i) The system facilitated the communication for obtaining information	3.9
(3-ii) The photos was helpful in obtaining the travel information	4.6
(3-iii) When I search the travel information, I want to use this system	3.9

shown in Table 2, the values for ease of operation (1-i), selection of categories (1-ii), and reply (1-iii) were low. One of the reasons for the low values was that the Android phone we had rented in the experiment had a low-resolution display, so it was difficult to operate outdoors because it was too small. Some participants pointed out the flaw on the questionnaire.

Next, we discussed the numbers of tweets and selected categories. At the 'Amusement park', where people enjoy the scenery, nine tweets were categorized to the landscape category. At the 'Japanese castle', the participants enjoyed some events so they often selected the chances, events and accidents categories. At the 'Shopping mall along the beach', the percentages of souvenirs and stores were higher than in the other areas. The posting experiment started upon arrival at the destination and the experimental period was one hour. Therefore, road signs, accommodations and traffic information were usually not selected.

As shown in Table 3, the values for items (2-i) and (2-iii) are higher for our system under condition (a) than the values under condition (b). From these results, we infer that information that was appropriately categorized and expressed is a supportive feature for users when they are searching tweets with using the location information on the map.

The results from the questionnaires on the proposed system are provided in Table 5. The evaluation method was same one that was used in Tables 2 and 3. The participants answered that the proposed system was helpful for searching and obtaining travel information. High evaluations were obtained for the functionality of the system; however, there were some comments in the free description fields on the questionnaires regarding the improvement of the interface.

5   Conclusion

In this article, we proposed a travel-information sharing system that aims to provide comprehensive and visual live information. From the results of two experiments and an analysis of the data, it is clear that users can detect the presence and actions of other users in the vicinity from the map plotted tweets. In addition, users' ability to search for tourist information is supported by and plotting information with symbols on a map and appropriately classifying information.

In the browsing experiments in this article, we did not compare our system to other systems in which photographs are posted to a photo-sharing service. We need to experiment using the reply and retweet function on our system in order to investigate the effect of users communicately directly through exchanging tweets. Furthermore, the low evaluation could be due the performance of the Android device, and therefore, it is necessary to conduct the experiment again using an Android device with better performance.

References

1. Google Places API - Google Developers. https://developers.google.com/places/. Accessed 29 October 2014
2. 4travel, Inc. http://4travel.jp/. Accessed 29 October 2014
3. Ushio, S., Ito, Y., Okada, K., Kitahara, T., Tsuji, H., Moriguchi, S., Narita, M., Kato, Y.: The digital travel diary system using the network service platform. In: Proceedings of the International Conference on Advanced Information Networking and Applications (WAINA), pp. 890–895 (2011)
4. Kisilevich, S., Krstajic, M., Keim, D., Andrienko, N., Andrienko, G.: Event-based analysis of people's activities and behavior using flickr and panoramio geotagged photo collections. In: 2010 14th International Conference on Information Visualisation (IV), pp. 289–296 (2010)
5. Popescu, A., Grefenstette, G., Moellic, P.: Mining tourist information from user-supplied collections. In: Proceedings of the 18th ACM Conference on Information and Knowledge Management (CIKM), pp. 1713–1716 (2009)
6. Tiwari, S., Kaushik, S.: Information enrichment for tourist spot recommender system using location aware crowdsourcing. In: IEEE 15th International Conference on Mobile Data Management (MDM), vol. 2, pp. 11–14 (2014)

Ubiquitous Healthcare Systems: Improving the Adherence Level within Diabetic Medication Using Cloud-Based Reminder System

Mohammed Kalkattawi[✉] and Tatsuo Nakajima

Department of Computer Science and Engineering,
Waseda University, Tokyo, Japan
{M.Kalkattawi,Tatsuo}@dcl.cs.waseda.ac.jp

Abstract. This research focuses on diabetic patients who undergo multiple daily injections therapy (MDI) for their diabetic management. MDI therapy is usually considered challenging and difficult to maintain. For this reason, patients might not able to maintain a good level of adherence to the insulin medication. As a step to improve the adherence level among diabetics, we would like to propose a reminder system that can promote a change in the patients' behavior. This paper is divided into two scopes: the first scope concerns the evaluation of current technologies within diabetic management; while the second scope focuses on testing the proposed system among a number of patients. The results from this usability study demonstrated that there was some improvement within the adherence level among participants. We concluded that these types of systems have the potential to ease the diabetic management and improve the adherence to insulin medication.

Keywords: Diabetes mellitus · Multiple daily injections · Medication adherence · Ubiquitous health · Mobile computing · Smart devices · Smart applications

1 Introduction

Diabetes mellitus occurs when the body, due to certain circumstances, loses the ability to control the blood glucose level. At this stage, the patient needs to rely on external resources—insulin or oral medication—to bring the blood glucose level closer to the normal values (i.e., 79 - 110 mg/dL). For insulin therapy, in particular, there are two common practices that have been available for some time: the Multiple Daily Injections therapy (MDI) and Insulin Pumping therapy. This research focuses mainly on the MDI therapy, and, specifically, concentrating on the adherence to daily insulin doses.

1.1 MDI Therapy Challenges

MDI (Fig. 1) involves taking a number of insulin shots on a daily basis (e.g., 4 or 5 times per day). MDI therapy depends on the management between two types of doses: Bolus, doses that are taken before meals or sometimes for glucose level adjustment, and Basal,

© Springer International Publishing Switzerland 2015
S. Yamamoto (Ed.): HIMI 2015, Part I, LNCS 9172, pp. 535–546, 2015.
DOI: 10.1007/978-3-319-20612-7_51

doses that are taken to lower the glucose level between meals and during sleep. Overall, MDI therapy is considered practical and flexible compared to its counterpart, the pump therapy. However, it is also considered highly challenging [1]. In order to maximize the outcomes from MDI therapy, the patients need to maintain a high level of adherence to the insulin medication. Timing, for example, is critical for insulin medication. The patient has to match daily routines (meals, exercise, sleep time, etc.) and insulin onset behavior. Some research has shown evidence of patients suffering from poor glucose control as a result of being incompetent with their insulin medication adherence [2, 3].

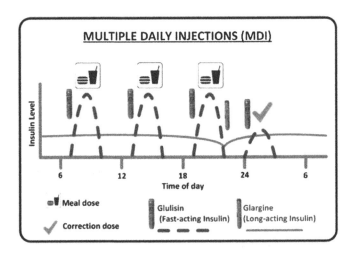

Fig. 1. Multiple daily injections

1.2   Insulin Glargine

Insulin Glargine is a long-acting type of insulin produced by SANOFI under the brand name "Lantus®". It can be used by both TYPE 1 and TYPE 2 patients for basal doses. Directions state that insulin Glargine should be taken once daily within a 24-hour period in a daily fixed amount. This is similar to hypertension and cardiac medications.

In this research, we choose Insulin Glargine as an example for our application for two reasons: First, it is compatible with the instrument that we are using within this research, and second, its nature and directions can be verified with the proposed application in this research.

1.3   The Research Goal

This research is utilizing a couple of ubiquitous technologies, such as cloud computing and smart devices, to provide a supporting system for MDI patients. The main objective is to provide a solution that can help maintaining a high level of adherence to the insulin Glargine medication. The research is giving an example in how we can utilize modern technologies to support MDI management. It followed the Wizard of Oz prototyping concepts in order to test the usability of the proposed system among a group of diabetic patients.

2 Related Work

2.1 Intelligent Insulin Pens

The first major upgrade was the creation of insulin pens in 1985 by *NOVO NORDISK* [4]. They could provide more practical and accurate solutions for MDI, The situation remained relatively unchanged until 2007 when *Eli Lilly* introduced their *HumaPen® Memoir™* model [5]. *HumaPen® Memoir™* was introduced with a memory feature that can record last few taken doses. The feature aimed to overcome double dosing, one of the major issues in MDI therapy. This was followed by another model from *NOVO NORDISK* in 2012, which applied the same feature but with a different concept [6]. *Pendiq GmbH* was the first company that introduced a full new technological solution for MDI instrument. The new *Pendiq®* intelligent insulin pen was introduced with some features that could overcome certain issues existing within MDI [7], such as insulin sensitivity and noncompliant dosing behavior.

2.2 Reminder Systems for Medications

After conducting some reviews for approximately 80 applications and other literature review, we found that most of these applications can be used as management tools to keep track of diabetic records; however, few of these applications have features like dosing and carbohydrates calculation (e.g., Rapidcalc app) or dose and blood checking reminders (e.g., Glucose Buddy app). Unfortunately, most of these applications lack intuitive features like automated data entry or data sync between devices [8]. Similarly, a lot of the commercial tools available within the market are not open source and lack cross compatibility between each other as well [9].

In general, recommendations from healthcare firms always suggest matching the medication time, such as insulin Glargine or hypertension medication, with daily routines (e.g., mealtime or bedtime); however, practices suggest also using reminder systems as well in order to act as a backup to the daily routine [10]. There are several methods that have been used as reminder systems. Some examples are calendars, smartphone apps, alarms and text messaging. Nevertheless, studies found that the most popular method among them is the use of smart devices [11]. Results from different research concluded that the use of short messages (SMS), calendars, apps and alarms managed to raise the adherence level among patients [12, 13]; on the other hand, the use of smart devices as reminder systems has its own drawbacks. First, they encourage the users to rely on them rather than promoting habitual behavior. Second, most of the apps and alarms in current smart devices are not customizable and they might not fit with the users' needs. Lastly, they lack a post-completion check or acknowledgment features. Even if the patient could respond to the reminder correctly, there is an issue of the patient forgetting whether he/she did respond to the notification correctly. Most of the studies, which evaluated the influence of reminder systems on adherence improvements, were relying on patients' self-reporting. Studies found that self-reporting can be overestimated and liable to alteration and human-errors [14]. For this reason, it is very important to include a reliable post-completion check system that can keep track of taken medications. For example, in the study that applied gamification concepts through the utilization of social media [15], patients are competing against each other in order to keep the highest rank of adherence level within a list. Other research recommends wearable computing and wireless networks to send reminders for medication and refilling and also keeping track of these actions [16].

3   Research Method

Following the above examples, we are proposing similar approaches to create a reminder system for basal MDI doses (Fig. 2). In order to make the reminders effective and encourage habitual directions, we would like to include the following features:

- Automated-snooze capability repeated within a period of time
- Automated post-completion check with log data.
- Cloud-based communication

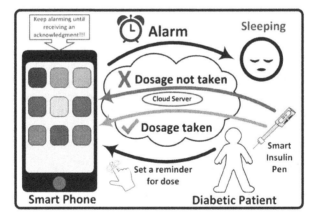

Fig. 2. Cloud-based reminder system

In order to evaluate the interaction between the suggested system and patients, we conducted two usability studies; each one of them lasted 3 weeks with 4 participants in each study (i.e., Total of 6 weeks with 8 participants). Details of the two studies are explained below.

3.1   Design

The two studies were composed of two parts. The first part was an oral interview. The questions focused on personal diabetic management, the use of technology within diabetic practices, and opinions about current technologies. The second part was a practical experiment divided into two parts. The first part of the experiment lasted 10 days. It focused on the interaction of the patient with the usual systems using intelligent insulin pens, and then measured its influence on the medication adherence level. The second part of the experiment also lasted 10 days; however, this time the focus was on the interaction between the patients and the suggested cloud-based reminder system, and then measuring its influence on the adherence to medication. The main equipment used for this experiment were:

1. 4 x Intelligent insulin pens – To keep data logs of administered doses
2. 4x portable laptops with pre-installed diabetic management software and remote access agent software – To verify the administration of daily doses
3. Smart reminders with cloud feature installed in the patient's personal devices – The device was pre-set to the patient's dose time and shared with the administrator through a shared cloud account.

3.2   Participants

Participants (Table 1) were recruited through either representatives from King Fahd Hospital in Jeddah, Saudi Arabia, or through personal communications from the Saudi diabetic community. There were 3 criteria for participant selection. First, the participant had to be between the age of 21 and 75. Second, they had to maintain a good level of physical and mental health. Third, the participant had to be under insulin Glargine therapy (i.e., Lantus®). Any other brands were excluded from this experiment. Finally, the participant had to have at least basic knowledge of using PCs and smart devices (i.e., Apple' iPad or iPhone, Android based devices, etc.). Any cases that did not meet these conditions were not considered for the study. The main reasons for having a small number of participants were the limitation in the number of equipment and amount of budget, and, also, all the participants were required to continue administration to minimize risk and provide any support in case of any malfunctions with the experiment equipment.

Table 1. List of participants

ID	Gender	Usage of smartphones	Age
P1	Male	High	21–39
P2	Male	Low	60–75
P3	Male	High	40–59
P4	Female	Average	40–59
P5	Female	High	40–59
P6	Male	Low	60–75
P7	Female	Average	21–39
P8	Female	Low	40–59

After getting approval from their primary care provider to proceed with the study, participants were provided with consent forms. After agreeing, they were enrolled in the study. All the participants completed the first part, the oral interviews; however, two participants withdrew from the second part of the study due to some concerns regarding the complexity of the intelligent insulin pens. Except for the withdrawn participants, all the other participants were rewarded with almost $ 20 for each week. In case there was any violation within the stated rules, a deduction penalty had to be applied on the given reward. The other withdrawn participants were rewarded with complimentary rewards for their participation with the interviews. All the participants were provided a sufficient amount of insulin Glargine covering the whole period. All the participants were provided with Internet data subscription in their smart devices to cover the experiment period.

3.3   Procedure and Data Collection

One day was dedicated for the introduction of the whole study, the oral interviews and tutorial for conducting the experiment. Participants were taught how to use the intelligent pens for dosing and changing the insulin cartridge; any other features were not covered in this experiment.

For the following 10 days, the first 3 days were considered a trial for the new system. After the three days, the participants were given the option to withdraw if they could not continue. After that, we proceeded with the experiment. Basically, the patients were asked to take their doses in the manner they had been doing. The directions stated that as soon as the participants would take their doses, they had to return the pen to its station and connect it through the provided laptop. This allowed for data collection on a daily basis through a remote agent.

For the next 10 days, the first three days were also set aside as a trial for the new setup. After that, participants were directed to follow the same dosing process as in the first experiment, but this time using the reminder system notifications (Fig. 3). The directions stated that participants should take a dose as soon as the reminder was activated, within 30 min after the reminder alarm. They were also allowed to take the dose within 30 min before the reminder alarm.

The administration of the dose was checked remotely through the management software. If the required dose was administered, the reminder (or the snooze) would be disabled, and then a confirmation message would be sent to the patient. If the administration of the dose could not be confirmed, snooze was activated for every 10 min until the confirmation of the dose could be accomplished, or until a period of 30 min would pass. After that, a message would be sent to the patients stating that "the dose was not administered within the appointed time and it should be administered as soon as seeing the sent message". Please note, for the second round of experiments, all system components were automated from the patients' prospective. Only the connectivity between the pen and laptop was not. The reason for this was the absence of the supporting technology within the intelligent pens. The doses verification and snooze activation processes were done manually through the administration side (i.e., It was blinded from the patients). Also, all the reminder system control was done totally through the

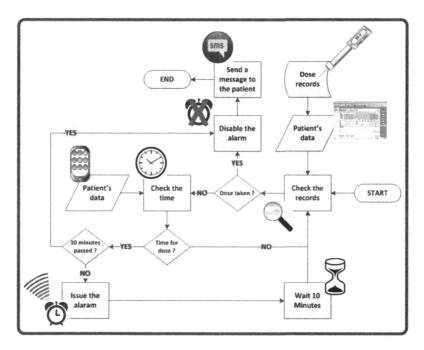

Fig. 3. 2nd experiment process

administration side. Any attempt from the patient's side was considered a violation of the experiment rules. The connectivity between the intelligent pens and the provided laptop had to be working at all times, except during dosing time. As soon as the patient would finish dosing, the pen had to be returned to its designated station. Failing to follow this was also considered a violation of the experiment directions.

After finishing the two experiments, we conducted one more oral interview to collect patients' feedback regarding the usability of the whole system, and also to understand the patient's behavior while interacting with the system.

3.4   Scoring

We measured the level of adherence during both experiments. We based these values on SANOFI's directions for insulin Glargine [17], "once a day" and "within 24-hour". If the patient managed to take the dose within the assigned period, a full score would be given for that day. If the patient took the dose outside the assigned time, a half point score would be given for that day. If the dose was completely absent during the whole day, no score would be given for that day. We made another measurement to evaluate the level of awareness among patients. We based these values on how fast the patient could respond to the reminder alarm (Table 2).

Table 2. Scale for the patient's awarness

Scores	Period of time	Patient's Awareness
5	Before the time	Mostly responded before the 1st alarm
4	On time	Mostly responded to the 1st alarm
3	10 min passed	Mostly responded to the 2nd alarm
2	20 min passed	Mostly responded to the 3rd alarm
1	30 min passed Or more than 30 min earlier	Mostly responded to the last alarm or miscalculated the assigned time

4   Results

4.1   Results from the Oral Interviews

The first question asked about the administration of daily doses. All the patients were taking at least 4 shots per day (i.e., one shot for the basal). All the patients reported no regular mistakes while administering the doses. Two of them were associating their dose time with one daily routine, while two others were using phone alarms to remind themselves about the dose. The others were just trying to keep the doses closer to an assigned time. We asked the participants about the other technologies for insulin delivery, such as insulin pumps. Only two of the participants said they would consider switching to another technology if it would be suitable for them and could offer more advanced features. The others preferred to stay on the MDI therapy. We asked about the experience in using intelligent insulin pens. All the participants reported that they never saw or used these types of pens before this interview. Four participants did not welcome the idea of replacing standard insulin pens with intelligent ones as they were concerned about complexity. The other four participants were willing to switch to these types of pens if they could assure a better administration for insulin doses. We asked about the use of smart devices and their utilization for diabetic management. Only one participant was using smartphones for diabetic management, on an irregular basis, as it required extra work from the patient's side.

4.2   Results from the Two Experiments

Observed data. Only two patients scored around the middle level in the adherence scale (i.e., above 3.5 in the scale). The other patients maintained a good level of adherence (i.e., above 6 in the scale). After applying the cloud-based reminder system (Fig. 4), we noticed a good improvement with the patients who were scoring low with in the first experiment. For the others, performance was either the same or slightly better.

As per the level of awareness (Fig. 5), three patients typically responded immediately after the 1st alarm. Only two cases required more than one alarm (i.e., two or three) to respond to the notification. We had only one participant who kept administering the medication before the alarm issuance (i.e., within 30 min before the alarm).

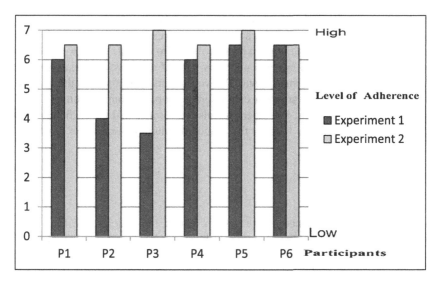

Fig. 4. Comparison between the adherence levels in both experiments

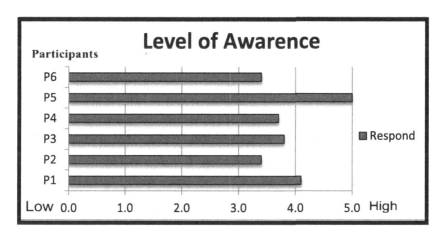

Fig. 5. Level of awareness

Patients' feedback. We asked the patients about the overall evaluation of the system. All the patients gave positive feedback, especially those with busy schedules and who could not match dosing with daily habits. For those who were able to match doses and routines, they insisted that the system could raise the assurance factor within themselves. One comment pointed out that the system was more reliable than usual habits because daily habits may change. Also, the system has the ability to confirm and acknowledging the administration of doses, while daily habits still depend on a patient's awareness and self-management. We also inquired about the main reasons for not administering the doses within the assigned time during both experiments. All the comments indicted that they were aware of the situation, but they could not proceed with administration. Either it was because of being outdoors or out of reach, or being involved with some social activities. Only one patient reported an oversleeping case, which prevented both the administration of the dose on time and hearing the alarm as well. When we asked about the replacement of standard systems with this kind of digital system (i.e., the use of intelligent pens along with smart devices), two patients were open to the idea. They appreciated how the digital solution can assure a proper administration of the dose, including the dosing process, but other patients were concerned about the complexity of the intelligent pens. They thought that standard solutions were more practical and faster.

5 Discussion

Judging from the performance of the system among the patients, we found all the people who were associating the dose time with an appointed time or a daily habit had a slightly better performance in the 2nd experiment. Nevertheless, based on the comments, the system kept the patients alerted and raised the assurance factor within themselves. On the other hand, people, who had busy routines, or had some difficulties with following an assigned time, had a better advantage from the system. So we can assume here this type of system can be an alternatively good method for those who are concerned about any sudden changes within their daily routines. However, for those who are maintaining a schedule that prevents them from being strict with their medication time, this kind of system can be essential for them. Since all the confirmation and snoozing processes are done automatically out of the user's control, it has the potential to keep the patient alerted and prevent missing doses incidents.

The patients appraised the use of regular smart devices rather than using specialized reminder devices. We noticed, within the data, the more the patient would be attached to his\her smart device, the faster his/her response would be. This gave us an idea that, in the future, this kind of system should have a customized level of alerts. For example, people who keep their devices away sometimes might need a shorter period between snooze alarms; similarly, people who suffer from deep sleep might need a louder or more noticeable notification to wake them up. Also, since this alarm is utilizing cloud services, it can be installed within multiple devices. The advantage here is that this kind of setup can overcome problems such as battery outage or inaccessibility.

Finally, while not directly related to our motivations, we noticed some negative feedback regarding the replacement of the standard MDI system with the intelligent pens. The use of intelligent pens was not greatly welcomed by some of our participants. The intelligent pens were criticized for being more complex than the standard pens. Although this feedback might not concern our scope, it does indirectly affect this system. The system requires digital instruments that can exchange data with smart devices for data processing. It cannot be accomplished with standard pens. Future developments of these kinds of pen should find a solution that can maintain a balance between simplicity and advanced operations. Future developments should also focus on creating solutions that would allow smoother communication through Bluetooth and wireless connectivity for data processing purposes.

6   Conclusion and Future Work

This paper proposed a cloud-based reminder system to be used by patients who are following MDI therapy for diabetic management. The features of the system were based on some aspects of the literature review done for this research. In order to maximize the outcomes, we believe the system should maintain an automated snooze feature, a post-completion acknowledgment and cloud-based services. The components of the system were composed mainly from intelligent insulin pens associated with smart devices. The study was divided into two parts: an oral interview and a practical experiment. The practical experiment first tests the regular setup for the patients, and then tests the setup after applying the cloud-based system. The results from the usability study showed there were some improvements after applying the system when comparing both setups. We concluded that the system could be a good alternative for people who rely on associating their dose time with daily routines or regular alarm/ notification systems. On the other hand, people whose schedules are very busy would benefit greatly from this kind of system.

We would like to point out that this study had some limitations. First, both the number of participants and time period were insufficient for a complete diabetic study, which relates the glycemic control with the system outcomes. These types of study require a longer period of time (i.e., between 2 to 3 months). Also, collaboration with diabetes related practitioners might be necessary. Second, the study was based on the Wizard of Oz prototyping method; we hope in the future we would able to make a full-automated system, which can be tested and used in an actual/real setting without restrictions or adjusted scenarios.

Acknowledgment.   I would like to thank all the participants and people who helped with the experiment. A special thanks to Ms.Faiga Kalkattawi for her help in the recruitment and coordination with the participants.

References

1. Doyle, E.A., Weinzimer, S.A., Steffen, A.T., Ahern, J.A., Vincent, M., Tamborlane, W.V.: A randomized, prospective trial comparing the efficacy of continuous subcutaneous insulin infusion with multiple daily injections using insulin glargine. Diab. Care **27**(7), 1554–1558 (2004)
2. Donnelly, L.A., Morris, A.D., Evans, J.M.: DARTS/MEMO collaboration, Adherence to insulin and its association with glycaemic control in patients with type 2 diabetes. QJM : Mon. J. Assoc. Phys. **100**(6), 345–350 (2007)
3. Brod, M., Rana, A., Barnett, A.H.: Adherence patterns in patients with type 2 diabetes on basal insulin analogues: missed, mistimed and reduced doses. Curr. Med. Res. Opin. **28**(12), 1933–1946 (2012)
4. Rex, J., Jensen, K.H., Lawton, S.A.: A review of 20 years' experience with the Novopen® Family of Insulin Injection Devices. Clin. Drug Investig. **26**(7), 367–401 (2006)
5. Ignaut, D.A., Venekamp, W.J.: HumaPen® Memoir™: a novel insulin-injecting pen with a dose-memory feature (2007)

6. Xue, L., Mikkelsen, K.H.: Dose accuracy of a durable insulin pen with memory function, before and after simulated lifetime use and under stress conditions. Expert Opin. Drug Deliv. **10**(3), 301–306 (2013)
7. Brown, A., et al.: CLOSERLOOK. In: The 47th Annual Meeting for European Association for the Study of Diabetes, Lisbon, Portugal, September 12–16, 2011
8. El-Gayar, O., Timsina, P., Nawar, N., Eid, W.: Mobile applications for diabetes self-management: status and potential. J. Diab. Sci. Technol. **7**(1), 247–262 (2013)
9. Grifantini, K.: Advances in management technology for diabetes: from personal reminders to digital doctors. IEEE Pulse **5**(3), 40–44 (2014)
10. Stawarz, K., Cox, A.L., Blandford, A.: Don't forget your pill!: designing effective medication reminder apps that support users' daily routines. In: Proceedings of the 32nd Annual ACM Conference on Human Factors in Computing Systems, ACM, pp. 2269 (2014)
11. Laffer, M.S., Feldman, S.R.: Improving medication adherence through technology: analyzing the managing meds video challenge. Skin Res. Technol. **20**(1), 62–66 (2014)
12. Patel, S., Jacobus-Kantor, L., Marshall, L., Ritchie, C., Kaplinski, M., Khurana, P.S., Katz, R.J.: Mobilizing your medications: an automated medication reminder application for mobile phones and hypertension medication adherence in a high-risk urban population. J. Diab. Sci. Technol. **7**(3), 630–639 (2013)
13. Vervloet, M., Dijk, L.V., Bakker, D., Souverein, P., Santen-Reestman, J., Vlijmen, B.V., Aarle, M., Hoek, L., Bouvy, M.: Short-and long-term effects of real-time medication monitoring with short message service (SMS) reminders for missed doses on the refill adherence of people with Type 2 diabetes: evidence from a randomized controlled trial. Diabet. Med. **31**(7), 821–828 (2014)
14. Straka, R.J., Fish, J.T., Benson, S.R., Suh, J.T.: Patient self-reporting of compliance does not correspond with electronic monitoring an evaluation using isosorbide dinitrate as a model drug. Pharmacother. J. Hum. Pharmacol. Drug Ther. **17**(1), 126–132 (1997)
15. De Oliveira, R., Cherubini, M., Oliver, N.: MoviPill: improving medication compliance for elders using a mobile persuasive social game. In: Proceedings of the 12th ACM International Conference on Ubiquitous Computing, ACM, pp. 251 (2010)
16. Li, J., Peplinski, S.J., Nia, S.M., Farajidavar, A.: An interoperable pillbox system for smart medication adherence. In: 2014 36th Annual International Conference of the IEEE Engineering in Medicine and Biology Society (EMBC), pp. 1386. IEEE (2014)
17. Mohan, V., John, M., Baruah, M., Bhansali, A.: Addressing barriers to effective basal insulin therapy. J. Assoc. Phys. India **62**(1 Suppl), 10–14 (2014)

Centralized Approach for a Unified Wireless Network Access

Jan David Nose[1], Jaromir Likavec[2], Christian Bischof[3],
and Arjan Kuijper[2,4]($\boxtimes$)

[1] Fraunhofer-Gesellschaft e.V., Competence Center LAN, Darmstadt, Germany
[2] Fraunhofer Institut für Graphische Datenverarbeitung (IGD), Darmstadt, Germany
[3] Scientific Computing and University Computing Center, Technische Universität Darmstadt, Darmstadt, Germany
[4] GRIS, Technische Universität Darmstadt, Darmstadt, Germany
arjan.kuijper@igd.fraunhofer.de

Abstract. In this paper, a concept is presented that allows to deploy a unified wireless network access for all employees in organizations with heterogeneous network environments. It is designed to be easy to implement and to maintain. Also, it focuses on usability, removing the need for manual actions to obtain network access when roaming between locations. The concept has been tested in the Fraunhofer-Gesellschaft, and has proven to solve its requirements. It can be deployed with only a small team thanks to the reduced complexity in the branch locations, and it can also be maintained without much effort since ongoing manual tasks have been avoided. Since it is based on open standards, it can easily be customized to match the requirements of the individual organization, or be extended with future improvements. For research and education organizations it is particularly useful that this concept can be integrated with eduroam seamlessly. This allows not only the own employees to roam between locations, but also guests from other participating institutions.

1 Introduction and Motivation

The Fraunhofer-Gesellschaft is one of Europes largest research organizations with approximately 22,000 employees that work in over 60 different institutes. It has unique structure where its institutes operate almost independently, similar to autonomous enterprises [4–6]. This includes total control over the institutes network foundation, with only a few restrictions, which has led to a variety of network infrastructures with different vendors, concepts and technologies in use. Especially wireless networks differ due to financial reasons and, often in smaller institutes, a lack of expertise.

The technological advance of the last ten years has led to a rising number of mo-bile devices people work with. These devices rely on a wireless network, and play a more and more vital role in the workings of employees. For this reason enterprises should consider providing a reliable wireless network that can be used by employees.

S. Yamamoto (Ed.): HIMI 2015, Part I, LNCS 9172, pp. 547–559, 2015.
DOI: 10.1007/978-3-319-20612-7_52

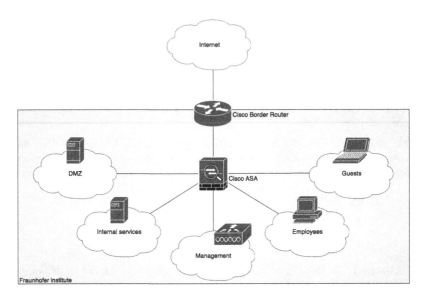

Fig. 1. Scheme of a generic network

Using the Fraunhofer-Gesellschaft as an example, this paper presents a concept how a unified wireless network access can be provided in institutions with multiple locations and heterogeneous network infrastructures. The solution must work independent of the local network infrastructure and it must not be vendor-dependent. To be applicable to research organizations and enterprises, it must also provide reasonable security for the users credentials.

Additionally, the concept is designed to be both easy to use and easy to maintain. The ease-of-use is important for acceptance by the employees, as well as for usability and productivity in general. The solution must be easy to maintain, since it should provide a unified access for all employees in all locations.

2 Prerequisites

This chapter discusses the perquisites in the Fraunhofer-Gesellschaft, and where those apply to other institutions as well. The problems of current solutions are shown, and consequently requirements for a new solution are established.

2.1 Generic Network Design in an Institute

The highly independent nature of the Fraunhofer-Gesellschafts institutes has led to a wide variety of network designs. The following description introduces a very generic network design and indicated the differences that exist in comparison to the institutes actual networks (Fig. 1).

First, it must be not noted that all institutes operate a similar border router and the same firewall appliance. This enables the creation and use of site-to-site VPN connections, and the deployment of a unified security concept for the whole society.

The institutes network is divided into several subnets. The details vary, but normally a certain set of subnets exists in every institute. Those include a subnet for employees and departments, four for the DMZ, and one for guests. The subnet for employees has mostly total access to internal resources and the internet, while the guest network is restricted from accessing any internal resources, and often also restricted with regard to internet access.

The implementation of this network design differs between institutes, since they have different requirements and equipment. Most institutes operate equipment by Cisco Systems [3], but hardware by Juniper Networks [7] and Extreme Networks is also in use. But even if two institutes operate the same hardware, software versions and configurations diverge greatly. This results in a wide variety of computer networks, as design, hardware and software differ between institutes. As a result, solutions for a unified wireless network access, provided by network vendors, are not applicable, since they work only with a set of institutes.

Although the analysis above is specific for the Fraunhofer institutes, similar net-works are operated by universities and enterprises. It is not always possible to maintain a homogeneous network throughout an organization, which makes it impossible to rely on a solution provided by only one vendor of network equipment.

2.2 Existing Wireless Network Access Methods

Currently, no unified solution for a wireless network access for all employees exists in the Fraunhofer-Gesellschaft. Most institutes operate wireless networks that offer access to the employees of that specific institute, and some even provide wireless networks for guests. But the details differ greatly, which proves to be problematic, especially when institutes cooperate closely and employees travel a lot between them.

Typically, a guest has to request access to a wireless network from the local IT department, where ideally a unique, temporary account is created for the guest. Most times, the wireless network itself is not secured with a key, but the account credentials have to be entered into a Captive Portal in the users internet browser. This solution can very easily be deployed, requires no additional hardware, but has a lot of down-sides.

First of all, the process of how to request access differs from institute to institute, and is most often not standardized. This makes it difficult for employees visiting other institutes to gain internet access. Second, the wireless network is unsecured, allowing to capture a users traffic and analyze it if the user does not take additional security measures like using a Virtual Private Network (VPN). Often, users are not aware of this, and leave their connections unsecured. Especially in enterprises and research organizations, this poses as a security thread to the whole organization as sensitive information could be captures.

Third, mobile devices like smartphones do not offer comfortable interfaces to enter the credentials, especially if they are complex. This reduces usability, especially if the connection is disconnected regularly for security reasons, and the user has to reenter his credentials.

All in all, these restrictions often led to the employee choosing cellular net-works over wireless local area networks, as they are easier to use with mobile devices, and do not require the effort to obtain and use temporary credentials. But cellular net-works are more expensive, provide less performance and are often unavailable inside buildings. This problem is not specific to the Fraunhofer-Gesellschaft.

In summary, the following problems or issues have to be solved by a new solution to provide an easy-to-use, truly unified wireless network access:

– In every institute a custom solution for wireless network access exists
– Manual actions by the IT department or the user are almost always necessary
– The guest network does not provide a satisfying user experience
– The guest network does not provide reasonable security

Analyzing these problems yields a set of requirements that are presented in the next section.

2.3   Requirements of a Unified Wireless Network Access

In the last section, the greatest problem with current solutions have been described. To solve those issues and to consider the technical distinctiveness of heterogeneous networks, the new solution needs to fulfill certain requirements. On the technical side, the concept must be applicable to all locations, which means it must be scalable and independent of vendor-specific technologies or protocols. Because the concept should be applicable to enterprises and research organizations, security is also an important concern. The necessary infrastruc-ture must provide an adequate level of security for both the users credentials and traffic.

Additionally, the concept must be easy to implement and later on to main-tain. The goal is to provide a unified access for all employees, which means that every location of an organization implements the solution and provides support for the local staff. Especially the maintenance and support requirements must be reduced to guarantee wide adaptation of the unified access method.

But most importantly, the solution must be easy to use. The first reason for this is that it must compete with cellular networks which work out-of-the-box. The second reason is that with over 22,000 employees in case of the Fraunhofer-Gesellschaft, tens of thousands of devices need to be configured. This is simply not possible in a reasonable amount of time if either a complex configuration or regular reconfiguration is required. Ideally, devices need to be configured only once, without the need to touch them again to access the network. This would result in a user experience similar to cellular networks, with the benefit of more performance and less cost.

To summarize, the requirements for a unified wireless network access are:

– It must be scalable
– It must be vendor-independent
– It must provide reasonable security

- It must be easy to implement
- It must be easy to maintain
- It must be easy to use
- It should remove the need for manual actions

3   Potential Solutions

After establishing the requirements, three different approaches are presented that would solve the given problem.

3.1   Unsecured Guest Network

First, the aforementioned unsecured guest network is a viable solution. An open wireless network allows all guests to connect, and configured properly requires them to establish a VPN connection to secure their traffic. This solution is supported by all network equipment available, and requires almost no additional effort. But the usability is very low, because users must connect to a VPN gateway before they can use the internet. Besides introducing additional effort on the user, it also drains the battery life of mobile devices faster.

3.2   Vendor-specific Solutions

Second, vendor-specific solutions are available to connect at least the majority of locations. Designs suggested by major network manufacturers are based on the idea of one or two main locations, and a bunch of branch offices. Since the Fraunhofer institutes operate highly independent, and have different requirements than typical branch offices, this approach is difficult to implement, and cannot provide a truly unified wireless network access to all employees.

3.3   RADIUS Roaming Network

Third, a solution based on a RADIUS roaming network can be deployed. This roaming networks acts as an authentication backend for local wireless networks. RADIUS is a very widespread protocol, and is supported by every wireless network equipment available today. In combination with WPA2-Enterprise, a secure and vendor-independent wireless network can be provided. One example of an RADIUS roaming network is eduroam (http://eduroam.org, [10]), which allows members of research and education facilities to use the service worldwide. eduroam has an hierarchical infrastructure (Fig. 2), where different parties interact to provide the service together. On the lowest level, individual institutions provide two functionalities. First, they manage user credentials and operate an authentication server to authenticate those users, and second they operate an access network that allows users to access internet services once they authenticated successfully. The first role is called an Identity Provider, while the second role is called Service Provider.

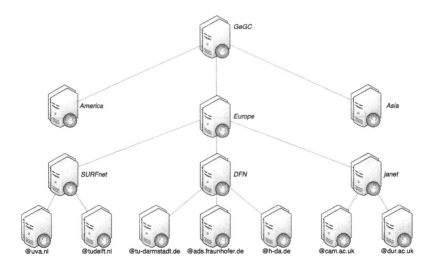

Fig. 2. Excerpt from eduroam hierarchy

Since RADIUS roaming networks are totally independent of vendors, and can be combined easily with secure wireless authentication methods, a solution based on such a network is the most appropriate choice for a unified wireless network access. eduroam proves that by providing network access to thousands of users worldwide.

4   Concept for a Unified Wireless Network Access

Looking back at the different solutions introduced in the last section, and the requirements summarized in the section before that, none of the presented solutions satisfy them all. But one does satisfy most of them, and that is the approach of a RADIUS roaming network. It is scalable, as shown during years of operation in eduroam, and it is vendor-independent, as it relies heavily on standardized technologies. However, it is not necessarily easy to implement in distributed environment. And although it is easy to use by the end-user, the administration is complex due to the high number of different components. The following section discusses how the concept of eduroam can be adapted for organizations like the Fraunhofer-Gesellschaft by reducing its complexity.

4.1   Introduction

Analyzing the roles defined by eduroam for the operation of the service, it becomes clear that the operation of an Identity Provider is more complex than that of a Service Provider. The reason for this is that most organizations and institutes already operate wireless access networks, which can easily be extended to provide access to roaming users. But managing user credentials and providing authentication endpoints can be much more difficult in large and distributed organizations.

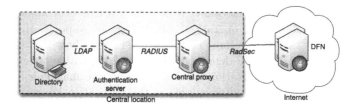

Fig. 3. Infrastructure of centralized IdP

The logical consequence is that to reduce the efforts required to deploy a unified wireless network access, it is necessary to reduce the complexity of the authentication solution. Therefore, we propose a design where one Identity Provider is responsible for the whole organization, while the single locations only provide the access networks. This approach requires a centralized authentication service, though. Figure 3 shows the central authentication infrastructure with its components and connections. The following section more clearly defines the role of the central authentication service.

4.2   Design

In this section, the different components of the concept are discussed. To achieve the goal of easy implementation and maintenance, the concept splits the responsibilities in a centralized authentication service and local service providers.

Centralized Authentication Service. The centralized authentication service consists of several components that need to be deployed and maintained. First, a user database has to exist that can be used to authenticate users. To provide network access to all employees, this requires that every user has an account in the central database. Depending on the deployment, this can either be an already existing account that is also used for other services, or a new account solely for this purpose. While the second option introduces additional over-head in managing a second account, it provides additional security benefits as the account credentials cannot be used to authenticate against other services of the organization.

Second, an authentication server is required. It must support authentication via the RADIUS protocol, and to secure the users credentials should require that authentications use the Extensible Authentication Protocol (EAP, [1]) with encryption of the users credentials. Due to the number of possible configurations and combinations regarding EAP, the secure configuration of an authentication server requires a lot of knowledge, which is one reason that is implementation and operation should be centralized. Not all locations may have the expertise to provide a secure configuration of an authentication server, especially when compatibility with a lot of client operating systems is required.

By reducing the number of authentication servers, ideally to only one central cluster, the required amount of effort to deploy a unified wireless network access is reduced significantly. Furthermore, a small team can be trained to handle the issues that arise during operation, which reduces response times to support requests and allows for a more stable usage. Especially with EAP methods with encryption, the local IT departments are no longer able to support their users with regard to authentication failures. Since all information is hidden from the network devices, and is only available at the authentication server, support requests must be directed at the maintainers of this server. This in return provides an even greater benefit to the locations, as the overhead of grating network access is fully outsourced and centralized.

Centralizing the authentication service has some additional benefits:

- The service can be used from day one by all employees in range of an access net-work.
- Focusing all efforts on a central service allows to deploy greater redundancy and achieve higher availability than it would have been possible if every location need-ed their own infrastructure.
- Since the locations only need to provide a wireless access network, the solution can be deployed very rapidly in many locations at once. This allows to scale the unified access very quickly over the whole organization.

Decentralized Service Provider. The responsibility of a service provider is to operate a wireless access network that users can connect to. Since most locations today already operate wireless networks, adding another one is no difficult task. Configuring it to communicate with the central authentication server can be more difficult, though. Experience has shown that several issues exist with the operation of wireless access networks with WPA2-Enterprise configurations. While the solution is very secure in terms of data layer encryption and privacy of user credentials, configuring such a network on a mobile device can be complex due to the large number of configuration parameters. In the operation of eduroam, for example, we have observed a high number of authentication requests that is spawned regularly by misconfigured clients, which try to reconnect constantly independently of the authentication servers response to the first request.

While it would technically suffice to install a central RADIUS server, against which the local wireless infrastructures authenticate directly, several risks exist with regard to this design in large deployments, the greatest being overloading the central authentication server. Especially in the context of roaming networks like eduroam, a huge performance improvement can be achieved if faulty requests are discarded or rejected before ever reaching the authentication server.

For this reason, a local RADIUS proxy is deployed. Its only purpose is to accept authentication requests from the local wireless infrastructure, and forward valid re-quests while rejecting faulty ones. This allows to greatly reduce the load on the central authentications servers, introduce load balancing and save bandwidth. The configuration of the server is identical for all its instances, so it is very easy to deploy and manage it using modern DevOps tools.

Deploying a local proxy has two additional benefits. First, it abstracts from the local infrastructure, and provides a single communication gateway. This makes it easy to configure firewall rules and secure the traffic between authentication server and institute. This is especially true since second, the local proxy provides an extensible connection to the authentication server. Independent of the location and its equipment, the connection between the authentication and proxy servers can be secured with state of the art technology without having to deal with restrictions by the local networking equipment.

Overall, in large deployments outweigh the benefits of this solution the additional cost of deploying and maintaining the local proxy. Using this approach, the deployment of the unified wireless network access is reduced to the deployment of the local proxy, and the configuration of a wireless access network.

Connecting Proxy and Authentication Server. Since the locations are most likely distributed, untrusted networks like the internet have to be used to communicate between them. This requires that additional security measures are taken to secure the privacy of RADIUS traffic, which is by its nature unencrypted.

The first solution would be to establish a VPN connection between the location and the main office, and tunnel all RADIUS traffic through it. A VPN link is most likely already established between the locations to encrypt sensitive traffic, which makes this approach very easy to deploy.

Alternatively, the protocol RadSec can be used. It is an extension of RADIUS, and used TCP and TLS to establish stateful, encrypted connections between RADIUS servers [11]. In case both sides support RadSec, no additional components are required to secure the traffic, which makes this a viable alternative to VPN in same cases

5 Implementation

The concept proposed in this paper has been implemented by the Fraunhofer-Gesellschaft as its unified wireless network access for roaming employees, and by connecting to the eduroam roaming network, even for guests from other research or education organizations [2,8]. Full details can be found in [9]. The field test provided valuable information about the assumptions made when designing the solution, and allowed to verify that the requirements where met. Figure 4 visualizes the final infrastructure. The following section discusses both the implementation and the operation of this field test.

5.1 Discussion of the Implementation

As a requirement, the implementation must be easy. Although this is generally true, a differentiation can be made between the implementation of the central and distributed parts of the concept. Since the separation of Identity Provider and Service Provider resulted in only a single authentication infrastructure, not

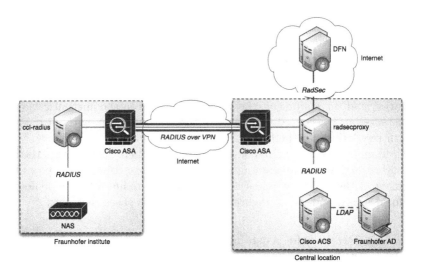

Fig. 4. Final infrastructure

maintained by the local IT department, the cost to implement the solution at the different locations weighs more than the cost to deploy the centralized authentication service.

The implementation of the distributed part is very straight forward. Since wireless networks are almost always already available, it is easy to add another one as the wireless access network employees and guests can use. This leaves the installation of the local RADIUS proxy as the biggest hurdle. Since its configuration is the same for every installation, this proxy can very easily be deployed automatically with the help of automation tools. Depending on the form of communication between the sites, additional firewall rules need to be configured, which concludes the implementation of the solution in a branch (Fig. 5). The implementation of the centralized authentication solution is more complex, as it has more dependencies. Also, it is unique to the organization. For the Fraunhofer-Gesellschaft, a user database already existed, which reduced the required effort to the deployment of an authentication server.

In summary, the deployment of this solution can be done in very little time after the necessary preparations have been made. The reason for this is the easy implementation of the role of Service Provider, which helps tremendously to reduce the overall effort to provide a unified network access to all employees.

5.2   Discussion of the Operation

Several requirements concerned the operation of the new concept, especially the ease of use and the removal of manual actions. For the operation of the service, two phases can be identified. First, an initial configuration must be performed to enable a device to use the service. Second, the device can use the service without interaction. For every stage the compliance with the requirements is analyzed separately.

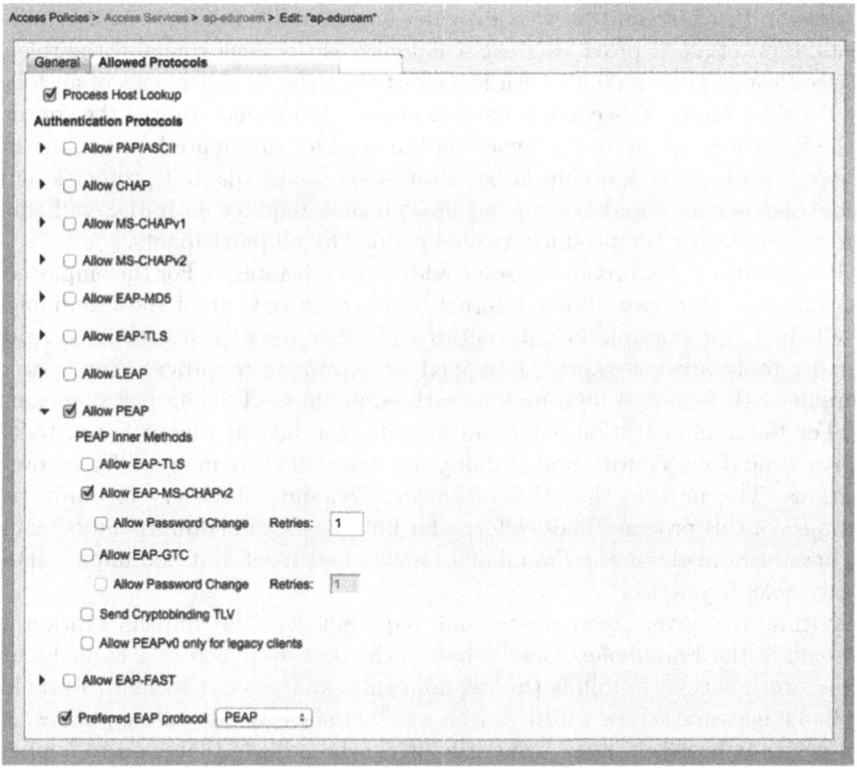

Fig. 5. Configuration of authentication types

In the first phase, the initial configuration, manual interaction is necessary. The employee needs at least the documentation of how to configure his device, and often requires assistance to perform all tasks required. And, as the configuration of advanced parameters is required, for example the EAP type, it does not fulfill the re-quirement to be easy. Those problems can only be partially addressed by the introduction of automated configuration tools. But since the configuration has to be done only once, and the solution provides strong security, the additional effort is worth it.

In comparison to the current solutions for guest access, the new concept provides great benefits to the local IT departments. The amount of manual interactions is significantly reduced and the service can be used more easily, for example without a captive portal. Furthermore, the local IT department can rely on the support of the central team to troubleshoot and solve problems that arise, in contrast to their own solutions for which they are responsible themselves.

6   Conclusions

With the introduction of a RADIUS roaming network, and the implementation of eduroam specifically, the defined goals are met. Additionally, the separation

of Identity Provider and Service Provider singlehandly fulfills several requirements. First of all, it provides great scalability, as the deployment of the role of
Service Provider can be done with less effort than the establishment of an Identity Provider requires. Second, it enables an easy implementation of the concept
in the institutes, again due to removing the need for distributed authentication
servers. Third, since eduroam is based on open standards and protocols, it is
vendor-independent, and last but not least it only requires an initial configuration, thus reducing the need for manual actions by all participants.

Participating in eduroam has some additional advantages. For the employees,
it means that they can obtain Internet access even outside of the Fraunhofer-
Gesellschaft, for example in universities and other research institutions. Additionally, tools are constantly developed or advanced to provide the user of
eduroam with help and information, with eduroam CAT being just one example. For the administration, eduroam provides the benefit that it is constantly
improved, and its security and stability are researched by many different organizations. The introduction of RadSec and Dynamic Discovery are only two
examples of this process. Those efforts, for both users and administrators, could
not have been made by the Fraunhofer-Gesellschaft itself, if it had implemented
its own roaming network.

Within the given restrictions and requirements, the implementation of
eduroam in the Fraunhofer- Gesellschaft is the best approach to a unified wireless network access. It fulfills the requirements, and meets the goal to provide
a reliable network access which can be used satisfactorily by all employees. As
the service is based on open standards, it can be adjusted later on to support
different authentication types or user directories, if the need arises. This, and its
modular design, provide a great platform to operate the service even if requirements change in the next years. Looking at the years of operation, the next
section proposes possible improvements and changes to the concept, followed by
an outlook on future enhancements to eduroam.

References

1. Aboba, B., Blunk, L., Vollbrecht, J., Carlson, J., Levkowetz, H.: Extensible Authentication Protocol (EAP). RFC 3748 (Proposed Standard), June 2004. http://www.
   ietf.org/rfc/rfc3748.txt, updated by RFC 5247
2. Aderhold, A., Wilkosinska, K., Corsini, M., Jung, Y., Graf, H., Kuijper, A.: The
   common implementation framework as service – towards novel applications for
   streamlined presentation of 3D content on the web. In: Marcus, A. (ed.) DUXU
   2014, Part II. LNCS, vol. 8518, pp. 3–14. Springer, Heidelberg (2014)
3. Cisco Systems Inc.: Installation and Upgrade Guide for Cisco Secure Access Control
   System 5.4, August 2013. http://www.cisco.com/en/US/docs/net_mgmt/cisco_
   secure_access_control_system/5.4/installation/guide/csacs_book.html. Accessed 11
   December 2013
4. Grosse-Puppendahl, T., Herber, S., Wimmer, R., Englert, F., Beck, S., von
   Wilmsdorff, J., Wichert, R., Kuijper, A.: Capacitive near-field communication
   for ubiquitous interaction and perception. In: ACM UbiComp 2014, pp. 231–242
   (2014). http://doi.acm.org/10.1145/2632048.2632053

5. Grosse-Puppendahl, T.A., Berghoefer, Y., Braun, A., Wimmer, R., Kuijper, A.: Opencapsense: A rapid prototyping toolkit for pervasive interaction using capacitive sensing. In: 2013 IEEE PerCom, pp. 152–159 (2013). http://doi. ieeecomputersociety.org/10.1109/PerCom.2013.6526726
6. Grosse-Puppendahl, T.A., Braun, A., Kamieth, F., Kuijper, A.: Swiss-cheese extended: an object recognition method for ubiquitous interfaces based on capacitive proximity sensing. In: 2013 ACM SIGCHI Conference on Human Factors in Computing Systems, CHI 2013, pp. 1401–1410 (2013). http://doi.acm.org/10. 1145/2470654.2466186
7. Juniper Networks Inc.: Juniper Networks Horizontal Campus Validated Design Guide, May 2012. http://www.juniper.net/us/en/local/pdf/design-guides/ jnpr-horizontal-campus-validated-design.pdf. Accessed 10 December 2013
8. Limper, M., Jung, Y., Behr, J., Sturm, T., Franke, T., Schwenk, K., Kuijper, A.: Fast and progressive loading of binary encoded declarative 3D web content. IEEE Comput. Graphics Appl. **33**(5), 26–36 (2013). http://dx.doi.org/10.1109/ MCG.2013.52
9. Nose, J.D.: Centralized approach for a site independent wireless network access. Technical report, Department of Computer Science, TU Darmstadt (2013)
10. Wierenga, K., Winter, S., Wolniewicz, T.: The eduroam architecture for network roaming, July 2013. http://tools.ietf.org/html/draft-wierenga-ietf-eduroam. Accessed 10 December 2013
11. Winter, S., McCauley, M., Venaas, S., Wierenga, K.: Transport Layer Security (TLS) Encryption for RADIUS. RFC 6614 (Experimental), May 2012. http:// www.ietf.org/rfc/rfc6614.txt

Proposal of Advance Care Planning Support System

Satomi Yamamoto[1]([✉]), Takashi Yoshino[1], Chigusa Kita[2], Misa Takeshima[2], and Takashi Kato[2]

[1] Faculty of Systems Engineering, Wakayama University, Wakayama, Japan
s165058@center.wakayama-u.ac.jp, yoshino@sys.wakayama-u.ac.jp
[2] Graduate School of Informatics, Kansai University, Osaka, Japan

Abstract. In terminal care, patients may not receive the treatment they want because they cannot express their will. We found that the "Advance Directive" and the "Living Will" are useful for determining the treatment in terminal care. However, patients being unable to respond to changes due to self-choices and share these self-choices when using a conventional format are some problems that remain. We propose an advance care planning support system that enhances the possibility of performing self-choices, collecting data about end-of-life care, confirming self-choices, and sharing the information with others using social networks.

Keywords: Terminal care · Advance care planning · Quality of death

1 Introduction

In step with the aging of the Japanese society, Ministry of Health, Labour and Welfare announced an "Integrated Community Care System [1]", a policy that regards elderly care at home. Meanwhile, a book about "Calm Death" became a best seller. In this way, the "Quality of Death" is becoming increasingly important. Recently, we found that an "Advance Directive" and a "Living Will" play an important role for patients in improving the "Quality of Death" in elderly medical practice. These previous reports contain directions about medical practice when a patient begins to face difficulties in making his own decisions and intentions clear. The documents can help the family and doctors to determine the treatment for the patient. However, even if elderly people wrote a living will, "it is only possible for heirs to know the result of the choice but unable to understand the reason for the choice" when using a conventional format [2]. Furthermore, a guideline announced by the Ministry of Health, Labour and Welfare warns that patients' will may vary and this must be taken into account [3].

We propose an advance care planning system that not only records the result of the patients' decision, but also the reasons behind their decision.

2 Related Work

Several studies on decision support in medical care are underway. Advance care planning is one of the methods of decision support [4,5].

© Springer International Publishing Switzerland 2015
S. Yamamoto (Ed.): HIMI 2015, Part I, LNCS 9172, pp. 560–568, 2015.
DOI: 10.1007/978-3-319-20612-7_53

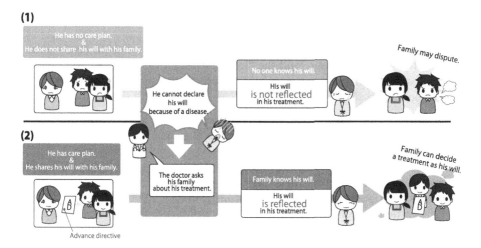

Fig. 1. Difference between presence and absence of advance directive.

The necessity for and the approach to advance care planning has been discussed recently. Many decision support systems for medical workers have been studied [6,7]. However, there are few decision support systems for common people. Thus, it was important to develop a "Patient's Decision-making Support System: PDSS", which is useful for advance care planning of common people [8].

Benjamin et al. developed "Making Your Wishes Known" [9] as an advance care planning support system for common people, which works on Adobe Flash Player[1]. Users can decide their advance directive by answering questions about terminal care. This system has numerous questions about terminal care. Because most questions are of objective type, it is easy for the users to answer these questions. However, this system does not collect the reasons behind the users' choices. Therefore, users' answers may not be used in an actual terminal care scenario. Our purpose is to enhance users' "Quality of Death" by supporting their self-choice in such a way that their family and doctor can select the treatment they want in case they cannot declare their will; this is illustrated in Fig. 1(2). Our system supports the users' self-choice and shares it with family and acquaintances. Furthermore, it records not only users' self-choice but also the reason behind their choice. Consequently, even if a patient is unable to declare his will, his or her family and the doctor could guess his or her will using this system and he or she could be treated accordingly in terminal care. One of the possible reasons for changes in a patient's self-choice could be a change in situation. Our system shows an example of self-choice and treatment presented to a user. If a family and doctor can know the patient's will in each situation, they could decide what treatment the patient wants.

---

[1] http://get.adobe.com/flashplayer/.

3   Design Policy

The design policy of our system is summarized in this section. In this system, there are two roles: the "user" and the "information provider". The "user" makes self-choices, and the "Information provider" records the questions about terminal care in the system.

Design policy 1 Encouraging user to make self-choices. We set this policy to collect enough data to help the user's family and doctor to decide his or her treatment in terminal care.

Design policy 2 Collecting enough useful data on self-choice and perception regarding terminal care. We set this policy to solve the problem in a conventional format as described in reference [2].
This system collects enough useful data of self-choice and general perception regarding terminal care to help decide the patient's treatment by recording the user's self-choice and the result of the choice.

Design policy 3 Providing information as a useful reference for self-choice. Sometimes, people may not make self-choices because of a lack of knowledge. We set this policy to help the user answer questions about terminal care.

Design policy 4 Considering variable self-choice. We set this policy to address the issue that the "patient's decision may vary," as stated in the guideline [3] announced by Ministry of Health, Labour and Welfare.

Design policy 5 Easy to share self-choice with others. In case a conventional format is used, the way to share the advance directive with family and acquaintances has been uncertain. Therefore, family and acquaintances may not be aware of the patient's will and the patient may not receive the treatment he or she wants. We set this policy to solve such a problem.

4   System Overview

4.1   Measures to Follow the Design Policies

The following measures apply to our design policies in Sect. 3.

- **Encouraging user to make self-choices.** We encourage users to make self-choices in our system by easily answering questions about terminal care. We developed our system as a web application. The user can answer the questions about terminal care anytime, anywhere, if they have a device which can access the web. Our system shows the question as a graphic image instead of a table. The image is that of a flower, where the color of its petals varies for every category.
- **Collecting enough useful data on self-choice and perception regarding terminal care.** The reason behind the self-choice is important to decide the treatment for a patient in terminal care using advance directive and living will. When answering a question about terminal care using this system, a user records a self-choice as well as a comment such as the reason for the self-choice and a request. Both the self-choice and the comment are mandatory fields.

– **Providing information as a useful reference for self-choice.** People may not make a self-choice because of a lack of knowledge if they are shown only the name of the symptoms and the treatments. When determining the treatment of a patient, their condition and situation that they're in is considered. Our system shows examples of true incidents to patients in terminal care. Thus, users may read understandable information. Users may refer to examples of actual self-choices and treatments during terminal care; these are introduced through books or news web sites, which an information provider experienced.

– **Considering variable self-choice.** Users can change their answers anytime in our system. However, people may not be aware of these changes when confirming the latest answer. Our system accumulates all the data answered by users. Users and their family and acquaintances can then comprehend the evolution of answers.

– **Easy to share self-choice with others.** Our system uses the function of sharing link in Facebook². A message personalized by the user and the URL of the shared page is posted in their timeline when they click the share button.

4.2   System Configuration

Figure 2 shows the system configuration. Our system consists of the server that stores the data and the terminal used by each user. The server stores the following data: user data, question data, and users' answers. The information provider creates the questions data, while users can answer the questions about terminal care and view their self-choices and statistical data. Users can share their self-choice with others using SNS. We use Facebook as SNS to create the sharing function.

5   Function for Users

5.1   Screen for Users

A user can access the system using his or her Facebook account. The system acquires the information of the user within Facebook, and then the system can use the user's basic information.

Figure 3 is the screen shown after the registration or login. A flower shown on a screen shows one category. The number of petals is the number of questions present in the category [10]. One petal shows one question. A question is shown when the user chooses a petal. The colored area of the petal corresponds to the number of answers of the user. A user knows at a glance the number of times the answer has been changed. A user can appreciate an answer with several changes and another with very little changes. An answer with several changes may be the answer that will tend to change more for a user.

---

² https://www.facebook.com/.

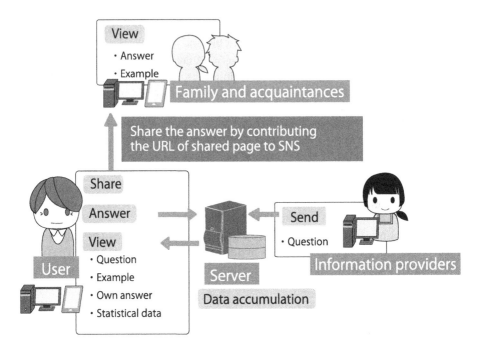

Fig. 2. System configuration

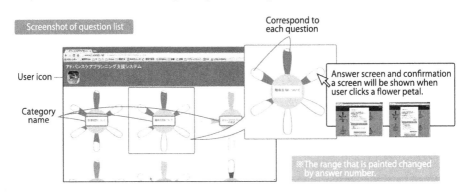

Fig. 3. Screen when logging in (Question list).

5.2   Answer Function to the Question

The top part of Fig. 4 an answer screen for a question.

Figure 5 is the actual case of Fig. 4, and the example of answer is in the bottom part of Fig. 4.

When the user clicks a petal, an answer is shown (Fig. 3). The user reads the case shown and a quoted article, and then answers. The user also gives the reason behind his or her choice and an impression on the quoted article in addition to the answer to the choices. The system requires a description for the reason.

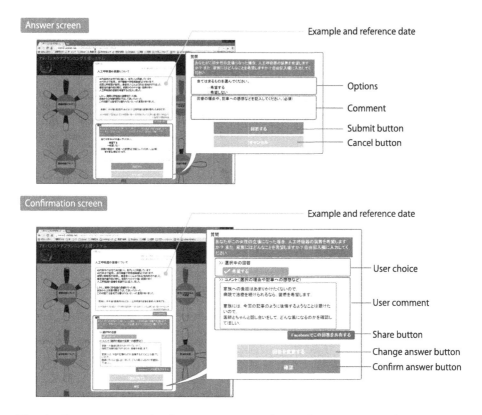

Fig. 4. Screen presented after a question choice (an answer and an answer confirmation).

5.3 Reconfirmation and Revision of an Answer

A user can reconfirm and revise any answer freely. The bottom part of Fig. 4 shows the reconfirmation screen of an answer and the revision screen of an answer. A user can check the contents of the answer and add a description on the confirmation screen.

When the answer was changed, all answers in the past are also stored. The user's family and acquaintance who share an answer can also kwon to answers in the past. In other words, the user's family and acquaintance can know the user's changeable self-selection.

5.4 Sharing an Answer

A user can share his or her answer with others by SNS (Facebook).

6 Function for Information Providers

An information provider shows questions to users. Anyone can prepare a question if they are registered as information providers.

566   S. Yamamoto et al.

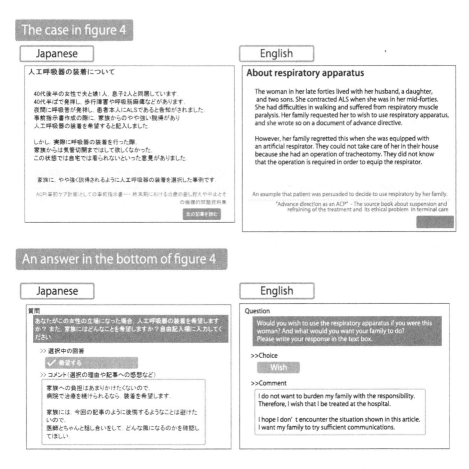

Fig. 5. Case shown in Fig. 4 and an example of an answer.

6.1   Registration Data

An information provider should make up the following items into a question data.

- Basic items of a question
- Actual case
- Cited reference

Basic items of a question are the title of the question, the category of the question, the question itself, the different choices for the answers, and the item of the choices. The categories of a question were extracted from the ending notebooks in the marketplace and the ending notebooks exhibited on the internet.

The form of the answer is one of the following.

- Choice between two
- Choice (one choice)

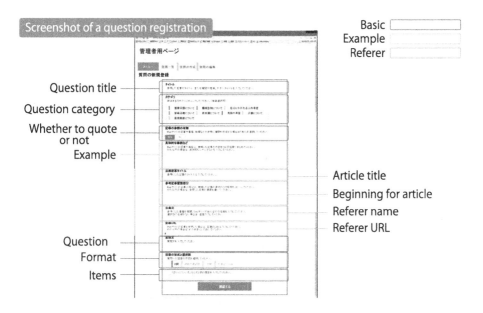

Fig. 6. Question registration screen.

- Choice (multiple selection)
- Seven-point scale
- Only description

The choices for the answers are input at the same time a question without "Only description" is added. An actual case is a one that occurred at a medical site, while the situation was developed by an information provider. We assume that the presentation of the situation in detail prompts a respondent to take self-choice more seriously.

6.2 Question Registration Screen

Figure 6 shows a registration screen of a question.

An information provider inputs the data in this screen, which is described in subsection 6.1. The red framed part shows the basic items of the question. The green framed part is an input part where an actual case is shown in detail to the respondent. The blue framed part is the quoted reference. The parts within the red and green frames are the required items.

7   Conclusion

We have developed an advance care planning support system. The proposed system is designed for changing self-choices. We plan to evaluate our system in the near future.

References

1. Ministry of Health, Labour and Welfare: Integrated Community Care System, 20 February 2015. http://www.mhlw.go.jp/stf/seisakunitsuite/bunya/hukushikaigo/kaigokoureisha/chiiki-houkatsu/
2. Ogusu, N.: The possibilities of life story recollection by the elderly to understand their desires in the last stage of their life. Jpn J. Nurs. Sci. **28**(2), 46–54 (2008)
3. Ministry of Health, Labour and Welfare: The first national guideline on terminal care and withdrawal of treatment in Japan, 20 February 2015. http://www.mhlw.go.jp/shingi/2007/05/s0521-11.html
4. Thomas, K., Lobo, B.: Advance Care Planning in End of Life Care, pp. 4–24. Oxford University Press, New York (2010)
5. Abe, Y.: Advance care planning featuring shared decision-making. Palliat. Care **22**(5), 416–419 (2012)
6. Fatima, I., Fahim, M., Guan, D., Lee, Y.-K., Lee, S.: Socially interactive CDSS for u- life Care. In: Proceedings of the 5th International Conference on Ubiquitous Information Management and Communication, vol. 95 (2011)
7. Matsumura, Y.: Development of a clinical decision support system using clinical laboratory test data. Clinicopathological **59**(5), 512–518 (2011)
8. Itai, k.: What is medical information system as "Patient's Decision making Support System:PDSS"?, Information ethics collection book, vol. 2, pp. 84–97. FINE Project of Kyoto University (2000)
9. Green, M.J., Levi, B.H.: Development of an interactive computer program for advance care planning. Health Expect **12**(1), 60–69 (2009)
10. Takeshima, M., Kita, C., Kato, T., Yoshino, T., Yamamoto, S.: Construction of creation ending note support system. In: The 77th national convention of IPSJ (2015)

User Studies

A Study of the Feature
of the Lovely Product Forms

Wen-chih Chang[✉] and Ching-An Hsu

National Taiwan University of Science and Technology, Taipei, Taiwan
wchang@mail.ntust.edu.tw

Abstract. The appealing points of a product are not only "good function" and "easy to use", but also "lovely form" for a consumer. Especially it is true for a window shopping or an internet shopping. Many studies have shown that a product looked lovely is more welcomed. If product features made products looked lovely are analyzed and singled out, product designers can easily apply them in the concept development stage. This study was conducted by two phases: a questionnaire survey and a feature analysis of product that looked lovelier. This paper concludes several important findings which are: 1. A structure scale for measuring form features is established. 2. The form features of the loveliest products, the form features of lovelier product between male and female, and the form features of lovelier product among different age groups are identified.

Keywords: Lovely form · Product feature · Feature analysis

1 Introduction

The appealing points of a product are not only "good function" and "easy to use", but also "lovely form" for a consumer. Successful story of Swatch is a good example. Especially it is true for a window shopping or an internet shopping [1]. Consumers are usually attracted by a product form first before they really buy and use it. A product form may become a most important factor to influence their purchase intent. Therefore, a product designer should fully understand the consumer preference of product form, so that these products would get extra winning edge in a competitive marketplace. Many studies have shown that a product looked lovely is more welcomed [2, 3]. Lorenz revealed that location proportion of eye, nose, mouth to face of baby animal is quite different from grow-up. Baby animals always looked lovey no matter how fearful when they grow up [4]. This may implies that specific features may cause lovely image. If product features made products looked lovely are analyzed and singled out, product designers can easily apply them in the concept development stage [5]. Furthermore, this study aims at exploring product features that make a product looked lovelier and their differences between male and female consumers as well as among the different age groups. It is hope that this study would help designers to know better the product feature that create lovelier image.

S. Yamamoto (Ed.): HIMI 2015, Part I, LNCS 9172, pp. 571–581, 2015.
DOI: 10.1007/978-3-319-20612-7_54

2   Research Method

This study was conducted by two phases: a questionnaire survey and a feature analysis of product that looked lovelier.

2.1   Questionnaire Survey

As for the questionnaire survey, 1000 photos of product for daily use were collected from 61 well known brands from their official websites. Several screening processes were then taken to eliminate those were not looked lovely. Finally, 33 product photos were selected as the sample of the survey.

For questionnaire design, a 9-point Likert scale was measured to indicate the extent of lovely image of these product samples. The questionnaire survey took place from December 2012 to February 2013 through internet and hard copy questionnaire for those ages over 45. Experimental variables include gender and age. A total of 254 valid questionnaires were collected. Among them, there were 95 males (41.1 %) and 136 (58.9 %) females. There were 5 (2 %) age under 19, 83 (36 %) age between 20–31, 62 (27 %) age between 32–43, 65 (28 %) age between 44–55, 17 (7 %) age over 5 in terms of age.

The outcome of the questionnaire survey included the lovely ranking of the product samples, the identification of the product samples with a significant lovely difference between male and female subjects through t-test, as well as among the different age group subjects through ANOVA and Sheffee.

2.2   Feature Analysis of Product that Looked Lovelier

In order to indicate the features of lovely products, a structure measuring scale modified from previous researchers [6–8] was established in advance. The product features are indicated by aspects of color treatment, form element, detail treatment and texture. There are 4–5 items for further indication of each aspect. For example, color treatment can be further indicated by items of warm-cold color, bright-dark color, number of colors, and relation between colors. For each item, there are 3 choices. In warm-cold color, 3 choices are mainly hue is cold colors, Hue is cold and warm colors in half-and-half, and mainly hue is warm colors. In bright-dark color, 3 choices are mainly brightness is dark colors, Brightness is dark and bright colors in half-and-half, and mainly brightness is bright colors. In number of color, 3 choices are mainly color scheme is single hue, Color scheme is between single hue and multiple hues, and mainly color scheme is multiple hues. In relation between colors, 3 choices are mainly color scheme is contrast colors, Color scheme is contrast and harmony colors in half-and-half, and mainly color scheme is harmony colors. One of them considered most appropriate to represent the feature of that item is picked. Six experienced designers together with the researchers used this scale to measure the features of product samples. The product feature of every item was decided by common consensus among these people.

3   Result of Research

3.1   Features of the Most Lovely Products

The statistic results of the questionnaire survey on the participants' ranking of lovely image of sample product are shown in Table 1. The top six most lovely products are sample 8 (M = 7.33), sample 9 (M = 7.21), sample 24 (M = 6.95), sample 11 (M = 6.62), sample 2 (M = 6.58), sample 3 (M = 6.58).

The feature of these 6 samples were picked as Table 2. If more than 4 samples are picked as feature of a item, that choice is considered as the indication of that item. The result of Table 2 was then concluded as Table 3 to show features of the loveliest products. It is noted that products with the following features are more likely to be considered as lovelier: (1) color treated mainly in cold and bright colors, color scheme is between single hue and multiple hues, and mainly color scheme is harmony colors; (2) In terms of form element, totally bionic, mainly organic, mainly symmetric, and form is between single shape and polymorph; (3) In terms of detail treatment, mainly rounded form, functional and decorative in half-and-half, more detail features, and graving type; (4) In terms of material treatment, mainly hard, mainly rough (matte), mainly consistent, not reflective, and not transparent.

Table 1. The ranking of lovely images on analyzed samples

Ranking	No.	Mean	Sample	Ranking	No.	Mean	Sample	Ranking	No.	Mean	Sample
1	8	7.33		12	18	6.22		21	17	5.91	
2	9	7.21		13	4	6.16		24	20	5.85	
3	24	6.95		14	14	6.12		25	25	5.74	
4	11	6.62		14	10	6.12		26	19	5.66	
5	2	6.58		16	16	6.09		27	26	5.64	
6	3	6.58		17	15	6.08		27	31	5.64	
7	32	6.34		18	21	6.05		29	28	5.45	
8	22	6.31		19	29	6.05		30	5	5.44	
9	30	6.28		20	7	5.96		31	6	5.42	
10	23	6.27		21	27	5.91		32	33	4.95	
11	1	6.24		21	13	5.91		33	12	4.56	

Table 2. A survey of form features on lovely images

			Form Features	Sample No.						Sum
				2	3	8	9	11	24	
C o l o r T r e a t m e n t	1	1	Mainly hue is cold colors	●	●	●	●	●		5*
		2	Hue is cold and warm colors in half-and-half							0
		3	Mainly hue is warm colors						●	1
	2	1	Mainly brightness is dark colors							0
		2	Brightness is dark and bright colors in half-and-half				●			1
		3	Mainly brightness is bright colors	●	●	●		●	●	5*
	3	1	Mainly color scheme is single hue	●	●					2
		2	Color scheme is between single hue and multiple hues			●	●	●	●	4*
		3	Mainly color scheme is multiple hues							0
	4	1	Mainly color scheme is contrast colors				●			1
		2	Color scheme is contrast and harmony colors in half-and-half						●	1
		3	Mainly color scheme is harmony colors	●	●	●		●		4*
F o r m	1	1	Totally bionic		●	●	●	●	●	5*
		2	Partly bionic	●						1
		3	No bionic							0
	2	1	Mainly geometric							0
		2	Geometric and organic in half-and-half	●						1

(*Continued*)

Table 2. (*Continued*)

		3	Mainly organic		•	•	•	•	•	5*
		1	Mainly symmetric		•	•	•	•	•	5*
	3	2	Symmetric and asymmetric in half-and-half							0
		3	Mainly asymmetric	•						1
		1	Mainly single shape							0
	4	2	Form is between single shape and polymorph	•	•	•	•			4*
		3	Mainly polymorph					•	•	2
D e a t i a l T r e a t m e n t	1	1	Mainly rounded form	•	•	•	•	•	•	6*
		2	Rounded and sharp in half-and-half							0
		3	Mainly sharp form							0
	2	1	Mainly functional							0
		2	Functional and decorative in half-and-half	•	•	•	•	•	•	6*
		3	Mainly decorative							0
	3	1	More detail features		•		•	•	•	4*
		2	Moderate detail features	•		•				2
		3	Less detail features							0
	4	1	Printing type							0
		2	Graving type	•	•	•	•	•	•	6*
		3	Pierced type							0
M a t e r i a l t r e a t m e n	1	1	Mainly soft							0
		2	Soft and hard in half-in-half					•		1
		3	Mainly hard	•	•	•	•		•	5*
	2	1	Mainly smooth		•					1
		2	Smooth and rough in half-in-half			•				1
		3	Mainly rough (matte)	•			•	•	•	4*
	3	1	Mainly consistent	•	•	•	•	•	•	6*
		2	Between consistent and diverse							0
		3	Mainly diverse							0
	4	1	Reflective		•					1
		2	Reflective and not reflective in half-in-half							0

Table 2. (*Continued*)

t										
	3	Not reflective	•		•	•	•	•	5*
	1	Transparent							0
5	2	Transparent and not transparent in half-in-half							0
	3	Not transparent	•	•	•	•	•	•	6*

Table 3. Corresponding form features to lovely images of samples

Category	Item	Form features
Color treatment	1	Mainly hue is cold colors
	2	Mainly brightness is bright colors
	3	Color scheme is between single hue and multiple hues
	4	Mainly color scheme is harmony colors
Form	1	Totally bionic
	2	Mainly organic
	3	Mainly symmetric
	4	Form is between single shape and polymorph
Detail treatment	1	Mainly rounded form
	2	Functional and decorative in half-and-half
	3	More detail features
	4	Graving type
Material treatment	1	Mainly hard
	2	Mainly rough (matte)
	3	Mainly consistent
	4	Not reflective
	5	Not transparent

3.2 The Difference Between Male and Female to Features of Lovelier Product

After t-test, statistic results show that there are significant effects to sample 4, sample 5, sample 28, and sample 33 between female and male subjects (see Table 4). It is noted that the average scores of female subject are higher than male subject. This indicates that female subjects have a stronger agreement of lovely image to these samples.

Comparing the feature of these 4 samples, female subjects are easier than male subjects to consider products with mainly bright color, mainly symmetrical form, mainly rounded and mainly decorative detail treatment as lovely. Products are with mainly hard, mainly smooth, mainly consistent, reflective, and not transparent in terms of material treatment (see Table 5). Comparing Tables 3 and 5, some items are different (items marked with *). This may indicate that female subjects have wilder reception of lovely features.

Table 4. Samples with significant level in t-test

No.	Sample	Male Mean	Male S.D.	Female Mean	Female S.D.	t-test	Sig.	Diff.	S.D.
4		5.74	1.93	6.45	1.48	-2.842	0.005*	-0.703	0.247
5		5.10	2.05	5.67	1.84	-2.104	0.037*	-0.570	0.271
28		4.92	2.14	5.82	1.96	-3.153	0.002*	-0.903	0.286
33		4.53	2.12	5.24	2.09	-2.371	0.019*	-0.701	0.296

Note: ⌈*⌋ indicates significant level <= 0.05

Table 5. Females agree form features with lovely images more than males

Category	Item	Form features
Color treatment	1	-
	2	Mainly brightness is bright colors
	3	-
	4	-
Form	1	-
	2	-
	3	Mainly symmetric
	4	-
Detail treatment	1	Mainly rounded form
	2	Mainly decorative*
	3	-
	4	-
Material treatment	1	Mainly hard
	2	Mainly smooth*
	3	Mainly consistent
	4	Reflective *
	5	Not transparent

Note: ⌈−⌋ indicates that the form feature does not exceed a half of samples

3.3   The Difference Among Different Female Age Groups to Features of Lovelier Product

After ANOVA analysis, statistic results show that there are significant different effects among different age groups (see Table 6). Further test of Sheffee, subjects of age group 44–55 (3) have higher scores than age group of 20–31 (1) to sample 5, sample 6, sample 10, sample 13, sample 14, sample 20, sample 26, sample 28, sample 31, sample 33 (3 > 1). (see Table 6). Subjects of age group 44–55 (3) have higher scores than age group of 32–43 (2) to sample 10, sample 13, sample 26, sample 28, sample 29 (3 > 2). Subject of age group 32–43 (2) have higher scores than age group of 20–31 (1) to sample 10, sample 24, sample 28 (2 > 1).

Comparing the feature of these samples, age group 44–55 are easier than age group of 20–31 that products with the following features are more likely to be considered as lovelier (see Table 7): (1) mainly bright color; (2) In terms of form element, totally bionic, mainly organic, mainly symmetric, and mainly polymorph; (3) In terms of detail treatment, mainly rounded form, functional and decorative in half-and-half, and graving type; (4) In terms of material treatment, mainly hard, mainly smooth, mainly consistent, reflective, and not transparent. Comparing the feature of these samples, there are similar results between age group of 44–55 and age group of 32–43. So are between age group 32–43 and age group of 20–31. This indicates that the older of female subjects the stronger reception of these features as lovely form.

Table 6. Age of female is significant by ANOVA analysis

No.	Sample	(1) 20-31	(2) 32-43	(3) 44-55	F	P	Scheffe
5		5.17	5.64	6.28	4.383	.015*	3>1
6		4.90	5.72	6.19	7.064	.001*	3>1
10		5.42	6.51	6.69	6.295	.003*	2>1 . 3>1
13		5.33	5.85	7.12	11.503	.000*	3>1 .3>2
14		5.17	6.24	6.79	7.985	.001*	3>1
20		5.17	5.85	6.69	11.235	.000*	3>1
24		6.69	7.64	7.12	3.114	.048*	2>1
26		5.10	5.55	6.69	9.250	.000*	3>1.3>2
28		4.73	5.97	6.95	18.704	.000*	2>1.3>1.3>2
29		5.19	5.85	6.90	9.523	.000*	3>1.3>2
31		4.85	5.79	6.29	5.829	.004*	3>1
33		4.60	5.45	5.79	4.022	.020*	3>1

Table 7. Different age of female's cognition of form feature on lovely images

Category	Item	3 > 1	3 > 2	2 > 1
Color treatment	1	–	–	–
	2	Mainly brightness is bright colors#	Mainly brightness is bright colors#	Mainly brightness is bright colors#
	3	–	–	Color scheme is contrast and harmony colors in half-and-half
	4	–	Mainly color scheme is contrast colors	–
Form	1	Totally bionic#	Totally bionic#	Totally bionic#
	2	Mainly organic#	Mainly organic#	Mainly organic#
	3	Mainly symmetric#	Mainly symmetric#	Mainly symmetric#
	4	Mainly polymorph#	Mainly polymorph#	Mainly polymorph#
Detail treatment	1	Mainly rounded form#	Mainly rounded form#	Mainly rounded form#
	2	Functional and decorative in half-and-half	Mainly decorative	Mainly decorative
	3	–	–	More detail features
	4	Graving type#	Graving type#	Graving type#
Material treatment	1	Mainly hard#	Mainly hard#	Mainly hard#
	2	Mainly smooth#	Mainly smooth#	Mainly smooth#
	3	Mainly consistent#	Mainly consistent#	Mainly consistent#
	4	Reflective#	Reflective#	Reflective#
	5	Not transparent#	Not transparent#	Not transparent#

Note: ⌈−⌋ indicates that the form feature does not exceed a half of samples

3.4 The Difference Among Different Male Age Groups to Features of Lovelier Product

After ANOVA analysis, statistic results show that there are significant different effects among different age groups. Further test of Sheffee, there are four relations among different age groups. They are 3 > 2, 1 > 2, 1 > 3, and 3 > 1 (see Table 8). Comparing the feature of these samples, the older of male subjects do not have stronger reception of these features as lovely form.

Table 8. Different age of male's cognition of form feature on lovely images

Category	Item	3 > 2	1 > 2	3 > 1	1 > 3
Color treatment	1	Mainly hue is cold colors	–	Mainly hue is cold colors#	Mainly hue is cold colors#
	2	Mainly brightness is bright colors	Mainly brightness is bright colors	Mainly brightness is bright colors#	Mainly brightness is bright colors#
	3	–	Mainly color scheme is single hue	–	Mainly color scheme is single hue
	4	–	Mainly color scheme is harmony colors	–	Mainly color scheme is harmony colors
Form	1	–	–	–	–
	2	–	Geometric and organic in half-and-half	–	–
	3	Mainly symmetric	–	Mainly symmetric	–
	4	Mainly polymorph	–	Mainly polymorph	–
Detail treatment	1	–	Mainly rounded form	–	Mainly rounded form
	2	–	Functional and decorative in half-and-half	–	Functional and decorative in half-and-half
	3	–	Moderate detail features	More detail features	–
	4	–	Graving type	–	Graving type
Material treatment	1	Mainly hard	–	Mainly hard	–
	2	–	Mainly rough (matte)	Mainly smooth	Mainly rough (matte)
	3	–	Mainly consistent	–	Mainly consistent
	4	–	Not reflective	Not reflective	Not reflective
	5	Not transparent	Not transparent	Not transparent#	Not transparent#

Note: ⌐–⌐ indicates that the form feature does not exceed a half of samples

4 Conclusions

1. Products with the following features are more likely to be considered as lovelier: (1) color treated mainly in cold and bright colors, Color scheme is between single hue and multiple hues, and mainly color scheme is harmony colors; (2) In terms of form element, Totally bionic, mainly organic, mainly symmetric, and Form is between single shape and polymorph; (3) In terms of detail treatment, mainly rounded form, Functional and decorative in half-and-half, More detail features, and Graving type; (4) In terms of material treatment, mainly hard, mainly rough (matte), mainly consistent, Not reflective, and Not transparent.

2. Female subjects are easier than male subjects to consider products with mainly bright color, mainly symmetrical form, mainly rounded and mainly decorative detail treatment as lovely. Products are with mainly hard, mainly smooth, mainly consistent, reflective, and not transparent in terms of material treatment. Female subjects have wilder reception of lovely features.

3. Products with the following features are more likely to be considered as lovelier: (1) mainly bright color; (2) In terms of form element, totally bionic, mainly organic, mainly symmetric, and mainly polymorph; (3) In terms of detail treatment, mainly rounded form, functional and decorative in half-and-half, and graving type; (4) In terms of material treatment, mainly hard, mainly smooth, mainly consistent, reflective, and not transparent. There are similar results between age group of 44–55 and age group of 32–43. So are between age group 32–43 and age group of 20–31. This indicates that the older of female subjects the stronger reception of these features as lovely form.

4. Unlike female, the older of male subjects do not have stronger reception of features as lovely form.

References

1. Kuo, B.S.: Research on the Relationship between the Product's Form and Emotion-A Case Study of Electric Kettles Design. Master's thesis, Graduate Institute of Industrial Design, National Yunlin University of Science and Technology (2006)
2. Liu, Y.C.: The influence of interaction of on lovely image using product. Master's thesis, Graduate Institute of Industrial Design, Tatung University (2009)
3. Wu, T.Y.: The effect of product forms on consumer's pleasurable affection. Doctoral thesis, Graduate Institute of Industrial Design, National Taiwan University of Science and Technology (2006)
4. Lorenz, K.: Studies in Animal and Human Behavior. Harvard University Press, Cambridge (1971)
5. Baxter, M.: Product Design - A Practical Guide to Systematic Methods of New Product Development. Chapman & Hall Publishing, London (1996)
6. Chen, K.S.: Style recognition and description. J. Des. **2**, 123–143 (1997)
7. Chou, C.J.: Creating A Multi-Kansei Image - Based on Formal Features. Master's thesis, Graduate Institute of Industrial Design, National Cheng Kung University (2001)
8. Ibid. 3

Induction of Human Behavior by Presentation of Environmental Acoustics

Eisuke Fujinawa[1], Sho Sakurai[1(✉)], Masahiko Izumi[1],
Takuji Narumi[1], Osamu Houshuyama[2], Tomohiro Tanikawa[1],
and Michitaka Hirose[1]

[1] The Graduate School of Information Science and Technology,
The University of Tokyo, 7-3-1 Hongo, Bunkyo-ku, Tokyo, Japan
{nawafuji,sho,masa,narumi,
tani,hirose}@cyber.t.u-tokyo.ac.jp
[2] NEC, Minato, Japan
houshu@bq.jp.nec.com

Abstract. Many conventional guidance systems utilize words and signals that need to be recorded by humans. However, these systems have the disadvantage of going unnoticed or being too intrusive when used in quiet places, such as a museum. Human behavior is known to change as a result of varying feelings and ambient sounds elicit pleasant and unpleasant feelings. We therefore hypothesized that creating a comfortable sound field at a particular location would induce human behavior. To induce human behavior with sound, we constructed a system that divides space without a physical barrier by focusing sound in a narrow area. Using this system, we examined the possibility of generating an acoustic field in a narrow target position and measured the output accuracy of the presented acoustic pressure. In addition, we tested whether humans were unconsciously guided by the effects of this system.

Keywords: Behavior induction · Virtual sound field · Parametric speaker · Evoking emotion · Acoustic AR

1 Introduction

Museums require the behavior of visitors to be stimulated in order to guide them to appropriate exhibited works or avoid congestion. Therefore, many guidance systems are utilized to induce human behavior. A typical example of a guidance system used in public spaces is a large-screen display and a speaker for audio assistance. However, it is now possible to present information individually through smartphones and various wearable devices. A user is required to gather the information that s/he needs for her/his behavior selection.

Many of these conventional guidance systems utilize words and signals. Thus, their meaning needs to be interpreted so that the appropriate behavior is selected. However, these types of guidance systems have the disadvantage of going unnoticed or being too intrusive in quiet spaces, such as museums. In addition, explicit information presented by these systems could ruin the mood of the exhibition.

© Springer International Publishing Switzerland 2015
S. Yamamoto (Ed.): HIMI 2015, Part I, LNCS 9172, pp. 582–594, 2015.
DOI: 10.1007/978-3-319-20612-7_55

Psychological studies have shown that human behavior is altered by ambient information. For example, the lighting in an environment affects the content of conversation and speaking volume [1, 2]. The arrangement of color in a classroom greatly influences students' achievement [3]. In addition, it is becoming clear that environmental lighting and temperature affects the amount of food consumed [4, 5]. The temperature of an object that people touch affects graciousness [6]. These findings show that seemingly meaningless information greatly affects human emotions, judgment, and behavior [7] and suggest that controlling the environmental information can control human emotions and behavior.

In this study, we focused on implicitly inducing human behavior in public spaces with environmental sound, such as environmental noise and background music (BGM). These sounds significantly affect pleasant/unpleasant feelings [8]. Therefore, we hypothesized that human behavior could be induced implicitly by creating comfortable/uncomfortable sound fields. This effect is evoked in the subject without their conscious attention to the sound and interpretation of the meaning of the sound. Therefore, this induction method using environmental sound balances the competing goals of guidance efficiency and maintaining the mood of a museum. Recently, sound presentation systems that can create sound fields within a narrow area have been developed [9–11]. These systems can be used to create local sound fields that induce appropriate human behavior in appropriate places. In order to create sound fields that divide space without a physical barrier, we constructed a system that can focus sound to a narrow area by using directional loudspeakers. We used this system to conduct an experiment and examined our ability to generate an acoustic field at a narrow target position. We also examined the output accuracy of the presented acoustic pressure. In addition, we tested whether humans were unconsciously guided by the effects of this system.

2 Inducing Human Behavior by Presenting Sensory Stimuli

Conventional guidance techniques instruct about appropriate routes or behaviors with explicit auditory or visual information, such as characters and symbols. For example, methods for presenting guidance information through mobile/wearable include devices that users carry [12, 13] and projectors embedded in the environment [14]. While the methods that use visual stimuli can present a lot of information, the user is always required to pay attention to the presented information. Auditory information is often used to make announcements in public spaces, including museums. Sound requires less attention than visual information in order to grasp the information. However, it is difficult to present different information to individuals because the same sound is usually presented to the entire space through a speaker.

Intuitive guidance techniques that do not use explicit symbols have been studied. For example, Yoshikawa et al. proposed a system for directing the pedestrian movement to one side of a passage by creating a vection field with a lenticular lens [15]. However, because this system could affect untargeted people in the space, it is difficult to induce the behavior of only a particular person. A haptic interface is sometimes used for realizing intuitive guidance. For example, Amemiya and Maeda proposed a navigation system that uses perceptual attraction forces [16]. Humans translate asymmetric acceleration into a one-directional force because of their perception characteristics. Their method, which utilizes these characteristics, can generate constant force by repeating one cycle of motion for navigation, even though it is a nongrounded device. Narumi et al. constructed a system called Thermotaxis, which controls the positions of humans in public spaces with thermal stimulation and which is based on the findings that temperature sensations are closely related to pleasure-displeasure feelings [17, 18]. Thermotaxis presents a virtual thermal field in which the temperature that is presented through a wearable device changes according to the position of each user. They showed that it is possible to control the position of users and the physical and psychological distance between the users with the temperature of the thermal stimuli [19]. In addition to thermal stimuli, haptic stimuli strongly affect emotions. Sakurai et al. proposed a method to evoke multiple emotions by presenting a wide variety of haptic stimuli, such as thermal stimulation, vibration stimulation, and pressure stimulation [20, 21]. Human behavior changes as a result of emotional changes that occur in response to various sensory stimuli because emotional states largely influence judgment and behavior changes [7].

However, a wearable device is required to be able to present personalized information or control stimuli when using these methods. However, it is possible that the user would pay attention to the wearable device itself rather than the stimuli presented through the device because wearing the device increases physical load.

As an example of a method that induces behavior through other senses, Maeda et al. proposed a system that induces walking courses with vestibular electrical stimulation [22]. The system controls the pedestrians walking direction according to perceived gravity acceleration that functions by passing weak electric current between electrodes placed behind the ears. While this approach does not require the user to direct their attention to the stimuli, it is difficult for the user to change direction by themselves due to the very strong forces. Moreover, the safety of the long-term use of this method has not been confirmed.

In this study, we aimed to realize a method for inducing human behavior unconsciously without the use of a wearable device. We assumed that it would be used in a museum and with a focus on auditory sensation. As previously mentioned, auditory sensations allow the presentation of information to humans without requiring their attention as much as that required for visual sensations. However, conventional methods that use auditory sensations have been used as a way to provide explicit information through announcements in the main language. Therefore, as is the case with the use of visual symbols, it is necessary to interpret the meaning of the presented information.

However, inexplicit sounds have also been shown to greatly influence pleasant/unpleasant feelings of humans and have various psychological effects [8]. In recent years, some approaches that use these findings have tried to influence human behavior. For example, there have been attempts to reduce the crime rate by playing classical music in a public space, such as a station [23]. In addition, a high-frequency sound called mosquito noise, which is only heard by the young, is used in convenience stores to suppress youth misbehavior [24].

Methods to manipulate behavior with sound have been incorporated in the field of art. For instance, Hein published a work called, "Invisible Labyrinth," which requires a participant to walk around an exhibition space while wearing headphones [25]. Noise comes from the headphones, and the volume of the noise changes according to the position of the participants in the space. This installation makes the participants move as if there is an invisible load in the exhibition space with nothing in it because all of the participants try to find a way to avoid hearing the unpleasant noise. Although this approach requires the wearing of a device and it is not necessarily involving the unconscious, these observations suggest that it is possible to induce a human to a specific position by affecting their feelings through the presentation of a sound. Based on these observations of induction of the position/movement of humans and in order to realize a method to induce the position/movement of the user, we propose a system to divide space into comfortable and uncomfortable areas by controlling the acoustic environment at arbitrary positions in the space.

3   Acoustic Research System for Inducing Human Behavior

3.1   Directional and Local Sound Presentation

Sound consists of vibration stimuli transmitted through air and that normally have no locality. Recently, studies have been conducted in order to synthesize a sound field by presenting sound to particular locations.

Many studies that have investigated synthesizing sound fields in a real environment have adopted methods that create focal points of sound by controlling the time required to reproduce and amplify the sounds, which are outputs from lined speaker arrays arranged side by side [9]. These methods can reproduce high-definition sound fields. However, these methods have a number of drawbacks: they are very expensive due to the requirement for a few hundred speaker arrays and the installation locations of the speaker arrays are limited.

Another method that can be used to present sound locally is to use directional loudspeakers, such as parametric speakers. Parametric speakers implement strong directivity and reflectivity due to their use of ultrasound as the carrier [10]. Ikefuji et al. developed a system for forming stereophonic sound [11], which consisted of units that include multiple parametric speakers and face in multiple directions. The ultrasounds, which are outputs from the unit, reflect off the floor, wall surfaces, ceiling, and mirrors that are set in the space and travel to the listener. The positions where the ultrasounds are reflected to, then seem to be the source of the sound. In addition, stereophonic sound can be reproduced by constructing several audio image locations.

Some studies have been conducted in order to provide new experiences through the high directivity of sound irradiated from parametric speakers. For example, Kimura et al. produced VITA, which is a space-filling display system that visualizes sound beams from a unit that includes multiple parametric speakers, which enable various spatial sound interactions with visual feedback [26]. Ueta et al. proposed a system named Juke Cylinder that enables users to feel like their body is made up of various instruments by irradiating the sound of the instruments to the user's hand from parametric speakers, which are incorporated in the chassis of the system [27].

The high directivity of the parametric speakers enables local presentation of sounds. Parametric speakers are commonly used for movement guidance in stations and for descriptions of exhibited works in museums because of their low cost and acoustic quality improvements. In the preceding cases, the direction of the parametric speakers is fixed so that sounds are presented in a certain direction. If the direction of the parametric speakers are controlled dynamically, the sound could be presented locally anywhere. This approach has the advantages of low cost and high flexibility for use in different situations.

Based on the studies and reviews described above, we constructed an acoustic research (AR) system to induce human behavior with parametric speakers.

3.2 Acoustic AR System to Create a Local Sound Field

We propose a system capable of inducing the feeling that there is an acoustic field by presenting different sounds with parametric speakers according to the position of the listener (Fig. 1). This system consists of two parametric speakers (Tristate Inc.), two pan-tilt camera platforms, a depth sensor (Microsoft Kinect), an A/D D/A converter (audio interface, M-AUDIO Profire 610), and a Laptop PC. The target area where the sound was presented was sandwiched between two parametric speakers, which were arranged on the ceiling. Each parametric speaker was rested on a pan-tilt camera platform. The directions of the camera platforms were controlled with servo-motors (Futaba FP-S3101). Hereafter, this system is collectively called the speaker unit. The speaker units were linked to the audio interface connected to a PC by a wired connection.

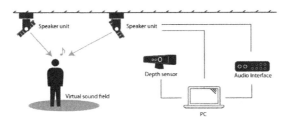

Fig. 1. The configuration of the acoustic research system

The system turned the parametric speakers in the direction of the listener's head in order to present sound depending on the position of the listener. First, the depth sensors detected the position of the listener's head. Next, the parametric speakers faced the user's head by manipulating the angle of the camera platform according to the detected coordinates. Each of the outputs from the speaker unit branched and sent audio sources from the audio interface. The type of sound and sound pressure of each audio source were controlled depending on the position of the user. In this way, this system made the listener feel that there was a sound field when the listener moved within the target space by changing the type of sound or loudness according to the position of the listener.

3.3 An Experiment to Investigate the Effectiveness of the AR System for Generating Virtual Sound Fields in a Space

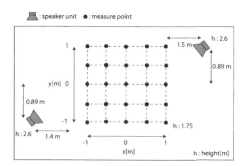

Fig. 2. Experimental setup

Table 1. Equipment and condition adopted in this experiment

Microphone	RION NL-20	Ambient noise level	40.1 dB
Equalization	16 bits	Sound source	White noise
Sampling frequency	44.1 kHz	Evaluated frequency	20–8,000 kHz
Carrier frequency	40 kHz		

In order to test whether our proposed system generated several virtual sound fields in which different sounds were provided to individuals sharing the space, the system's ability to generate acoustic fields at a narrow target position was evaluated. In addition, we evaluated how the generated acoustics were localized in order to investigate whether this system could generate high locality of an acoustic field at the target position.

Figure 2 shows the environment of the performance evaluation. The target area for generating the sound fields was set to be 200 cm^2 between the speaker units. In this experiment, sound pressure was measured at the 35 points where it was picked up vertically and horizontally at 50-cm intervals in the target area. Hereafter, these 35 points are called measuring points. In addition, ultrasound was irradiated toward 9 points where it was picked up vertically and horizontally at 100-cm intervals within the 35 points. Hereafter, these 9 points are called target points. When the sound was output to each irradiating point, the sound pressure was measured at each of the measuring points. Through this procedure, the system was examined according to whether sound pressure increased locally only at each target point. Table 1 shows the equipment and conditions adopted in this experiment.

3.4   Results and Discussion

Figure 3 shows the sound pressure level distribution at each of the 9 target points through linear interpolating of the values of the sound pressures at each of 35 measuring points. The average sound pressures at 9 target points were 55 dB.

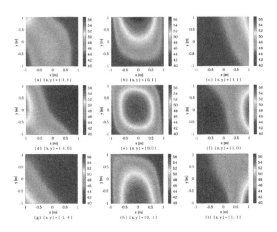

Fig. 3. Sound pressure level distribution during sound output to each target point using the constructed acoustic AR system

The average at a position 100 cm away from each target point was 47 dB, which dropped by an average of 8.0 dB. According to the index about acoustic perception, sound at about 55 dB is considered loud and annoying, and sound at about 45 dB can be heard but it is not bothersome [28]. Depending on this index, our system could present different sounds to each individual when the individuals were at a distance of 100 cm.

The change in sound pressure in the x-direction in the experimental area was slow compared to the change in the y-direction. Thus, it is thought that the presented sound wave passed target points adjacent to the x-direction of the experimental area due to the smallness of the incident angle of the presented sound waves to the x-y plane. Setting the speakers to a higher position would solve this problem.

The maximum difference between the sound pressures of each target point was 4.7 dB. This result indicated that variations of sound pressures fell within the value of the target points anywhere. Based on Figure 5, possible reasons for this varying of the sound pressures were the decay distance of the parametric speakers and the control of the direction of the misalignment of the camera platform. The former case was issued by placing the parametric speakers so that the distances between each of the speakers did not differ much. With the camera platform, more accurate calibration or controlling the angle helps with the latter case.

The results suggested the effectiveness of our system in generating a virtual sound field.

4 Inducing Human Behavior with the Acoustic AR System

4.1 Experimental Hypothesis, Settings, and Procedures

We investigated whether human behavior was induced by dividing a space into comfortable/uncomfortable areas with an acoustic AR system. In this experiment, the system divided a space into a high sound pressure/low sound pressure area. It makes humans in the space feel that these two areas are different places. Through psychological effects of the sound that differently affect different people, sound is classified as pleasant or unpleasant [8, 29]. The difference between pleasant/unpleasant depending on the presented sound also affects human behavior and behavioral cognition [30, 31]. These findings suggest that a high sound pressure area with a pleasant sound and a low sound pressure area with an unpleasant sound were considered relatively comfortable. We hypothesized that humans stay in these comfortable areas longer than in the other areas.

Figure 4 shows the environment of this experiment. A space in front of four pictures, which were projected by a single focus projector, is set as the area of movement of a participant. The details of the four pictures are described later. The area of movement for the participant was divided into 7 areas (hereafter referred to as point-areas) every 50 cm in the horizontal direction. The time that the participant stayed in each area was measured.

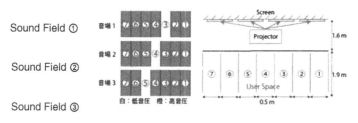

Fig. 4. Experimental environment for inducing the position of participants (Left: Conditions for sound fields, Right: Experimental environment)

This experiment used the two following types of sounds to induce the position of the participant: White noise as a sound, which would be perceived as unpleasant (hereafter referred to as WN conditions) and jazz music, which was considered a pleasant sound (hereafter referred to as BGM conditions). In addition, a trial of silence was set up for comparison of the effects of the two types of sound (hereafter referred to as S conditions). Table 2 shows the conditions of each sound.

Figure 4 shows the type of generated sound fields that were used in the experiment.

In order to make sure no participants determined the purpose of this experiment, the participants were asked to watch four pictures of tarot cards and choose their favorite picture and second favorite picture as a dummy task. The task was set because repeating more than one trial would cause the participants to move in a narrow space for the experiment without a sense of question. Sixty-eight types of tarot cards were used in this experiment to disperse the preference for pictures that have quality that can be appreciated.

Table 2. Experimental conditions for sounds used in the experiment

Condition	Used sound (SF, Q)
WN	White noise (44.1 kHz, 16 bits)
BGM	Jazz (44.1 kHz,16 bits)
S	Silent

Each participant underwent 6 trials in the WN condition (2 trials on each sound field distribution shown in Figure 4) 6 trials in the BGM condition (2 trials on each sound field distribution shown in Figure 4), and 3 trials in the S conditions, for a total of 15 trials of the above task. Each trial was 1-minute long, and the time that the participant stayed in each area was measured. After the end of 15 trials, the participants were asked to listen to the noise and jazz music that were used in this experiment once again with headphones, and they rated the comfort level of the sounds with a 7-point Likert scale. In addition, they were asked whether they noticed a difference in each trial. The participants included 9 males and 1 female. All of them were in their twenties.

4.2   Results

We investigated the effects on inducing human behavior at each acoustic space in the WN and BGM conditions. We calculated the average time that a participant stayed at a low sound pressure area in 6 trials of the WN conditions and of the BGM conditions, and the average time they stayed at point-area 3, point-area 4, and point-area 5 of all 3 trials in the S condition. The average times of each participant in each of the calculated conditions were further averaged over all of the participants (Fig. 5.)

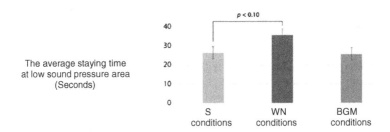

Fig. 5. The average staying time at each low sound pressure area in each sound condition

The average staying times in each of the conditions were as follows: 35.8 s (WN conditions), 25.7 s (BGM conditions), and 26.5 s (S conditions). *t*-Tests showed a marginally significant difference between average staying time under WN conditions and S conditions ($p < 0.10$.) There was no significant difference between the BGM and S conditions ($p = 0.31$.)

The participants evaluated that the white noise that was used in the WN conditions was rather uncomfortable (average score was 2.8), and the jazz music that was used in the BGM conditions was rather comfortable (average score was 5.3). According to the questionnaire after all the trials, 7 participants noticed a difference in the sound pressure and 2 participants felt like the sound pressure was different. In addition, 1 participant moved to the low sound pressure area while watching the presented pictures.

4.3   Discussion

This study showed that the time spent in the low sound pressure areas increased in the WN condition. Because white noise was evaluated as an uncomfortable sound, these results were consistent with the hypothesis that the participants felt pleasant feelings in areas of low sound pressure when uncomfortable sound occurred, and they stayed there longer.

However, the results showed that the average time participants stayed in the low sound pressure area decreased about 1 s in the BGM condition. Because the jazz music was evaluated as a comfortable sound, these results were consistent with the hypothesis that participants stayed at low sound pressure areas a shorter amount of time when comfortable sounds occurred. However, there was no significant difference in the staying time. This result might be because the difference in the presented sound pressure was not enough to lose the pleasant feelings evoked by the comfortable BGM.

As for a method to induce behavior with comfortable sounds, selecting the type of sound according to the context of the user's experience is important. At this time, the sound does not relate to the place or the setting of the experiment. Specific sounds are preferred in a certain context. For example, loud techno would be preferred in a discotheque. In contrast, calming classical music would be popular at expensive restaurants. Similarly, whether the sound being heard is in line with the context of the experience or not could influence the feelings of comfort.

Moreover, we attempted to induce human behavior with only binary sound pressure that differed vastly from each other. However, high sound pressure does not always produce feelings of comfort as in the above-mentioned examples. It is possible that separating the sound pressure of the presented sound into several steps could induce the user to the area where the appropriate sound pressure is located.

The size of the sound fields could also affect the induction of human behavior. Because the width of each area for the participants' movements was only 50 cm, there was a possibility that they passed soon without noticing changes in sound pressure at each low sound pressure area compared to the other area, depending on their walking pace. Therefore, the difference in the effects of inducing human behavior in our proposed method due to the size of acoustic field needs to be investigated.

5 Conclusion

In this paper, we proposed a method to induce human behavior without interpreting presented information by dividing a space into a comfortable area and an uncomfortable area with acoustic field generation techniques.

First, we created a nonwearable system that presented sound locally and created acoustic fields virtually by using multiple directional loudspeakers. We tested whether the system generated acoustic fields at narrow target positions. In an attempt to generate and control the right sound field at each location we also examined how the generated acoustic field was localized by comparing acoustic pressure measures between the target position and other positions. This test showed the following: Sound pressure decreases by 8.0 dB on average at a distance of 100 cm from the location where the sound is presented and the dispersion of sound pressure fell within a 200-cm square. These results suggested that the system was able to present sound locally with an accurate output of acoustic pressure.

Next, we investigated whether dividing a space into comfortable/uncomfortable areas with the acoustic AR system induced human behavior. As a result, the time that participants stayed in the low sound pressure area increased when an uncomfortable sound was presented. This suggested that our system could change the behavior of visitors and increase their sojourn time at a target position. Although the effect of inducing behavior was not seen when a comfortable sound was presented, human behavior could possibly be induced by considering the condition of the acoustic field or a relationship between the experience of the users and sound.

Although this study intended to use a confined narrow area as the target area, our proposed method has the potential to induce not only the position of visitors but also their direction and trajectory. In addition, it is thought that our proposed methods would change the distance between people interactively by adapting our method for multiple users. In the future, we will examine whether the system is capable of inducing human behavior in a highly public area, such as an exhibition space, by constructing acoustic fields that suit the exhibition content.

References

1. Sanders, M., Gustanski, J., Lawton, M.: Effect of ambient illumination on noise level if groups. J. Appl. Psychol. **59**, 527–528 (1974)
2. Gifford, R.: Light, decor, arousal, comfort and communication. J. Environ. Psychol. **8**, 177–189 (1988)
3. Barrett, P., et al.: A holistic, multi-level analysis identifying the impact of classroom design on pupils' learning. JBE **59**, 678–689 (2013)
4. Sommer, R.: Personal Space: Behavioral Basis of Design. Englewood Cliff, Prentice- Hall (1969)
5. Brobeck, J.R.: Food intake as a mechanism of temperature regulation. Yale J. Biol. Med. **20**, 545–552 (1948)
6. Williams, L.E., Bargh, J.A.: Experiencing physical warmth promotes interpersonal warmth. Science **322**(5901), 606–607 (2009)

7. Yoshida, S., Sakurai, S., Narumi, T., Tanikawa, T., Hirose, M.: Manipulation of an emotional experience by real-time deformed facial feedback. In: AH 2013, pp. 35–42 (2013)

8. Dubé, L., Chebat, J.-C., Morin, S.: The effects of background music on consumers' desire to affiliate in buyer-seller interactions. Psychol. Mark. **12**, 305–319 (1995)

9. Shinagawa, K., Horio, K., Takemura, H., Mizoguchi, H.: Sound spot generation and evaluation by large scale panel loudspeaker array. In: Proceedings of 2008 IEEE International Conference on Systems, Man and Cybernetics (SMC 2008), pp. 1164–1168 (2008)

10. Croft, J.J., Norris, J.O.: Theory, history, and the advancement of parametric loudspeaker. White paper of American Technology Corporation (2001)

11. Ikefuji, D., Nakayama, M., Nishiura. T., Yamashita, Y.: Fundamental study of moving sound image design with curved-type parametric loudspeaker. In: 7th Forum Acusticum 2014 (FA2014), Paper ID: R05D_3 (2014)

12. Varoudis, T.: Ambient displays: influencing movement patterns. In: Campos, P., Graham, N., Jorge, J., Nunes, N., Palanque, P., Winckler, M. (eds.) INTERACT 2011, Part IV. LNCS, vol. 6949, pp. 52–65. Springer, Heidelberg (2011)

13. Beyer, G., Kottner, F., Schiewe, M., Haulsen, I., Butz, A.: Squaring the circle: how framing influences user behavior around a seamless cylindrical display. In: Proceedings of the SIGCHI Conference on Human Factors in Computing Systems, pp. 1729–1738. ACM, April 2013

14. Narumi, T., Hada, Y., Asama, H., Tsuji, K.: Pedestrian route guidance system using moving information based on personal feature extraction. In: Proceedings of IEEE International Conference on Multisensor Fusion and Integration for Intelligent Systems, pp. 94–99, August 2008

15. Yoshikawa, H., Hachisu, T., Fukushima, S., Furukawa, M., Kajimoto, H.: "Vection field" for pedestrian traffic control. In: SIGGRAPH 2011 E-tech, Article No. 21 (2011)

16. Amemiya, T., Maeda, T.: Directional force sensation by asymmetric oscillation from a double-layer slider-crank mechanism. Trans. ASME. J. Comput. Inf. Sci. Eng. **9**(1), 011001 (2009)

17. Stolwijk, J.A.: Responses to the thermal environment. Fed. Proc. **36**(5), 1655 (1977)

18. Narumi, T., Akagawa, T., Seong, Y.A., Hirose, M.: Thermotaxis. In: SIGGRAPH 2009: Posters, p. 18. ACM, August 2009

19. Narumi, T., Akagawa, T., Seong, Y.A., Hirose, M.: An entertainment system using thermal feedback for increasing communication and social skills. In: Chang, M., Kuo, R., Kinshuk, Chen, G.-D., Hirose, M. (eds.) Learning by Playing. LNCS, vol. 5670, pp. 184–195. Springer, Heidelberg (2009)

20. Sakurai, S., Ban, Y., Katsumura, T., Narumi, T., Tanikawa, T., Hirose, M.: Communious mouse: a mouse interface to experience emotions in remarks on the web by extending and modulating one's body image. In: SIGGRAPH Asia 2014 E-Tech, Article 4, p. 3 (2014)

21. Sakurai, S., Katsumura, T., Narumi, T., Tanikawa, T., Hirose, M.: Evoking emotions in a story using tactile sensations as pseudo-body responses with contextual cues. In: Yamamoto, S. (ed.) HCI 2014, Part I. LNCS, vol. 8521, pp. 241–250. Springer, Heidelberg (2014)

22. Maeda, T., Ando, H., Amemiya, T., Nagaya, N., Sugimoto, M., Inami, M.: Shaking the world: galvanic vestibular stimulation as a novel sensation interface. In: SIGGRAPH 2005 E-Tech, Article 17 (2005)

23. London, J.: Third-party uses of music and musical pragmatics. J. Aesthet. Art Criticism **66** (3), 253–264 (2008)

24. Compound Security Systems Ltd. http://www.compoundsecurity.co.uk/. Accessed 12 February 2015

25. Hein, J.: Invisible Labyrinth. http://www.jeppehein.net/pages/project_id.php?path= works&id=125. Accessed 12 February 2015
26. Kimura, K., Houshuyama, O., Narumi, T., Tanikawa, T., Hirose, M.: Sound-power visualization system for real-world interaction based on ultrasonic power transmission. In: Proceedings of ACE2011, Article 60, p. 8 (2011)
27. Ueta, M., Houshuyama, O., Narumi, T., Sakurai, S., Tanikawa, T., Hirose, M: Juke cylinder: sound image augmentation to metamorphose hands into a musical instrument. In: Proceedings of ACE 2012, pp. 453–460 (2012)
28. Davis, H.: The articulation area and the social adequacy index for hearing. Laryngoscope **58** (8), 761–778 (1948)
29. Sweeney, J.C., Fiona, W.: The role of cognitions and emotions in the mu- sic-approach-avoidance behavior relationship. J. Serv. Mark. **16**(1), 51–69 (2002)
30. North, A.C., Hargreaves, D.J.: The effect of music on atmosphere and purchase intentions in a cafeteria. J. Appl. Psychol. **28**(24), 2254–2273 (1998)
31. Yalch, R.F., Spangenberg, E.: An environmental psychological study of foreground and background music as retail atmospheric factors. In: AMA Educators' Conference Proceedings. American Marketing Association, pp. 106–110 (1988)

Modeling User's Sentiment in User Segmentations: An Argumentation Approach for User Centered Design

María Paula González[1,2](✉), Carlos I. Chesñevar[1,2], and Ramon Brena[3]

[1] Department of Computer Science and Engineering, Universidad Nacional del Sur,
Av. Alem 1253, 8000 Bahía Blanca, Argentina
{mpg,cic}@cs.uns.edu.ar
[2] National Council of Scientific and Technical Reseach CONICET,
Buenos Aires, Argentina
[3] Escuela de Posgrado en Ingeniera y Ciencias, Tecnolgico de Monterrey, Campus
Monterrey CETEC Torre Sur. Av. E. Garza Sada 2501, 64849 Monterrey, Mexico
ramon.brena@itesm.mx

Abstract. User segmentation is a practice of clustering an audience based on mutually exclusive subsets of individuals that are similar in specific ways. Nowadays user segmentation is crucial not only for the industry but also for the field of User Centered Design, where achieving an accurate understanding of the user's behavior in the current e-scenario is becoming a complex task. The segmentation could be based on demographic issues, social-economical features, psychographic data, physical characteristics and psychological profiles, etc. This paper proposes a novel strategy for the automatic detection of critical segmentation factors that divide users focused on their feelings and opinions towards a particular topic. Given a topic and on the basis of user's text-based opinions posted at Web 2.0 services (such as social networks, microblogging platforms, online review systems, online news media, etc.), our proposal introduces an argument-oriented methodology that integrates argumentation theory, sentiment analysis and opinion mining including the computational treatment of incomplete, contradictory or potentially inconsistent information. The mining process is characterized in terms of dialectical analysis of opinions (atomic or more complex opinions constructed by an aggregation mechanism) according to a preference criterion given by topic and feature specificity. As a result, an "opinion analysis tree" rooted in the first original topic is automatically constructed and visualized, in which any node models a user segmentation, showing the factor that define the segmentation as well as the particularities that group the subset. This way, traditional problems associated with the subjective interpretation of user's opinions expressed in natural language are minimized. Besides, instead of defining a user's statistical sample, all available information is considered and possible, not evident critical segmentation factors could be discovered, thus enhancing a rational decision making process.

© Springer International Publishing Switzerland 2015
S. Yamamoto (Ed.): HIMI 2015, Part I, LNCS 9172, pp. 595–606, 2015.
DOI: 10.1007/978-3-319-20612-7_56

Keywords: User centered design · User segmentation · Sentiment analysis · Sentiment mining · Argumentation theory

1 Introduction and Motivation

Audience segmentation is a practice of clustering an audience based on mutually exclusive subsets of individuals that are similar in specific ways to make up hypothetical archetypes of actual users. Audience segmentation has been defined as "the process of identifying groups of customers who are relatively homogenous in their response to marketing stimuli, so that the market offering can be tailored more closely to meet their needs" [3]. The goal is to find new, previously unaddressed target groups of customers to better design communication strategies catering them in an suitable way according with their specific needs to increase their satisfaction and loyalty. The segmentation could be based on demographic issues (i.e. age, gender, region, ethnic); social-economical features (i.e. sector, services access, income); psychographic data (i.e. lifestyle, values, attitudes, interests, activities, opinions), physical characteristics (disabilities, perceptual abilities, motor skills abilities), psychological profiles, and all other measurable criteria that will affect the target.

With the advent of the Digital Society, the idea that people behave differently during the purchase process has been extended beyond the business industry to other fields, i.e. social networks targeting, citizens centered services and e-government [2], web site personalization [25], etc. In particular, audience segmentation provides key insights to the field of User Centered Design (UCD), where achieving an accurate understanding of the user's behavior is becoming a complex task [15]. An adequate user classification will enhance the later definition of user profiles, flexible targeting requirements, personalized design, test cases design, and prediction of user navigation patterns and habits, among others (UCD) oriented activities. From the UCD perspective user behavior includes issues regarding web usage, such as frequency of use, importance of functions and data usage and usage flow plus the most traditional items listed above (demographic issues, social-economical features, physical characteristics, psychological profiles, etc.). The involved users should represent the intended users, and the validity and reliability of the segmentation has to be guaranteed.

Many problems have been described regarding audience segmentation, including the criteria for segmentation itself: which data to select, how many clusters to produce and how to evaluate the clustering results. In particular, from an UCD perspective, being capable to deal with the users' emotions and modelling their feeling as a part of the user profile definition is a central problem to solve. Indeed the definition of accurate segmentation criteria as a previous step to perform each segment calculation becomes a very complex task when dealing with emotions as part of the psychological profiles, due to the complexity and the numerous cultural and emotional-biased variables that have to be taken into account [19]. Additionally, even though some proposals deal with vagueness and uncertainty (see Sect. 4), coping with the treatment of incomplete, contradictory or potentially inconsistent information is still a challenge to achieve.

This paper proposes a novel strategy for the automatic detection of critical segmentation factors that divide users focused on their feelings and opinions towards a particular topic. Given a topic and on the basis of user's text-based opinions posted at Web 2.0 services (such as social networks, microblogging platforms, online review systems, online news media, etc.), our proposal introduces an argument-oriented methodology that integrates argumentation theory, sentiment analysis and opinion mining including the computational treatment of incomplete, contradictory or potentially inconsistent information. The mining process is characterized in terms of dialectical analysis of opinions (atomic or more complex opinions constructed by aggregation mechanism) according to a preference criterion given by topic and feature specificity. As a result, an "opinion analysis tree" rooted in the first original topic is automatically constructed and visualized, on which any node models a user segmentation, showing the factor that defines the segmentation as well as the particularities that group the subset. This way, traditional problems associated with the subjective interpretation of user's opinions expressed in natural language are minimized. Besides, instead of defining a user's statistical sample, all available information is considered and possible not evident critical segmentation factors could be discovered, thus enhancing a rational decision making process.

This paper is structured as follows. First, in Sect. 2 we give an overview of the novel argumentative approach that underlies our proposal. Then, Sect. 3 describes the integration of these algorithms and their graphical results when defining user profiles from an UCD perspective. Section 4 discusses some related work. Finally, Sect. 5 concludes by summarizing the main implications of this proposal and discussing future work.

2   Mining Opinions and Users' Feelings. An Argumentative Approach

Social networks have grown exponentially in use and impact on the society as a whole. The scientific study of emotions in opinions associated with a given topic has become relevant, consolidating a new area known as *sentiment analysis* [8,17]. In particular, microblogging platforms such as Twitter have become important tools to assess public opinion on different issues. Recently, some approaches for assessing Twitter messages have been developed, identifying sentiments associated with relevant keywords or hashtags. However, such approaches have an important limitation, as they do not take into account contradictory and potentially inconsistent information which might emerge from relevant messages. This limitation can be overcome by using an argumentative perspective [1,22].

In the above context a novel argument-based framework which allows to mine opinions from Twitter based on incrementally generated queries was proposed [5,11]. The notion of opinion is modelled as a collection of atomic opinions. Given a query Q (corresponding to one or more keywords or hashtags), this novel approach allows to collect those distinguished tweets referring to Q, according to an aggregation criterion (also provided as an input). This collection of tweets is

called a *Twitter-based argument* A for Q, associated with a *prevailing sentiment*
(computed on the basis of the tweets involved).[1] By expanding Q in different
ways, more specific arguments can be obtained which might be in conflict with
A. These counter-arguments might be in turn in conflict with other more specific arguments. This will result in the characterization of an "opinion tree",
rooted in the first original query. "Conflict trees" emerged by considering distinguished nodes in this "opinion tree", resembling dialectical trees as those used
traditionally in defeasible argumentation [22].

The computation of the "opinion trees" finishes in finite time, as the maximum depth level is eventually reached. Additionally, branches cannot extend
infinitely, as the query length is always finite (a finite set of terms), and as
the set of feature values is always finite as well. Therefore the algorithm will
eventually stop, providing an opinion analysis tree as an output.

Intuitively, a conflict tree depicts all possible ways of extending the original
query Q such that every extension (child node in the tree) corresponds to a sentiment change. Note that this approach to opinion trees is more generic than the
one used for dialectical trees in argumentation [9]), in the sense that for a given
argument, the children nodes will correspond to more specific arguments that
are not necessarily in conflict with the parent argument. The novel framework
includes a lattice-based characterization [5] which uses equivalence classes to
minimize the representation space to be analyzed when contrasting arguments.
This formal lattice-based characterization also introduces the definition of an
effective procedure to compute conflict superior lattices, which can be regarded
as a generalization of conflict trees. A Java prototype[2] was developed as a beta
version of a software tool for performing the mining process.

2.1 Formalizing a Twitter-Based Framework Using Arguments

A query Q is any set of descriptors used for filtering some relevant tweets from
the set of existing tweets based on a given criterion C. In order to abstract away
how such selection is performed, an aggregation operator $Agg(Q, C)$ is defined.
There are several alternative definitions for $Agg(Q, C)$. For instance, requiring
that those tweets T were retweeted more than n times, requiring that every user
that posted tweets T has at least m followers, etc.

A TB-argumentation framework is a 5-tuple $(Tweets, C, S, Sent, Conflict)$,
where

- Tweets is the set of available tweets,
- C is a selection criterion,
- S is a non-empty set of possible sentiments. A possible range for S could be
  positive, negative and neutral (as done for example in commercial platform
  sentiment140.com), or any other particular discrete range as anger and hap-
  piness; boredom and excitement, etc.,

---

[1] Several software tools have been recently developed for such an association, such as
www.sentiment140.com or tweetsentiments.com.

[2] Available to download from http://cs.uns.edu.ar/~cic/twitter.zip.

– *Sent* and *Conflict* are sentiment prevailing and conflict mappings[3].

A TB-argument for a query Q is a 3-uple $< Arg, Q, Sent >$, where Arg corresponds to a bunch of tweets associated with a query Q, obtained through $Agg(Q, C)$ and $Sent$ is the prevailing sentiment associated with $Agg(Q, C)$.

Example 1. Consider a TB-framework $(Tweets, C, S, Sent, Conflict)$, where $Q = \{$"Windows 8", "stability"$\}$, C is defined as all tweets after Nov. 1, 2014, and $S = \{$pos, neg, neutral$\}$, such that: $Conflict(pos)=\{$neg, neutral$\}$, $Conflict(neg) =\{$pos, neutral$\}$ and $Conflict(neutral) =\{$pos,neg$\}$. Then $Arg = Agg(Q, C)$ is the set of all possible tweets containing $\{$"Windows 8", "stability"$\}$ that have been published since Nov. 1, 2014. Suppose that $Sent(AggTweets(Q, C)) =$ negative (i.e., the prevailing sentiment involved is negative). Then $< Arg; \{$"Windows 8", "stability'$\}$,negative$>$ is a TB-argument.

Suppose that a TB-argument supporting the query $Q = \{$"Windows 8"$\}$ is obtained with a prevailing negative sentiment. If the original query Q is extended in some way into a new query Q that is more specific than Q (i.e. $Q = Q \cup \{d\}$, for some descriptor d), it could be the case that a TB-argument supporting Q has a different (possibly conflicting) prevailing sentiment. For example, more specific opinions about Windows 8 are related to other topics, like for example usability, mobile devices, users with disabilities issues, etc. To explore all possible relationships associated with TB-arguments returned for a specified query Q and criteria C, we can define an algorithm to construct an opinion tree recursively as follows:

Algorithm BuildOpinionTree
Input: Q
Output: Opinion Tree rooted in $< Arg, Q, Sent >$

1. We start with a TB-argument A obtained from the original query Q (i.e., $< Arg, Q, Sent >$), which will be the root of the tree.
2. Next, we compute within A all relevant descriptors that might be used to "extend" Q, by adding a new element ($NewTerm$) to the query, obtaining $Q' = Q \cup \{NewTerm\}$.
3. Then, a new argument for Q' is obtained, which will be associated with a subtree rooted in the original argument A.

Note that for any query Q, the algorithm *BuildOpinionTree* finishes in finite time: given that a tweet may not contain more than 140 characters, the number of contained descriptors is finite, and therefore the algorithm will eventually stop, providing an opinion tree as an output.

Figure 1 illustrates how the construction of an opinion tree for the query $Q = \{$"Windows 8"$\}$ looks like. Distinguished symbols $+, -, =$ are used to denote positive, negative and neutral sentiments, respectively. Note that the original

---

[3] See formal definitions in [5].

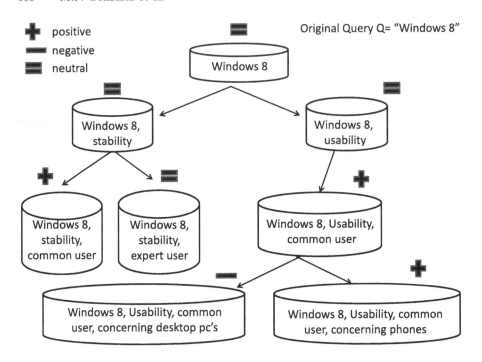

Fig. 1. Opinion Tree for query $Q= \{$"Windows 8"$\}$

query Q has cardinality 1, and further levels in the opinion tree refer to incrementally extended queries (e.g. {"Windows 8", "stability"}, or {"Windows 8", "usability", "common users"}). Leaves correspond to arguments associated with a query Q which cannot be further expanded, as the associated number of tweets is too small for any possible query $Q \cup \{d\}$, for some d. Furthermore, we can identify some subtrees in the Opinion Tree rooted in {"Windows 8"} which consist of nodes having all the same sentiment. In other words, further expanding a query into more complex queries does not change the prevailing sentiment associated with the root node. In other cases, expanding some queries results in a sentiment change (e.g. from {"Windows 8"} into {"Windows 8", "stability", "common user"} or {"Windows 8", "usability", "common user"}). This situation will allow us to characterize the "Conflict trees" described above. For all the formal definition regarding the notions discussed in this Section see [5,11].

3   The Proposal

Based on the construction of an "opinion tree" as shown in Sect. 2, the framework depicted in Fig. 2 proposes a novel strategy for the automatic detection of critical segmentation factors that divide users focused on their feelings and opinions towards a particular topic. The framework is composed by (1) a Natural Language Processing (NLP) Component used to extract terms, relations and entities, to parse text and do semantic annotation and semantic analysis, aiming to go beyond current implementation focused on Twitter; (2) a Users Opinions Knowledge base (UOK) generated by the NLP component which comprises a knowledge base storing users opinions; (3) an Argument Component divided in three parts- to cope with the computation of the "opinion tree" on the basis of the information stored in UOK. The Argument Component is formed by (a) an Argument Generation Component to analyze (given a context C) opinions in order to generate pro and con arguments based on the information stored in UOK; (b) an Argument Assessment Component to carried out with the construction of "opinion tree" as shown in Sect. 2.1; and (c) an Argument Visualization Component based on graphic user interfaces (GUI), the component enables to visualize dialectical analysis of arguments to support and facilitate the interpretation of results (discovered segmentation criteria plus segments graphically represented).

Note that users' opinions and feelings are automatically extracted and summarized directly form the users' text-based opinions posted at Web 2.0 services, such as social networks. This way the cultural-bias commonly present in subjective expert's interpretation of user's opinions expressed in natural language is minimized (as the one expressed in questionnaires typically used in UCD methods to collate data when defining psychological profiles). Besides, instead of defining a user's statistical sample, all real available information coming from real users is considered, stressing the most relevant UCD principles. In addition, note that the incorporation of an Argument Visualization Component enhances the graphical representation of results, thus enhancing their comprehension and significance for non experts in argumentation. While outputs of the computation can be seen as segmentation criteria results, the graphical representation adds awareness and valuable evidence supporting these results.

It must be remarked that the novel strategy replaces the need of supposing probable segmentation criteria as a previous step to perform each segment calculation when dealing with emotions by an automated computation of all available information in the web 2.0 source (as Twitter in the current implementation of the framework). Indeed, factors determining internal branches of the computed trees showed more specific segmentation criteria that the one expressed in the root of the tree (for example "stability", "usability" or "common user" in Fig. 1). This way, novel and non-evident or unexplored segmentation criteria should emerge, thus showing the real factors that are determining some of the user's feeling toward a topic without previous conjectures or assumptions. In addition, the automatic calculation provides a reasonable resource to re-calculate the same query in different moments of time, thus providing evidence about the user's opinions evolution upon time.

The methodology is independent of any particular user definition process, making possible to include it in any of the practices currently performed to define psychographic and psychological factors as part of any user profile modelling. While information in the internal nodes of the computed "opinion tree" summarizes novel and unknown segmentation criteria, results in any branch

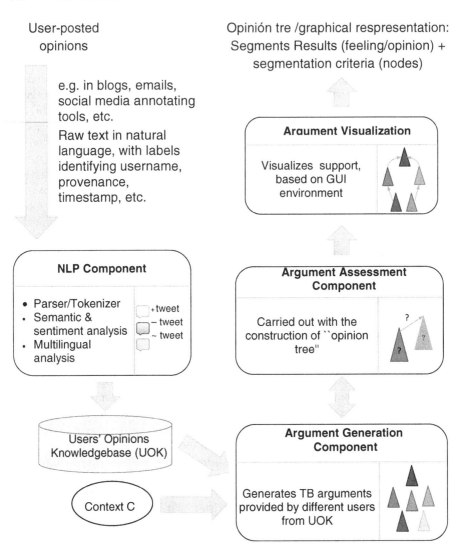

Fig. 2. The proposed framework for processing user's feelings and opinions towards a particular topic

(e.g. positive, negative, neutral in the present implementation) show users' opinions and feeling towards these criteria. Moreover, the graphical representation of the obtained "opinion tree" can be seen as the evidence that supports final conclusions regarding the original query Q represented at the top of the tree. Even though the current implementation of the proposal focuses on text-based opinions posted on Twitter, the discussed ideas can be considered in the case of other data sources such as any user's text-based Web 2.0 services.

4   Related Work

The idea of capturing essential intrinsic user behaviour values for enriching user profiles with user perceptual preferences characteristics was discussed in [19]. These authors focused on the definition of a comprehensive user profiling, incorporating the User Perceptual Preference Characteristics, that serves as the core element for filtering Web-based raw content. The final goal is related to web-based personalized environments. In contrast to our proposal, no argument-oriented methodology was included in this approach.

Among user's segmentation techniques two are especially important: data-driven analysis and Personas segmentation. Regarding data-driven analysis, contrast between UCD segmentation (qualitative approach) and statistical based methods (quantitative approach) were discussed. For example, [24] analyzes the precariousness of arising premature qualitative conclusions based on the statistical treatment of data coming from survey responses. He points out the disparity on the significance of small average differences in a large enough sample statistically treated versus these significance for practical, decision-making purposes in individual cases or in small UCD samples, where effect size and likelihood of classification error are more important. Reference [24] suggests that if statistical patterns regarding users segmentation were treated as hypothesis to be tested with more behavioral UCD research, the gap between both approaches would be smoothed, as they can be seen as complementary to each other. Respecting our approach, although a huge number of cases can be automatically computed, note that the richness of qualitative perspectives based on final user's opinions and feelings expressed in their natural language persist.

There have been many other efforts for automatizing the process of customer and user segmentation. For example, [14] proposes an interesting automatic architecture to search and to select customer segmentation based on dataming techniques, including the use of real world data and visualisation methods like Intelligent Icons [13] to present final results. In particular, soft computing, a family of data mining techniques, has been recently started to be exploited in the area of customer segmentation and it stands out as a potential area that may be able to shape the future of segmentation research, including fuzzy tools, RST, ANN and EM approaches [12]. Both fuzzy tools and RST can work with descriptive and numeric data, while ANN and EM can work only with numeric data [7]. Respecting the fuzzy tools of soft computing that enable to work with vagueness and uncertainty, the treatment of incomplete, contradictory or potentially inconsistent information is based on fuzzy clustering and not in the argument-oriented methodology discussed in this paper. Besides, the application of soft computing presents some critical issues regarding the usage of them in a specific problem domain [18], as feature evaluation and dimensionality reduction, and choice of metrics and evaluation. Note that the nature of our proposal is not related with these problems.

Some approaches suggest the use of personas as a better way of modelling real user in UCD, where the term *persona* refers to fictional characters created to represent archetypical groups of users [6]. Even though the use of personas offers several benefits used in combination to scenarios and user's stories in UCD processes [21], research suggests that because personas are fictional, it is difficult to determine how many –if any– users are represented by a persona, and thus is difficult to know whether a persona is relevant for intended users [4,23]. Besides, [4] and [23] argue that personas cannot be adequately verified or falsified and therefore have no demonstrable validity. In addition, empirical results have described different limitations of the personas method in real projects [16,20,23]. More specifically, [24] discusses by means of an instructive real case common fallacies in the evolving practice of segmentation and use of personas. Regarding our proposal, it must be remarked that it does not deal with hypothetic user data but with real social networks usage, and consequently the use of personas was not considered.

It must be remarked that the dialectical analysis of TB-arguments that underlies the proposal aims at modeling the possible space of alternatives associated with different (incrementally more specific) queries. In contrast, the dialectical analysis in standard argumentation frameworks [22] aims at determining the ultimate status of a given argument at issue (in terms of some acceptability semantics).

5   Conclusion and Future Work

This paper outlines the use of a novel strategy for the automatic detection of novel critical segmentation factors that divide users focused on their feelings and opinions towards a particular topic. To achieve this, a new framework including the strategy described in Sect. 3 was presented. The process is characterized in terms of dialectical analysis of opinions (atomic or more complex opinions constructed by aggregation mechanism) according to a preference criterion given by topic and feature specificity. As a result, an "opinion analysis tree" rotted in the first original topic is automatically constructed and visualized, on which any node models a user segmentation, showing the factor that define the segmentation as well as the particularities that group the subset. Our final goal is to enhance users'profile creation by adding to traditional construction process novel tools to support the computational treatment of incomplete, contradictory or potentially inconsistent information, as well as novel mechanisms to discover segmentation issues when dealing with psychographic and psychological factors, among others. To the best of our knowledge, no other approach has been developed in a similar direction.

Future work includes the needed of more experimentation and the inclusion of the proposal in real UCD oriented projects to empirically establish the scope of the results discussed here. A deeper comparison with alternatives belonging to the soft computing approach (as those provided by Google Analytics) must be analyzed. Besides, based on a previous Java implementation for analyzing the Twitter microblogging platform [11], we are currently implementing a first prototype of our proposal where atomic opinions to be handled in this specification are richer than tweets, requiring to focus search on particular text-based collections of information items (Google snipets, Amazon book reviews, etc.). We are also working the analysis of the usability features involved in the specification, in order to provide a suitable interface through which the user can define features to be considered in an interactive way. Regarding this, our goal is the deployment of a web service which can be included as intelligent decision making tool during the user profile modeling process.

Finally, an the extension of the framework shown in Sect. 3 is under consideration to incorporate an Organization Ontology Component to provide an ontology defining domain knowledge, such as information sources, concept hierarchies, social relations, etc.; and a Trust and Reputation Component to implements a trust and reputation system to weight arguments based on provenance and domain knowledge. In particular, the inclusion of the ontology model discussed at [10] will be explored.

Acknowledgments. This research is funded by Projects LACCIR R1211LAC004 (Microsoft Research, CONACyT and IDB), PIP 112-200801-02798, PIP 112-200901-00863 (CONICET, Argentina), PGI 24/ZN10, PGI 24/N006, PGI 24/N029 (SGCyT, UNS, Argentina) and Universidad Nacional del Sur.

References

1. Besnard, P., Hunter, A.: The Elements of Argumentation. The MIT Press, London (2008)
2. Hall, N., Jucuite, R., Blakemore, M., McDonal, N.: Delivering Citizen-centric public services through technology-facilitated organizational change. In: Nixon, P.G., Koutrakou, V.N., Rawal, R. (eds.) Understanding E-Government in Europe, pp. 19–38. Routletge, Taylor and Francis, London (2010)
3. Garneau, P., Brennan, R., Baines, P.: Contemporary Strategic Marketing. Palgrave Macmillan, Basingstoke (2008)
4. Chapman, C., Milham, R.: The personas new clothes: methodological and practical arguments against a popular method. In: Human Factors and Ergonomics Society Annual Conference (2006)
5. Chesñevar, C.I., González, M.P., Grosse, K., Maguitman, A.G.: A first approach to mining opinions as multisets through argumentation. In: Chesñevar, C.I., Onaindia, E., Ossowski, S., Vouros, G. (eds.) AT 2013. LNCS, vol. 8068, pp. 195–209. Springer, Heidelberg (2013)
6. Cooper, A.: The Inmates Are Running the Asylum. Macmillan Publishing Co., Inc., Indianapolis (1999)
7. Duntsch, I., Gediga, G.: Rough set data analysis. Encyclopaedia Comput. Sci. Technol. **43**, 281–301 (2000)
8. Feldman, R.: Techniques and applications for sentiment analysis. Commun. ACM **56**(4), 82–89 (2013)
9. García, A.J., Simari, G.R.: Defeasible logic programming: An argumentative approach. TPLP **4**(1–2), 95–138 (2004)
10. García, A.J., Chesñevar, C.I., Simari, G.R.: Ontoarg: a decision support framework for ontology integration based on argumentation. Expert Syst. Appl. **40**(5), 1858–1870 (2013)

11. Grosse, K., Chesñevar, C.I., Maguitman, A.G.: An argument-based approach to mining opinions from twitter. In: Proceedings of the First International Conference on Agreement Technologies, AT 2012, Dubrovnik, Croatia, October 15–16, 2012, pp. 408–422 (2012)

12. Hiziroglu, A.: Soft computing applications in customer segmentation: state-of-art review and critique. Expert Syst. Appl. **40**, 6491–6507 (2013)

13. Wei, L., Lonardi, S., Shieh, J., Sirowy, S., Keogh, E., Xiaopeng, X.: Intelligent icons: Integrating lite-weight data mining and visualization into GUI operating systems. In: Proceedings of the ICDM Conference (2006)

14. Lefait, T., Kechadi, G.: Customer segmentation architecture based on clustering techniques. In: Fourth International Conference on Digital Society, ICDS 2010 (2010)

15. Karlsson, A., Liu, M., Osvalder, Y.: Considering the importance of user profiles in interface design. In: Matrai, R. (ed.) User Interfaces, pp. 61–80. InTech Publishing, Croatia (2010)

16. Long, F.: Real or imaginary: The effectiveness of using personas in product design. In: Proceedings of the Irish Ergonomics Society Annual Conference (2009)

17. Martineau, J.: Identifying and isolating text classification signals from domain and genre noise for sentiment analysis. Ph.D. thesis, University of Maryland, Baltimore County, USA (2011)

18. Mitra, P., Mitra, S., Pal, S.K.: Data mining in soft computing framework: a survey. IEEE Trans. Neural Netw. **13**, 3–14 (2002)

19. Lekkas, Z., Mourlas, C., Samaras, G., Panagiotis, G., Tsianos, N.: Capturing essential intrinsic user behaviour values for the design of comprehensive web-based personalized environments. Comput. Hum. Behav. **24**(4), 1434–1451 (2008)

20. Portigal, S.: Toward a model of innovation. Interactions **15**, 28–36 (2008)

21. Pruitt, J., Adlin, T.: The Persona Lifecycle : Keeping People in Mind Throughout Product Design. Morgan Kaufmann, San Francisco (2006)

22. Rahwan, I., Simari, G.: Argumentation in Artificial Intelligence. Springer, Berlin (2009)

23. Rnkk, K.: An empirical study demonstrating how different design constraints, project organization, and contexts limited the utility of personas. In: Hawaii International Conference on System Sciences (2005)

24. Siegel, D.: The mystique of numbers: belief in quantitative approaches to segmentation and persona development. In: Proceedings of the 28th of the International Conference Extended Abstracts on Human Factors in Computing Systems (2010)

25. Van Velsen, L.S.: User-centered desing for personalization. Ph.D. thesis, University ogf Twente (2011)

Voice Control System and Multiplatform Use: Specialist Vs. Generalist?

Soyoung Jung[1(✉)], Kwan Min Lee[2], and Frank Biocca[1,3]

[1] Syracuse University, S.I. Newhouse School of Public Communicatoin,
201 University Ave., Syracuse, NY 13202, USA
sjung01@syr.edu
[2] University of Southern California, Annenberg School for Communication
and Journalism, Los Angeles, CA 90007, USA
[3] Interaction Science, SungKyunKwan University, Sungkyunkwan-Ro,
Jongno-Gu, Seoul, Korea

Abstract. How do participants respond to and prefer either a common voice agent that follows them across platforms or a community of specialist agents connected to specific hardware platform. This study examines users' gender as it relates to preference for voice-control system (VCS). The participants experiences a VCS agent that followed them across platforms such as from a smart pone to a personal cloud computing (PCC) or smart TV. One group met a different specialist agents that were tied to different devices. This study pits the effect of specialization by interface against the principle of consistency design principle with regards to voice agents. However, we found a strong gender effect, females preferred a single, generalist female agent across platforms while males tended to prefer different, specialist female agents embodying different platform.

Keywords: Voice control system · Voice agent · Multi-platform · Clouding · Specialist vs. Generalist · CASA HCI

1 Introduction

How do users perceived their relationships with voice agents that embody and represent interaction with a device? In a recently released movie "Her" (2013), a lonely man develops a relationship with a talking operating system, named "Samantha." This scientific fiction dramatizes the well, established research evidence that users have conscious and unconscious social responses to synthesized voices and agents (Nass, Steuer, Tauber, & Reeder, 1993; Nass, Steuer, & Tauber, 1994; Reeves & Nass, 1996; Nass & Lee, 2001).

But what kind of interaction would be best for users and voice agents in a multi-platform or multi-device environment? Would users prefer and respond more strongly to a single, consistent voice agent that follows users across platforms? Or would they prefer and trust specialist agents who "specialize" in their interaction with a particular platform. This study compares two types of voice agent control systems—specialized agent vs. consistent (generalist) agent—while crossing the multiplatform environment of user devices, focusing on how users accept and evaluate the two different types of interactive agents.

© Springer International Publishing Switzerland 2015
S. Yamamoto (Ed.): HIMI 2015, Part I, LNCS 9172, pp. 607–616, 2015.
DOI: 10.1007/978-3-319-20612-7_57

The study explores both theoretical and practical implications for voice agent studies. Also, the theoretical approach can enhance the study of affective or cognitive source orientation with the gender effect.

1.1   Voice Control System (VCS)

Popularity. Voice interaction has been seen an ideal for interacting with technologies. The revolutionary speech interpretation and response interface "Siri," an artificial-intelligent, "assistant" (Trautschold, Ritchie, & Mazo, 2011), has drawn world wide attention to this kind of interaction (Watson 2012). More generally voice control systems with natural speech-based user interfaces, like Siri, Google now, and Microsoft Cortana, have gained wide circulation in interface interactions.

Define applications. The VCS is a type of voice control application (app.), which allow the users use their voice to send messages, schedule meetings, place phone calls, and more. Ask VCS to do things just by talking the way users talk. VCS process voice to text, interpret what users are requesting, appear to understand what the users mean, execute tasks, and even provide conversational interaction on accumulated database. The accumulated database help VCS to assist the users.

Siri and system. The current systems such as Siri have achieved a successful threshold of recognition: they enhance users' experience of the multi-tasking ability of the interfaces, the ease of use and practicality of voice, as well as with the apparent "personality" of the voice interface. According to this increasing popularity, voice agent has been augmenting several application areas including texting, scheduling meetings, searching, emailing but also other applications areas (Pirani et al. 2014; Jaramillo et al. 2014).

Different types.
Users on mobile. Furthermore, the popularity of smartphone has led to an escalated use of VCS, because of the ability to control devices with less hand interaction (Jaramillo et al., 2014). Moreover, mobility of smartphone encourages people to use more VCS. By using mobile VCS, users can send execute commands and messages while they are on the move. Pirani and et al argue that the use of mobile devices have generally encouraged users to use VCS in a variety of settings (2014).

1.2   Agents in Multiplatform and Cloud Computing Environments

Cross platform. Owing to the increasing worldwide popularity of voice control system (VCS) in smartphones, there is a diffusion and adoption in the use of voice intelligent personal agent (IPA) across different interface platforms. So users experience agents as they navigate across platforms from phone to their TV or laptop computer.

Different apps. For example internet-connected smart television (TV) provides interactive features, including all kinds of applications available on the Web.

Why multeplatform. With increased functionalities, however, interactive elements interfere with screen-obscuring content, which may harm the quality of the watching experience when using the system (Berglund and Johansson 2004). Berglund et al. (2004) suggested new user interface and service solutions with speech and dialogue for interactive TV navigation. These has been pursued in several systems. Voice agent interactions can be seen in automobiles and other platforms.

Cloud computing. Cloud computing also creates and environment relevant to agents. Users are interacting with their data across many platforms. Private cloud computing (PCC) storage is a service used to store synchronous data. This allows end users to access their data from multiple platforms, "anytime, anywhere" from iCloud, Skydrive, and Evernote (Armbrust 2010). Cloud-computer users save their photos, documents, and email on the virtual storage of their cloud service so that they can use the synchronous data wirelessly while they switch among platforms, such as a laptop, desktop, tablet personal computer (PC), or even a smart TV. Moreover, Ye and Huang (2011) have introduced a framework for a cloud-based smart home.

Agents that share some "familiarity" with user data across platforms make consistency of interaction of potential value in this environment. The agent moves across platforms like the data. Given the utility of such cross-platform and VCS app, this study will examine to what extent the attitude towards a general cross platform agent clashes with the specialized voice agent and how this can affect user perception of the agent, the device, and the information provides.

2 Theoretical Approach

2.1 Computers Are Social Actor

There is a research base on user responses to computers as social actors. Nass and Lee (2001) examine the computer-synthesized speech and its personalities. According to "Computers are Social Actors" or "CASA" theory (Nass, Steuer, Tauber, & Reeder, 1993; Nass, Steuer, & Tauber, 1994; Reeves & Nass, 1996), when humans interact with computers, users perceive the computers as social actors regardless of the interfaces. Therefore, researchers who subscribe to CASA theory, tend to apply social psychological theories and principles to human-computer interaction (HCI).

2.2 Consistency-Attraction and Specialization

There is an existing body of research in social psychology and HCI regarding how people perceive "generalists" and "specialist" be it people or interfaces.

Nass and Lee (2001), examined how similarity and consistency-attraction works for computer-synthesized speech in HCI studies. Consistency-attraction is the idea that people prefer consistent characteristics while they interact because if people have interaction with inconsistent characteristics, this creates a cognitive load and makes it hard to predict what will happen when they engage with others (Field 1994; Fiske and Taylor 1991; Thomas and Johnstone Thomas and Johnston 1981). When users perceived a social presence from a computer, users were preferred to a consistent computer synthesized voice and text (Nass and Lee 2001). People with a tendency towards anthropomorphism are more likely to prefer same (generalist) voice agent than those with a less tendency towards anthropomorphism. It is assumed individuals who tend to anthromorphize perceive the voice agent as a social actor.

Media Specialization. At the same time, there is perceived social value in "specialization." Findings in previous study show that the devices that have "specialized" functions are seen as superior to devices that have "generalized" functions be they monitors, sensors, and other devices (Nass and Moon 2000; Reeves and Nass 1996; Sundar and Nass 2000; Sundar and Nass 2001). As specialized computer devices become more common, this value for specialization is more frequently applied to media technologies and becomes more important and salient feature. Moreover, Reeves and Nass found that only labeling as a "specialized" device or introduced as specialized media has significant effects on users in their work on the media equation (1996). The attributions relating to specialization and generalization have affect on perceivers' attitude and evaluation toward technology and media (Leshner et al. Brewer 1998; Nass et al. 1996, 1994; Nass and Steuer 1993). For example, Nass and et al. examined the attribution of specialization and generalization in TV set in 'Technology and Role: a tale of two TV' and a specialist TV set is evaluated as having a better screen and better content deliver TV set than a generalist TV set, even though they are both same physically. Not only the TV set but Web agent, web site and computer were also examined to testify the credibility of specialist effect (Koh and Sundar 2010).

Media Integration. However, Reeves and Nass (1996) doubted that specialization would cause conflicts to occur when integrating across different functions in the media equation. Also, they worried that using a "single" media appliance could "create a sense of commonality across the different functions" (p. 152). These two significant design principles—specialization and consistency—would be competing principles. This study's purpose is to investigate the effects of specialization and consistency and to determine which principle is more effective as voice agent interfaces cross platforms.

2.3   Research Question

In the crossing-multiplatform situation (between smartphones and smart TV), would a specialist (varied agent; Siri and Sori) or generalist (consistent agent; Siri and Siri) voice agent be perceived as more effective in users' evaluation of the social perception of the agent, the agent's usability, and their attitudes towards to the quality of the interface and the viewing experience?

  Individual differences: Given that social interaction is affected by gender patterns, would the gender of the users and two different agents affect the evaluation of the agent, the usability tests of the voice control system, and the viewing experience?

Hypothesis 1. When users experience a voice agent for the first time, the gender of the user lead to differences in the social perception of the agents.

Hypothesis 2: When users experience agents across platforms, they will perceive specialist agents as more social, usable, and effective than a generalist agent.

Hypothesis 3. The gender of the user (male or female) will respond differently to specialist or generalist agents.

3   Method

3.1   Experiment Design

For this experiment a between-subject design was used with two factors: Type of agent with two levels, consistent or specialized voice agent, and the second factor, user gender with two levels, male vs. female.

3.2   Participants

A total of 36 participants were recruited via an online bulletin boards for payment. Participants blocked by gender, 18 males and 18 females, and randomly assigned to one of two voice agent conditions.

3.3   Materials

Three interfaces were created (See Fig. 1). First, we used a common phone interface featuring a voice agent called, Siri. We created two interactive, smart television interfaces, one featuring the same agents as the phone, Siri, the other using a new voice agent, Sori. Both Sori' and Siri were played in female Korean synthesized voices, and based on translated scripts from the American version of Siri. Sori has a similar conversational repertoire as Siri, except that Sori introduces herself as a specialist.

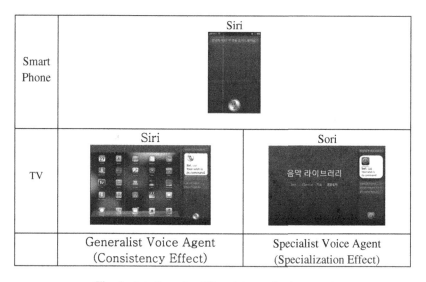

Fig. 1. Interfaces by different type of voice agent.

Procedure. Users entered the lab and were instructed that they would evaluate a new interface. All participants were introduced to a smart phone using the voice agent, Siri. The participants were escorted to a simulated living room with a one-way mirror, and then, they were guided to the sofa. The participants received an iPhone- featured device that featured the voice agent, Siri, but the device was controlled via a Wizard of Oz technique, meaning that when subjects interact with computer system they believe that the system works autonomously, but the researcher behind a the one way mirror remotely manipulates functions.

Brief instructions on how to control the voice- recognition system were given to participants, along with four tasks—listening to music, watching news, scheduling, and calling. After completing the four tasks with the iPhone and Siri, each participant went out to answer a questionnaire using a computer. During the first phase of the experiment, all participants experienced the Korean version of Siri.

After filling out the questionnaire, half of the male or female participants were randomly assigned to interact with the same agent, the Korean Siri, for the voice-control system for the smart TV while the other half of the participants were assigned to new agent Sori for the voice-control system for the smart TV.

The participants faced a smart TV and controlled the smart TV with voice agent to finish tasks, which was manipulated by a researcher from outside of the simulated room using the same Wizard of Oz technique used in the first phase of the study. As in the first phase of the study instructions on how to use VCS were given, and the four tasks were explained. In the both conditions the agents greeted the participants, but the specialist agent condition, Sori added that she was a specialist for smart TVs. After completing the four tasks with different contents on the smart TV, each participant went out to answer a questionnaire on a computer.

After completing all of the tasks and the questionnaire, all of the participants were debriefed regarding the purpose of the study, thanked for their participation, and dismissed.

3.4   Measures

In order to observe the evaluation of agents both on the smartphone and on the smart TV, we measured **social perception** of the agent using: social presence (Cronbach's $\alpha = .82$, and Cronbach's $\alpha = .8$), social attraction (Cronbach's $\alpha = .83$, and Cronbach's $\alpha = .87$), and perception of likability (Cronbach's $\alpha = .91$ and Cronbach's $\alpha = .87$) of the agent, i.e., the social presence was measured by five statements, such as "I focused on the interaction with the voice control system," and "I felt that I was really communicating with the agent." In order to evaluate the agent on 10-point scales, 15 questions were asked (Fig. 2).

The assessment of the **overall usability** of the voice control systems was measured using five sub-scales: usefulness (Cronbach's $\alpha = .93$, and Cronbach's $\alpha = .91$), ease of use (Cronbach's $\alpha = .93$ and Cronbach's $\alpha = .93$), ease of learning (Cronbach's $\alpha = 91$, Cronbach's $\alpha = .89$), satisfaction (Cronbach's $\alpha = .91$ and Cronbach's $\alpha = .84$), The sub-scales of 19 questions about usability were asked using 10-point scales: "It helps me be more effective," "It is simple to use,".

Attitudes towards the experience and product were measured using content evaluation was inquired about using three questions, i.e., "I am satisfied with the content" (Cronbach's α = .92, and Cronbach's α = .91); viewing experience, 10-point semantic differential scales were used with the following adjectives: enjoyed, excited, and had fun (Cronbach's α = .90 and Cronbach's α = .80), and buying intention (Cronbach's α = .86, and Cronbach's α = .84).

4 Results

4.1 Results of Experiment 1

The first phase of the experiment was a control condition. An independent t-test was executed to examine the effects of the participants' gender with regard to the voice-control system in the smartphone control setting across all ten measures in the area of social perception, usability, and attitudes towards the experience and product. There were no significant differences across for gender for any of the 10 measures[1]. So the groups were similar in their responses to voice agents in first phase of the study.

A two-way, between-groups ANOVA was conducted to explore the impact of gender on the type of agent, generalist or specialized, experienced when viewing the smart television No significant differences were found in the mean scores between the groups. The results do not support hypothesis 2. However, most items had either a significant interaction effect or a marginal interaction effect. Hypothesis 3 was supported by the most of results.

---

[1] To test hypothesis 1, a questionnaire on the agent, usability, and viewing experience with regard to gender differences was administered. The results indicated that the participants' gender had no significant effect on the evaluation of the agent from experiment 1; social presence towards for males (M = 6.43, SD = 1.45) and females M = 6.58, SD = 1.33; t (34) = -.334 p = .74 (two-tailed); social attraction towards the voice agent for males (M = 6.12, SD = 2.02) and females (M = 6.74, SD = 1.76) $t(34)$ = -.96 p = .34 (two-tailed); and perception of likability about voice agent for males (M = 7.23, SD = 1.21) and females (M = 7.8, SD = 1.36) t (34) = -1.32 p = .19 (two-tailed). The result of the usability test did not show significant differences based on subjects' gender. Consider the following results the usefulness for male (M = 7.55, SD = 1.27) and female M = 8.0, SD = 1.15; t = (34) = -.247 p = .676 (two-tailed); ease of use (M = 8.0, SD = 1.27) and female M = 8.61, SD = 1.07; t = (34) = -1.55 p = .12 (two-tailed); ease of learning (M = 8.63, SD = 1.21) and female M = 8.93, SD = 0.95; t (34) = -.837 p = .40 (two-tailed); satisfaction (M = 7.63, SD = 1.21) and female M = 7.88, SD = 1.46; t = (34) = -.569 p = .57 (two-tailed); buying intention for male (M = 6.94, SD = 1.40) and female M = 7.15, SD = 1.55; $t(34)$ = -.421 p = .676 (two-tailed). Also, consider the following results for viewing experience and content evaluation satisfaction: enjoyable viewing experience (M = 7.00, SD = 1.71) and female M = 7.14, SD = 1.87; t (34) = -.421 p = .80 (two-tailed); content evaluation satisfaction (M = 7.81, SD = 1.33) and female M = 7.78, SD = 1.51; t (34) = 0.05 p = 0.95 (two-tailed). The summary of experiment 1 is that gender has no significant effect on 10 dependent variables.

The evaluation of the agent. The result indicated that the participants' genders had no significant main effect on the evaluation of the two agents (Fs < 1), but the interaction effect between gender and agent was statistically significant on evaluation of the agent and marginally significant with regard to the social presence $F(1,32) = 3.16$, p < 0.08 multivariate partial eta squared = .09, social attraction $F(1,32) = 4.39$, p < 0.05 multivariate partial eta squared = .012, and perception of likability $F(1,32) = 3.16$, p < 0.08 multivariate partial eta squared = .09. According to the results, hypothesis 3 is accepted.

Usability. The same analysis was submitted. The results had no significant main effect ps < .10; however, interaction effects were found for usefulness, $F(1,32) = 4.19$, p < 0.05 multivariate partial eta squared = .11; satisfaction $F(1,32) = 3.19$, p < 0.08 multivariate partial eta squared = .012; and buying intention, $F(1,32) = 4.23$, p < 0.05 multivariate partial eta squared = .12. According to the results, hypothesis 3 is accepted.

Results of Experiment 1
Viewing experience and content evaluation. Similar results were produced: there was no significant main effect. However, a significant interaction effect was found for both viewing experience $F(1,32) = 5.84$, p < 0.05 multivariate partial eta squared = .04 and content evaluation $F(1,32) = 3.10$, p < 0.08 multivariate partial eta squared = .08.

5 Conclusion

5.1 Discussion

Is there a difference in how people perceive specialist or generalized voice agents. Are they more comfortable with an agent that is consistent and follows them around platforms or an agent that is specialized for a particular platform? In this study we find no gender differences in how they evaluate one voice agent in one interface. But the answer to the question appears to be that gender has a strong effect on all dimension of how individual perceive a generalized voice agent of a specialized voice agent.

While there was no main effect for the type of voice agent, user's gender significantly affected the social perception of the agent, the agent's usability, and the users perception of the experience and value of the product. Generally, females responded more favorably to a consistent, female agent. They seemed to respond negatively to a new specialized agent, tending to score this new female agent lower. Males, on the other hand, tended to prefer, new specialized female agents.

The interaction effect can be explained by "affect and cognition" – the rational and emotional ways of dealing with social interaction (Forgas 2008). Also, in previous research on computers as social actors individuals show social responses towards computers that are highly influenced by human social categories, especially gender (Nass and Moon 2000; Reeves and Nass 1996; Sundar and Nass 2000; Sundar and Nass 2001).

Affect and Cognition. Considerable research has been done on the interplay between affect and cognition – rational and emotional ways of dealing with objects and individuals. This distinction (Forgas 2008) has important implications for relational exchanges as encounters between principles and agents (service providers) (Singh and Sirdeshmukh 2000). Affective characteristics of an entity might contain likability and familiar information, whereas cognitive characteristics of a spokesperson might include credibility, expertise, trustworthiness. In general, when social interaction occurs, research suggests that females use a "peripheral route" that uses less of a main message and the affective characteristics, while males who uses "central route" that emphasis on message content.

Categorical Perception. Individuals receive first impressions automatically by relying upon the category to which a social object has been assigned. Categorical perception helps to memory for social information (Brewer 1998). In the cognitive-psychology view, labels have significant effects on how people perceive social objects. Media specialization suggests that people show a categorical perception that relies on the labels assigned to media (Nass et al. 1996). The label or representation of the social category for example specialist label come into a tendency to be biased in their perceptions (Ashforth and Humphrey 1997). Once an object has been categorized, individuals tend to interpret additional cues in line with the categorization, and they may not pay attention to inconsistent information (Hamilton, Sherman & Ruvolo, 1990). For example, when an individual is labeled by definition (e.g., Cindy is a specialist), people perceive him or her based on the central attribute of the social category (e.g., expertise) whether or not that person actually possesses the attribute. That is, the label initiates the central attribute (expertise) assigned to the representation of the category. However, when the research was conducted, the Korean version of Siri had not yet been produced and the smart TV with the voice control system had just emerged. Therefore, participants lacked experience with the machines and the novel attitude could be observed with regard to both voice control systems, Siri and Sori. In sum, this research suggests that there are gender differences as relates to response to two different voice control agents, specialist and generalist (consistent agent,): females gave a better evaluation to the consistent agent, and males preferred the specialist agent.

References

Armbrust, M., Fox, A., Griffith, R., Joseph, A.D., Katz, R., Konwinski, A., et al.: A view of cloud computing. Commun. ACM **53**(4), 50–58 (2010)

Ashforth, B.E., Humphrey, R.H.: The ubiquity and potency of labeling organizations. Organ. Sci. **8**(1), 43–58 (1997)

Berglund, A., Johansson, P.: Using speech and dialogue for interactive TV navigation. Univers. Access Inf. Soc. **3**(3), 224–238 (2004)

Brewer, M.B.: Category-based vs. person-based perception in intergroup contexts. Eur. Rev. Soc. psychol. **9**(1), 77–106 (1998)

Brody, L.R., Hall, J.A.: Gender and Emotion. Guilford Press, New York (1993)

Bullis, C., Horn, C.: Get a little closer: further examination of nonverbal comforting strategies. Commun. Rep. **8**(1), 10–17 (1995)

Field, S.: Screenplay: The Foundations of Screenwriting. Bantam Doubleday Dell, New York (1994)

Fiske, S.T., Taylor, S.E.: Social Cognition. McGraw-Hill, New York (1991)

Forgas, J.P.: Affect and cognition. Perspect. Psychol. Sci. **3**(2), 94–101 (2008)

Hamilton, D.L., Sherman, S.J., Ruvolo, C.M.: Stereotype-based expectancies: effects on information processing and social behavior. J. Soc. Issues **46**, 35–60 (1990)

Hawkins, J.: Computers and girls: rethinking the issues. Sex Roles **13**(3–4), 165–180 (1985)

Kiesler, S., Sproull, L., Eccles, J.S.: Pool halls, chips, and war games: women in the culture of computing. Psychol. Women Q. **9**(4), 451–462 (1985)

Nass, C., Lee, K.M.: Does computer-synthesized speech manifest personality? Experimental tests of recognition, similarity-attraction, and consistency-attraction. J. Exp. Psychol. Appl. **7**(3), 171 (2001)

Nass, C., Reeves, B., Leshner, G.: Technology and roles: a tale of two TVs. J. Commun. **46**(2), 121–128 (1996)

Nass, C., Steuer, J., Tauber, E.: Computers are social actors. In: Paper Presented to CHI 1994 Conference of the ACM/SIGCHI, Boston, MA, USA (1994)

Nass, C.I. Steur, J.S., Tauber, E., Reeder, H.: Anthropomorphism, agency, and ethopoeia: computers as social actors. In: Proceedings of the International CHI Conference, Amsterdam, The Netherlands (1993)

Nass, C., Moon, Y.: Machines and mindlessness: social responses to computers. J. Soc. Issues **56** (1), 81–103 (2000)

Reeves, B., Nass, C.: How people treat computers, television, and new media like real people and places: CSLI Publications and Cambridge University Press (1996)

Singh, J., Sirdeshmukh, D.: Agency and trust mechanisms in consumer satisfaction and loyalty judgments. J. Acad. Mark. Sci. **28**(1), 150–167 (2000)

Sundar, S.S., Nass, C.: Source orientation in human–computer interaction: programmer, networker, or independent social actor? Commun. Res. **27**(6), 683–703 (2000)

Sundar, S.S., Nass, C.: Conceptualizing sources in online news. J. Commun. **51**(1), 52–72 (2001)

Thomas, F., Johnston, O.: Disney Animation: The Illusion of Life. Abbeville Press, New York (1981)

Trautschold, M., Ritchie, R., Mazo, G.: Multitasking and Siri. iPhone 4S Made Simple, 179–188 (2011)

Watson, C.A.: Technology Trends and Predictions: Is a Flying Car in Our Future? (2012)

Whitley, B.E.: Gender differences in computer-related attitudes and behavior: a meta-analysis. Comput. Hum. Behav. **13**(1), 1–22 (1997)

Ye, X., Huang, J.: A framework for cloud-based smart home. In: 2011 International Conference on Computer Science and Network Technology (ICCSNT), vol. 2, pp. 894–897. IEEE, December 2011

This Study of Hand Anthropometry and Touchscreen Size of Smartphones

Yu-Cheng Lin[1]([✉]) and Ming-Hung Lin[2]

[1] Overseas Chinese University, Taichung, Taiwan, R.O.C.
yclin@ocu.edu.tw
[2] Electronic Systems Research Department, National Chung-Shan Institute
of Science and Technology, Taoyuan, Taiwan, R.O.C.

Abstract. With the development of communication technology, smartphone becomes an important personnel device that everyone must have. As the introduction of 3rd Generation mobile telecommunication, the technology of touch screen was started to be applied on the mobile phones and an indispensable component on a 3G smartphone that is built in advanced computing capability like digital cameras, GPS and web-browser. Most of modern smartphones include high-resolution touchscreens for display and control and the size of touchscreen becomes larger and larger. However, the question is that a larger screen is convenient to every user? The aim of this study is to realize the relationship between touchscreen sizes of smartphones and user's relative hand dimensions based on the operation time, operation error rate and subjective thumb fatigue. One hundred subjects, including 50 males and 50 females were invited to attend the experiment. The experiment design includes 4 touchscreen sizes. The hand length and hand width were both divided into 4 categories respectively. The results indicated there is a rapid increasing trend from 3.5 in. screen to 5.7 in. screen for smaller hand length/width and the trend decreases firstly slight and then increases for large hand length/width. Touchscreen size from 4.6 in. to 5.0 in. is suggested for most people because this interval of screen size is relatively suitable based on the analysis of hand dimensions and 3 performance evaluation indices. Too large touchscreen (5.7 in.) is hard to use for any hand length or width.

Keywords: Touchscreen · Anthropometry · Hand dimension · Smartphone

1 Introduction

Since Apple launched iPhone, the innovation and function improvement on smart/ mobile devices is faster and faster. One of the most important evolvement from previous mobile phone to smartphone is the application of touchscreen to remove the traditional keypad. Nowadays the functions of smartphone are very powerful, just like a simple handhold PC without keyboard. Full touchscreen operation allows the use of smartphones more intuitive. Moreover, the request for screen size, resolution and color authenticity/saturation of touchscreen is increasing with the development on smartphone. Four years ago, Samsung and Sony started to lunch large screen smartphones. Furthermore, Apple also lunched iPhone 6 and iPhone 6 plus with 4.7

© Springer International Publishing Switzerland 2015
S. Yamamoto (Ed.): HIMI 2015, Part I, LNCS 9172, pp. 617–626, 2015.
DOI: 10.1007/978-3-319-20612-7_58

and 5.5 in. touchscreens last year. However, what is the appropriate screen size for users? To observe users who are using smartphones, it is very common that the size of touchscreen is not suitable for the user's hand dimensions. However it is difficult to operate with single hand if the touchscreen is too large. On the other hand, too small touchscreen is not suitable for large hands. Thus, the operation error may be increased and performance may be reduced if the size of touchscreen is not appropriate to user's hand. Hare indicated that People cannot use hands to operate too small input devices [1]. The mobility convenience of mobile devices is a major reason that let users frequently bring them in dynamic mobile environment. Users must frequently use single hand to operate the mobile device in order to deal with other things with the other hand [2]. For example, it is very common that consumers handle and use the smartphone with one hand and take something with the other hand. In the field survey, most people use single hand to operate mobile phone. An experimental result conducted by Karlson [3] also confirmed that people prefer to use one-handed operation is better than a two-handed operation in the subjective rating.

Shneiderman [4] pointed out that the user's finger is the most direct control tools on the touchscreen. Parhi et al. [5] explored the target size on the small touchscreen and indicated that the icon size (target) from 9.2 mm to 9.6 mm was better for touch tasks. Colle and Hiszem [6] pointed out that users preferred the recognition touch area of 20 mm × 20 mm in public information kiosks.

The handheld device should match the characteristics of the hand shape [7]. Hand anthropometry would affect the preferred size and shape of the grip area and movement of fingers would also affect the size and the layout of the buttons [8]. In order to make the input operation more stable, the gripping stability of mobile phone must also be consideration as well as movement range of operating finger and posture of handhold [7]. Furthermore, most people use thumb to operate the smartphone when they take the smartphone with single hand. However, Wobbrock et al. [9] indicated that using forefinger to operate had better performance on input time and error rate compared with thumb after compare thumb operation and forefinger operation if people use one hand to hold phone and use the other hand to operate it. Lin [10] studied the relation small to touchscreen sizes (3.2, 3.7 and 4.27 in.) and hand dimensions. The result shows there are obvious differences between touchscreen size in both error rate and subjective thumb fatigue. He also found that the people whose hand length between 15.5 to 17.4 cm or hand width between 8.6 cm to 9.8 cm had longer operation time regardless of screen size. Thus, the relationship between operating performance and user's hands should be emphasized, especially for the larger and larger size of touchscreen.

The purpose of this study was to try to realize the relationship between the small to large touchscreen size of smartphone and the dimension of hand based on 3 evaluation indices, the operation time, operation error rate and subjective fatigue on thumb. Since most people likes to use smartphone with single hand, only one hand operation was considered in this study. That is, subjects must use dominant hand to handle the phone and user the thumb to operate on the touchscreen.

2   Methodology

This study used four smartphones whose touchscreen sizes are different as experimental equipment. The screen sizes are 3.5 in., 4.6 in., 5.0 in. and 5.7 in. respectively. Although the widths of the 4 smartphones are different due to their touchscreen sizes, the distances between edge of touchscreen and body for each smartphone are as similar as possible. All operation systems are Andriod. A 3D hand scanning system was employed to measure hand dimensions, including hand length, palm length, forefinger length, hand width, palm width, thumb length and thumb width that is shown in Table 1.

Table 1. Hand dimensions and definitions

Dimensions	Definition
Hand length	The distance from top of middle finger to bottom of hand
Palm length	The distance from bottom of middle finger to bottom of hand
Forefinger length	The distance from top of forefinger to bottom of forefinger
Hand width	The width of hand including thumb
Palm width	The width of palm without thumb
Thumb length	The distance from top of thumb to first dorsal interosseous
Thumb width	The width of thumb

In order to let the thumb be able to touch every point on the screen, a click app program was developed. This app program can display a 4 mm x 4 mm block randomly for 500 times and subjects have to touch the block within 1 s. If the subject didn't touch the screen on the right bock within 1 s or clicked on a wrong location, one error was counted. After 500 times, the app program calculates the error rate and total operating time automatically. Each subject had to complete 12 rounds.

One hundred college students, including 50 males and 50 females, were invited to attend the experiment. Every subject had extensive experience in operating the Android smartphone. Totally 12 rounds (3 repeats/round) of test were conducted for each subject and as least 15 min of rest time was needed for fatigue recovery. Before the experiment, subject was asked to handle the smartphone with comfortable sitting posture and put the arm on a table. Neither the holding method nor the posture could be changed during the experiment progress. Operation time and error rate were collected by app program automatically. After each experimental round, a subjective evaluation about the thumb fatigue that was numbered from 1 to 10 according to the degree feeling was conducted.

3   Results and Discussions

3.1   Simple Statistical Summary

Table 2 lists the statistical summaries categorized by touchscreen size. The ANOVA were conducted to test difference between touchscreen sizes. There are significant differences on operation time, error rate and subjective thumb fatigue between screen sizes. The Duncan post hoc test was applied to realize the significant difference between any two sizes and the result is shown in Table 3. The performances of 5.7 in. touchscreen are worst whether in operation time, error rate and subjective thumb fatigue and there is an obvious gape between 5.0 in. and 5.7 in. touchscreens. That is, the 5.7 in. touchscreen are too large to handle and operate with single hand for all people. The 3.5 in. and 4.6 in. screens are no obvious difference for most people since they belongs to the same group except error rate. Thus, user can choose larger screen since there is no clear difference between 3.5 and 4.6 in. touchscreens.

Table 2. The statistical summary categorized bytouchscreen size ($\alpha = 0.05$).

Evaluation index	3.5 in.		4.6 in.		5.0 in.		5.7 in.		Sig.
	Mean	Std.	Mean	Std.	Mean	Std.	Mean	Std.	
Operation time (sec.)	161.9	18.0	161.2	15.1	163.5	17.8	177.2	21.6	*
Error rate (%)	4.6 %	1.6 %	3.3 %	0.9 %	3.9 %	0.9 %	8.2 %	3.8 %	*
Subjective fatigue	3.12	1.29	3.30	1.24	3.58	1.22	8.36	2.41	*

Table 3. The Duncan post hoc test result.

Evaluation index	3.5 in.	4.6 in.	5.0 in.	5.7 in.
Operation time (s)	A	A	B	C
Error rate (%)	A	B	B	C
Subjective fatigue	A	A	B	C

3.2 Touchscreen Size and Hand Length

The hand length and hand width were chosen to further analysis in this study since the they are the most critical dimensions in hand anthropometry, Frist, the data was divided into 4 groups according to the hand length, i.e. 15.5–17.0 cm, 17.0–18.5 cm, 18.5–20.0 cm and 20.0–21.5 cm. The mean dimensions and post hoc multiple comparison results are listed in Table 4. For larger hand length (18.5–20.0 cm and 20.0–21.5 cm hand length categories), the operation time and error rate is better when using 4.6 in. and 5.0 in. touchscreens. On the other hand, for shorter hand length (15.5–17.0 cm and 17.0–18.5 cm), the operation time and error rate is better when using 3.5 in. or 4.6 in. touchscreens. However, the subjective fatigue is always relative small when operating with 3.5 in. screen no matter what hand length category is. According to the result, 5.7 in. screen is too large to use for any hand length category, especially small hand length. It is not suggested to use the smartphone with 5.7 in. screen.

As illustrated in Fig. 1, there is an increasing trend from 3.5 in. screen to 5.7 in. screen for smaller hand length (15.5–17.0 cm and 17.0–18.5 cm), no matter which evaluation index is. On the contrary, the trend decreases firstly and then increases for large hand length category. The longer the user's hand, the easier he touches every

Table 4. Statistical data and multiple comparison test result of touchscreen size based on the hand length category.

Evaluation index	Screen size		Hand length			
			15.5-17.0 cm	17.0-18.5 cm	18.5-20.0 cm	20.0-21.5 cm
Operation time (sec.)	3.5 inch	mean	169.24	162.38	159.67	161.40
		group	(D)	(B,C)	(B)	(B)
	4.6 inch	mean	168.69	164.21	158.33	156.74
		group	(D)	(C)	(A)	(A)
	5.0 inch	mean	172.66	167.88	158.97	157.82
		group	(F)	(E)	(A,B)	(A)
	5.7 inch	mean	197.84	183.07	170.44	161.93
		group	(H)	(G)	(F)	(B)
Error rate	3.5 inch	mean	4.65%	4.43%	4.57%	5.84%
		group	(C)	(C)	(C)	(D)
	4.6 inch	mean	4.48%	3.48%	3.07%	2.88%
		group	(C)	(B)	(A)	(A)
	5.0 inch	mean	5.85%	4.50%	3.01%	3.09%
		group	(D)	(C)	(A)	(A)
	5.7 inch	mean	9.84%	8.56%	7.77%	6.96%
		group	(H)	(G)	(F)	(E)
Subjective fatigue	3.5 inch	mean	3.77	3.44	2.67	3.01
		group	(D)	(C)	(A)	(B)
	4.6 inch	mean	4.38	3.98	2.57	2.50
		group	(E,F)	(D)	(A)	(A)
	5.0 inch	mean	4.61	4.11	2.89	3.04
		group	(F)	(E)	(B)	(B)
	5.7 inch	mean	9.37	8.88	7.78	7.46
		group	(J)	(I)	(H)	(G)

location on the screen. Longer hand and fingers are helpful to increase operation performance. The long operation time for smaller hand length may indicate that the person who has smaller hand length must use more time to move his thumb and touch the screen. However, if the screen is too small, user still has little difficult to operate the smartphone. Thus, in spite of the 5.7 in. touchscreen, the touchscreen size and hand length have a positive relationship in general. In other words, larger touchscreen size is more appropriate to larger hand length if the screen size is not very large.

Although no significant difference in the error rate was found, the change in trend is similar with the change trend of the subjective thumb fatigue. Moreover, the 3.2-in. screen for large hand length category is especially highest than others. Thus, in spite of the operation time, the touchscreen size and hand length have a positive relationship. In other words, larger touchscreen size is more appropriate to larger hand length. The long operation time for smaller hand length may indicate that the person who has smaller hand length must use more time to move his thumb and touch the screen.

3.3 Touchscreen Size and Hand Width

Like above analysis, the data was also divided into 4 groups according to the hand width, i.e. 8.5–9.5 cm, 9.5–10.5 cm, 10.5–11.5 cm and 11.5–12.5 cm. The mean

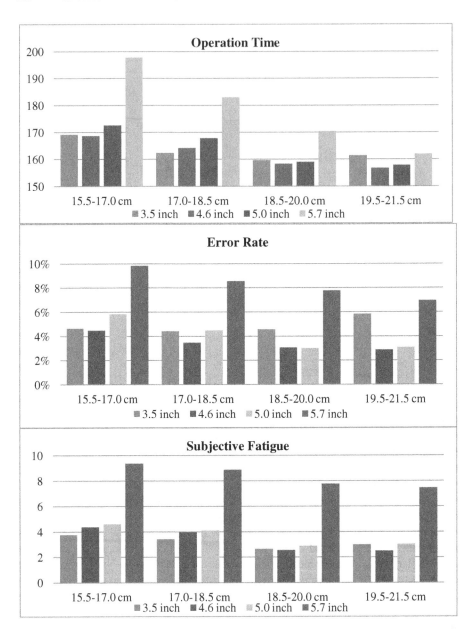

Fig. 1. The bar charts of operation time, error rate and subjective fatigue divided by touchscreen size and hang length.

Table 5. Statistical data and multiple comparison test result of touchscreen size based on the hand width category.

Evaluation index	Screen size		Hand width			
			8.5-9.5 cm	9.5-10.5 cm	10.5-11.5 cm	11.5-12.5 cm
Operation time (sec.)	3.5 inch	mean	164.54	161.42	161.22	165.48
		group	(D)	(C)	(C)	(D)
	4.6 inch	mean	169.25	162.21	158.46	158.04
		group	(E)	(C)	(B)	(A,B)
	5.0 inch	mean	176.36	169.12	156.47	155.36
		group	(F)	(E)	(A)	(A)
	5.7 inch	mean	199.21	182.85	169.44	161.72
		group	(H)	(G)	(E)	(C)
Error rate	3.5 inch	mean	4.45%	4.49%	4.63%	5.91%
		group	(D)	(D)	(D)	(E)
	4.6 inch	mean	4.76%	3.53%	2.85%	2.78%
		group	(D)	(C)	(A)	(A)
	5.0 inch	mean	5.96%	4.62%	2.99%	2.87%
		group	(E)	(D)	(A,B)	(A)
	5.7 inch	mean	10.17%	8.96%	7.37%	6.62%
		group	(I)	(H)	(G)	(F)
Subjective fatigue	3.5 inch	mean	3.81	3.39	2.71	2.98
		group	(D)	(C)	(A,B)	(B)
	4.6 inch	mean	4.39	4.01	2.60	2.42
		group	(E,F)	(D)	(A)	(A)
	5.0 inch	mean	4.58	4.12	2.97	2.99
		group	(F)	(D,E)	(B)	(B)
	5.7 inch	mean	9.45	8.90	7.88	7.26
		group	(I)	(H)	(G)	()

dimensions and post hoc multiple comparison results are listed in Table 5. Based on the results, for larger hand width (10.5–11.5 cm and 11.5–12.5 cm hand width categories), the operation time and error rate is better when using 4.6 in. and 5.0 in. touchscreens. For narrower hand width (8.5–9.5 cm and 9.5–10.5 cm), the operation time and error rate is better when using 3.5 in. or 4.6 in. touchscreens. However, the subjective fatigue is smaller if operating with smaller touchscreen (3.5 in. and 4.7 in.) no matter what hand length category is. Furthermore, according to this result, 5.7 in. touchscreen is also too large to use for any hand width category, especially narrow hand width.

There is also a rapid increasing trend illustrated in Fig. 2 from 3.5 in. screen to 5.7 in. screen for smaller hand length (8.5–9.5 cm and 9.5–10.5 cm) in spite of the evaluation indices. On the contrary, the trend slightly decreases and then increases with the increase of screen size. If a user has wider hands, he can handle a large screen smartphone more stable than the people whose hands are narrower. Stable handling is helpful to reduce the occurrence of operation error and fatigue. Thus, in spite of the 5.7 in. touchscreen that is not suggested, the touchscreen size and hand width also have a positive relationship in general. In other words, larger touchscreen size is more appropriate to the people who have narrower hands.

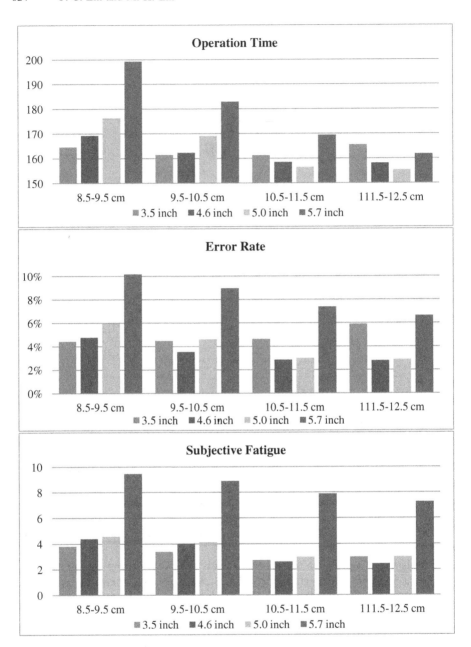

Fig. 2. The bar charts of operation time, error rate and subjective fatigue divided by touchscreen size and hang width.

4   Conclusion

In order to realize the relationship between touchscreen sizes and hand basic dimensions, this study recruited 100 subjects to attend the experiment. The operation time and error rate were calculated by the experimental app program. The subjective fatigue on thumb was asked after each test round. The statistical test shows there are always significant differences between touchscreen sizes, i.e. 3.5, 4.6, 5.0 and 5.7 in. no matter which evaluation index is applied.

The data of hand length and hand width were both divided into 4 categories respectively. The operation time and error rate is better for larger hand length (18.5–20.0 cm and 20.0–21.5 cm) when using 4.6 and 5.0 in. screens and it is worse for shorter hand length (15.5–17.0 and 17.0–18.5 cm) when using 5.0 in. touchscreen and above. There is a rapid increasing trend from 3.5 in. screen to 5.7 in. screen for smaller hand length (15.5–17.0 and 17.0–18.5 cm), no matter which evaluation index is. However, the trend decreases firstly slight and then increases for large hand length. Longer hand and fingers are helpful to increase operation performance. If the screen is too small, user still has little difficult to operate the smartphone.

The analysis results of hand width and screen size are similar. For larger hand width (10.5–11.5 and 11.5–12.5 cm hand width), the operation time and error rate is better when using 4.6 in. and 5.0 in. touchscreens and that is poorer for narrower hand width (8.5–9.5 and 9.5–10.5 cm) when using 5.0 and 5.7 in. touchscreens. There is also a rapid increasing trend from 3.5 in. screen to 5.7 in. screen for smaller hand length (8.5–9.5 and 9.5–10.5 cm) in spite of the evaluation indices. The trend slightly decreases and then increases with the increase of screen size. If a user has wider hands, he can handle a large screen smartphone more stable than the people whose hands are narrower.

According to the result, touchscreen size from 4.6 in. to 5.0 in. is suggested for most people because this interval of screen size is relatively suitable based on the analysis of hand dimensions and 3 performance evaluation indices. A 5.7 in. screen is too large to handle and operate for any hand length or width so it is not suggested to use the smartphone with 5.7 in. touchscreen.

Acknowledgment. The authors would like to acknowledge Ministry of Science and Technology of the Republic of China for financially supporting this research (MOST 103-2221-E-240-003-).

References

1. Hare, C.B.: Redefining user input on handheld. In: 3G Mobile Communication Technologies, pp. 388–393 (2002)
2. Pascoe, J., Ryan, N., Morse, D.: Using while moving: HCI issues in fieldwork environments. ACM Trans. Comput. Hum. Interact. **7**(3), 417–437 (2000)
3. Karlson, A.K. Bederson, B.B., Contreras-Vidal, J.L.: Understanding one handed use of mobile devices. In: Handbook of Research on User Interface Design and Evaluation for Mobile Technology. Idea Group Reference (2007)

4. Shneiderman, B., Plaisant, C.: Designing the User Interface: Strategies for Effective Human-Computer Interaction. Addison Wesley, Reading (2005)
5. Parhi, P.K., Amy K., Bederson, B.B.: Target size study for one-handed thumb use on small touchscreen devices. In: Proceedings of the 8th Conference on Human-Computer Interaction with Mobile Devices and Services, pp.12–15 (2006)
6. Colle, H.A., Hiszem, K.J.: Standing at a kiosk: effects of key size and spacing on touch screen numeric keypad performance and user preference. Ergonomics **47**(13), 1406–1423 (2004)
7. Hirotaka, N.: Reassessing current cell phone designs: using thumb input effectively. In: CHI 2003, New Horizons (2003)
8. Lee, M.W., Myung, H.Y., Jung, E.S., Freivalds, A.: High touch: ergonomics in a conceptual design process - case studies of a remote controller and personal telephones. Int. J. Ind. Ergon. **19**(3), 239–248 (1997)
9. Wobbrock, J.O., Myers, B.A., Aung, H.H.: The performance of hand postures in front-and back-of-device interaction for mobile computing. Int. J. Hum. Comput. Stud. **66**(12), 857–875 (2008)
10. Lin, C.-Y.: The relationship between touchscreen sizes of smartphones and hand dimensions. In: Stephanidis, C., Antona, M. (eds.) Universal Access in Human-Computer Interaction. Applications and Services for Quality of Life. LNCS, vol. 8011, pp. 643–650. Springer, Heidelberg (2013)

Internet Users' Legal and Technical Perspectives on Digital Legacy Management for Post-mortem Interaction

Cristiano Maciel[1(✉)], Vinicius Carvalho Pereira[1], and Monica Sztern[2]

[1] Universidade Federal de Mato Grosso (UFMT) – Laboratório de Ambientes Virtuais Interativos (LAVI), Cuiabá, MT, Brazil
{crismac,viniciuscarpe}@gmail.com
[2] Rio de Janeiro, RJ, Brazil
monica.sztern@gmail.com
http://www.monicasztern.jur.adv.br

Abstract. Digital assets are produced in large scale by technology users, especially after the advent of the Internet. This paper aims to analyze Brazilian users' experience with *Google Inactive Accounts*, under technical, legal and cultural perspectives. Regarding legal aspects, Brazilian laws are still inceptive. Some projects are being designed or analyzed by governmental institutions, and the right to oblivion is one of the main controversial points. The experiment was part of an exploratory research by means of questionnaires, which were answered by web software engineers, who are users of that application too. The answers were organized into four main categories: (a) inheritance rights; (b) the Right to be Forgotten; (c) temporal contact information; and (d) technical stalemates. All those data were analyzed according to a literature review on technical and legal issues regarding death, legacy and technology, so as to better understand the advantages and disadvantages of the options provided by *Google Inactive Accounts*.

Keywords: Digital legacy management · Post-mortem · Legal issues

1 Introduction

Digital assets are produced in large scale by technology users, especially after the advent of the Internet. Those assets consist not only of texts and photos stored in personal computers; they are also worldwide spread in application servers, such as e-mail managers and social networks. Most users do not think it is important to manage their data considering the event of death, and many feel uncomfortable to use applications of the kind [7]. That uneasiness might be due to death-related taboos and beliefs societies harbor [19], directly influencing the way people face computational modelling of aspects related to death, mortality and mourning.

Recently, Google launched *Google Inactive Accounts* [13], enabling the management of user account data so that photos, emails and documents have a destination when their accounts are no longer used. This implies, among other things, making a digital testament to provide a fate for the legacy after the user`s death. Options in this system are: setting a time limit for the account to become inactive; defining a cell phone

© Springer International Publishing Switzerland 2015
S. Yamamoto (Ed.): HIMI 2015, Part I, LNCS 9172, pp. 627–639, 2015.
DOI: 10.1007/978-3-319-20612-7_59

number and alternative email address for alerts when the inactive time period runs out; notification of contacts; data sharing; and account exclusion. Considering memories are narrative texts based on data (such as mementos or mental images), not data themselves, *Google Inactive Accounts* provides the user with different procedures to narrate his posthumous identity. This means actively defining some cornerstones to treat digital legacy, instead of abandoning data to their own fate.

Such a solution has its advantages and limitations. Among the advantages is the fact that it (a) doesn't allow the digital legacy to be lost. These days, a large part of what we do is on the internet, stored on normally distant servers and password protected; (b) permits deletion of inactive accounts which in the near future could pollute and/overload the internet; and (c) provides the user with the option of keeping, or not, every digital thing that was built up during his lifetime.

From that discussion, many human values emerge and need to be taken into account when dealing with "inheritance", such as privacy, trust, ethics and interpersonal conflicts. On the other hand, legal questions need to be discussed and often the available technology is ahead of the lawmakers. Thus, in this article we ask: to what extent can the technical and cultural issues found by software engineers and interaction designers, faced with *Google Inactive Accounts*, contribute to the discussion of legal aspects related to the digital legacy? As the objective of this study, we intend to raise legal questions that emerged from applications that permit the configuration of a posthumous digital legacy, from the viewpoint of engineers.

For this study, our multidisciplinary research group, composed of specialists in Computer Sciences, Linguistics and Law, made a literature review about wills, inheritance [9, 12], legislation on digital legacy and Human-Computer Interaction (HCI) aspects related to this issue [4, 15, 19]. Among the researches our review analyzed, some papers were related to volition on digital legacy [19] and posthumous interaction [18].

The experiment was part of an exploratory research by means of questionnaires, which were answered by web software engineers. This research was intended to elicit advantages and disadvantages of the options provided by *Google Inactive Accounts*. The data collected were categorized and analyzed, leading us to important discussions on legal and technical implications of that tool, under software developers' view, who are users of that application too. From the qualitative data analysis, we come up with legal and technical recommendations. These recommendations are useful for human-computer interaction designers and software engineers who, along with the market, can propose or improve computational solutions that are compatible with users concerns. On the other hand, since this is a multidisciplinary study and because we understand that technology directly affects and modifies other areas of knowledge, we believe that the contributions given here may also be useful in the field of law, where regulations need to be created and/or adapted to deal with the digital legacy.

2 Literature Review

In this section, we will discuss, based on Brazilian legislation, the Right to be Forgotten, aspects related to inheritance rights, the Internet Civil Mark, digital wills and some studies that have been carried out on posthumous digital legacy.

Inheritance rights, in relation to civil law, vary greatly from one country to another especially when it comes to cases where this is no will (which is very frequent in terms of digital assets). This becomes even more complex if taking into account, in the case of digital legacies, the global spread of users, software companies and servers. Seeing the many different facets that this discussion presents in this sphere, we opted, in this study, to focus on the Brazilian judicial system since the researchers and the questionnaire respondents are all Brazilian.

Currently, the Brazilian Civil Code [7], in article 1788, is the statutory basis for inheritance rights: "*Art. 1.788. A person dying with no will transmits the inheritance to the legitimate heirs; the same applies to the assets that were not contemplated in the will; and the legitimate inheritance subsists if the will lapses or is judged to be null.*"

In other words, after death, in the hypothesis that no will was made or, even if one has been made and no express mention has been made of rights, this right is passed on to the legitimate heirs. It is clear, therefore, that if a person makes a will before dying which expressly determines his/her wishes with respect to a particular right, this must be obeyed unless the will is judged to be null or has expired.

However, there is a bill of law, No. 4099/2012 [3], which has already been approved by the Constitution and Justice Commission, which has been awaiting Federal Senate approval since October 2013. This bill proposed the inclusion of the following paragraph into article 1788 of the Civil Code [1]: "*Single paragraph – It is to be transmitted to the heirs all the content of digital accounts and files belonging to the author of the inheritance.*" It is worth mentioning here the justification given for the Bill of Law [3]: "*...there have been cases taken to the courts of situations where the families of deceased persons wish to obtain access to the files or accounts stored by internet services and the solutions have been very contradictory, leading to different, and sometimes unfair, handling of cases in similar situations (...) The best thing is to ensure that inheritance law covers these situations, regulating and unifying their treatment, making it clear that the heirs will receive in the inheritance access and total control of these digital accounts and files (...)*".

Despite the social aspect being considered in this justification for the Bill of Law, there are some deeper issues that need to be considered. Firstly, it is necessary to consider the hermeneutic effects that approval of this paragraph in article 1788 of the Civil Code may imply. Indeed, the *caput* of the article mentioned proposes that the rights may only be transmitted to the legitimate heirs if they have not already been made the objects of the will or, further, if the will is judged null or expired. Thus, it is correct to state that if the will maker includes a clause in the will on the non-transmission of rights, such as passwords to access internet accounts, his wishes must be respected unless exceptions apply (annulment or lapsing of the will).

However, with the addition of the single paragraph, another exception is created which is independent from any previous analysis: the content of the digital accounts and files must be transmitted to the heirs regardless of the data owner's wishes. This premise ignores the deceased's privacy, as well as any possible disinterest when alive to have accounts accessed posthumously.

Currently, in order to gain access to such content, heirs must bring declaratory action suits in the knowledge that there is no consensus of understanding on this issue.

The most common result, when access is authorized, is the removal of the deceased's profiles and content (photos, videos, texts) which have not been shared with family.

Precisely due to the fact there is no specific legislation on this issue, its regulamentation is casuistic. So, for example, in the case of Facebook, as stated in the Terms of Use, in case of user death the family is required to send the death certificate in order for the account to be deleted. In this case, the decision to delete is in the hands of the family who "inherit" the possibility to destroy data whilst not holding legal ownership of it. It is also worth noting that this solution is conditional to the existence of documents which prove death; in Brazil, this is the Death Certificate.

Secondly, we must not leave out of our consideration the Right to be Forgotten. This is not a new topic within international legal doctrines. In the countries of the European Union, the Right to be Forgotten resulted in the application of rules which govern personal data protection, in particular the principles of consent and purpose,[1] expressly stated in the European Council Directive 95/46/CE of October 24th 1995 [8]. Based on these principles, the European data protection agencies have used the Right to be Forgotten as the basis for removing data available on the internet when they no longer serve the purposes for which they were collected and stored. This position has already been adopted by the data protection agencies of France (*Comission Nationale de L'informatique et des Libertés*), Italy (*Garante per la Protezione dei Dati Personali*) and Spain (*Agencia Española de Protección de Datos — AEPD*), in response to requests from people to intervene for the deletion of personal data on the internet.

This movement has been gaining greater attention due to the ease with which information can be kept and circulated on the internet and how it can be used to create overexposure of rumors, facts and news even when the events that originated this information may have taken place long ago. This issue became even more relevant with the publication of Announcement 531 of the VI Civil Rights Movement promoted by the Federal Justice Council [7]. The text, a doctrinal guidance document based on the Civil Code, places the Right to be Forgotten within the realm of personal rights: "The tutelage of human dignity in an information society includes the Right to be Forgotten". In this way, announcement 531 draws on an interpretation of the Civil Code in relation to personal rights by stating that people have the right to be forgotten by the public and press.

Thirdly, the passing of Law no. 12.965, known as the Internet Civil Mark [2], has added another even more unconstitutional aspect to Bill of Law no. 4099/2012, since it establishes, as a basic principle, the right of privacy (Article 3°, II) and protection of personal data, in the form of a law (Article 3°, II). Among user rights and guarantees, in Chap. 2, Article 7°, II, is the assurance for the user of "non-violation of the intimacy of private life, its protection and compensation for material or moral damages resulting from such violation" and in Ch. XI, "*permanent deletion of personal data that has been supplied to a particular internet application, on request, at the termination of the relationship between the parties...*".

---

[1] The principle of consent establishes the need for prior consent from the owner to collect, store and handle his/her personal data. Whilst the principle of purpose requires data to be kept and used in strict adherence to the specific purposes for its collection.

On the other hand, studies into HCI show that users' desire in relation to "forgetting" their data, in the form of posthumous erasure, is in line with the Bills of Law on posthumous data in Brazil. Studies by [14, 18], despite using different methodologies and distinct profiles of research subjects, point towards similar results: most users wish to have their data deleted after death, but practically none of them had already given thought to this before being approached for the survey.

Respecting users' wishes in terms of the fate of their data has also been discussed from the point of view of volition [20] and posthumous interaction [18]. The authors propose that the software models the fate options for the dead user's data and enable this choice to be made upon accepting the terms of use. Today, most systems ignore cases of death or set a policy that has little flexibility for the fate of digital legacies in the terms of use (which cannot be changed by the user), and which is not necessarily adequate for the legal system in the country where the user lives. On the other hand, those which include in the terms of use some kind of rule in relation to user death do so in a way which is not clear.

Google's initiative is in line with the proposal to respect volition in terms of the digital legacy even though it doesn't directly mention the word "death" in its interface. The term "inactive account" suggests the company, with the aim of achieving greater support, opted not to use a taboo term to designate the application and its functions. Even so, what the application offers is the possibility to make a digital will, which is a testamentary instrument that cannot be disassociated from death. To make such a statement, we used a definition of will which transcends local judicial systems: "It constitutes a mandate to the executor" [12].

However, ensuring these "last wishes and intentions" (which in this study are elements of volition) are carried out by technical means within legality, meeting the cultural demands of each society, is a challenge in the universe of digital assets for a number of reasons as raised by Edwards and Harbinja [9]:

- The difficulty of defining what digital assets are, given the multiplicity of elements that can be placed in this category: e-mails, ebooks, music and downloaded movies, posts in social media, score and fictional money in games, reputation in virtual communities, photos posted (or shared) by third parties;
- The disparity between the terms of use of each service provider and local legislation;
- The difference of judicial systems between the jurisdictions where the deceased user lived, where the heir lives, where the software company is based and where the providers that store the information are located;
- The conflicts of interest between stakeholders (the deceased user, heirs and the software companies);
- Respecting the deceased user's privacy in the case of no will being made or a will which clearly states which data should or shouldn't be inherited by others;
- The difficulty of separating what is a digital asset (an e-mail for example) and what is the information that the digital asset holds, it being controversial how to decide if some information is something that can be left in a will for others.

Such dilemmas on the preservation or destruction of a deceased user's data, which generate heated discussions in terms of ethics and law, have been worked on in an almost homogeneous way from a technical viewpoint: "forgetting-by-selection" and "remembering-by default", instead of the other way around [22]. This shows that, from the company's viewpoint, the standard option is to store data since the technical procedures to do this are becoming less and less complex thanks to technological evolution. The possible financial gains via big data analytics and curatorship services for deceased users' data are still being estimated.

A proposal made by Brubaker et al. [4] to deal with these challenges consists of shifting the focus from inheritance to stewardship. Such a paradigm shift would imply treating deceased users' data not as a legacy or property to be transmitted to others but as a set of social symbols which would be administered and curated by a steward. On one hand, this approach takes into account the dilemma that in a digital universe it is difficult to separate which data constitute the user's identity and which constitute his assets; on the other, this does not discard the need for legislation that regulates the steward's actions in a way which is analogous to that of the executor of a will.

Faced with so many conflicts between technical, legal and cultural aspects related to digital wills, we carried out the present study as detailed in the next section.

3   Methodology

In this research, an exploratory study was performed using questionnaires for a target population of web software engineers with knowledge of HCI so as to answer the following research question: to what extent can the technical and cultural issues found by software engineers, dealing with *Google Inactive Accounts*, contribute to the discussion of legal aspects related to the digital legacy?

The questionnaire contained the interface of *Google Inactive Accounts* [13] and instructions for the respondents to reflect on the advantages and disadvantages of this functionality based on the options available in this tool. This tool gives optional measures to be taken by the user, regarding the management of his account: (a) setting a timeout period, after which the account can be treated as inactive; (b) being alerted via text message and optionally email before the timeout period ends; (c) adding trusted contacts who should be made aware that the user is no longer using his account; (d) selecting data to be shared with the aforementioned trusted contacts; and (d) allowing Google to delete the account.

The participants of the survey were 25 students on a specialization course in Web Systems Engineering invited as volunteers during a classroom activity. All participants are graduates in the area of Computers. The group consisted of 23 men and 2 women. The average age was 33 years. All were resident in the Brazilian state of Mato Grosso. For the purposes of standardization and anonymity, each survey subject is identified by the letter "E" followed by a number.

From the interpretive analysis of the responses to the survey, we found thematic patterns that we categorized as follows: (a) inheritance rights; (b) the Right to be Forgotten; (c) temporal contact information; and (d) technical stalemates. From this, we intend to articulate cultural, technological and legal aspects of the fate of the digital legacy.

4 Data Analysis

To begin the discussion, we must mention that the lack of a legal framework for the digital legacy was mentioned more than once by the survey subjects. E5 states that it is an advantage that *Google Inactive Accounts* allows "at least this option since there are no policies on personal data that circulate on the internet after a person's death". On the other hand, a problem was pointed out on the lack of legal norms governing data of this nature: that different systems can develop distinct policies for deceased users' data. According to E11, "Does the service have a link with other accounts of other profiles that the user might have? Probably not, as this is a Google resource. Therefore, I believe that other companies should make this resource available or pass this function on to a competent organ".

In the same tone, E15 questions the lack of backing in real-world civil documents for decisions on the fate of virtual legacy, stating a disadvantage of *Google Inactive Accounts* as "not having the option to link with legal documents (death certificate)".

Inheritance Rights. The Brazilian Civil Code deals with inheritance rights in article 1784 [1]. In few words it deals with the transmission of assets of a deceased person on to the heirs. The deceased's assets consist of possessions, rights and obligations held during life and transmitted to heirs. The Civil Code, when dealing with inheritance and its transmission, does not mention only the tangible assets and, therefore, the intangible assets may also be considered as also being covered by the law. E1 states, "from the moment that the user agrees to use the service he will be "delegating" the use of his data to another person in his trust, thus, should unforeseen events occur such as death or other problems, even bad health, this information can be recovered and preserved by another user". The ideas of delegation, recovery and preservation mentioned above ratify that digital data is a kind of property that is owned and transmitted by inheritance where the heir is responsible for its management.

The terms "inheritance", "heir" and "legacy" are found in the specialized literature on this topic [4, 9, 12] and were used frequently by the engineers in the survey. For E9, for example, a limitation of data exclusion is "the fact that a virtual legacy that the person built up will cease to exist". Understanding his digital data as being a possession to be passed on to his offspring in the same way as material assets in a will, E20 states that "with the aim of giving him the digital inheritance as a gift, he gave his telephone number and email address".

The affective value of these assets and the attachment that they evoke, complicating factors when discussing the value of these data and the impacts of their transmission to others or their destruction, were mentioned by E1: "I have dear ones that I've lost, I keep their photos, videos and other belongings. I can't imagine ever destroying these memories. I'm human, I miss them". E20, showing not just emotional worth but also economic value of digital assets, adds: "by offering this option, the user can decide who the digital heirs of the content will be, which sometimes can be of great economic and affective importance".

Another problem introduced into the discussion is the fact that the heir is not consulted before any data is destroyed. According to E9, one disadvantage to the

Google Inactive Accounts system is "not having an "heir" who can administer or even authorize the actual destruction of your data". In the real world, there are a number of cases in which the future heir must be consulted before disposing of a person's assets.

E19 sees an advantage in the fact that the "user leaves his/her profile as "inheritance" so that the other person can decide what to do with the profile". In this comment, it is clear that it's the heir who will be deciding what will be done with the deceased's data. However, there was no mention in the responses of another problem which is linked to digital assets: what if the heir does not wish to take what the deceased user has left him? As an example of this, we can take a user's intimate conversations on social networks, log registers of sites associated with illicit practices or even pornographic videos and photos. Is the heir (or even the executor) obliged to deal with these data? And how can the heir's right to receive digital assets or not be made compatible with the user's right to express volition [20] with regards to the fate of his legacy? According to E11, "giving the user greater autonomy over his/her information" is the advantage brought by this application.

Concern is shown by E1 with the limits of control that the heir must have over the data, running the risk of altering them in such a way as to taint the deceased user's reputation: "as the new user will preserve an individual's information who has died or suffers from serious health problems, he must be aware of the issue of privacy since, for example, sometimes these new user will, over time, be able to change what was agreed with the old user who entrusted him completely". Similar cases occur when login names and passwords for email accounts and social networks are inherited allowing the user to impersonate the deceased and act in bad faith.

The Right to be Forgotten. The Right to be Forgotten has generated discussions on the field of technologies [7]. For example, for E3, "the main advantage is having personal information excluded from the web". E9 sees as an advantage the possibility of "eliminating information and data that is no longer managed by the person". E20 is in line with these opinions and relates them to data privacy: "I may possess documents that I would never like other people to have access to, even after my death, and in this case it would be clear and well defined that after becoming inactive I would want their total destruction".

As well as this, E2 puts forward another aspect of privacy related to the Right to be Forgotten, which would "make your information unavailable on the web preventing insurance scams etc.". Here, we can see a concern with the user's right to protect himself, in life, against unauthorized use of his data as mentioned by Farrugia [11].

Furthermore, in the previous category cases were mentioned where the heir might not wish to receive any kind of data from the deceased user, whereas we now discuss cases where the user does not wish some particular data to be shared with the heirs as mentioned by E12: "What if the information there makes someone sad or upset when they discover something that the person hasn't told them?" In this case, one should respect that "there are data that I would like my family and friends to inherit and other data that I wouldn't". However, when this survey was made, *Google Inactive Accounts* did not allow the user the possibility to make this kind of choice; it is up to him to delete everything or leave everything to one or more heirs. For E18, "There is a lack of options in the tool that would make it possible to take different actions for different services". E24 exemplifies this situation, stating that "There should be the option for the user to choose which information must be excluded and which must be kept. The user may, for example, want his profile on Google + to be excluded but his blog and Youtube videos preserved". The possibility of the user choosing the content he wishes to pass on to the heirs is discussed by Maciel and Pereira [19].

E9 shows concern for the symbolic value of information by commenting that "There is information within Google apps that should not be lost since it adds symbolic value to the groups and relationships established between users". E9 further suggests that the service "could be more wide-ranging and allow types of data that add symbolic value to be mapped by the user onto his circle of relationships, offering the option to keep or delete each one of the connections". Such a solution is very interesting but complex from the computer modelling point of view since it requires dealing with an intangible legacy, dealt with by Khalid and Dix [15] from the viewpoint of an Extended Episodic Experience, which would include not only digital assets but also the user's social and affective relationships within digital environments.

On the other hand, the possibility of controlling these data by the definition of a period of non-use of the account, as proposed by Maciel [20], is also modelled by the Google service which was seen as a benefit by the engineers. For E5, one advantage of the service is "being able to set the period of time for the account expiration due to inactivity".

Another problem in this respect, according to E8, is that "The user does not usually know when he is going to die so he may expose information which at that moment he would not wish to share." The unpredictability of death would impede, in this case, the user to previously delete from his legacy that which he would not like to be passed on to another by means of Google's tool.

From another perspective, E12 relates the preservation of the digital legacy to digital mourning [21] by questioning "to what extent would it be interesting to keep the information of someone who is no longer with us; to keep remembering this person could do good or bad (...), I have come across people who have died but their profiles on Facebook and Orkut are still alive. Or even receive an email from a friend who had died. So it would prevent this kind of situation." However, this is a complex area since digital mourning could involve suffering or may provide a way of getting over a loved one's death by forming a community of mourners or by producing digital memories [16].

Temporality of Contact Information. A central issue in the discussion of passing on digital assets is related to the moment and the way the heir's information and the sharing procedures are registered on the system. Many participants showed concern with the modification of information that is used to control the transmission of the legacy. E2, when analyzing the service which requests a telephone number to contact the user with the aim of confirming activity on the system, states that "telephone numbers change constantly, it's possible to configure the service and be excluded from the network without receiving an alert on your cell phone".

E20 goes further by stating that the nominated heir could also change email address and be unable to be contacted by the tool: "... he didn't think his son would change email address and telephone number and this would mean everything would be lost in the digital ocean". If changing the user's own contact data is already a problem, this becomes even more serious when there is no control over the designated heir changing his data.

Still on the topic of temporality, E16 raises the issue of the case of the heir dying before the user: "How can it be ensured that the person nominated has not died too, in this case how could the person be contacted?" According to the Brazilian legal system, in cases such as this, the will should propose a substitute for the heir, something which very rarely happens. If there is no substitute, the inheritance is then transmitted to the necessary heirs.

Many other engineers also question the possibility of undue data exclusion when, for example, the user does not access the account for some time due to health reasons or incarceration. For E6, "Should the user be unable to access the internet, Google would exclude the account and there would be no way to reverse the process (in the case of imprisonment)". E16 shows concern in this way: "How to ensure that the user who, for reasons of serious illness but still alive, has been unable to access his profile for a long time would not have it cancelled".

For E14, one limitation is that "There may be a need to access the account and the account has already been deactivated". Access of this nature can be requested by judicial means in case of family members who feel they have the right to receive the deceased user's data. E15 exemplifies why the possibility of "excluding files such as videos for example is problematic. Often this video may be useful to people and, because of the exclusion, people will not have this content at their disposal anymore". E2 exemplifies cases such as this: "Google deletes your information and it becomes impossible to track it, making it unavailable for a lawsuit for example". On the other hand, in case the family wishes to close the deceased's account, E24 understands that this application brings advantages to the extent that "in case of death it avoids turmoil for the family who try to cancel the Google account. With this resource, the process would be more bureaucratic".

Technical Stalemates. Software engineers, given their academic and professional backgrounds, are concerned with the benefits to the company, in this case Google. E2 comments that: "Google provides more space on its servers and the active users gain more innovation resources". For E9, one advantage for the company is "being able to measure the real number of active users".

Despite this being a Google service, E24 raises an issue: "It's for Google products only. Other services like Facebook, Twitter, Instagram or email accounts with other providers will remain active". E25 adds: "As well as Google, I have contacts in many other places and data stored in these other places. To be really effective, the data would have to be integrated. It's not enough for just Google to provide palliative solutions. This raises the question: How to integrate everything? There is a long way to go until there is a solution of a kind that really meets the demands". This difficulty of integration was mentioned in category "a" of our study (inheritance rights), since the lack of legislation on this topic means each software company has to define its own policy for data treatment of deceased users. However, this is an issue that also involves technical aspects, such as those of category "e" of our study (technical stalemates), given the difficulty of designing solutions that integrate data of very different natures in different systems, belonging to different companies.

In this sense, it's worth highlighting that some companies have invested in this market niche. *LegacyLocker.com,* for example, offers software that functions as a repository of account data, which are forwarded, after death, to the nominated heirs. E6, though, shows a concern with the fact that the *Google Inactive Accounts* service is "optional" for users: "If the user does not define the settings, the account will not be deactivated". With the existence of more interactive terms of use, this could be mitigated, increasing user engagement when defining the fate of his digital legacy. This design solution was also proposed by E18 for system modelling: "The system should force users to set the options of inactive accounts, both new and old ones". In this sense, solutions that lead to more interactive terms of use [17] and solutions that allow the user to configure his prior volition in terms of the posthumous digital legacy are required [19].

The possibility of the system to induce a user to losing data, due to modelling problems, is also raised by the engineers. E8 alerts to the fact that the user "could have his account excluded should he make an error in the time limit setting and does not opt to be advised by cell phone; his contacts may not see the message". In this sense, solutions that provide usability and communicability to the system are fundamental. Given the complexity of the treatment of this topic, according to E11, "some of the options, such as *notify contacts, advise me and share*, require of the user a certain level of maturity in decision taking; and what if the user shares by mistake?". E20 reminds us that if the system "is badly configured, it could result in undesired actions. This is why all the decisions to be taken must be well detailed and easy to understand".

In this sense, E11 states "I do not consider "EXCLUSION" to be an option. Will the person who opts for exclusion have all the content permanently deleted? I prefer to consider the option <u>Deactivation</u> of content, making it unavailable and inaccessible on the internet, however, in the case of safeguards of requests by a relative or competent organ, this content could be reactivated or accessed".

E16 sees an advantage in "allowing the nominated family members to transform the profile into an internet memorial", since Google accounts are connected to the profiles. Brubaker et al. [5] and Lopes et al. [16] have discussed such possibilities. Some social networks are beginning to implement services that offer memorials for deceased users. Facebook, for example, has already presented an option to transform a normal profile into a digital memorial after filling out a form called "*Facebook Memorialization Request*" [10] to prove the death of the user.

Finally, regardless of the categories raised in this study, the fact that we are studying this topic is a theoretical exercise on a very controversial issue, especially when stimulating the study subjects into making this reflection. For E20, the existence of the *Google Inactive Accounts* service, regardless of its limitations, also brings benefits since "by having this option, the user has to analyze how to act on the digital documents belonging to him and how these should be treated when he becomes inactive. This is an issue that people do not stop to think about and safeguard themselves (...)".

5   Conclusion

In this paper, we sought to raise the legal issues that emerge from the availability of configuring a posthumous digital legacy in applications such as *Google Inactive Accounts* from the viewpoint of software engineers. From the interpretive analysis of the survey responses, there was discussion of inheritance rights, the Right to be Forgotten, temporality of contact information and technical stalemates of the tool.

From the legal point of view, as happens in many areas and not just with inheritance, the legislation has not kept up with the changes in society and, especially, with technological developments. Until recently, the concern with transmission of assets was limited to those of a material nature. Only now have legislators begun to take the first steps towards regulating the transmission of non-material assets. This is a very controversial issue, as seen in the analysis of the survey results.

There are now more doubts than certainties. The validity and future regulamentation of the Internet Civil Mark [3], which establishes the right to privacy as a basic principle, will bring more solutions to the problems of transmitting non-material rights in the case of death. However, as has been occurring, the answers to the problems will be given casuistically, analyzing the characteristics of each case so as to reach the most appropriate solution within the legal framework.

It can be seen, throughout analyses of the responses, that there are a number of concerns with how to deal with this topic. However, no mention was found of how to define the responsibilities of the heir of a digital asset.

It is worth highlighting that, as a limitation of this study, despite having considered bibliographies of international authors, has focused on Brazil since it is necessary to carry this out in accordance with the legal norms of each country.

The dilemmas imposed by the issues discussed in this study are fundamental for systems development to consider cultural and legal aspects of death and legacy. The HCI area can greatly collaborate by questioning solutions, testing them and proposing ways of dealing with death, mortality and the management of digital legacy.

References

1. Brasil: Código Civil Brasileiro. Lei no 10.406 (2002). http://www.soleis.com.br/ebooks/0-civil.htm
2. Brasil: Lei no 12.965. Marco Civil da Internet (2013). http://www.planalto.gov.br/ccivil_03/_ato2011-2014/2014/lei/l12965.htm
3. Brasil. Projeto de Lei nº 4099 (2012). http://www.camara.gov.br/proposicoesWeb/fichadetramitacao?idProposicao=548678
4. Brubaker, J.R., Dombrowski, L., Gilbert, A., Kusumakaulika, N., Hayes, G.R.: Stewarding a legacy: responsibilities and relationships in the management of post-mortem data. In: Proceedings of CHI 2014. Toronto, Canada, 26 April–1 May 2014
5. Brubaker, J.R., Hayes, G.R., Dourish, J.P.: Beyond the grave: Facebook as a site for the expansion of death and mourning. Inf. Soc. **29**(3), 152–163 (2013)
6. Carrol, E., Romano, J.: Your Digital Afterlife: When Facebook, Flickr and Twitter are Your estate, What's Your Legacy?, 216 pp. New Riders Pub, Berkeley (2010)
7. Brasil: Conselho da Justiça Federal. AGUIAR JR., Ruy Rosado de (Coord. Geral Evento). MOREIRA, Rogério Meneses Fialho (Coord. Parte Geral). Enunciados Aprovados. In: VI Jornada de Direito Civil. Brasília: Conselho da Justiça Federal, Centro de Estudos Judiciários, cap. 5. 180 pp (2013). http://www.cjf.jus.br/cjf/CEJ-Coedi/jornadas-cej/vijornada.pdf

8. European Council Directive 95/46/CE. http://eur-lex.europa.eu/legal-content/PT/TXT/?uri= CELEX:31995L0046. Accessed 24 Oct 1995
9. Edwards, L., Harbinja. E. "What Happens to my Facebook Profile when I Die?": legal issues around transmission of digital assets on death. In: Maciel, C., Pereira, V.C. (eds.) Digital Legacy and Interaction: post mortem issues, pp. 115–144. Springer, London (2013)
10. Facebook Memoralization Request. https://www.facebook.com/help/contact/305593649477238
11. Farrugia. R.: Post-Mortem data protection in the age of big data and its threat to personal autonomy. Thesis, Tilburg Institute for Law, Technology and Society, 113 pp (2014)
12. Field, C.: The Drafting of Wills, 217 pp. SiberInk, Cape Town (2013)
13. Google Inactive Account. https://www.google.com/settings/account/inactive
14. Grimm, C., Chiasson, S.: Survey on the fate of digital footprints after death. In: Workshop on Usable Security (USEC), Internet Society (2014)
15. Khalid, Haliyana, Dix, Alan: Extended episodic experience in social mediating technology: our legacy. In: Meiselwitz, Gabriele (ed.) SCSM 2014. LNCS, vol. 8531, pp. 452–461. Springer, Heidelberg (2014)
16. Lopes, A.D., Maciel, C., Pereira, V.C.: Virtual homage to the dead: an analysis of digital memorials in the social web. In: Proceedings of HCI International 2014, Heraklion, Crete, Greece, pp. 67–78 (2014)
17. Luger, E.A., Moran, S., Roddem, T.: Consent for all: revealing the hidden complexity of terms and conditions. In: CHI 2013, Paris, France, pp 2687–2696 April 27–May 2 2013
18. Maciel, C., Pereira, V.C.: The internet generation and its representations of death: considerations for posthumous interaction projects. In: Proceedings of the 11th Brazilian Symposium on Human Factors in Computing Systems (IHC 2012). Brazilian Computer Society, Porto Alegre, Brazil, pp. 85–94 (2012)
19. Maciel, C., Pereira, V. C.: The fate of digital legacy in software engineers' view: technical and cultural aspects. In: Maciel, C., Pereira, V.C. (eds.) Digital Legacy and Interaction: Post-Mortem Issues, 1st edn. HCI, pp. 1–30. Springer, Switzerland (2013)
20. Maciel, C.: Issues of the Social Web interaction project faced with afterlife digital legacy. In: Proceedings of IHC+CLIHC 2011, pp. 3–12. ACM Press (2011)
21. Massimi, M., Baecker, R.M.: A death in the family: opportunities for designing technologies for the bereaved. In: Proceedings of the CHI 2010, pp. 1821–1830. ACM Press, New York (2010)
22. Mayer-Schonberger, V.: Delete: The Virtue of Forgetting in the Digital Age. Princeton University Press, Princeton (2009)

Analysis Using Purchasing Data in Japan

Ryota Morizumi[⊠] and Yumi Asahi

Department of Engineering, Graduate School of Integrated Science
and Technology, Shizuoka University, Shizuoka, Japan
cm230025@gmail.com, asahi@sys.eng.shizuoka.ac.jp

Abstract. Purchasing style of Japanese consumers have made their own development. Purchase of goods with a large amount once a month or once a few weeks is a kind of global standard. On the contrary, purchase of goods with a small amount once in couple of days is common in purchasing style of Japanese consumers. Purchase of goods with a large amount in a weekend is recently getting to increase however the interval is a week at the longest.

Japanese supermarkets have various features to respond to such a unique purchasing style. First, in the rest of the world, stores are located in the extensive sites on the suburbs but, in Japan, stores are located in the town. Secondly, Japanese supermarkets handle a small amount of products which are subdivided. Furthermore, even if in the same category, supermarkets handle different kinds of products by different manufacturers. In this way, purchasing style of Japanese consumers have made their own development.

The analysis was carried out using the purchasing data of all customers who visited stores and distribution data of members-only coupon.

As the analysis, the authors have found that member registration rate of customers is very high. Its registration rate is as high as 70 %. Also, utilization rate of the coupons as member's privileges is low and, when the members pay in the stores, 70 % of them don't use the coupons.

In future task, how to analyze the member information which is not customer information.

Keywords: Comparative analysis · Marketing strategy · Membership system · Purchasing style

1 Introduction

Purchasing style of Japanese consumers have made their own development. Purchase of goods with a large amount once a month or once a few weeks is a kind of global standard. On the contrary, purchase of goods with a small amount once in couple of days is common in purchasing style of Japanese consumers. Purchase of goods with a large amount in a weekend is recently getting to increase however, the interval is a week at the longest.

As a background, there are a variety of factors. Firstly, it can be mentioned that motorization in Japan has not developed as Europe and America. Therefore, it is difficult to buy goods with a large amount. Secondly, it can be mentioned that Japanese residence is narrow. Japanese residence is narrower than Western residence. Residence in downtown is narrow in particularly. Therefore, even if it's bought in large quantities,

© Springer International Publishing Switzerland 2015
S. Yamamoto (Ed.): HIMI 2015, Part I, LNCS 9172, pp. 640–647, 2015.
DOI: 10.1007/978-3-319-20612-7_60

there is no place to keep. Thirdly, it can be mentioned that Japanese seek a fresh. Japanese tend to buy a fresh thing. Culture to eat raw fish, such as represented in sushi is its symbol. Therefore, in order to get fresh things, it is to the frequent shopping.

Retailing of Japan has various features to accommodate Japanese purchasing. According to L.P. Bucklin, it shows the four factors as distribution results that consumer seek: spatial convenience, lot size, delivery time and width and depth of assortment. In four factors of L.P. Bucklin, purchase of goods with a small amount once in couple of days has strongly demanded spatial convenience and lot size. As a result, retailings of Japan are improved spatial convenience to make small scale store in comparison with Europe and American. Also, lot size is smaller than Europe and American. Furthermore Japanese tendency to want to select products in comparison from the instruments that number also strong. Distribution style of Japan is making small scale store and preparing small lot of goods widely. Compared with store of Europe and American are located in the extensive sites on the suburbs and assorted at large lot of goods, it is inefficient. In order to perform efficient management, retailing is common to become large scale by M&A. As a result, Market becomes oligopoly. And leading market share increases. In actuality, in Australia, top five companies account for about 90 % of the market. Also, in America, top eight companies account for about 40 % of the market. On the contrary, in Japan, top five companies account only 7 % on the market. As a background, it was born to various operating styles to accommodate spatial convenience. Specifically, there is convenience store with improved temporal convenience by being open 24 h. Also, it is a factor that the government had been factor also had been protecting a small retailing to restrict the opening of large-scale stores by legal regulations. However, in recent years, these legal regulations have been abolished one after another by the deregulation. As a result of, case to overlap with each of management style has increased because retailing pursues the convenience. Specifically, convenience store is sold fresh food and supermarket is extended the operating hours. Therefore, market of retailing has become highly competitive. In addition, growth of online market is also more vigorously competition in recent years. Under such fierce competition, the retailing has been introduced a membership system in order to survive. The purpose of membership system is to enclose the customer by member benefits, such as coupon. However, if a membership benefit is functioning effectively, membership system is meaningless.

The purpose of the research is to discover more effective method of membership system by analyzing the actual data.

2 Data Used for the Analysis

The data that can be used for the analysis was offered from All Japan Foods Co., Ltd. There are two data that can be used for the analysis.

2.1 Store Data Used for the Analysis

It is used 5 stores in Hokkaido area and Tokyo area respectively to analysis. Data of store shows in Table 1.

Table 1. Store data

Area	Address	Shop area	Daily turnover
Hokkaido	Higasi-ku, Sapporo City, Hokkaido	879m^2	¥2,210,000
Hokkaido	Higasi-ku, Sapporo City, Hokkaido	1,285m^2	¥3,140,000
Hokkaido	Kita-ku, Sapporo City, Hokkaido	879m^2	¥1,740,000
Hokkaido	Bunkyodai, Ebetsu City, Hokkaido	244m^2	¥280,000
Hokkaido	Asahi, Ebetsu City, Hokkaido	482m^2	¥440,000
Tokyo	Higashitateishi, kaushika-ku, Tokyo	125m^2	¥390,000
Tokyo	Nishisakado, Sakado City, Saitama	330m^2	¥570,000
Tokyo	Higurashi, Matsudo City, Chiba	115m^2	¥290,000
Tokyo	Yashio, Shinagawa-ku, Tokyo	214m^2	¥490,000
Tokyo	Kumizawa, Totsuka-ku, Yokohama City, Kanagawa	198m^2	¥400,000

Area of Hokkaido is located in the north of Japan. Public transportation of Hokkaido is not much development. Therefore, motorized society is developing into Hokkaido in Japan relatively. On the contrary, public transportation of Tokyo is highly developed to be the center of Japan. Therefore, there are a lot of people who don't have a car.

Also, it is found that shop area is proportional to the daily turnover.

2.2 Purchasing Data of All Customers

It is indicated below about the outline of data.

Term: Jul.2013 ～ Jun.2014
Area: Hokkaido area and Tokyo area, 5 each
Number of data: about 18.6 million cases

Data1 is receipt data. Including information is sale date, sale time, membership number (members only), large classification code, middle classification code, jancode, using coupon flag (members only), and coupon number (members only).

2.3 Ticketing Data of Member-Only Coupon

It is indicated below about the outline of data.

Term: Jul.2013 ～ Jun.2014
Area: Hokkaido area and Tokyo area, 5 each
Number of data: about 9.1 million cases

Data2 is ticketing data of member-only coupon. Including information is membership number, month and years, middle classification code, coupon code, regular price, coupon price, number of sheets, number that was used.

Data2 is distribution data of members-only coupon. Supermarket that was used in the analysis is issued 20 items coupon to customers every month. The contents of the coupon is determined from past purchase history. If there is not 20 items purchasing history, related Products of purchase history is added. Still, if there is not 20items, featured Products of the shop is added (Fig. 1).

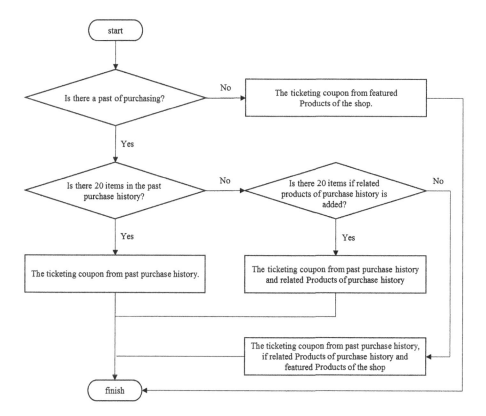

Fig. 1. Flow chart of coupon ticketing

3   Result of Analysis

3.1   Comparison of Each Store

As a result, it was found that next thing. Firstly, member ratio is high. About 70 % of the customer is a member. Secondly, the average purchase price and the average purchase items is there is a difference of 2 times in the members and non-members. For example, in "Higashi-ku, Sapporo City, Hokkaido", while average purchase price of member is 2038 yen, average purchase price of nonmember is 1075 yen. Thirdly, the one with the wide store area, there are a lot of average purchase price and average purchase items. Specifically, while Average purchase price of "Higashi-ku, Sapporo City, Hokkaido" which area is 1285 m^2 is 2124 yen, Average purchase price of "Higurashi, Matsudo City, Chiba" which area is 115 m^2 is 901 yen (Table 2).

Table 2. Comparison of each store

Area		Average purchase price	Average purchase items	Member, nonmember ratio
Higashi-ku, Sapporo City, Hokkaido	Member	¥2,038	8.9	0.8
	Nonmember	¥1,075	3.8	0.2
	Total	¥1,822	7.8	
Higashi-ku, Sapporo City, Hokkaido	Member	¥2,124	9.0	0.8
	Nonmember	¥1,189	3.8	0.2
	Total	¥1,910	7.8	
Kita-ku, Sapporo City, Hokkaido	Member	¥2,016	9.4	0.7
	Nonmember	¥1,203	4.9	0.3
	Total	¥1,778	8.1	
Bunkyodai, Ebetsu City, Hokkaido	Member	¥986	5.4	0.8
	Nonmember	¥598	2.7	0.2
	Total	¥900	4.8	
Asahi, Ebetsu City, Hokkaido	Member	¥1,328	7.4	0.7
	Nonmember	¥826	4.1	0.3
	Total	¥1,191	6.5	
Higashitateishi, kaushika-ku, Tokyo	Member	¥1,003	5.4	0.6
	Nonmember	¥580	2.8	0.4
	Total	¥820	4.3	
Nishisakado, Sakado City, Saitama	Member	¥1,202	7.0	0.7
	Nonmember	¥696	4.0	0.3
	Total	¥1,061	6.1	
Higurashi, Matsudo City, Chiba	Member	¥901	5.1	0.6
	Nonmember	¥558	3.0	0.4
	Total	¥771	4.3	
Yashio, Shinagawa-ku, Tokyo	Member	¥1,102	5.8	0.7
	Nonmember	¥614	3.1	0.3
	Total	¥951	5.0	
Kumizawa, Totsuka-ku, Yokohama City, Kanagawa	Member	¥997	6.0	0.7
	Nonmember	¥633	3.7	0.3
	Total	¥881	5.2	

3.2   Comparison of Each Day

It is the same as comparison of store about the trend of members and non-members. It is worthy of special mention that average purchase price and average purchase items of holiday has not changed significantly from average purchase price and average purchase items of weekday. Specifically, while average purchase price of weekday is 1440 yen, average purchase price of holiday is 1783 yen. Purchase price of holiday is purchase price of weekday of about 1.23 times. We have expected that average purchase price and average purchase items of holiday is increased as compared to the weekend (Table 3).

Table 3. Comparison of each day

Day		Average purchase price	Average purchase items	Member, nonmember ratio
Sunday	Member	¥1,631	8.7	0.7
	Nonmember	¥881	3.9	0.3
	Total	¥1,423	7.4	
Monday	Member	¥1,633	7.6	0.7
	Nonmember	¥889	3.7	0.3
	Total	¥1,433	6.5	
Tuesday	Member	¥1,593	7.8	0.7
	Nonmember	¥858	3.7	0.3
	Total	¥1,394	6.7	
Wednesday	Menber	¥1,608	7.6	0.7
	Nonmember	¥869	3.7	0.3
	Total	¥1,408	6.5	
Thursday	Member	¥1,676	7.6	0.7
	Nonmember	¥914	3.7	0.3
	Total	¥1,476	6.6	
Friday	Member	¥1,730	7.8	0.7
	Nonmember	¥904	3.7	0.3
	Total	¥1,488	6.8	
Saturday	Member	¥1,935	8.0	0.7
	Nonmember	¥1,022	3.9	0.3
	Total	¥1,678	7.4	

Table 4. Comparison of time zone

Time zone			Average purchase price	Average purchase items	Member, nonmember ratio
Zone1	~11:59	Member	¥1,834	8.6	0.8
		Nonmember	¥888	3.5	0.2
		Total	¥1,598	7.3	
Zone2	12:00 ~ 14:59	Member	¥1,747	8.0	0.7
		Nonmember	¥844	3.5	0.3
		Total	¥1,504	6.8	
Zone3	15:00 ~ 17:59	Member	¥1,687	7.9	0.7
		Nonmember	¥924	3.8	0.3
		Total	¥1,490	6.8	
Zone4	18:00~	Member	¥1,510	7.2	0.7
		Nonmember	¥952	4.0	0.3
		Total	¥1,332	6.2	
Total		Member	¥1,689	7.9	0.7
		Nonmember	¥907	3.8	0.3
		Total	¥1,474	6.8	

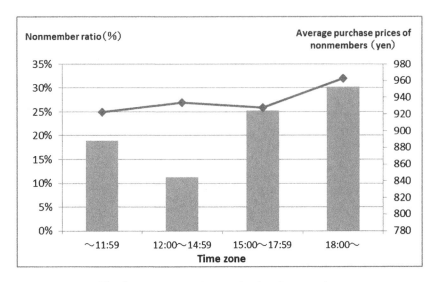

Fig. 2. Average purchase and ratio of nonmember

Table 5. Utilization ratio of coupon

Area	Average monthly visit number of times	Average monthly coupon number of uses	Utilization ratio
Higasi-ku, Sapporo City, Hokkaido	10.5	3.7	35.2%
Higasi-ku, Sapporo City, Hokkaido	10.8	3.8	35.5%
Kita-ku, Sapporo City, Hokkaido	9.4	3.6	38.7%
Bunkyodai, Ebetsu City, Hokkaido	10.4	3.9	43.3%
Asahi, Ebetsu City, Hokkaido	9.3	4.0	40.6%
Higashitateishi, kaushika-ku, Tokyo	11.6	4.7	37.5%
Nishisakado, Sakado City, Saitama	13.9	5.2	37.5%
Higurashi, Matsudo City, Chiba	9.5	3.9	41.2%
Yashio, Shinagawa-ku, Tokyo	12.9	4.9	37.7%
Kumizawa, Totsuka-ku, Yokohama City, Kanagawa	9.4	3.8	41.0%
Total	10.7	4.0	37.7%

3.3 Comparison of Time Zone

It is the same as comparison of store about the trend of members and non-members. It is worthy of special mention that the purchase price and ratio of nonmembers of zone4 has increased slightly. Specifically, average purchase price and ratio of nonmember is the highest in the all times zone. If it seems that main customers of zone4 is a single person of the work way back, it is considered that member ratio of single person is low (Table 4 and Fig. 2).

3.4 Utilization Ratio of Coupon

As a result, it was found next thing. Average monthly visit member of times is about 10 times. On the contrary, average monthly coupon member of uses is 3 times (Table 5).

4 Conclusion

4.1 Conclusion

The authors analyzed purchasing data of all customers and ticketing data of member-only coupon. The purpose of the analysis was to clarify the different between member and nonmember and the problems of usage of coupons.

As a result of the analysis, it was clarified that member ratio was very high and coupon is not used sufficiently.

4.2 Further Task

As a result of analysis, it was clarified that coupon is not used sufficiently. All Japan Foods Co., Ltd that was offered in this time dose not be collected customer information. It is easy to become member by being not collected customer information. The purpose of membership system is to acquire and analyze customer information. In future task, how to analyze the member information which is not customer information.

References

1. Abe, S., Murakami, T.: Comparative study of global marketing systems: Analysis of Convergence and Divergence, Tokyo (2003)
2. Oba, M.: The research on the store selection factors and store integrated evaluation index of consumer. In: Survey Reports on Business Administration Trends, 32(2), pp. 1–13
3. Economic and Social REserch Institute.: Japan's distribution system: Theory and Empirical, Economic analysis (1999)
4. Uzuhara, Z.: Marketing innovation of the Japan-US distribution industry, Tokyo (2007)

Changing Drinking Behavior and Beverage Consumption Using Augmented Reality

Eiji Suzuki, Takuji Narumi$^{(\boxtimes)}$, Sho Sakurai, Tomohiro Tanikawa,
and Michitaka Hirose

The University of Tokyo, 7-3-1 Hongo, Bunkyo, Tokyo, Japan
{eiji,narumi,sho,tani,hirose}@cyber.t.u-tokyo.ac.jp

Abstract. The main aim of this paper is to investigate whether our augmented reality (AR) system (which changes the appearance of a cup) can implicitly change individuals' beverage consumption via affecting volume perception for long periods. Recent studies have revealed that the consumption of food and beverages is influenced by both their actual volume and external factors during eating and drinking. Previous research has confirmed that the apparent height of the cup is a vital factor in changing drinking behavior with regard to one sip. Therefore, in this paper, we conducted a user study to confirm whether our AR system can change drinking behavior and beverage consumption and whether the effect can be sustained over the course of one hour. The results showed that the total amount of beverage consumed in one hour can be changed from about −14 % to about 25 % compared to normal. By comparing this result and that of previous research, we showed that the total beverage consumption in one hour is proportional to the amount consumed in one mouthful, and the effect of our method on changing the total beverage consumption continues over the course of one hour.

Keywords: Volume perception · Beverage consumption · Augmented reality · Human food interaction · Health

1 Introduction

All over the world, obesity has become a serious public health problem that needs to be addressed [5]. Its incidence should be curbed because it increases the risk of many medical conditions, both physical and mental. It increases the risk of contracting diseases, which not only decreases quality of life but also increases the costs of national health coverage. Some countries have been facing the crisis of a deficit-ridden health insurance system. Thus, there is a compelling need for methods of reducing the incidence of obesity. To promote the treatment and prevention of illnesses caused by obesity, it is essential to establish healthy eating habits. One of the significant factors contributing to obesity is believed to be the excessive consumption of sugar-sweetened beverages. Such beverages are the main cause of excess energy intake in children. Striegel-Moore et al. revealed that the consumption of sugar-sweetened drinks had a significant association with body mass index, which may lead to a "high-risk of overweight" [17].

© Springer International Publishing Switzerland 2015
S. Yamamoto (Ed.): HIMI 2015, Part I, LNCS 9172, pp. 648–660, 2015.
DOI: 10.1007/978-3-319-20612-7_61

Numerous methods to promote physical activity and draw people's attention to the amount of food that they are eating have been proposed to decrease rates of obesity [7, 8]. However, strong willpower and constant positivity are frequently required to increase people's physical activities and improve their diets. Although those methods can lead to dietary improvements, they typically do not solve the problem of how to maintain the effort. These dietary improvement methods often require continuous effort on the part of the consumer to actually change their eating habits. Sustaining a highly conscious effort to adequately control the eating activity is difficult.

On the other hand, recent psychological and economic studies have revealed that the amount of food consumed is influenced by both the characteristics of the food itself and environmental factors during eating. For example, if a person decides to eat a certain quantity of soup, the size of the bowl acts as a contextual cue [19]. These contextual cues can be modified with augmented reality (AR). AR has great potential for enhancing and modifying individuals' perception of real life experiences. Since human senses are highly interconnected, perception through one sensory system is changed by stimuli that are simultaneously received through other senses. This phenomenon is referred to as "cross-modality" [16]. As a result, retaining the impression from an eating experience can be modified significantly by changing stimuli through only one modality. For example, recent AR research has shown that changing appearance using AR changes individuals' perception of smell [9] and taste [11, 12]. Moreover, some researchers have focused on changing environmental factors such as the apparent size of food as a cue to affect the perception of satiety. Narumi et al. have proposed the "augmented satiety" method for food-volume augmentation, using shape deformation processing in real time [10]. They showed that their system could change consumption volume from about -10 % to about 15 % by changing only the food's apparent size without changing perceived fullness. Meanwhile, this system can only be applied to the case of solid food and cannot be applied to beverages. Thus, to undermine the effects of sugar-sweetened beverage on obesity, another technique that is applicable to liquid food and beverages is required.

Another psychological research study revealed that beverage consumption is influenced by the shape of containers such as glasses and cups. Raghubir et al. explain that this is caused by an illusion of volume perception such as in the case of the Fick illusion (vertical–horizontal illusion) [14]. Therefore, an illusion that affects volume perception, if used in the context of the volume of a beverage, can likely be utilized to change drinking behavior. In line with this, the authors implemented an "illusion cup" system (Fig. 1), which can overlay virtual cups of varied shapes onto a real cup, and confirmed that the apparent height of the cup is a vital factor in changing drinking behavior with regard to one sip [18]. However, previous research has not confirmed whether the system can change beverage consumption for long periods of time. Therefore, in this paper, we conducted an experiment that aimed to confirm the effect of the illusion cup system on beverage consumption over the course of one hour.

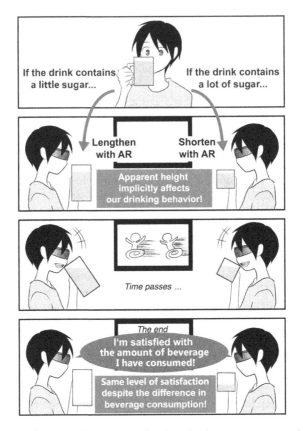

Fig. 1. Concept of our system for changing beverage consumption

2 Beverage Consumption and Environmental Factors

As mentioned earlier, humans cannot accurately evaluate the volume or nutritional value of the food they consume. Hence, humans estimate consumption volume by using indirect cues such as stomach and bowel distension, elevated blood-glucose levels, and the apparent size of the food. These evaluations are not exact because some cues are evaluated relative to an individual's surroundings.

Therefore, food and beverage consumption is affected by several external cues such as the apparent volume [10] and size of the cutlery [1, 6, 12, 16]. Some of these cues evoke visual illusions, which change individuals' estimation of the food volume. Individuals' consumption varies according to the perceived volume. Therefore, this change in volume estimation affects food and drink consumption. For example, in the context of beverage consumption, Attwood et al. showed that (1) participants were 60 % slower to consume an alcoholic beverage from a straight glass compared to a curved glass, (2) participants also misjudged the half-way point of a curved glass to a greater degree than they did in the case of a straight glass, and (3) there was a trend toward a positive association between the degree of error and total drinking time [1].

This effect, however, was not observed for non-alcoholic beverages. Attwood et al. explained that this effect was caused by misjudgments of the remaining amount. Moreover, when we drink from two kinds of cups with different shapes but the same capacity, we unconsciously consume more from the tall narrow glass than the short wide glass [14]. Raghubir et al. explained that this is caused by a difference in the perceived beverage volume owing to the vertical–horizontal illusion, in which people tend to focus on the vertical dimension of an object at the expense of the horizontal dimension. Because of this illusion, people perceive that a long narrow glass contains a larger volume of a beverage than does a short wide glass, despite the fact that the two glasses have the same capacity. Raghubir et al. also showed that the perceived volume of a beverage negatively affects the perceived consumption of the beverage. In short, people perceive that they have drunk more from a short wide glass than from a long narrow glass even though they have consumed the same volume from the two glasses. Based on these facts, it is assumed that people unconsciously try to maintain consistent satisfaction from drinking beverages and change their actual consumption when the apparent volume changes. Therefore, the apparent volume of beverages can influence drinking behavior. Girao also showed that the elongation of a glass positively influences the perceived volume of the beverage contained in it, while indirectly and inversely affecting the perceived beverage consumption [6].

As stated earlier, the perception of satiety is influenced by several factors. Controlling these contextual cues by evoking an illusion effect with human-computer interaction techniques may allow us to control (i.e., enhance or weaken) perception of satiety without conscious effort. This can be accomplished without changing the actual volume of the beverage. Thus, our previous study proposed a system that can elongate and contract the apparent height of a cup to implicitly control beverage intake by using the perceptual effects of illusion and AR technology [18]. We showed that this system could implicitly change the volume of one sip of a beverage from about -22 % to about 18 % by changing only the apparent height of the cup by ± 30 %, using AR. This study examined only the effect of AR on one mouthful of beverage. Although it is assumed that the total consumption of a beverage is proportional to the amount consumed in one mouthful, the effect of the method on changing the total consumption should be confirmed. Thus, we decided to conduct an experiment that investigates the effect of the illusion cup system on beverage consumption over the course of one hour.

3 AR System to Deform the Apparent Shape of a Cup

People often estimate size and shape relatively; thus, volume perception is assessed according to the size of neighboring objects such as food, dishes, cutlery, and a person's hand. Therefore, we needed to design an AR system that changes the shape of a cup consistently with its surroundings.

We constructed a system that can shorten/lengthen the apparent height of a cup, using an absolute AR setup. The system deforms only the appearance of the cup in the captured image in real time, using an image-based deformation technique. The equipment consists of a laptop, a video see-through head-mounted display (head-mounted display + webcam), a blue tablecloth, and a cup. The shape of the cup is almost cylindrical and it has a handle. Its height is 9.6 cm. The diameter of its top is 7.1 cm and that of its base is 6.5 cm. Its capacity is about 280 cm^2. The cylindrical part of the cup is white and the handle is orange. We used this type of cup because its cylindrical shape is suitable for changing only its height. Although we used this cup for the experiments in this research, we believe our method can also be used with other types of containers such as glasses or plastic bottles. Users of this system have to wear only a video see-through head-mounted display and need to be drinking a beverage (Fig. 2). Figure 3 shows the flow of the image processing method for shortening/lengthening the height of the cup. Each step is discussed in greater detail in the subsequent sections.

Captured Image   Composed Image

Fig. 2. Augmented reality system that changes the apparent height of the cup

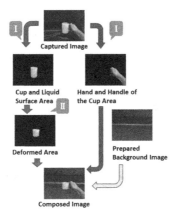

Fig. 3. Image processing for shortening/lengthening the height of the cup.

3.1 Extraction of the Cup and the User's Hand in the Captured Image

First, the captured image was converted from RGB space into HSV space, and the relevant areas of the cup and user's hand were extracted from the captured image based on the hue and saturation. The cup and liquid surface were extracted from one area of the image, and the user's hand and the handle of the cup were extracted from a separate area; these groupings were chosen because of the similarity of the colors of the extracted items. Then, we calculated the centroid of the cup and the liquid surface area.

We created a blue background using chroma keying, which facilitates color extraction, as shown in Fig. 2. A blue tablecloth is often used to cover a dining table, and is not an unusual item in an eating setup. Previous research [7] has also used this kind of setup. Thus, we considered it acceptable for an initial user study designed to test the effectiveness of the proposed system.

3.2   Changing the Height of the Cup

Next, we deformed the cup and the liquid surface area. We detected the edges of this area with a Sobel filter, and obtained the gradients of the cup by using the generalized Hough transform. Then, the cup was lengthened or shortened in the direction parallel to the gradients (Fig. 4). At this point, the deformation was performed without changing the centroid of the area. This is because the difference between center-of-gravity perception via haptic sensation and via vision may contribute to a feeling of strangeness and weaken the effect of our AR method on consumption volume. Some research has shown that when appearance is changed using AR, individuals' haptic perception changes [2–4]. Indeed, Omosako et al. showed that changing apparent shape using AR affects center-of-gravity perception [13]. Therefore, we decided to keep the position of the centroid unchanged so that such an effect would be avoided.

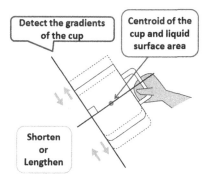

Fig. 4. Changing the height of the cup without changing its centroid.

Finally, we overlaid the shortened/lengthened cup, hand and handle images over the background image which we prepared in advance.

4   User Study on the Effect of Changing Cup Height on Beverage Consumption Over Long Periods of Time

Previous research [18] has clarified that our system, which involves using AR to change the height of a cup, can change drinking behavior with regard to one sip. The study confirmed that people drank about 18 % more with a cup whose appearance was lengthened by 30 %, and they drank about 22 % less with a cup whose appearance was shortened by 30 %. Although these results show that the system can change the pace of drinking, it remains unclear whether it can change beverage consumption for long periods. Humans may change their drinking behavior with a different pace of drinking. Therefore, using our AR system, we conducted a new user study that measures beverage volume consumed over the course of one hour in order to examine whether the method can affect beverage consumption for long periods.

4.1 Experimental Design

The study consisted of 15 male subjects. The subjects' ages ranged from 20 to 23 years and the average age was 21.5 years. The subjects were screened to ensure that they were in good health, had no food allergies/restrictions, were not currently dieting for weight loss or trying to gain weight, were not depressed, and were not using any medication known to affect one's appetite. The subjects were not informed of the actual purpose of the study.

The experiment used a within-subjects design. On three separate days, subjects came to our laboratory to drink juice. Although out of all existing beverages, carbonated drinks are the major cause of people becoming overweight, in this study, we used apple juice (Kokusan Tsugaru 100 % by Koshin Milk Products Co. Ltd.). This is because apple juice remains unchanged for a long period of time (and would therefore remain unchanged throughout the experiment), whereas carbonated drinks change in terms of taste (they lose their carbonation) in a short period of time.

During each testing session, the subjects were presented with a cup belonging to one of three conditions: Short condition (×0.70), Normal condition (×1.0), and Long condition (×1.3) (Fig. 5). To eliminate any effect of presentation order of apparent size, the presentation order was randomly assigned and balanced across subjects. The days on which the subjects were tested were separated by at least two days in order to prevent any satiation effects. We kept the temperature and humidity in the laboratory between 25[°C] and 28[°C] and 55[%] and 65[%], respectively, as these levels are believed to be comfortable levels of temperature and humidity in the summer.

Fig. 5. Appearance of the cup in the Short (left), Normal (center), and Long (right) conditions

To prevent the subjects from knowing the true purpose of the study, we told them that the study's purpose was to measure fatigue from wearing an HMD. If participants only wore an HMD and drank juice when they wanted, they would have tended to focus too much attention on the juice; this may have prevented us from measuring natural consumption. Therefore, it was necessary to give the subjects a task to perform. However, a visual burden would dilute the effect of our method. Consequently, we asked the subjects to sit and listen to radio news. The news they listened to had been broadcasted the previous night; thus, on each day of testing, the news the subjects heard was different.

When the remaining juice in the subjects' cups had been reduced to less than half, we poured more juice in order to prevent the remaining quantity from affecting subjects' consumption volume. We measured total consumption by measuring the weight of the cup just before pouring in more juice and before and after the trial. Moreover, we placed an electrical scale under the tablecloth so that the subjects could not see it (Fig. 6). We measured how many sips the subjects drank and how much juice was consumed in each sip. However, these values were subject to an unavoidable error of some grams because the measurements were made through the tablecloth.

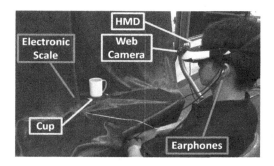

Fig. 6. A user sitting and listening to radio news with the help of earphones

To compare the effect of the cup's appearance change in each condition, we measured "rate of change" (RC), which was defined as follows:

$$\text{Rate of Change} = \frac{\text{Consumption Volume in \{Long, Short\} condition}}{\text{Consumption Volume in Normal condition compared with that in \{Long, Short\} condition}}$$

This formula for RC was also used in our previous study [18]. We hypothesized that the RC would be larger than 1.0 in the Long condition and smaller than 1.0 in the Short condition.

4.2 Procedure

The subjects were asked to keep their activity level on the three days prior to all three testing session days as similar as possible. Further, the subjects were instructed to not consume any food or drink for two hours before the experiment. The subjects kept a brief record of their activity patterns on the day before each testing session day and on each testing session day. Prior to each testing session, the subjects recorded their daily routine and we made sure that they had followed the prescribed protocol before each session, namely, at least two hours had passed since they eaten or drunk anything and their activity level had been similar to that in the days before the earlier testing sessions (e.g., no all-night work or strenuous exercise). If the subjects' activity patterns differed from those of the day prior to the previous testing session(s), we postponed the testing session for at least one day.

We told the subjects that they could drink as much juice as they wanted, that they should hold the handle when they drank, that they should put the cup in the same place (which was actually on the electrical scale), and that they should not look around. Next, subjects were set up with the HMD and earphones. Then, we put the cup filled with juice in front of them. After the subjects had finished all the experiments, we asked them what they thought the difference among the three testing sessions was and what they thought the purpose of the experiment was. The subjects also answered a free-response questionnaire.

4.3   Results and Discussion

Average juice consumption and the standard error of the mean in each experimental condition were as follows: Short, 219.9 ± 35.5[g]; Normal, 242.9 ± 40.0[g]; and Long, 280.8 ± 35.4[g]. The average RC and its standard error were 0.94 ± 0.18 in the Short condition and 1.21 ± 0.13 in the Long condition.

We conducted Thompson's rejection tests for each condition. As a result, one subject's RC in the Short condition and another subject's RC in the Long condition were rejected. In the case of the former, the subject's physical condition ratings before the Short condition were largely different from his/her prior testing session ratings. Although we confirmed that the ratings did not have a difference of more than 30[mm], most of the ratings before the Short condition were still different by a little less than 30 [mm] from those of the prior testing session. Thus, we considered that this subject's data were not valid because of this difference in his physical condition.

In the case of the other subject whose data was not considered valid, the number of sips he took was 7 in the Short condition and 8 in the Normal condition, but only 1 in the Long condition. Moreover, he was exposed to the Long condition on the third day, which was the day he answered the free-response questionnaire. His response to one of the free-response questions was that the flavor of the juice caused bad feelings. This suggests that this subject's feelings toward the juice became more negative and that he deliberately reduced consumption on the third day due to these negative feelings. Therefore, we excluded all the data of these two subjects from our analysis.

The other 13 subjects' average juice consumption and the standard error of the mean in each experimental condition were as follows: Short, 206.0 ± 38.1[g]; Normal, 251.0 ± 45.8[g]; and Long, 283.7 ± 40.9[g]. The average RC and its standard error were 0.86 ± 0.083 in the Short condition and 1.25 ± 0.11 in the Long condition (Fig. 7). In other words, the subjects consumed 14 % more in the Long condition than in the Normal condition and 22 % less in the Short condition than in the Normal condition. We used paired t-tests with the Bonferroni-Holm correction. The tests revealed

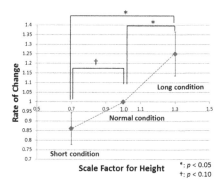

Fig. 7. Average RC in consumption volume in one hour and the SE in each height condition.

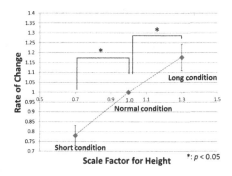

Fig. 8. Average RC in a sip and the SE in each height condition (from [19]).

significant differences in the RC between the Long and Normal ($p = 0.0496$) and Long and Short conditions ($p = 0.0242$). It also showed a marginally significant difference in the RC between the Short and Normal conditions ($p = 0.0595$). The average and standard error of number of sips, and volume consumed in a sip were as follows: Short, 6.6 ± 1.1[times] and 34.8 ± 3.5[g]; Normal, 7.7 ± 1.2[times] and 38.6 ± 4.4[g]; and Long: 7.3 ± 1.0[times], 44.2 ± 4.5[g]. However, as mentioned earlier, these results contain error. We normalized these two results based on the results under the Normal condition and conducted z-tests on them; the tests showed no significance.

Across all the conditions, no significant differences were found before the testing session with regard to ratings of hunger, thirst, nausea, tiredness, and prospective consumption (Fig. 9). Furthermore, there were also no significant differences across all the conditions with regard to these ratings after each testing session. These results indicated that our experimental design was valid. These results also showed that our illusory cup system maintains perceived satisfaction obtained from drinking even after the subjects have drunk the beverage. This is particularly compelling given that consumption is only influenced by the visual augmentation of the cup. Our results suggest that increasing the apparent length of a cup affects beverage intake and the perception of satisfaction; further, this effect holds true even when the beverage amount remains

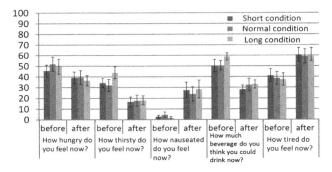

Fig. 9. Ratings of physical conditions before and after the testing session in the experimental conditions (Average ± SE).

the same. Only two subjects noticed the difference in the height of the cup between the three days and none of them answered that they were conscious of their consumption volume. Therefore, we could confirm that the proposed AR system does not require the user's effort or awareness.

Our results suggested that changing the apparent height of a cup can affect beverage consumption over the course of one hour. Figure 8 illustrates the average RC and its standard error in the previous study [18]. In that study, subjects consumed 18 % more in one sip in the Long condition than in the Normal condition and 22 % less in the Short condition than in the Normal condition. An independent t-test between the RC in the Short condition in the previous study and that in this study revealed no significant difference. The same test conducted between the RC in the Long condition in the previous study and that in this study also showed no significant difference. Therefore, it is assumed that our method has the same effect on beverage volume consumed in one sip and beverage volume consumed over the course of one hour, although the variance of consumption volume is larger because of the longer time span of measuring in the latter case.

5   Conclusion

In this paper, we aimed to confirm whether the illusion cup system, which involves changing the appearance of a cup using AR, can change beverage consumption over long periods. We conducted an experiment to investigate the effect of the illusion cup system on beverage consumption over the course of one hour. Our results showed that the system could change beverage consumption over the course of one hour from about −14 % to about 25 % by changing only the apparent height of the cup. By comparing these results and those of previous research [18], we showed that the total beverage consumption in one hour is proportional to the amount consumed in one mouthful, and the effect of the method on changing total consumption continues over the course of one hour.

The ability to control the subjects' beverage consumption with minimal effort is a conspicuous advantage of our system. However, this study does have some limitations.

First, the illusionary effect of the cup may decrease when we drink a beverage without looking at the cup. On the other hand, some research has indicated that the illusion effect of cutlery was enhanced while the subjects watched TV, since the effect worked in peripheral vision [20]. Thus, we need to assess the effect of our method when the subject is watching TV. Second, users of our method need to wear an HMD. As an alternative method, projection-based AR can be used for changing contextual cues. Recently, there have been many studies that have brought interactive surface techniques to dining tables [15]. By projecting patterns that evoke optical illusions onto cups with these techniques, we may be able to develop an augmented satiety method for beverages that does not require wearing any special apparatus.

While the current study is the first step toward designing an AR-based method that can help individuals regulate their beverage consumption, and while it no doubt has its limitations, we believe that the proposed system can help individuals more effortlessly control their beverage consumption. This should have significant effects on promoting nutritional health.

Acknowlegement. This work was partially supported by the MEXT, Grant-in-Aid for Young Scientists (A), 24680012, and the JST/CREST "Lifelog Infrastructure for Food" project.

References

1. Attwood, A.S., et al.: Glass shape influences consumption rate for alcoholic beverages. PLoS ONE **7**(8), e43007 (2012)
2. Ban, Y., Narumi, T., Tanikawa, T., Hirose, M.: Modifying an Identified Size of Objects Handled with Two Fingers Using Pseudo-Haptic Effects. In: ICAT/EGVE/EuroVR, pp. 1–8 (2012)
3. Ban, Y., Kajinami, T., Narumi, T., Tanikawa, T., Hirose, M.: Modifying an identified curved surface shape using pseudo-haptic effect. In: Haptics Symposium (HAPTICS 2012), pp. 211–216. IEEE (2012)
4. Ban, Y., Kajinami, T., Narumi, T., Tanikawa, T., Hirose, M.: Modifying an identified angle of edged shapes using pseudo-haptic effects. In: Isokoski, P., Springare, J. (eds.) EuroHaptics 2012, Part I. LNCS, vol. 7282, pp. 25–36. Springer, Heidelberg (2012)
5. Consultation, W.: Obesity: preventing and managing the global epidemic. World Health Organization Technical report series 894 (2000)
6. Girao, V.I.M.: Glasses' makeup: the simple and the combined effect of color and shape on perceived volume and beverage intake (2009)
7. Maitland, J., Chalmers, M.: Designing for peer involvement in weight management. In: Proceedings of the 2011 Annual Conference on Human Factors in Computing Systems, pp. 315–324. ACM (2011)
8. Nakazato, N., Narumi, T., Takeuchi, T., Tanikawa, T., Suwa, K., Hirose, M.: Influencing driver behavior through future expressway traffic predictions. In: Proceedings of the 2014 ACM International Joint Conference on Pervasive and Ubiquitous Computing: Adjunct Publication, pp. 127–130. ACM (2014)
9. Nambu, A., Narumi, T., Nishimura, K., Tanikawa, T., Hirose, M.: Visual-olfactory display using olfactory sensory map. In: Virtual Reality Conference (VR), pp. 39–42. IEEE (2010)

10. Narumi, T., Ban, Y., Kajinami, T., Tanikawa, T., Hirose, M.: Augmented perception of satiety: controlling food consumption by changing apparent size of food with augmented reality. In: Proceedings of the 2012 ACM Annual Conference on Human Factors in Computing Systems, pp. 109–118. ACM (2012)
11. Narumi, T., Miyaura, M., Tanikawa, T., Hirose, M.: Simplification of olfactory stimuli in pseudo-gustatory displays. IEEE Trans. Vis. Comput. Graph. **20**(4), 504–512 (2014)
12. Narumi, T., Nishizaka, S., Kajinami, T., Tanikawa, T., Hirose, M.: Meta cookie+: an illusion-based gustatory display. In: Shumaker, R. (ed.) VAMR 2011, Part III. LNCS, vol. 6773, pp. 260–269. Springer, Heidelberg (2012)
13. Omosako, H., Kimura, A., Shibata, F., Tamura, H.: Shape-cog illusion: psychophysical influence on center-of-gravity perception by mixed-reality visual stimulation. In: Virtual Reality Workshops (VR), pp. 65–66. IEEE (2012)
14. Raghubir, P., Krishna, A.: Vital dimensions in volume perception: Can the eye fool the stomach? J. Mark. Res. **36**(3), 313–326 (1999)
15. Sakurai, S., Narumi, T., Ban, Y., Tanikawa, T., Hirose, M.: Affecting our perception of satiety by changing the size of virtual dishes displayed with a tabletop display. In: Shumaker, R. (ed.) VAMR 2013, Part II. LNCS, vol. 8022, pp. 90–99. Springer, Heidelberg (2013)
16. Shimojo, S., Shams, L.: Sensory modalities are not separate modalities: plasticity and interactions. Curr. Opin. Neurobiol. **11**(4), 505–509 (2001)
17. Striegel-Moore, R.H., et al.: Correlates of beverage intake in adolescent girls: the National Heart, Lung, and Blood Institute Growth and Health Study. J. Pediatr. **148**(2), 183–187 (2006)
18. Suzuki, E., Narumi, T., Sakurai, S., Tanikawa, T., Hirose, M.: Illusion cup: interactive controlling of beverage consumption based on an illusion of volume perception. In: Proceedings of the ACM 5th Augmented Human International Conference, Article No: 41, pp. 1–8 (2014)
19. Wansink, B., et al.: Bottomless bowls: why visual cues of portion size may influence intake. Obes. Res. **13**(1), 93–100 (2005)
20. Wansink, B., Cashman, M.: Mindless Eating. Books on Tape, New York (2006)

Learning to Manage Nextgen Environments: Do Student Controllers Prefer to Use Datalink or Voice?

Alice Winter[✉], John Sweet, Yuri Trujillo, Adriana Miramontes,
Sam Curtis, Karen Sanchez, Kim-Phuong L. Vu,
and Thomas Z. Strybel

Center for Human Factors in Advanced Aeronautics Technologies, Department
of Psychology, California State University, Long Beach, 1250 N Bellflower
Blvd, Long Beach, CA 90840, USA
{alicebwinter, johnsweethf, trujillo.yuri2319,
adrianajmiramontes, scurtis925, ksanz89}@gmail.com,
{kim.vu, thomas.strybel}@csulb.edu

Abstract. The Next Generation Air Transportation (NextGen) system will introduce new automation tools to help air traffic controllers manage the projected increase in air traffic. As automation tools are gradually implemented, there will be a period of time where some air traffic will be managed with traditional voice-based tools and others will be managed with automation tools. The present study examined whether ATCo students prefer to use voice or Datalink more often to solve conflicts, and determine if there were any situations where Datalink was particularly beneficial to students. The present study is an archival analysis of data collected from 50 student ATCos who took part in one of four semesters of an ATCo training internship offered by the Center for Human Factors in Advanced Aeronautics Technologies (CHAAT). We found that students were more likely to use Datalink to resolve conflicts during the midterm than at the final, suggesting early reliance on tools during learning. However, at the final exam, students used voice and Datalink equally often, and indicated that they preferred voice over Datalink. The preference for voice is likely due to it being a more efficient method of controller-pilot communication than Datalink.

Keywords: ATC-pilot communication · ATC training · Nextgen tools · Datalink

1 Introduction

The goal of the Next Generation Air Transportation (NextGen) system is to introduce new tools and concepts of operations that will accommodate the projected increase in air traffic in the National Air Space (NAS) [1]. To ensure safety in the current system, each airspace sector has a maximum number of aircraft that are allowed to enter the sector [2]. The reason for this limit is to ensure that cognitive resources of air traffic controllers (ATCos) are not exceeded, as this would produce an unacceptable amount

© Springer International Publishing Switzerland 2015
S. Yamamoto (Ed.): HIMI 2015, Part I, LNCS 9172, pp. 661–667, 2015.
DOI: 10.1007/978-3-319-20612-7_62

of workload, and therefore compromise safety [2]. To accommodate the projected increase in traffic density, NextGen has proposed the introduction of new automation tools that will assist ATCos in handling more aircraft while keeping cognitive workload at an acceptable level.

Datalink or data communications is one NextGen tool that is designed to help ATCos manage more aircraft in their sector. Datalink allows both vertical and lateral conflict resolutions and trajectory changes to be communicated between pilots and air traffic controllers through non-verbal methods. As such, Datalink can decrease the amount of miscommunication on the party line because only the intended recipient will receive the message, and the message, being shown on a visual display, can be referenced at a later time. Datalink can also decrease the working memory load of pilots because the system can be integrated with the flight management system of the aircraft, and the pilot can simply execute the appropriate clearance. Datalink is also likely to be implemented with other automation tools designed to reduce ATCo workload. One tool is conflict detection, which alerts the ATCos when two Datalink equipped aircraft are in conflict prior to a loss of separation. Conflict detection will reduce the need for ATCos to scan the radar display for conflicts. Another tool is the conflict probe that would alert an ATCo if potential route changes using a third tool, the trial planner, would result in new conflicts [3].

Prevot et al. [4] conducted a study that examined whether ATCos can successfully employ Datalink for managing conflicts in their sector. Air traffic control participants were tested under three levels of simulated traffic density: 1X (current traffic density), 2X (twice the current traffic density), or 3X (three times the current traffic density). Prevot et al. found that ATCos were able to use the Datalink tools effectively, and that Datalink tools were most beneficial to the ATCos when the traffic density was 2X and 3X compared to current day traffic levels.

Although Datalink offers ATCos the benefits described earlier, it also has drawbacks. ATCos are typically slower at issuing Datalink clearances because they must navigate through computer menus to give a command rather than voicing the clearance [5]. The delays in Datalink communications may also not be acceptable when clearances need to be executed immediately. Additionally, although Datalink reduces party chatter, it also eliminates the immediate feedback of the pilot acknowledging the clearance. This may compel the ATCo to be more vigilant when monitoring the radar to make sure clearances were indeed executed appropriately. Because traditional voice communication between ATCo and pilot provides immediate feedback that the pilot received the clearance (correctly or incorrectly), it may be preferred in times of urgency.

In present study, we examined what communication method student controllers preferred when they were learning how to manage traffic. Data from 4 semesters of students participating in a radar internship at the Center for Human Factors in Advanced Aeronautics Technologies (CHAAT) were analyzed. We wanted to answer the following questions: In general, do students prefer to use Datalink or Voice to resolve conflicts? Does the preferred method change over a semester of training? Are there situations where Datalink is specifically helpful in assisting conflict resolution?

2 Methods

2.1 Participants

A total of 50 air traffic controller students' data were included for analyses from four semesters of data collection over the period of Fall 2011 to Spring 2013. Demographics were available for 44 participants. There were 37 males and 7 females, and the mean age of the students was 24.75 yrs, with a standard deviation of 2.74 yrs.

2.2 Simulation Environment

Participants were tested and trained on scenarios using the Multi Aircraft Control System (MACS) software, a medium-fidelity simulator [6]. MACS simulated Indianapolis Center (ZID-91), which includes overflights as well as departures from, and arrivals to, Louisville International Airport. Aircraft in the sector were piloted by other students in the class during the semester who were trained to make flight changes using simplified menus provided by MACS. The NextGen equipped aircraft included the following tools: trial planner, conflict probe, and Datalink. The conflict probe uses algorithms to detect conflicts between pairs of Datalink equipped aircraft. Datalink is a digital communication tool that allows ATCos to digitally handoff, change frequency, and deliver various clearances to aircraft in a text-based format. The trial planner is a tool that allows ATCos to make changes in the aircraft's route visually on the radar display by "clicking and dragging". The route change can uploaded directly to the aircraft's flight management system through Datalink.

2.3 Procedure

Each internship class consisted of 3.25 h of radar simulation training and 1.5 h of class lecture. A retired, radar-certified air traffic controller taught all components of the internship. In the first 8 weeks of the internship, students were instructed on basic air traffic management techniques, such as issuing speed, altitude, and heading clearances. Students were tested twice, once at the midterm and once at the end of the internship (i.e., the final test). For each test session, participants were tested on scenarios that consisted of 0 %, 50 %, and 100 % Datalink equipped aircraft. The data included in the present study is only from the 50 % equipage scenarios from the midterm and final exam because those scenarios were the only scenarios in which participants would issue both voice and Datalink clearances. In the 50 % scenario, there were 2 planned conflicts between a Datalink equipped and non-Datalink equipped aircraft. How the students resolved these planned conflicts were evaluated to answer some of our research questions.

2.4 Data Coding

To answer the question of which method ATCo students used to resolve conflicts, we recorded whether the ATCo student moved the Datalink equipped or unequipped aircraft to solve the conflict. If the students moved the Datalink equipped aircraft, this would indicate that they preferred to resolve the conflict using Datalink. Conversely, if the students moved the unequipped aircraft, this would indicate that they preferred voice.

Students were also asked about their preference for using Datalink versus voice in a debriefing session that occurred after the final exam. In particular, there were two questions concerning preference between voice and Datalink that were analyzed through content analysis. The first question was "Which method did you prefer to solve conflicts?" The second was, "Are there tasks that are specifically difficult to perform without Datalink?" To assess inter-rater reliability, two researchers categorized the answers independently. The agreement rate was 98 %. For the 3 discrepancies out of the total 150 questions, a third rater resolved the discrepancy.

3   Results

As with any study examining data collected in courses over multiple semesters, slight differences in the instruction and testing were evident across the semesters. Due to this, we set our alpha level at .10 for a more liberal criterion. However, all students included in this analysis were trained on air traffic management with both Datalink and voice over a course of 16 weeks.

3.1   Which Communication Method Do Student ATCos Use More Often to Solve Conflicts?

To assess which method ATCo students use more often to solve conflicts, and if this changes over time, a Chi-square contingency test found that preference for moving aircraft with voice or Datalink changed between the midterm and final exam, $\chi^2 = (1, N = 95) = 2.879$, p = .090. Participants moved more aircraft using Datalink than voice at the midterm, but at the final, the number of voice and Datalink clearances was roughly equal, as shown in Table 1.

Table 1. Number of Datalink and Voice Aircraft Moved to Resolve Conflicts at the Midterm and Final.

Exam	Voice	Datalink
Midterm	12	28
Final	26	29
Total	38	57

3.2   Which Communication Method Do Student ATCos Prefer to Use to Solve Conflicts?

As shown in Fig. 1, more students preferred to solve conflicts using voice (52 %) compared to Datalink (20 %). For the participants who indicated, "It depends" (12 %), they stated preferring using Datalink for conflicts that were further out and voice when the conflict was perceived as closer.

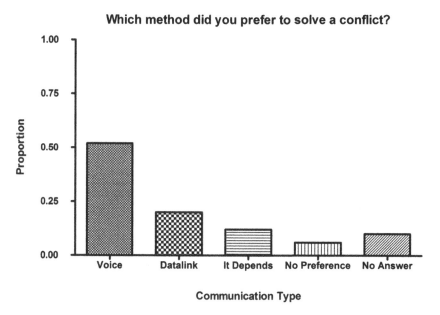

Fig. 1. Proportion of responses for preferred method of conflict resolution

3.3 Are There Tasks that Are Specifically Difficult to Perform Without Datalink?

As shown in Fig. 2, 54 % of the student ATCos indicated that vectoring was more difficult to perform without Datalink. Because conflict detection was only available between two Datalink equipped aircraft, 16 % of the students also indicated that detecting conflicts was more challenging without Datalink.

4 Discussion

The main goal of our study was to examine student ATCos' preferences between traditional voice-based communication and Datalink, which method they use more often to solve conflicts, and if this changes over a semester of training. In terms of performance, we found that students were more likely to use Datalink during their midterm (after 8 weeks of training), but at the final, they used Datalink and voice equally often. The early preference for Datalink observed during the mid-term may be a result of the students relying on advanced tools to help them with air traffic management while becoming proficient with voice communications.

When students were directly asked which method they preferred during the debriefing session, more students indicated that they prefer voice over Datalink.

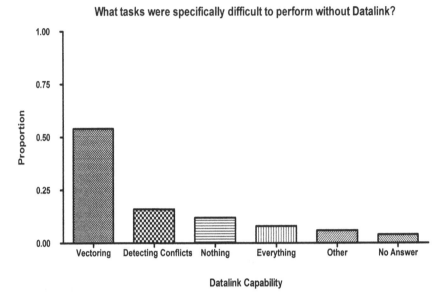

Fig. 2. Proportion of responses for tasks that are difficult to perform without Datalink

The preference for voice over Datalink may be due to the fact that once phraseology is mastered, voice communications can be faster than Datalink [5]. Some students responded that "it depends". For these students, they indicated favoring Datalink when the conflict was farther out and voice if the conflict was closer, again suggesting that the main benefit of voice was that it was a more efficient method of managing traffic. As mentioned earlier, sending a Datalink message typically entails a longer waiting period for the ATCo to know that the pilot acknowledged the clearance, which may compel ATCos to use voice based communications in times of urgency.

We also wanted to determine if there were any situations where Datalink might be favored. In the debriefing, the majority of ATCo students indicated that vectoring was more difficult to do without Datalink. When an ATCo gives a vector by voice, it can involve multiple calls to the pilot, giving them heading vectors and then putting them back on their original flight plan. This process can be taxing for the ATCos. Moreover, many ATCos indicated that vectoring is much easier to do with Datalink because they can visualize the route when using the trial planner that was implemented in the studies we analyzed.

In summary, we found that students were more likely to use Datalink to solve a conflict during their midterm than at their final exam. At the final, though, no performance difference was found. The majority of students reported favoring voice over Datalink to solve conflicts. However, even among students who preferred voice, many ATCo students saw the benefit of using Datalink to give trajectory changes to aircraft. It is important to note that the data from our study is from ATCo students, and that preferences for ATCos who have been working in the field may be different.

Acknowledgments. This project was supported by NASA cooperative agreement NNX09AU66A, Group 5 University Research Center: Center for Human Factors in Advanced Aeronautics Technologies (Brenda Collins, Technical Monitor).

References

1. Joint Planning and Development Office (JPDO) Concept of operations for the next generation air transportation system version 3.2 (2010). http://jpe.jpdo.gov/ee/docs/conops/NextGen_ConOps_v3_2.pdf. Accessed 3 July 2013
2. Prevot, T., Homola, J.R., Martin, L.H., Mercer, J.S., Cabrall, C.D.: Toward Automated Air Traffic Control—Investigating a Fundamental Paradigm Shift in Human/Systems Interaction. Int. J. Hum Comput. Interact. **28**(2), 77–98 (2012)
3. Rorie, R., Kiken, A., Morgan, C., Billinghurst, S., Morales, G., Monk, K., Vu, K.-P.L., Strybel, T., Battiste, V.: A preliminary investigation of training order for introducing nextgen tools. In: Salvendy, G., Smith, M.J. (eds.) HCII 2011, Part II. LNCS, vol. 6772, pp. 526–533. Springer, Heidelberg (2011)
4. Prevot, T., Homola, J., Mercer, J., Mainini, M., Cabrall, C.: Initialevaluation of nextgen airground operations with ground-based automated separation assurance. In: Proceedings of the 8th FAA Eurocontrol R&D Seminar (2009).
5. Battiste, H., Choi, W., Mirchi, T., Sanchez, K., Vu, K.-P.L., Chiappe, D., Strybel, T.Z.: The effects of early training with automation tools on the air traffic management strategies of student ATCOs. In: Yamamoto, S. (ed.) HCI 2013, Part II. LNCS, vol. 8017, pp. 13–21. Springer, Heidelberg (2013)
6. Prevot, T.: Exploring the many perspectives of distributed air traffic management: The Multi Aircraft Control System: MACS. In: International Conference on Human-Computer Interaction in Aeronautics, HCI-Aero 2002, 23–25 October, MIT, Cambridge (2002)

An Observation of Human Comprehension Through Wood Joints Assembly of a Cube Puzzle

Thongthai Wongwichai[1] and Takamitsu Tanaka[2](✉)

[1] Graduate School of Engineering, Iwate University, 4-3-5 Ueda,
Morikoa, Iwate, Japan
pang_design@hotmail.com
[2] Iwate University, 2-18-33 Ueda, Morikoa, Iwate, Japan
taktak@iwate-u.ac.jp

Abstract. In Japan, cube puzzle toys are traditionally made of jointed wood. This paper explores the personal decision-making process necessary to correctly assemble a cube puzzle toy. Participants from Iwate Prefecture were divided into two groups, based on a questionnaire that assessed their skill level in assembling construction kits. The participants were presented with an unassembled toy and their actions, together with all of the conditions necessary for interpretation of the puzzle, were recorded with a VDO camera. As a result of the observations, new variables were developed to create three cube puzzle sets and customize the difficulty level associated with each puzzle. Furthermore, new information about how people define shapes was revealed during the observational stage of the study.

Keywords: Signifier · Physical constraint · Affordance

1 Introduction

The interlocking puzzle has been a popular toy around the globe for a very long time. The configuration and functional techniques associated with various puzzles have been developed by manufacturers, artisans, and researchers over many years [1, 2]. An important factor for toy developers to consider is why people do or do not understand the correct way to assemble a wooden puzzle without using color or markings to indicate the required solution. The origin of this consideration lies in the relationship between the burr and notch. However, we believe that the number of components and shape of the pieces are not the primary factors that confuse players who encounter a burr puzzle. In general, we assume that difficulty arises from a constellation of variables associated with the design stage of a puzzle.

To test this hypothesis, we propose a design method that considers three types of a cube puzzle with the same number of components. Different variables were used to create shapes that affect a player's perceptions. For our puzzle, we expected results to be connected with a phenomenal reciprocity between a player and strategies for assembling the cube puzzle. Our aim was to illuminate the process of understanding the correct way to assemble a puzzle. This paper discusses the techniques participants used to successfully complete cube puzzles, speculates how inferences were made about

© Springer International Publishing Switzerland 2015
S. Yamamoto (Ed.): HIMI 2015, Part I, LNCS 9172, pp. 668–677, 2015.
DOI: 10.1007/978-3-319-20612-7_63

shapes, and explores how people contend with more difficult challenges. Data were derived from questionnaire answers and recordings made with a VDO camera.

Section 2 summarizes our design process, which applied variables to the manufacture of a cube puzzle toy. Section 3 explains our observational design and the objective of the questionnaires. The results of our observations are presented in Sect. 4. The article concludes with results of our observations regarding the design of a cube puzzle with discussing in our future work in Sect. 5.

2 The Design Process

This section describes the design process used to create three cubes of a puzzle toy. First, the traditional Japanese method was used to create the general shape of a cube puzzle. More than 200 different kinds of joints used in the manufacture of wooden furniture and structures may be incorporated into the puzzle. Second, we developed a method to create three types of a cube puzzle that has the same amount of components. However, different variables were implemented in order to create shapes that would influence a player's perception. Variables such as signifier, physical constraint, and affordance, from the fundamental psychological concepts posed by Norman [3], were applied during the design phase. However, we discovered a new way to use these variables in our research study.

In general, we opted for traditional techniques associated with Japanese joints to design the cube puzzle toy. We designed the core of the puzzle as a center burr in order to allow for joining with other notches. However, when they are separated by a single piece, most notches may not match with the core burr, as shown in Fig. 1.

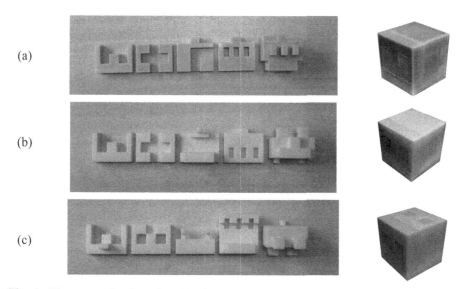

Fig. 1. The conventional version (a), the developed version (b), and the advance version (c) including a completed shape in three sets of cube puzzles.

Therefore, the first step of selection plays an important role in finding a signifier for the next step of the puzzle's composition.

The conventional version or a simple level designed by Tanaka [4] of the cube puzzle included a core with three burrs that matched a piece with three notches, as shown in Fig. 2. The unambiguous burrs and notches in this design made strong use of a signifier a clear cue was presented to the player. Furthermore, when the first side was completed, an even more salient signifier appeared on another side of the puzzle. This new variable, which is different from fundamental psychological conceptualizations, is necessary to navigate the correct construction of the puzzle.

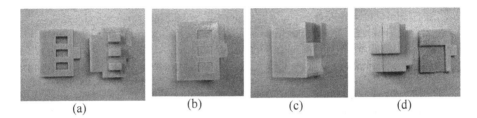

| (a) | (b) | (c) | (d) |

Fig. 2. (a) The first signifiers indicated by three burrs and notches. (b) Completed configuration of three burrs and notches. (c) The next signifier continuing to appear in another side. (d) New signifiers of next burr appeared to match another notch.

To design a cube puzzle of the developed version or a moderate level designed by the author, rather than use a signifier to compose a joint in the first step, we used another variable, "physical constraints," to limit the possible action between burr and notch. This variable generated moderate difficulty because it manifests as an ambiguous form. Therefore, players must interpret a shape and compose the correct configuration, as shown in Fig. 3.

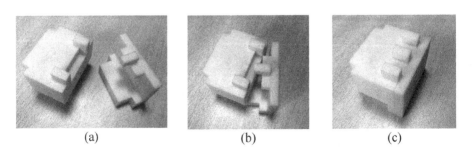

| (a) | (b) | (c) |

Fig. 3. From (a)–(c). A design using the "physical constraints" variable

(a)   (b)

(c)   (d)

Fig. 4. From (a)–(d). A design using an "Affordance" allowing many possible actions to compose their items.

To design the advance version or a difficult level designed by the author, we introduced another variable, called "an affordance." This variable increases the possible actions of the puzzle's various components. In general, the burr-and-notch form is designed to serve as a joint in many directions, as shown in Fig. 4, but including additional variables—signifier, physical constraint, and affordance—allows for different levels of difficulty. This hypothesis is tested in the next section.

3   Observations

In this section, we describe the process and objectives of the questionnaire that was used in the first stage of the study.

Before testing commenced, 20 participants filled out a questionnaire intended to determine their higher and lower spatial abilities. The questionnaire was divided into three parts:

1. General Information (gender, age, nationality, course of study)
2. Specific Information (experience, type, and frequency of encountering assembly)
3. Participant Ability (three items)

- Inspired by the models of mental imagery developed by Shepard and Metzler [5], we tested for perceptual ability when an object was rotated to another position. We believe this measurement relates to the human ability to perceive and differentiate forms, as shown in Fig. 5.

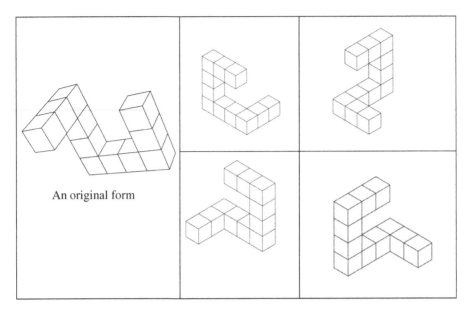

Fig. 5. Example of an identifiable form. Participants were required to choose true or false for each image.

- The correlation of burr and notch, which tests the ability to understand addition and subtraction made to a particular configuration. Participants were required to choose true or false for the forms shown in Figs. 6 and 7.

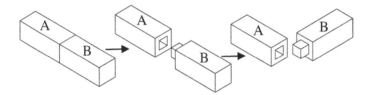

Fig. 6. Example of correlation assembly between part A and part B

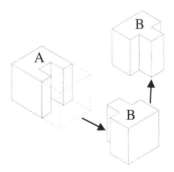

Fig. 7. Example of a missing shape (B) derived from subtraction (A)

- Predicting an absent form tested participants' abilities to define missing parts. This assessment related to the process of finding a signifier during assembly, as shown in Figs. 8 and 9.

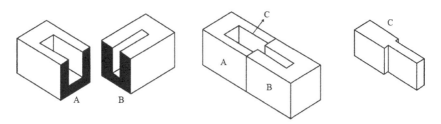

Fig. 8. Example of a void shape (C) derived from a combination of notches formed by part A and part B.

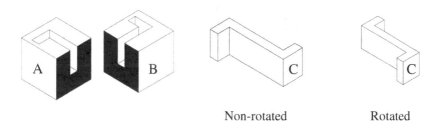

Non-rotated   Rotated

Fig. 9. Example of a void shape (C), which might be non-rotated or rotated, derived from a combination of notches formed by part A and part B.

Results of the questionnaire are detailed in the next section.

4   Results of the Observations

Before presenting the results of our observations, we offer a brief overview of the demographics, prior experience, and general ability of the participants.

Demographics. Of the 20 people who participated in this study, 8 participants were men and 12 participants were women. Participants ranged in age from 20 to 30 years old and hailed from Thailand, Japan, Taiwan, and China. All participants studied the fields of engineering, industrial design, or education.

Specific Information. Participants who studied engineering or industrial design had more experience solving puzzles than people who studied education.

Participant's Ability. The scale used to measure ability totaled 24 points. It can be divided participants into two groups which are the skillful and unskillful groups.

After completed a questionnaire, all participants composed three sets of cube puzzles. We recorded their actions by VDO camera. An average time of this experiment has shown in Fig. 10.

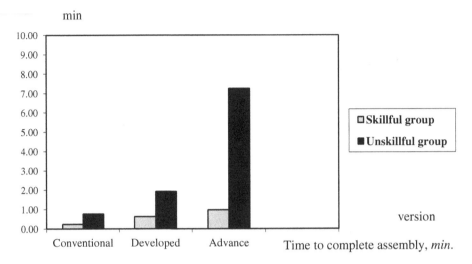

Fig. 10. Bar graph shows an average of assembly time between skillful and unskillful groups.

It's clearly seen in Fig. 10 that the average time of skillful and unskillful group of three cases are different. Skillful group spent time to compose less than unskillful group. However, the different time between skillful and unskillful group in developed and advance version are wider than in conventional version. It's interestingly that different time between skillful and unskillful in the advance version is dramatically wider than other two cases. Therefore, it was clear that the different variables (signifier, physical constraint, and affordance) affected the difficulty level of the three cube puzzles. Furthermore, Engineering and Industrial design students, a skillful group, spent a slight time to compose all sets of puzzles which received a high score from a questionnaire. On the contrary, Educational students, an unskillful group, spent a long time and received a low score from a questionnaire.

Table 1 shows an explanation of participant's behavior to investigate the causes that how participants define the shape and how develop more difficulty in their levels.

As a result, it can be concluded that a personal ability and the difficult levels of cube puzzle are important causes considered to why people do or do not understand the correct way to assemble a cube puzzle toy. Personal ability and the object are interacted with each other and reveal their perception-action activity that we can observe in a specific environment.

Table 1. Participant's behavior

Stage of assembly	Explanation of participant's behavior		
Before assembly	-All skillful participants tended to consider the shape of an item before selection. -None of the unskillful participants considered the shape of all items before selection.		
Start assembly	-For the conventional version, all skillful participants chose an unambiguous match of burr and notch.		
	-For the conventional version, most unskillful participants chose an unambiguous match of burr and notch, similar to participants in the skillful group.		
	-For the developed and advance version, at first, all skillful participants chose a complex shape, trying to match a burr and notch.		
	-For the developed and advance version, at first, most unskillful participants chose a simple shape and tried to match burr and notch.		

(Continued)

Table 1. (*Continued*)

Stage of assembly	Explanation of participant's behavior	
During assembly	- For the developed and advance version, some skillful participants explored the complex shape, which had 3 notches, and then created 3 burrs derived from 2 pieces to forge a relationship.	
	-For the conventional version, some unskillful participants did not compose by following the signifier.	
	-For the developed and advance version, some unskillful participants started to compose a complex shape, but could not understand how to join the pieces.	
Development of ability	-Some unskillful participants understood the relationship of the burr and notch better by trying to form a complex shape in the first stage of selection. -In contrast to initial observations, some unskillful participants started composing from a core piece earlier in the process.	

5　Conclusion

This paper explored why people do or do not understand the correct way to assemble a cube puzzle and how players define shapes when tasked with constructing a puzzle. We identified new variables that contribute to the difficulty of a puzzle tested by a small group of participants. However, the numbers of participants will be assured more accuracy. It may be explored new information about participant's behavior and expanded for other files of researches.

References

1. Song, P., Fu, C.-W., Cohen-Or, D.: Recursive interlocking puzzles. In: Journal ACM Transactions on Graphics (TOG), vol. 31, issue 6, Article no. 128 (2012)

2. Xin, S.-Q., Lai, C.-F., Fu, C.-W., Wong, T.-T., He, Y., Cohen-Or, D.: Making burr puzzles from 3D models. In: ACM Transactions on Graphics (SIGGRAPH), vol. 30, issue 4, Article 97 (2011)
3. Norman, D.: Design of Everyday Things: Revised and Expanded. New York: Basic Books, London: MIT Press (UK edition) (2013)
4. Tanaka, T., Tachibana, M., Hirata, I.: development of teaching material volume calculations using a wooden puzzle. In: HCI International 2014 Conference Proceedings, 22 June 2014
5. Shepard, R.N., Metzler, J.: Mental rotation of three dimensional objects. Science **171**, 701–703 (1971)

The Research of the Influence of Customer Perceived Value to Customer Satisfaction in Mobile Games

Kailiang Zhang[✉] and Yumi Asahi

Faculty of Engineering, Shizuoka University, Shizuoka, Japan
zhang.kailiang.14@cii.shizuoka.ac.jp,
tyasahi@ipc.shizuoka.ac.jp

Abstract. With the popularity of LTE technology, the mobile industry is booming and the market size of the mobile industry is expanding. The major Internet companies have entered the mobile gaming market, resulting in an increasingly competitive market. Under this background, mobile games have then become an emerging market in online game industry in the past few years. The scholars studying mobile games are focused on the technology development level, few studies on consumer behavior. The paper study is behavior intention of mobile games based on Customer Perceived Value. The research results in this paper have practical meaning for mobile game developers and operators. Through the use of Customer Perceived Value, analyze the behavior features of Chinese and Japanese users. Then they can enhance customer satisfaction and customer loyalty by properly managing Customer Perceived Value.

Keywords: Mobile game · Customer perceived value · Customer satisfaction · Customer loyalty

1 Introduction

1.1 Research Background

Despite being the world's largest mobile game market, Japanese mobile game market has faced slower growth since 2013, when the market began to be saturated. By comparison, however, in Chinese mobile game market, Internet companies have devoted more energy to developing mobile games successively since the second half of 2013. As a large quantity of mobile games are launched in the market, mobile games will be undoubtedly become the new growth point of mobile internet.

According to Japanese authoritative market research agency cyber-z's report (Fig. 1): Japanese mobile game market size in 2014 was 658.4 billion yen, 2015 growth forecast to 746.2 billion yen (Growth rate of 13 %), and it will growth forecast to 823.8 billion yen in 2016 (Growth rate of 10 %). Chinese mobile game market size in 2014 was 380 billion yen, 2015 growth forecast to 574 billion yen (Growth rate of 51 %), and it will growth forecast to 778 billion yen in 2016 (Growth rate of 36 %).

The mobile game developed based on the application of social networking service is an interactive behavior that enhances the exchange between people through games.

© Springer International Publishing Switzerland 2015
S. Yamamoto (Ed.): HIMI 2015, Part I, LNCS 9172, pp. 678–687, 2015.
DOI: 10.1007/978-3-319-20612-7_64

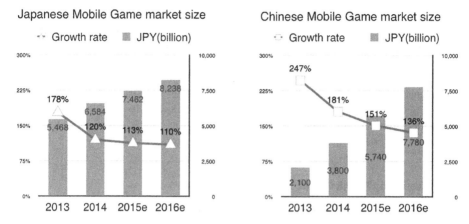

Fig. 1. Mobile game market's revenue growth rate comparison between Japan and China [11]

Both Line of Japan and WeChat of China have attracted a large number of users. In Japan, Line has 49 million users, taking up 37.6 % of Japanese population. With the number of monthly active users arriving at 438 million, WeChat has developed into the necessity of Chinese mobile phone users. Supported by the broad customer base, Line and WeChat have established their respective mobile phone platform as its important source of income. For instance, Line achieved a year-on-year growth of 104.2 % in the third quarter of 2014.

Chinese mobile game industry started late compared with that of Japan, but its market size expands rapidly. The internet process of Chinese society and economy has laid a foundation for the application and user attraction of mobile internet. In China that witnesses an explosive growth in the number of smart phone users, mobile game shows a promising prospect.

1.2 The Raising of Questions

As shown by these astonishing data, the development of mobile games hits bottlenecks: the problems such as the severely homogenous game, the short life cycle, the high churn rate, and low payment rate have perplexed the developers and operators of mobile game. Different from the massively multiplayer online game (MMOG) with the life cycle of five to seven years, present mobile game products have a shorter life cycle, normally reaching 6 months.

How to upgrade the customer loyalty of mobile games has become a concern of mobile game industry as well as a conundrum that every game developer has to solve while improving their competitive strengths.

Since Philip Kotler who is honored as the *Father of Modern Marketing* proposed the question of how enterprises should develop competitive strengths in the 1980s, neither academic community nor business community has ceased the exploration on this question. Afterwards, since Kotler put forward the concept of *Marketing 3.0* in 2010, customer orientation has been mentioned and studied frequently. Customer perceived value is the real value of the products or services that enterprises provide for customers. Only when the largest perceived value is created for customers, can customer satisfaction be improved and customer loyalty be built to sustain the competitive edge of enterprises.

The research focus is the influence that customer perceived value of mobile phone has on customer satisfaction and loyalty, and meanwhile, the customer perceived value management method of mobile games is presented accordingly. Besides, suggestions on the development and operation of mobile game enterprises are proposed to help enterprises understand their competitive edges in market.

1.3   Research Objective and Significance

The research is intended to explore the customer perceived value management method of mobile games. Below are the specific research objectives:

1. Analyze the influence that customer perceived value of mobile games has on customer satisfaction;
2. Analyze the influence that customer perceived value of mobile games has on customer loyalty;
3. Make a comparative analysis about the influence that customer perceived value of Chinese and Japanese mobile game users has on customer loyalty;
4. Explore the method to manage customer perceived value of mobile games.

After consulting a large amount of literature, the author finds that customer perceived value has not been widely applied as a research tool in a specific industry in China and Japan yet. Currently, there is little attention paid to the systematic study on the customer perceived value in mobile game industry. Thus, this study is intended to expand the application scope of customer perceived value theory, and introduce it into the study on mobile game industry.

1.4   Research Methods

1. Literature research method
   The meanings of mobile game, customer perceived value, customer satisfaction and customer loyalty are made clear by means of literature research and theoretical analysis in an attempt to provide theoretical support for research.

2. Questionnaire survey
   In order to conduct a preliminary study on the mechanism in which customer perceived value exercises an influence over customer loyalty, energy is devoted to making an experimental survey and analyzing the survey result to further confirm the questionnaire items before questionnaire research, which is intended to guarantee the referential value of the data obtained in the formal questionnaire survey.

3. Empirical analysis
   Based on literature research, the theoretical model regarding the influence of customer perceived value on customer loyalty and satisfaction is built and relevant

hypotheses are presented. Additionally, SPSS 22.0 software is utilized to make reliability, validity, correlation, regression and factor analyses on the survey data for the purpose of verifying the hypotheses proposed herein and bringing forward relevant management suggestions.

2 Literature Review

2.1 Concept of Customer Perceived Value

Scholars from home and abroad have made numbers of studies on the concept of customer perceived value, but there is still a lack of a unified definition. As indicated by the definition of customer perceived value given by Philip Kotler, customer perceived value = total customer value + total customer cost. Total customer value refers to the benefits that customers expect to achieve from a certain product or service, and total customer cost to the estimated expenses arising from customer's evaluation, obtainment and use of the product or service.

From this study, a conclusion that the core of customer perceived value is the trade-off between perceived benefits and perceived sacrifices is drawn. Thus, there are two approaches to elevating customer perceived value, raising perceived benefits or lessening perceived sacrifices. However, due to individual difference, customers vary from each other in the perceived value of the same products or services.

2.2 Dimensions of Customer Perceived Value

According to the studies on the dimensions of customer perceived value in a large amount of literature, the dimensions of customer perceived value will change with products and markets though the customer perceived values in different industries and domains have different compositions and the customer perceived values at home and abroad vary in composition model. On the whole, however, these dimensions of customer perceived value mainly reflect two aspects including perceived benefits and sacrifices, and different scholars have developed different understandings of the embodiments of perceived benefits and sacrifices.

According to the description on the dimensions of customer perceived value in *Marketing 3.0* of Philip Kotler, and the previous research achievements regarding perceived value theory of online games, the hypothesis that the perceived value of mobile games encompasses at least 5 dimensions is proposed, including functional value, emotional value, social value, monetary cost, and non-monetary cost. Meanwhile, empirical study is conducted to verify and study the relationship between these dimensions and customer satisfaction and loyalty.

2.3 Concept of Customer Satisfaction and Loyalty

In 1988, American scholar Fornell combined structural equation with mental path of satisfaction formation to propose a new satisfaction model, which has laid a foundation for the building of national satisfaction index models in countries worldwide. Based on this model, SCSB was presented by Sweden and then ACSI and ECSI were developed successively. In 2009, Japan put forward Japanese Customer Satisfaction Index (JCSI for short), which has been widely applied in different industries. The theoretical model of this study is also derived from JCSI, with the major factors including expectation, perceived quality, perceived value, satisfaction, complaints and loyalty. Of these factors, expectation, perceived quality and perceived value are factors that create satisfaction, and then satisfaction will lead to complaints and loyalty (Fig. 2).

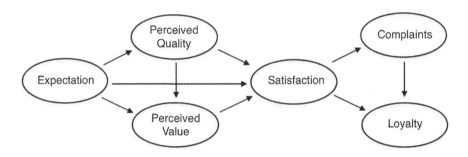

Fig. 2. Japanese customer satisfaction index

2.4 The Building of Theoretical Model

The theoretical model of this study is built based on the review and analysis of relevant literature and theories (Fig. 3).

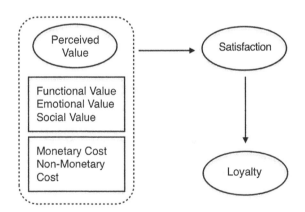

Fig. 3. Academic framework

3 Research Methods

3.1 Research Objective

The research respondents are mainly constituted by smart phone users. Since the questionnaire survey is implemented in both China and Japan, the author focuses attention on college students or the youth in the society, most of whom are smart phone users often playing mobile games and able to provide data support and reference for this study.

The respondents of this study are the mobile game users in the social circle of the author, and the questionnaire survey is made through paper questionnaire, the third-party questionnaire platform, online chatting tools, and email, and the data are collected by various approaches such as interview.

3.2 Questionnaire Design

This study explores the influence that customer perceived value exerts on customer satisfaction and loyalty, as well as the interactive mechanism of all influencing factors by means of questionnaire. The questions relevant to customer perceived value, customer satisfaction, and customer loyalty in this study are derived from previous research achievements.

The questionnaire is made up of ten parts. The first part asks whether the respondents have smart phones and when they use smart phones. The second part is about the name of user's favorite mobile game. The third part makes a survey on the recreational value of the mobile game. The fourth part pays attention to emotional value of the mobile game. The fifth part relates to the social value of the mobile game. The sixth part revolves around user's perception on the monetary cost of the mobile game. The seventh part investigates user's perception on the non-monetary cost of the mobile game. The eighth part focuses attention on users' satisfaction with the mobile game. The ninth part lays stress on user's loyalty to the mobile game. The final part collects the information regarding demographic characteristic variables such as gender and age of users, as well as the behavioral characteristic variables of game players, such as game-playing time and the favorite mobile game type (Table 1).

4 Data Analysis

4.1 Collection of Experimental Survey Data and Sample Description

The respondents of the experiment are the Japanese college students that the author got acquainted with while participating in the exchange activity in Japan. The respondents from different universities are randomly and representatively selected. This survey, carried out in the form of paper questionnaire, involves 30 respondents, and 5 questionnaires are found ineffective because they are obviously inauthentic or the respondents are not mobile game players. As a result of this, there only are 25 effective

Table 1. Resource of scales

Variable	Measurement items	Scale
Functional value	FV1	I think mobile game contains diverse contents and plots
	FV2	I consider it is easy to operate and learn mobile game
	FV3	I find mobile game has wonderful scenes, music and role design
	FV4	I think there are clear game objectives in play process
Emotional value	EV1	Playing games can kill time
	EV2	Game achievements can pleasure me
	EV3	Game achievements can excite me
Social value	SV1	Game achievements can help me show off my skills in front of friends and achieve satisfaction
	SV2	Playing this game can give me a sense of identity in the society
	SV3	Playing this game can help me make new friends and expand my social circle
	SV4	Playing this game can help me interact and contact with friends that I cannot meet frequently in real life
Monetary cost	MC1	I buy props and rare cards to make myself distinctive and attract other's attention when playing games
	MC2	I pay money to improve the speed of game progress and reduce the efforts that need to make
Non-monetary cost	NMC1	I pay time for role upgrade and game experiencing
	NMC2	I pay time for the interaction with friends
	NMC3	I devote much energy to playing games so as not to be far inferior to friends in skills
Customer satisfaction	CS1	I feel satisfied with the game I am now playing
	CS2	I don't regret having paid money for playing games
Customer loyalty	CL1	I will continue to play the game that I am now playing
	CL2	I will pay for the game that I am now playing as before
	CL3	I will recommend this mobile game to other friends

questionnaires, with the effective collection rate standing at 87.3 %. The basic descriptive statistical data of effective samples are shown in Fig. 4.

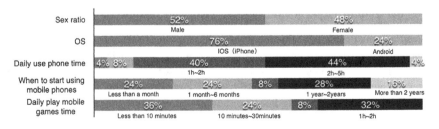

Fig. 4. Sample constitutes

4.2   Reliability Analysis

Reliability analysis is intended to analyze the consistency level of the results obtained by one evaluation method and meanwhile judge the reliability of the evaluation through the degree of consistency. The reliability of the test result is closely associated with the degree of the influence that the errors exert on the test result.

According to reliability analyses, Cronbach alpha (α) is the index that depends most heavily on evaluation reliability. Developed by Cronbach in 1951, α is frequently applied to estimating the systematic variations on the variable of every factor. The higher the reliability coefficient α is, the more systematic the variables of the factor will be.

American statistician Hair et al. (1988) insisted that when Cronbach $\alpha > 0.7$, the data are highly reliable, and when the number of items in measurement is smaller than 6 and Cronbach $\alpha > 0.6$, the data are reliable.

The internal consistency coefficients of all variables and corresponding measured items are calculated by means of SPSS 22.0 software, with the calculation result shown in Table 2. All the internal consistency coefficients (Cronbach α) of the variables designed in this study are greater than 0.6, which suggests that the variables of the study are highly reliable.

Table 2. Cronbach α analysis of questionnaire

Variable	Cronbach α	Measurement items
Functional value	0.655	FV1
		FV2
		FV3
		FV4
Emotional value	0.865	EV1
		EV2
		EV3
Social value	0.774	SV1
		SV2
		SV3
		SV4
Monetary cost	0.98	MC1
		MC2
Non-monetary cost	0.723	NMC1
		NMC2
		NMC3

4.3   Exploratory Factor Analysis

Firstly, there is a need to make factor analysis on customer perceived value. When KMO is 0.546, factor analysis can be performed.

According to principal component analysis, 3 factors are extracted from customer perceived value. It is found that the cumulative explanatory variance is 0.672, greater than 0.5, which implies that these 3 factors can embody sample information effectively. The factor loading matrix derived from the maximum rotation of variance is shown in Table 3. According to factor connotation analysis, factors 1, 2 and 3 have reflected customer perceived value of mobile games, which proves that customer perceived value of mobile games include at least three dimensions, namely, functional value, emotional value and social value.

Table 3. Exploratory factor analysis

	Component		
	1	2	3
FV1	0.311	-0.389	0.521
FV2	-0.052	-0.097	0.802
FV3	-0.14	0.243	0.777
FV4	0.243	-0.025	0.651
EV1	0.179	0.822	-0.151
EV2	0.047	0.943	0.075
EV3	0.412	0.785	0.096
SV1	0.744	0.178	0.05
SV2	0.674	-0.008	0.463
SV3	0.834	0.21	-0.186
SV4	0.76	0.098	0.099
	Social Value	**Emotional Value**	**Functional value**

5   Research Limitations and Future Research Plan

5.1   Research Limitations

In this paper, some achievements have been made by studying and empirically analyzing the influence that customer perceived value of mobile games has on customer satisfaction. This study, however, still shows varieties of deficiencies as a result of insufficient time, energy and ability.

1. There is a lack of samples since experimental investigation is the only focus.
2. Little consideration is given to the effect of control variables such as income and educational level and the influencing factors such as frequency of play and game type on satisfaction and loyalty of mobile game customers.
3. The difference between mobile game users of China and those of Japan fails to be analyzed comprehensively from the perspective of game development history.

5.2   Future Research Orientation

Based on the abovementioned research limitations, the study on customer perceived value of mobile games can be conducted from following angles:

1. To expand sample size and diversify the source of respondents. Currently, preparations have been made to conduct a questionnaire survey on the coastal regions of Mainland China and carry out group analysis and research based on user

background in March 2015. Meanwhile, the difference in the influence that customer perceived value factors has on customer satisfaction is verified with the hope of helping game developers develop the satisfactory games for customers in different regions.
2. To extend association study. Customer perceived value involves the contents of the disciplines such as consumer psychology, marketing and management. Therefore, in the future, focus can be placed on interdisciplinary study to make the improved theory and model more adaptable to different disciplines.

References

1. Kamiyama, S.: Analysis of the theme park customers satisfied (397), 38–53 (2011)
2. Ono, J.: According JCSI customer satisfaction model. Mark. J. **30**(1), 20–34 (2010)
3. Kotler, P.: Marketing Analysis, Planning and Control. Prentice Hall, Englewood Cliffs (1985)
4. Kotler, P.: Kotler's Marketing 3.0 the new law times of social media. Asahi Shimbun Publications Inc. (2010)
5. Kotler, P., Keller, K.L.: A Framework for Marketing Management, 12th edn. Prentice Hall, Englewood Cliffs (2002)
6. Zhang, F.: Empirical study of customer perceived value elements online game. Zhejiang University, Zhejiang (2005)
7. Smith, J.B., Colgate, M.: Customer value creation: a practical framework. J. Mark. Theory Prac. **15**(1), 7–23 (2007)
8. Xiong, Z.: Effects of the value of repeat purchase behavior online game customer perception. Anhui University, Anhui (2010)
9. Yen, Y.-S.: The impact of perceived value on continued usage intention in social networking sites. In: 2011 2nd International Conference on Networking and Information Technology, IPCSIT, vol. 17, pp. 217–223 (2011)
10. Zhou, S.X.: Gratifications, loneliness, leisure boredom and self-esteem as predictors of SNS-game addiction and usage pattern among Chinese College students. The Chinese University of Hong Kong University, Hong Kong, May 2010
11. Mobile Game market's Revenue Growth Rate Comparison between Japan and China (2014). http://cyber-z.co.jp/news/pressreleases/2014/0730_1659.html
12. Japanese Customer Satisfaction Index (2009). http://www.service-js.jp/

Author Index